# the
# Unofficial
# Guide® to

## the Best RV and Tent
## Campgrounds in
## the Great Lakes States

### Illinois, Indiana, Michigan,
### Minnesota, Ohio & Wisconsin

## Other Titles in the Unofficial Guide
## Best RV and Tent Campgrounds Series

California & the West

Florida & the Southeast

Mid-Atlantic States

The Northeast

Northwest & Central Plains

Southwest & South Central Plains

U.S.A.

# Other Unofficial Guides

Beyond Disney: The Unofficial Guide to Universal, SeaWorld,
and the Best of Central Florida

Inside Disney: The Incredible Story of Walt Disney World
and the Man Behind the Mouse

Mini Las Vegas: The Pocket-Sized Unofficial Guide to Las Vegas

Mini-Mickey: The Pocket-Sized Unofficial Guide to Walt Disney World

The Unofficial Guides to Bed & Breakfasts and Country Inns:
California   Great Lakes   New England
Northwest   Rockies   Southeast   Southwest

The Unofficial Guides to the Best RV and Tent Campgrounds:
California & the West   Florida & the Southeast   Great Lakes
Mid-Atlantic States   Northeast   Northwest   Southwest   U.S.A.

The Unofficial Guide to Branson, Missouri

The Unofficial Guide to Chicago

The Unofficial Guide to Cruises

The Unofficial Guide to Disneyland

The Unofficial Guide to Disneyland Paris

The Unofficial Guide to Florence, Rome, and the Heart of Italy

The Unofficial Guide to the Great Smoky and Blue Ridge Region

The Unofficial Guide to Golf Vacations in the Eastern U.S.

The Unofficial Guide to Hawaii

The Unofficial Guide to Las Vegas

The Unofficial Guide to London

The Unofficial Guide to New Orleans

The Unofficial Guide to New York City

The Unofficial Guide to Paris

The Unofficial Guide to San Francisco

The Unofficial Guide to South Florida, including Miami and the Keys

The Unofficial Guides to Traveling with Kids:
California   Florida   Mid-Atlantic   New England and New York
Walt Disney World

The Unofficial Guide to Walt Disney World

The Unofficial Guide to Walt Disney World for Grown-Ups

The Unofficial Guide to Washington, D.C.

The Unofficial Guide to the World's Best Diving Vacations

# the Unofficial Guide® to

# the Best RV and Tent Campgrounds in the Great Lakes States

## 1st Edition

Illinois, Indiana, Michigan,
Minnesota, Ohio & Wisconsin

Jackie Sheckler Finch

**Hungry Minds™**

Best-Selling Books • Digital Downloads • e-Books • Answer Networks • e-Newsletters
Branded Web Sites • e-Learning

*New York, NY • Indianapolis, IN • Cleveland, OH*

Please note that price fluctuate in the course of time, and travel information changes under the impact of many factors that influence the travel industry. We therefore suggest that you write or call ahead for confirmation when making your travel plans. Every effort has been made to ensure the accuracy of information throughout this book and the contents of this publication are believed correct at the time of printing. Nevertheless, the publishers cannot accept responsibility for errors or omissions or for changes in details given in this guide or for the consequences of any reliance on the information provided by the same. Assessments of attractions and so forth are based upon the author's own experience and therefore, descriptions given in this guide necessarily contain an element of subjective opinion, which may not reflect the publisher's opinion or dictate a reader's own experience on another occasion. Readers are invited to write to the publisher with ideas, comments, and suggestions for future editions.

Your safety is important to us, so we encourage you to stay alert and be aware of your surroundings. Keep a close eye on cameras, purses, and wallets, all favorite targets of thieves and pickpockets.

**Published by Hungry Minds, Inc.**
909 Third Avenue
New York, NY 10022

Produced by Menasha Ridge Press
COVER DESIGN BY MICHAEL J. FREELAND
INTERIOR DESIGN BY MICHELE LASEAU


Unofficial Guide is a registered trademark of Hungry Minds, Inc.

ISBN 0-7645-6255-X

ISSN 1536-965X

Manufactured in the United States of America

10 9 8 7 6 5 4 3 2

# Contents

# Introduction

## Why Unofficial?

The material in this guide has not been edited or in any way reviewed by the campgrounds profiled. In this "unofficial" guide we represent and serve you, the consumer. By way of contrast with other campground directories, no ads were sold to campgrounds, and no campground paid to be included. Through our independence, we're able to offer you the sort of objective information necessary to select a campground efficiently and with confidence.

## Why Another Guide to Campgrounds?

We developed *The Unofficial Guide to the Best RV and Tent Campgrounds in the Great Lakes States* because we recognized that campers are as discriminating about their choice of campgrounds as most travelers are about their choice of hotels. As a camper, you don't want to stay in every campground along your route. Rather, you prefer to camp only in the best. A comprehensive directory with limited information on each campground listed does little to help you narrow your choices. What you need is a reference that tells you straight out which campgrounds are the best, and that supplies detailed information, collected by independent inspectors, that differentiates those campgrounds from all of the also-rans. This is exactly what *The Unofficial Guide to the Best RV and Tent Campgrounds* delivers.

## The Choice Is All Yours

Life is short, and life is about choices. You can stay in a gravel lot, elbow to elbow with other campers, with tractor-trailers roaring by just beyond the fence, or with this guide, you can spend the night in a roomy, shaded site, overlooking a sparkling blue lake. The choice is yours.

The author of this guide combed the Great Lakes states inspecting and comparing hundreds of campgrounds. The objective was to create a hit parade of the very best, so that no matter where you travel, you'll never have to spend another night in a dumpy, gravel lot.

The best campgrounds in each state are described in detail in individual profiles so you'll know exactly what to expect. In addition to the fully profiled campgrounds, we provide a Supplemental Directory of Campgrounds that lists hundreds of additional properties that are quite adequate, but that didn't make the cut for the top 350 in the guide. Thus, no matter where you are, you'll have plenty of campgrounds to choose from. None of the campgrounds appearing in this guide, whether fully profiled or in the supplemental list, paid to be included. Rather, each earned its place by offering a superior product. Period.

### *Letters, Comments, and Questions from Readers*

Many who use the Unofficial Guides write to us with questions, comments, and reports of their camping experiences. We appreciate all such input, both positive and critical. Readers' comments are frequently incorporated into revised editions of the Unofficial Guides and have contributed immeasurably to their improvement. Please write to:

*The Unofficial Guide to the Best RV and Tent Campgrounds*
P.O. Box 43673
Birmingham, AL 35243
UnofficialGuides@menasharidge.com

For letters sent through the mail, please put your return address on both your letter and envelope; the two sometimes become separated. Also include your phone number and email address if you are available for a possible interview.

## How to Use This Guide

Using this guide is quick and easy. We begin with this introduction followed by "Campground Awards," a list of the best campgrounds for RVers, tenters, families, and more. Then we profile the best 350 campgrounds in the Great Lakes states. Next is a supplemental list of hundreds of additional campgrounds including details about prices, hookups, and more. Bringing up the rear is an alphabetical index of all campgrounds included in the guide.

Both the profiled section and the supplemental directory are ordered alphabetically, first by state and then by city. To see what campgrounds are available:

- Find the section covering the state in question.

- Within that section, look up the city alphabetically.

- Under the city, look up the campgrounds alphabetically.

You can choose and locate campgrounds in four different ways.

1. **Use the Map**  If a city appears with a black, solid bullet on our map, at least one of our profiled or listed campgrounds will be located there. The converse is also the case: if the city has a hollow, outlined bullet, you can assume that we do not cover any campgrounds in that city.

2. **Check the Campground Profiles**  In the section where we profile campgrounds, look up any city where you hope to find a campground. If the city isn't listed, it means we do not profile any campgrounds there.

3. **Check the Supplemental Directory of Campgrounds**  Check for the same city in the supplemental listings.

4. **Use the Index**  If you want to see if a specific campground is profiled or listed in the guide, look up the name of the campground in the alphabetical index at the back of the book.

When looking up campgrounds, remember that the best campgrounds are found in the profiled section; always check there first before turning to the Supplemental Directory of Campgrounds.

# Understanding the Profiles

Each profile has seven important sections:

**Campground Name, Address, and Contact Information** In addition to the street address, we also provide phone and fax numbers as well as website and email addresses.

**Ratings** Using the familiar one- to five-star rating with five stars being best, we offer one overall rating for RV campers and a second overall rating for tent campers. The overall rating for each type of camper is based on a rough weighted average of the following eight individually rated categories:

| Category | Weight |
| --- | --- |
| Beauty | 15% |
| Site Privacy | 10% |
| Site Spaciousness | 10% |
| Quiet | 15% |
| Security | 13% |
| Cleanliness/upkeep | 13% |
| Insect Control | 10% |
| Facilities | 14% |

*Beauty* This rates the natural setting of the campground in terms of its visual appeal. The highest ratings are reserved for campgrounds where the beauty of the campground can be enjoyed and appreciated both at individual campsites and at the campground's public areas. Views, vistas, landscaping, and foliage are likewise taken into consideration.

*Site Privacy* This category rates the extent to which the campsites are set apart and/or in some way buffered (usually by trees and shrubs) from adjacent or nearby campsites. The farther campsites are from one another the better. This rating also reflects how busy the access road to the campsites is in terms of traffic. Campgrounds that arrange their sites on a number of cul-de-sacs, for example, will offer quieter sites than a campground where the sites are situated off of a busy loop or along a heavily traveled access road.

*Site Spaciousness* This rates the size of the campsite. Generally, the larger the better.

*Quiet* This rating indicates the relative quietness of the campground. There are three key considerations. The first is where the campground is located. Campgrounds situated along busy highways or in cities or towns are usually noisier, for example, than rural or wilderness campgrounds removed from major thoroughfares. The second consideration relates to how noise is managed at the campground. Does the campground forbid playing of radios or enforce a "quiet time" after a certain hour? Is there someone on site at night to respond to complaints about other campers being loud or unruly at a late hour? Finally, the rating considers the extent to which trees, shrubs, and the natural topography serve to muffle noise within the campground.

*Security* This rating reflects the extent (if any) to which management monitors the campground during the day and night. Physical security is also included in this rating: Is the campground fenced? Is the campground gated? If so, is the gate manned? Generally, a campground located in a city or along a busy road is more exposed to thieves or vandals than a more remote campground, and should more actively supervise access.

*Cleanliness*    This rates the cleanliness, serviceability, and state of repair of the campground, including grounds, sites, and facilities.

*Insect Control*    This rating addresses questions regarding insect and pest control. Does management spray or take other steps to control the presence of mosquitoes and other insect pests? Does the campground drain efficiently following a rain? Are garbage and sewage properly collected and disposed of?

*Facilities*    This rates the overall variety and quality of facilities to include bath house/toilets, swimming pool, retail shops, docks, pavilions, playgrounds, etc. If the quality of respective facilities vary considerably within a given campground, inconsistencies are explained in the prose description of the campground.

**Campground Description** This is an informative, consumer-oriented description of the campground. It includes what makes the campground special or unique and what differentiates it from other area campgrounds. The description may additionally include the following:

- The general layout of the campground.

- Where the campground is located relative to an easily referenced city or highway.

- The general setting (wilderness, rural, or urban).

- Description of the campsites including most and least desirable sites.

- Prevailing weather considerations and best time to visit.

- Mention of any unusual, exceptional, or deficient facilities.

- Security considerations, if any (gates that are locked at night, accessibility of campground to non-campers, etc.).

**Basics**    Key information about the campground including:

- *Operated By* Who owns and/or operates the campground.

- *Open* Dates or seasons the campground is open.

- *Site Assignment* How sites are most commonly obtained (first-come, first served; reservations accepted; reservations only; assigned on check-in, etc. Deposit and refund policy.

- *Registration* Where the camper registers on arrival. Information on how and where to register after normal business hours (late arrival).

- *Fee* Cost of a standard campsite for one night for RV sites and tent sites respectively. Forms of payment accepted. Uses the following abbreviations for credit cards: V = VISA, AE = American Express, MC = MasterCard, D = Discover, CB = Carte Blanche, and DC = Diner's Club International.

- *Parking* Usual entry will be "At campsite" or "On road," though some campgrounds have a central parking lot from which tent campers must carry their gear to their campsite.

**Facilities**   This is a brief data presentation that provides information on the availability of specific facilities and services.

- *Number of RV Sites*  Any site where RVs are permitted.
- *Number of Tent-Only Sites*  Sites set aside specifically for tent camping, including pop-up tent trailers.
- *Hookups*  Possible hookups include electric, water, sewer, cable TV, phone, and Internet connection. Electrical hookups vary from campground to campground. Where electrical hookups are available, the amperage available is stated parenthetically, for example: "Hookups: Electric (20 amps), water."
- *Each Site*  List of equipment such as grill, picnic table, lantern pole, fire pit, water faucet, electrical outlet, etc., provided at each campsite.
- *Dump station, laundry, pay phone, restrooms and showers, fuel, propane, RV service, general store, vending, playground*  Are these items or services available on site? Their respective fields indicate the answer.
- *Internal Roads*  Indicates the road type (gravel, paved, dirt), and condition.
- *Market*  Location and distance of closest supermarket or large grocery store.
- *Restaurant*  Location and distance of closest restaurant.
- *Other*  Boat ramp, dining pavilion, miniature golf, tennis court, lounge, etc.
- *Activities*  Activities available at the campground or in the area.
- *Nearby Attractions*  Can be natural or manmade.
- *Additional Information*  The best sources to call for general information on area activities and attractions. Sources include local or area chambers of commerce, tourist bureaus, visitors and convention authorities, forest service, etc.

**Restrictions**   Any restrictions that apply, including:

- *Pets*  Conditions under which pets are allowed or not.
- *Fires*  Campground rules for fires and fire safety.
- *Alcoholic Beverages*  Campground rules regarding the consumption of alcoholic beverages.
- *Vehicle Maximum Length*  Length in feet of the maximum size vehicle the campground can accommodate.
- *Other*  Any other rules or restrictions, to include minimum and maximum stays; age or group size restrictions; areas off-limits to vehicular traffic; security constraints such as locking the main gate during the night; etc.

**How to Get There**   Clear and specific directions, including mileage and landmarks, for finding the campground.

## Supplemental Directory of Campgrounds

If you're looking for a campground within the territory covered in this guide and can't find a profiled campground that is close or convenient to your route, check the Supplemental Directory of Campgrounds. This directory of hundreds of additional campgrounds is organized alphabetically by state and city name. Each entry provides the campground's name, address, reservations phone, fax, website, number of sites, average fee per night, and hookups available.

To Alaska

BRITISH COLUMBIA

ALBERTA

SASKATCHEWAN

MANITOBA

Vancouver
Victoria
Seattle
Olympia
Calgary
Saskatoon
Regina
Winnipeg
Grand Forks
Fargo

WASHINGTON
Spokane
Yakima
Portland
Salem
Eugene
Medford

Lewiston
Missoula
Great Falls
Helena
Butte
Billings

MONTANA

NORTH DAKOTA
Bismarck

OREGON
IDAHO
Boise
Idaho Falls

Sheridan

Rapid City

SOUTH DAKOTA
Pierre
Sioux Falls

Eureka
Redding
Chico
Twin Falls
Pocatello

WYOMING

Casper

Sioux City

Reno
Carson City
Great Salt Lake
Salt Lake City
Provo

Laramie
Fort Collins
Cheyenne

NEBRASKA
Lincoln

Sacramento
San Francisco
San Jose
Monterey
Fresno

NEVADA

UTAH
Grand Junction
Boulder
Denver
Colorado Springs
Pueblo

COLORADO

KANSAS
Salina
Wichita

CALIFORNIA
Bakersfield
Santa Barbara
Los Angeles
Las Vegas
St. George
Colorado
Flagstaff
Santa Fe

OKLAHOMA
Oklahoma City

Palm Springs
San Diego
Mexicali
Phoenix
Tucson
Las Cruces

ARIZONA
Albuquerque
Amarillo
Lubbock

NEW MEXICO
Roswell
Abilene
Dallas

UNITED STATES
MEXICO

PACIFIC OCEAN

Hermosillo
Chihuahua
El Paso
Odessa
Del Rio
Laredo
Monterrey
Saltillo

TEXAS
Waco
Austin
San Antonio
Corpus Christi

Rio Grande

MEXICO

Missouri
CANADA
UNITED STATES

Barrow
Fort Yukon
Nome
Fairbanks
ALASKA
CANADA
Anchorage
Cordova
Juneau
Unalaska
RUSSIA
Bering Sea
PACIFIC OCEAN

0    500 mi
0    500 km

6

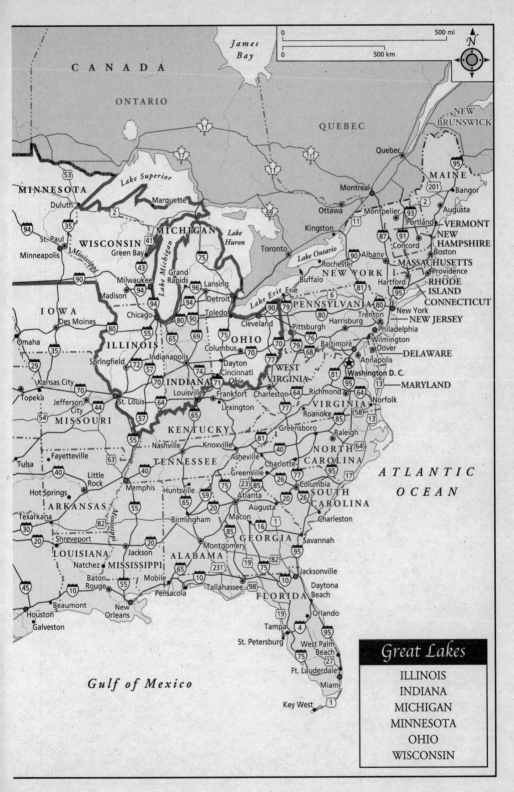

James Bay

CANADA

ONTARIO

QUEBEC

NEW BRUNSWICK

500 mi
500 km
N

Lake Superior

MINNESOTA
Duluth
Marquette

Quebec
MAINE
201
Bangor
Augusta

WISCONSIN
Green Bay
MICHIGAN
Lake Huron
69
Montreal
Ottawa
Montpelier
Portland
VERMONT
NEW HAMPSHIRE
Concord
Boston

St-Paul
Minneapolis
Madison
Milwaukee
Grand Rapids
Lansing
Detroit
Kingston
Toronto
Lake Ontario
Rochester
Albany
MASSACHUSETTS
Providence
Hartford
RHODE ISLAND
CONNECTICUT

IOWA
Des Moines
Chicago
Toledo
Lake Erie
Erie
Buffalo
NEW YORK
New York
NEW JERSEY

Omaha
ILLINOIS
Springfield
Indianapolis
Cleveland
Columbus
OHIO
Dayton
Cincinnati
PENNSYLVANIA
Pittsburgh
Harrisburg
Trenton
Philadelphia
Wilmington
Dover
DELAWARE

Kansas City
Jefferson City
St. Louis
INDIANA
Louisville
Frankfort
Charleston
WEST VIRGINIA
Baltimore
Annapolis
Washington D. C.
MARYLAND

Topeka
MISSOURI
Lexington
KENTUCKY
Nashville
Knoxville
Richmond
VIRGINIA
Roanoke
Norfolk

Tulsa
Fayetteville
TENNESSEE
Asheville
Greensboro
Raleigh
NORTH CAROLINA

Little Rock
Hot Springs
Memphis
Huntsville
Greenville
Charlotte
Columbia
SOUTH CAROLINA
ATLANTIC OCEAN

Texarkana
ARKANSAS
Birmingham
Atlanta
Augusta
Charleston

Shreveport
Jackson
Macon
GEORGIA
Savannah

LOUISIANA
Natchez
MISSISSIPPI
ALABAMA
Montgomery
Jacksonville

Baton Rouge
Mobile
Tallahassee
Daytona Beach

Beaumont
Houston
Galveston
New Orleans
Pensacola
FLORIDA
Orlando

Tampa
St. Petersburg
West Palm Beach

Gulf of Mexico
Ft. Lauderdale
Miami

Key West

**Great Lakes**

ILLINOIS
INDIANA
MICHIGAN
MINNESOTA
OHIO
WISCONSIN

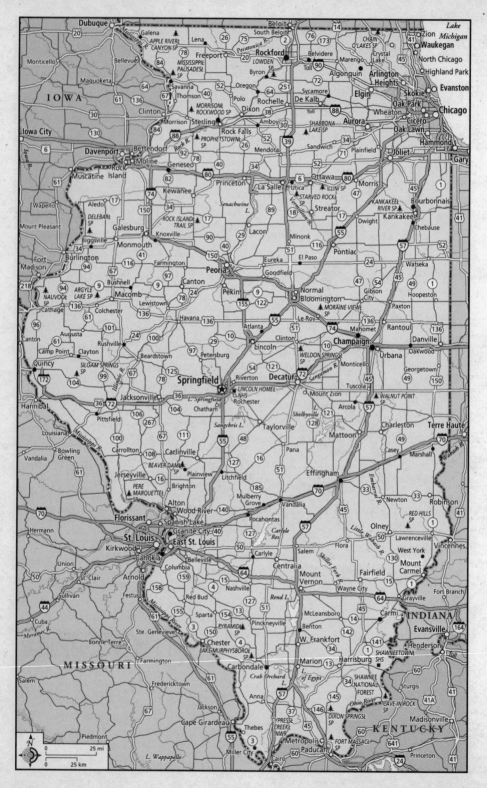

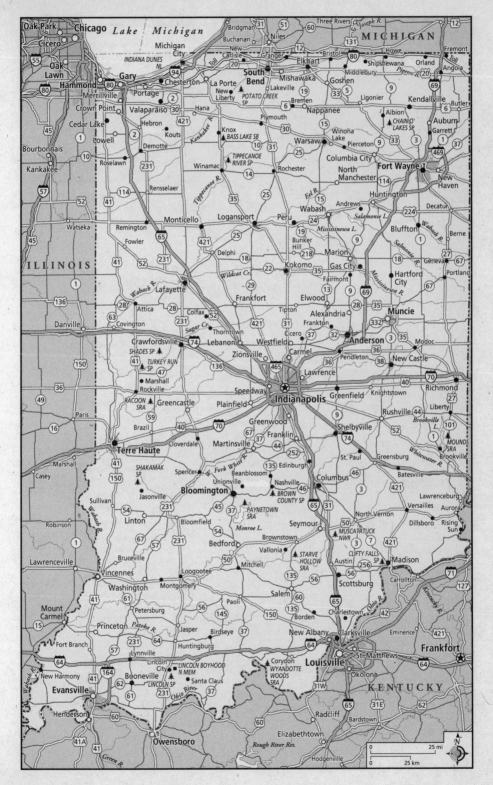

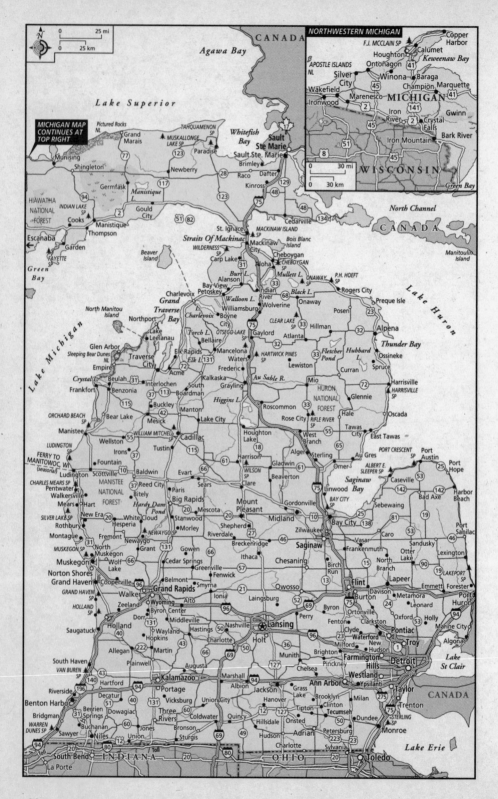

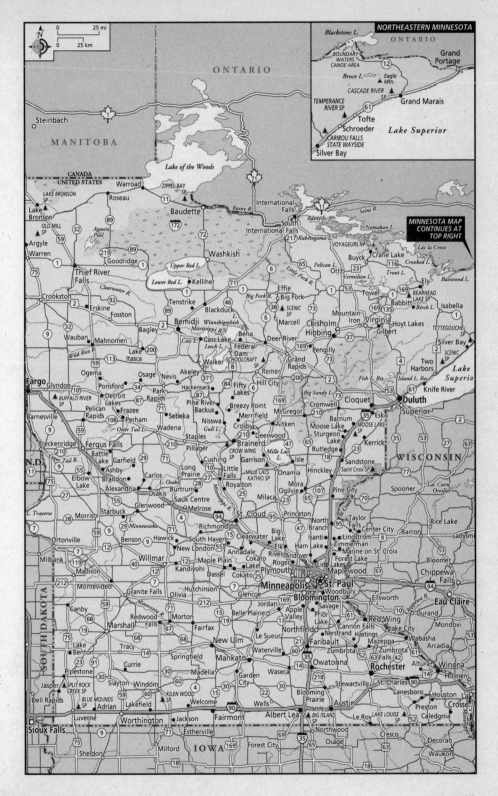

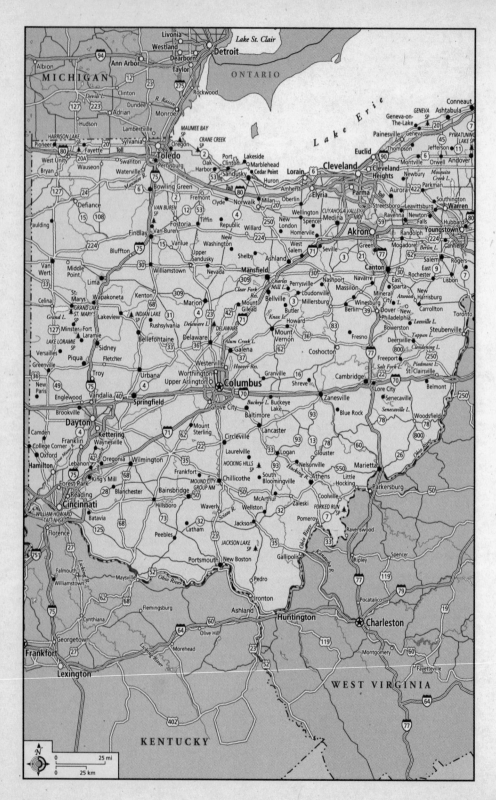

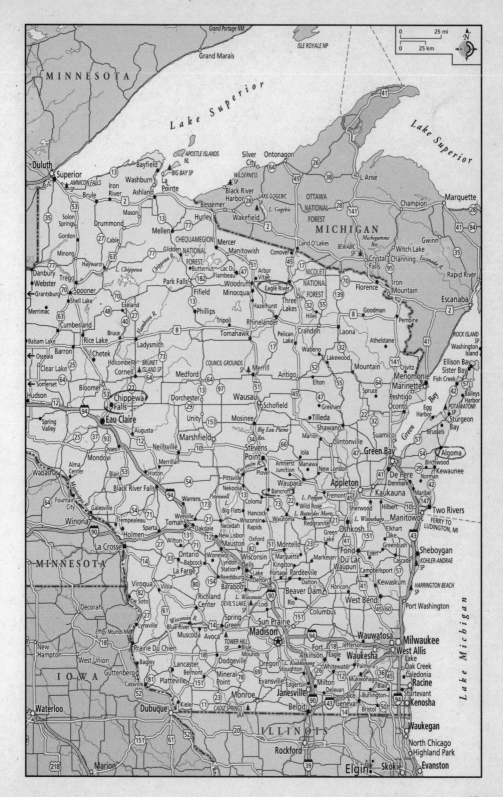

# Campground Awards

## ILLINOIS

### Best RV Camping
Casey KOA, Casey
O'Connell's Yogi Bear's Jellystone Park Camp
Resort, Amboy

### Best Tent Camping
Casey KOA, Casey
O'Connell's Yogi Bear's Jellystone Park Camp
Resort, Amboy

### Most Beautiful Campgrounds
Casey KOA, Casey
Green River Oaks Camping Resort, Amboy
Kickapoo State Park, Oakwood
Lincoln Trail State Park, Marshall
Mississippi Palisades, Savanna
Pine Lakes Camping and Fishing Resort, Pittsfield

### Most Private Campsites
Casey KOA, Casey
O'Connell's Yogi Bear's Jellystone Park Camp
Resort, Amboy

### Most Spacious Campsites
Casey KOA, Casey
O'Connell's Yogi Bear's Jellystone Park Camp
Resort, Amboy

### Quietest Campgrounds
Casey KOA, Casey
O'Connell's Yogi Bear's Jellystone Park Camp
Resort, Amboy

### Most Secure Campgrounds
O'Connell's Yogi Bear's Jellystone Park Camp
Resort, Amboy
Goodfield's Yogi Bear's Jellystone Park Camp
Resort, Goodfield

Galesburg East Best Holiday, Knoxville
Lena KOA, Lena
Rainmaker Campground, Litchfield
Cedarbrook RV & Camper Park, Mulberry Grove
Tomahawk RV Park, Pocahontas
Rock Cut State Park, Rockford

### Cleanest Campgrounds
Casey KOA, Casey
Lena KOA, Lena
Cedarbrook RV & Camper Park, Mulberry Grove
LaSalle-Peru KOA, Utica

### Best Campground Facilities
Cedarbrook RV & Camper Park, Mulberry Grove
Casey KOA, Casey

### Best Rural, Farm, or Ranch Settings
Casey KOA, Casey
Cedarbrook RV and Camper Park, Mulberry
Grove
Green River Oaks Camping Resort, Amboy

### Best Urban and Suburban Settings
Granite City KOA, Granite City
Tin Cup RV Park, Mahomet

### Best Mountain Settings
Buckskin Mountain State Park, Parker

### Best Waterfront Settings
Geneseo Campground, Geneseo
Green River Oaks Camping Resort, Amboy
Pine Lakes Camping and Fishing Resort, Pittsfield

### Most Romantic Campgrounds
Casey KOA, Casey

## ILLINOIS (continued)

### Most Romantic Campgrounds (continued)
Cedarbrook RV and Camper Park, Mulberry Grove
Green River Oaks Camping Resort, Amboy
Springfield Best Holiday Springfield

### Best Family-Oriented Campgrounds
Goodfield's Yogi Bear's Jellystone Park Camp-Resort, Goodfield
O'Connell's Yogi Bear's Jellystone Park Camp-Resort, Amboy

### Best Swimming Pools
Green River Oaks Camping Resort, Amboy
O'Connell's Yogi Bear's Jellystone Park Camp Resort, Amboy
Benton Best Holiday Trav-L Park, Benton
Casey KOA, Casey

Kankakee South KOA, Chebanse
Hickory Hills Campground, El Paso
Palace Campgrounds, Galena
Goodfield's Yogi Bear's Jellystone Park Camp Resort, Goodfield
Granite City KOA, Granite City
Galesburg East Best Holiday, Knoxville
Lena KOA, Lena
River Road Camping & Marina Inc., Oregon
Springfield Best Holiday, Springfield
Maple Aire Crow Valley Campground, Sterling
Ruffit Park, Sterling
LaSalle-Peru KOA, Utica
Okaw Valley Campground, Vandalia

## INDIANA

### Best RV Camping
South Bend East KOA Camping Resort, South Bend
Twin Mills Camping Resort, Howe
Yogi Bear's Jellystone Park Camp-Resort, Fremont
Woods-N-Waters , Columbus

### Best Tent Camping
South Bend East KOA Camping Resort, South Bend
Twin Mills Camping Resort, Howe
Yogi Bear's Jellystone Park Camp-Resort, Fremont
Woods-N-Waters , Columbus

### Most Beautiful Campgrounds
Twin Mills Camping Resort, Howe
Yogi Bear's Jellystone Park Camp-Resort, Fremont
Woods-N-Waters , Columbus

### Most Private Campsites
South Bend East KOA Camping Resort, South Bend
Twin Mills Camping Resort, Howe
Yogi Bear's Jellystone Park Camp-Resort, Fremont
Woods-N-Waters , Columbus

### Most Spacious Campsites
Woods-N-Waters , Columbus
Twin Mills Camping Resort, Howe

South Bend East KOA Camping Resort, South Bend
Yogi Bear's Jellystone Park Camp-Resort, Fremont

### Quietest Campgrounds
South Bend East KOA Camping Resort, South Bend
Twin Mills Camping Resort, Howe
Yogi Bear's Jellystone Park Camp-Resort, Fremont
Woods-N-Waters , Columbus

### Most Secure Campgrounds
Thousand Trails & NACO Indian Lakes, Batesville
Hidden Lake Campground, Fairmount
Yogi Bear's Jellystone Park Camp-Resort, Fremont
Twin Mills Camping Resort, Howe
Little Farm on the River RV Park Camping Resort, Rising Sun
South Bend East KOA Camping Resort, South Bend
Gordon's Camping, Kendallville

### Cleanest Campgrounds
Thousand Trails & NACO Indian Lakes, Batesville
Woods-N-Waters , Columbus
Yogi Bear's Jellystone Park Camp-Resort, Fremont
Little Farm on the River RV Park Camping Resort, Rising Sun
South Bend East KOA Camping Resort, South Bend

## INDIANA (continued)

### Best Campground Facilities
Yogi Bear's Jellystone Park Camp-Resort, Fremont
Woods-N-Waters, Columbus
South Bend East KOA Camping Resort, South Bend

### Best Rural, Farm, or Ranch Settings
Eby's Pines Campground, Bristol
Lake Monroe Village Recreation Resort, Bloomington
South Bend East KOA Camping Resort, South Bend
Woods-N-Waters, Columbus
Yogi Bear's Jellystone Park Camp-Resort at Barton, Lake Fremont

### Best Urban and Suburban Settings
The Last Resort RV Park & Campground, Nashville

### Best Waterfront Settings
Lakeview Campground, Rochester
Manapogo Park, Orland
Thousand Trails & NACO Indian Lakes, Batesville

### Most Romantic Campgrounds
Crawfordsville KOA, Crawfordsville
Ely's Pines Campground, Bristol
Old Mill Run Park, Thorntown
Woods-N-Waters Columbus

### Best Family-Oriented Campgrounds
Honey Bear Hollow Campground, Peru
Lake Rudolph Campground & RV Resort, Santa Claus
Manapogo Park, Orland
South Bend East KOA Camping Resort, South Bend

Twin Mills Camping Resort, Howe
Yogi Bear's Jellystone Park Camp-Resort at Barton Lake, Fremont
Yogi Bear's Jellystone Park Camp-Resort, Plymouth

### Best Swimming Pools
Thousand Trails & NACO Indian Lake, Batesville
Eby's Pines Campground, Bristol
Broadview Lake Camping Resort, Colfax
Woods-N-Waters, Columbus
Lake Holiday Yogi Bear Jellystone Park Camp-Resort, DeMotte
Miami Camp, Frankton
Yogi Bear's Jellystone Park Camp-Resort, Fremont
Mar-brook Campground, Gas City
Sports Lake Camping Resort, Gas City
Twin Mills Camping Resort, Howe
Clifty Falls State Park, Madison
The Last Resort RV Park & Campground, Nashville
Honey Bear Hollow Campground, Peru
Lake Rudolph Campground & RV Resort, Santa Claus
South Bend East KOA Camping Resort, South Bend
Old Mill Run Park, Thorntown
Versailles State Park, Versailles
Lake Monroe Village Recreation Resort, Bloomington
Crawfordsville KOA, Crawfordsville
Gordon's Camping, Kendallville
Lafayette AOK Campground, Lafayette
Yogi Bear's Jellystone Park Camp-Resort, Plymouth

## MICHIGAN

### Best RV Camping
Petoskey KOA, Petoskey
Monroe County KOA Kampground, Petersburg
Poncho's Pond, Ludington
Indian River RV Resort & Campground, Indian River
Yogi Bear's Jellystone Park Camp-Resort, Indian River
Frankenmuth Jellystone Park, Frankenmuth

Vacation Trailer Park, Benzonia
Vacation Station RV Park, Ludington

### Best Tent Camping
St. Ignace/Mackinac Island KOA, St. Ignace
Petoskey KOA, Petoskey
Monroe County KOA Kampground, Petersburg
Poncho's Pond, Ludington
Indian River RV Resort & Campground, Indian River

## MICHIGAN (continued)

**Best Tent Camping** (continued)
Yogi Bear's Jellystone Park Camp-Resort,
   Indian River
Frankenmuth Jellystone Park, Frankenmuth
Vacation Station RV Park, Ludington

**Most Beautiful Campgrounds**
Camp Cadillac, Cadillac
Castle Rock Mackinac Trail Campark, St. Ignace
Double R Ranch Camping Resort, Smyrna
Fort Trodd Family Campground. Resort Inc.,
   Port Huron
Holiday Park Campground, Traverse City
Indian River RV Resort & Campground,
   Indian River
Interstate State Park, Taylors Falls
Monroe County KOA Kampground, Petersburg
Oak Grove Resort Campgrounds, Holland
Petoskey KOA, Petoskey
Poncho's Pond, Ludington
St. Ignace/Mackinac Island KOA, St. Ignace
Vacation Station RV Park, Ludington
Yogi Bear's Jellystone Park Camp-Resort, I
   ndian River
Vacation Station RV Park, Ludington·

**Most Private Campsites**
St. Ignace/Mackinac Island KOA, St. Ignace
Fort Trodd Family Campground Resort Inc.,
   Port Huron
Petoskey KOA, Petoskey
Monroe County KOA Kampground, Petersburg
Poncho's Pond, Ludington
Indian River RV Resort & Campground,
   Indian River
Yogi Bear's Jellystone Park Camp-Resort, I
   ndian River
Oak Grove Resort Campgrounds, Holland
Frankenmuth Jellystone Park, Frankenmuth
Vacation Station RV Park, Ludington

**Most Spacious Campsites**
Fort Trodd Family Campground Resort Inc.,
   Port Huron
Frankenmuth Jellystone Park, Frankenmuth
Indian River RV Resort & Campground, Indian
   River
Monroe County KOA Kampground, Petersburg
Oak Grove Resort Campgrounds, Holland
Petoskey KOA, Petoskey
Poncho's Pond, Ludington

St. Ignace/Mackinac Island KOA, St. Ignace
Yogi Bear's Jellystone Park Camp-Resort,
   Indian River
Vacation Station RV Park, Ludington

**Quietest Campgrounds**
St. Ignace/Mackinac Island KOA, St. Ignace
Fort Trodd Family Campground Resort Inc.,
   Port Huron
Petoskey KOA, Petoskey
Monroe County KOA Kampground, Petersburg
Poncho's Pond, Ludington
Indian River RV Resort & Campground,
   Indian River
Yogi Bear's Jellystone Park Camp-Resort,
   Indian River
Oak Grove Resort Campgrounds, Holland
Frankenmuth Jellystone Park, Frankenmuth
Vacation Station RV Park, Ludington

**Most Secure Campgrounds**
Frankenmuth Jellystone Park, Frankenmuth
Yogi Bear's Jellystone Park Camp-Resort,
   Indian River
Poncho's Pond, Ludington
Harbortown RV Resort, Monroe
Petoskey KOA, Petoskey
Vacation Station RV Park, Ludington
Port Huron KOA, Port Huron

**Cleanest Campgrounds**
Frankenmuth Jellystone Park, Frankenmuth
Trails Campground, Frederic
Oak Grove Resort Campgrounds, Holland
Indian River RV Resort & Campground,
   Indian River
Poncho's Pond, Ludington
Harbortown RV Resort, Monroe
Monroe County KOA Kampground, Petersburg
Petoskey KOA, Petoskey
Fort Trodd Family Campground Resort Inc.,
   Port Huron
St. Ignace/Mackinac Island KOA, St. Ignace
Driftwood Shores Resort & RV Park, Thompson
Headwaters Camping & Cabins, Waters
Vacation Station RV Park, Ludington

**Best Campground Facilities**
Poncho's Pond
Petoskey KOA, Petoskey
Monroe County KOA Kampground, Petersburg

## MICHIGAN (continued)

Indian River RV Resort & Campground, Indian River

Harbortown RV Resort, Monroe

Frankenmuth Jellystone Park, Frankenmuth

Vacation Station RV Park, Ludington

Port Huron KOA, Port Huron

### Best Rural, Farm, or Ranch Settings

Crystal Lake Best Holiday Trav-L Park, Ludington

Higgins Hills RV Park Roscommon,

Oak Shores Resort Campground, Vicksburg

Rockey's Campground, Albion

Yogi Bear's Jellystone Park Camp-Resort, Grayling

### Best Urban and Suburban Settings

Dutch Treat Camping & Recreation, Zeeland

Frankenmuth Jellystone Park, Frankenmuth

Jerry's Campground, Montague

Lakeside Camp Park, Cedar Springs

Oak Grove Resort Campgrounds, Holland

Palace Campgrounds, Galena

### Best Waterfront Settings

Mackinaw Mill Creek Camping, Mackinaw City

River Park Campground and Trout Pond, Grayling

River Pines RV Park & Campground, Ontonagon

Tee Pee Campground, Mackinaw City

Vacation Trailer Park, Benzonia

### Most Romantic Campgrounds

Indian Lake Travel Resort, Manistique

Lake Leelanau RV Park, Lake Leelanau

Michigamme Shores Campground Resort, Champion

Poncho's Pond Ludington

Wandering Wheels Campground, Munising

### Best Family-Oriented Campgrounds

Benton Harbor/St. Joseph KOA, Benton Harbor

Monroe County KOA Campground, Petersburg

River Ridge Campground, Midland

Spaulding Lake Campground, Niles

Yogi Bear's Jellystone Park of Holly, Holly

### Best Swimming Pools

Campers Cove RV Park, Alpena

Benton Harbor/St. Joseph KOA, Benton Harbor

Vacation Trailer Park, Benzonia

Greenbriar Golf & Camping, Brooklyn

Camp Cadillac, Cadillac

Oak Shores Campground, Decatur

Hungry Horse Campground, Dorr

Snow Lake Kampground, Fenwick

Frankenmuth Jellystone Park, Frankenmuth

Gaylord Michaywe Wilderness Resort, Gaylord

Yogi Bear's Jellystone Park Camp-Resort, Grayling

Countryside Campground, Harrison

Whispering Waters Campground & Canoe Livery, Hastings

Oak Grove Resort Campgrounds, Holland

Yogi Bear's Jellystone Park Camp-Resort, Holly

Houghton Lake Travel Park, Houghton Lake

Sandyoak RV Park, Houghton Lake

Wooded Acres Family Campground, Houghton Lake

Indian River RV Resort & Campground, Indian River

Yogi Bear's Jellystone Park Camp-Resort, Indian River

Poncho's Pond, Ludington

Mackinaw Mill Creek Camping, Mackinaw City

Hide-A-Way Campground, Mears

Sandy Shores Campground & Resort, Mears

Silver Lake Yogi Bear's Jellystone Park Camp-Resort, Mears

River Ridge Campground, Midland

Valley Plaza RV Park, Midland

Harbortown RV Resort, Monroe

Shardi's Hide-Away, Mt. Pleasant

Wandering Wheels Campground, Munising

Petoskey KOA, Petoskey

Double R Ranch Camping Resort, Smyrna

St. Ignace/Mackinac Island KOA, St. Ignace

Timber Ridge Campground, Traverse City

Traverse City South KOA, Traverse City

Oak Shores Resort Campground, Vicksburg

Dutch Treat Camping & Recreation, Zeeland

Leisure Valley Campground, Decatur

Vacation Station RV Park, Ludington

Port Huron KOA, Port Huron

## MINNESOTA

### Best RV Camping
St. Cloud Campground and RV Park, St. Cloud
El Rancho Manana , Richmond
Lakeshore RV Park & Fruit Farm, Ortonville
Stony Point Resort Campground and RV Park,
Cass Lake

### Best Tent Camping
Interstate State Park, Taylors Falls
Timberline Campground, Sturgeon Lake
St. Cloud Campground and RV Park, St. Cloud
El Rancho Manana , Richmond
Lakeshore RV Park & Fruit Farm, Ortonville

### Most Beautiful Campgrounds
Eagle Cliff Campground and Lodging Inc.,
Lanesboro
El Rancho Manana , Richmond
Interstate State Park, Taylors Falls
Itaska State Park Lake, Itaska
Lakeshore RV Park & Fruit Farm, Ortonville
Silver Rapids Lodge, Ely
St. Cloud Campground and RV Park, St. Cloud
St. Croix State Park, Hinckley
Sullivan's Resort and Campground, Brainerd
Timberline Campground, Sturgeon Lake

### Most Private Campsites
Timberline Campground, Sturgeon Lake
St. Cloud Campground and RV Park, St. Cloud
El Rancho Manana , Richmond
Lakeshore RV Park & Fruit Farm, Ortonville

### Most Spacious Campsites
El Rancho Manana , Richmond
Lakeshore RV Park & Fruit Farm, Ortonville
St. Cloud Campground and RV Park, St. Cloud
Timberline Campground, Sturgeon Lake
Vagabond Village, Park Rapids

### Quietest Campgrounds
Timberline Campground, Sturgeon Lake
St. Cloud Campground and RV Park, St. Cloud
El Rancho Manana , Richmond
Lakeshore RV Park & Fruit Farm, Ortonville

### Most Secure Campgrounds
Grand Casino Hinckley RV Resort, Hinckley
Fletcher Creek Campground, Little Falls
El Rancho Manana , Richmond
Silver Lake RV Park, Rochester
St. Cloud Campground and RV Park, St. Cloud

### Cleanest Campgrounds
Grand Casino Hinckley RV Resort, Hinckley
Eagle Cliff Campground and Lodging Inc.,
Lanesboro
Lakeshore RV Park & Fruit Farm, Ortonville
Rochester KOA, Rochester
Silver Lake RV Park, Rochester
St. Cloud Campground and RV Park, St. Cloud
Timberline Campground, Sturgeon Lake

### Best Campground Facilities
St. Cloud Campground and RV Park, St. Cloud
Lakeshore RV Park & Fruit Farm, Ortonville
Grand Casino Hinckley RV Resort, Hinckley

### Best Rural, Farm, or Ranch Settings
El Rancho Manana, Richmond
Fritz's Resort and Campground, Nisswa
Lakeshore RV Park & Fruit Farm, Ortonville
Old Barn Resort Preston,
Silver Rapids Lodge, Ely
St. Cloud Campground and RV Park, St. Cloud
Whitewater State Park, Altura

### Best Urban and Suburban Settings
Town & Country Campground, Savage

### Best Waterfront Settings
Cokato Lake Campground, Cokato Lake
Don and Mayva's Crow Wing Lake Campground,
Brainerd
Eagle Cliff Campground and Lodging Inc.,
Lanesboro
Gull Lake Campground, Bemidji
Shores of Leech Lake Campground & Marina,
Walker
Stone Point Resort Campground and RV Park,
Cass Lake
Two Rivers Park, Royalton

### Most Romantic Campgrounds
Country Campground, Detroit Lakes
Old Barn Resort, Preston
St. Croix Haven Campground, Hinckley
Stony Point Campground and RV Park, Cass Lake
Sullivan's Resort and Campground, Brainerd
Timberline Campground, Sturgeon Lake

### Best Family-Oriented Campgrounds
Bemidji KOA, Bemidji
El Rancho Manana, Richmond
Gull Lake Campground, Bemidji

## MINNESOTA (continued)

Itaska State Park, Lake Itaska
Kiester's Campground, Waseca
Lakeshore RV Park and Fruit Farm, Ortonville
Vagabond Village Park, Rapids

### Best Swimming Pools
Albert Lea-Austin KOA Kampground, Albert Lea
Hickory Hills Campground, Albert Lea
Sun Valley Resort and Campground, Alexandria
Beaver Trails Campgrounds, Austin
Bemidji KOA, Bemidji
Gull Lake Campground, Bemidji
Nodak Lodge , Bena
Don and Mayva's Crow Wing Lake Campground, Brainerd
Sullivan's Resort and Campground, Brainerd
Cloquet/Duluth KOA, Cloquet
Cokato Lake Campground, Cokato Lake
Camp Faribo, Faribault
Grand Casino Hinckley RV Resort, Hinckley
St. Croix Haven Campground, Hinckley
Money Creek Haven , Houston

South Isle Family Campground, Isle
Fletcher Creek Campground, Little Falls
Hilltop Family Campground, Ogilvie
Lakeshore RV Park & Fruit Farm, Ortonville
Vagabond Village, Park Rapids
Pokegama Lake RV Park and Golf Course, Pine City
Pipestone RV Campground, Pipestone
Old Barn Resort, Preston
Rochester KOA, Rochester
Town & Country Campground, Savage
Lazy D Campground, St. Charles
St. Cloud Campground and RV Park, St. Cloud
Timberline Campground, Sturgeon Lake
Wildwood RV Park and Campground, Taylors Falls
Pioneer Campsite, Wabasha
Moonlight Bay Resort and Campground on Leech Lake, Walker
Kiesler's Campground, Waseca
Winona KOA, Winona

## OHIO

### Best RV Camping
Indian Creek Camping Resort, Geneva-On-The Lake
Cross Creek Camping Resort, Delaware
Bear Creek Resort Ranch KOA, Canton
Dayton Tall Timbers KOA Resort, Brookville

### Best Tent Camping
Indian Creek Camping Resort, Geneva-On-The Lake
Cross Creek Camping Resort, Delaware
Bear Creek Resort Ranch KOA, Canton

### Most Beautiful Campgrounds
Alum Creek State Park Delaware
Bear Creek Resort Ranch KOA, Canton
Caesar Creek State Park Waynesville
Cross Creek Camping Resort, Delaware
Indian Creek Camping Resort, Geneva-On-The Lake
Rocky Fork State Park Hillsboro
Shawnee State Park Portsmouth

### Most Private Campsites
Indian Creek Camping Resort, Geneva-On-The Lake

Cross Creek Camping Resort, Delaware
Bear Creek Resort Ranch KOA, Canton

### Most Spacious Campsites
Bear Creek Resort Ranch KOA, Canton
Cross Creek Camping Resort, Delaware
Indian Creek Camping Resort, Geneva-On-The Lake

### Quietest Campgrounds
Indian Creek Camping Resort, Geneva-On-The Lake
Cross Creek Camping Resort, Delaware
Bear Creek Resort Ranch KOA, Canton

### Most Secure Campgrounds
Yogi Bear's Jellystone Park Camp-Resort, Aurora
Dayton Tall Timbers KOA Resort, Brookville
Indian Creek Camping Resort, Geneva-On-The Lake
Thousand Trails-Wilmington, Wilmington

### Cleanest Campgrounds
Yogi Bear's Jellystone Park Camp-Resort, Aurora
Dayton Tall Timbers KOA Resort, Brookville
Bear Creek Resort Ranch KOA, Canton

## OHIO (continued)

### Cleanest Campgrounds (continued)
Cross Creek Camping Resort, Delaware

Indian Creek Camping Resort, Geneva-On-The Lake

Thousand Trails-Wilmington, Wilmington

### Best Campground Facilities
Yogi Bear's Jellystone Park Camp-Resort, Aurora

Indian Creek Camping Resort, Geneva-On-The Lake

Dayton Tall Timbers KOA Resort, Brookville

Cross Creek Camping Resort, Delaware

Bear Creek Resort Ranch KOA, Canton

### Best Rural, Farm, or Ranch Settings
Buckeye Lake KOA, Buckeye Lake

Camp Toodik Family Campground, Cabins, & Canoe Livery, Loudonville

Cross Creek Camping Resort, Delaware

Indian Creek Camping Resort, Geneva-On-The Lake

Scenic Hills RV Park, Berlin

Spring Valley Campground, Cambridge

### Best Waterfront Settings
Alum Creek State Park Campground, Delaware

Bear Creek Resort Ranch KOA, Canton

Camp Toodik Family Campground, Cabins, & Canoe Livery, Loudonville

Deerland Resort, Jackson

East Harbor State Park, Port Clinton

### Most Romantic Campgrounds
Bear Creek Resort Ranch KOA, Canton

Carthage Gap Campground, Athens

Dayton Tall Timbers KOA Resort, Brookville

Deerland Resort, Jackson

Indian Creek Camping Resort, Geneva-On-The-Lake

Spring Valley Campground, Cambridge

### Best Family-Oriented Campgrounds
Buckeye Lake KOA Buckeye, Lake

Cross Creek Camping Resort, Delaware

Pleasant View Recreation, Van Buren

Wapakoneta/Lima KOA, Wapakoneta

Yogi Bear's Jellystone Park Camp-Resort, Aurora

### Best Swimming Pools
Yogi Bear's Jellystone Park Camp-Resort, Aurora

Dayton Tall Timbers KOA Resort, Brookville

Buckeye Lake KOA, Buckeye Lake

Butler Mohican KOA, Butler

Hillview Acres Campground, Cambridge

Spring Valley Campground, Cambridge

Bear Creek Resort Ranch KOA, Canton

Cross Creek Camping Resort, Delaware

Berkshire Lake Campground, Galena

Indian Creek Camping Resort, Geneva-On-The Lake

Yogi Bear's Jellystone Park Camp-Resort, Jackson

Camp Toodik Family Campground, Cabins & Canoe Livery, Loudonville

The Landings Family Campground, Marietta

Mt. Gilead Campground, Mt. Gilead

Maple Lakes Recreational Park, Seville

Whispering Hills Recreation Inc., Shreve

Pleasant View Recreation, Van Buren

Wapakoneta/Lima South KOA, Wapakoneta

Spring Valley Frontier Campground, Waynesville

Hidden Acres Campground, West Salem

Town & Country Camp Resort, West Salem

Thousand Trails-Wilmington, Wilmington

## WISCONSIN

### Best RV Camping
Neshonoc Lakeside Campground, West Salem

Yogi Bear's Jellystone Park Camp-Resort, Warrens

Buffalo Lake Camping Resort, Montello

Kilby Lake Campground, Montello

Hidden Valley RV Resort and Campground, Milton

Wagon Trail Campground, Ellison Bay

Frontier Wilderness Campground, Egg Harbor

Vista Royalle Campground, Bancroft

### Best Tent Camping
Neshonoc Lakeside Campground, West Salem

Yogi Bear's Jellystone Park Camp-Resort, Warrens

Kilby Lake Campground, Montello

Heaven's Up North Family Campground, Lakewood

Hixton-Alma Center KOA, Hixton

Wagon Trail Campground, Ellison Bay

Frontier Wilderness Campground, Egg Harbor

## WISCONSIN (continued)

Hickory Hills Campground, Edgerton

Vista Royalle Campground, Bancroft

### Most Beautiful Campgrounds

Frontier Wilderness Campground, Egg Harbor

Heaven's Up North Family Campground, Lakewood

Hixton-Alma Center KOA, Hixton

Kilby Lake Campground, Montello

Neshonoc Lakeside Campground, West Salem

Potawatomi State Park Daisy Field Campground Sturgeon Bay

Vista Royalle Campground, Bancroft

Wagon Trail Campground, Ellison Bay

Wyalusing State Park Bagley

Yogi Bear's Jellystone Park Camp-Resort, Warrens

### Most Private Campsites

Neshonoc Lakeside Campground, West Salem

Yogi Bear's Jellystone Park Camp-Resort, Warrens

Kilby Lake Campground, Montello

Hidden Valley RV Resort and Campground, Milton

Heaven's Up North Family Campground, Lakewood

Hixton-Alma Center KOA, Hixton

Wagon Trail Campground, Ellison Bay

Frontier Wilderness Campground, Egg Harbor

Hickory Hills Campground, Edgerton

Vista Royalle Campground, Bancroft

### Most Spacious Campsites

Frontier Wilderness Campground, Egg Harbor

Heaven's Up North Family Campground, Lakewood

Hickory Hills Campground, Edgerton

Hidden Valley RV Resort and Campground, Milton

Hixton-Alma Center KOA, Hixton

Kilby Lake Campground, Montello

Neshonoc Lakeside Campground, West Salem

Vista Royalle Campground, Bancroft

Wagon Trail Campground, Ellison Bay

Yogi Bear's Jellystone Park Camp-Resort, Warrens

### Quietest Campgrounds

Neshonoc Lakeside Campground, West Salem

Yogi Bear's Jellystone Park Camp-Resort, Warrens

Kilby Lake Campground, Montello

Hidden Valley RV Resort and Campground, Milton

Heaven's Up North Family Campground, Lakewood

Hixton-Alma Center KOA, Hixton

Wagon Trail Campground, Ellison Bay

Frontier Wilderness Campground, Egg Harbor

Hickory Hills Campground, Edgerton

Vista Royalle Campground, Bancroft

### Most Secure Campgrounds

Vista Royalle Campground, Bancroft

Hickory Hills Campground, Edgerton

Hidden Valley RV Resort and Campground, Milton

Kilby Lake Campground, Montello

Buffalo Lake Camping Resort, Montello

Yogi Bear's Jellystone Park Camp-Resort, Warrens

Neshonoc Lakeside Campground, West Salem

### Cleanest Campgrounds

Vista Royalle Campground, Bancroft

Hickory Hills Campground, Edgerton

Frontier Wilderness Campground, Egg Harbor

Wagon Trail Campground, Ellison Bay

Hixton-Alma Center KOA, Hixton

Heaven's Up North Family Campground, Lakewood

Hidden Valley RV Resort and Campground, Milton

Kilby Lake Campground, Montello

Leon Valley Campground , Sparta

Yogi Bear's Jellystone Park Camp-Resort, Warrens

Neshonoc Lakeside Campground, West Salem

### Best Campground Facilities

Yogi Bear's Jellystone Park Camp-Resort, Warrens

Wagon Trail Campground, Ellison Bay

Vista Royalle Campground, Bancroft

Neshonoc Lakeside Campground, West Salem

Kilby Lake Campground, Montello

Hidden Valley RV Resort and Campground, Milton

Hickory Hills Campground, Edgerton

Frontier Wilderness Campground, Egg Harbor

### Best Rural, Farm, or Ranch Settings

Door County Camping Retreat, Egg Harbor

Heaven's Up North Family Campground, Lakewood

Rice Lake-Haugen KOA, Rice Lake

Tunnel Trail Campground, Wilton

Vista Royalle Campground, Bancroft

### Best Urban and Suburban Settings

Buffalo Lake Camping Resort, Montello

## WISCONSIN (continued)

### Best Waterfront Settings
Kilby Lake Campground, Montello
Lake Chippewa Campground, Hayward
Lake Lenwood Beach and Campground, West Bend
O'Neil Creek Campground & RV Park, Chippewa Falls
Wilderness Campground, Montello

### Most Romantic Campgrounds
Frontier Wilderness Campground, Egg Harbor
Hixton-Alma Center KOA, Alma Center
Pine Aire Resort & Campground, Eagle River
Wagon Wheel Campground, Ellison Bay
Wyalusing State Park, Bagley

### Best Family-Oriented Campgrounds
Hickory Hills Campground, Edgerton
Hidden Valley RV Resort and Campground, Milton
Jellystone Park at Fort Atkinson, Fort Atkinson
Westward Ho Camp Resort, Fond de Lac
Yogi Bear's Jellystone Park Camp Resort, Warrens
Yogi Bear's Jellystone Park Camp-Resort, Fremont

### Best Swimming Pools
Timber Trail Campground, Algoma
Yogi Bear's Jellystone Park Camp-Resort, Bagley
Baileys Grove Travel Park and Campground, Baileys Harbor
Turtle Creek Campsite, Beloit
Parkland Village Campground, Black River Falls
Happy Acres Kampground, Bristol
Quietwoods South Camping Resort, Brussels
Yogi Bear's Jellystone Park Camp-Resort, Caledonia
Chetek River Campground, Chetek
Coloma Camperland, Coloma

Hickory Hills Campground, Edgerton
Camp-Tel Family Campground, Egg Harbor
Door County Camping Retreat, Egg Harbor
Frontier Wilderness Campground, Egg Harbor
Westward Ho Camp Resort, Fond du Lac
Jellystone Park at Fort Atkinson, Fort Atkinson
Rivers Edge Campground & Resort, Galesville
Hixton-Alma Center KOA, Hixton
Cedar Valley Campground, Kewaunee
Kewaunee Village RV Park, Kewaunee
Heaven's Up North Family Campground, Lakewood
Maple Heights Campground, Lakewood
Edgewater Acres Campground, Menomonie
Hidden Valley RV Resort and Campground, Milton
Lakeland Camping Resort, Milton
Buffalo Lake Camping Resort, Montello
Kilby Lake Campground, Montello
Wilderness Campground, Montello
Oakdale KOA, Oakdale
Osseo Camping Resort, Osseo
Rice Lake-Haugen KOA, Rice Lake
Aqualand Camp Resort, Sister Bay
Leon Valley Campground , Sparta
Quietwoods North Camping Resort, Sturgeon Bay
Yogi Bear's Jellystone Park Camp-Resort, Sturgeon Bay
Turtle Lake RV Park, Turtle Lake
Yogi Bear's Jellystone Park Camp-Resort, Warrens
Timber Trail Campground, West Bend
Neshonoc Lakeside Campground, West Salem
Tunnel Trail Campground, Wilton
Yogi Bear's Jellystone Park Camp-Resort, Fremont
Rivers Edge Campground, Stevens Point

# Illinois

The "Land of Lincoln" has a welcome blend of history and outdoor activities, along with much more to keep anyone happy. Bordered on almost all sides by water, Illinois is awash with water sports. It's also home to the grasslands that inspired poet Carl Sandburg and the mighty "Windy City" of Chicago. Sandburg's ashes are scattered under **Remembrance Rock** in his hometown of **Galesburg,** just as he requested.

Historic stops across Illinois trace the political career of Abraham Lincoln on the **Lincoln Heritage Trail.** In **Springfield, Lincoln's Tomb State Historic Site** contains the tomb of Lincoln, his wife, and three of their four children. Near Chicago, **Oak Park** showcases the **Frank Lloyd Wright Home and Studio** where the architect's love for the prairie is evident in his creations. Superman may not really exist, but his legendary home of **Metropolis** honors the man of steel with monuments to the super hero.

In **Chicago,** the **Field Museum** is home to Sue, the largest and most complete T. Rex ever found. Once the largest Mississippi River port north of St. Louis, **Galena** has a vibrant downtown and some of the finest period architecture in the Midwest. John Deere settled in the village of **Grand Detour** and developed his famed steel plow. See Deere's restored homestead and other farming memorabilia at the **John Deere Historic Site.** A huge manmade pile of earth, Monk's Mound is the remnant of a prehistoric civilization at **Cahokia Mounds State Historic Site** in **Collinsville.**

At **Starved Rock State Park** in **La Salle,** Mother Nature presents an unusual show—in the spring, water cascades from the park's many canyons; in the winter, the falls become crystal icefalls. A 55-mile trail that begins in **Elmhurst,** the **Illinois Prairie Path** is a bicyclist's dream. Near **Mount Vernon,** the 19,000-acre **Rend Lake** draws campers, swimmers, boaters, and anglers, as does the **Shawnee National Forest** that covers most of the southern tip of Illinois. **Horseshoe Lake** and **Union County Wildlife Refuge** near **Cairo** attract one of the nation's largest gatherings of geese each winter.

The twin cities of **Champaign/Urbana** are separated by a single street but united in a wealth of attractions, such as the **University of Illinois** and the **John Philip Sousa Library and Museum.** The Amish brought their way of life to **Arcola** and **Arthur** where quilts are still made by hand and baked goods tempt with homemade goodness.

## The following facilities accept payment in checks or cash only:

Benton Best Holiday Trav-L Park, Benton

Hickory Hills Campground, El Paso

Palace Campgrounds, Galena

Lake Le-Aqua-Na State Park, Lena

Rainmaker Campground, Litchfield

Lincoln Trail State Park, Marshall

Kickapoo State Park, Oakwood

River Road Camping & Marina Inc., Oregon

Tomahawk RV Park, Pocahontas

Valley View Campground, Quincy

Rock Cut State Park, Rockford

Schuy-Rush Lake & Campground, Rushville

Mississippi Palisades State Park, Savanna

Ruffit Park, Sterling

Sycamore RV Resort, Sycamore

Hickory Holler Campground, West York

# Campground Profiles

## AMBOY

### Green River Oaks Camping Resort

P.O. Box 131, Amboy 61310. T: (815) 857-2815

🚐 ★★★★          ▲ ★★★★

Beauty: ★★★★
Spaciousness: ★★★★
Security: ★★★★
Insect Control: None

Site Privacy: ★★★★
Quiet: ★★★★
Cleanliness: ★★★★
Facilities: ★★★★

A river runs through Green River Oaks, located three miles southwest of Amboy. Two creeks also meander through the campground, and giant oaks and pines help account for its beauty and its name. Two heated pools are an unusual plus, but swimming is not allowed in Arrow Lake. A schedule of events is always posted so campers can know what's going on. Arranged in a series of loops, the campground offers mostly grassy sites with an average site width of 35 feet. All sites are back-in and most are shady. More than half the sites are occupied by seasonal residents. Seasonals sites are clumped together in sections—one sizable group by each pool. The remaining RV sites are in rows by themselves. Tent sites are in a separate area with privacy and more grassy and shady surroundings.

### BASICS

**Operated by:** Mike Ciaccio. **Open:** May 1–Oct. 15. **Site Assignment:** Reservations are required w/ 1-night deposit; refunds w/ 7-day notice, plus $5 service charge. **Registration:** At campground office. **Fee:** $30 (cash, check, credit cards). **Parking:** At site.

### FACILITIES

**Number of RV Sites:** 225. **Number of Tent-Only Sites:** 10. **Hookups:** Electric (30 amps), water, sewer. **Each Site:** Picnic table. **Dump Station:** Yes. **Laundry:** Yes. **Pay Phone:** Yes. **Rest Rooms and Showers:** Yes. **Fuel:** No. **Propane:** Yes. **Internal Roads:** Paved, in good condition. **RV Service:** No. **Market:** 3 mi. northeast in Amboy. **Restaurant:** 3 mi. northeast in Amboy. **General Store:** Yes. **Vending:** Yes. **Swimming Pool:** Two. **Playground:** Yes. **Other:** Sports court, tennis courts, 18-hole mini-golf, softball field, shuffleboard, horseshoes, fishing lake, family center. **Activities:** Swimming, fishing, lumberjack breakfasts on weekends (Memorial Day through Labor Day), planned weekend activities. **Nearby Attractions:** Flea markets, Amboy Depot Museum, wood carvings at Amboy City Park East, scenic drive, bike trail. **Additional Information:** Blackhawk Waterways CVB, (800) 678-2108.

### RESTRICTIONS

**Pets:** Leash only. **Fires:** Fire pits only. **Alcoholic Beverages:** Permitted. **Vehicle Maximum Length:** 40 ft. **Other:** 2-night min. on weekends, 3-night min. on holidays, w/ all 3 nights paid at least a month in advance.

### TO GET THERE

From I-88 take the Sugar Grove Rte. 30 West Exit. Go to Rte. 52, turn south to Main St. in downtown Amboy. Turn west and go to the west end of town. Take Rockyford Rd. to the left and go 3 mi. to Sleepy Hollow Rd. and turn right into Green River Oaks. Sleepy Hollow Rd. has poor shoulders.

## AMBOY

### O'Connell's Yogi Bear's Jellystone Park Camp Resort

970 Green Wing Rd., Amboy 61310. T: (800) FOR-YOGI; F: (815) 857-2916; www.jellystoneamboy.com; reservations@mail.jellystoneamboy.com.

🚐 ★★★★                     ▲ ★★★★

Beauty: ★★★★          Site Privacy: ★★★★
Spaciousness: ★★★★     Quiet: ★★★★
Security: ★★★★★        Cleanliness: ★★★★
Insect Control: None      Facilities: ★★★★

O'Connell's Yogi Bear's Yellowstone Park Camp Resort is a destination. Folks come to visit because they know they can count on a clean, secure campground with enough recreation and programs to wear anyone out. Campers are escorted to their sites when they arrive or can opt for express check-in on Fridays for reservations paid in full in advance. A rolling, grassy campground with shaded and open sites, O'Connell's is a rural facility, five miles east of Amboy, laid out in a series of loops. The typical site width for the 275 pull-throughs is 40 feet. Tent sites are away from RVs and offer more shade and privacy. Because the campground is so large, it features multiple facilities, such as three outdoor pools, three spas, three kiddie pools, three laundromats, and five large rest room/shower combinations. Laundromats and showers are open 24 hours a day. Security is tops owing to a locked entrance gate with gate codes and regular patrols of the area. To ensure safety and quiet, the enforced speed limit is 7 mph, quiet hours are from 11 p.m. to 7 a.m., no bicycle riding is permitted after dusk, and visitor checkout time is 11 p.m.

### BASICS

**Operated by:** Jane & Daniel O'Connell. **Open:** Apr. 7–Oct. 25. **Site Assignment:** Reservations w/ 1-night deposit; refund (minus $10) or a certificate of credit for full amount of deposit w/ 14-day notice. Holiday weekends require pre-pay, 1 month in advance, & a 3-night min. stay; there is a 2-night min. for weekend camping. **Registration:** At campground office. **Fee:** $40 (cash, check, credit cards). **Parking:** At site.

### FACILITIES

**Number of RV Sites:** 635. **Number of Tent-Only Sites:** 250. **Hookups:** Electric (30, 50 amps), water, sewer. **Each Site:** Picnic table. **Dump Station:** Yes. **Laundry:** Yes. **Pay Phone:** Yes. **Rest Rooms and Showers:** Yes. **Fuel:** No. **Propane:** Yes. **Internal Roads:** Paved, in good condition. **RV Service:** Yes. **Market:** 5 mi. west in Amboy. **Restaurant:** 5 mi. west in Amboy. **General Store:** Yes. **Vending:** Yes. **Swimming Pool:** Yes. **Playground:** Yes. **Other:** Two lakes, spas, kiddie pools, mini-golf, soccer & softball fields, snack bar, ranger station, game room, pavilion, banquet center, swimming beach, horseshoes, movies, Green River, hiking trails, RV sales. **Activities:** Swimming, fishing, hiking, haywagon rides, boating (rental kayak & paddleboats available), planned daily activities, Sunday church services. **Nearby Attractions:** Flea markets, festivals, Ambody Depot Museum, wood carvings at Amboy City Park East, scenic drive, bike trail. **Additional Information:** Blackhawk Waterways CVB, (800) 678-2108.

### RESTRICTIONS

**Pets:** Leash only. **Fires:** Fire pits only. **Alcoholic Beverages:** Permitted. **Vehicle Maximum Length:** None. **Other:** Spa for 18 years & older.

### TO GET THERE

From junction Hwy. 52 and Main St., drive 1.5 mi. east on Main St., then 2.5 mi. southeast on Shaw Rd., then 1 mi. north on Green Wing Rd. Roads are wide and well maintained with good shoulders.

## BENTON

### Benton Best Holiday Trav-L Park

Rte. 1, Whittington 62897. T: (618) 439-4860

🚐 ★★★★                     ▲ ★★★

Beauty: ★★★          Site Privacy: ★★★
Spaciousness: ★★★     Quiet: ★★★★
Security: ★★★★        Cleanliness: ★★★★
Insect Control: None    Facilities: ★★★★

Tall oak trees shade Benton Best Holiday Trav-L-Park, located five miles north of Benton. Level campsites with a typical width of 25 feet and easy access from the interstate make this a popular stop for travelers. With 20 pull-throughs, the sites are mostly shaded and grassy with gravel pads for RVs. A big pavilion is a draw for camping clubs. Primitive tent camping is provided on the perimeters of the campground, where tenters have more privacy away from RVs. Quiet time from 11 p.m. to 7 a.m. is enforced, as is a 5 mph speed limit. Laid out in a series of loops, the campground has security provided by owners who live on the site and offer regular patrols. It also has 20 seasonal campers. Many campers come for the 1,900-acre Rend Lake Recreation Area nearby for fishing, boating, and swimming. Although it is open year-round, the campground offers limited facilities from Nov. through Apr. 1.

## BASICS

**Operated by:** Phil & Mary Poninski. **Open:** All year. **Site Assignment:** Reservations w/ no deposit for non-holidays; for holidays, 1-night deposit required; refund w/ 7-day notice. **Registration:** At campground office. **Fee:** $21 (cash, check). **Parking:** At site.

## FACILITIES

**Number of RV Sites:** 97. **Number of Tent-Only Sites:** 23. **Hookups:** Electric (30, 50 amps), water, sewer. **Each Site:** Picnic table, fire ring. **Dump Station:** Yes. **Laundry:** Yes. **Pay Phone:** Yes. **Rest Rooms and Showers:** Yes. **Fuel:** No. **Propane:** No. **Internal Roads:** Gravel, in good condition. **RV Service:** No. **Market:** 5 mi. south in Benton. **Restaurant:** 5 mi. south in Benton. **General Store:** Yes. **Vending:** Yes. **Swimming Pool:** Yes. **Playground:** Yes. **Other:** Game room, pavilion, basketball, horseshoes, shuffleboard, video games, sports field. **Activities:** Swimming, bingo, & hayrides on holiday weekends. **Nearby Attractions:** Rend Lake Recreation Area, tennis, golf, Benton Civic Center, marina, winery, antiques, Old Franklin County Jail, Franklin County Garage 1910s Museum. **Additional Information:** Southern Tourism Development Office, (618) 998-9397.

## RESTRICTIONS

**Pets:** Leash only. **Fires:** Fire ring only. **Alcoholic Beverages:** Permitted. **Vehicle Maximum Length:** None..

## TO GET THERE

From junction of I-57 and Hwy. 154, take Exit 77, drive 0.25 mi. east on Hwy. 154, then 0.5 mi. south on Hwy. 37. Roads are wide and well maintained with good shoulders.

## CASEY
## Casey KOA

P.O. Box 56, Casey 62420. T: (800) 554-9206; www.koa.com.

🚐 ★★★★                    ⛺ ★★★★

Beauty: ★★★★              Site Privacy: ★★★★
Spaciousness: ★★★★        Quiet: ★★★★
Security: ★★★★            Cleanliness: ★★★★★
Insect Control: None      Facilities: ★★★★

The owners of the Casey KOA wax the campground's rest room floors. That's an indication of the attention to detail shown at the campground. Arranged in a series of loops, the campground offers an average site width of 30 feet, along with 45 pull-throughs. Each site is level, has a tree, and offers a good combination of gravel for an RV and grass for the picnic table. A major plus is the short distance and easy access from the interstate. Travelling campers will find this a good place for an overnight stay—it is a popular stopping-off point for people going to Branson, which is one day away. Located three miles north of Casey, the campground also is a good place to come as a destination, because of its recreation facilities and planned activities. Owners sell RVs and offer on-site service. The best RV site is 11, because it is close to the pool, rec room, and other activities. The most popular site for tent campers is 53, because it is more private and tenters can walk to the lake.

## BASICS

**Operated by:** Gene & Patti Shanks. **Open:** Mar. 1–Oct. 31. **Site Assignment:** Reservations accepted w/ 1-night deposit, refunded for cancellations w/ 24-hour notice, or 72-hour notice for holidays. **Registration:** At campground office. **Fee:** $23 (cash, check, credit cards). **Parking:** At site.

## FACILITIES

**Number of RV Sites:** 79. **Number of Tent-Only Sites:** 2. **Hookups:** Electric (20, 30, 50 amps), water, sewer. **Each Site:** Picnic table, fire ring. **Dump Station:** Yes. **Laundry:** Yes. **Pay Phone:** Yes. **Rest Rooms and Showers:** Yes. **Fuel:** No. **Propane:** Yes. **Internal Roads:** Gravel, in good condition. **RV Service:** Yes. **Market:** 3 mi. south in Casey. **Restaurant:** 3 mi. south in Casey. **General Store:** Yes. **Vending:** Yes. **Swimming Pool:** Yes. **Playground:** Yes. **Other:** Game room, stocked fishing lake, horseshoes, basketball, volley-ball. **Activities:** Fishing, boating (rental rowboats & paddleboats available), Sunday pancake breakfast, weekly planned activities. **Nearby Attractions:** Amish country, Lincoln log cabin, antique malls, golf course, outlet shopping. **Additional Information:** Arthur Information Center, (800) 722-6474.

### RESTRICTIONS

**Pets:** Leash only. **Fires:** Fire ring only. **Alcoholic Beverages:** Permitted. **Vehicle Maximum Length:** None.

### TO GET THERE

From I-70 and Hwy. 49 junction, take Exit 129, drive 0.25 mi. north on Hwy. 49, then 0.25 mi. west on CO 1250 N. Roads are wide and well maintained; all except the county road have broad shoulders.

## CHEBANSE
### Kankakee South KOA

425 East 6000 South Rd., Chebanse 60922. T: (815) 939-4603; www.koa.com.

🚐 ★★★                    ▲ ★★★

Beauty: ★★★              Site Privacy: ★★★
Spaciousness: ★★★        Quiet: ★★★★
Security: ★★★            Cleanliness: ★★★
Insect Control: None      Facilities: ★★★

KOA Kankakee South offers the best of both worlds—ease of access to the interstate, yet a quiet location off the main highway. Six miles south of Kankakee, the campground is shielded from road noise by a row of oak trees and bushes. Farm fields ring the campground. Quiet hours are enforced from 11 p.m. to 7 a.m. The speed limit is a strict 4 mph. Laid out in a series of loops, the campground has gravel, shaded RV sites. The typical site width is 30 feet and 90 percent of the sites offer pull-through access. Only an hour from Chicago, the campground attracts many Chicagoans looking for some country peace. The best RV sites are in row 40, because these offer concrete pads and sewer hookups. Tent sites are located in a back area, where they have more privacy, greenery, and quiet. Security is good, with an owner who lives on the site and offers regular campground patrols.

### BASICS

**Operated by:** Sam Kwak. **Open:** Apr. 1–Oct. 31. **Site Assignment:** Reservations w/ 1-night

deposit; refund w/ 24-hour notice. **Registration:** At campground office. **Fee:** $15 (cash, credit cards). **Parking:** At site.

### FACILITIES

**Number of RV Sites:** 59. **Number of Tent-Only Sites:** 22. **Hookups:** Electric (30 amps), water, sewer. **Each Site:** Picnic table, fire ring. **Dump Station:** Yes. **Laundry:** Yes. **Pay Phone:** Yes. **Rest Rooms and Showers:** Yes. **Fuel:** No. **Propane:** Yes. **Internal Roads:** Gravel, in good condition. **RV Service:** No. **Market:** 6 mi. north in Kankakee. **Restaurant:** 6 mi. north in Kankakee. **General Store:** Yes. **Vending:** No. **Swimming Pool:** Yes. **Playground:** Yes. **Other:** Pool table, basketball court, volleyball, sports field, video games, picnic shelter. **Activities:** Swimming. **Nearby Attractions:** Golf, canoe trips, Friday night stock-car races, scenic drive, antique mall, skydiving, Model Railroad Museum. **Additional Information:** Kankakee County CVB, (900) 74-RIVER.

### RESTRICTIONS

**Pets:** Leash only. **Fires:** Fire ring only. **Alcoholic Beverages:** At sites only. **Vehicle Maximum Length:** 40 ft.

### TO GET THERE

Take Exit 308 off I-57 onto US 45/32. Drive 3 mi. south on US 45/52, then 0.5 mi. east on Rd. 6000 to Kankakee South KOA. Roads wide and well maintained with decent shoulders.

## EFFINGHAM
### Camp Lakewood

1217 West Rickelman Ave., Effingham 62401. T: (217) 342-6233

🚐 ★★★                    ▲ ★★★

Beauty: ★★★              Site Privacy: ★★★★
Spaciousness: ★★★★       Quiet: ★★★★
Security: ★★★★           Cleanliness: ★★★★
Insect Control: None      Facilities: ★★★

Camp Lakewood has many good things going for it, but it doesn't offer swimming. For campers who expect that as a normal part of their camping recreation, it may be hard to do without. Located on the north shores of Lake Pauline, one mile north of Effingham, the campground has 45 pull-throughs and the typical site width is 25 feet. Sites are generally gravel and shady. Camp Lakewood is conveniently located near the interstate and city restaurants, shopping, and movies. Security is good, with owners who live on the grounds, providing regular patrols, and city police nearby who keep an eye on the property. Campers are given a good first impression when escorted to their sites instead of just being handed a map with a red line indicating where to go. Tent sites are set off in a more primitive area. The price also is right; very economical for such a clean campground in a good location. But for some campers all the positive aspects might not balance out that one missing element—swimming.

## BASICS

**Operated by:** Deb & Gary Gregory. **Open:** All year. **Site Assignment:** Reservations w/ no deposit. **Registration:** At campground office. **Fee:** $18.50 (cash, check, credit cards). **Parking:** At site.

## FACILITIES

**Number of RV Sites:** 65. **Number of Tent-Only Sites:** 10. **Hookups:** Electric (30, 50 amps), water, sewer, cable TV. **Each Site:** Picnic table, fire ring. **Dump Station:** Yes. **Laundry:** Yes. **Pay Phone:** Yes. **Rest Rooms and Showers:** Yes. **Fuel:** No. **Propane:** No. **Internal Roads:** Gravel, in good condition. **RV Service:** No. **Market:** 1 mi. south in Effingham. **Restaurant:** 1 mi. south in Effingham. **General Store:** Yes. **Vending:** No. **Swimming Pool:** No. **Playground:** Yes. **Other:** Boat ramp, game room, fishing dock, horseshoes. **Activities:** Fishing, boating (rental rowboats available). **Nearby Attractions:** Golf, mini-golf, movie theater, outlet mall, marina, art galleries, restaurants. **Additional Information:** Effingham CVB, (800) 772-0750.

## RESTRICTIONS

**Pets:** Leash only. **Fires:** Fire ring only. **Alcoholic Beverages:** At sites only. **Vehicle Maximum Length:** None.

## TO GET THERE

From I-57 and I-70, take Effingham Exit 160. Turn north on Rte. 33/32. Go about 0.25 mi. to Ford Ave. and turn right. Follow signs 1 mi. to Camp Lakewood Campground. Roads are wide and well maintained, with broad shoulders.

# EL PASO

## Hickory Hills Campground

RR 1 Box 157, Secor 61771. T: (888) 801-4469; F: (309) 744-2407; www.hickoryh@elpaso.net.

 ★★★           ★★★

| | |
|---|---|
| Beauty: ★★★ | Site Privacy: ★★★ |
| Spaciousness: ★★★ | Quiet: ★★★★ |
| Security: ★★★★ | Cleanliness: ★★★★ |
| Insect Control: None | Facilities: ★★★ |

Hickory Hills Campground is what it sounds like—a grassy rural facility with a lot of trees. The typical site width is 25 feet and the campground has ten pull-throughs. About half of the sites are occupied by seasonal campers. Located four miles west of El Paso, the campground is level with a mix of grassy and gravel sites, along with shady or open ones. Many campers are repeats who come for the family atmosphere and recreation. Safety measures are enforced, including a 5 mph speed limit. Anyone driving a golf cart must be licensed and all golf carts must be insured if they are driven on the road. Quiet time is 10 p.m. to 8 a.m. on weekdays and midnight to 8 a.m. on weekends. The campground has one entrance road and owners who live on site providing a regular patrol of the campgrounds.

## BASICS

**Operated by:** Bryan & Ficki Outinen. **Open:** Apr. 1–Nov. 1. **Site Assignment:** Reservations w/ no deposit; holiday weekends require 1-night deposit. **Registration:** At campground office. **Fee:** $22 (cash, check). **Parking:** At site.

## FACILITIES

**Number of RV Sites:** 179. **Number of Tent-Only Sites:** 110. **Hookups:** Electric (20, 30 amps), water, sewer. **Each Site:** Picnic table, fire ring. **Dump Station:** Yes. **Laundry:** Yes. **Pay Phone:** Yes. **Rest Rooms and Showers:** Yes. **Fuel:** No. **Propane:** Yes. **Internal Roads:** Gravel, in good condition. **RV Service:** No. **Market:** 4 mi. east in El Paso. **Restaurant:** 4 mi. east in El Paso. **General Store:** Yes. **Vending:** Yes. **Swimming Pool:** Yes. **Playground:** Yes. **Other:** Mini-golf, rec hall, video games, horseshoes, volleyball, basketball, fishing stream, hiking trails, sports field. **Activities:** Swimming, fishing, hiking, planned weekend activities. **Nearby Attractions:** Nature center, zoo, museum, casino, antique shops, art galleries, botanical garden, golf. **Additional Information:** Peoria Area CVB, (800) 747-0302.

## RESTRICTIONS

**Pets:** Leash only. **Fires:** Fire ring only. **Alcoholic Beverages:** Permitted. **Vehicle Maximum Length:** None.

## TO GET THERE

From junction of I-39 and US 24, take Exit 14, drive 4 mi. west on US 24, then 0.25 mi. south on a county road. Roads are wide and well maintained with adequate shoulders.

## GALENA

### Palace Campgrounds

11357 Rte. 20 West, Galena 61036. T: (815) 777-2466; F: (815) 777-3739; www.palacecampground.com; palace@galenalink.net.

🚐 ★★★★    ▲ ★★★★

| | |
|---|---|
| Beauty: ★★★★ | Site Privacy: ★★★★ |
| Spaciousness: ★★★★ | Quiet: ★★★ |
| Security: ★★★★ | Cleanliness: ★★★★ |
| Insect Control: None | Facilities: ★★★★ |

Palace Campgrounds is a rural campground that is rapidly becoming an urban campground as the city of Galena, grows out to meet it. That means the campground is surrounded by city amenities such as restaurants and gas stations. A restaurant and hotel/motel is located next door. Bordered by farm fields in the back, the campground features rolling hills, woods, and a tree-lined road. The typical site width is 28 feet with eight pull-throughs. Laid out in a series of loops, the campground has gravel sites for RVs and grassy ones for tents. Some RV sites are open, others shady. Free fishing is available at the four-acre pond. Tent sites are off by themselves, away from RVs in a more secluded, natural area. The campground is fenced with one major entrance/exit road. and speed bumps on interior roads help keep traffic speeds down.

### BASICS

**Operated by:** Teenie McCarthy. **Open:** Apr. 1–Oct. 31. **Site Assignment:** Reservations w/ $10 deposit, 1-night deposit required on holidays; refund w/ 10-day notice. **Registration:** At campground office. **Fee:** $23 (cash, check). **Parking:** At site.

### FACILITIES

**Number of RV Sites:** 133. **Number of Tent-Only Sites:** 100. **Hookups:** Electric (30, 50 amps), water, sewer. **Each Site:** Picnic table, fire ring. **Dump Station:** Yes. **Laundry:** Yes. **Pay Phone:** Yes. **Rest Rooms and Showers:** Yes. **Fuel:** No. **Propane:** No. **Internal Roads:** Gravel, in good condition. **RV Service:** No. **Market:** 1 mi. east in

Galena. **Restaurant:** Next door. **General Store:** No. **Vending:** Yes. **Swimming Pool:** Yes. **Playground:** Yes. **Other:** Basketball, snack bar, arcade, mini-golf, rec hall, pool table, outdoor movies, wading pool, fishing pond, sports field, horseshoes. **Activities:** Swimming, fishing, Saturday night hayrides, planned weekend activities. **Nearby Attractions:** Historic Galena, go-cart track, golf, riverboat casino, antique shops, fishing, flea markets, trail rides, cave tours, mountain resort, Alpine slide & chair lift rides. **Additional Information:** Galena/Jo Davies County CVB, (800) 747-9377.

### RESTRICTIONS

**Pets:** Leash only. **Fires:** Fire ring only. **Alcoholic Beverages:** Permitted. **Vehicle Maximum Length:** 40 ft. **Other:** Must be at least 21 to reserve a site.

### TO GET THERE

From the west edge of Galena, drive 1 mi. west on US 20. US 20 has no shoulders and a steep hill coming out of Galena.

## GENESEO

### Geneseo Campground

22978 Illinois Hwy. 82, Geneseo 61254. T: (309) 944-6465; F: (309) 944-8879; www.fulltiming-america.com/geneseo; w6465@geneseo.net.

🚐 ★★★★    ▲ ★★★

| | |
|---|---|
| Beauty: ★★★★ | Site Privacy: ★★★ |
| Spaciousness: ★★★ | Quiet: ★★★★ |
| Security: ★★★★ | Cleanliness: ★★★★ |
| Insect Control: None | Facilities: ★★★★ |

A rural campground adjacent to the historic Hennepin Canal, Geneseo Campground offers grassy, mostly shaded sites. The campground has 25 pull-through sites and a typical site width of 24 feet. Rustic cabins with air conditioning are a popular plus. Along with being a quiet spot, the biggest thing Geneseo Campground has going for it is its location adjacent to the Hennepin Canal. Listed in the National Register of Historic Places, the canal joins the Mississippi and Illinois Rivers. There are 32 of the original 33 locks still visible on the canal. Located within walking distance of the campground is one of the five locks restored to working condition and one of the six remaining aqueducts that carry the Hennepin across larger rivers and streams. You can rent a canoe or kayak for a Hennepin Canal trip that begins and ends at the campground. Fully watered, the canal also is a good fishing spot.

## BASICS

**Operated by:** Craig & Shari Weber. **Open:** Apr. 1–Oct. 31. **Site Assignment:** Reservations w/ 1-night deposit; refund w/ 7-day notice. **Registration:** At campground office. **Fee:** $16 (cash, check, credit cards). **Parking:** At site.

## FACILITIES

**Number of RV Sites:** 63. **Number of Tent-Only Sites:** 0. **Hookups:** Electric (20, 30, 50 amps), water, sewer, phone. **Each Site:** Picnic table, fire ring. **Dump Station:** Yes. **Laundry:** Yes. **Pay Phone:** Yes. **Rest Rooms and Showers:** Yes. **Fuel:** No. **Propane:** Yes. **Internal Roads:** Gravel, in good condition. **RV Service:** No. **Market:** 2 mi. south in Geneseo. **Restaurant:** 2 mi. south in Geneseo. **General Store:** Yes, limited. **Vending:** No. **Swimming Pool:** No. **Playground:** Yes. **Other:** Sports field, horseshoes, rental cabins, rec room, fishing stream, badminton, hiking trails, volleyball. **Activities:** Fishing, canoeing & kayaking (rental canoes & kayaks available), hiking. **Nearby Attractions:** Victorian architecture, antiques, arts & crafts, golf, Grand Illinois Trail, Hennepin Canal, Bishop Hill, John Deere Museum, Rock Island Arsenal, riverboat cruises, casinos, Niabi Zoo, Wacky Waters, Geneseo Historical Museum, community swimming pool. **Additional Information:** Henry County Tourism Council, (309) 937-1255.

## RESTRICTIONS

**Pets:** Leash only. **Fires:** Fire ring only. **Alcoholic Beverages:** Permitted. **Vehicle Maximum Length:** None.

## TO GET THERE

From junction of I-80 and Hwy. 82, take Exit 19 and drive 1.25 mi. north on Hwy. 82. Follow blue camping signs through town, pick up Hwy. 82 again and drive 2 mi. north. Roads are wide and well maintained with some narrow shoulders.

## GOODFIELD

### Goodfield's Yogi Bear's Jellystone Park Camp Resort

P.O. Box 92, Goodfield 61742. T: (800) 558-2954, ext. 116; F: (309) 965-2156; www.campjellystone.com.

 ★★★★           ★★★★

Beauty: ★★★          Site Privacy: ★★★★
Spaciousness: ★★★★          Quiet: ★★★★
Security: ★★★★★          Cleanliness: ★★★★
Insect Control: Yes          Facilities: ★★★★

Located 20 miles northwest of Bloomington, Goodfield's Yogi Bear's Jellystone Park Resort offers open and shaded grassy sites on a rolling terrain. Arranged in a series of loops, the rural campground has a typical site width of 30 feet with 20 pull-throughs. The campground offers separate sections for about 100 seasonal campers. Primitive areas for tent campers are scattered around the perimeter of the campground offering more privacy and natural beauty. Most popular tent sites are by the lake and by the ravine. Best RV sites are 113–122 because they are pull-throughs with small trees for shade. Safety measures include a speed limit of 5 mph that is strictly enforced, no bike riding after dark, and some restrictions for children. Quiet hours are between 10:30 p.m. and 8 a.m., visitors must leave by 10 p.m., and no generators are allowed in the campground. The owners live on site and a guard helps control access and makes regular patrols of the campgrounds.

## BASICS

**Operated by:** Bruce & Kathy Watkins. **Open:** All year. **Site Assignment:** Reservations w/ 1-night deposit; refunds (minus $5) w/ 7-day notice. **Registration:** At campground office. **Fee:** $26 (cash, check, credit cards). **Parking:** At site.

## FACILITIES

**Number of RV Sites:** 387. **Number of Tent-Only Sites:** 200. **Hookups:** Electric (30, 50 amps), water, sewer. **Each Site:** Some picnic tables, fire sites. **Dump Station:** Yes. **Laundry:** Yes. **Pay Phone:** Yes. **Rest Rooms and Showers:** Yes. **Fuel:** No. **Propane:** Yes. **Internal Roads:** Gravel, in fair condition. **RV Service:** No. **Market:** 7 mi. north in Eureka. **Restaurant:** 3 mi. south in Goodfield. **General Store:** Yes. **Vending:** Yes. **Swimming Pool:** Yes. **Playground:** Yes. **Other:** Stocked fishing lake, mini-golf, bocci ball court, volleyball, horseshoes, softball, rec hall, chapel, clubhouse, hiking trails, boat dock. **Activities:** Swimming, fishing, hiking, boating (rental paddleboats, rowboats available) planned weekend activities. **Nearby Attractions:** Horse racing track, historic sites, museums, art galleries, antique shops, zoo, casino, golf, Prairie Aviation Museum, dinner theater, Factory Outlet

Mall. **Additional Information:** Bloomington-Normal Area CVB, (800) 433-8226.

## RESTRICTIONS

**Pets:** Leash only. **Fires:** Fire pits only. **Alcoholic Beverages:** At sites only. **Vehicle Maximum Length:** 65 ft. **Other:** 3-day min. stay on holidays.

## TO GET THERE

From junction of I-74 and Hwy. 117, take Exit 112 and drive 1 mi. north on Hwy. 117, then 0.75 mi. east on Timberline Rd. Roads are wide and well maintained with broad shoulders.

## GRANITE CITY

### Granite City KOA

3157 West Chain of Rocks Rd., Granite City 62040. T: (618) 931-5160; www.koa.com.

🚐 ★★★★　　　　Ａ ★★★

| | |
|---|---|
| Beauty: ★★★ | Site Privacy: ★★★ |
| Spaciousness: ★★★ | Quiet: ★★★★ |
| Security: ★★★★ | Cleanliness: ★★★★ |
| Insect Control: None | Facilities: ★★★★ |

It's sort of a trade-off. At Granite City KOA, you are 11 miles north of downtown St. Louis on historic Rte. 66. It's an easy place to use as a base for all the wonderful St. Louis area attractions. But, since it is in the city limits, you cannot have a campfire at Granite City KOA. You can use a grill for cooking but no open fires are permitted in the city limits. Granite City KOA does have a lot of other amenities going for it, though. A rural/urban campground laid out in a series of loops, Granite City KOA offers mostly wooded, grassy, or gravel, level sites. There are few open sites available. The typical site width is 35 feet and there are 70 pull-throughs. A secluded area set aside for tents is shaded with big elm and maple trees, offering privacy. There are no scheduled activities. With all St. Louis has to offer, most campers don't seem to mind.

## BASICS

**Operated by:** Cuvar Family. **Open:** Mar. 15–Nov. 1. **Site Assignment:** Reservations accepted w/ 1-night deposit of $10 on credit card by mail; refund w/ 24-hour notice. **Registration:** At campground office. **Fee:** $23 (cash, credit cards). **Parking:** At site.

## FACILITIES

**Number of RV Sites:** 80. **Number of Tent-Only Sites:** 50. **Hookups:** Electric (20, 30, 50 amps), water, sewer. **Each Site:** Picnic table. **Dump Station:** Yes. **Laundry:** Yes. **Pay Phone:** Yes. **Rest Rooms and Showers:** Yes. **Fuel:** No. **Propane:** Yes. **Internal Roads:** Paved/gravel, in good condition. **RV Service:** No. **Market:** 3 mi. south in Granite City. **Restaurant:** 3 mi. south in Granite City. **General Store:** Yes. **Vending:** No. **Swimming Pool:** Yes. **Playground:** Yes. **Other:** Basketball, horseshoes, game room, rental cabins, recreation field, pavilion, badminton. **Activities:** Swimming. **Nearby Attractions:** St. Louis Arch, raceway, bike trails, historic sites, museums, zoo, riverboat gambling, Six Flags, Busch Stadium, Laclede's Landing. **Additional Information:** St. Louis Convention & Visitors Commission, (800) 916-0040.

## RESTRICTIONS

**Pets:** Leash only. **Fires:** None. **Alcoholic Beverages:** Permitted. **Vehicle Maximum Length:** None.

## TO GET THERE

From junction I-270 and Hwy. 3, take Exit 3A, drive 0.25 mi. south on Hwy. 3, then 0.5 mi. east on Chain of Rocks Rd. Roads are wide and well maintained with broad shoulders.

## KNOXVILLE

### Galesburg East Best Holiday

1081 US Hwy. 150 East, Knoxville 61448. T: (309) 289-CAMP; F: (309) 289-0079; .

🚐 ★★★★　　　　Ａ ★★★

| | |
|---|---|
| Beauty: ★★★ | Site Privacy: ★★★ |
| Spaciousness: ★★★ | Quiet: ★★★★ |
| Security: ★★★★★ | Cleanliness: ★★★★ |
| Insect Control: None | Facilities: ★★★★ |

Located in a secluded country setting with farm fields around it, Galesburg East Best Holiday Trav-L-Park offers a quiet, secure facility. With easy access from the Hwy., the campground has level, shady spots with an average width of 25 feet and 55 pull-throughs. Tent sites are somewhat separated from RVs and offer more shade and grass. Campers often stay at Galesburg East to do geneaology work in the area and enjoy the local festivals. A welcome touch in the hot summer is the air-conditioned laundry and store. Security is tops thanks to lights on buildings, security cameras, owners who live on the property, and regular patrols of the campground, which is seven miles east of Galesburg.

## BASICS

**Operated by:** Stan & Judy Herrick. **Open:** Apr. 1–Nov. 1. **Site Assignment:** Reservations w/ 1-night deposit; refund w/ 24-hour notice. **Registration:** At campground headquarters. **Fee:** $20 (cash, credit cards). **Parking:** At site.

## FACILITIES

**Number of RV Sites:** 58. **Number of Tent-Only Sites:** 10. **Hookups:** Electric (30, 50 amps,) water, sewer. **Each Site:** Picnic table, fire ring. **Dump Station:** Yes. **Laundry:** Yes. **Pay Phone:** Yes. **Rest Rooms and Showers:** Yes. **Fuel:** No. **Propane:** Yes. **Internal Roads:** Gravel, in fair condition. **RV Service:** Next door. **Market:** 7 mi. west in Galesburg. **Restaurant:** 3 mi. west in Knoxville. **General Store:** Yes. **Vending:** No. **Swimming Pool:** Yes. **Playground:** Yes. **Other:** Fishing pond, lounge w/ TV, enclosed shelter, heated swimming pool. **Activities:** Fishing. **Nearby Attractions:** Carl Sandburg's Birthplace, Bishop Hill Swedish colony, scenic drive, golf, railroad museum, Wolf Covered Bridge spanning Spoon River. **Additional Information:** Galesburg Area CVB, (309) 343-1194.

## RESTRICTIONS

**Pets:** Leash only. **Fires:** Fire ring only. **Alcoholic Beverages:** At sites only. **Vehicle Maximum Length:** 40 ft.

## TO GET THERE

From Exit 54 on US 150, drive 1 mi. east to the campground. Roads are wide and well maintained with broad shoulders.

## LENA

### Lake Le-Aqua-Na State Park

8542 North Lake Rd., Lena 61048. T: (815) 369-4282; www.dnr.state.il.us.

| 🚐 ★★ | ⛺ ★★★★ |
|---|---|
| Beauty: ★★★★ | Site Privacy: ★★★ |
| Spaciousness: ★★★ | Quiet: ★★★★ |
| Security: ★★★★ | Cleanliness: ★★★★ |
| Insect Control: None | Facilities: ★★ |

Six miles south of the Illinois-Wisconsin state line, Lake Le-Aqua-Na State Park was dedicated as a state park in 1958. The unusual name is the result of a contest to name the park; it's a combination of the town name of Lena and the Latin word for water, aqua. Oak, hickory, walnut, and other hardwood trees grow in abundance here, along with large tracts of pines. Campsites are grouped into three designated areas. Class A facilities include gravel pads, conveniently located water hydrants, a dumping station, and a shower building with flush toilets. Class B facilities offer vehicular access and the use of the shower building. Big Buck Campground is separate from the other areas and is maintained for equestrians. It is accessed from the county roads bordering the park. Alcohol is prohibited in the campgrounds. The average site width is 20 feet and there are three pull-throughs. The campground offers a mix of shady and open sites. The best RV sites are 42 and 43, because they are the biggest. The best tent sites are Hickory Hill sites 1–7 and 150–153 because they are more wooded and offer more privacy. Internal roads in the park are often twisty with no shoulders. Some of the hilly terrain makes it difficult for RVs to maneuver, but the views are worth it.

## BASICS

**Operated by:** State of Illinois. **Open:** All year. **Site Assignment:** 28 sites available for reservations; 1-night deposit required, plus $5 reservation fee; refund w/ 7-day notice. **Registration:** At campground office. **Fee:** $11 (cash, check). **Parking:** At site.

## FACILITIES

**Number of RV Sites:** 141. **Number of Tent-Only Sites:** 30. **Hookups:** Electric (30, 50 amps). **Each Site:** Picnic table, fire ring. **Dump Station:** Yes. **Laundry:** No. **Pay Phone:** Yes. **Rest Rooms and Showers:** Yes. **Fuel:** No. **Propane:** No. **Internal Roads:** Paved, in good condition. **RV Service:** No. **Market:** 3 mi. south in Lena. **Restaurant:** 3 mi. south in Lena. **General Store:** Yes. **Vending:** Yes. **Swimming Pool:** No. **Playground:** Yes. **Other:** Lake w/ beach, hiking trails, boat ramp, boat dock, equestrian trail. **Activities:** Swimming, fishing, boating (rental rowboats & paddleboats available), hiking. **Nearby Attractions:** Lena Area Historical Museum, Stagecoach Trail, Stephenson–Black Hawk Trail, *Field of Dreams* movie site, cheese companies, golf, casino. **Additional Information:** Northern Illinois Tourism Development Office, (815) 547-3740.

## RESTRICTIONS

**Pets:** Leash only. **Fires:** Fire ring only. **Alcoholic Beverages:** Not permitted. **Vehicle Maximum Length:** None. **Other:** 2-week stay limit.

## To Get There

From junction US 20 and Hwy. 73, drive 5 mi. north on Hwy. 73 and Lake Park Rd. US 20 is well maintained but narrow with no shoulders.

## LENA

### Lena KOA

10982 West Hwy. 20, Lena 61048. T: (815) 369-2612; F: (815) 369-5338; www.koa.com; reservations@lenakoa.com.

 ★★★         ▲ ★★★

| | |
|---|---|
| Beauty: ★★★ | Site Privacy: ★★★ |
| Spaciousness: ★★★ | Quiet: ★★★★ |
| Security: ★★★★★ | Cleanliness: ★★★★★ |
| Insect Control: None | Facilities: ★★★ |

Surrounded by cornfields and woods, Lena KOA is a quiet, family campground one mile north of Lena. The typical site width is 27 feet and the campground has 25 pull-throughs. There is a mixture of wooded and open sites. A Kamping Kitchen, with three cooking stations with sinks and electric stoves, plus six picnic tables, provides cooking and eating facilities for campers to use. Tent sites are grassy with wooden platforms for tents. RV sites are grassy with gravel pads for RVs. The best RV sites are M6–11, because they are long sites offering easy in and out; L1–5, because they are away from the road and closer to the woods; and I1–5, because they are long, level, have 50 amps electricity and a variety of trees. Tent sites are spacious and level, with a short walk to rest rooms and showers. Campers are escorted to their sites when they check in. Security is good thanks to an owner who lives on the grounds, a staffed office from 8 a.m. to 9 p.m., enforced quiet time from 10 p.m. to 7 a.m., and regular patrols of the campground.

## BASICS

**Operated by:** Denny Drake & Bonnie Phillips. **Open:** May 1–Nov. 1. **Site Assignment:** Reservations w/ $20 deposit; refund (minus $5 service fee) w/ 3-day notice. **Registration:** At campground office. **Fee:** $26 (cash, check, credit cards). **Parking:** At site.

## FACILITIES

**Number of RV Sites:** 83. **Number of Tent-Only Sites:** 5. **Hookups:** Electric (30, 50 amps), water, sewer, phone, Internet. **Each Site:** Picnic table, fire ring. **Dump Station:** Yes. **Laundry:** Yes.

**Pay Phone:** Yes. **Rest Rooms and Showers:** Yes. **Fuel:** No. **Propane:** Yes. **Internal Roads:** Gravel, in good condition. **RV Service:** No. **Market:** 1 mi. north in Lena. **Restaurant:** 1 mi. north in Lena. **General Store:** Yes. **Vending:** Yes. **Swimming Pool:** Yes. **Playground:** Yes. **Other:** Video arcade, rec room, volleyball, horseshoes, basketball, sports field, pavilion, Kamping Kitchen. **Activities:** Swimming, biking (rental low-rider bikes available), planned activities on weekends. **Nearby Attractions:** Lena Area Historical Museum, Stagecoach Trail, *Field of Dreams* movie site, Stephenson–Black Hawk Trail, cheese companies, golf, casino. **Additional Information:** Northern Illinois Tourism Development Office, (815) 547-3740.

## RESTRICTIONS

**Pets:** Leash only. **Fires:** Fire ring only. **Alcoholic Beverages:** At sites only. **Vehicle Maximum Length:** 45 ft.

## To Get There

From junction of Hwy. 73 and US 20, drive 0.25 mi. east on US 20. US 20 has no shoulders so be careful turning into the campground.

## LITCHFIELD

### Rainmaker Campground

865 Rainmaker Tr., Litchfield 62056. T: (217) 532-6370

🚐 ★★★         ▲ ★★

| | |
|---|---|
| Beauty: ★★★ | Site Privacy: ★★★ |
| Spaciousness: ★★★ | Quiet: ★★★★ |
| Security: ★★★★★ | Cleanliness: ★★★★ |
| Insect Control: None | Facilities: ★★★ |

The fourth generation of campers are now visiting Rainmaker Campground, six miles east of Litchfield. And the same owners are there who started it almost four decades ago. Prices must not have changed much over those years because the campground is a real bargain—$10 for an RV or tent site. Seasonals campers have taken up 140 of the sites and seem to spend considerable time fixing up their second homes with flowers, shrubs, and decorations. The owners don't charge storage if RVs are left year-round on the site. The campground is a destination. Very few RVs would drive those country roads just for an overnight place to stay. The drive is pretty but the winding, narrow roads can get tiresome. RV sites are gravel with a choice of open or shaded. Typical site width is 25 feet and there are five pull-throughs in front of the shower facility. Those are the most popular RV sites. Tent campers can use any of the RV sites which puts them at a bit of a disadvantage if they want privacy. The family campground has solid security measures—owners who live on the grounds, regular patrols, a security camera, and an access gate that is locked from 11 p.m. to 6 a.m.

### BASICS

**Operated by:** Rex & June Brawley. **Open:** Apr. 1–Oct. 31. **Site Assignment:** Reservations w/ no deposit. **Registration:** At campground office. **Fee:** $10 (cash, check). **Parking:** At site.

### FACILITIES

**Number of RV Sites:** 220. **Number of Tent-Only Sites:** 0. **Hookups:** Electric (20, 30 amps), water, sewer. **Each Site:** Picnic table, fire ring. **Dump Station:** Yes. **Laundry:** No. **Pay Phone:** Yes. **Rest Rooms and Showers:** Yes. **Fuel:** No. **Propane:** Yes. **Internal Roads:** Paved/gravel, in good condition. **RV Service:** Yes. **Market:** 6 mi. west in Litchfield. **Restaurant:** 6 mi. west in Litchfield. **General Store:** Yes. **Vending:** No. **Swimming Pool:** No. **Playground:** Yes. **Other:** Fishing pond, Lake Yeager, nature trails, horseshoes, volleyball, tetherball, basketball, bait, boat ramp, boat dock, rec hall, pavilion, adults room, recreation field. **Activities:** Swimming, fishing, boating, hiking, Sunday church services, planned weekend activities. **Nearby Attractions:** Golf, drive-in theater, nature conservation area, Sportsman's Family Fun Park, nature trails, water sports, swimming. **Additional Information:** Central Illinois Tourism Development Office, (217) 525-7980.

### RESTRICTIONS

**Pets:** Leash only. **Fires:** Fire ring only. **Alcoholic Beverages:** Permitted. **Vehicle Maximum Length:** None.

### TO GET THERE

From junction of I-55 and Hwy. 16, take Exit 52, drive 5.5 mi. east on Hwy. 16, then 4 mi. northwest on Parsons. The country roads are very winding and narrow at times.

## MAHOMET
## Tin Cup RV Park

1715 East Tincup Rd., Mahomet 61853. T: (217) 586-3011

| 🚐 ★★★ | 🏕 ★★★ |
|---|---|
| Beauty: ★★★ | Site Privacy: ★★★ |
| Spaciousness: ★★★ | Quiet: ★★★★ |
| Security: ★★★★ | Cleanliness: ★★★★ |
| Insect Control: Yes | Facilities: ★★★ |

At first glance, Tin Cup RV Park looks like a golf course. The slopes of the grassy campground are so well maintained they could be a golf green. Located in the small town of Mahomet, eight miles west of Champaign, the campground offers a country setting just down the road from the Champaign Country Forest Preserve. A favorite with golfers, the campground also has an updated golf driving range with a ball dispenser. Most sites offer shade with mature trees. Typical site width is 30 feet and the campground has 18 pull-throughs. Laid out in a series of loops, the campground has mostly gravel pads on grassy sites for RVs. Best RV sites are 33–40 because they are spacious and well shaded and offer easy access. Primitive sites are set aside in three acres of woods where RVs aren't allowed to camp. The tent sites are promoted as being unlimited but could probably accommodate an estimated 700 tent campers. However, the tent area is never filled up so tent campers have a bit more privacy and rustic surroundings. Security is good with a co-owner who lives on the premises and provides regular patrols of the area. Set back from the road, the campground is quiet. Many campers probably spend their days at the nearby 18-hole golf course.

### BASICS

**Operated by:** Stephen Robinson. **Open:** All year. **Site Assignment:** Reservations w/ no deposit. **Registration:** At campground office. **Fee:** $22 (cash, check, credit cards). **Parking:** At site.

### FACILITIES

**Number of RV Sites:** 65. **Number of Tent-Only Sites:** 700. **Hookups:** Electric (30 amps), water, sewer. **Each Site:** Picnic table, fire ring. **Dump Station:** Yes. **Laundry:** No. **Pay Phone:** Yes. **Rest Rooms and Showers:** Yes. **Fuel:** No. **Propane:** No. **Internal Roads:** Paved/gravel, in good condition. **RV Service:** No. **Market:** 0.5 mi. west on Mahomet. **Restaurant:** 0.5 mi. west on Mahomet. **General Store:** No. **Vending:** Yes. **Swimming Pool:** No. **Playground:** Yes. **Other:** Golf driving range w/ ball dispenser, sports field. **Activities:** None on-site. **Nearby Attractions:** Golf course, fishing lakes, swimming area, Early American Museum, University of Illinois, hiking trails, paved bike trails. **Additional Information:** Mahomet Chamber of Commerce, (217) 586-3165.

## RESTRICTIONS

**Pets:** Leash only. **Fires:** Fire ring only. **Alcoholic Beverages:** At sites only. **Vehicle Maximum Length:** 40 ft.

## TO GET THERE

From junction of I-57 and I-74, take Exit 174 and drive 5 mi. northwest on I-74, then 0.5 mi. north on Prairie View Rd., then 0.5 mi. west on Tincup Rd. Roads are wide and well maintained with broad shoulders.

## MARSHALL
### Lincoln Trail State Park

RR 1 Box 117, Marshall 62441. T: (217) 826-2222; www.dnr.state.il.us.

🚐 ★★★          ⛺ ★★★★

Beauty: ★★★★          Site Privacy: ★★★★
Spaciousness: ★★★★     Quiet: ★★★★
Security: ★★★★         Cleanliness: ★★★★
Insect Control: None    Facilities: ★★★

Officially dedicated in 1958, Lincoln Trail State Park was named after the trail Abraham Lincoln's family followed en route from Indiana to Illinois in 1831. With 3,000 markers showing the way, the trail winds through Kentucky, Indiana, and Illinois. Located five miles south of Marshall, the 1,023-acre park centers around the 146-acre Lincoln Trail Lake. Two campgrounds, Plainview and Lakeside, offer amenities, including mostly gravel, open sites with 23 pull-throughs. For those who wish to be atuned to nature without the distractions of modern conveniences, Lakeside Campground also includes a camping area for tents. Tent sites offer more privacy, grass, and shade. A full-service concession stand near the boat docks offers a wide variety of refreshments and supplies, as well as boat and dock rentals.

The Beech Tree Trail is just a half mile long, extending from the boat dock parking lot and concession stand, past the large picnic shelter, and on to the campground. The trail includes a series of stairways and foot bridges, which provide an excellent view of the beech maple forest contained within the nature preserve. Now, if only Lincoln Trail State Park had someplace nice to swim.

## BASICS

**Operated by:** State of Illinois. **Open:** All year. **Site Assignment:** First come, first served. **Registration:** At campground office. **Fee:** $11 (cash, check). **Parking:** At site.

## FACILITIES

**Number of RV Sites:** 208. **Number of Tent-Only Sites:** 24. **Hookups:** Electric (20, 30, 50 amps). **Each Site:** Picnic table, fire ring. **Dump Station:** Yes. **Laundry:** No. **Pay Phone:** Yes. **Rest Rooms and Showers:** Yes. **Fuel:** No. **Propane:** No. **Internal Roads:** Paved, in good condition. **RV Service:** No. **Market:** 5 mi. north in Marshall. **Restaurant:** On site. **General Store:** No. **Vending:** Yes. **Swimming Pool:** No. **Playground:** Yes. **Other:** Lincoln Trail Lake, boat ramp, boat dock, hiking trails. **Activities:** Fishing, hiking, boating (rental motorboats, canoes, paddleboats, & rowboats available). **Nearby Attractions:** The Archer House former stagecoach stop, Clark County Museum, Stone Arch Bridges, hunting, Amish country, antique shops, golf. **Additional Information:** Central Illinois Tourism Development Office, (217) 525-7980.

## RESTRICTIONS

**Pets:** Leash only. **Fires:** Fire ring only. **Alcoholic Beverages:** Permitted. **Vehicle Maximum Length:** 60 ft. **Other:** 2-week stay limit.

## TO GET THERE

From junction US 40 and Hwy. 1, drive 5 mi. south on Hwy. 1, then 1 mi. west on blacktop road. Roads are wide and well maintained with good shoulders.

## MULBERRY GROVE

### Cedarbrook RV & Camper Park

1109 Mulberry Grove Rd., Mulberry Grove 62262.
T: (618) 326-8865

🚐 ★★★★          ▲ ★★★★

Beauty: ★★★★          Site Privacy: ★★★★
Spaciousness: ★★★     Quiet: ★★★★
Security: ★★★★★        Cleanliness: ★★★★★
Insect Control: None   Facilities: ★★★★

Not only are the rest rooms at Cedarbrook RV and Camper Park very clean, they are also decorated: scatter rugs lay on the floor, a fan supplies cooling breezes, and a fancy bottle of liquid soap adorns the sink. The owners obviously care. The secluded wilderness setting eight miles west of Vandalia, features nine pull-through sites—the most popular with RVs—and an average site width of 25 feet. A wooded ravine and a small lake for fishing and swimming add to the amenities, but there are no scheduled activities. RV sites are generally gravel with a mixture of sunny and shady places. Tent sites are more primitive and grassy. The campground has a gate for security, owners who live on the grounds, and regular patrols of the area.

### BASICS

**Operated by:** Howard & Donna Kunder. **Open:** Apr. 1–Nov. 1. **Site Assignment:** Reservations w/ 1-night deposit; refund w/ 24-hour notice. **Registration:** At campground office. **Fee:** $18 (cash, credit cards). **Parking:** At site.

### FACILITIES

**Number of RV Sites:** 57. **Number of Tent-Only Sites:** 15. **Hookups:** Electric (20, 30, 50 amps), water, sewer. **Each Site:** Picnic table, fire ring. **Dump Station:** Yes. **Laundry:** Yes. **Pay Phone:** Yes. **Rest Rooms and Showers:** Yes. **Fuel:** No. **Propane:** Yes. **Internal Roads:** Gravel, in good condition. **RV Service:** No. **Market:** 8 mi. east in Vandalia. **Restaurant:** 1 mi. north in Mulberry Grove. **General Store:** Yes. **Vending:** Yes. **Swimming Pool:** No. **Playground:** Yes. **Other:** Small lake, clubhouse w/ complete kitchen, horseshoes, ping-pong, volleyball, TV, pool table. **Activities:** Swimming in lake, fishing. **Nearby Attractions:** Carlyle Lake, biggest man-made lake in Illinois; Vandalia, first capitol of Illinois; scenic drives. **Additional Information:** Crawford County Tourism Council, (800) 445-7006.

### RESTRICTIONS

**Pets:** Leash only. **Fires:** Fire ring only. **Alcoholic Beverages:** Permitted. **Vehicle Maximum Length:** None.

### TO GET THERE

From I-70, take Exit 52, drive 1 mi. south. Roads are wide and well maintained with broad shoulders.

## OAKWOOD

### Kickapoo State Park

10906 Kickapoo Park Rd., Oakwood 61858. T: (217) 442-4915; www.dnr.state.il.us.

🚐 ★★★          ▲ ★★★★

Beauty: ★★★★          Site Privacy: ★★★
Spaciousness: ★★★     Quiet: ★★★★
Security: ★★★★        Cleanliness: ★★★
Insect Control: None   Facilities: ★★★

Easily reached by I-74, Kickapoo State Park has a wealth of natural beauty and outdoor activities. Oddly, that is not how it all started. Once a scarred wasteland ravaged by strip-mine operations, Kickapoo State Park's 2,842 acres now provide an outdoor playground with something to appeal to every member of the family. For campers, Kickapoo has two major campgrounds for tent and RV camping. Campers occupying electrical sites are required to pay for the availability of electricity even if the service is not used. A limited number of walk-in sites are available for primitive campers. Sites are mostly shaded and level. The park is said to be the first in the nation built on strip-mined land and one of the first to be subsidized through public contributions. The spoil piles and mine pits left behind after nearly a century (1850–1940) of mining were the base from which nature had to recover to transform Kickapoo State Park into the outdoor playground it is today. The park has 22 deep-water ponds providing a total of 221 acres of water for boaters, canoeists, and anglers.

### BASICS

**Operated by:** State of Illinois. **Open:** All year. **Site Assignment:** Some sites available for reservations; 1-night deposit, plus $5 for reservation; refund w/ 7-day notice. **Registration:** At campground office. **Fee:** $11 (cash, check). **Parking:** At site.

Facilities**Number of RV Sites:** 108. **Number of Tent-Only Sites:** 75. **Hookups:** Electric (20, 50 amps). **Each Site:** Picnic table, fire ring. **Dump Station:** Yes. **Laundry:** No. **Pay Phone:** Yes. **Rest Rooms and Showers:** Yes. **Fuel:** No. **Propane:** No. **Internal Roads:** Paved, in good condition. **RV Service:** No. **Market:** 1 mi. south in Oakwood. **Restaurant:** 1 mi. south in Oakwood. **General Store:** No. **Vending:** No. **Swimming Pool:** No. **Playground:** Yes. **Other:** Vermilion River, lakes, ponds, horseshoes, boat ramp, shelters, hiking trails, mountain bike trails. **Activities:** Fishing, boating (rental boats available), canoeing, hiking, hunting, scuba diving. **Nearby Attractions:** Danville Stadium, Vermilion County Museum, Middle Fork National Scenic River, Vermilion County War Museum Society, antique & arts & crafts stores. **Additional Information:** Danville Area CVB, (800) 383-4386.

## RESTRICTIONS

**Pets:** Leash only. **Fires:** Fire ring only. **Alcoholic Beverages:** Not permitted. **Vehicle Maximum Length:** None. **Other:** 2-week stay limit.

## TO GET THERE

From Oakwood, drive 1 mi. north on New Town Rd. Roads are wide and well maintained with mostly broad shoulders.

## OREGON
## Lake LaDonna Family Campground

1302 Harmony Rd., Oregon 61061. T: (815) 732-6804

| 🚐 ★★★ | 🛖 ★★★ |
|---|---|
| Beauty: ★★★ | Site Privacy: ★★★ |
| Spaciousness: ★★★ | Quiet: ★★★ |
| Security: ★★★★ | Cleanliness: ★★★ |
| Insect Control: None | Facilities: ★★★ |

Campers often stop and ask if they have to be veterans to stay at Lake LaDonna Family Campground. They don't, of course. But the campground is dedicated to veterans and has the nation's first Vietnam Memorial Wall. The 80-foot wall was built in 1982 by the owner, himself a Vietnam vet whose limp attests to his war injuries. Flags fly everywhere, POW and MIA signs are prominently displayed, and military branch symbols are affixed to RVs and campers. Special memorial services also are held several times a year to honor veterans. Laid out in a series of loops, the campground has well-shaded grassy and gravel sites. The average site width is

28 feet, with 50 pull-throughs. The campground has 135 seasonal campers. The campground's white sand beach and spring-fed lake are its biggest draws. The lake has a 16-foot waterfall, a boardwalk with huge thatched huts for shade, a diving board, and a life guard on duty.

## BASICS

**Operated by:** Lamont Gaston. **Open:** Apr. 15–Oct. 15. **Site Assignment:** Reservation required, w/ 1-night deposit; full refund w/ 1-week notice; cancellations w/ 24-hour notice receive half the deposit amount. **Registration:** At campground office. **Fee:** $25 (cash, check, credit cards). **Parking:** At site.

## FACILITIES

**Number of RV Sites:** 351. **Number of Tent-Only Sites:** 6. **Hookups:** Electric (20, 30, 50 amps), water. **Each Site:** Picnic table. **Dump Station:** Yes. **Laundry:** No. **Pay Phone:** Yes. **Rest Rooms and Showers:** Yes. **Fuel:** No. **Propane:** Yes. **Internal Roads:** Paved, in good condition. **RV Service:** No. **Market:** 5 mi. north in Oregon. **Restaurant:** 5 mi. north in Oregon. **General Store:** Yes. **Vending:** Yes. **Swimming Pool:** No. **Playground:** Yes. **Other:** Manmade lake, beach, rope swing dock, boardwalk, basketball court, lodge, video game arcade, pool tables, pinball, juke box, fast-food restaurant, amphitheater. **Activities:** Swimming, planned activities. **Nearby Attractions:** Go-karts, mini-golf, bumper boats, ultralight flying lessons, shooting gallery, 4 state parks, paddlewheel boat, 48-ft. tall Black Hawk statue overlooking Rock River. **Additional Information:** Northern Illinois Tourism Development Office, (815) 547-3740.

## RESTRICTIONS

**Pets:** Leash only. **Fires:** Fire pits only. **Alcoholic Beverages:** Permitted. **Vehicle Maximum Length:** 40 ft. **Other:** 2-night min. for weekends, 3-night min. on holiday weekends.

## TO GET THERE

From Rte. 64 west, turn left at the 3rd stoplight (Rte. 2) in Oregon. Continue south to edge of town. Follow signs to White Pines State Park by turning right onto Pines Rd. Continue on Pines Rd., following signs to White Pines State Park. Two miles before the state park, turn right off Pines Rd. onto Harmony Rd. Lake LaDonna is 0.5 mile on right on Harmony Rd., marked by a large, lighted sign. Road is well maintained with sufficient shoulders.

## OREGON

### River Road Camping & Marina

3922 River Rd., Oregon 61061. T: (815) 234-5383; F: (815) 234-5386; www.gocampingamerica.com/riverroadcpmar/index.html.

🚐 ★★               ▲ ★★

| | |
|---|---|
| Beauty: ★★ | Site Privacy: ★★ |
| Spaciousness: ★★ | Quiet: ★★★ |
| Security: ★★★★ | Cleanliness: ★★ |
| Insect Control: None | Facilities: ★★ |

The Rock River is the centerpiece of River Road Camping and Marina, five miles north of Oregon. Most people come for water recreation and the most popular sites are right by the river, especially sites 36–41 that are around a big oak tree and near the boat launch. Sites on the river also get a cooling breeze which can be a welcome relief in a Midwest summer. The campground tends to get crowded, so reservations are recommended. Laid out in a series of loops, the rural campground has a typical site width of 26 feet and offers 30 pull-throughs. RV sites are level with a mix of grass and gravel with shaded or open areas. A primitive area is set aside for tent campers, offering more privacy, shade, and grass. A creek runs through the campground, winding through some of the sites. Security measures are good with owners living in the campground, a regular patrol of the area, and entrance gates that are locked from 10 p.m. to 8 a.m. on weekdays and 11 p.m. to 8 a.m. on weekends.

#### BASICS

**Operated by:** Al & Ada Overton. **Open:** Apr. 15–Oct. 30. **Site Assignment:** Reservations w/ 1-night deposit; 2-night min.; 3-night min. on holidays, paid in advance. No refunds. **Registration:** At campground office. **Fee:** $26 (cash, check). **Parking:** At site.

#### FACILITIES

**Number of RV Sites:** 150. **Number of Tent-Only Sites:** 200. **Hookups:** Electric (30 amps), water. **Each Site:** Picnic table, fire ring. **Dump Station:** Yes. **Laundry:** Yes. **Pay Phone:** Yes. **Rest Rooms and Showers:** Yes. **Fuel:** Yes. **Propane:** Yes. **Internal Roads:** Paved, in good condition. **RV Service:** No. **Market:** 5 mi. south in Oregon. **Restaurant:** 5 mi. south in Oregon. **General Store:** Yes. **Vending:** Yes. **Swimming Pool:** Yes. **Playground:** Yes. **Other:** Rock River, Spring

Creek, game room, boat dock, boat launch, horseshoes, basketball, pavilion, badminton, sports field, volleyball. **Activities:** Swimming, waterskiing, fishing, boating (rental pontoons, rowboats, & canoes available), planned weekend activities. **Nearby Attractions:** Go-karts, mini-golf, bumper boats, ultralight flying lessons, shooting gallery, 4 state parks, paddlewheel boat, 48-ft. tall Black Hawk statue overlooking Rock River. **Additional Information:** Northern Illinois Tourism Development Office, (815) 547-3740.

#### RESTRICTIONS

**Pets:** Leash only. **Fires:** Fire ring only. **Alcoholic Beverages:** Permitted. **Vehicle Maximum Length:** 40 ft.

#### TO GET THERE

From junction of Hwy. 2 and Hwy. 64, drive 0.5 mi. east on Hwy. 64, then 4 mi. north on River Rd. Roads are wide and well maintained with broad shoulders.

## PITTSFIELD

### Pine Lakes Camping & Fishing Resort

RR 3, Box 3077, Pittsfield 62363. T: (877) 808-PINE; F: (217) 285-1439; pinelake@adams.net.

🚐 ★★★★            ▲ ★★★★

| | |
|---|---|
| Beauty: ★★★★ | Site Privacy: ★★★★ |
| Spaciousness: ★★★★ | Quiet: ★★★★ |
| Security: ★★★★ | Cleanliness: ★★★★ |
| Insect Control: None | Facilities: ★★★★ |

Pine Lakes Camping and Fishing Resort in Pittsfield, has natural beauty—to begin with, 45-acre Pine Lake with a pretty shoreline, a ravine, and sandy swimming beach. The campground also has little touches to add to its scenic attractions—flower gardens, flower boxes, large wooden carvings, and a totem pole. Laid out in a series of loops, the campground's typical site width is 35 feet and it has 16 pull-throughs. RV sites are a mixture of grass and gravel. Many RV sites have concrete pads and picnic tables covered with wooden canopies. RVs have a choice of shady or open sites. A primitive site for tents offers more privacy, trees, and grass. The best RV sites are in the 400 section along the lake, and the heavily-shaded 100 section. The speed limit is 7.5 mph, no bicycles or golf carts are allowed after dark (bike helmets are encouraged), and each vehicle must exhibit a camper or visitor pass. Security and noise regulations are enforced. Bug zappers are not permitted and quiet hours are 11 p.m. to 8 a.m. Children must be on their site during quiet hours unless accompanied by an adult. A security gate guards the entrance to the campground and the area is patrolled.

## BASICS

**Operated by:** Jim & Marsha. **Open:** All year, limited winter facilities. **Site Assignment:** Reservations w/ 1-night deposit; refunds (minus $7 service charge) w/ 14-day notice; cancellations within 3–14 days will be issued credit for current season; 2-night min. reservation, 3-night min. for holiday weekends. **Registration:** At campground office. **Fee:** $21 (cash, check, credit cards). **Parking:** At site.

## FACILITIES

**Number of RV Sites:** 130. **Number of Tent-Only Sites:** 50. **Hookups:** Electric (20, 30, 50 amps), water, sewer, cable TV. **Each Site:** Picnic table, fire ring. **Dump Station:** Yes. **Laundry:** Yes. **Pay Phone:** Yes. **Rest Rooms and Showers:** Yes. **Fuel:** No. **Propane:** Yes. **Internal Roads:** Paved/gravel, in good condition. **RV Service:** No. **Market:** 0.5 mi. south in Pittsfield. **Restaurant:** 0.5 mi. south in Pittsfield. **General Store:** Yes. **Vending:** Yes. **Swimming Pool:** No. **Playground:** Yes. **Other:** Pine Lake, sandy swimming beach, arcade, fish-cleaning building, tetherball, horseshoes, volleyball, basketball, hiking trail, outdoor movies, bait shop. **Activities:** Swimming, fishing (no license required), boating (rental rowboats, canoes, & paddleboats), rental golf carts, hiking, planned activities. **Nearby Attractions:** Hunting, horseback riding, golf, antique shops, craft shops, ostrich farm, geneaology resources, apple orchard. **Additional Information:** Western Illinois Tourism Development Office, (309) 837-7460.

## RESTRICTIONS

**Pets:** Leash only. **Fires:** Fire ring only. **Alcoholic Beverages:** At sites only. **Vehicle Maximum Length:** None. **Other:** Pole fishing only, limit 4 catfish & 4 bass a day; no private boats or motors allowed; no boats on water before dawn or after dusk; swimming beach open 10 a.m. to dusk.

## TO GET THERE

From junction of I-72/US 36 and Pittsfield/New Salem Rd., take Exit 31 and drive 4.5 mi. south on Pittsfield/New Salem Rd. Roads are wide and well maintained with broad shoulders.

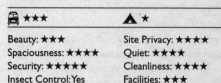

# POCAHONTAS
## Tomahawk RV Park

119 Tomahawk Dr., Pocahontas 62275. T: (618) 669-2781

🚐 ★★★                    ▲ ★

Beauty: ★★★              Site Privacy: ★★★★
Spaciousness: ★★★★       Quiet: ★★★★
Security: ★★★★★          Cleanliness: ★★★★
Insect Control: Yes       Facilities: ★★★

Small camping clubs love Tomahawk RV Park because of its large rec hall with kitchen facilities for get togethers. Other nice touches are concrete patios and wooden canopies over picnic tables at some RV sites. But the campground, ten miles east of Highland, has a high percentage of seasonal campers. About 100 of the sites are taken by seasonals. The campground also doesn't have a special section for tent campers. Tents are allowed on RV sites but those don't allow for the type of private setting most tent campers are seeking. Typical site width is 28 feet and the campground has 15 pull-throughs. RV sites are primarily gravel and open. Best RV sites are 5–8 because they are the most level. Other sites have a slight slope to them. Security and quiet measures are strictly enforced, including a 5 mph speed limit. Quiet hours are 11 p.m. to 7 a.m., the swimming beach is open noon to 7:30 p.m. on weekdays and 10:30 a.m. to 7:30 p.m. on weekends. The campground has security gates, security lights, an owner who lives on the premises, regular patrols, motion sensor lights, and a driveway warning bell for approaching vehicles.

## BASICS

**Operated by:** Ron Griffith. **Open:** All year. **Site Assignment:** Reservations w/ no deposit. **Registration:** At campground office. **Fee:** $16 (cash, check). **Parking:** At site.

## FACILITIES

**Number of RV Sites:** 135. **Number of Tent-Only Sites:** 0. **Hookups:** Electric (20, 30 amps), water. **Each Site:** Picnic table, fire ring. **Dump Station:** Yes. **Laundry:** Yes. **Pay Phone:** Yes. **Rest Rooms and Showers:** Yes. **Fuel:** No. **Propane:** Yes. **Internal Roads:** Gravel, in good condition. **RV Service:** Limited. **Market:** 10 mi. west in Highland. **Restaurant:** 10 mi. west in Highland. **General Store:** Yes. **Vending:** No. **Swimming Pool:** No. **Playground:** Yes. **Other:** 2 lakes, swimming beach, horseshoes, bait & tackle shop, rec hall, pavilion, coin games, basketball, sports field, volleyball. **Activities:** Swimming, fishing, planned activities. **Nearby Attractions:** Carlyle Lake, antique shops, boating, scenic drives, Louis Latzer Homestead. **Additional Information:** Illinois Bureau of Tourism, (800) 226-6632.

## RESTRICTIONS

**Pets:** Leash only. **Fires:** Fire ring only. **Alcoholic Beverages:** Permitted. **Vehicle Maximum Length:** None. **Other:** No mini-bikes or motorcycles are to be ridden inside camp area; no fishing license required but fee of $3 per pole to fish in either lake.

## TO GET THERE

From junction of I-70 and Hwy. 143, take Exit 30 and drive 6 mi. east on Hwy. 143, then 1 mi. south on Jamestown Rd. Roads are wide and well maintained with adequate shoulders. Entry road to campground is narrow.

## QUINCY

### Valley View Campground

2300 Bonansinga Dr., Quincy 62301. T: (217) 222-7229

🚐 ★★                   ⛺ ★★

Beauty: ★★                Site Privacy: ★★★
Spaciousness: ★★★        Quiet: ★★★
Security: ★★             Cleanliness: ★★
Insect Control: Yes       Facilities: ★★

Valley View Campground, two miles west of Quincy, has great potential, but needs some work. A closed swimming pool is an eyesore and the whole campground could use a general spiffing up. Arranged in a series of loops, the hilly campground offers grassy sites—some shaded, some open—in a rural setting. The campground has a typical site width of 30 feet and offers no pull-through sites. Boat launching ramps to the Mississippi River and the many lakes and streams surrounding Quincy are accessible across from the campground. Most popular RV sites are 18–24 because they are more level and easier to back into. Most popular tent sites are by the shelter house. Many campers come from the area or are construction workers in the area for the summer. Some campers are also overnighters passing through. A manager lives on the site and city police regularly patrol the campground.

## BASICS

**Operated by:** Bob Mays. **Open:** All year. **Site Assignment:** Reservations w/ no deposit. **Registration:** At campground office. **Fee:** $20 (cash, check). **Parking:** At site.

## FACILITIES

**Number of RV Sites:** 36. **Number of Tent-Only Sites:** 100. **Hookups:** Electric (30, 50 amps), water, sewer. **Each Site:** Picnic table, fire ring. **Dump Station:** Yes. **Laundry:** Yes. **Pay Phone:** Yes. **Rest Rooms and Showers:** Yes. **Fuel:** No. **Propane:** No. **Internal Roads:** Paved/gravel, in fair condition. **RV Service:** No. **Market:** 2 mi. east in Quincy. **Restaurant:** 2 mi east in Quincy. **General Store:** No. **Vending:** Yes. **Swimming Pool:** No. **Playground:** Yes. **Other:** Pavilion, sports field, television lounge. **Activities:** None on-site. **Nearby Attractions:** Historic district, 7 museums, Mississippi River, Quinsippi Island, public marina, boating, fishing, swimming, hunting. **Additional Information:** Quincy CVB, (800) 978-4748.

## RESTRICTIONS

**Pets:** Leash only. **Fires:** Fire ring only. **Alcoholic Beverages:** At sites only. **Vehicle Maximum Length:** 40 ft.

## TO GET THERE

From junction of I-172 and US 24W, take Exit 19 and drive 3 mi. west and 4 mi. south on US 24. Entrance to campground is through a mobile home park with rough roads, speed bumps, and a steep hill going down to the campground.

## ROCKFORD

### Rock Cut State Park

7318 Harlem Rd., Loves Park 61111. T: (815) 885-3311; dnr.state.il.us.

🚐 ★★★                   ⛺ ★★★★

Beauty: ★★★★            Site Privacy: ★★★
Spaciousness: ★★★        Quiet: ★★★
Security: ★★★★★          Cleanliness: ★★★★
Insect Control: None      Facilities: ★★★

Chiseled out of the state's far northern region, Rock Cut State Park got its name from the blasting operations that railroad crews conducted during the 1859 construction of the Kenosha-Rockford Rail Line. It's an area of rolling plains and two lakes. Pierce Lake, with 162 acres, is a retreat for people wanting to fish, ice fish, or ice skate. The 50-acre Olson Lake is especially for swimmers. Laid out in a series of one-way loops, the wilderness campground, two miles north of Loves Park, offers grassy sites for tent campers and gravel pads for RVs with hookups. Sitting on a point overlooking Pierce Lake, site 20 is the most popular for tents. Reservations are not accepted for the site so campers often start arriving around noon, looking to see if the site will be vacated at the 3 p.m. check-out time. For RVs, the 400 loop of sites on the even side are the most popular because of the trees and privacy. The campground has a mix of shady and open sites for RVs but offers no pull-throughs. Security is excellent with a gate that is locked at 10 p.m. and regular patrols of the grounds. A big sign at the entrance warns visitors "Don't get locked in" because the park closes at 10 p.m. Rock Cut has speed bumps as well as speed checked by radar. The campground is very serious about its one-way entrance and exit—nails will chew up the tires of any vehicle that tries to go "in" the "out" or vice versa.

## BASICS

**Operated by:** State of Illinois. **Open:** All year. **Site Assignment:** Reservations w/ 1-night deposit plus $5; refund (minus $5) w/ 3-day notice. **Registration:** At campground office. **Fee:** $11 (cash, check). **Parking:** At site.

## FACILITIES

**Number of RV Sites:** 220. **Number of Tent-Only Sites:** 60. **Hookups:** Electric (30, 50 amps). **Each Site:** Picnic table, grill. **Dump Station:** Yes. **Laundry:** No. **Pay Phone:** Yes. **Rest Rooms and Showers:** Yes. **Fuel:** No. **Propane:** No. **Internal Roads:** Paved, in good condition. **RV Service:** No. **Market:** 2 mi. south in Loves Park. **Restaurant:** On site. **General Store:** Yes. **Vending:** Yes. **Swimming Pool:** No. **Playground:** Yes. **Other:** Pierce Lake, Olson Lake, swimming beach, hiking trails, boat launch, equestrian trails, fishing pier, concession stand, bait shop. **Activities:** Fishing, swimming, hiking, boating (rental rowboats & paddleboats). **Nearby Attractions:** Museums, BMX track, bowling, golf, nature preserve, tennis, Magic Waters, horseback riding, theater, speedway, antique & art shops. **Additional Information:** Rockford Area CVB, (800) 521-0849.

## RESTRICTIONS

**Pets:** Leash only. **Fires:** In grills only; ground fires prohibited. **Alcoholic Beverages:** Not permitted.

**Vehicle Maximum Length:** 40 ft. **Other:** 2-week stay limit.

## TO GET THERE

From junction of US 51 and Hwy. 173, drive 3 mi. west on Hwy. 173. Roads are wide and well maintained with good shoulders.

## RUSHVILLE
### Schuy-Rush Lake & Campground

RR 3, Rushville 62681. T: (217) 322-6628; www.rushville.org.

🚐 ★★            ⛺ ★★★

| | |
|---|---|
| Beauty: ★★★ | Site Privacy: ★★★ |
| Spaciousness: ★★★ | Quiet: ★★★★ |
| Security: ★★★★ | Cleanliness: ★★★ |
| Insect Control: None | Facilities: ★★ |

The centerpiece of Schuy-Rush is a 225-acre lake which has been stocked with bass, channel cat, walleye, blue gill, and crappie fish. Laid out in a series of loops, the rural campground three miles south of Rushville, offers a mix of grassy and gravel sites with 12 pull-throughs. Tent sites are set away from RVs in a woodsy area for more privacy and shade. The campground does a great deal of repeat business and is especially busy around holidays and the annual gas engine show in June. Best RV sites are 1–20 near the showers and rest rooms. Favorite tent sites are in the primitive area in the woods. The road leading to the back RV sites is narrow and winding on a steep hill. Security measures are good with a manager who lives on site, gates that are locked from 10 p.m. to 6 a.m., security patrols, plus regular drive-throughs by city police.

## BASICS

**Operated by:** City of Rushville. **Open:** Apr. 1–Nov. 1. **Site Assignment:** Reservations w/ 1-night deposit; no refund. **Registration:** At campground office. **Fee:** $10 (cash, check). **Parking:** At site.

## FACILITIES

**Number of RV Sites:** 81. **Number of Tent-Only Sites:** 100. **Hookups:** Electric (20, 30 amps), water. **Each Site:** Picnic table, fire ring. **Dump Station:** Yes. **Laundry:** No. **Pay Phone:** No. **Rest Rooms and Showers:** Yes. **Fuel:** No. **Propane:** No. **Internal Roads:** Paved, in good condition. **RV Service:** No. **Market:** 3 mi. north in Rushville. **Restaurant:** 3 mi. north in Rushville. **General Store:** No. **Vending:** Yes. **Swimming Pool:** No.

**Playground:** Yes. **Other:** Schuy-Rush Lake, hiking trails, boat ramp, baseball. **Activities:** Fishing, boating, hiking, planned activities. **Nearby Attractions:** Community theater, genealogical center, hunting, antique shops, golf, Schuyler County Jail Museum, art galleries, nature preserve, tennis. **Additional Information:** Rushville Area Chamber of Commerce, (217) 322-3689.

## RESTRICTIONS

**Pets:** Leash only. **Fires:** Fire ring only. **Alcoholic Beverages:** At sites only. **Vehicle Maximum Length:** None.

## TO GET THERE

Take US 67 out of Rushville and drive 3 mi. south. Entrance road to campground is sloping and has narrow shoulders.

## SAVANNA

### Mississippi Palisades State Park

16327 A IL Rte. 84, Savanna 61074. T: (815) 273-2731; www.dnr.state.il.us.

🚐 ★★★                          ⛺ ★★★★

| | |
|---|---|
| Beauty: ★★★★ | Site Privacy: ★★★★ |
| Spaciousness: ★★★★ | Quiet: ★★★★ |
| Security: ★★★★ | Cleanliness: ★★★★ |
| Insect Control: None | Facilities: ★★ |

Palisades is the word used to describe a line of lofty, steep cliffs usually seen along a river. Mississippi Palisades, three miles north of Savanna, handsomely lives up to its name. Caves are evident, as are dangerous sink holes—limestone caves that go straight down. Atop the bluffs, erosion has carved intriguing rock formations, such as Indian Head and Twin Sisters—which bears keen resemblance to a pair of human figures. With sites in both shaded and open areas, the campground is in demand. Because of its popularity, reservations are not accepted. RV sites have gravel pads and are generally open; 12 are pull-throughs. The best RV site is 64, on the corner of a one-way road and away from tent campers. The best tent site is 25, private and grassy and located over the edge of a hill so no headlights hit it. Three primitive walk-in sites are also tucked into Mississippi Palisades. By hiking about a half mile, you'll be able to enjoy rustic camping along the park's serene northern trails. Natural beauty abounds, but Mississippi Palisades sure could use a good swimming spot.

## BASICS

**Operated by:** State of Illinois. **Open:** All year. **Site Assignment:** First come, first served. **Registration:** At campground office. **Fee:** $11 (cash, check). **Parking:** At site.

## FACILITIES

**Number of RV Sites:** 110. **Number of Tent-Only Sites:** 121. **Hookups:** Electric (20, 30, 50 amps). **Each Site:** Picnic table, fire ring. **Dump Station:** Yes. **Laundry:** No. **Pay Phone:** Yes. **Rest Rooms and Showers:** Yes. **Fuel:** No. **Propane:** No. **Internal Roads:** Paved, in good condition. **RV Service:** No. **Market:** 3 mi. south in Savanna. **Restaurant:** 3 mi. south in Savanna. **General Store:** Yes. **Vending:** Yes. **Swimming Pool:** No. **Playground:** Yes. **Other:** Mississippi River, boat ramp, boat dock, hiking trails. **Activities:** Fishing, boating, hiking, hunting, nature programs, slide shows. **Nearby Attractions:** Antique mall, marinas, Savanna-Sabula Bridge, playhouse, scenic drives, golf. **Additional Information:** Northern Illinois Tourism Development Office, (815) 547-3740.

## RESTRICTIONS

**Pets:** Leash only. **Fires:** Fire ring only. **Alcoholic Beverages:** Not permitted. **Vehicle Maximum Length:** None. **Other:** 2-week stay limit.

## TO GET THERE

From junction of US 52 and SR 84, drive 2 mi. north on SR 84. The state road is narrow and winding with limited shoulders.

## SPRINGFIELD

### Mr. Lincoln's Campground

3045 Stanton St., Springfield 62703. T: (800) 657-1414; F: (217) 529-6725.

🚐 ★★★                          ⛺ ★★★

| | |
|---|---|
| Beauty: ★★★ | Site Privacy: ★★★ |
| Spaciousness: ★★★ | Quiet: ★★★ |
| Security: ★★★★ | Cleanliness: ★★★★ |
| Insect Control: None | Facilities: ★★★ |

Location is everything, and Mr. Lincoln's Campground sure has it. The urban campground in Springfield, is in the midst of more historical sites and recreational opportunities than most other facilities dream of. First and foremost, the area is filled with Abraham Lincoln attractions. The campground also is on the bus line to downtown and the White Oaks Mall. In addition to being the only campground in Lincoln's hometown, the facility also offers the area's largest RV center with parts and service. The campground is laid out in a series of loops, with 30 feet the typical site width. All RV sites have gravel pads, some are shady, and others open. There are 15 pull-throughs. The tent area is separated from RVs and offers more shade and privacy. Because it has a large yard, 51 is the best RV site. All tent sites are similar—secluded, quiet, and tree-lined. The campground has good security measures including a manager staying on the premises, regular staff patrols, one entrance/exit, and patrols by city police. The campground also is completely fenced.

## BASICS

**Operated by:** Sue Johnson. **Open:** All year. **Site Assignment:** Reservations w/ 1-night deposit; refund w/ 24-hour notice. **Registration:** At campground office. **Fee:** $21 (cash, check, credit cards). **Parking:** At site.

## FACILITIES

**Number of RV Sites:** 42. **Number of Tent-Only Sites:** 108. **Hookups:** Electric (30, 50 amps), water, sewer, cable TV. **Each Site:** Picnic table, fire ring. **Dump Station:** Yes. **Laundry:** Yes. **Pay Phone:** Yes. **Rest Rooms and Showers:** Yes. **Fuel:** No. **Propane:** Yes. **Internal Roads:** Gravel, in fair condition. **RV Service:** Yes. **Market:** Across street. **Restaurant:** 0.5 mi. in either direction. **General Store:** Yes. **Vending:** Yes. **Swimming Pool:** No. **Playground:** No. **Other:** Horseshoes, volleyball, softball, sauna, sports field, rec room, coin games, badminton, movies, RV parts & accessory store. **Activities:** Local tours. **Nearby Attractions:** Lincoln historical sites, golf, theaters, shopping center, antique malls, lake, universities, walking tours, Old State Capitol, Museum of Funeral Customs, zoo, botanical gardens, wildlife sanctuary. **Additional Information:** Springfield CVB, (800) 545-7300.

## RESTRICTIONS

**Pets:** Leash only. **Fires:** Fire ring only. **Alcoholic Beverages:** Permitted. **Vehicle Maximum Length:** 45 ft.

## TO GET THERE

From junction of I-55 and Stevenson Dr., take Exit 94 and drive 1 mi. west on Stevenson Dr., then 1 block north on Stanton St. Roads are wide and well maintained with broad shoulders.

# SPRINGFIELD
## Springfield Best Holiday

P.O. Box 11231, Springfield 62629. T: (217) 483-9998

🚐 ★★★★                    ▲ ★★★★

Beauty: ★★★              Site Privacy: ★★★★
Spaciousness: ★★★         Quiet: ★★★★
Security: ★★★★            Cleanliness: ★★★★
Insect Control: No         Facilities: ★★★★

Located 15 minutes from downtown Springfield, the campground is a popular spot for folks enjoying the area's historical attractions. The campground also gets many repeat campers who come mainly for the facilities and activities. Arranged in a series of loops, the campground offers a rural setting with mostly pull-through sites. Typical site width is 30 feet and sites are a mixture of gravel and grass. Most sites are wooded and shady but some are open. RVs favor the sites in the 90s section because they are pull-throughs and offer 50 amps electricity. Tent sites are fairly isolated from the general campground, offering more privacy, grass, and trees. Security is good, with owners who live on the grounds, regular patrols, and the presence of state police from headquarters two miles away.

## BASICS

**Operated by:** N. J. & Joyce Bucklin. **Open:** Apr. 1–Nov. 1. **Site Assignment:** Reservations w/ 1 night deposit. No refunds. **Registration:** At campground office. **Fee:** $21 (cash, check, credit cards). **Parking:** At site.

## FACILITIES

**Number of RV Sites:** 105. **Number of Tent-Only Sites:** 20. **Hookups:** Electric (30, 50 amps), water, sewer. **Each Site:** Picnic table, grill. **Dump Station:** Yes. **Laundry:** Yes. **Pay Phone:** Yes. **Rest Rooms and Showers:** Yes. **Fuel:** No. **Propane:** No. **Internal Roads:** Gravel, in good condition. **RV Service:** Yes. **Market:** 5 mi. west in Chatham. **Restaurant:** 5 mi. west in Chatham. **General Store:** Yes. **Vending:** Yes. **Swimming Pool:** Yes. **Playground:** Yes. **Other:** Mini-golf, tennis, rec room, baseball, basketball. **Activities:** Swimming, planned weekend activities. **Nearby Attractions:** Lincoln-related historical sites, Illinois State Museum, Children's Zoo, Frank Lloyd Wright Home, scenic drive, bike trail, golf. **Additional Information:** Springfield CVB, (800) 545-7300.

## RESTRICTIONS

**Pets:** Leash only. **Fires:** Fire pits only. **Alcoholic Beverages:** Permitted. **Vehicle Maximum Length:** None.

## TO GET THERE

On I-55 Frontage Rd., 1 mi. south of Springfield, between Exits 88 and 83. Roads are wide and well maintained with broad shoulders.

## STERLING

## Maple Aire Crow Valley Campground

23807 Moline Rd., Sterling 61081. T: (815) 626-5376

🚐 ★★                               🔺 ★

| | |
|---|---|
| Beauty: ★★ | Site Privacy: ★★ |
| Spaciousness: ★★ | Quiet: ★★ |
| Security: ★★ | Cleanliness: ★★ |
| Insect Control: None | Facilities: ★★ |

Maple Aire Crow Valley Campground is a work in progress. In fact, even the name is changing. The Maple Aire part was just added and the original Crow Valley may eventually be dropped. The new owner hopes to implement a bunch of improvements—a laundry, gate house, electric pedestals, more sites, better hookups. The rural campground offers open, grassy RV sites with concrete pads to park on, an average site width of 28 feet, and seven pull-throughs. At press time, roads in the area are under construction and may be considerably improved. The Rock River is the centerpiece of the campground and activities. The most popular sites are by the river, and many local people like to come for the fishing and boating. The campground is conveniently located off I-88, five miles west of Rock Falls. However, the campground is so close to the interstate that the noise of cars and trucks whizzing by can be heard in the campground.

## BASICS

**Operated by:** Mike & Beth Johnson. **Open:** Apr. 15–Oct. 15. **Site Assignment:** Reservations w/ 1-night deposit; refunds w/ 7-day notice. **Registration:** At campground office. **Fee:** $20 (cash, credit cards). **Parking:** At site.

## FACILITIES

**Number of RV Sites:** 100. **Number of Tent-Only Sites:** 0. **Hookups:** Electric (30 amp), water. **Each Site:** Picnic table, fire ring. **Dump Station:**

Yes. **Laundry:** No. **Pay Phone:** No. **Rest Rooms and Showers:** Yes. **Fuel:** No. **Propane:** No. **Internal Roads:** Gravel, in poor condition. **RV Service:** No. **Market:** 5 mi. east in Rock Falls. **Restaurant:** 5 mi. east in Rock Falls. **General Store:** No. **Vending:** No. **Swimming Pool:** Yes. **Playground:** Yes. **Other:** Rock River, boat ramp, basketball, volleyball, badminton, horseshoes, shuffleboard, sports field. **Activities:** Fishing, swimming. **Nearby Attractions:** Bison ranch, Dillon Home Museum, bike trails, Behren's Country Village. **Additional Information:** Northern Illinois Tourism Development Office, (815) 547-3740.

## RESTRICTIONS

**Pets:** Leash only. **Fires:** Fire ring only. **Alcoholic Beverages:** At sites only. **Vehicle Maximum Length:** None.

## TO GET THERE

From junction of I-88 and Hwy. 2/30, take Exit 36, drive 1 mi. west on Moline Rd. The road is in fair condition with adequate shoulders.

## STERLING

## Ruffit Park

24832 Rock Falls Rd., Sterling 61081. T: (815) 626-0221

🚐 ★★★                               🔺 ★★

| | |
|---|---|
| Beauty: ★★ | Site Privacy: ★★★ |
| Spaciousness: ★★★ | Quiet: ★★★ |
| Security: ★★★★ | Cleanliness: ★★★ |
| Insect Control: None | Facilities: ★★★ |

Ruffit Park Camping Resort offers easy access from the interstate and good parking with about 50 pull-through sites. The grassy campground five miles west of Sterling, offers shaded or open sites with a typical site width of 28 feet. Laid out in a series of loops, the campground has 34 seasonal campers. The fast-flowing Elkhorn Creek runs through the park and is filled with game fish. Favorite campsites are by the river. Quiet hours from 11 p.m. to 7 a.m. are enforced, as is a 5 mph speed limit. In the Gaumer family for over three decades, the campground is bordered by a small cemetery. For security measures, the owners live on site, offer regular patrols, and have a gate that is shut at night.

## BASICS

**Operated by:** Gaumer Family. **Open:** May 1–Oct. 1. **Site Assignment:** Reservations w/ 1-night deposit; refund w/ 7-day notice. **Registration:** At campground office. **Fee:** $16 (cash, check). **Parking:** At site.

## FACILITIES

**Number of RV Sites:** 100. **Number of Tent-Only Sites:** 25. **Hookups:** Electric (30, 50 amps), water. **Each Site:** Picnic table, fire ring. **Dump Station:** Yes. **Laundry:** Yes. **Pay Phone:** Yes. **Rest Rooms and Showers:** Yes. **Fuel:** No. **Propane:** No. **Internal Roads:** Paved/gravel, in fair condition. **RV Service:** No. **Market:** 5 mi. east in Sterling. **Restaurant:** 5 mi. east in Sterling. **General Store:** Yes. **Vending:** Yes. **Swimming Pool:** Yes. **Playground:** Yes. **Other:** Basketball, hiking trails, horseshoes, game room, wading pool, fishing stream, basketball, badminton, sports field, volleyball. **Activities:** Swimming, fishing, hiking. **Nearby Attractions:** Bison ranch, Dillon Home Museum, bike trails, Behren's Country Village, golf, John Deere Museum, casino. **Additional Information:** Northern Illinois Tourism Development Office, (815) 547-3740.

## RESTRICTIONS

**Pets:** Leash only. **Fires:** Fire ring only. **Alcoholic Beverages:** Not permitted. **Vehicle Maximum Length:** None.

## TO GET THERE

From junction of I-88 and Hwy. 2/30, take Exit 36 and drive 0.25 mi. east on Hwy. 2/30. Roads are wide and well maintained with broad shoulders.

## SYCAMORE

### Sycamore RV Resort

375 East North Ave., Sycamore 60178. T: (815) 895-5590; F: (815) 895-5729; www.sycamorervresort.com.

🚐 ★★★      ⛺ n/a

Beauty: ★★★      Site Privacy: ★★★
Spaciousness: ★★★      Quiet: ★★★★
Security: ★★★      Cleanliness: ★★★★
Insect Control: None      Facilities: ★★★

Sycamore RV Resort is surprisingly quiet, especially since it is located right in the town of Sycamore. Surrounded on three sides by water and woods, the campground has a natural buffer to keep out urban noises. The owners also enforce rules to keep the peace. Beach hours are 11 a.m. to 6 p.m. and no scheduled activities are

planned. The campground also does not allow motorcycle campers or tent campers. All fishing in the two lakes is catch-and-release only and stops at dusk. Laid out in a series of loops, the campground has a typical site width of 30 feet and 15 pull-throughs. RVs park in a level gravel site with a choice of trees or open. Most popular RV sites are 22–46 because they are located along the lake. The campground tends to be crowded and reservations are recommended. Sycamore's annual pumpkin festival in Oct. and other town activities and attractions are located within walking distance.

## BASICS

**Operated by:** Dale & Anita Cappel. **Open:** Apr. 1–Nov. 1. **Site Assignment:** Reservations w/ no deposit. **Registration:** At campground office. **Fee:** $22 (cash, check). **Parking:** At site.

## FACILITIES

**Number of RV Sites:** 56. **Number of Tent-Only Sites:** 0. **Hookups:** Electric (30, 50 amps), water, sewer, phone, Internet. **Each Site:** Picnic table, fire ring. **Dump Station:** Yes. **Laundry:** Yes. **Pay Phone:** Yes. **Rest Rooms and Showers:** Yes. **Fuel:** No. **Propane:** Yes. **Internal Roads:** Gravel, in good condition. **RV Service:** No. **Market:** 3 blocks in Sycamore. **Restaurant:** 2 blocks in Sycamore. **General Store:** Yes. **Vending:** Yes. **Swimming Pool:** No. **Playground:** Yes. **Other:** 2 spring-fed lakes, swimming beach, boat launch, badminton, sports field, volleyball. **Activities:** Swimming, fishing, boating (rental paddleboats & rowboats). **Nearby Attractions:** Golf, speedway, nature trail, Northern Illinois University, historic district walking tour. **Additional Information:** Northern Illinois Tourism Development Office, (815) 547-3740.

## RESTRICTIONS

**Pets:** Leash only. **Fires:** Fire ring only. **Alcoholic Beverages:** At sites only. **Vehicle Maximum Length:** 40 ft. **Other:** No tent camping; no camping motorcyclists.

## TO GET THERE

From junction of Hwy. 64 and Hwy. 23, drive 0.5 mi. north on Hwy. 23, then 200 yards east on East North Ave. Roads are wide and well maintained with adequate shoulders.

# UTICA

## LaSalle-Peru KOA

756 North 3150th Rd., Rte. 2, Utica 61373. T: (800) KOA-9498; www.koa.com.

🚐 ★★★★          ⛺ ★★★★

| | |
|---|---|
| Beauty: ★★★★ | Site Privacy: ★★★ |
| Spaciousness: ★★★ | Quiet: ★★★★ |
| Security: ★★★★ | Cleanliness: ★★★★★ |
| Insect Control: None | Facilities: ★★★ |

LaSalle-Peru KOA is a clean, quiet campground out in the country. No highway noise or passing trains disturb the setting. Located one-and-a-half hours from Chicago, the campground is a popular getaway for city dwellers wanting some peace and quiet, along with good recreation facilities. Quiet hours are enforced between 10 p.m. and 7 a.m. Bicycle riding is not allowed after dark and generators are not permitted at any time. Another rule enforcing the quiet time requires that pets be confined in an enclosed vehicle or tent at night. If campers leave the campground, they must take their pets with them. Sites are mostly grassy and shady, with a common width of 30 feet. Laid out in a series of loops, the campground has 40 pull-through sites. The laundry uses soft water and the camp store offers rental videos. TV reception varies between excellent and poor. Prime time reception is usually better. Tent sites offer some privacy from RVs, grass, and shade from tall oak trees.

### BASICS

**Operated by:** Denny & Ginny Lazar. **Open:** Apr. 1–Oct. 15. **Site Assignment:** Reservations w/ no deposit. **Registration:** At campground office. **Fee:** $29 (cash, credit cards). **Parking:** At site.

### FACILITIES

**Number of RV Sites:** 65. **Number of Tent-Only Sites:** 40. **Hookups:** Electric (20, 30 amps), water, sewer. **Each Site:** Picnic table, fire ring. **Dump Station:** Yes. **Laundry:** Yes. **Pay Phone:** Yes. **Rest Rooms and Showers:** Yes. **Fuel:** No. **Propane:** No. **Internal Roads:** Gravel, in good condition. **RV Service:** Yes. **Market:** 4 mi. south in Utica. **Restaurant:** 2 mi. south in Utica. **General Store:** Yes. **Vending:** Yes. **Swimming Pool:** Yes. **Playground:** Yes. **Other:** Small fishing creek, game room, horseshoes, recreation field, badminton, volleyball. **Activities:** Swimming, fishing, planned weekend activities. **Nearby Attractions:** Antique shops, golf, stock car races, horseback riding, I & M Canal State Trail, LaSalle County Historical Society, Matthiessen State Park, Starved Rock State Park. **Additional Information:** Heritage Corridor Visitors Bureau, (800) 746-0550.

### RESTRICTIONS

**Pets:** Leash only. **Fires:** Fire ring only. **Alcoholic Beverages:** Permitted. **Vehicle Maximum Length:** None. **Other:** No visitors, everyone must be a registered guest; if friends or family are visiting, they must register on a separate campsite.

### TO GET THERE

From junction of I-80 and SR 178, take Exit 81, drive north 1.5 mi. on SR 178 to North 3150th Rd., drive west 0.5 mi. Roads are wide and well maintained with broad shoulders.

# VANDALIA

## Okaw Valley Campground

RR 2 Box 55A, Brownstown 62418. T: (888) 470-3968

🚐 ★★★          ⛺ ★★★

| | |
|---|---|
| Beauty: ★★★★ | Site Privacy: ★★★★ |
| Spaciousness: ★★★★ | Quiet: ★★★ |
| Security: ★★★ | Cleanliness: ★★★★ |
| Insect Control: None | Facilities: ★★★ |

A partially shaded campground on rolling terrain five miles east of Vandalia, Okaw Valley Campground is a popular overnight destination with travelers passing through on I-70. The campground is located 330 miles, or about a day's drive, from Branson. The typical site width is 30 feet and the campground has 25 pull-throughs. Arranged in a series of loops, the rural campground offers both shady and open sites, with mostly gravel spots for RVs. There is a section for tent sites away from RVs, as well as a primitive tent site featuring more grass, trees, and privacy. A five-acre lake allows boating and fishing but no swimming. No license is required to fish in the lake; the catch is mostly bass, catfish, and bluegill. The TV lounge and laundromat are open 24 hours a day. A service sink on the north wall outside the washrooms is provided for washing pots, pans, and dishes. A 5 mph speed limit is enforced, as is a 10 p.m. to 7 a.m. quiet time.

## BASICS

**Operated by:** Dennis & Vikki Ramsey. **Open:** Apr. 1–Nov. 1. **Site Assignment:** Reservations w/ 1-night deposit; refunds w/ 24-hour notice. **Registration:** At campground office. **Fee:** $22 (cash, check, credit cards). **Parking:** At site.

## FACILITIES

**Number of RV Sites:** 51. **Number of Tent-Only Sites:** 40. **Hookups:** Electric (20, 30 amps), water, sewer. **Each Site:** Picnic table, fire ring. **Dump Station:** Yes. **Laundry:** Yes. **Pay Phone:** Yes. **Rest Rooms and Showers:** Yes. **Fuel:** No. **Propane:** Yes. **Internal Roads:** Gravel, in good condition. **RV Service:** No. **Market:** 3 mi. east in Brownstown. **Restaurant:** 5 mi. west in Vandalia. **General Store:** Yes. **Vending:** No. **Swimming Pool:** Yes. **Playground:** Yes. **Other:** Lake, volleyball, basketball, TV lounge, game room, horseshoes, boat dock, adults room, rec room, sports field, pavilion. **Activities:** Swimming, fishing, boating (rental paddleboats & rowboats), biking (rental bikes), planned activities. **Nearby Attractions:** Vandalia State House, Fayette County Museum, Steam Engine Museum, golf, rollerskating, stock car races, Alwerdt's Gardens. **Additional Information:** Vandalia Chamber of Commerce, (618) 283-2728.

## RESTRICTIONS

**Pets:** Leash only. **Fires:** Fire ring only. **Alcoholic Beverages:** Permitted. **Vehicle Maximum Length:** None.

## TO GET THERE

From junction of I-70 and US 40, take Exit 68 and drive 1,000 feet north on US 40, then 0.25 mi. west on frontage road. Roads are wide and well maintained with broad shoulders.

# WEST YORK

## Hickory Holler Campground

9876 East 2000th Ave., West York 62478. T: (618) 563-4779

| 🚐 ★★★ | 🅰 ★★★ |
|---|---|
| Beauty: ★★★ | Site Privacy: ★★★★ |
| Spaciousness: ★★★★ | Quiet: ★★★★ |
| Security: ★★★★ | Cleanliness: ★★★★ |
| Insect Control: Yes | Facilities: ★★★ |

A quiet, rural campground (eight miles north of West York) with an emphasis on Christian activities, Hickory Holler Campground offers spacious, peaceful surroundings. The typical site width is 40 feet with grassy sites and a good mixture of shaded and open areas. As the name implies, Hickory Holler is blessed with mature hickory trees. Gospel sing-alongs are held in an old remodeled cattle barn and nightly campfires offer community get-togethers. Despite the absence of a swimming pool, the campground offers a lot of varied activities and clean surroundings for a low fee (the $13 rate is about half what other area campgrounds charge). Primitive sites for tent campers feature trees and privacy from RV campers. Security lights, an owner who lives on the grounds, and regular patrols add to campground security.

## BASICS

**Operated by:** Leola Guyer. **Open:** All year. **Site Assignment:** Reservations w/ 1-night deposit, refunds w/ 24-hour notice. **Registration:** At campground office. **Fee:** $13 (cash, check). **Parking:** At site.

## FACILITIES

**Number of RV Sites:** 100. **Number of Tent-Only Sites:** 15. **Hookups:** Electric (20, 30, 50 amps), water, sewer. **Each Site:** Picnic table, fire ring. **Dump Station:** Yes. **Laundry:** Yes. **Pay Phone:** No. **Rest Rooms and Showers:** Yes. **Fuel:** No. **Propane:** No. **Internal Roads:** Gravel, in good condition. **RV Service:** No. **Market:** 12 mi. south in Robinson. **Restaurant:** 7 mi. north in West Union. **General Store:** Yes. **Vending:** Yes. **Swimming Pool:** No. **Playground:** Yes. **Other:** Mini-golf, rec hall, video games, pool table, 2 lakes. **Activities:** Fishing, boating (rental paddleboats available), nightly community campfires, monthly gospel sing-alongs, talent night. **Nearby Attractions:** Crawford County Historical Museum, military museum, Lincoln Trail College, parks. **Additional Information:** Springfield CVB, (800) 545-7300.

## RESTRICTIONS

**Pets:** Leash only. **Fires:** Fire ring only. **Alcoholic Beverages:** Not permitted. **Vehicle Maximum Length:** 40 ft.

## TO GET THERE

From Marshall, drive 18 mi. south on Rte. 1 to Annapolis Rd. Drive 4 mi. west of Rte. 1 on Rte. 33 to Hickory Holler Campground. Roads are wide and well maintained with broad shoulders.

# Indiana

Home of cool icons like James Dean and the Indy 500, the Hoosier State offers unique treats from its "crossroads of America." For starters, the May speedway extravaganza in Indianapolis boasts some of the fastest speeds, smoothest racecars, and most skilled drivers in the racing world. Indianapolis also is home to 113 city parks, including the 250-acre White River State Park right in the heart of the city.

The short life of James Dean is celebrated in his hometown of **Fairmount** where the *Rebel Without a Cause* star is buried. A continuously changing artwork is seen at the **Indiana Dunes** where winds swirl the sand into surreal landscapes. Howl with the wolves at **Wolf Park** in **Lafayette** or hike through the scenic hills of 195,000-acre **Hoosier National Forest.** See the many species of coral and prehistoric ocean life in the fossil bed at **Falls of the Ohio State Park** in **Clarksville** or enjoy the unusual limestone formations and waterfalls at **McCormick's Creek State Park,** east of **Spencer.**

Spelunking is special in Indiana where an electric boat takes visitors through **Bluespring Caverns** in **Bedford.** Hear the story of how **Marengo Cave** was discovered by two youngsters or see the cave where Daniel Boone's brother, Squire, is buried in **Corydon.** An underground mountain and huge helicties mark the passages of Wyandotte caves.

Rent a pontoon boat and cruise **Bloomington's Lake Monroe** to catch a glimpse of a nesting bald eagle, or head to **Madison** to experience the timeless treasure of this beautifully preserved river town. **Auburn's** history as a luxury car manufacturer is recalled at the **Auburn Cord Duesenberg Museum** while **Columbus** has architectural landmarks designed by the master, including I. M. Pei.

**French Lick** and next door neighbor, **West Baden, were** early resorts and health centers because of the abundant artisan springs. Take a ride on the historic 1920s railroad and visit the amazing **West Baden Springs Hotel,** whose domed atrium was once considered the Eighth Wonder of the World. In **Nashville,** the area's beauty led to the establishment of an artists colony that still thrives today, along with the **Little Nashville Opry** which showcases top country music stars. Remnants of a Utopian community draws visitors to **New Harmony,** and the nation's first theme park thrills families at **Holiday World and Splashin' Safari** in **Santa Claus.** Home to one of the world's largest Amish communities, **Shipshewana** also has what is said to be the biggest flea market in America.

*The following facilities accept payment in checks or cash only:*

Broadview Lake Camping Resort, Colfax

Miami Camp, Frankton

Mar-brook Campground, Gas City

Sports Lake Camping Resort, Gas City

Bixler Lake Campground, Kendallville

Oak Lake Family Campground, Roselawn

Gordon's Camping, Kendallville

# Campground Profiles

## BATESVILLE

### Thousand Trails & NACO
### Indian Lakes

7234 East Hwy. 46, Batesville 47006. T: (800) 427-3392; www.1000trails.com.

★★★★     ▲ ★★

Beauty: ★★★★
Spaciousness: ★★★★
Security: ★★★★★
Insect Control: None

Site Privacy: ★★★★
Quiet: ★★★★
Cleanliness: ★★★★★
Facilities: ★★★★

Thousand Trails NACO-Indian Lakes is part of a nationwide network of 57 campground resorts for members of a private camping club. Membership options with annual dues allow members to camp at every preserve in the system or choose only a favorite region. Nonmembers are allowed a get-acquainted visit and will be invited, but not required, to attend a presentation regarding membership offerings. Located eight miles east of Batesville, the campground is on a preserve of wooded land, open spaces. and several lakes. The typical site width is 35 feet and the campground has 100 pull-throughs. Sites are mostly shaded from mature oak, maple, and ash trees. Members have access to a wide array of recreational opportunities, including indoor and outdoor swimming pools and a wading pool, as well as a boat ramp and dock. Quiet time is enforced from 11 p.m. to 8 a.m. when outside patio and decorative lights must be turned off. Golf carts also are prohibited during quiet hours. Speed limit is 15 mph on the main road and five mph in the camping areas. Security measures are great with a gate that requires a code to get in, a manager on site and regular patrols.

## BASICS

**Operated by:** Thousand Trails Inc. **Open:** May 1–Nov. 1. **Site Assignment:** Reservations w/ 1-night deposit; refund w/ 24-hour notice. **Registration:** At campground office. **Fee:** $25 (cash, check, credit cards). **Parking:** At site.

## FACILITIES

**Number of RV Sites:** 1,200. **Number of Tent-Only Sites:** 0. **Hookups:** Electric (30 amps), water. **Each Site:** Picnic table, fire ring. **Dump Station:** Yes. **Laundry:** Yes. **Pay Phone:** Yes. **Rest Rooms and Showers:** Yes. **Fuel:** Yes. **Propane:** Yes. **Internal Roads:** Paved, in great condition. **RV Service:** No. **Market:** 8 mi. west in Batesville. **Restaurant:** 8 mi. west in Batesville. **General Store:** Yes. **Vending:** Yes. **Swimming Pool:** Yes. **Playground:** Yes. **Other:** Indian Lake, adult lounge, ballfield, rental cabins, gazebos, golf course, horseshoes, basketball, shuffleboard, tennis, lodges, mini golf, nature trail, volleyball, amphitheater, game room, boat ramp, boat dock, coin games, trading post. **Activities:** Swimming, boating, hiking, scheduled activities. **Nearby Attractions:** Metamora antique village, covered bridge, riverboat casinos, museums, historic homes, Cincinnati Zoo. **Additional Information:** Batesville Chamber of Commerce, (812) 934-3101.

## RESTRICTIONS

**Pets:** Leash only. **Fires:** Fire ring only. **Alcoholic Beverages:** At sites only. **Vehicle Maximum Length:** None. **Other:** 14-day stay limit.

## TO GET THERE

From junction I-74 and Hwy. 46, take Exit 156 and drive 3.5 mi. west on Hwy. 46. Roads are wide and well maintained with broad shoulders.

## BEANBLOSSOM

## Bill Monroe Memorial Music Park & Campground

5163 IN 135N, Bean Blossom 46160. T: (800) 414-4677; www.beanblossom.com.

🚐 ★★★                          ⛺ ★★★

Beauty: ★★★              Site Privacy: ★★
Spaciousness: ★★★       Quiet: ★★
Security: ★★★★            Cleanliness: ★★★★
Insect Control: None      Facilities: ★★★

This countryside campground is the home of Bill Monroe's famous "Bean Blossom Bluegrass Festival," the longest running annual bluegrass festival in the world. Its wooded amphitheater, with a seating capacity of 5,000, also features other music festivals when camping sites are at a premum. A Pickin' Parlor is a popular site for impromptu music sessions by campers and performers, as are campsites and the parking lot. For music lovers, it's the place to be when events are going on. For folks who want to sleep, it might be a bit noisy during festivals. An on-site museum tells the story of bluegrass and displays some of Monroe's memorabilia, along with the Bluegrass Hall of Fame room. Hillside vistas and natural ambience like cows grazing in nearby fields add a country touch. Air-conditioned showers and restrooms are a welcome respite during hot, humid Hoosier summers. The best sites for tenters are on Miller Hill and Rude Dog where the spots are bigger and shaded. Best places for RVs are sites 43–115 in the woods. The typical site width is 35 feet and the campground offers eight pull-throughs. Located five miles north of Nashville, the campground provides good security with one entry road and regular patrols.

### BASICS
**Operated by:** Dwight Dillman. **Open:** All year. **Site Assignment:** Reservations accepted w/ full payment; no refund. **Registration:** At campground office. **Fee:** $16 (cash, check, credit cards). **Parking:** At site.

### FACILITIES
**Number of RV Sites:** 237. **Number of Tent-Only Sites:** 300. **Hookups:** Electric (30, 50 amps), water. **Each Site:** Grill, picnic table, fire ring. **Dump Station:** Yes. **Laundry:** No. **Pay Phone:**

Yes. **Rest Rooms and Showers:** Yes. **Fuel:** No. **Propane:** No. **Internal Roads:** Gravel, in good condition. **RV Service:** No. **Market:** Walking distance. **Restaurant:** Food concessions during festivals. **General Store:** No. **Vending:** Yes. **Swimming Pool:** No. **Playground:** Yes. **Other:** Small fishing lake, fitness trail, cabins, gift shop. **Activities:** Fishing, biking. **Nearby Attractions:** Brown County State Park, Nashville artist colony w/ more than 350 specialty shops, scenic drives, winter skiing, Little Nashville Opry, golf, Indiana University. **Additional Information:** Brown County CVB, (800) 753-3255.

### RESTRICTIONS
**Pets:** Leash only. **Fires:** Fire rings, campfires. **Alcoholic Beverages:** At sites only. **Vehicle Maximum Length:** 40 ft.

### TO GET THERE
Take I-65 to Exit 68 in Columbus, Indiana. Take Hwy. 46 west 15 mi. to Nashville, Indiana. Bean Blossom is 5 mi. north of Nashville on IN 135. Roads are wide and well maintained with adequate shoulders, but the area is known for its winding roads and steep hills.

## BLOOMINGTON

## Lake Monroe Village Recreation Resort

8107 South Fairfax Rd., Bloomington 47401. T: (812) 824-CAMP; www.lakemonroevillage.com.

🚐 ★★★★                          ⛺ ★★★★

Beauty: ★★★★            Site Privacy: ★★★★
Spaciousness: ★★★★     Quiet: ★★★★
Security: ★★★★            Cleanliness: ★★★★
Insect Control: None      Facilities: ★★★★

Arriving at Lake Monroe Village Recreation Resort, visitors are greeted with a smile and escorted on a tour of the facilities. Campers have a choice of any available sites and are allowed to see them before choosing. Located eight miles southeast of Bloomington, the campground has 30 seasonal campers, 25 pull-through sites, and a typical site width of 24 feet. Laid out in a series of loops, the rural campground offers open and shaded sites. The chlorine-free pool uses electronic purification. Other water recreation choices are an adults-only hot tub and a baby pool. Security measures include surveillance cameras and gates at the entrance and exit. Speed limit is five mph and quiet times are from 11 p.m. to 8 a.m. Little touches such as stone walls used as terraces between some sites add to the beauty and quietness of the campground.

## BASICS

**Operated by:** Sandy & Nelson Cicchitto. **Open:** All year. **Site Assignment:** Reservations w/ 1-night deposit; refund w/ 7-day notice. **Registration:** At campground office. **Fee:** $30 (cash, check, credit cards). **Parking:** At site.

## FACILITIES

**Number of RV Sites:** 125. **Number of Tent-Only Sites:** 50. **Hookups:** Electric (20, 30, 50 amps), water, sewer. **Each Site:** Picnic table, fire ring. **Dump Station:** Yes. **Laundry:** Yes. **Pay Phone:** Yes. **Rest Rooms and Showers:** Yes. **Fuel:** No. **Propane:** Yes. **Internal Roads:** Gravel, in good condition. **RV Service:** No. **Market:** 6 mi. north in Bloomington. **Restaurant:** 1.5 mi. north in Fairfax. **General Store:** Yes. **Vending:** Yes. **Swimming Pool:** Yes. **Playground:** Yes. **Other:** Pavilion, baseball, hot tub, volleyball, basketball, horseshoes, rec hall, rental cabins, badminton, sports field. **Activities:** Swimming. **Nearby Attractions:** Lake Monroe, Indiana University, golf, antiques, arts & crafts, boating, fishing, museums, historic homes, bike park, speedway, horseback riding, wineries. **Additional Information:** Bloomington/Monroe County CVB, (800) 800-0037.

## RESTRICTIONS

**Pets:** Leash only. **Fires:** Fire ring only. **Alcoholic Beverages:** At sites only. **Vehicle Maximum Length:** None.

## TO GET THERE

From junction of Hwy. 45 and Hwy. 31, drive 6 mi. south on Hwy. 37, then 1.8 mi. east on Smithville Rd., then 1.25 mi. south on Fairfax Rd. Roads are wide and well maintained with broad shoulders.

## BRISTOL

### Eby's Pines Campground

14583 SR 120, Bristol 46507. T: (574) 848-4583; F: (574) 848-7291; www.Ebyspines.com; Ebyspinescamp@juno.com.

 ★★★★          ▲ ★★★★

Beauty: ★★★★          Site Privacy: ★★★★
Spaciousness: ★★★★          Quiet: ★★★★

Security: ★★★          Cleanliness: ★★★★
Insect Control: None          Facilities: ★★★★

Harry Eby was a conservationist with a particular fondness for trees. Campers can now enjoy his legacy at Eby's Pines Campground, located three miles east of Bristol. Most of the trees, of course, are pines—white pine, scotch pine and red pine. Laid out in a series of loops, the campground sites are level, mostly shaded and grassy with gravel parking spots. The typical site width is 40 feet; there are 96 seasonal campers and 69 pull-through sites. Best RV spots are 71–76 because they are located by the fishing pond, shower facilities, and swimming pools. The best tent sites are in the Poplars section because they are surrounded by poplar trees and have privacy from RVs. For being so close to the interstate, the campground is surprisingly quiet and peaceful with the pines, the ponds, and the Little Elkhart River providing a natural buffer. At one time a tree farm, the campground has a nicely equipped new camp store and Amish hand-built, rustic log camping cabins that can be rented. A large 2,400-square-foot heated pool has a double tube slide, water umbrella, and—most importantly—a certified lifeguard on duty.

## BASICS

**Operated by:** Barry Lang. **Open:** Apr. 1–Oct. 31. **Site Assignment:** Reservations w/ 1-night deposit; refunds (minus $6) w/ 48-hour notice. **Registration:** At campground office. **Fee:** $28 (cash, credit cards). **Parking:** At site.

## FACILITIES

**Number of RV Sites:** 330. **Number of Tent-Only Sites:** 13. **Hookups:** Electric (30 amps), water, sewer. **Each Site:** Picnic table, fire ring. **Dump Station:** Yes. **Laundry:** Yes. **Pay Phone:** Yes. **Rest Rooms and Showers:** Yes. **Fuel:** No. **Propane:** Yes. **Internal Roads:** Paved/gravel, in good condition. **RV Service:** No. **Market:** 3 mi. west in Bristol. **Restaurant:** 3 mi. west in Bristol. **General Store:** Yes. **Vending:** Yes. **Swimming Pool:** Yes. **Playground:** Yes. **Other:** Basketball, tennis, volleyball, roller skating, horseshoes, rec room, video games, rental cabins, fishing pond, hiking trail, spa pool, pavilion, sports field. **Activities:** Swimming, fishing, hiking, scheduled weekend activities. **Nearby Attractions:** Amish country, Shipshewana Flea Market, golf, RV History Museum, antique shops, arts & crafts shops, museums, historic homes, Notre Dame University. **Additional Information:** Amish Country/Elkhart County Visitors Center, (800) 860-5949.

<u>RESTRICTIONS</u>

**Pets:** Leash only. **Fires:** Fire ring only. **Alcoholic Beverages:** At sites only. **Vehicle Maximum Length:** 40 ft.

<u>TO GET THERE</u>

From junction of I-80/90 (Indiana Turnpike) and Hwy. 13, take Exit 101 and drive 1 mi. south on Hwy. 13, then 3 mi. west on Hwy. 120. Roads are wide and well maintained with broad shoulders.

## CLOVERDALE
### Cloverdale RV Park

2789 East CR 800S, Cloverdale 46120. T: (888) 298-0035; cdalervp@ccrtc.com.

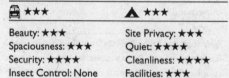

Beauty: ★★★
Spaciousness: ★★★
Security: ★★★★
Insect Control: None
Site Privacy: ★★★
Quiet: ★★★★
Cleanliness: ★★★★
Facilities: ★★★

Cloverdale RV Park is a nice, quiet, comfortable place to stay and hosts many return campers. That's why reservations are strongly recommended. Laid out in a series of loops, the campground has 50 pull-throughs and a typical site width of 35 feet. The rural campground two miles north of Cloverdale, has a fishing pond but doesn't allow swimming or boating. Regulations to keep the campground quiet and safe are strictly enforced. Quiet times are between 9 p.m. and 8 a.m. and children must be accompanied by an adult in public areas at all time. The campground has a eight mph speed limit which might be better set at five mph. Children camping are more concerned about play than about watching for cars. Security measures include one entrance; an exit is closed at night so vehicles have to drive by the office to enter. Owners live on site and provide regular patrols.

<u>BASICS</u>

**Operated by:** Dan & Cher Nickerson. **Open:** All year. **Site Assignment:** Reservations accepted w/ 1-night deposit; refund w/ 48-hour notice. **Registration:** At campground office. **Fee:** $22 (cash, check, credit card). **Parking:** At site.

<u>FACILITIES</u>

**Number of RV Sites:** 52. **Number of Tent-Only Sites:** 20. **Hookups:** Electric (30 amps), water, sewer, telephone. **Each Site:** Picnic table, fire ring. **Dump Station:** Yes. **Laundry:** Yes. **Pay Phone:** Yes. **Rest Rooms and Showers:** Yes. **Fuel:** No. **Propane:** No. **Internal Roads:** Gravel, in good condition. **RV Service:** No. **Market:** 2 mi. south in Cloverdale. **Restaurant:** 2 mi. south in Cloverdale. **General Store:** Yes. **Vending:** Yes. **Swimming Pool:** No. **Playground:** Yes. **Other:** Rec room, fax & copy service, fishing pond, horseshoes, basketball, nature trail, coin games, sports field. **Activities:** Fishing, hiking. **Nearby Attractions:** Covered bridges, raceway, antiques, Victory Field, zoo, Cataract Falls. **Additional Information:** Putnam County CVB, (800) 829-4639.

<u>RESTRICTIONS</u>

**Pets:** Leash only. **Fires:** Fire ring only. **Alcoholic Beverages:** At sites only. **Vehicle Maximum Length:** None. **Other:** No clotheslines permitted on sites.

<u>TO GET THERE</u>

From junction of I-70 and US 231, take Exit 41, drive 0.8 mi. north on US 231 to CR 800S, drive east 0.5 mi. Roads are wide and well maintained with broad shoulders.

## COLFAX
### Broadview Lake Camping Resort

4850 South Broadview Rd., Colfax 46035. T: (765) 324-2622

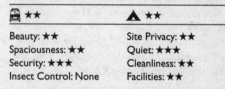

Beauty: ★★
Spaciousness: ★★
Security: ★★★
Insect Control: None
Site Privacy: ★★
Quiet: ★★★
Cleanliness: ★★
Facilities: ★★

Located two miles north of Colfax, Broadview Lake Camping Resort is set back from major roads and surrounded by cornfields. Almost every site has a tree including quite a few tall maples. A primitive camping area is bordered on two sides by a creek. The typical site width is 30 feet; there are four pull-throughs and 70 seasonal campers. Most sites are grassy and a few have gravel pads for RVs. Speed limit is five mph. Campers and visitors over the age of ten must buy a fishing pass at $5 a day for campers and $6 for visitors. No swimming or wading is allowed in the lake or creeks.

## BASICS

**Operated by:** Fred & Karen Culross. **Open:** Apr. 1–Oct. 15. **Site Assignment:** Reservations w/ no deposit. **Registration:** At campground office. **Fee:** $15 (cash). **Parking:** At site.

## FACILITIES

**Number of RV Sites:** 100. **Number of Tent-Only Sites:** 30. **Hookups:** Electric (30 amps), water, sewer. **Each Site:** Picnic table, fire ring. **Dump Station:** Yes. **Laundry:** No. **Pay Phone:** Yes. **Rest Rooms and Showers:** Yes. **Fuel:** No. **Propane:** No. **Internal Roads:** Paved/gravel, in fair condition. **RV Service:** No. **Market:** 13 mi. north in Frankfort. **Restaurant:** 2 mi. south in Colfax. **General Store:** Yes. **Vending:** Yes. **Swimming Pool:** Yes. **Playground:** Yes. **Other:** Stocked fishing lake, game room, rec hall, badminton, horseshoes, volleyball, sports field. **Activities:** Swimming, fishing, scheduled weekend activities. **Nearby Attractions:** Golf, Purdue University, antiques, Tippecanoe Battlefield, Wolf Park, Fort Quiatenon, museums, historic homes. **Additional Information:** Greater Lafayette CVB, (800) 872-6648.

## RESTRICTIONS

**Pets:** Leash only. **Fires:** Fire ring only. **Alcoholic Beverages:** Permitted. **Vehicle Maximum Length:** 38 ft. **Other:** Tents may not remain in one spot for longer than 5 days; limit of 6 catfish per day per person; limit of 2 poles per person.

## TO GET THERE

From junction of I-65 and Hwy. 28, take Exit 158 and drive 2.5 mi. west on Hwy. 28, then 3 mi. south on US 52, then 0.25 mi. west on Broadview Rd./CR 800W. Roads are wide and well maintained with broad shoulders, with one bad curve on Broadview Rd.

## COLUMBUS

### Woods–Waters

8855 South 300 West, Columbus 47201. T: (800) 799-3928

🚐 ★★★★          ▲ ★★★★

| | |
|---|---|
| Beauty: ★★★★ | Site Privacy: ★★★★ |
| Spaciousness: ★★★★ | Quiet: ★★★★ |
| Security: ★★★★ | Cleanliness: ★★★★★ |
| Insect Control: None | Facilities: ★★★★ |

Woods–Waters offers a quiet country setting close to the interstate and other attractions. Located five miles south of Columbus, the rural campground has level gravel sites with a typical site width of 35 feet. The campground has 15 seasonal campers and 15 pull-throughs. Situated in a forest, the campground is well maintained and decorated with flowers, as well as a wishing well and a wooden swing with a canopy. The bathrooms are not only extremely clean, but brightened with wallpaper, artificial flowers, framed paintings, and plenty of mirrors over the sink, along with a full-length mirror on the wall. A well-stocked campstore with friendly folks makes it an even more pleasant place. Security and safety measures are good with a five mph speed limit, quiet hours from eight p.m. to 7 a.m., a year-round resident manager, and three deputy sheriffs who are seasonal campers at the campground.

## BASICS

**Operated by:** Larry & Betty York. **Open:** All year. **Site Assignment:** Reservations w/ 1-night deposit; refund w/ 7-day notice. **Registration:** At campground office. **Fee:** $22 (cash, check, credit cards). **Parking:** At site.

## FACILITIES

**Number of RV Sites:** 100. **Number of Tent-Only Sites:** 10. **Hookups:** Electric (30, 50 amps), water, sewer. **Each Site:** Picnic table, fire ring. **Dump Station:** Yes. **Laundry:** Yes. **Pay Phone:** Yes. **Rest Rooms and Showers:** Yes. **Fuel:** No. **Propane:** Yes. **Internal Roads:** Gravel, in good condition. **RV Service:** No. **Market:** 5 mi. north in Columbus. **Restaurant:** 5 mi. north in Columbus. **General Store:** Yes. **Vending:** No. **Swimming Pool:** Yes. **Playground:** Yes. **Other:** Game room, movies clubhouse, lounge, coin games, pavilion, nature trail, fishing lake, basketball, badminton, sports field, volleyball, horseshoes. **Activities:** Swimming, fishing, hiking, scheduled weekend activities. **Nearby Attractions:** Columbus architecture tour, museums, historic homes, golf, Brown County & Nashville, crafts shops, antiques, Indianapolis Zoo, Indy 500. **Additional Information:** Columbus Area Visitor Center, (800) 468-6564.

## RESTRICTIONS

**Pets:** Leash only. **Fires:** Fire ring only. **Alcoholic Beverages:** At sites only. **Vehicle Maximum Length:** None.

## To Get There

From junction of I-65 and Hwy. 58 (Ogilville), take Exit 64, drive 0.5 mi. west on Hwy. 58, then 1 mi. south on CR 300W. Roads are wide and well maintained with broad shoulders, except for CR 300W which has narrow shoulders.

## CRAWFORDSVILLE

### Crawfordsville KOA

1600 Lafayette Rd., Crawfordsville 47933. T: (317) 362-4190; www.koa.com; cvillkoa@tetc.com.

🚐 ★★★★                    ▲ ★★★★

Beauty: ★★★★            Site Privacy: ★★★★
Spaciousness: ★★★★     Quiet: ★★★
Security: ★★★★           Cleanliness: ★★★★
Insect Control: No         Facilities: ★★★★

Crawfordsville KOA is conveniently located, clean, and secure. It also offers spacious spots, almost all of which are pull-throughs, with a typical site width of 48 feet. Laid out in a series of loops, the rural campground offers a choice of shady or open, grassy or gravel sites. Large patches of iris and peonies brighten the campgrounds, as do shrubs and other landscaping. Located two miles north of Crawfordsville, the campground is convenient to several popular local festivals—Feast of the Hunters Moon, Strawberry Festival, Covered Bridge Festival, to name a few—so be sure there is an open space if you know when you want to stay there. Easy access and good roads pull a lot of travelers from the interstate looking for a night's rest. Security is good with one entrance road and owners who live on site.

### Basics

**Operated by:** Richard Nelson. **Open:** Mar. 15–Nov. 25. **Site Assignment:** Reservations accepted w/ no deposit. **Registration:** At campground office. **Fee:** $23 (cash, check, credit cards). **Parking:** At site.

### Facilities

**Number of RV Sites:** 60. **Number of Tent-Only Sites:** 7. **Hookups:** Electric (30, 50 amps), water, sewer, cable TV. **Each Site:** Picnic table, fire ring. **Dump Station:** Yes. **Laundry:** Yes. **Pay Phone:** Yes. **Rest Rooms and Showers:** Yes. **Fuel:** No. **Propane:** Yes. **Internal Roads:** Paved/gravel, in good condition. **RV Service:** Yes. **Market:** 2 mi. south in Crawfordsville. **Restaurant:** 2 mi. south in Crawfordsville. **General Store:** Yes. **Vending:** Yes. **Swimming Pool:** Yes. **Playground:** Yes. **Other:** RV supply store, rec room, horseshoes, pavilion, volleyball, coin games, sports field, rental cabins. **Activities:** Swimming. **Nearby Attractions:** Ben Hur Museum, antiques, Old Jail Museum, 42 covered bridges, golf, canoe trips. **Additional Information:** Crawfordsville CVB, (800) 866-3973.

### Restrictions

**Pets:** Leash only. **Fires:** Fire ring only. **Alcoholic Beverages:** Permitted. **Vehicle Maximum Length:** 38 ft.

### To Get There

From junction of I-74 and US 231, take Exit 34, then drive 1 mi. south on US 231. Roads are wide and well maintained with good shoulders.

## DEMOTTE

### Lake Holiday Yogi Bear Jellystone Park Camp-Resort

11780 West SR 10, DeMotte 46310. T: (219) 345-3132; F: (219) 345-4422; www.jellystonedemotte.com.

🚐 ★★★                     ▲ ★★

Beauty: ★★★             Site Privacy: ★★★
Spaciousness: ★★★       Quiet: ★★★
Security: ★★★★           Cleanliness: ★★★★
Insect Control: None       Facilities: ★★★

Located right off I-65 in DeMotte, this campground offers convenience and easy access with the feel of a country setting in a city location. Sites are level and mostly shaded with a typical site width of 40 feet. Laid out in a series of loops, Lake Holiday has five pull-through sites and 115 seasonal campers. As with most Yogi Bear resorts, the campground has many activities and recreation facilities. Speed limit is five mph, but at the time of our visit, golf carts were zipping around much faster As a family campground, Lake Holiday requires that shirts and shoes be worn in the ranger station and restaurant, that alcoholic beverages be kept in a covered container or at campsites and that children under seven are not to be in restrooms unless accompanied by an adult. Security measures include an on-site manager, regular ranger patrols, and a security gate that requires a card to open. The gate is manned 24 hours a day.

## BASICS

**Operated by:** Jim Rose. **Open:** Apr. 1–Oct. 31. **Site Assignment:** Reservations paid in full; refund (minus $5) w/ 5-day notice. **Registration:** At campground office. **Fee:** $29 (cash, check, credit cards). **Parking:** At site.

## FACILITIES

**Number of RV Sites:** 674. **Number of Tent-Only Sites:** 20. **Hookups:** Electric (30 amps), water, sewer. **Each Site:** Picnic table, fire ring. **Dump Station:** Yes. **Laundry:** Yes. **Pay Phone:** Yes. **Rest Rooms and Showers:** Yes. **Fuel:** No. **Propane:** Yes. **Internal Roads:** Paved/gravel, in good condition. **RV Service:** No. **Market:** 1 block in DeMotte. **Restaurant:** On site. **General Store:** Yes. **Vending:** Yes. **Swimming Pool:** Yes. **Playground:** Yes. **Other:** Lake Holiday, swimming beach, sports area, rec hall, waterslide, splash boats, mini-golf, rental golf carts, horseshoes, tennis, basketball, volleyball, shuffleboard, pool tables, video games. **Activities:** Swimming, fishing, canoeing, scheduled activities. **Nearby Attractions:** Golf, dragstrip, Amish Acres, antiques, historic sites, museums, Indiana Beach. **Additional Information:** DeMotte Chamber of Commerce, (219) 987-5800.

## RESTRICTIONS

**Pets:** Leash only. **Fires:** Fire ring only. **Alcoholic Beverages:** Permitted. **Vehicle Maximum Length:** 40 ft.

## TO GET THERE

From junction of I-65 and Hwy. 10, take Exit 230 (DeMotte-Roselawn Exit), drive 1 block west on Hwy. 10. Roads are wide and well maintained with broad shoulders.

## FAIRMOUNT
### Hidden Lake Campground

11460 SR 37, Fairmount 46928. T: (765) 948-4862; hiddnlake@aol.com.

| 🚐 ★★ | 🏕 ★★ |
|---|---|
| Beauty: ★★ | Site Privacy: ★★ |
| Spaciousness: ★★★ | Quiet: ★★★ |
| Security: ★★★★★ | Cleanliness: ★ |
| Insect Control: Yes | Facilities: ★★ |

A '57 Chevy rests at the bottom of a lake at Hidden Lake Campground. It seems a fitting memento for a campground outside actor James

Dean's hometown. The sunken auto is used for scuba diving and lessons. A cabin cruiser also is sunk there to further interest scuba divers in the 100-foot-deep lake. The best things about the campground are its proximity to Fairmount (about eight miles), its spring-fed lake, and its security system. Video cameras are placed in several locations and the owner lives on site to help monitor quiet and safety. The campground has one entrance and exit. An air-conditioned gameroom is a welcome spot on humid Hoosier summers. The typical site width is 35 feet and the campground offers ten pull-throughs. Unfortunately, the campground is not as well maintained as others we've seen. At the time of our visit, it was long overdue for an intensive cleaning. Junk cars need to be towed off, buildings need painting, and trash and brush need to be removed. After all, this is the area where the "King of Cool" once roamed. With some work, this could be a cool campground.

## BASICS

**Operated by:** Colin Johnstone. **Open:** Apr. 1–Oct. 15. **Site Assignment:** Reservations accepted, no deposit. **Registration:** At campground office. **Fee:** $22.50 (cash, check, credit cards). **Parking:** At site.

## FACILITIES

**Number of RV Sites:** 125. **Number of Tent-Only Sites:** 36. **Hookups:** Electric (20, 30 amps), water. **Each Site:** Fire ring. **Dump Station:** Yes. **Laundry:** No. **Pay Phone:** Yes. **Rest Rooms and Showers:** Yes. **Fuel:** No. **Propane:** No. **Internal Roads:** Gravel, in fair condition. **RV Service:** No. **Market:** 8 mi. south in Elwood. **Restaurant:** 8 mi. south in Elwood. **General Store:** No. **Vending:** Yes. **Swimming Pool:** No. **Playground:** Yes. **Other:** Spring-fed lake, sandy beach, rec hall, video games, horseshoes, volleyball, badminton. **Activities:** Swimming, fishing, scuba diving, rental kayak & paddleboats available. **Nearby Attractions:** Fairmount (home of actor James Dean), museums, boating, James Dean's final resting place. **Additional Information:** Grant County CVB, (800) 662-9474.

## RESTRICTIONS

**Pets:** Leash only. **Fires:** Fire ring only. **Alcoholic Beverages:** At sites only. **Vehicle Maximum Length:** None.

## TO GET THERE

From junction of I-69 and Hwy. 26, take Exit 55, drive 9 mi. west on Hwy. 26, then 3 mi.

south on Hwy. 37. Roads are wide and well maintained with adequate shoulders.

## FRANKTON
## Miami Camp

8851 West 400N, Frankton 46044. T: (765) 734-1365; www.campgrounds.com/icoa; miamicamp@worldnet.att.net.

🚐 ★★         🅰 ★★

| | |
|---|---|
| Beauty: ★★ | Site Privacy: ★★ |
| Spaciousness: ★★ | Quiet: ★★★★ |
| Security: ★★★ | Cleanliness: ★★ |
| Insect Control: Yes | Facilities: ★★ |

Miami Camp got its name from its location, the site of an old Miami Indian encampment in a grove of huge sycamore trees along a half mile of Pipe Creek. All the sites are wooded with abundant shade and a mix of grassy and gravel sites. The local health department sprays for mosquitos when necessary. Laid out in a series of loops, the campground offers a large, shady, primitive area where tenters have more natural surroundings and privacy away from RVs. Miami Camp has two pull-through sites and access to pizza delivery from seven miles away. The larger city of Anderson, is 11 miles south. Living on site, the owner enforces quiet and safety rules. Pets must be in the units at night.

BASICS

**Operated by:** Millie Burkhart. **Open:** Apr. 15–Oct. 15. **Site Assignment:** Reservations accepted w/ no deposit. **Registration:** At campground office. **Fee:** $19 (cash, check). **Parking:** At site.

FACILITIES

**Number of RV Sites:** 50. **Number of Tent-Only Sites:** 50. **Hookups:** Electric (20, 30, 50 amps), water, sewer. **Each Site:** Picnic table, fire ring. **Dump Station:** Yes. **Laundry:** No. **Pay Phone:** Yes. **Rest Rooms and Showers:** Yes. **Fuel:** No. **Propane:** No. **Internal Roads:** Gravel, in fair condition. **RV Service:** No. **Market:** 7 mi. north in Elwood. **Restaurant:** 7 mi. north in Elwood. **General Store:** No. **Vending:** Yes. **Swimming Pool:** Yes. **Playground:** Yes. **Other:** Hiking trails, horsehoes, volleyball, badminton, bocce ball, fishing creek. **Activities:** Swimming, fishing, hiking. **Nearby Attractions:** Antiques, fine arts center, Historic Military Armor Museum, horse race

track. **Additional Information:** Madison County CVB, (800) 533-6569.

RESTRICTIONS

**Pets:** Leash only. **Fires:** Fire ring only. **Alcoholic Beverages:** At sites only. **Vehicle Maximum Length:** None.

TO GET THERE

From south junction of Hwy. 13, Hwy. 37 and CR 400N, drive 1.25 mi. east on CR 400N. Roads are wide and well maintained with adequate shoulders.

## FREMONT
## Yogi Bear's Jellystone Park Camp-Resort

140 Lane 201, Fremont 46737. T: (219) 833-1114; www.jellystonesbest.com.

🚐 ★★★★       🅰 ★★★★

| | |
|---|---|
| Beauty: ★★★★ | Site Privacy: ★★★★ |
| Spaciousness: ★★★★ | Quiet: ★★★★ |
| Security: ★★★★★ | Cleanliness: ★★★★★ |
| Insect Control: Yes | Facilities: ★★★★★ |

The campground's name indicates that it is a resort, and that is a good way to describe Yogi Bear's Jellystone Park Camp-Resort at Barton Lake. Located seven miles west of Fremont, the campground offers enough activities to keep families happily busy for days. With its snack bar and well-stocked campstore, it is possible for campers to come, park their vehicles, and not leave the campground for little errands. Campers have a choice of open or shady spots with 35 feet being the typical site width. Sites are generally grassy with concrete patios. The facility has 216 seasonal campers and 50 pull-through sites. Swimmers have a choice of a sandy beach at Barton Lake, a heated outdoor pool or an indoor solarium pool. Tent campers can choose a rustic area with more greenery and privacy from RVs or tents may be put on any of the RV sites. Security is tops with a locked card-coded gate, surveillence cameras, regular patrols, and owners who live on site.

BASICS

**Operated by:** The Barry & Corcimiglia families. **Open:** Apr. 15–Nov. 1. **Site Assignment:** Reservations w/ 1-night deposit; refund w/ 7-day notice.

**Registration:** At campground office. **Fee:** $38 (cash, check, credit cards). **Parking:** At site.

## FACILITIES

**Number of RV Sites:** 460. **Number of Tent-Only Sites:** 25. **Hookups:** Electric (30, 50 amps), water, sewer. **Each Site:** Picnic table, fire ring. **Dump Station:** Yes. **Laundry:** Yes. **Pay Phone:** Yes. **Rest Rooms and Showers:** Yes. **Fuel:** No. **Propane:** Yes. **Internal Roads:** Paved, in excellent condition. **RV Service:** Yes. **Market:** 7 mi. east in Fremont. **Restaurant:** 7 mi. east in Fremont. **General Store:** Yes. **Vending:** Yes. **Swimming Pool:** Yes. **Playground:** Yes. **Other:** Fishing lake, rental cabins, spa, snack bar, volleyball, basketball, arcade building, horseshoes, mini-golf, boat launch, rec hall, pavilion, sandy beach. **Activities:** Swimming, fishing, boating (rental rowboats, paddleboats available), movies, scheduled activities. **Nearby Attractions:** Outlet shopping malls, water slide, Amish area, flea market, amusement park, car musuem, lakes, golf, antiques, arts & crafts shops. **Additional Information:** Amish County/Elkhart County Visitors Center, (800) 860-5949.

## RESTRICTIONS

**Pets:** Leash only. **Fires:** Fire ring only. **Alcoholic Beverages:** At sites only. **Vehicle Maximum Length:** None. **Other:** Campfires must be extinguished by midnight.

## TO GET THERE

From I-80/90 (Indiana Turnpike), take Exit 144 to Hwy. 120, drive 3.25 mi. west on Hwy. 120, then 0.5 mi. north on CR 300 W. Roads are wide and well maintained with broad shoulders.

## GARRETT
## Indian Springs Campground

981 CR 64, Garrett 46738. T: (219) 357-5194; F: (219) 357-5194; indiansprings@ctlnet.com.

🚐 ★★                    ⛺ ★★

| | | |
|---|---|---|
| Beauty: ★★ | Site Privacy: ★★ |
| Spaciousness: ★★★ | Quiet: ★★★★ |
| Security: ★★★★ | Cleanliness: ★★ |
| Insect Control: Yes | Facilities: ★★ |

Indian Springs Campground is blessed with three lakes—two for fishing, one for fishing and swimming—and an abundance of mature oak and hickory trees. Laid out in a series of loops, the campground offers 15 pull-throughs and an average site width of 35 feet. Most sites are grassy and shaded. A separate section is set aside for tent campers, away from RVs. Security is good with a traffic control gate requiring a pass. Owners live on site and the campground is patrolled regularly. A game room is a good addition but needs to be spiffed up in our opinion. If you go, be careful entering and exiting the campground because of a hill that makes it difficult to see oncoming traffic. Also be cautious of a narrow bridge crossing at the campground entrance.

## BASICS

**Operated by:** Karen & Kenneth Steele; Kathy, Deborah, Dale, & Don Moore. **Open:** All year. **Site Assignment:** Reservations accepted w/ 1-night deposit; refund (minus $5 fee) w/ 48-hour notice. **Registration:** At campground office. **Fee:** $23 (cash, check, credit cards). **Parking:** At site.

## FACILITIES

**Number of RV Sites:** 400. **Number of Tent-Only Sites:** 17. **Hookups:** Electric (20, 30, 50 amps), water, sewer. **Each Site:** Picnic table, fire ring. **Dump Station:** No. **Laundry:** Yes. **Pay Phone:** Yes. **Rest Rooms and Showers:** Yes. **Fuel:** No. **Propane:** Yes. **Internal Roads:** Gravel, in fair condition. **RV Service:** No. **Market:** 4 mi. north in Garrett. **Restaurant:** 4 mi. north in Garrett. **General Store:** Yes. **Vending:** Yes. **Swimming Pool:** No. **Playground:** Yes. **Other:** 3 small lakes, hiking trails, basketball, volleyball, horseshoes, game room. **Activities:** Swimming, fishing, boating (rental pontoon, rowboats, canoes, paddleboats available), church services, hiking, scheduled weekend activities. **Nearby Attractions:** Amish communities, nation's 2nd largest genealogy library, Lincoln Museum, zoo, Auburn Cord Duesenberg Museum. **Additional Information:** Fort Wayne/Allen County CVB, (800) 767-7752.

## RESTRICTIONS

**Pets:** Leash only. **Fires:** Fire ring only. **Alcoholic Beverages:** At sites only. **Vehicle Maximum Length:** None. **Other:** Pet owners must show proper vaccination records.

## TO GET THERE

From junction of I-69 and Hwy. 8, take Exit 129, drive 3 mi. west on Hwy. 8, then 5 mi. south on Hwy. 327, then 0.5 mi. west on CR 64. Roads are in good condition with adequate shoulders.

# GAS CITY
## Mar-brook Campground

6690 East 600 South, Marion 46953. T: (765) 674-4383

🚐 ★★★                    ⛺ ★★★

Beauty: ★★★              Site Privacy: ★★★
Spaciousness: ★★★         Quiet: ★★
Security: ★★★★            Cleanliness: ★★★
Insect Control: Yes        Facilities: ★★★

Mar-brook Campground is so close to I-69 that you can almost read the license plates on vehicles speeding by. The convenience of such easy access comes with a price, though. Highway noise is very loud, particularly during rush hours. The noise is less noticeable on the back side of the campground. The typical site width is 22 feet, with 15 pull-throughs. Laid out in a loop, the riverside park offers mostly shady spots. Security measures are good with one entrance road, owners who live on site, and regular patrols. Safety also is emphasized in the family campground, located four miles west of Gas City. No motor bike riding is allowed, bicycles must be put up when the dusk to dawn lights come on, and bikes are not allowed at any time on the hill in front of the recreation building. Children under 13 are not allowed in the pool unsupervised and small children are not to go to the restrooms alone. To make sure the rules are understood, campers must read and sign a copy of the regulations.

### BASICS
**Operated by:** Paul & Joyce Martin. **Open:** Apr. 15–Oct. 15. **Site Assignment:** Reservations w/ 1-night deposit; refund w/ 4-day notice. **Registration:** At campground office. **Fee:** $17 (cash, check). **Parking:** At site.

### FACILITIES
**Number of RV Sites:** 160. **Number of Tent-Only Sites:** 30. **Hookups:** Electric (20, 30 amps), water, sewer. **Each Site:** Picnic table, fire ring. **Dump Station:** Yes. **Laundry:** Yes. **Pay Phone:** Yes. **Rest Rooms and Showers:** Yes. **Fuel:** No. **Propane:** Yes. **Internal Roads:** Paved/gravel, in fair condition. **RV Service:** No. **Market:** 4 mi. east in Gas City. **Restaurant:** 4 mi. east in Gas City. **General Store:** Yes. **Vending:** Yes. **Swimming Pool:** Yes. **Playground:** Yes. **Other:** Mississinewa River, hiking trails, horseshoes, basketball court, recreation field, volleyball, arcade, mini-golf. **Activities:** Swimming, fishing, hiking, scheduled weekend activities. **Nearby Attractions:** James Dean hometown, museums, golf, antiques, Mississinewa Battlefield. **Additional Information:** Grant County CVB, (800) 662-9474.

### RESTRICTIONS
**Pets:** Leash only. **Fires:** Fire ring only. **Alcoholic Beverages:** At sites only. **Vehicle Maximum Length:** None. **Other:** No cotton garments, suntan oil, or lotion allowed in pool.

### TO GET THERE
From junction of I-69 and Hwy. 22, take Exit 59, drive 0.25 mi. east on Hwy. 22, then 1 mi. south on CR 700E, then 1 mi. southwest on CR 600S. The county road is narrow and rough in spots.

# GAS CITY
## Sports Lake Camping Resort

7230 East 400 South, Marion 46953. T: (765) 998-2558; F: (765) 674-9229.

🚐 ★★★                    ⛺ ★★★

Beauty: ★★★              Site Privacy: ★★★
Spaciousness: ★★★         Quiet: ★★★★
Security: ★★★★            Cleanliness: ★★★
Insect Control: None       Facilities: ★★★

With two golf courses nearby, Sports Lake Camping Resort is a popular campground for golfers and other sports enthusiasts. Located two miles east of Gas City, the campground also offers many recreational opportunities on site. Not surprisingly, about half the sites are occupied by seasonal campers and only two full hookups spots remain. A heavily wooded lakeside campground in a secluded rural area, Sports Lake offers a common site width of 30 feet with ten pull-throughs. A five mph speed limit is strictly enforced and motorists who try to enter the exit will find their tires in trouble from a one-way apparatus. Security features include an electric gate that is closed from 10 p.m. to 8 a.m. The owner lives nearby and helper campers also assist in keeping an eye on the campground. About the only noise is what drifts over from the Friday night races nearby. Best spots for RVs are 1A–10A because they are larger pull-throughs. Favorite sites for tent campers are in the woods.

## BASICS

**Operated by:** Randy & Peggy Richards. **Open:** Apr. 15–Oct. 15. **Site Assignment:** Reservations accepted w/ 1-night deposit; no refunds. **Registration:** At campground office. **Fee:** $25 (cash, check). **Parking:** At site.

## FACILITIES

**Number of RV Sites:** 150. **Number of Tent-Only Sites:** 25. **Hookups:** Electric (20, 30 amps), water, sewer. **Each Site:** Picnic table, fire ring. **Dump Station:** Yes. **Laundry:** No. **Pay Phone:** No. **Rest Rooms and Showers:** Yes. **Fuel:** No. **Propane:** No. **Internal Roads:** Gravel, in fair condition. **RV Service:** No. **Market:** 2 mi. west in Gas City. **Restaurant:** 2 mi. west in Gas City. **General Store:** Yes. **Vending:** Yes. **Swimming Pool:** Yes. **Playground:** Yes. **Other:** Rec hall, pavilion, fishing lake, mini-golf, shuffleboard, badminton, sports field, horseshoes, volleyball. **Activities:** Swimming, fishing, boating (rental rowboats, paddleboats available), scheduled weekend activities. **Nearby Attractions:** James Dean's hometown, golf, antiques, museums, Mississinewa Battlefield. **Additional Information:** Grant County CVB, (800) 662-9474.

## RESTRICTIONS

**Pets:** Leash only. **Fires:** Fire ring only. **Alcoholic Beverages:** At sites only. **Vehicle Maximum Length:** None. **Other:** Visitors must park in the lot outside & pay $2 each to visit; no swimming in the lake.

## TO GET THERE

From junction of I-69 and Hwy. 22, take Exit 59, drive 0.5 mi. east on Hwy. 22, then 1 mi. north on CR 700E, then 0.25 mi. east on CR 400S. Roads are wide and well maintained with narrow shoulders in spots.

## HOWE

### Twin Mills Camping Resort

1675 West SR 120, Howe 46746. T: (219) 562-3212; www.twinmillscamping.com.

🚐 ★★★★          ▲ ★★★★

Beauty: ★★★★          Site Privacy: ★★★★
Spaciousness: ★★★★          Quiet: ★★★★
Security: ★★★★★          Cleanliness: ★★★★
Insect Control: Yes          Facilities: ★★★★

Twin Mills Camping Resort has the beauty and paved roads of a state park, along with the facilities of a private resort. The result is a winning combination for campers. Located two miles east of Howe, the campground has wooded and open sites with a typical site width of 35 feet. Each site is plainly marked with a white pole and red number sign. Mature pine trees and other greenery add to the privacy, quiet, and attractiveness. Laid out in a series of loops, the campground has 280 seasonals and 20 pull-through sites. Most popular sites are in Campers Cove which is close to the activities. A full-time recreation director keeps the activities going. A five mph speed limit and one-way roads help with safety. Security measures are tops with a key-card gate, one entrance/exit road, owners who live on site, surveillance cameras, and regular patrols of the campground.

## BASICS

**Operated by:** Dave & Vicki Cagley. **Open:** Apr. 15–Oct. 15. **Site Assignment:** Reservations w/ 1-night deposit; refund (less $5) w/ 48-hour notice. **Registration:** At campground office. **Fee:** $32 (cash, check, credit cards). **Parking:** At site.

## FACILITIES

**Number of RV Sites:** 559. **Number of Tent-Only Sites:** 10. **Hookups:** Electric (30 amps), water, sewer. **Each Site:** Picnic table, fire ring. **Dump Station:** Yes. **Laundry:** Yes. **Pay Phone:** Yes. **Rest Rooms and Showers:** Yes. **Fuel:** Yes. **Propane:** Yes. **Internal Roads:** Paved, in good condition. **RV Service:** Yes. **Market:** 2 mi. east in Howe. **Restaurant:** 2 mi. east in Howe. **General Store:** Yes. **Vending:** Yes. **Swimming Pool:** No. **Playground:** Yes. **Other:** Lake beach, mini-golf, biking & hiking trails, shuffleboard, basketball, horseshoes, volleyball, game room, coin games, rec hall, rental cabins, pavilion, nature lookout, boat dock, badminton. **Activities:** Swimming, hiking, fishing, boating (rental rowboats, canoes available), scheduled weekend activities. **Nearby Attractions:** Amish community, flea market, antique mall, auto museum, golf, arts & crafts, Borkholder Dutch Village. **Additional Information:** LaGrange County CVB, (800) 254-8090.

## RESTRICTIONS

**Pets:** Leash only. **Fires:** Fire ring only. **Alcoholic Beverages:** At sites only. **Vehicle Maximum Length:** None.

## TO GET THERE

From junction of I-80/90 and Hwy. 9, take Exit 121, drive 2.5 mi. south on Hwy. 9, then 1.75

mi. west on Hwy. 120. Roads are wide and well maintained with broad shoulders.

## KENDALLVILLE
### Bixler Lake Campground

211 Iddings St., Kendallville 46755. T: (219) 347-1064

🚐 ★★★　　　　　🏕 ★★★

| | |
|---|---|
| Beauty: ★★★ | Site Privacy: ★★★ |
| Spaciousness: ★★★ | Quiet: ★★★ |
| Security: ★★★ | Cleanliness: ★★★ |
| Insect Control: None | Facilities: ★★★ |

Located in the woods and wilds, yet close to town and separated by a 120-acre lake, Bixler Lake Campground is a popular spot with local campers and with groups that can be in adjoining sites. Despite the lengthy directions, Bixler Lake Campground is easy to find with signs to point the way. But much of the access travel must be done on residential streets which can be narrow with inadequate shoulders. The campground offers a choice of grassy or gravel sites, shady or open, 20 pull-throughs. Rates are surprisingly low and discounts are given to groups with ten units or more. The campground offers wheelchair-accessible rest rooms and showers. Security is good with a check-in point, as well as regular patrols by local officers.

### BASICS
**Operated by:** Kendallville Parks & Recreation Dept. **Open:** May 15–Oct. 15. **Site Assignment:** Reservations accepted w/ no deposit. **Registration:** At campground office. **Fee:** $14 (cash, check). **Parking:** At site.

### FACILITIES
**Number of RV Sites:** 80. **Number of Tent-Only Sites:** 20. **Hookups:** Electric (20, 30, 50 amps), water. **Each Site:** Picnic table, fire ring. **Dump Station:** Yes. **Laundry:** No. **Pay Phone:** Yes. **Rest Rooms and Showers:** Yes. **Fuel:** No. **Propane:** No. **Internal Roads:** Paved/gravel, in good condition. **RV Service:** No. **Market:** 2 mi. west in Kendallville. **Restaurant:** 2 mi. west in Kendallville. **General Store:** No. **Vending:** Yes. **Swimming Pool:** No. **Playground:** Yes. **Other:** Fishing lake, swimming beach, boat launch, fishing piers, volleyball, duck pond, nature trails, observation platforms, herb garden, butterfly plots, beekeeping display, recreation field, tennis court.

**Activities:** Fishing, swimming, boating (rental paddleboats available), scheduled weekend activities. **Nearby Attractions:** Windmill museum, golf, nation's 2nd largest genealogy library, Lincoln Museum, zoo, Auburn Cord Duesenberg Museum. **Additional Information:** Fort Wayne/Allen County CVB, (800) 767-7752.

### RESTRICTIONS
**Pets:** Leash only. **Fires:** Fire ring only. **Alcoholic Beverages:** Not permitted. **Vehicle Maximum Length:** None. **Other:** 14-day stay limit.

### TO GET THERE
From junction of US 6 and US 3, drive 1.3 mi. east on US 6 to Fair St., then 0.4 mi. south to Wayne St., 500 feet east to Park Ave., and finally 0.4 mi. south to Lake Park Dr. Roads are well maintained, residential streets, some narrow with poor shoulders.

## KENDALLVILLE
### Gordon's Camping

9500 South 600E, Wolcottville 46755. T: (219) 351-3383; www.gordonscamping.com; info@gordonscamping.com.

🚐 ★★★　　　　　🏕 ★★★

| | |
|---|---|
| Beauty: ★★★ | Site Privacy: ★★★ |
| Spaciousness: ★★★ | Quiet: ★★★ |
| Security: ★★★★★ | Cleanliness: ★★★★ |
| Insect Control: None | Facilities: ★★★ |

Calling itself "the cure for summertime blues," Gordon's Camping has enough recreation and activities to keep most anyone happy. Located 35 miles north of Kendallville, the campground also is convenient to many attractions. So, not surprisingly, Gordon's is popular. Offering wooded sites on rolling terrain, Gordon's has 150 pull-throughs and some sites as large as 50 feet wide. Sites are mostly shady and grassy. The best sites for tents are along the pond in the Black Willow section where it is quieter and more natural. The best sites for RVs are in the Black Walnut and Tulip Tree sections because the sites offer 50 amp electricity, are pull-throughs, and feature more shade. Security is tops with a traffic-control gate requiring a pass, owners who live on site, and regular patrols of the campground.

## BASICS

**Operated by:** Jerry & Sandi Bubb. **Open:** May 13–Oct. 15. **Site Assignment:** First come; first served. **Registration:** At campground office. **Fee:** $25 (cash, check). **Parking:** At site.

## FACILITIES

**Number of RV Sites:** 300. **Number of Tent-Only Sites:** 0. **Hookups:** Electric (20, 30, 50 amps), water. **Each Site:** Picnic table, fire ring. **Dump Station:** Yes. **Laundry:** Yes. **Pay Phone:** Yes. **Rest Rooms and Showers:** Yes. **Fuel:** No. **Propane:** Yes. **Internal Roads:** Paved/gravel, in good condition. **RV Service:** No. **Market:** 8 mi. south in Kendallville. **Restaurant:** 8 mi. south in Kendallville. **General Store:** Yes. **Vending:** Yes. **Swimming Pool:** Yes. **Playground:** Yes. **Other:** Mini-golf, hiking trails, pavilion, video rental, basketball, volleyball, horseshoes, kids' fishing pond, coin games, wading pool, sports field. **Activities:** Swimming, boating (rental rowboats available), biking (rental bikes available), church services, scheduled activities, rental cabins. **Nearby Attractions:** Golf, Auburn Cord Duesenberg Museum, zoo, nation's 2nd largest geneaology library, windmill museum. **Additional Information:** Fort Wayne/Allen County CVB, (800) 767-7752.

## RESTRICTIONS

**Pets:** Leash only. **Fires:** Fire ring only. **Alcoholic Beverages:** Permitted. **Vehicle Maximum Length:** None.

## TO GET THERE

From junction of US 20 and Hwy. 3, drive 7 mi. south on Hwy. 3, then 1.25 mi. east on CR 600S. Roads are well maintained but narrow with adequate shoulders.

## LAFAYETTE

### Lafayette AOK Campground

225 East 300 South, Lafayette 47909. T: (765) 474-5030

| 🚐 ★★★★ | ⛺ ★★★★ |
|---|---|
| Beauty: ★★★ | Site Privacy: ★★★ |
| Spaciousness: ★★★ | Quiet: ★★★ |
| Security: ★★★★ | Cleanliness: ★★★★ |
| Insect Control: None | Facilities: ★★★★ |

It is no typo and your eyes aren't playing tricks. This is the Lafayette AOK Campground, not a KOA, but that is a common misconception. Campers often think they are pulling into a KOA.

Laid out in a series of loops, the Lafayette AOK offers a choice of shaded or open sites in a rolling terrain. The typical site width is 30 feet and the campground has mostly pull-through sites and 50 seasonals. The best RV sites are in the first row in the campground which offers easier access and more trees. The best tent sites are in a corner of the grounds with more woods, shade, and privacy. A five mph speed limit is enforced as are quiet times from 10 p.m. to 8 a.m. No outside clotheslines are permitted but laundry facilities are open 24 hours a day. Security includes one entrance/exit road, a manager living on site, and seasonal campers who keep an eye on their area.

## BASICS

**Operated by:** Ted Riehle. **Open:** All year. **Site Assignment:** Reservations w/ 1-night deposit; refund w/ 24-hour notice. **Registration:** At campground office. **Fee:** $24 (cash, check, credit card). **Parking:** At site.

## FACILITIES

**Number of RV Sites:** 76. **Number of Tent-Only Sites:** 150. **Hookups:** Electric (30, 50 amps), water, sewer, cable TV, phone. **Each Site:** Picnic table. **Dump Station:** Yes. **Laundry:** Yes. **Pay Phone:** Yes. **Rest Rooms and Showers:** Yes. **Fuel:** No. **Propane:** Yes. **Internal Roads:** Paved/gravel, in good condition. **RV Service:** No. **Market:** 0.25 mi. north in Lafayette. **Restaurant:** 0.25 mi. east in Lafayette. **General Store:** Yes. **Vending:** Yes. **Swimming Pool:** Yes. **Playground:** Yes. **Other:** Coin games, pool table, exercise machines, horseshoes, recreation field, rec hall, game room, hiking trails, creek. **Activities:** Swimming, hiking. **Nearby Attractions:** Tippecanoe Battlefield, Wolf Park, Fort Quiatenon, golf, Purdue University, museums, historic homes, antiques, Indiana Beach amusement park. **Additional Information:** Greater Lafayette CVB, (800) 872-6648.

## RESTRICTIONS

**Pets:** Leash only. **Fires:** Fire ring only. **Alcoholic Beverages:** Permitted. **Vehicle Maximum Length:** None.

## TO GET THERE

From junction of I-65 and Hwy. 38, take Exit 168, drive 1.25 mi. west on Hwy. 38, then 4 mi. west on CR 475E and CR 350S, then 0.5 mi. north on CR 100E, then 0.9 mi. west on CR 300S. Roads are wide and well maintained with broad shoulders.

## MADISON

### Clifty Falls State Park

1501 Green Rd., Madison 47250. T: (812) 273-8885;
F: (812) 265-6662; www.state.in.us/dnr.

🚐 ★★★                           ▲ ★★★★

Beauty: ★★★★              Site Privacy: ★★★
Spaciousness: ★★★          Quiet: ★★★★
Security: ★★★★             Cleanliness: ★★★★
Insect Control: None        Facilities: ★★★

It's easy to see where Clifty Falls State Park got its name. With four plunging waterfalls, 70-foot gorges, sheer cliffs, and a narrow valley, Clifty Falls shows the awesome forces of nature at work. The park is popular with campers who like to hike in the area. Winter and spring hiking show the falls at their best. July through Nov. offer meager falls and the easiest hiking in Clifty Creek's wonderful stone bed. A muddy, rock-strewn, 600-foot tunnel piercing the hillside beneath Oak Grove is the most prominent remnant of the Madison and Indianapolis Railroad, begun in 1852 and abandoned in bankruptcy. It is passable on foot with flashlight. Security is good, with passes needed to enter the campground and a ranger on patrol. Despite the lack of water hookups and laundry, Clifty Falls has a dedicated following of campers, both RV and tents. The natural beauty, the programs, and the security are the main draws.

### BASICS

**Operated by:** Indiana Dept. of Natural Resources. **Open:** All year. **Site Assignment:** Written reservations w/ 1-night deposit; no refunds. **Registration:** At campground office. **Fee:** $12 (check, credit cards). **Parking:** At site.

### FACILITIES

**Number of RV Sites:** 140. **Number of Tent-Only Sites:** 60. **Hookups:** Electric (30 amps). **Each Site:** Picnic table, fire ring. **Dump Station:** Yes. **Laundry:** No. **Pay Phone:** Yes. **Rest Rooms and Showers:** Yes. **Fuel:** No. **Propane:** No. **Internal Roads:** Paved, in good condition. **RV Service:** No. **Market:** 1 mi. east in Madison. **Restaurant:** Yes. **General Store:** Yes. **Vending:** Yes. **Swimming Pool:** Yes. **Playground:** Yes. **Other:** Nature center, inn w/ indoor swimming pool, picnic shelters, tennis court. **Activities:** Swimming, hiking, guided nature walks, summer

weekday programs & evening activities offered by naturalist. **Nearby Attractions:** Scenic drives, golf, historic Madison, Ohio River, Lanier State Historic Site, vineyards, marina. **Additional Information:** Madison Area CVB, (800) 559-2956.

### RESTRICTIONS

**Pets:** Leash only. **Fires:** Fire rings & grills only. **Alcoholic Beverages:** At sites only. **Vehicle Maximum Length:** 35 ft. **Other:** 14-day stay limit.

### TO GET THERE

From Madison, drive 1 mi. west on IN 56/62. Roads are generally wide and well maintained. Shoulders are often poor. The area is popular for its scenic, hilly, winding roads but they can be difficult to maneuver.

## NASHVILLE

### The Last Resort RV Park & Campground

2248 East SR 46, Nashville 47448. T: (812) 988-4675

🚐 ★★★★                          ▲ ★★★★

Beauty: ★★★★              Site Privacy: ★★★★
Spaciousness: ★★★★        Quiet: ★★★★
Security: ★★★★             Cleanliness: ★★★★
Insect Control: None        Facilities: ★★★★

Location is everything. And The Last Resort RV Park & Campground has a prime spot to be a campground. The Last Resort is in the midst of beautiful Brown County, two-and-a-half miles east of Nashville, Indiana, but it offers the peacefulness and beauty of a woodland setting. Situated atop a hill, and surrounded by ravines, the campground has both open and shaded sites that are level and grassy with gravel parking spots. Laid out in a loop, the campground has 16 seasonals, 18 pull-through sites and a typical site width of 35 feet. Nice touches include private shower stalls, each with a door and a curtain. Speed limit is five mph and quiet hours are 10 p.m. to 8 a.m.; generators are not permitted at any time. Sites 114–117 are popular because they back up into the woods and are away from the main activity. Security includes one entrance/exit road and an on-site manager. The campground is particularly lovely when autumn foliage is showing peak colors.

## BASICS

**Operated by:** Frank & Dot Moser. **Open:** Apr. 1–Nov. 1. **Site Assignment:** Reservations w/ 1-night deposit; refund w/ 7-day notice. **Registration:** At campground office. **Fee:** $25 (cash, check, credit cards). **Parking:** At site.

## FACILITIES

**Number of RV Sites:** 80. **Number of Tent-Only Sites:** 36. **Hookups:** Electric (30, 50 amps), water, sewer, cable TV. **Each Site:** Picnic table, fire ring. **Dump Station:** Yes. **Laundry:** Yes. **Pay Phone:** Yes. **Rest Rooms and Showers:** Yes. **Fuel:** No. **Propane:** Yes. **Internal Roads:** Paved/gravel, in good condition. **RV Service:** No. **Market:** 2.5 mi. west in Nashville. **Restaurant:** 2.5 mi. west in Nashville. **General Store:** Yes. **Vending:** Yes. **Swimming Pool:** Yes. **Playground:** Yes. **Other:** Rec room, horseshoes, recreation field, pavilion, coin games, basketball, hiking trails. **Activities:** Swimming, hiking, scheduled weekend activities. **Nearby Attractions:** Brown County State Park, Nashville artist colony w/ more than 350 specialty shops, scenic drives, winter skiing, Little Nashville Opry, golf, Indiana University. **Additional Information:** Brown County CVB, (800) 753-3255.

## RESTRICTIONS

**Pets:** Leash only. **Fires:** Fire ring only. **Alcoholic Beverages:** At sites only. **Vehicle Maximum Length:** None.

## TO GET THERE

From junction of I-65 and Hwy. 46, take Exit 68, drive 14 mi. west on Hwy. 46. Roads are wide and well maintained with broad shoulders.

## ORLAND

## Manapogo Park

5495 W 760N, Orland 46776. T: (260) 833-3902; www.manapogo.com.

| 🚐 ★★★★ | ⛺ ★★★★ |
|---|---|
| Beauty: ★★★ | Site Privacy: ★★★★ |
| Spaciousness: ★★★★ | Quiet: ★★★★ |
| Security: ★★★★ | Cleanliness: ★★★★ |
| Insect Control: Yes | Facilities: ★★★★ |

A wooded, grassy campground, Manapogo Park centers around 425-acre Lake Pleasant. Located four miles east of Orland, Indiana, the campground has a typical site width of 50 feet. The campground has 247 seasonal campers and no pull-through sites. A five mph speed limit is enforced for vehicles and bicycles. Bicycles may not be ridden after sundown and motorcycles may be used only for entering or leaving the campground, when idle speed is required. A separate section for tent campers allows more greenery and privacy from RVs. Overnight sites are generally placed together instead of being scattered throughout the park's seasonals. Security measures include entrance gates that require a $5 deposit fee for cards, refundable upon return of the card. The campground owner lives on site and provides regular patrols.

## BASICS

**Operated by:** John West. **Open:** 3rd week in Apr.–1st week in Oct. **Site Assignment:** Reservations w/ 1-night deposit; refund (minus $5) w/ 5-day notice. **Registration:** At campground office. **Fee:** $32. **Parking:** At site.

## FACILITIES

**Number of RV Sites:** 304. **Number of Tent-Only Sites:** 15. **Hookups:** Electric (30 amps), water, sewer. **Each Site:** Picnic table, fire ring. **Dump Station:** Yes. **Laundry:** Yes. **Pay Phone:** Yes. **Rest Rooms and Showers:** Yes. **Fuel:** Yes. **Propane:** Yes. **Internal Roads:** Paved/gravel, in good condition. **RV Service:** No. **Market:** 4 mi. west in Orland. **Restaurant:** 4 mi. west in Orland. **General Store:** Yes. **Vending:** Yes. **Swimming Pool:** No. **Playground:** Yes. **Other:** Lake Pleasant, swimming beach, pavilion, boat piers, boat ramp, basketball, volleyball, shuffleboard, horseshoes, rental cabins, fish-cleaning station, rec room, coin games, mini-golf, fishing pond. **Activities:** Swimming, fishing, boating (rental fishing boats, paddleboats, canoes & water bikes available), scheduled weekend activities. **Nearby Attractions:** Golf, Shipshewana flea market, factory outlet stores, amusement park, car museum, go-cart raceway, antiques, arts & crafts shops. **Additional Information:** Amish County/Elkhart County Visitors Center, (800) 860-5949.

## RESTRICTIONS

**Pets:** Leash only; walking of pets in park is not allowed; pets must be carried or transported in vehicle to the designated walking area near the dump station. **Fires:** Fire ring only. **Alcoholic Beverages:** Permitted but must be kept in covered container if taken off campsite. **Vehicle Maximum Length:** None. **Other:** No golf carts or mopeds permitted, except for park staff.

## To Get There

From junction of Hwy. 327 and Hwy. 120, drive 3.25 mi. east on Hwy. 120, then 0.75 mi. north on CR 650W, then 1 mi. east on CR 760N. Roads are wide and well maintained with broad shoulders, except for a narrow section and steep curve on CR 760N.

## PERU

### Honey Bear Hollow Campground

4252 West 200 N, Peru 46970. T: (765) 473-4342; F: (765) 473-5366; jelly@netusal.net.

🚐 ★★★★          ⛺ ★★★★

| | |
|---|---|
| Beauty: ★★★ | Site Privacy: ★★★★ |
| Spaciousness: ★★★★ | Quiet: ★★★★ |
| Security: ★★★★ | Cleanliness: ★★★★ |
| Insect Control: Yes | Facilities: ★★★★ |

The entryway to Honey Bear Hollow Campground lets guests know that the owners care about the facility. A small pond and water display along with flowers and other greenery add a nice welcoming touch. Well-tended flower barrels also decorate bathroom entrances. Laid out in a series of loops, the campground has a typical site width of 30 feet with 50 seasonal campers and pull-through sites for all overnight campers. Locted four miles north of Peru, Indiana, the campground has a well-stocked camp store and is surrounded by woods. Sites are mostly shady and grassy with gravel pads to park on. Quiet time is 11 p.m. to 8 a.m. and there is a curfew for children under age 18. Security measures include an alarm system, one entrance/exit and owners who live on site.

## BASICS

**Operated by:** Dawn Thomas & her parents, Bob & Toni Billetz. **Open:** All year. **Site Assignment:** Reservations w/ 1-night deposit; refund (minus $5) w/ 7-day notice; no refunds on holiday weekends. **Registration:** At campground office. **Fee:** $23 (cash, check, credit cards). **Parking:** At site.

## FACILITIES

**Number of RV Sites:** 105. **Number of Tent-Only Sites:** 5. **Hookups:** Electric (30, 50 amps), water. **Each Site:** Picnic table, fire ring. **Dump Station:** Yes. **Laundry:** Yes. **Pay Phone:** Yes. **Rest Rooms and Showers:** Yes. **Fuel:** No. **Propane:** Yes. **Internal Roads:** Gravel, in good condition. **RV

**Service:** No. **Market:** 4 mi. south in Peru. **Restaurant:** 4 mi. south in Peru. **General Store:** Yes. **Vending:** Yes. **Swimming Pool:** Yes. **Playground:** Yes. **Other:** Rec hall, pavilion, fishing pond, mini-golf, horseshoes, volleyball, game room, disc golf course, cartoons & video games. **Activities:** Swimming, fishing, scheduled weekend activities. **Nearby Attractions:** Grissom Air Museum, historic homes, glass museum, golf, Big Top Circus & Hall of Fame Museum, antiques, arts & crafts shops. **Additional Information:** Howard County Convention & Visitors Commission, (800) 837-0971.

## RESTRICTIONS

**Pets:** Leash only. **Fires:** Fire ring only. **Alcoholic Beverages:** At sites only. **Vehicle Maximum Length:** None. **Other:** No fireworks of any kind, including sparklers, are permitted.

## To Get There

From junction of US 31 and Bypass US 24, go 1 mi. north on US 31, then 1.25 mi. west on CR 200N. Roads are wide and well maintained with broad shoulders, except for CR 200N which is narrow with small shoulders.

## PLYMOUTH

### Yogi Bear's Jellystone Park Camp-Resort

7719 Redwood Rd., Plymouth 46563. T: (219) 936-7851

🚐 ★★★★          ⛺ ★★

| | |
|---|---|
| Beauty: ★★★ | Site Privacy: ★★★★ |
| Spaciousness: ★★★★ | Quiet: ★★★★ |
| Security: ★★★★ | Cleanliness: ★★★★ |
| Insect Control: None | Facilities: ★★★★ |

Yogi Bear's Jellystone Park Camp-Resort is owned by the people who live there, the Marshall County Membership Corp. That helps keep the campground well maintained and attractive. People take pride in what they own. For example, lights in the main bathroom are triggered to come on when somone comes in; the water faucet in the sink releases a certain amount of water when a person's hands are under it. Those measures are both convenient and energy saving. The facilities also are very clean and nicely decorated. A 5.5 mph speed limit is enforced and campers are warned if they "exceed the speed limit at Yogi Bear, you'll find yourself walking." Laid out in a series of loops, the campground has 946 owner/campers, leaving 150 sites for visitors and 32 spots in the primitive tent area which is used only on Labor Day weekend. Located four miles west of Plymouth, Indiana, the campground has ten pull-through sites and a typical site width of 40 feet. Security measures are excellent with a controlled gate entry system and 24-hour security on the premises.

## BASICS

**Operated by:** Marshall County Membership Corp. **Open:** May 1–Oct. 1. **Site Assignment:** Reservations w/ 1-night deposit; refund (minus 10 percent) w/ 10-day notice. **Registration:** At campground office. **Fee:** $32 (cash, check, credit cards). **Parking:** At site.

## FACILITIES

**Number of RV Sites:** 1,096. **Number of Tent-Only Sites:** 32. **Hookups:** Electric (30 amps), water, sewer. **Each Site:** Picnic table, fire ring. **Dump Station:** Yes. **Laundry:** Yes. **Pay Phone:** Yes. **Rest Rooms and Showers:** Yes. **Fuel:** No. **Propane:** Yes. **Internal Roads:** Paved/gravel, in good condition. **RV Service:** No. **Market:** 3 mi. east in Plymouth. **Restaurant:** 3 mi. east in Plymouth. **General Store:** Yes. **Vending:** Yes. **Swimming Pool:** Yes. **Playground:** Yes. **Other:** Snack bar, gameroom, fishing pond, pavilion, rec hall, rental cabins, tennis, basketball, mini-golf, horseshoes, adults room, recreation field, coin games, wading pool, boat dock. **Activities:** Swimming, fishing, boating (rental kayaks & paddleboats available), scheduled activities. **Nearby Attractions:** Golf, Amish Acres, Culver Military Academy, University of Notre Dame, Studebaker Museum, College Football Hall of Fame, Trail of Courage, antiques, arts & crafts, historic homes. **Additional Information:** Marshall County CVB, (800) 626-5353.

## RESTRICTIONS

**Pets:** Leash only. **Fires:** Fire ring only. **Alcoholic Beverages:** At sites only. **Vehicle Maximum Length:** None. **Other:** Roller skates, skateboards, & roller blades are not allowed.

## TO GET THERE

From junction of Hwy. 17 and US 30, drive 4 mi. west on US 30. Roads are wide and well maintained with broad shoulders.

## REMINGTON
### Caboose Lake Campground

3657 West US 24, Remington 47977. T: (800) 726-6982; www.cabooselake.com; cabooselake@yahoo.com.

🚐 ★★                    ⛺ ★★

Beauty: ★★                 Site Privacy: ★★
Spaciousness: ★★           Quiet: ★★
Security: ★★★★             Cleanliness: ★★★
Insect Control: None        Facilities: ★★

Caboose Lake Campground, located two miles east of Remington, Indiana, is a work in progress. Already, the campground has a great location—a stone's throw off I-65, right on the travel route for snowbirds and other folks heading north or south. Starting with a nice little lake, the owners (a father/daughter team) have some great plans, including the addition of a brand new comfort station, go-kart track, mini-golf, and rental cabooses and cabins. As a new facility, Caboose Lake has planted lots of small trees that don't offer much shade yet. Sites are level and grassy with a typical site width of 40 feet and six pull-throughs. Favorite RV and tent sites are ones facing the lake. Security measures include a five mph speed limit, regular patrols, and an owner who lives on site. Open all year, Caboose Lake is an easy stopping-off point for travelers. However, you can't be this close to an interstate without hearing the rumbling noise of trucks and autos.

## BASICS

**Operated by:** Douglas McGill & Christiane Palladino. **Open:** All year. **Site Assignment:** Reservations w/ 1-night deposit; refund w/ 1-week notice. **Registration:** At campground office. **Fee:** $20 (cash, check, credit card). **Parking:** At site.

## FACILITIES

**Number of RV Sites:** 38. **Number of Tent-Only Sites:** 10. **Hookups:** Electric (20, 30, 50 amps), water, sewer. **Each Site:** Picnic table, fire ring. **Dump Station:** Yes. **Laundry:** No. **Pay Phone:** Yes. **Rest Rooms and Showers:** Yes. **Fuel:** No. **Propane:** Yes. **Internal Roads:** Gravel, in good condition. **RV Service:** No. **Market:** 2 mi. west in Remington. **Restaurant:** 0.5 mi. west in Remington. **General Store:** No. **Vending:** Yes.

**Swimming Pool:** No. **Playground:** Yes. **Other:** Caboose Lake, pavilion, swimming beach, volleyball, horseshoes. **Activities:** Swimming, fishing, boating (rental paddleboats, sailboats & fishing boats available), scheduled activities. **Nearby Attractions:** Purdue University, Wolf Park, Lake Shafer, Indiana Beach amusement park, Tippecanoe Battlefield & Museum. **Additional Information:** Greater Lafayette CVB, (800) 872-6569.

## RESTRICTIONS

**Pets:** Leash only. **Fires:** Fire ring only. **Alcoholic Beverages:** At sites only. **Vehicle Maximum Length:** None.

## TO GET THERE

From junction of I-65 and US 24E, take Exit 201, drive 500 feet east on US 24. Roads are wide and well maintained with broad shoulders.

## RISING SUN

### Little Farm on the River RV Park Camping Resort

1343 East Bellview Ln., Rising Sun 47040. T: (812) 438-4500; F: (812) 438-9135; www.littlefarmrv resort.com; littlefarmrv@hotmail.com.

🚐 ★★★          ⛺ ★★★

| | |
|---|---|
| Beauty: ★★★ | Site Privacy: ★★ |
| Spaciousness: ★★★ | Quiet: ★★★ |
| Security: ★★★★★ | Cleanliness: ★★★★★ |
| Insect Control: None | Facilities: ★★★★ |

The good thing about Little Farm on the River RV Park Camping Resort is that it's new. Sparkling clean facilities still have the fresh smell of construction and the owner is energetic and enthusiastic. The bad thing about Little Farm on the River is that it's new. More than 300 trees have been planted and still have some growing to do for adequate shade in the upper camp sites. At press time, facilities are still being constructed and activities are being added. Located a mile east of Rising Sun, Indiana, the country campground is situated on the Ohio River with a natural sand bank and towering trees alongside the river bank—the prime camping spots. Autumn and spring would be best times for a stay—the flowering dogwood and pear trees and 3,000 newly planted flower bulbs put on quite a spring show. A series of three loops offers spacious grassy or gravel

sites, pull-through or back-in spots. Open all year, the campground has underground water hookups so water is available even in freezing temperatures. Security is tops with an on-site manager, as well as both county and town police patrolling every hour all night and the Dept. of Natural Resources keeping a watch from the river. Some campers will enjoy the campground's close proximity to three riverboat gambling casinos.

## BASICS

**Operated by:** Little Farm on the River LLC. **Open:** All year. **Site Assignment:** Reservations w/ 1-night deposit; full refund w/ 7-day notice. **Registration:** At campground headquarters. **Fee:** $21.50 (check, credit cards, cash). **Parking:** At sites & headquarters.

## FACILITIES

**Number of RV Sites:** 142. **Number of Tent-Only Sites:** 41. **Hookups:** Electric (20, 30, 50 amps), water, sewer. **Each Site:** Fire ring, picnic table. **Dump Station:** Yes. **Laundry:** Yes. **Pay Phone:** Yes. **Rest Rooms and Showers:** Yes. **Fuel:** No. **Propane:** Yes. **Internal Roads:** Gravel, in good condition. **RV Service:** Yes. **Market:** 1 mi. west in Rising Sun. **Restaurant:** 1 mi. west in Rising Sun. **General Store:** Yes. **Vending:** Yes. **Swimming Pool:** No. **Playground:** Yes. **Other:** Stocked fishing pond, rec room, pool table, card table, free Internet access, pavilion, TV, basketball court, RV storage & cleaning, baby animal petting zoo, Native American artifact display, shuffleboard court, tetherball, horseshoes, badminton, volleyball, free shuttle to Grand Victoria Casino & historic district of Rising Sun. **Activities:** Fishing, bike riding (rental bikes available), horseback riding (rental horses available), bingo, poker, crafts, fishing tournament. **Nearby Attractions:** Scenic river drive, golf, historic Rising Sun, Ohio River, marina, 3 riverboat casinos. **Additional Information:** Rising Sun/Ohio County Convention & Tourism Bureau (888) RSNGSUN.

## RESTRICTIONS

**Pets:** Leash only. **Fires:** Fire rings & grills only. **Alcoholic Beverages:** Permitted. **Vehicle Maximum Length:** None.

## TO GET THERE

From US 50 in Aurora, drive east 7 mi. to East Bellview Ln. The state highway is wide and well maintained; Bellview Ln. was recenly paved by the county.

## ROCHESTER

### Lakeview Campground

7781 East 300 North, Rochester 46975. T: (219) 353-8114; F: (219) 353-8114; www.perfect-matrix.com/lakeview; lakeview@medt.com.

🚐 ★★★                    ⛺ ★★★

| | |
|---|---|
| Beauty: ★★★★ | Site Privacy: ★★★★ |
| Spaciousness: ★★★★ | Quiet: ★★★★ |
| Security: ★★★★ | Cleanliness: ★★★ |
| Insect Control: Yes | Facilities: ★★★ |

Campers don't have to worry about getting a lake-front site at Lakeview Campground. Each site is on Barr Lake. Located seven miles northeast of Rochester, Indiana, the campground has a surprising amount of shade for lakefront sites. Laid out in a half loop, the campground has a typical site width of 30 feet with 45 seasonals and eight pull-through sites. Lakeview is well maintained with freshly painted buildings, a mowed bank that goes down to a small creek, and a colorful mini-golf setup with a little teepee, windmill, log cabin, bridge, and other gizmos to offer challenge. Tents have a separate area with more greenery and privacy from RVs. Security includes one entrance/exit road, surveillance cameras and owners who live on site. Quiet hours are 11 p.m. to 8 a.m.

#### BASICS

**Operated by:** Jim, Roberta, & Jeff Bever. **Open:** Apr. 15–Oct. 15. **Site Assignment:** Reservations w/ 1-night deposit; refund w/ 48-hour notice. **Registration:** At campground office. **Fee:** $25 (cash, check, credit cards). **Parking:** At site.

#### FACILITIES

**Number of RV Sites:** 105. **Number of Tent-Only Sites:** 25. **Hookups:** Electric (30 amps), water, sewer. **Each Site:** Picnic table, fire ring. **Dump Station:** Yes. **Laundry:** No. **Pay Phone:** Yes. **Rest Rooms and Showers:** Yes. **Fuel:** No. **Propane:** No. **Internal Roads:** Gravel, in good condition. **RV Service:** No. **Market:** 7 mi. southwest in Rochester. **Restaurant:** 7 mi. southwest in Rochester. **General Store:** Yes, limited. **Vending:** No. **Swimming Pool:** No. **Playground:** Yes. **Other:** Barr Lake, swimming beach, mini-golf, pavilion, volleyball, basketball, hiking trails, rec hall, badminton, sports field, fish-cleaning house. **Activities:** Swimming, fishing, boating (rental rowboats, canoes, paddleboats available), hiking, scheduled weekend activities. **Nearby Attractions:** Golf, outlet stores, Rounds Barn Museum, Fulton County Museum, antiques, Living History Village. **Additional Information:** Fulton County Historical Society, (219) 223-4436.

#### RESTRICTIONS

**Pets:** Leash only. **Fires:** Fire ring only. **Alcoholic Beverages:** Permitted. **Vehicle Maximum Length:** None.

#### TO GET THERE

From junction of Hwy. 31 and Hwy. 14, drive 6.5 mi. east on Hwy. 14 to Athens, then 3 mi. north on CR 650E, then 1 mi. east on CR 300N. Roads are wide and well maintained with broad shoulders.

## ROSELAWN

### Oak Lake Family Campground

5310 East 900 North, Fair Oaks 47943. T: (219) 345-3153

🚐 ★★★                    ⛺ n/a

| | |
|---|---|
| Beauty: ★★ | Site Privacy: ★★ |
| Spaciousness: ★★ | Quiet: ★★★ |
| Security: ★★★★ | Cleanliness: ★★★ |
| Insect Control: Yes | Facilities: ★★★ |

Located on the outskirts of Roselawn, Indiana, Oak Lake Family Campground is an RV park only. Sites are mostly grassy and shady with a typical site width of 35 feet. The campground has 40 pull-throughs and 175 seasonal campers. The camp area is heavily wooded with oaks trees; wild roses, berries, and mushrooms decorate the grounds. For RV clubs, Oak Lake has two clusters of sites set around a central bonfire pit. A small lake offers fishing, a sandy beach for swimming, and a fun island with a footbridge. Limited supplies are available at the camp store which also offers a small gift shop and lending library. Fast-food items include hot sandwiches and pizza and, in season, fresh farm vegetables. Security measures include a locked laundry room (key is available at office), owners who live on site and provide regular patrols, and a security gate which is locked at night. Campers need a plastic entry card to enter the security gate.

#### BASICS

**Operated by:** Paul & Allegra McCurtain. **Open:** Apr. 15–Oct. 15. **Site Assignment:** Reservations w/ 1-night deposit; refund w/ 7-day notice. **Registration:** At campground office. **Fee:** $24 (cash, check). **Parking:** At site.

## FACILITIES

**Number of RV Sites:** 250. **Number of Tent-Only Sites:** 0. **Hookups:** Electric (30, 50 amps), water, sewer. **Each Site:** Picnic table, fire ring. **Dump Station:** Yes. **Laundry:** Yes. **Pay Phone:** Yes. **Rest Rooms and Showers:** Yes. **Fuel:** No. **Propane:** No. **Internal Roads:** Paved/gravel, in good condition. **RV Service:** Yes. **Market:** 1.5 mi. north in Roselawn. **Restaurant:** 1.5 mi. north in Roselawn. **General Store:** Yes, limited. **Vending:** Yes. **Swimming Pool:** No. **Playground:** Yes. **Other:** Oak Lake, swimming beach, hiking trails, island, footbridge, duck pond, baby animal pen, recreation building, rental cabins, badminton, volleyball, picnic shelter, pavilion, coin games. **Activities:** Swimming, fishing, hiking, scheduled weekend activities. **Nearby Attractions:** Indiana Beach, museums, historic sites, antiques, golf, arts & crafts shops. **Additional Information:** North Newton Chamber of Commerce, (219) 345-2525.

## RESTRICTIONS

**Pets:** Leash only. **Fires:** Fire ring only. **Alcoholic Beverages:** At sites only. **Vehicle Maximum Length:** 40 ft.

## TO GET THERE

From junction of I-65 and Hwy. 10, take Exit 230 (Roselawn) exit, drive 0.25 mi. west on CR 900N. Roads are wide and well maintained with broad shoulders.

## SANTA CLAUS

## Lake Rudolph Campground & RV Resort

78 North Holiday Blvd., Santa Claus 47579. T: (877) 478-3657; F: (812) 937-4470; www.lakerudolph.com.

🚐 ★★★★          ▲ ★★★★

| | |
|---|---|
| Beauty: ★★★ | Site Privacy: ★★★ |
| Spaciousness: ★★★ | Quiet: ★★★ |
| Security: ★★★★ | Cleanliness: ★★★★ |
| Insect Control: None | Facilities: ★★★★ |

A touch of Christmas lives year-round at Lake Rudolph Campground & RV Resort. Located in the small Indiana town of Santa Claus, Lake Rudolph got its name from, of course, the famed red-nosed reindeer. Sections of the two big loops are named Dasher, Kringer, and Prancer. Next door to Holiday World Theme Park & Splashin' Safari Water Park, the campground is a summertime favorite with folks who like to be a free shuttle ride or a ten-minute walk from their campsite and the amusement park. The spacious, forested campground with its southern Indiana hills features beautiful fall foliage and a quieter refuge when the theme park starts closing down after Labor Day. The best sites for RVs are 2, 11, 17, 35, 37, 39, and 92 in the Dasher section because they are easier to back in (no pull-through sites are available). Sites have gravel pads with a grassy area; no two lots are the same. Tenters favor sites 125–130 in the Dasher section for the huge pine, maple and oak trees. Though open all year, the freezing temperatures, snow, and lack of on-site water make Lake Rudolph a good-weather option for all but the most hardy—or those who want to experience Santa Claus in his true element.

## BASICS

**Operated by:** Koch Development Corp. **Open:** All year. **Site Assignment:** Reservations w/ 1-night deposit; refunds w/ 48-hour notice, 10-day notice on RV & cabin rentals. **Registration:** At campground headquarters. **Fee:** $20 (credit cards, cash), $75 for cabin, $59 for RV rental. **Parking:** At sites or at headquarters parking lot.

## FACILITIES

**Number of RV Sites:** 200. **Number of Tent-Only Sites:** 50. **Hookups:** Electric (30, 50 amps), water, sewer. **Each Site:** Fire ring, picnic table. **Dump Station:** Yes. **Laundry:** Yes. **Pay Phone:** Yes. **Rest Rooms and Showers:** Yes. **Fuel:** No. **Propane:** Yes. **Internal Roads:** Paved, in good condition. **RV Service:** No. **Market:** 0.25 mi. west in Santa Claus. **Restaurant:** 0.25 mi. west in Santa Claus. **General Store:** Yes. **Vending:** Yes. **Swimming Pool:** Yes. **Playground:** Yes. **Other:** Game room, billiard room, basketball, horseshoes, volleyball, nature trail, fishing lake, mini-golf, free shuttle to Holiday World Theme Park & Splashin' Safari Water Park, cabin rentals, RV rentals. **Activities:** Fishing, bingo, occasional cookouts, special Halloween weekends w/ hayrides & other activities. **Nearby Attractions:** Holiday World Theme Park & Splashin' Safari Water Park, golf, Santa Claus post office, Lincoln Boyhood National Memorial, caves, Lincoln State Park, Young Abe Lincoln Outdoor Drama. **Additional Information:** Santa

Claus–Lincoln City Area Visitors Bureau, (800) GO-SANTA.

## RESTRICTIONS

**Pets:** Leash only (not in rentals). **Fires:** Fire rings & grills only. **Alcoholic Beverages:** At sites only. **Vehicle Maximum Length:** 40 ft. **Other:** Rentals 2-night min. stay, holiday weekends 3-day min. stay.

## TO GET THERE

Take Exit 63 off I-64, travel 7 mi. south on SR 162, turn right at Holiday World parking lot, then go 200 yards and turn right into campgrounds. Roads are wide and well maintained.

## SOUTH BEND
## South Bend East KOA Camping Resort

50707 Princess Way, Granger 46530. T: (219) 277-1335; www.southbendeastkoa.com; marshkoa@aol.com.

🚐 ★★★★          ⛺ ★★★★

Beauty: ★★★★           Site Privacy: ★★★★
Spaciousness: ★★★★      Quiet: ★★★★
Security: ★★★★★         Cleanliness: ★★★★★
Insect Control: None     Facilities: ★★★★

Little touches add up to some pleasing results at the South Bend KOA Camping Resort in the town of Granger, Indiana. Pink rose bushes are planted to help conceal a propane tank, framed pictures and artificial flowers brighten the restrooms, and clean, private shower rooms have lights that turn on when the door is closed. An urban campground with level shaded sites, the facility has no seasonal campers, 40 pull-throughs and a typical site width of 24 feet. The rec room is modem friendly for computer users. A five mph speed limit is enforced for safety and to prevent vehicles from kicking up dust. Security measures include owners who live on site, a traffic control gate, and surveillance cameras. A list of campground guidelines is nicely worded with more than a list of the usual "no's." Instead, the campground requests that "we don't want any of our trees or guests strangled, so please no clotheslines." If campers are not satisfied within one hour of check in, registration fees are refunded.

## BASICS

**Operated by:** Terry & Beverlee Marsh. **Open:** Mar. 15–Nov. 15. **Site Assignment:** Reservations w/ 1-night deposit; refund w/ 7-day notice. **Registration:** At campground office. **Fee:** $30 (cash, check, credit cards). **Parking:** At site.

## FACILITIES

**Number of RV Sites:** 88. **Number of Tent-Only Sites:** 12. **Hookups:** Electric (30, 50 amps), water, sewer, cable TV. **Each Site:** Picnic table, fire ring. **Dump Station:** Yes. **Laundry:** Yes. **Pay Phone:** Yes. **Rest Rooms and Showers:** Yes. **Fuel:** No. **Propane:** Yes. **Internal Roads:** Paved/gravel, in good condition. **RV Service:** No. **Market:** Two blocks in Granger. **Restaurant:** Two blocks in Granger. **General Store:** Yes. **Vending:** Yes. **Swimming Pool:** Yes. **Playground:** Yes. **Other:** Game room, basketball, volleyball, horseshoes, mini-golf, nature trail, rental cabins, pavilion w/ kitchen, coin games, badminton, sports field, adults room. **Activities:** Swimming, hiking, scheduled weekend activities. **Nearby Attractions:** College Football Hall of Fame, golf, Studebaker National Museum, Notre Dame University, zoo, Amish acres, RV museum, Shipshewana Flea Market, antiques, St. Mary's College, historic homes. **Additional Information:** South Bend/Mishawaka CVB, (800) 282-2330.

## RESTRICTIONS

**Pets:** Leash only. **Fires:** Fire ring only. **Alcoholic Beverages:** Permitted. **Vehicle Maximum Length:** None.

## TO GET THERE

From junction of I-80/90 (Indiana Turnpike), take Exit 83 and drive 0.5 mi. to Hwy. 23, then 2 mi. north on Hwy. 23, then 0.3 mi. north on Princess Way. Roads are wide and well maintained with broad shoulders.

## THORNTOWN
## Old Mill Run Park

8544 West 690 North, Thorntown 46071. T: (765) 436-7190; www.frontiernet.net/~oldmill; oldmill@frontiernet.net.

🚐 ★★★★          ⛺ ★★★★

Beauty: ★★★★           Site Privacy: ★★★★
Spaciousness: ★★★★      Quiet: ★★★★
Security: ★★★★          Cleanliness: ★★★★
Insect Control: Yes      Facilities: ★★★★

Little touches like coordinated wallpaper in the bathrooms, an entrance way decorated with day lilies, and a mill water fountain make this campground stand out. Mature trees and newly planted ones are mingled to ensure future shade. Campers have a choice of open or shaded areas and mostly pull-through sites. Laid out in a series of loops, Old Mill Run Camp has 197 seasonal campers and a separate section for tents. The average site width is 35 feet and sites are mostly grassy with patios. As a family campground located one mile west of Thorntown, Old Mill doesn't allow alcohol at any activities or facilities, including walking around the park with it. Quiet hours are 11 p.m. to 7 a.m. Clotheslines are not permitted in the park, nor are mopeds, four-wheelers, or motorized bikes. Electric golf carts are permitted for seasonal campers age 21 and up. The best RV sites are 216–248 because they are bigger, offer cable TV, and cement pads. The best tent sites are P13–P24 because they are behind the pond and provide more greenspace and privacy. A security patrol, an owner who lives on site, and one entrance/exit to the campground help assure campers' safety.

## BASICS

**Operated by:** Ralph & Sandy Christman. **Open:** Apr. 1–Oct. 15. **Site Assignment:** Reservations w/ no deposit. **Registration:** At campground office. **Fee:** $24 (cash, check, credit card). **Parking:** At site.

## FACILITIES

**Number of RV Sites:** 347. **Number of Tent-Only Sites:** 25. **Hookups:** Electric (30 amps), water, sewer, cable TV, phone. **Each Site:** Picnic table, fire ring. **Dump Station:** Yes. **Laundry:** Yes. **Pay Phone:** Yes. **Rest Rooms and Showers:** Yes. **Fuel:** No. **Propane:** Yes. **Internal Roads:** Gravel/paved, in good condition. **RV Service:** No. **Market:** 9 mi. east in Lebanon. **Restaurant:** 1 mi. east in Thorntown. **General Store:** Yes. **Vending:** No. **Swimming Pool:** Yes. **Playground:** Yes. **Other:** Mini-golf, horseshoes, rental cabin, rally area, shelter house, 2 fishing ponds, hot tub, 5-hole golf course, basketball, volleyball, shuffleboard, Sugar Creek, coin games, sports field, badminton. **Activities:** Swimming, fishing, scheduled activities, Sunday church services. **Nearby Attractions:** Indianapolis Zoo, Children's Museum, Indianapolis Motor Speedway, antiques, museums, historic sites. **Additional**

**Information:** Boone County Chamber of Commerce, (765) 482-1320.

## RESTRICTIONS

**Pets:** Leash only. **Fires:** Fire ring only. **Alcoholic Beverages:** At sites only. **Vehicle Maximum Length:** None. **Other:** Limit of 6 fish per day.

## TO GET THERE

From I-65W, take Exit 146, drive 6.5 mi. west on Hwy. 47, then 1 mi. north on CR 825W. Roads are wide and well maintained with broad shoulders.

## VERSAILLES

### Versailles State Park

Box 205, US 50, Versailles 47042. T: (812) 689-6424; www.state.in.us/dnr.

🚐 ★★★     ⛺ ★★★

| | |
|---|---|
| **Beauty:** ★★★★ | **Site Privacy:** ★★★ |
| **Spaciousness:** ★★★ | **Quiet:** ★★★ |
| **Security:** ★★★★ | **Cleanliness:** ★★★★ |
| **Insect Control:** None | **Facilities:** ★★★ |

At 5,905 acres, Versailles State Park is the second largest state park in Indiana. It also has the second busiest state park swimming pool, a 25-meter pool with a 100-foot waterslide. In peak summer time, the park, campgrounds, and pool are overrun with visitors. Hillsides with limestone outcroppings, ravines, upland wooded areas, fields, and a 230-acre lake help make this one of the state's prettiest parks. Oct. is a peak time for fall foliage, as well as the annual Bluegrass Festival. At the entrance to the park, you can drive over Busching Bridge, one of the two remaining covered bridges in Ripley County. Located two miles east of Versailles, Indiana, the park is one of the few state parks to offer horseback riding. The horseback trails are open year-round but the saddle barn is open only Apr. through Oct. The park also has more than six miles of scenic hiking trails marked for skilled and beginning hikers. All camping sites will accommodate both RVs and tents. Security measures are strict with passes needed to enter the campground; the area is patrolled by rangers.

## BASICS

**Operated by:** Indiana Dept. of Natural Resources. **Open:** All year. **Site Assignment:** Written reservations w/ 1-night deposit, no refunds. **Registra-**

tion: At campground office. **Fee:** $12 (check, credit cards). **Parking:** At site.

## FACILITIES

**Number of RV Sites:** 226. **Number of Tent-Only Sites:** 0. **Hookups:** Electric (30 amps). **Each Site:** Picnic table, fire ring. **Dump Station:** Yes. **Laundry:** No. **Pay Phone:** Yes. **Rest Rooms and Showers:** Yes. **Fuel:** No. **Propane:** No. **Internal Roads:** Paved, in good condition. **RV Service:** No. **Market:** 2 mi. west in Vincennes. **Restaurant:** 2 mi. west in Vincennes. **General Store:** Yes. **Vending:** Yes. **Swimming Pool:** Yes. **Playground:** Yes. **Other:** Boat ramp (only electric trolling motors permitted), nature center, picnic shelters. **Activities:** Hiking, fishing, boating (rental rowboats, paddleboats, & canoes available), summer weekday programs, nature walks & evening activities offered by naturalist. **Nearby Attractions:** Scenic drives, 27-mi. Hoosier Hills Bicycle Route, golf, Ripley County Historical Society. **Additional Information:** Ripley County Tourism Bureau, (888) 747-3827.

## RESTRICTIONS

**Pets:** Leash only. **Fires:** Fire rings & grills only. **Alcoholic Beverages:** At sites only. **Vehicle Maximum Length:** 35 ft. **Other:** 14-day stay limit.

## TO GET THERE

From junction of US 421 and US 50, drive 1 mi. east on US 50. Roads are wide and well maintained with adequate shoulders.

# Michigan

Outdoor recreation is a way of life in the Wolverine State, especially if it involves a jaunt in your automobile of choice. In the "Motor City" of **Detroit,** Henry Ford and his Model-T gave highway travelers the wheels to hit the road. The state is also home to the original "Big Mac"—the **Mackinac Bridge** that joins Michigan's Lower Peninsula to its rugged Upper Peninsula. Ironically, **Mackinac Island** enforces a "no-cars" ban on its picturesque shores. Visitors take a ferry, catamaran, or plane to the tiny island, often to marvel at the 1887 **Grand Hotel** and its sweeping 600-foot-long white veranda topped by a sky-blue ceiling.

Blessed with two national forests, two national lakeshores, and a national park, Michigan also shares **four Great Lakes** and nearly 100 state parks, as well as magnificent sand dunes. Guarding the shores are more than 100 lighthouses. Despite those guardian lights, the 38,000 square miles of Great Lakes bottomlands are still the final resting place of more than 3,000 shipwrecks, attracting scuba divers and glass-bottomed boats.

For a taste of Dutch heritage, stop by **Holland,** where shopkeepers still scrub cobblestone sidewalks, America's only authentic Dutch windmill still twirls, and a profusion of colorful tulips dazzle visitors each May. To get the feel of Munich, head to **Frankenmuth,** home of **Bronner's Christmas Wonderland.** With a showroom bigger than four football fields, Bronner's is said to be the world's largest Christmas shop.

The cereal capital of the world, **Battle Creek** showcases breakfast food history. **Petoskey** draws rockhounds seeking stone remnants of an extinct coral that inhabited the shallow waters there 350 million years ago. In **Cheboygan,** one of the Great Lake's largest cattail marshes serves as a nesting site for 54 bird species. **Grand Haven** offers its special singing sands—when walked upon, the small sand particles create a peculiar whistling music. A fish ladder sculpture in **Grand Rapids** helps salmon jump over a six-foot dam to reach their spawning ground.

In **Sault Ste. Marie,** huge freighters pass through the town's greatest attraction, the **Soo Locks.** In winter, icefishing shacks pop up on Michigan waterways as anglers cut through the ice to tempt the fish. With a name that means "heaven," **Ishpeming** has become a well-known ski center. As the largest island in Lake Superior, **Isle Royale** is 99% wilderness. Along with its wealth of activities, Isle Royale is a great place for those seeking solitude and a chance to get closer to Michigan's natural beauty.

**The following facilities accept payment in checks or cash only:**

Clearwater Campground, Ortonville

Cottonwood Resort, Quincy

Happi Days Campground, Frederic

Indian Lake Travel Resort, Manistique

Jerry's Campground, Montague

Leisure Valley Campground, Decatur

Rockey's Campground, Albion

Sandyoak RV Park, Houghton Lake

Spaulding Lake Campground, Niles

Trails Campground, Frederic

Tri-Lakes Trails Campground, Marshall

Waffle Farm Campground, Coldwater

Withii Trailer Camp, Harrison

**The following facilities have 20 or fewer sites:**

Driftwood Shores Resort & RV Park, Thompson

Honcho Rest Campground, Elk Rapids

Jack's Landing Resort, Hillman

Just-In-Time Campgrounds, Ithaca

River Pines RV Park & Campground, Ontonagon

Waterways Campground, Cheboygan

Whitefish Hill Mobile Home & RV Park, Rapid River

# Campground Profiles

## ALBION

### Rockey's Campground

19880 27½ Mile Rd., Albion 49224. T: (877) 762-5397; F: (517) 857-4455.

🚐 ★★★★          🏕 ★★★

Beauty: ★★★★
Spaciousness: ★★★★
Security: ★★★★
Insect Control: ★★★★

Site Privacy: ★★★★
Quiet: ★★★★
Cleanliness: ★★★★
Facilities: ★★★

A rural campground on a chain of five lakes, Rockey's Campground is located about six-and-a-half miles south of Albion. The secluded campground offers open or shaded sites, with a typical site width of 35 feet. The campground has 50 seasonal campers and and no pull-through sites. A large building is available for groups, and a cement boat ramp is popular with boaters. Sites are level and grassy with gravel pads. The best sites are those closest to the water. Be aware that no large dogs are permitted. Facilities are very clean and well maintained. About half of sites are occupied by seasonals, and many other regulars return year after year, so reservations are recommended. For security measures, owners and staff members seem to keep a close watch on the campground while also being friendly and helpful.

### BASICS

**Operated by:** Brian & Vicki Mead. **Open:** May 15–Oct. 1. **Site Assignment:** Reservations w/ 1-night deposit; refund (minus $5) w/ 7-day notice. **Registration:** At campground office. **Fee:** $20 (cash, check). **Parking:** At site.

### FACILITIES

**Number of RV Sites:** 100. **Number of Tent-Only Sites:** 0. **Hookups:** Electric (20, 30 amps), water. **Each Site:** Picnic table, fire ring. **Dump Station:** Yes. **Laundry:** No. **Pay Phone:** Yes. **Rest Rooms and Showers:** Yes. **Fuel:** No. **Propane:** Yes. **Internal Roads:** Gravel, in good condition. **RV Service:** No. **Market:** 5 mi. south in Albion. **Restaurant:** 5 mi. south in Albion. **General Store:** Yes, limited. **Vending:** Yes. **Swimming Pool:** No. **Playground:** Yes. **Other:** Bass Lake, sandy beach, lake swimming, game room, mini-golf, boat ramp, sports field, horseshoes, rental cottage. **Activities:** Swimming, fishing, boating (rental rowboats, canoes available), scheduled weekend activities. **Nearby Attractions:** Whitehouse Nature Center, antiques, Albion's Historic Walkway, Albion College Observatory, Bobbitt Visual Arts Center, children's museum, Star Commonwealth, golf, Brueckner Museum & Gladstone Cottage. **Additional Information:** Greater Albion Chamber of Commerce, (517) 629-5533.

## RESTRICTIONS
**Pets:** No large dogs. **Fires:** Fire ring only. **Alcoholic Beverages:** Permitted. **Vehicle Maximum Length:** None.

## TO GET THERE
From the junction of I-94 and 28 Mile Rd., take Exit 121 and drive 7 mi. north on 28 Mile Rd. Roads are mostly wide and well maintained w/ adequate shoulders.

## ALLEGAN
### Tri-Ponds Family Camp Resort
3687 Dumont Rd., Allegan 49010. T: (616) 673-4740

🚐 ★★★★          ⛺ ★★★★

Beauty: ★★★           Site Privacy: ★★★★
Spaciousness: ★★★★    Quiet: ★★★★
Security: ★★★★        Cleanliness: ★★★★
Insect Control: ★★★★  Facilities: ★★★★

Circling several small ponds in Allegan, Tri-Ponds Family Camp Resort offers open and shaded campsites. Sites are level with a typical site width of 35 feet. The campground has 26 seasonal campers and eight pull-through sites. An activities and crafts director is on staff and worship services are held on Sunday. No license is necessary to fish in the ponds. The campground is well maintained and clean, with a great deal of attention put into keeping bathrooms and shower facilities in tip-top shape. Security is good with owners who make sure the campground is safe and quiet for campers.

## BASICS
**Operated by:** Paul & Dotty VanDrunen. **Open:** May 1–Oct. 31. **Site Assignment:** Reservations w/ 1-night deposit; refund w/ 2-week notice. **Registration:** At campground office. **Fee:** $24 (cash, check, credit cards). **Parking:** At site.

## FACILITIES
**Number of RV Sites:** 86. **Number of Tent-Only Sites:** 15. **Hookups:** Electric (20, 30 amps), water, sewer. **Each Site:** Picnic table, fire ring. **Dump Station:** Yes. **Laundry:** Yes. **Pay Phone:** Yes. **Rest Rooms and Showers:** Yes. **Fuel:** No. **Propane:** No. **Internal Roads:** Paved, in good condition. **RV Service:** No. **Market:** 2 mi. **Restaurant:** 2 mi. **General Store:** Yes. **Vending:** Yes. **Swimming Pool:** No. **Playground:** Yes. **Other:** Pond, swimming beach, rec hall, horse-

shoes, hiking trails, volleyball, sports field, activities & craft director. **Activities:** Swimming, fishing, scheduled activities. **Nearby Attractions:** Golf, antiques, bowling, horseback riding, Old Jail Museum, orchards, parks, Allegan State Game Area, arts & crafts, skiing. **Additional Information:** Allegan Area Chamber of Commerce, (616) 673-2479.

## RESTRICTIONS
**Pets:** Leash only. **Fires:** Fire ring only. **Alcoholic Beverages:** Not permitted. **Vehicle Maximum Length:** None.

## TO GET THERE
From the junction of Hwy. 222 and Hwy. 40/89, drive 3 mi. northwest on Hwy. 40/89, then 2 mi. north on 36th St., then 0.5 mi. west on Dumont Rd. Roads are mostly wide and well maintained w/ narrow shoulders in places. Dumont Rd. is paved but only in fair condition.

## ALPENA
### Campers Cove RV Park
5005 Long Rapids Rd., Alpena 49707. T: (888) 306-3708; www.camperscovecampground.com.

🚐 ★★★★          ⛺ ★★★★

Beauty: ★★★★         Site Privacy: ★★★★
Spaciousness: ★★★★   Quiet: ★★★★
Security: ★★★★       Cleanliness: ★★★★
Insect Control: Yes  Facilities: ★★★★

Located on a lake seven miles west of Alpena, Campers Cove RV Park has 45 waterfront sites. Sites are mostly grassy and shaded with a typical site width of 50 feet. Some sites have places to tie up boats on the inland waterway for easy access to Thunder Bay River. A sauna is available by request only and takes half an hour to heat. No children ages 12 and under are permitted in the sauna unless accompanied by an adult. The indoor heated pool has adults-only swim times. Laid out in a series of loops, the campground has level sites with 15 seasonal campers and ten pull-throughs. Rustic tent sites are in a separate area with more green space and privacy. Speed limit is 5.6 mph and quiet times are 11 p.m. to 8 a.m. Security measures include one entrance/exit road, owners who live on site, and regular patrols of the campground.

## BASICS

**Operated by:** Bruce, Jo, & Jill Canady. **Open:** May 1–Oct. 1. **Site Assignment:** Reservations w/ $25 deposit; refund (minus $5) w/ 15-day notice. Deposits made a year in advance are non refundable. **Registration:** At campground office. **Fee:** $27 (cash, check, credit cards). **Parking:** At site.

## FACILITIES

**Number of RV Sites:** 80. **Number of Tent-Only Sites:** 20. **Hookups:** Electric (20, 30, 50 amps), water, sewer, cable TV, phone. **Each Site:** Picnic table, fire ring. **Dump Station:** Yes. **Laundry:** Yes. **Pay Phone:** Yes. **Rest Rooms and Showers:** Yes. **Fuel:** No. **Propane:** Yes. **Internal Roads:** Paved/gravel, in good condition. **RV Service:** No. **Market:** 7 mi. east in Alpena. **Restaurant:** 7 mi. east in Alpena. **General Store:** Yes. **Vending:** Yes. **Swimming Pool:** Yes. **Playground:** Yes. **Other:** Lake Winyah, sauna, game room, TV lounge, pavilion, mini-golf, shuffleboard, basketball, volleyball, nature area, stocked fishing pond, badminton, sports field, coin games, boat ramp, boat dock. **Activities:** Swimming, boating (rental canoes, kayaks, paddleboats, & rowboats available), biking (rental bicycles, fun cycles, & electric scooters available), fishing. **Nearby Attractions:** Wildlife sanctuary, planetarium, golf, museums, historic homes, dinosaur gardens, charter boat fishing, lighthouses, beaches, underwater park, diving, rockhound areas, sinkholes, antiques. **Additional Information:** Alpena Area CVB, (800) 4-ALPENA.

## RESTRICTIONS

**Pets:** Leash only. **Fires:** Fire ring only. **Alcoholic Beverages:** Permitted. **Vehicle Maximum Length:** None.

## TO GET THERE

From the junction of US 23 and Long Rapids Rd., drive 6 mi. west on Long Rapids Rd. (Johnson St.). Roads are wide and well maintained w/ broad shoulders.

## BELMONT

### Grand Rogue Campgrounds Canoe & Tube Livery

6400 West River Dr., Belmont 49306. T: (616) 361-1053; F: (616) 972-1071; www.grandrogue.com.

🚐 ★★★★      ⛺ ★★★★

Beauty: ★★★★          Site Privacy: ★★★★
Spaciousness: ★★★★     Quiet: ★★★★

Security: ★★★★          Cleanliness: ★★★★
Insect Control: ★★★★     Facilities: ★★★

Located on the Grand and Rogue Rivers in Belmont, Rogue River Campgrounds Canoe & Tube Livery is minutes away from Grand Rapids attractions. Sites are grassy and partly shaded with a typical site width of 40 feet. The campground is adjacent to an 18-hole golf course and lighted driving range. Located in a secluded lake and riverside setting, the campground offers canoe and tube trips from one to four hours long. Be aware that alcohol is not permitted on paddlesport trips. The campground also has a tour train that runs along the river and through 75 acres of wooded trails. A large pavilion is available for use to campers. Campground staff is friendly and helpful, escorting campers to sites upon check-in. They will help park the camping unit or park it for you.

## BASICS

**Operated by:** Tom & Joan Briggs. **Open:** May 1–Oct. 15. **Site Assignment:** Reservations w/ $26 deposit; refund (minus $2) w/ 5-day notice. **Registration:** At campground office. **Fee:** $24 (cash, check, credit cards). **Parking:** At site.

## FACILITIES

**Number of RV Sites:** 82. **Number of Tent-Only Sites:** 10. **Hookups:** Electric (20, 30 amps), water, phone. **Each Site:** Picnic table, fire ring. **Dump Station:** Yes. **Laundry:** Yes. **Pay Phone:** Yes. **Rest Rooms and Showers:** Yes. **Fuel:** No. **Propane:** No. **Internal Roads:** Gravel, in good condition. **RV Service:** No. **Market:** 3 mi. **Restaurant:** 3 mi. **General Store:** Yes, limited. **Vending:** Yes. **Swimming Pool:** No. **Playground:** Yes. **Other:** Lake, river, pavilion, horseshoes, sports field, boat ramp, float trips, golf, basketball, hiking trails, volleyball. **Activities:** Swimming, fishing, boating (rental canoes, kayaks available), scheduled weekend activities. **Nearby Attractions:** Gerald B. Ford Museum, Fredrick Meijer Gardens, zoo, Michigan Adventure Amuseument Park, Roger B. Chaffee Planetarium, golf, tennis, rivers & lakes, antiques, Wooden Shoe Factory. **Additional Information:** Grand Rapids/Kent County CVB.

## RESTRICTIONS

**Pets:** Leash only. **Fires:** Fire ring only. **Alcoholic Beverages:** Not on river activities. **Vehicle Maximum Length:** None.

## To Get There

From north junction of I-96 and US 131, take Exit 91 and drive 1.5 mi. north on US 131, then 4 mi. east on West River Dr. Roads are mostly wide and well maintained w/ adequate shoulders.

## BENTON HARBOR

### Benton Harbor/St. Joseph KOA

3527 Coloma Rd., Riverside 49084. T: (616) 849-3333; www.koa.com; bhstjoekoa@qtm. net.

🚐 ★★★★     ⛺ ★★★★

| | |
|---|---|
| Beauty: ★★★ | Site Privacy: ★★★ |
| Spaciousness: ★★★★ | Quiet: ★★★★ |
| Security: ★★★★ | Cleanliness: ★★★★ |
| Insect Control: ★★★★ | Facilities: ★★★★ |

With easy interstate access and a big roster of activities, Benton Harbor/St. Joseph KOA is a popular camping spot. Reservations are recommended, especially for busy weekends and peak season. The area is known for having a festival almost every summer and early fall weekend. The campground offers level, grassy sites with a choice of open or shaded. The typical site width is 45 feet. The campground has 12 seasonal campers and 16 pull-through sites. A small pond offers a chance to dunk a worm, but don't count on catching much. Lake Michigan is only five minutes away with great fishing and other water activities. The hot tub is a nice touch, but sometimes it gets crowded. Quiet time is enforced beginning at 11 p.m., and rowdy people can be ejected. Security is also good with regular patrols and owners who keep a close watch on the campground. The goal is to have a nice, family-oriented campground, and it seems to be working at Benton Harbor/St. Joseph KOA.

### BASICS

**Operated by:** Ginter & Ursela Bansen. **Open:** Apr. 15–Oct. 15. **Site Assignment:** Reservations w/ 1-night deposit; refunds (minus $5) w/ 3-day notice. **Registration:** At campground office. **Fee:** $30 (cash, check, credit cards). **Parking:** At site.

### FACILITIES

**Number of RV Sites:** 115. **Number of Tent-Only Sites:** 18. **Hookups:** Electric (20, 30 amps), water, sewer. **Each Site:** Picnic table, fire ring. **Dump Station:** Yes. **Laundry:** Yes. **Pay Phone:** Yes. **Rest Rooms and Showers:** Yes. **Fuel:** No. **Propane:** Yes. **Internal Roads:** Paved, in good condition. **RV Service:** No. **Market:** 3 mi. west. **Restaurant:** 3 mi. west. **General Store:** Yes. **Vending:** Yes. **Swimming Pool:** Yes. **Playground:** Yes. **Other:** Fishing pond, sauna, hot tub, rental cabins, tennis, basketball, volleyball, shuffleboard, mini-golf, movies, rec hall, badminton, sports field, hiking trails, horseshoes. **Activities:** Swimming, fishing, hiking, scheduled activities. **Nearby Attractions:** Lake Michigan, fruit farms, charter boats, golf, Deer Forest, Curious Kids' Museum, Krasl Art Center, nature center, wineries, atomic plants, tennis, historic walking tour, antiques, arts & crafts. **Additional Information:** St. Joseph Today, (616) 982-0032.

### RESTRICTIONS

**Pets:** Leash only. **Fires:** Fire ring only. **Alcoholic Beverages:** Permitted. **Vehicle Maximum Length:** None. **Other:** Only one sleeping unit per site.

### To Get There

From the junction of I-196 and Coloma-Riverside Rd., take Exit 4 and drive 1 block east on Coloma-Riverside Rd. Roads are wide and well maintained w/ broad shoulders.

## BENZONIA

### Vacation Trailer Park

2080 Benzie Hwy., Benzonia 49616. T: (800) 482-5101; F: (231) 882-4687; www.vacationtrailer.com; vacation@benzie.com.

🚐 ★★★★     ⛺ ★★★

| | |
|---|---|
| Beauty: ★★★★ | Site Privacy: ★★★★ |
| Spaciousness: ★★★★ | Quiet: ★★★★ |
| Security: ★★★★ | Cleanliness: ★★★★ |
| Insect Control: ★★★★ | Facilities: ★★★★ |

Nestled into the natural beauty of the Betsie River, Vacation Trailer Park offers camping and activities on the designated scenic river. Located less than a mile from West Benzonia, the campground is rolling and grassy with a typical site width of 30 feet. Vacation Trailer Park has 20 seasonal campers and five pull-through sites with a choice of open or shaded. A canoe livery service lets you rent a canoe and paddle down the Betsie River right past your camp site. The best sites for RVs are right on the river. Tents are permitted on any sites except the river ones to prevent erosion and problems with water pipes. Vacation Trailer Sales is located only 100 yards up the road and carries a complete line of RV parts and accessories. The campground general store also has a nice selection of fishing and hunting supplies. The campground provides 24-hour security with night managers on site and regular patrols of the campground.

## BASICS

**Operated by:** Bill & Betty Workman. **Open:** Mar. 1–Dec. 1. **Site Assignment:** Reservations w/ 1-night deposit; no refund but camping credit for 1 year. **Registration:** At campground office. **Fee:** $25 (cash, check, credit cards). **Parking:** At site.

## FACILITIES

**Number of RV Sites:** 100. **Number of Tent-Only Sites:** 0. **Hookups:** Electric (20, 30, 50 amps), water, sewer, cable TV. **Each Site:** Picnic table, fire ring. **Dump Station:** Yes. **Laundry:** Yes. **Pay Phone:** Yes. **Rest Rooms and Showers:** Yes. **Fuel:** No. **Propane:** No. **Internal Roads:** Gravel, in good condition. **RV Service:** Yes. **Market:** 0.25 mi. north to West Benzonia. **Restaurant:** 0.25 mi. north to West Benzonia. **General Store:** Yes. **Vending:** Yes. **Swimming Pool:** Yes. **Playground:** Yes. **Other:** Betsie River, rec room, coin games, boat docks, fishing guide, fish-cleaning station, basketball, badminton, horseshoes, canoe launch area, rental RVs, rental cabins, hiking trails, volleyball, sports field. **Activities:** Swimming, hiking, fishing, boating (rental canoes, kayaks available), float trips. **Nearby Attractions:** Lake Michigan, Crystal Mountain, Point Betsie Lighthouse, marinas, golf, downhill ski runs, snowmobile & cross-country ski trails, antiques, arts & crafts, Benzie Area Historical Museum, Gwen Frostic Prints. **Additional Information:** Benzie Area Visitors Bureau, (800) 882-5801.

## RESTRICTIONS

**Pets:** Leash only. **Fires:** Fire ring only. **Alcoholic Beverages:** At sites only. **Vehicle Maximum Length:** None.

## TO GET THERE

From south junction of Hwy. 115 and US 31, drive 1 mi. north on US 31. Roads are wide and well maintained w/ broad shoulders.

## BROOKLYN

### Greenbriar Golf & Camping

14820 Wellwood, Brooklyn 49230. T: (517) 592-6952; www.michcampgrounds.com/greenbriar.

🚐 ★★★★     ⛺ ★★★

| | |
|---|---|
| Beauty: ★★★★ | Site Privacy: ★★★ |
| Spaciousness: ★★★ | Quiet: ★★★★ |
| Security: ★★★★ | Cleanliness: ★★★★ |
| Insect Control: ★★★★ | Facilities: ★★★ |

The name says it all. Greenbriar Golf & Camping offers golf and camping with an 18-hole golf course and watered fairways. Located five minutes from Michigan International Speedway in Brooklyn, the campground is also near Wampler's Lake and Irish Hills attractions. With a rolling, grassy terrain, the campground offers a choice of open or shaded sites with a typical site width of 30 feet. There are ten pull-throughs and 15 seasonals. A children's fishing pond provides catch-and-release fishing. Golf and camping packages are available. A pavilion and clubhouse are comfortable gathering spots. Facilities are clean and well maintained. Grounds are nicely landscaped and mowed, as would be expected for a golf course.

## BASICS

**Operated by:** Arthur & Thelma Babian. **Open:** Apr. 1–Nov. 1. **Site Assignment:** Reservations w/ 1-night deposit; refund (minus $5) w/ 7-day notice. **Registration:** At campground office. **Fee:** $30 (cash, check, credit cards). **Parking:** At site.

## FACILITIES

**Number of RV Sites:** 82. **Number of Tent-Only Sites:** 18. **Hookups:** Electric (20, 30, 50 amps), water. **Each Site:** Picnic table, fire ring. **Dump Station:** Yes. **Laundry:** Yes. **Pay Phone:** Yes. **Rest Rooms and Showers:** Yes. **Fuel:** No. **Propane:** No. **Internal Roads:** Gravel, in good condition. **RV Service:** No. **Market:** 1 mi. **Restaurant:** 1 mi. **General Store:** Yes. **Vending:** Yes. **Swimming Pool:** Yes. **Playground:** Yes. **Other:** 18-hole golf course, club house, children's fishing pond, pavilion, game room, putting green, basketball, horseshoes, volleyball, sports field. **Activities:** Golf, swimming, fishing. **Nearby Attractions:** Irish Hills, Michigan International Speedway, Irish Hills Towers, Mystery Hill, Prehistoric Forest, St. Joseph's Shrine, Stagecoach Stop, Cambridge Historical Park, Hidden Lake Gardens, state parks, antiques. **Additional Information:** Jackson County Visitors Bureau, (517) 764-4440.

## RESTRICTIONS

**Pets:** Leash only. **Fires:** Fire ring only. **Alcoholic Beverages:** Permitted. **Vehicle Maximum Length:** None.

## TO GET THERE

From the junction of US 12 and Hwy. 124, drive 1.5 mi. north on Hwy. 124 to Wellwood Rd. Roads are wide and well maintained w/ broad shoulders.

## BUCHANAN

## Fuller's Resort & Campground on Clear Lake

1622 East Clear Lake Rd., Buchanan 49107. T: (616) 695-3785; F: (616) 695-4066; www.fullersresort.com; justjeffmc@aol.com.

 ★★★                    ▲ ★★★

| | |
|---|---|
| Beauty: ★★★★ | Site Privacy: ★★★ |
| Spaciousness: ★★★ | Quiet: ★★★★ |
| Security: ★★★★ | Cleanliness: ★★★ |
| Insect Control: ★★★★ | Facilities: ★★★ |

Fuller's Resort & Campground on Clear Lake offers a quiet country setting. Located in Buchanan, the campground has 110 seasonal campers, so it is best to make reservations. Sites are level and mostly shaded, with four pull-throughs and a typical site width of 30 feet. The campground features an eight-acre spring-fed lake with 400 feet of clean sandy beach. The best sites are closest to the lake. A primitive area for tents offers more green space and privacy. A rental log cabin nestled in the woods features a fieldstone fireplace. Two modern cottages can be rented right on the lakeside. A shaded picnic area is a nice addition. A family-oriented campground under strict supervision, Fuller's Resort boasts 16 flavors of ice cream in its concession stand.

## BASICS

**Operated by:** Jeff & Rene McNeil. **Open:** Apr. 15–Oct. 15. **Site Assignment:** Reservations w/ 1-night deposit; refund (minus $5) w/ 2-week notice. **Registration:** At campground office. **Fee:** $20 (cash, check, credit cards). **Parking:** At site.

## FACILITIES

**Number of RV Sites:** 140. **Number of Tent-Only Sites:** 30. **Hookups:** Electric (20, 30 amps), water, sewer. **Each Site:** Picnic table, fire ring. **Dump Station:** Yes. **Laundry:** Yes. **Pay Phone:** Yes. **Rest Rooms and Showers:** Yes. **Fuel:** No. **Propane:** Yes. **Internal Roads:** Gravel, in good condition. **RV Service:** No. **Market:** 3 mi. **Restaurant:** 3 mi. **General Store:** Yes. **Vending:** Yes. **Swimming Pool:** No. **Playground:** Yes. **Other:** Clear Lake, sandy beach, rental log cabins & cottages, recreation barn, coin games, boat ramp, basketball, sports field, horseshoes, volleyball. **Activities:** Swimming, fishing, boating (rental rowboats, canoes, & paddleboats available), scheduled weekend activities. **Nearby Attractions:** Amish Acres, golf, antiques, Berrien County Museum, Deer Forest, Bear Cave, Apple Valley Market, nature center, zoo, Kamm's Brewery, musuems, Andrews University. **Additional Information:** Buchanan Area Chamber of Commerce, (616) 695-3291.

## RESTRICTIONS

**Pets:** Leash only. **Fires:** Fire ring only. **Alcoholic Beverages:** Permitted. **Vehicle Maximum Length:** None.

## TO GET THERE

From the junction of US 12 and Bakertown Rd., drive 2 mi. north on Bakertown Rd., then 1 mi. west on Elm Valley, then 1 mi. northwest on East Clear Lake Rd. Roads are mostly wide and in fair condition w/ narrow shoulders in spots.

## BYRON

## Myers Lake United Methodist Campground

10575 Silver Lake Rd., Byron 48418. T: (800) 994-5050; F: (810) 266-6037; www.michcampgrounds.com/myerslake; myerslak@shianet.org.

 ★★★                    ▲ ★★★

| | |
|---|---|
| Beauty: ★★★★ · | Site Privacy: ★★★★ |
| Spaciousness: ★★★★ | Quiet: ★★★★ |
| Security: ★★★★ | Cleanliness: ★★★ |
| Insect Control: ★★★ | Facilities: ★★★ |

Located on the banks of a 100-acre lake in Byron, Myers Lake United Methodist Campground offers good, clean, family fun in a quiet rural facility. The campground features family, group, and church camping in an alcohol-free environment. Sites are mostly grassy and shaded, with a typical site width of 30 feet. The campground has only 18 water and electric sites; the rest are electric-only, so reservations are recommended. The best RV sites are the lakeview ones with 50 amp electricity and water hookups. The sites overlook the clear, spring-fed lake and nature trail. Special sites with 20 amp electricity for tenters, overlooking the lake and outdoor chapel, are also available on holiday weekends. The lake has a 75 hp limit. Centrally located near the cities of Brighton, Flint, and Lansing, the campground is owned by the United Methodist Church, but is open to the public. Basic safety and security rules are enforced, but few campers seem to need to be reminded. Church services are held on Sunday.

## BASICS

**Operated by:** Detroit Conference, The United Methodist Church. **Open:** May 1–Oct. 15. **Site Assignment:** Reservations w/ 1-night deposit; refund (minus $5) w/ 3-day notice. **Registration:** At campground office. **Fee:** $25 (cash, check, credit cards). **Parking:** At site.

## FACILITIES

**Number of RV Sites:** 126. **Number of Tent-Only Sites:** 0. **Hookups:** Electric (20, 30, 50 amps), water. **Each Site:** Picnic table, fire ring. **Dump Station:** Yes. **Laundry:** Yes. **Pay Phone:** Yes. **Rest Rooms and Showers:** Yes. **Fuel:** No. **Propane:** Yes. **Internal Roads:** Gravel, in good condition. **RV Service:** No. **Market:** 5 mi. **Restaurant:** 5 mi. **General Store:** Yes. **Vending:** Yes. **Swimming Pool:** No. **Swimming Pool:** No. **Playground:** Yes. **Other:** Myers Lake, sandy beach, rec hall, pavilion, coin games, boat dock, boat ramp, basketball, sports field, horseshoes, volleyball, tetherball, softball, rental cabins. **Activities:** Swimming, fishing, boating (rental pontoons, rowboats, kayaks, & paddleboats available), scheduled weekend activities. **Nearby Attractions:** Children's Museum, Crossroads Village & Huckleberry Railroad, *Genesee Belle* cruises, Flint Cultural Center, Genesee Recreation Area, Alfred P. Sloan Museum, Flint Institute of Arts, Longway Planetarium, golf, antiques, arts & crafts. **Additional Information:** Flint Area CVB, (800) 253-5468.

## RESTRICTIONS

**Pets:** Leash only. **Fires:** Fire ring only. **Alcoholic Beverages:** Not permitted. **Vehicle Maximum Length:** None.

## TO GET THERE

From the junction of US 23 and Silver Lake Rd., take Linden-Fenton Exit 79 and drive 10 mi. west on Silver Lake Rd. Road is mostly wide and well maintained w/ narrow shoulders in places.

## CADILLAC

### Camp Cadillac

10621 East 34 Rd., Cadillac 49601. T: (800) 927-3124; F: (231) 775-9724; www.campcadillac.com; vcs@netonecom.net.

🚐 ★★★★                    ▲ ★★★★

| | |
|---|---|
| Beauty: ★★★★ | Site Privacy: ★★★★ |
| Spaciousness: ★★★★ | Quiet: ★★★★ |
| Security: ★★★★ | Cleanliness: ★★★★ |
| Insect Control: ★★★★ | Facilities: ★★★★ |

Adjacent to state forest land, Camp Cadillac has the privacy and feel of a park with the conveniences of a modern campground. Located two miles east of Cadillac, the campground offers level, grassy, and mostly shaded sites with a typical site width of 45 feet. Laid out in a series of loops, the rural campground has nine pull-through sites. A large roster of activities, including the popular barrel train and petting zoo, makes this a favorite spot for families. Friendly owners, sparkling-clean rest rooms, and a nice family atmosphere keeps campers coming back. Many people also use Camp Cadillac as a base to enjoy all the area has to offer. The best RV sites are by the pool and facilities. The best tent sites are in the more wooded, private areas. Security measures include owners who live on site and keep a close watch on the campground.

## BASICS

**Operated by:** Tim & Angie Vaughan. **Open:** Apr. 15–Oct. 15. **Site Assignment:** Reservations w/ 1-night deposit; refund (minus $5) w/ 7-day notice. **Registration:** At campground office. **Fee:** $30 (cash, check, credit cards). **Parking:** At site.

## FACILITIES

**Number of RV Sites:** 105. **Number of Tent-Only Sites:** 10. **Hookups:** Electric (20, 30, 50 amps), water, sewer, phone. **Each Site:** Picnic table, fire ring. **Dump Station:** Yes. **Laundry:** Yes. **Pay Phone:** Yes. **Rest Rooms and Showers:** Yes. **Fuel:** No. **Propane:** Yes. **Internal Roads:** Gravel, in good condition. **RV Service:** No. **Market:** 2 mi. west in Cadillac. **Restaurant:** 2 mi. west in Cadillac. **General Store:** Yes, limited. **Vending:** Yes. **Swimming Pool:** Yes. **Playground:** Yes. **Other:** Clam river, petting zoo, rec hall, coin games, pond fishing, basketball, movies, badminton, sports field, horseshoes, hiking trails, volleyball, rental cabins, rental RVs. **Activities:** Swimming, hiking, fishing, scheduled activities. **Nearby Attractions:** Johnny's Wild Game & Fish Park, golf, hunting, bike path, walkway, scenic drives, pontoon boat rides, natural history museum, Shay Steam Locomotive, historic walking tour, antiques, arts & crafts, Shrine of the Pines. **Additional Information:** Cadillac Area Visitors Bureau, (800) 225-2537.

## RESTRICTIONS

**Pets:** Leash only; 1 dog per site. **Fires:** Fire ring only. **Alcoholic Beverages:** At sites only. **Vehicle Maximum Length:** None. **Other:** No extra tents on same site.

## TO GET THERE

From north junction of Hwy. 55 and US 131, drive 2.4 mi. north on US 131, then 2 mi. east on East Boon Rd./E 34 Rd. Roads are mostly wide and well maintained w/ adequate shoulders.

## CEDAR SPRING

### Lakeside Camp Park

13677 White Creek Ave., Cedar Springs 49319.
T: (616) 696-1735

| 🚐 ★★★★ | 🔺 ★★★ |
|---|---|
| Beauty: ★★★★ | Site Privacy: ★★★★ |
| Spaciousness: ★★★★ | Quiet: ★★★★ |
| Security: ★★★★ | Cleanliness: ★★★★ |
| Insect Control: ★★★★ | Facilities: ★★★★ |

Located 17 miles north of Grand Rapids, Lakeside Camp Park offers convenience and easy access from the interstate. In a suburban setting, the campground features a five-acre private lake with a nice sandy swimming beach and off-shore raft and fishing dock. The lake is stocked annually with trout, bass, catfish, perch, and panfish. No fishing license is required. Laid out in a series of loops, the campground has grassy, level, lakeside sites with a typical site width of 30 feet. Sites offer a choice of open or shaded, with nine pull-throughs and 62 seasonal campers in a separate area from daily or weekend campers. The best sites are closest to Lake Waller. A recreation building has seating for 80 and can be used by small or large groups camping at Lakeside. A speed limit of 7.5 mph is enforced and owners keep a close watch on the campground for security.

## BASICS

**Operated by:** Richard & Diane Lupico. **Open:** May 1–Oct. 1. **Site Assignment:** Reservations w/ 1-night deposit; refund w/ 2-week notice. **Registration:** At campground office. **Fee:** $21 (cash, check, credit cards). **Parking:** At site.

## FACILITIES

**Number of RV Sites:** 155. **Number of Tent-Only Sites:** 0. **Hookups:** Electric (20, 30 amps), water, sewer. **Each Site:** Picnic table, fire ring. **Dump Station:** Yes. **Laundry:** Yes. **Pay Phone:** Yes. **Rest Rooms and Showers:** Yes. **Fuel:** No. **Propane:** No. **Internal Roads:** Gravel, in good condition. **RV Service:** No. **Market:** One block. **Restaurant:** One block. **General Store:** Yes. **Vending:** Yes. **Swimming Pool:** No. **Playground:** Yes. **Other:** Waller Lake, swimming beach, volleyball, basketball, game room, golf range, coin games, pavilion, boat ramp, badminton, sports field. **Activities:** Swimming, fishing, boating (rental rowboats, kayaks, & paddleboats available), scheduled weekend activities. **Nearby Attractions:** Grand Rapids, golf, botanical gardens, pro baseball, Van Andel Museum, Gerald Ford Museum, Old Kent Baseball Stadium, antiques. **Additional Information:** Cedar Springs Chamber of Commerce, (616) 696-3260.

## RESTRICTIONS

**Pets:** Leash only. **Fires:** Fire ring only. **Alcoholic Beverages:** Permitted. **Vehicle Maximum Length:** None.

## TO GET THERE

From the junction of US 31 and Hwy. 46, take Exit 104 and drive 100 yards east on Hwy. 46, then 0.25 mi. south on White Creek Ave. Roads are wide and well maintained w/ adequate shoulders.

## CEDARVILLE
### Cedarville RV Park Campground

634 Grove St., Cedarville 49719. T: (800) 906-3351; www.michcampgrounds.com/cedarville; cedarr@northernway.net.

🚐 ★★★★                    ⛺ ★★★★

| | |
|---|---|
| Beauty: ★★★★ | Site Privacy: ★★★ |
| Spaciousness: ★★★ | Quiet: ★★★★ |
| Security: ★★★★ | Cleanliness: ★★★★ |
| Insect Control: ★★★★ | Facilities: ★★★★ |

Located on the shores of Lake Huron in the midst of Les Cheneaux Islands, Cedarville RV Park Campground offers beautiful views. The campground also has seven deep-water docks and 35 other boat docks, as well as a boat launch. A fish-cleaning building helps give the campground its sparkling facilities. Just three blocks away from downtown Cedarville, the campground offers level, mostly open sites, with a typical site width of 25 feet. There are 9 pull-throughs and 12 seasonal campers. Reservations are recommended during prime vacation time since the campground is a popular spot with water sports enthusiasts, as well as campers visiting the local attractions. Security measures include owners who live on site and keep a close watch on the campground. Although they won't tolerate any misbehavior, owners are very friendly and helpful.

### BASICS
**Operated by:** Jon & Sharrie Steinbach. **Open:** May 1–Oct. 31. **Site Assignment:** Reservations w/ 1-night deposit; refund (minus $7.50) w/ 1-week notice. **Registration:** At campground office. **Fee:** $22 (cash, check, credit cards). **Parking:** At site.

### FACILITIES
**Number of RV Sites:** 75. **Number of Tent-Only Sites:** 2. **Hookups:** Electric (20, 30, 50 amps), water, sewer. **Each Site:** Picnic table, fire ring. **Dump Station:** Yes. **Laundry:** Yes. **Pay Phone:** Yes. **Rest Rooms and Showers:** Yes. **Fuel:** No. **Propane:** No. **Internal Roads:** Gravel, in good condition. **RV Service:** No. **Market:** 6 blocks. **Restaurant:** 4 blocks. **General Store:** No. **Vending:** No. **Swimming Pool:** No. **Playground:** No. **Other:** Lake Huron, rec hall, boat dock, boat ramp, rental cabins, fish-cleaning building. **Activities:** Swimming, fishing, boating (rental rowboats & kayaks

available). **Nearby Attractions:** Castle Rock, Mackinac Bridge, Mackinac Island, Mackinaw City, Deer Ranch, golf, casino, Fort De Baude Indian Museum, Marquette Mission Park & Museum of Ojibwa Culture, New France Discovery Center & Father Marquette National Memorial, Soo Locks, Ft. Millimackinac, Tahqomen Falls. **Additional Information:** St. Ignace Tourism Assoc., (800) 338-6660.

### RESTRICTIONS
**Pets:** Leash only. **Fires:** Fire ring only. **Alcoholic Beverages:** Permitted. **Vehicle Maximum Length:** None.

### TO GET THERE
From the junction of I-75 and Hwy. 134, take Exit 359 and drive 17 mi. east on Hwy. 134 through Cedarville, then 1 block south on Lake St. Roads are wide and well maintained w/ adequate shoulders.

## CHAMPION
### Michigamme Shores Campground Resort

Box 6, Champion 49814. T: (906) 339-2116; www.michigammeshores.com.

🚐 ★★★★                    ⛺ ★★★★

| | |
|---|---|
| Beauty: ★★★★ | Site Privacy: ★★★★ |
| Spaciousness: ★★★★ | Quiet: ★★★★ |
| Security: ★★★★ | Cleanliness: ★★★★ |
| Insect Control: ★★★★ | Facilities: ★★★★ |

Michigamme Shores Campground Resort has a great location—two-and-a-half miles west of Champion, on the shores of Lake Michigamme, in the heart of Upper Michigan's moose country. Facilities are very clean and well maintained, showing close attention to detail. Sites are mostly gravel and shaded, with a typical site width of 30 feet and eight pull-throughs. A separate area for tents provides more green space and privacy. The best sites are as close to the lake as possible. Lake Michigamme encompasses 4,360 acres, or almost seven square miles. The lake has more than 20 islands and depths of 50 feet. Michigamme Shores is the closest resort to moose country, and winter sports enthusiasts can catch cross-country ski trails right at the campground. Miles of groomed trails through the UP's snow-covered backcountry are available for snowmobiling or skiing. Hunters can walk or take a short drive to some of the best hunting in the UP. Hikers can enjoy the wilderness and a bevy of animals and birds.

## BASICS

**Operated by:** Woody & Pat Taylor. **Open:** All year. **Site Assignment:** Reservations w/ 1-night deposit; refund w/ 2-week notice. **Registration:** At campground office. **Fee:** $26 (cash, check, credit cards). **Parking:** At site.

## FACILITIES

**Number of RV Sites:** 80. **Number of Tent-Only Sites:** 20. **Hookups:** Electric (20, 30, 50 amps), water, sewer. **Each Site:** Picnic table, fire ring. **Dump Station:** Yes. **Laundry:** Yes. **Pay Phone:** Yes. **Rest Rooms and Showers:** Yes. **Fuel:** No. **Propane:** Yes. **Internal Roads:** Paved, in good condition. **RV Service:** No. **Market:** 2 mi. east in Champion. **Restaurant:** 2 mi. east in Champion. **General Store:** Yes. **Vending:** Yes. **Swimming Pool:** No. **Playground:** Yes. **Other:** Michigamme Lake, sandy beach, rec hall, coin games, basketball, tennis, badminton, sports field, horseshoes, hiking trails, volleyball, boat dock,. **Activities:** Swimming, fishing, boating (rental canoes, rowboats, motorboats, pontoons, paddleboats available), hiking. **Nearby Attractions:** Walking tours, Historical Museum, Marquette Maritime Mueum, Presque Isle Park, Upper Peninsula Children's Museum, golf, waterfalls, ghost towns, Pictured Rocks National Lakeshore, rock hounding, Copper Harbor & Keweenaw Peninsula. **Additional Information:** Marquette County CVB.

## RESTRICTIONS

**Pets:** Leash only. **Fires:** Fire ring only. **Alcoholic Beverages:** Permitted. **Vehicle Maximum Length:** None.

## TO GET THERE

From west edge of Champion, drive 2.5 mi. west on US 41/Hwy. 28. Roads are wide and well maintained w/ broad shoulders.

## CHEBOYGAN

### Waterways Campground

P.O. Box 262, Cheboygan 49721. T: (888) 882-7066

🚐 ★★★          ⛺ ★★★

| | |
|---|---|
| Beauty: ★★★ | Site Privacy: ★★★ |
| Spaciousness: ★★★ | Quiet: ★★★★ |
| Security: ★★★★ | Cleanliness: ★★★★ |
| Insect Control: None | Facilities: ★★★ |

One of the newest campgrounds on the inland waterway, Waterways Campground is nestled on the shores of the Cheboygan River. Located two miles south of Cheboygan, the campground offers level sites arranged in upper and lower levels. Sites are grassy with gravel parking spots and have a typical site width of 30 feet. The campground has 11 seasonal campers, mostly open sites, and ten pull-throughs. Bouquets of fresh-cut flowers in the clean bathroom are a nice touch. Apple trees are scattered around the property, which is located across from a marina. A tent area is separate from RVs and offers more privacy and green space. The best RV sites are 42–50 because they are in the back of the campground, offer full hookup, and have cable TV. The speed limit is five mph and security measures include one entrance/exit road, one-way streets, owners who live on site, and regular campground patrols.

## BASICS

**Operated by:** Ron & Jan Ramsey. **Open:** May 1–Nov. 1. **Site Assignment:** Reservations w/ 1-night deposit; refund w/ 48-hour notice. **Registration:** At campground office. **Fee:** $23 (cash, check, credit cards). **Parking:** At site.

## FACILITIES

**Number of RV Sites:** 50. **Number of Tent-Only Sites:** Tent area. **Hookups:** Electric (30, 50 amps), water, sewer, cable TV. **Each Site:** Picnic table, fire ring. **Dump Station:** Yes. **Laundry:** No. **Pay Phone:** No. **Rest Rooms and Showers:** Yes. **Fuel:** No. **Propane:** No. **Internal Roads:** Gravel, in good condition. **RV Service:** No. **Market:** 2 mi. north in Cheboygan. **Restaurant:** 2 mi. north in Cheboygan. **General Store:** Yes. **Vending:** Yes. **Swimming Pool:** No. **Playground:** Yes. **Other:** Cheboygan River, horseshoes, game room, recreation field, boat ramp, boat dock, basketball, badminton, hiking trails, volleyball. **Activities:** Fishing, boating (rental pontoon, rowboats, paddleboats available), scheduled weekend activities. **Nearby Attractions:** Opera House, golf, archery range, Cross of the Woods Shrine, Mackinaw City, Mackinac Island, museums, antiques, beaches, state & city parks, 42 mi. of continuous inland waterway. **Additional Information:** Cheboygan Area Chamber of Commerce, (800) 968-3302.

## RESTRICTIONS

**Pets:** Leash only. Large or multiple pets must have prior approval. **Fires:** Fire ring only. **Alcoholic**

**Beverages:** Permitted. **Vehicle Maximum Length:** None.

## TO GET THERE

From the junction of Hwy. 27 and Hwy. 33, drive 0.25 mi. south on Hwy. 33. Roads are wide and well maintained w/ broad shoulders.

# COLDWATER

## Waffle Farm Campground

790 North Union Rd., Coldwater 49036. T: (517) 278-4315; www.wafflefarm.com.

🚐 ★★★★          ▲ ★★★★

| | |
|---|---|
| Beauty: ★★★★ | Site Privacy: ★★★★ |
| Spaciousness: ★★★★ | Quiet: ★★★★ |
| Security: ★★★★ | Cleanliness: ★★★★ |
| Insect Control: None | Facilities: ★★★★ |

A lakeside campground with open and shaded sites, Waffle Farm Campground got its name from the owner's grandmother, Myra Waffle, who started the camping business in 1925 with primitive camping and two wooden boats for rent. The camp sites are now spread over more than one-and-a-half miles of water frontage, mainly Craig Lake and part of Morrison Lake. The two lakes are part of a group totaling over 1,074 acres known as the Randall-Morrison Chain. The campground has 240 seasonal campers, 25 pull-throughs, and a typical site width of 30 feet. Seasonal campers are mostly in a separate area from other campsites. Tent campers have a section with more green space and privacy. Quiet hours are 11 p.m. to 8 a.m. Speed limit is 10 mph, a bit fast for a family campground. Security includes a guard on weekends.

## BASICS

**Operated by:** Loyd Green Jr. & Family. **Open:** Apr. 15–Oct. 15. **Site Assignment:** Reservations w/ $20 deposit; refund (minus $5) w/ 7-day notice. **Registration:** At campground office. **Fee:** $24 (cash, check). **Parking:** At site.

## FACILITIES

**Number of RV Sites:** 370. **Number of Tent-Only Sites:** 25. **Hookups:** Electric (20, 30, 50 amps), water, sewer. **Each Site:** Picnic table, fire spot. **Dump Station:** Yes. **Laundry:** No. **Pay Phone:** Yes. **Rest Rooms and Showers:** Yes. **Fuel:** Yes. **Propane:** Yes. **Internal Roads:** Gravel, in good condition. **RV Service:** No. **Market:** 3 mi.

south in Coldwater. **Restaurant:** 3 mi. south in Coldwater. **General Store:** Yes. **Vending:** Yes. **Swimming Pool:** No. **Playground:** Yes. **Other:** Lake, swimming beach, pavilion, arcade, mini golf, driving range, fish-cleaning stand, club area, boat ramp, boat landing, rental cottages, rec room, sports field, hiking trails. **Activities:** Swimming, fishing, hiking, boating (rental rowboats, paddleboats available). **Nearby Attractions:** Bowling, golf, summer theater, Branch County Historical Society, antiques, drive-in theaters, motor speedway, historic homes, museums, arts & crafts shops. **Additional Information:** Branch County Tourism Bureau, (800) 968-9333.

## RESTRICTIONS

**Pets:** Leash only. **Fires:** Fire ring only. **Alcoholic Beverages:** Permitted. **Vehicle Maximum Length:** None.

## TO GET THERE

From the junction of I-69 and US 12, drive 3.5 mi. north on I-69, take Exit 16, then 2.75 mi. west on Jonesville Rd., then 0.75 mi. north on Union City Rd. Roads are wide and well maintained w/ broad shoulders.

# DECATUR

## Leisure Valley Campground

40851 CR 669, Decatur 49045. T: (616) 423-7122

🚐 ★★★★          ▲ ★★★

| | |
|---|---|
| Beauty: ★★★★ | Site Privacy: ★★★★ |
| Spaciousness: ★★★★ | Quiet: ★★★★ |
| Security: ★★★★ | Cleanliness: ★★★★ |
| Insect Control: ★★★★ | Facilities: ★★★★ |

A grassy campground with open and shaded sites, Leisure Valley Campground is located three miles south of Decatur. Sites are level with a typical site width of 35 feet. The campground has 30 seasonal campers. A clubhouse with a kitchen is available. Campsites are adjacent to a small lake and five ponds. The lake is stocked with bass, bluegill, and perch. The best camp sites are closest to the water. A small island is a nice picnic spot. Facilities are very clean and well maintained, and the owners provide security to keep the campground a quiet, family-oriented place.

## BASICS

**Operated by:** Gale & Josie Congdon. **Open:** Apr. 1–Oct. 31. **Site Assignment:** Reservations w/ 1-

night deposit; refund (minus $5) w/ 7-day notice. **Registration:** At campground office. **Fee:** $20 (cash, check). **Parking:** At site.

## FACILITIES

**Number of RV Sites:** 108. **Number of Tent-Only Sites:** 0. **Hookups:** Electric (20, 30 amps), water, sewer, phone. **Each Site:** Picnic table, fire ring. **Dump Station:** Yes. **Laundry:** Yes. **Pay Phone:** Yes. **Rest Rooms and Showers:** Yes. **Fuel:** No. **Propane:** Yes. **Internal Roads:** Gravel, in good condition. **RV Service:** No. **Market:** 2 mi. north in Decatur. **Restaurant:** 2 mi. north in Decatur. **General Store:** Yes. **Vending:** Yes. **Swimming Pool:** Yes. **Playground:** Yes. **Other:** Swimming lake, rec hall, pavilion, coin games, boat dock, mini golf, basketball, shuffleboard, badminton, horseshoes, volleyball, hiking trails, rental trailers. **Activities:** Swimming, fishing, boating (rental canoes, rowboats, paddleboats available), scheduled weekend activities, hiking. **Nearby Attractions:** Golf, stock car racing, winery tours, playhouses, Palisades Nuclear Plant, Deer Forest, antiques, arts & crafts. **Additional Information:** Decatur Chamber of Commerce, (616) 423-7014.

## RESTRICTIONS

**Pets:** Leash only. **Fires:** Fire ring only. **Alcoholic Beverages:** Permitted. **Vehicle Maximum Length:** None.

## TO GET THERE

From the junction of Hwy. 51 and George St., drive 3 mi. south on George St., then 0.25 mi. west on Valley Rd. Roads are mostly wide and well maintained w/ adequate shoulders. Access road is in fair condition.

## DECATUR

### Oak Shores Campground

86882 CR 215, Decatur 49045. T: (616) 423-7370; www.michcampgrounds.com/oakshores/decatur.

| 🚐 ★★★★ | 🅰 ★★★★ |
|---|---|
| Beauty: ★★★ | Site Privacy: ★★★★ |
| Spaciousness: ★★★★ | Quiet: ★★★★ |
| Security: ★★★★ | Cleanliness: ★★★ |
| Insect Control: ★★★★ | Facilities: ★★★★ |

Located on a private 75-acre lake in Decatur, Oak Shores Campground offers a choice of sites ranging from full sun to full shade. Sites are level and grassy with a typical site width of 30 feet. There are 95 seasonal campers and 30 pull-through sites. The best sites are closest to Knickerbocker Lake. A separate primitive tent area provides more green space and privacy. Along with other playgrounds, Oak Shores offers a fenced-in Little Tykes playground with more size-appropriate equipment. A large rec hall is available for dancing and club activities. Owners provide security measures and try to make sure the campground maintains a peaceful, family-oriented atmosphere. From all the camping families that keep returning, their efforts must be working.

## BASICS

**Operated by:** Joe & Mary Lou Schantz. **Open:** Apr. 15–Oct. 15. **Site Assignment:** Reservations w/ 1-night deposit; refund (less $5) w/ 2-week notice. **Registration:** At campground office. **Fee:** $25 (cash, check, credit cards). **Parking:** At site.

## FACILITIES

**Number of RV Sites:** 220. **Number of Tent-Only Sites:** 10. **Hookups:** Electric (20, 30 amps), water, sewer, phone. **Each Site:** Picnic table, fire ring. **Dump Station:** Yes. **Laundry:** Yes. **Pay Phone:** Yes. **Rest Rooms and Showers:** Yes. **Fuel:** No. **Propane:** Yes. **Internal Roads:** Gravel, in good condition. **RV Service:** No. **Market:** 5 mi. **Restaurant:** 5 mi. **General Store:** Yes. **Vending:** Yes. **Swimming Pool:** Yes. **Playground:** Yes. **Other:** Knickerbocker Lake, sandy beach, coin games, rental cabins & travel trailers, sports field, whirlpool, game room, adult game room, pavilion, tennis, shuffleboard, rec hall, horseshoes, volleyball, basketball. **Activities:** Swimming, fishing, boating (rental canoes, kayaks, rowboats, paddleboats available), scheduled weekend activities. **Nearby Attractions:** Golf, stock car racing, winery tours, playhouses, Palisades Nuclear Plant, Deer Forest, antiques, arts & crafts. **Additional Information:** Decatur Chamber of Commerce, (616) 423-7014.

## RESTRICTIONS

**Pets:** Small pets only; on leash. **Fires:** Fire ring only. **Alcoholic Beverages:** Permitted. **Vehicle Maximum Length:** None.

## TO GET THERE

From the junction of I-94 and Hwy. 51, take Exit 56 and drive 10 mi. southwest on Hwy. 51, then 0.25 mi. north on CR 215. Roads are mainly wide and well maintained w/ adequate shoulders.

## DECATUR

### Timber Trails RV Park

84981 47½ St., Decatur 49045. T: (616) 681-9836

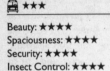 ★★★  ▲ ★★★★

| | |
|---|---|
| Beauty: ★★★★ | Site Privacy: ★★★★ |
| Spaciousness: ★★★★ | Quiet: ★★★★ |
| Security: ★★★★ | Cleanliness: ★★★★ |
| Insect Control: ★★★★ | Facilities: ★★★ |

With lakefront sites on the 289-acre Lake of the Woods, Timber Trails RV Park offers a full slate of water activities. Located in the lower peninsula seven miles north of Decatur, the campground is just a few miles from Lake Michigan. Campsites are level and grassy with a choice of open or shade. The best sites are on the lakefront. The typical site width is 30 feet, and the campground has three pull-through sites. Group RV and tent sites are available. Facilities are clean and well maintained, and the location is scenic. Those facts are all the good news. The bad news is that most of the campsites are taken by seasonal campers. About 25 sites are available for non-seasonal campers, so reservations are recommended. Also, be aware that no pets are allowed in the campground.

#### BASICS

**Operated by:** Gary & Deborah Douglas. **Open:** May 1–Sept. 30. **Site Assignment:** Reservations w/ 1-night deposit; refund w/ 14-day notice. **Registration:** At campground office. **Fee:** $22 (cash, check, credit cards). **Parking:** At site.

#### FACILITIES

**Number of RV Sites:** 107. **Number of Tent-Only Sites:** 10. **Hookups:** Electric (20, 30 amps), water. **Each Site:** Picnic table, fire ring. **Dump Station:** Yes. **Laundry:** Yes. **Pay Phone:** Yes. **Rest Rooms and Showers:** Yes. **Fuel:** No. **Propane:** Yes. **Internal Roads:** Gravel, in good condition. **RV Service:** None. **Market:** 6 mi. north in Decatur. **Restaurant:** 6 mi. north in Decatur. **General Store:** Yes, limited. **Vending:** Yes. **Swimming Pool:** No. **Playground:** Yes. **Other:** Lake of the Woods, sandy beach, volleyball, horseshoes, shuffleboard, game room, boat dock, sports field, badminton, boat slips. **Activities:** Swimming, fishing, boating (rental rowboats, canoes, paddleboats available). **Nearby Attractions:** Golf, stock car racing, winery tours, playhouses, Palisades Nuclear Plant, Deer Forest, antiques, arts & crafts. **Additional**

**Information:** Decatur Chamber of Commerce, (616) 423-7014.

#### RESTRICTIONS

**Pets:** No pets allowed. **Fires:** Fire ring only. **Alcoholic Beverages:** Permitted. **Vehicle Maximum Length:** None.

#### TO GET THERE

From the junction of I-94 and Hwy. 51, take Exit 56 and drive 8 mi. south on Hwy. 51, then 0.75 mi. north on 47½ St. Roads are mostly wide and well maintained w/ broad shoulders.

## DORR

### Hungry Horse Campground

2016 142nd St., Dorr 49323. T: (616) 681-9836; www.hungryhorsecampground.com; hhorse@accn.org.

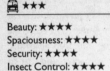 ★★★★  ▲ ★★★★

| | |
|---|---|
| Beauty: ★★★★ | Site Privacy: ★★★★ |
| Spaciousness: ★★★★ | Quiet: ★★★★ |
| Security: ★★★★ | Cleanliness: ★★★★ |
| Insect Control: ★★★★ | Facilities: ★★★★ |

Located 15 miles south of Grand Rapids in Dorr, Hungry Horse Campground offers a quiet rural setting. Laid out in a series of loops, the campground has level, grassy sites with a choice of open or shade. The typical site width is 30 feet, and the campground has 30 seasonal campers and 31 pull-through sites. Hungry Horse is nicely landscaped with flower beds, hanging baskets, and many perennial and annual flowers. Someone has a green thumb and spends a great deal of time keeping the grounds in tip-top shape. The playground with wooden structures is a nice addition. A heated wading pool is also popular with smaller youngsters. Rules are enforced to keep the campground well maintained and quiet. For example, long hair on swimmers in the swimming pool must be braided or tied back. Bicycles can be ridden on campground roads only, and quiet hours are enforced from 10 a.m. to 8 p.m. Motorcycles and all terrain vehicles also can't be ridden in the campgrounds. A ten mph speed limit is enforced but seems a bit high for such a family-oriented facility.

#### BASICS

**Operated by:** Norm & Nancy Fifelski. **Open:** May 1–Oct. 1. **Site Assignment:** Reservations w/ 1-night deposit; refund (minus $10) w/ 3-day notice.

**Registration:** At campground office. **Fee:** $28 (cash, check, credit cards). **Parking:** At site.

## FACILITIES

**Number of RV Sites:** 85. **Number of Tent-Only Sites:** 5. **Hookups:** Electric (20, 30 amps), water, sewer. **Each Site:** Picnic table, fire ring. **Dump Station:** Yes. **Laundry:** Yes. **Pay Phone:** Yes. **Rest Rooms and Showers:** Yes. **Fuel:** No. **Propane:** Yes. **Internal Roads:** Paved/gravel, in good condition. **RV Service:** No. **Market:** 3 mi. east. **Restaurant:** 3 mi. east. **General Store:** Yes. **Vending:** Yes. **Swimming Pool:** Yes. **Playground:** Yes. **Other:** Pavilion, rec room, shuffleboard, badminton, sports field, horseshoes, hiking trails, volleyball, coin games, wading pool. **Activities:** Swimming, hiking, scheduled weekend activities. **Nearby Attractions:** Gerald B. Ford Museum, Fredrick Meijer Gardens, zoo, Michigan Adventure Amusement Park, Roger B. Chaffee Planetarium, golf, tennis, rivers & lakes, antiques, Wooden Shoe Factory. **Additional Information:** Grand Rapids/Kent County CVB, (800) 678-9859.

## RESTRICTIONS

**Pets:** Leash only. **Fires:** Fire ring only. **Alcoholic Beverages:** At sites only. **Vehicle Maximum Length:** None.

## TO GET THERE

From the junction of US 131 and 142nd Ave., take Exit 68 and drive 4 mi. west on 142nd Ave. Roads are wide and well maintained w/ adequate shoulders.

## ELK RAPIDS
### Honcho Rest Campground

8988 Cairn Hwy., Elk Rapids 49629. T: (231) 264-8548; F: (231) 264-6849.

| 🚐 ★★★ | 🏕 n/a |
|---|---|
| Beauty: ★★★ | Site Privacy: ★★★ |
| Spaciousness: ★★★ | Quiet: ★★★ |
| Security: ★★★★ | Cleanliness: ★★★★ |
| Insect Control: ★★★★ | Facilities: ★★★ |

Located on the east shore of Bass Lake in Elk Rapids, Honcho Rest Campground offers a choice of shaded or open sites with a typical site width of 30 feet. Honcho Rest has 25 seasonal campers and two pull-through sites. Campsites have cement pads and patios. Across the street is a nine-hole golf course and Elk Lake. One mile away is Lake Michigan. The campground is clean and well maintained with seasonal spots also kept attractive. The number of seasonal campers does seem to continue growing, so reservations are recommended. Security measures are good with a main gate that is closed from 11 p.m. to 6 a.m.

## BASICS

**Operated by:** Robert & Johanna Wilder. **Open:** May 1–Oct. 15. **Site Assignment:** Reservations w/ 1-night deposit; refund w/ 2-week notice. **Registration:** At campground office. **Fee:** $26 (cash, check, credit cards). **Parking:** At site.

## FACILITIES

**Number of RV Sites:** 50. **Number of Tent-Only Sites:** 0. **Hookups:** Electric (20, 30, 50 amps), water, sewer, cable TV. **Each Site:** Picnic table, fire ring. **Dump Station:** Yes. **Laundry:** Yes. **Pay Phone:** Yes. **Rest Rooms and Showers:** Yes. **Fuel:** No. **Propane:** Yes. **Internal Roads:** Gravel, in good condition. **RV Service:** No. **Market:** Two blocks. **Restaurant:** Two blocks. **General Store:** No. **Vending:** Yes. **Swimming Pool:** No. **Playground:** Yes. **Other:** Bass Lake, boat dock, sports field. **Activities:** Swimming, fishing, boating (rental rowboats, canoes available). **Nearby Attractions:** Golf course, Lake Michigan, Elk Lake, marina, Guntzviller's Spirit of the Woods Museum, antiques, arts & crafts, fishing, swimming, watersports. **Additional Information:** Elk Rapids Chamber of Commerce, (231) 264-8202.

## RESTRICTIONS

**Pets:** Leash only. **Fires:** Fire ring only. **Alcoholic Beverages:** Permitted. **Vehicle Maximum Length:** None. **Other:** No tents allowed.

## TO GET THERE

From the junction of US 31 and Ames St. in Elk Rapids, drive 1.25 mi. southeast on Ames St. Roads are wide and well maintained w/ adequate shoulders.

## FENWICK
### Snow Lake Kampground

644 East Snow Lake Rd., Fenwick 48834. T: (517) 248-3224

| 🚐 ★★★★ | 🏕 ★★★★ |
|---|---|
| Beauty: ★★★★ | Site Privacy: ★★★★ |
| Spaciousness: ★★★★ | Quiet: ★★★★ |
| Security: ★★★★ | Cleanliness: ★★★★ |
| Insect Control: ★★★★ | Facilities: ★★★★ |

Located 28 miles from Grand Rapids in Fenwick, Snow Lake Kampground is a Christian family resort. The rural campground has open or shaded sites with a typical site width of 40 feet. The campground has 200 seasonal campers so reservations are recommended. Sites are mostly gravel with 25 pull-throughs. A new rally area features a new bathhouse and an enclosed pavilion. Facilities are very clean and well maintained. A nice touch is a kiddie pool for youngsters who might be too small for the regular heated pool. Sunday church services are held in the Little Church in the Wildwood. The best sites are those closest to Snow Lake. Owners keep a close watch on the campground and provide security measures. Without being nagging or intrusive, owners also enforce guidelines to keep Snow Lake Kampground a clean, quiet, safe, family-oriented facility.

## BASICS

**Operated by:** Ronald & Marie Sellers. **Open:** May 1–Oct. 1. **Site Assignment:** Reservations w/ 1-night deposit; refund w/ 5-day notice. **Registration:** At campground office. **Fee:** $28 (cash, check, credit cards). **Parking:** At site.

## FACILITIES

**Number of RV Sites:** 252. **Number of Tent-Only Sites:** 5. **Hookups:** Electric (20, 30, 50 amps), water, sewer, phone. **Each Site:** Picnic table, fire ring. **Dump Station:** Yes. **Laundry:** Yes. **Pay Phone:** Yes. **Rest Rooms and Showers:** Yes. **Fuel:** No. **Propane:** No. **Internal Roads:** Gravel, in good condition. **RV Service:** No. **Market:** 3 mi. north. **Restaurant:** On site. **General Store:** Yes. **Vending:** Yes. **Swimming Pool:** Yes. **Playground:** Yes. **Other:** Snow Lake, rec room, coin games, wading pool, boat dock, mini-golf, basketball, shuffleboard, sports field, horseshoes, volleyball, pavilion. **Activities:** Swimming, fishing, boating (rental rowboats, kayaks, paddleboats available), scheduled weekend activities. **Nearby Attractions:** Gerald B. Ford Museum, Fredrick Meijer Gardens, zoo, Michigan Adventure Amusement Park, Roger B. Chaffee Planetarium, golf, tennis, rivers & lakes, antiques, Wooden Shoe Factory. **Additional Information:** Grand Rapids/ Kent County CVB, (800) 678-9859.

## RESTRICTIONS

**Pets:** Leash only. **Fires:** Fire ring only. **Alcoholic Beverages:** Not permitted. **Vehicle Maximum Length:** 40 ft.

## TO GET THERE

From the junction of Hwy. 57 and Hwy. 66, drive 3 mi. south on Hwy. 66, then 0.75 mi. east on Snow Lake Rd. Roads are mostly wide and well maintained w/ adequate shoulders.

# FRANKENMUTH

## Frankenmuth Jellystone Park

1339 Weiss St., Frankenmuth 48734. T: (989) 652-6668; F: (989) 652-3461; www.frankenmuthjellystone.com.

| 🚐 ★★★★ | 🛖 ★★★★ |
|---|---|
| Beauty: ★★★★ | Site Privacy: ★★★★ |
| Spaciousness: ★★★★ | Quiet: ★★★★ |
| Security: ★★★★★ | Cleanliness: ★★★★★ |
| Insect Control: Yes | Facilities: ★★★★★ |

Located in the heart of the number one tourist attraction in Michigan, Frankenmuth Jellystone Park is a popular spot with reservations recommended. A bonus is that it's possible to park at the campground and walk to many attractions. It is 1,000 yards to Bronner's Christmas Wonderland and three-quarter mile to most shopping areas. There are sidewalks from the park to downtown. Laid out in a series of loops, sites are mostly open, level, and grassy with concrete pads or gravel to park on. The campground has no seasonal campers. The typical site width is 30 feet, and there are 48 pull-through sites. Cleanliness and security are tops. Security measures include a card-coded gate, ranger patrols, and an owner who lives on site. The downside to the campground's convenient location is that it must abide by city ordinances concerning campfires. So if you enjoy spending a quiet evening by your private campfire, this is not the place. Campers are welcome to use charcoal or gas grills at their sites but wood campfires are permitted only in designated rings off the sites. Community campfire rings are located between the rec hall and bathrooms and next to the pool. Campfires must be extinguished by 11 p.m., and flames should never be higher than two feet.

## BASICS

**Operated by:** Erv Banes. **Open:** All year. **Site Assignment:** Reservations w/ $35 deposit; refund (minus $5) w/ 7-day notice. **Registration:** At campground office. **Fee:** $40 (cash, credit cards). **Parking:** At site.

## FACILITIES

**Number of RV Sites:** 250. **Number of Tent-Only Sites:** 20. **Hookups:** Electric (20, 30, 50 amps), water, sewer. **Each Site:** Picnic table. **Dump Station:** Yes. **Laundry:** Yes. **Pay Phone:** Yes. **Rest Rooms and Showers:** Yes. **Fuel:** No. **Propane:** Yes. **Internal Roads:** Paved, in great condition. **RV Service:** No. **Market:** Next door. **Restaurant:** Next door. **General Store:** Yes. **Vending:** Yes. **Swimming Pool:** Yes. **Playground:** Yes. **Other:** Game room, hot tub, activity room, rec hall, snack bar, mini golf, pavilion, rental cabins, coin games, basketball, badminton, movies, horseshoes, volleyball. **Activities:** Swimming, scheduled activities. **Nearby Attractions:** Bronner's Christmas Wonderland, golf, paddlewheel boat, winery, antiques, arts & crafts, Bavarian shops, cheese haus, Military & Space Museum. **Additional Information:** Frankenmuth Chamber of Commerce, (800) FUN-TOWN.

## RESTRICTIONS

**Pets:** Leash only. **Fires:** Designated community fire rings only. **Alcoholic Beverages:** At sites only. **Vehicle Maximum Length:** None. **Other:** Children under 16 not permitted in hot tub. Limit of one guest family per site per day. Guests are not permitted on holiday & Halloween event weekends.

## TO GET THERE

From the junction of I-75 and M-83 (Birch Run Rd.), take Exit 136, drive 2 mi. east on Birch Run Rd., drive 5 mi. north on Gera Rd., drive 1 block north on Weiss St. Roads are wide and well maintained w/ broad shoulders.

# FRANKENMUTH
## Pine Ridge RV Campground

11700 Gera Rd., Birch Run 48415. T: (989) 624-9029

| 🚐 ★★★ | 🏕 n/a |
|---|---|
| Beauty: ★★★ | Site Privacy: ★★★ |
| Spaciousness: ★★★★ | Quiet: ★★★★ |
| Security: ★★★★ | Cleanliness: ★★★★ |
| Insect Control: None | Facilities: ★★★ |

Located about four miles south of Frankenmuth, Pine Ridge RV Campground has the benefit of being conveniently close to "Little Bavaria" without being restricted under city campfire codes. Individual campsites are permitted to have wood campfires in fire rings. Laid out in a series of loops, the campground is mostly shaded with mature trees. Sites are grassy with gravel parking spots. The campground has 150 pull-through sites and no seasonal campers. Tents are not permitted. The best site is 61, but it is often reserved a year or two in advance. This end site has a beautiful yard with tall trees, offers pull-through access, and is a quiet spot. Site 147 is also popular because it is across from the clubhouse. The typical site width is 40 feet. Security measures are great with a card-coded gate, a manager who lives on site, and regular patrols of the campground.

## BASICS

**Operated by:** Norman Wooten. **Open:** Apr. 15–Nov. 15. **Site Assignment:** Reservations w/ 1-night deposit; refund w/ 7-day notice. **Registration:** At campground office. **Fee:** $30 (cash, check, credit cards). **Parking:** At site.

## FACILITIES

**Number of RV Sites:** 201. **Number of Tent-Only Sites:** 0. **Hookups:** Electric (20, 30, 50 amps), water, sewer. **Each Site:** Picnic table, fire ring. **Dump Station:** Yes. **Laundry:** Yes. **Pay Phone:** Yes. **Rest Rooms and Showers:** Yes. **Fuel:** No. **Propane:** Yes. **Internal Roads:** Paved/gravel, in good condition. **RV Service:** No. **Market:** Walking distance. **Restaurant:** Walking distance. **General Store:** Yes, limited. **Vending:** No. **Swimming Pool:** No. **Playground:** Yes. **Other:** Pavilion, rec hall, basketball, volleyball. **Activities:** None. **Nearby Attractions:** Bronner's Christmas Wonderland, golf, paddlewheel boat, winery, antiques, arts & crafts, Bavarian shops, cheese haus, Military & Space Museum. **Additional Information:** Frankenmuth Chamber of Commerce, (800) FUN-TOWN.

## RESTRICTIONS

**Pets:** Leash only. **Fires:** Fire ring only. **Alcoholic Beverages:** At sites only. **Vehicle Maximum Length:** None. **Other:** No tents allowed.

## TO GET THERE

From the junction of I-75 and M-83 (Birch Run Rd.), take Exit 136 and drive 2 mi. east on Birch Run Rd., then 0.4 mi. north on Gera Rd. Roads are wide and well maintained w/ broad shoulders.

## FREDERIC

### Happi Days Campground

7486 West Batterson Rd., Frederic 49733. T: (989) 348-6115; hapidays@freeway.net.

🚐 ★★　　　　　🏕 ★★

| | |
|---|---|
| Beauty: ★★ | Site Privacy: ★★ |
| Spaciousness: ★★ | Quiet: ★★★★ |
| Security: ★★★ | Cleanliness: ★★ |
| Insect Control: ★★ | Facilities: ★★ |

Happi Days Campground has so much potential. It's in a great location with a lot to do in the area. Sites are level and shaded in a quiet wooded area surrounded by pines and hardwoods. The roads to it are good. You can walk next door for a home-cooked breakfast or lunch in the comfortable Happi Days Diner, which has an interesting collection of 1950s memorabilia, including old 45 records, photos of Elvis, James Dean, Marilyn Monroe, and much more. The campground has a friendly owner (who is also the diner's cook). Laid out in a loop, the campground has one seasonal camper, 30 pull-through sites, and two group camping areas. Security is good, with an owner who lives on site and provides regular patrols of the campground. However, Happi Days Campground needs a good cleaning.

#### BASICS

**Operated by:** Gilmar Smith. **Open:** All year. **Site Assignment:** Reservations w/ 1-night deposit; refund w/ 7-day notice. **Registration:** At campground office. **Fee:** $18 (cash, check). **Parking:** At site.

#### FACILITIES

**Number of RV Sites:** 40. **Number of Tent-Only Sites:** 50. **Hookups:** Electric (50 amps), water. **Each Site:** Picnic table, fire ring. **Dump Station:** Yes. **Laundry:** Yes. **Pay Phone:** No. **Rest Rooms and Showers:** Yes. **Fuel:** No. **Propane:** Yes. **Internal Roads:** Dirt, in fair condition. **RV Service:** No. **Market:** 8 mi. south in Grayling. **Restaurant:** Next door. **General Store:** No. **Vending:** No. **Swimming Pool:** No. **Playground:** Yes. **Other:** Horseshoes, volleyball, rental cabins. **Activities:** None. **Nearby Attractions:** Au Sable River, fishing, canoeing, hunting, Wellington Farm Park, state parks, golf, fish hatchery, bowling, antiques, arts & crafts. **Additional Information:** Grayling Area Visitors Council, (800) 937-8837.

#### RESTRICTIONS

**Pets:** Leash only. **Fires:** Fire ring only. **Alcoholic Beverages:** Permitted. **Vehicle Maximum Length:** None.

#### TO GET THERE

From the junction of I-75 and Hwy. 93, take Exit 259 and drive 1.5 mi. west on Hwy. 93, then 4 mi. north on Old 27, then 1 block west on Batterson Rd. Roads are wide and well maintained w/ broad shoulders.

## FREDERIC

### Trails Campground

4066 Old 27 North, Frederic 49733. T: (517) 348-8692

🚐 ★★★　　　　　🏕 ★★★

| | |
|---|---|
| Beauty: ★★★ | Site Privacy: ★★★ |
| Spaciousness: ★★★ | Quiet: ★★★★ |
| Security: ★★★★ | Cleanliness: ★★★★★ |
| Insect Control: None | Facilities: ★★ |

Trails Campground offers a quiet little place at a low price. It has few activities, but the campground is very clean and would be a nice spot to stay while enjoying all the recreational opportunities in the Au Sable River area. Laid out in a series of loops, the campground offers grassy, level sites with a choice of shade or open. There are 18 seasonal campers and no pull-through sites. Mature white pines, red pines, aspens and maples add a woodland effect. Located two miles south of Frederic, the campground has well maintained, decorated bathrooms, including shower stalls with woodland scenes and nice wooden counters. The best tent sites are in the back against the woods where there is more privacy and green space. Security measures include one entrance/exit road and owners who live on site and patrol the campground. Rules are fairly short and concise, including "use good judgment" and "no activities that will disturb or endanger other patrons."

#### BASICS

**Operated by:** Jim & Ruth Thompson. **Open:** All year. **Site Assignment:** Reservations w/ no deposit. **Registration:** At campground office. **Fee:** $18 (cash, check). **Parking:** At site.

#### FACILITIES

**Number of RV Sites:** 40. **Number of Tent-Only Sites:** 23. **Hookups:** Electric (20 amps), water. **Each Site:** Picnic table, fire ring. **Dump Station:** Yes. **Laundry:** Yes. **Pay Phone:** Yes. **Rest Rooms and Showers:** Yes. **Fuel:** No. **Propane:** No. **Internal Roads:** Dirt, in good condition. **RV Service:** No. **Market:** 8 mi. south in Grayling. **Restaurant:** 2 mi. north in Frederic. **General Store:** No. **Vending:** Yes. **Swimming Pool:** No. **Playground:** Yes. **Other:** Horseshoes, volleyball. **Activities:** None. **Nearby Attractions:** Au Sable River, fishing, canoeing, hunting, Wellington Farm Park, state parks, golf, fish hatchery, bowling, antiques, arts & crafts. **Additional Information:** Grayling Area Visitors Council, (800) 937-8837.

## RESTRICTIONS

**Pets:** Leash only. **Fires:** Fire ring only. **Alcoholic Beverages:** Permitted. **Vehicle Maximum Length:** None.

## TO GET THERE

From the junction of I-75 and Hwy. 93, take Exit 259, drive 1.5 mi. west on Hwy. 93, then 4 mi. north on Old 27. Roads are wide and well maintained w/ broad shoulders.

## GAYLORD

## Gaylord Michaywe Wilderness Resort

5101 Campfires Parkway, Gaylord 49735. T: (517) 939-8723

| 🚐 ★★★ | 🏕 ★★★ |
|---|---|
| Beauty: ★★★ | Site Privacy: ★★★ |
| Spaciousness: ★★★ | Quiet: ★★★ |
| Security: ★★★★ | Cleanliness: ★★★ |
| Insect Control: No | Facilities: ★★★ |

Nestled in 80 acres of birch, aspen, and pine, Gaylord Michaywe is bordered by the north branch of the Au Sable River. Laid out in a series of loops, the campground has 40 pull-through sites and a typical site width of 35 feet. The campground offers level, shaded, riverside sites. A five mph speed limit is strictly enforced with first-time offenders kicked out. "Kids always have right of way," campground rules state. Quiet hours are from 10 p.m. to 8 a.m. In season, campers can pick morel mushrooms, wild strawberries, raspberries, blueberries, and blackberries on the property. Security includes a traffic control gate, one entrance/exit, an owner who lives on site, and regular patrols of the campground.

## BASICS

**Operated by:** John Dohan. **Open:** May 1–Oct. 15. **Site Assignment:** Reservations w/ 1-night deposit; refund w/ 7-day notice. **Registration:** At campground office. **Fee:** $33 (cash, check, credit cards). **Parking:** At site.

## FACILITIES

**Number of RV Sites:** 120. **Number of Tent-Only Sites:** 3. **Hookups:** Electric (20, 30, 50 amps), water, sewer. **Each Site:** Picnic table, fire ring. **Dump Station:** Yes. **Laundry:** Yes. **Pay Phone:** Yes. **Rest Rooms and Showers:** Yes. **Fuel:** No. **Propane:** Yes. **Internal Roads:** Gravel, in good condition. **RV Service:** No. **Market:** 3 mi. west in Gaylord. **Restaurant:** 3 mi. west in Gaylord. **General Store:** Yes. **Vending:** Yes. **Swimming Pool:** Yes. **Playground:** Yes. **Other:** Au Sable River, golf driving nets, rental cabins, mini golf, basketball, volleyball, rental cabins, game room, child-sitting service, horseshoes, shuffleboard, sports field, hiking trails. **Activities:** Swimming, fishing, scheduled weekend activities. **Nearby Attractions:** Golf, bowling, ice skating, Bottle Cap Museum, canoeing, horseback riding, elk viewing, Otsego County Historical Museum, antiques. **Additional Information:** Gaylord Area Information Center, (800) 345-8621.

## RESTRICTIONS

**Pets:** Leash only. **Fires:** Fire ring only. **Alcoholic Beverages:** At sites only. **Vehicle Maximum Length:** None.

## TO GET THERE

From the junction of I-75 and Old 27, take Exit 279 and drive 2 mi. south on Old 27, then 0.5 mi. east on Charles Brink Rd. Roads are wide and well maintained w/ broad shoulders.

## GRAYLING

## River Park Campground and Trout Pond

2607 Peters Rd., Grayling 49738. T: (888) 517-9092; F: (517) 348-1638; www.riverparkcampground.com; riverpark@voyager.net.

| 🚐 ★★★★ | 🏕 ★★★ |
|---|---|
| Beauty: ★★★ | Site Privacy: ★★★★ |
| Spaciousness: ★★★★ | Quiet: ★★★★ |
| Security: ★★★★ | Cleanliness: ★★★★ |
| Insect Control: ★★★★ | Facilities: ★★★ |

Surrounded by hundreds of acres of state land, River Park Campground and Trout Pond is located on the east branch of the Au Sable River in Grayling. The campground offers level, grassy, shaded spots with a wealth of pine, maple, and oak trees. The typical site width is 40 feet. River Park has 40 seasonal campers and no pull-through sites. Laid out in a series of loops, the campground has a separate area for tent campers with more green space and privacy. The trout pond is stocked two or three times each summer with rainbow trout. No throwbacks are allowed—you have to keep what you catch and pay 40 cents per inch for the fish. Most of the trout measure from 10 inches up to 21 inches. River Park is open year-round and attracts winter enthuiasts who like being able to snowmobile from their campsite or ski out of the campground. Water is turned off at individual campsites during the winter, but the bathhouse is kept heated and open. Security includes owners who live on site, one entrance/exit road, and regular patrols of the campground.

## BASICS

**Operated by:** Dennis & Maureen Fyock. **Open:** All year. **Site Assignment:** Reservations w/ 1-night deposit; refund w/ 7-day notice. **Registration:** At campground office. **Fee:** $20 (cash, check, credit cards). **Parking:** At site.

## FACILITIES

**Number of RV Sites:** 58. **Number of Tent-Only Sites:** 10. **Hookups:** Electric (30 amps), water. **Each Site:** Picnic table, fire ring. **Dump Station:** Yes. **Laundry:** Yes. **Pay Phone:** Yes. **Rest Rooms and Showers:** Yes. **Fuel:** No. **Propane:** Yes. **Internal Roads:** Paved, in good condition. **RV Service:** No. **Market:** 6 mi. south in Grayling. **Restaurant:** 6 mi. south in Grayling. **General Store:** Yes, limited. **Vending:** No. **Swimming Pool:** No. **Playground:** Yes. **Other:** Au Sable River, shuffleboard, horseshoes, rec hall, sports field, coin games, basketball, shuffleboard, fishing pond. **Activities:** Swimming, fishing. **Nearby Attractions:** Wellington Farm Park, state parks, golf, fish hatchery, bowling antiques, arts & crafts, fishing, canoeing, hunting. **Additional Information:** Grayling Area Visitors Council, (800) 937-8837.

## RESTRICTIONS

**Pets:** Leash only. **Fires:** Fire ring only. **Alcoholic Beverages:** Permitted. **Vehicle Maximum Length:** None.

## TO GET THERE

From the junction of US 41 and 10th Ave., drive behind the K-Mart Shopping Center. Roads are wide and well maintained w/ broad shoulders.

## GRAYLING

## Yogi Bear's Jellystone Park Camp-Resort

370 West Four Mile Rd., Grayling 49738. T: (989) 348-2157; www.michcampground.com/yogibears.

🚐 ★★★★          ⛺ ★★★

| | |
|---|---|
| Beauty: ★★★★ | Site Privacy: ★★★★ |
| Spaciousness: ★★★★ | Quiet: ★★★★ |
| Security: ★★★★ | Cleanliness: ★★★★ |
| Insect Control: ★★★★ | Facilities: ★★★★ |

With easy access to the interstate and a well-recognized name, Yogi Bear's Jellystone Park Camp-Resorts in Grayling, is a popular stopping spot. The campground also is a destination for families because of its large roster of recreational activities. Located in a wooded, rural setting, the campground is laid out in a series of loops and offers grassy, mostly shaded sites. The typical site width is 45 feet, and the campground has 130 seasonal campers and no pull-through sites. Quiet hours are enforced from 11 p.m. to 8 a.m. and the campground doesn't allow ATVs anywhere in the campground or in adjacent private property. Security measures include a five mph speed limit, one entrance/exit road, owners who live on site, and patrols of the campground.

## BASICS

**Operated by:** Gregory & Marlene Schoo. **Open:** May 1–Sept. 31. **Site Assignment:** Reservations w/ 1-night deposit; refund w/ 7-day notice. **Registration:** At campground office. **Fee:** $32 (cash, check, credit cards). **Parking:** At site.

## FACILITIES

**Number of RV Sites:** 230. **Number of Tent-Only Sites:** 0. **Hookups:** Electric (20, 30 amps), water, sewer. **Each Site:** Picnic table, fire ring. **Dump Station:** Yes. **Laundry:** Yes. **Pay Phone:** Yes. **Rest Rooms and Showers:** Yes. **Fuel:** No. **Propane:** No. **Internal Roads:** Dirt, in good condition. **RV Service:** No. **Market:** 10 mi. north in Grayling. **Restaurant:** 10 mi. north in Grayling. **General Store:** Yes. **Vending:** Yes. **Swimming**

**Pool:** Yes. **Playground:** Yes. **Other:** Mini Golf, coin games, outdoor cartoon theatre, shuffleboard, horseshoes, rec hall, game room, sports field, rental cabins, hiking trails, horseshoes. **Activities:** Swimming, hiking, scheduled activities. **Nearby Attractions:** Au Sable River, fishing, canoeing, hunting, Wellington Farm Park, state parks, golf, fish hatchery, bowling, antiques, arts & crafts, horseback riding. **Additional Information:** Grayling Area Visitors Council, (800) 937-8837.

## RESTRICTIONS

**Pets:** Leash only. **Fires:** Fire ring only. **Alcoholic Beverages:** At sites only. **Vehicle Maximum Length:** 32 ft.

## TO GET THERE

From the junction of I-75 and Four Mile Rd., take Exit 251 and drive 4.5 mi. east on Four Mile Rd. Roads are wide and well maintained w/ broad shoulders.

## HARRISON
## Countryside Campground

805 Byfield Dr., Harrison 48625. T: (989) 539-5468; country@glccomputers.com.

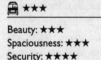 ★★★          ▲ ★★

| | |
|---|---|
| Beauty: ★★★ | Site Privacy: ★★★ |
| Spaciousness: ★★★ | Quiet: ★★★ |
| Security: ★★★★ | Cleanliness: ★★★★ |
| Insect Control: None | Facilities: ★★★ |

Located one mile west of Harrison, Countryside Campground has a nice combination of town conveniences and country peacefulness. Laid out in a series of loops, the campground has four seasonal campers, 20 pull-through sites, and a typical site width of 35 feet. A major plus is the campground's proximity to 20 lakes within 20 miles. Situated on rolling hills with a forest of pine trees, the campground offers a choice of shaded or open spots. Sites are grassy and level. The best sites are 14–24 because they surround a wooded area and offer more privacy. Pull-through sites also are popular because of their convenience. Families with children often prefer sites 8–13 located near the playground and swimming pool. Security measures include one-way roads past the office and owners who keep a close eye on the campground.

## BASICS

**Operated by:** Bob & Sylvia Kern. **Open:** May 1–Oct. 15. **Site Assignment:** Reservations w/ 1-night deposit; refund w/ 2-week notice. **Registration:** At campground office. **Fee:** $21 (cash, check, credit cards). **Parking:** At site.

## FACILITIES

**Number of RV Sites:** 55. **Number of Tent-Only Sites:** 0. **Hookups:** Electric (30 amps), water, sewer. **Each Site:** Picnic table, fire ring. **Dump Station:** Yes. **Laundry:** Yes. **Pay Phone:** Yes. **Rest Rooms and Showers:** Yes. **Fuel:** No. **Propane:** No. **Internal Roads:** Gravel, in good condition. **RV Service:** No. **Market:** Yes, limited. **Restaurant:** Two blocks. **General Store:** 1.5 mi. south in Harrison. **Vending:** Yes. **Swimming Pool:** Yes. **Playground:** Yes. **Other:** Rental cabins, horseshoes, volleyball, basketball, badminton, sports field, rental bikes. **Activities:** Swimming. **Nearby Attractions:** Golf, cambling casino, river rafting, hunting, hiking, canoeing, boating, fishing, museums, antiques, Amish area. **Additional Information:** Clare County CVB, (800) 715-3550.

## RESTRICTIONS

**Pets:** Leash only. **Fires:** Fire ring only. **Alcoholic Beverages:** At sites only. **Vehicle Maximum Length:** None.

## TO GET THERE

From the junction of Business 27 and Hwy. 61 in Harrison, drive 0.75 mi. west on Hwy. 61/Main St., then 0.25 mi. north on Byfield Dr. Roads are wide and well maintained w/ broad shoulders.

## HARRISON
## Wilson State Park

910 North First St., Harrison 48625. T: (517) 539-3021; www.michigandnr.com.

🚐 ★★★          ▲ ★★★★

| | |
|---|---|
| Beauty: ★★★★ | Site Privacy: ★★★ |
| Spaciousness: ★★★ | Quiet: ★★★ |
| Security: ★★★★ | Cleanliness: ★★★ |
| Insect Control: Yes | Facilities: ★★ |

Located in Harrison, Wilson State Park is known for its sandy beach on Budd Lake and its muskie fishing. The campground also is unusual because it is in town and provides easy access to local attractions, restaurants, and shops. The campground is right across the street from the county fairground. Reservations are a must during fair time (the last weekend of July and first week of Aug.). Sites are grassy and mostly shaded with no seasonal campers and four pull-through sites. The best sites for RVs are 25 because it is big, 125 because it overlooks the lake, and 134 because it is a pull-through close to the beach. Tents are permitted on any sites. Because of the lake and woods, the campground is quiet despite its location off such a busy street. Park rangers also ensure that the noise level at campsites is kept down so as not to disturb other campers. Security is tops with one entrance/exit road, a state park sticker required on vehicles, and regular patrols by park rangers and county police.

## BASICS

**Operated by:** State of Michigan. **Open:** Apr. 1–Dec. 1. **Site Assignment:** Reservations are accepted w/ a $2 fee; refund w/ 48-hour notice. **Registration:** At campground office. **Fee:** $14 (cash, check, credit cards). **Parking:** At site.

## FACILITIES

**Number of RV Sites:** 160. **Number of Tent-Only Sites:** 0. **Hookups:** Electric (30 amps). **Each Site:** Picnic table, fire ring. **Dump Station:** Yes. **Laundry:** No. **Pay Phone:** Yes. **Rest Rooms and Showers:** Yes. **Fuel:** No. **Propane:** No. **Internal Roads:** Paved/gravel, in good condition. **RV Service:** No. **Market:** Next door. **Restaurant:** Next door. **General Store:** No. **Vending:** Yes. **Swimming Pool:** No. **Playground:** Yes. **Other:** Budd Lake, swimming beach, pavilion, boating ramp, fishing lake, horseshoes, volleyball, recreation field, rental cabin. **Activities:** Swimming, fishing, boating. **Nearby Attractions:** Golf, gambling casino, river rafting, hunting, hiking, caoeing, museums, antiques, Amish area. **Additional Information:** Clare County CVB, (800) 715-3550.

## RESTRICTIONS

**Pets:** Leash only. **Fires:** Fire ring only. **Alcoholic Beverages:** At sites only. **Vehicle Maximum Length:** 40 ft. **Other:** 15-day stay limit.

## TO GET THERE

From US 27, take the Harrison exit, drive 3.5 mi. west. Roads are wide and well maintained w/ broad shoulders.

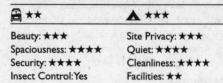

# HARRISON
## Withii Trailer Camp

1820 Hampton Rd., Harrison 48625. T: (989) 539-3128

| 🚐 ★★ | ⛺ ★★★ |
|---|---|
| Beauty: ★★★ | Site Privacy: ★★★ |
| Spaciousness: ★★★★ | Quiet: ★★★★ |
| Security: ★★★★ | Cleanliness: ★★★★ |
| Insect Control: Yes | Facilities: ★★ |

Located one mile north of Harrison, Withii Trailer Park has 20 lakes within a 20 miles proximity. The campground itself offers little recreation or activities, but the area is rich in swimming, boating, hiking, hunting and fishing. Laid out in a horseshoe, the campground has 50 seasonal campers and ten pull-through sites. Spots are grassy, level, and mostly shaded with a typical site width of 40 feet. Under the same ownership since 1970, the campground also has several mobile homes in an adjoining park. Campers are asked not to walk between the mobile homes since they are private residences. Showers are well maintained and clean with private dressing rooms. Safety and security measures include a five mph speed limit, no riding of motorized vehicles in the park, no generators permitted, and children under age ten are not allowed in rest rooms unless accompanied by an adult. Although the campground is open year-round, be prepared for frigid cold and deep snow during winter. No fires are permitted when fire rings are hidden by snow, and roads are kept open "to the best of our ability" during winter seasons.

## BASICS

**Operated by:** Allen & Pat Tomes. **Open:** All year. **Site Assignment:** Reservations w/ 1-night deposit; refund w/ 2-week notice. **Registration:** At campground office. **Fee:** $20 (cash). **Parking:** At site.

## FACILITIES

**Number of RV Sites:** 88. **Number of Tent-Only Sites:** 6. **Hookups:** Electric (20, 30, 50 amps), water, sewer. **Each Site:** Picnic table, fire ring. **Dump Station:** Yes. **Laundry:** No. **Pay Phone:** No. **Rest Rooms and Showers:** Yes. **Fuel:** No. **Propane:** No. **Internal Roads:** Gravel, in good condition. **RV Service:** No. **Market:** 1 mi. south in Harrison. **Restaurant:** 1 mi. south in Harrison. **General Store:** No. **Vending:** No. **Swim-**

ming **Pool:** No. **Playground:** Yes. **Other:** Horse-shoes, recreation field. **Activities:** None. **Nearby Attractions:** Golf, gambling casino, river rafting, hunting, hiking, canoeing, boating, fishing, musuems, antiques, Amish area. **Additional Information:** Clare County CVB, (800) 715-3550.

### RESTRICTIONS

**Pets:** Leash only. **Fires:** Fire ring only. **Alcoholic Beverages:** At sites only. **Vehicle Maximum Length:** 35 ft. **Other:** No bare feet in rest rooms.

### TO GET THERE

From the junction of Hwy. 61 and Business US 27, drive 1.25 mi. north on Business US 27, then 200 yards west on Hampton Rd. Roads are wide and well maintained w/ broad shoulders.

## HASTINGS

## Whispering Waters Campground & Canoe Livery

1805 North Irving Rd., Hastings 49058. T: (800) 985-7019; F: (616) 945-8722; www.michcamp grounds.com/whisperingwaters; whisper@iserv.net.

| 🚐 ★★★★ | 🛖 ★★★★ |
|---|---|
| Beauty: ★★★★ | Site Privacy: ★★★★ |
| Spaciousness: ★★★★ | Quiet: ★★★★ |
| Security: ★★★★ | Cleanliness: ★★★★ |
| Insect Control: ★★★★ | Facilities: ★★★★ |

A river runs through it. Whispering Waters Campground & Canoe Livery is is a wooded rolling campground on the high bank of the Thornapple River. Located in South Central Michigan in Hastings, the campground offers level, mostly shaded sites with a typical site width of 35 feet. The campground has 20 seasonal campers and 20 pull-through sites. A tent area on the river offers more green space and privacy. No motors are permitted on the river. A huge front porch at the campground building is a nice gathering spot, as is a commons area that features comfortable chairs, a microwave, TV, and library. Basic regulations for safety and security are enforced, including no alcohol on the river. The campground also doesn't tolerate rowdy behavior.

### BASICS

**Operated by:** Roger & Uta Wilmont. **Open:** Last Friday of Apr. through first Sunday of Oct. **Site Assignment:** Reservations w/ 1-night deposit;

refund (minus $5) w/ 2-week notice. **Registration:** At campground office. **Fee:** $24 (cash, check, credit cards). **Parking:** At site.

### FACILITIES

**Number of RV Sites:** 115. **Number of Tent-Only Sites:** 3. **Hookups:** Electric (20, 30, 50 amps), water, sewer, phone. **Each Site:** Picnic table, fire ring. **Dump Station:** Yes. **Laundry:** Yes. **Pay Phone:** Yes. **Rest Rooms and Showers:** Yes. **Fuel:** No. **Propane:** Yes. **Internal Roads:** Gravel, in good condition. **RV Service:** No. **Market:** 3 mi. **Restaurant:** 3 mi. **General Store:** Yes. **Vending:** Yes. **Swimming Pool:** Yes. **Playground:** Yes. **Other:** Thornapple River, swimming beach, rec room, pavilion, shuffleboard, badminton, sports field, horseshoes, hiking trails, volleyball, rental cabins, adults room. **Activities:** Swimming, fishing, hiking, boating (rental canoes available), scheduled weekend activities. **Nearby Attractions:** Riding ranch, golf, hot air ballooning, Gilmore Car Museum, Cheesbrough Rake Factory, Gun Lake, skydiving school, state parks, Kalamazoo Air Zoo, Historic Charleton Park Village & Museum. **Additional Information:** Barry County Chamber of Commerce, (616) 945-2454.

### RESTRICTIONS

**Pets:** Leash only. **Fires:** Fire ring only. **Alcoholic Beverages:** At sites only. **Vehicle Maximum Length:** None.

### TO GET THERE

From the west junction of Hwy. 43 and Hwy. 37, drive 3 mi. north on Hwy. 37, then 0.5 mi. north on Irving Rd. Roads are mostly wide and well maintained w/ adequate shoulders.

## HILLMAN

## Jack's Landing Resort

5966 Tennis Rd., Hillman 49746. T: (517) 742-4370; www.jackslanding.com.

| 🚐 ★★★ | 🛖 ★★★ |
|---|---|
| Beauty: ★★★★ | Site Privacy: ★★★ |
| Spaciousness: ★★★ | Quiet: ★★★ |
| Security: ★★★★ | Cleanliness: ★★★ |
| Insect Control: Yes | Facilities: ★★★ |

Located seven miles southeast of Hillman, Jack's Landing Resort has a beautiful view of Fletcher Pond. But don't let the name fool you. The "pond" offers 9,000 acres of premier fishing for pike, bass, and panfish. Wildlife viewing includes sights of eagles, osprey, loons and many ducks. The campground has level, open or shaded sites. It has no pull-throughs. From Jan. 4–Mar. 18, the campground offers ice fishing, with heated ice fishing shanties and a snow plow to keep the area open. The best RV site is 25 because it offers 50 amp hookup. The best tent site is 44 because it is set back in the woods and offers more privacy. Security measures include a five mph speed limit, one entrance/exit road, an owner who lives on site, and occasional campground patrols.

### BASICS

**Operated by:** Dean & Annie Robinson. **Open:** May 1–Oct. 31. **Site Assignment:** Reservations w/ 1-night deposit; refund w/ 7-day notice. **Registration:** At campground office. **Fee:** $22 (cash, check, credit cards). **Parking:** At site.

### FACILITIES

**Number of RV Sites:** 14. **Number of Tent-Only Sites:** 16. **Hookups:** Electric (20, 30, 50 amps), water. **Each Site:** Picnic table, fire ring. **Dump Station:** Yes. **Laundry:** No. **Pay Phone:** Yes. **Rest Rooms and Showers:** Yes. **Fuel:** Yes. **Propane:** Yes. **Internal Roads:** Gravel, in fair condition. **RV Service:** No. **Market:** 7 mi. west in Hillman. **Restaurant:** On site. **General Store:** Yes. **Vending:** Yes. **Swimming Pool:** No. **Playground:** Yes. **Other:** Fletcher Pond, marina, bar, rental cabins, lodge rooms, boat slips, boat launch, sports field, horseshoes, hiking trails, fish-cleaning hut. **Activities:** Fishing, swimming, boating (rental motorboats, pontoons available), hiking. **Nearby Attractions:** Golf, charter boat fishing, Lake Huron, elk viewing, Pigeon River Country State Forest, lighthouses, antiques, shipwreck sanctuary, museums, historic homes. **Additional Information:** Hillman Area Chamber of Commerce, (517) 742-3739.

### RESTRICTIONS

**Pets:** Leash only. **Fires:** Fire ring only. **Alcoholic Beverages:** Permitted. **Vehicle Maximum Length:** None.

### TO GET THERE

From the junction of Hwy. 451 and Hwy. 32, drive 2 mi. east on Hwy. 32, then 5 mi. south on Jack's Landing Rd. The highway is wide and well maintained w/ broad shoulders but Jack's Landing Rd. is bumpy gravel.

## HILLMAN
### Lyons' Landing & Campground

24553 Landing Rd., Hillman 49746. T: (517) 742-4756

★★        ★★★★

| | |
|---|---|
| Beauty: ★★★★ | Site Privacy: ★★★ |
| Spaciousness: ★★★ | Quiet: ★★★ |
| Security: ★★★ | Cleanliness: ★★★ |
| Insect Control: None | Facilities: ★★ |

Fishing reigns at Lyons' Landing, eight miles northeast of Hillman. No wonder, the campground is located on a 8,970-acre reservoir. A dam built in 1930 to generate electric power went through an area where the Upper South Branch of the Thunder Bay River ran through a large swamp. The result was an ideal fish habitat among flooded timber stumps and a dark bottom. Fletcher's is famous for its northern pike and largemouth bass. Because it is shallow, about seven to ten feet deep with some deeper creekbeds, the water warms up quickly to give an early start to bass fishing. Campground sites are grassy, open, and shaded with 30 pull-throughs and a typical site width of 35 feet. No swimming is allowed, nor are jet skis or water skis. Security includes one entrance, owners who live on site, and "no hesitation at calling law enforcement, if needed," according to campground rules.

### BASICS

**Operated by:** Craig & Cathy Lyons. **Open:** All year. **Site Assignment:** Reservations w/ 1-night deposit; refund w/ 7-day notice. **Registration:** At campground office. **Fee:** $12 (cash, check, credit cards). **Parking:** At site.

### FACILITIES

**Number of RV Sites:** 75. **Number of Tent-Only Sites:** 10. **Hookups:** Electric (20, 30 amps). **Each Site:** Picnic table, fire ring. **Dump Station:** Yes. **Laundry:** No. **Pay Phone:** Yes. **Rest Rooms and Showers:** Yes. **Fuel:** No. **Propane:** No. **Internal Roads:** Gravel, in fair condition. **RV Service:** No. **Market:** 8 mi. northeast in Hillman. **Restaurant:** 8 mi. northeast in Hillman. **General Store:** Yes. **Vending:** No. **Swimming Pool:** No. **Playground:** Yes. **Other:** Fletcher's Floodwaters, pavilion, boat ramp, boat dock, shuffleboard, sports field, horseshoes, volleyball, fish-cleaning hut, heated ice shanties in winter. **Activities:** Fishing, boating (rental boats available). **Nearby Attractions:** Golf, charter boat fishing, Lake Huron, elk viewing, Pigeon River Country State Forest, lighthouses, antiques, shipwreck sanctuary, museums, historic homes. **Additional Information:** Hillman Area Chamber of Commerce, (517) 742-3739.

### RESTRICTIONS

**Pets:** Leash only. **Fires:** Fire ring only. **Alcoholic Beverages:** Permitted. **Vehicle Maximum Length:** None.

### TO GET THERE

From Hillman, drive 4 mi. southwest on Hwy. 32, then 3 mi. south on Farrier Rd., then 1 mi. east on Landing Rd. Highway is wide and well maintained w/ broad shoulders. Landing Rd. is bumpy gravel.

## HOLLAND

### Oak Grove Resort Campgrounds

2011 Ottawa Beach Rd., Holland 49424. T: (616) 399-9230; www.michcampgrounds.com/oakgrove.

🚐 ★★★★      ▲ n/a

| | |
|---|---|
| Beauty: ★★★★ | Site Privacy: ★★★★ |
| Spaciousness: ★★★★ | Quiet: ★★★★ |
| Security: ★★★★ | Cleanliness: ★★★★★ |
| Insect Control: ★★★★ | Facilities: ★★★★ |

Oak Grove Resort Campground fills the wish list many campers have of the ideal spot to visit. Located within walking distance of Lake Macatawa and Lake Michigan beaches, the Holland campground is in the midst of a wealth of vacation recreation. Oak Grove itself is sparkling-clean, well arranged, friendly, secure, and a pleasure to visit. Beautiful landscaping touches such as flowers, shrubs, and mowed sites show close attention to detail. A large 24 × 50 heated pool and hot tub are a nice treat for those not ready to jump into the cold waters of Lake Michigan. The campground is also one mile before Holland State Park and offers access to miles of paved bike trails. Sites are level, wooded, and mostly shaded, with a typical site width of 35 feet. All sites have full hookups, and there are 80 seasonal campers. Mid-May brings the annual Tulip Festival, a glorious event which means reservations are strongly recommended for the campground. Be aware that no tents are allowed. Also note that the office building is closed on Sunday and that the security gate closes each night at 10 p.m.

### BASICS

**Operated by:** Ron & Betty, Rod & Maria Vandenberg. **Open:** May 1–Oct. 1. **Site Assignment:** Reservations w/ 1-night deposit; refund (minus $10) w/ 2-week notice. **Registration:** At campground office. **Fee:** $36 (cash, check, credit cards). **Parking:** At site.

### FACILITIES

**Number of RV Sites:** 135. **Number of Tent-Only Sites:** 0. **Hookups:** Electric (30, 50 amps), water, sewer, cable TV. **Each Site:** Picnic table, fire ring. **Dump Station:** Yes. **Laundry:** Yes. **Pay Phone:** Yes. **Rest Rooms and Showers:** Yes. **Fuel:** No. **Propane:** No. **Internal Roads:** Paved, in good condition. **RV Service:** No. **Market:** Two blocks. **Restaurant:** Two blocks. **General Store:** Yes. **Vending:** Yes. **Swimming Pool:** Yes. **Playground:** Yes. **Other:** Rec hall, hiking trails, rental cabins, whirlpool, horseshoes, basketball. **Activities:** Swimming, hiking. **Nearby Attractions:** Lake Macatawa, Lake Michigan, bike trails, Cappon House Museum, De Klomp Wooden Shoe & Delftware Factory, Dutch Village, Holland Museum, tulip gardens, Windmill Island, antiques, arts & crafts. **Additional Information:** Holland Area CVB, (800) 506-1299.

### RESTRICTIONS

**Pets:** Leash only. **Fires:** Fire ring only. **Alcoholic Beverages:** Not permitted. **Vehicle Maximum Length:** None. **Other:** No tents allowed.

### TO GET THERE

From the junction of US 31 and Lakewood Blvd., drive 1.5 mi. west on Lakewood Blvd., then 1.5 mi. west on Douglas, then 3 mi. west on Ottawa Beach Rd. Roads are mostly wide and well maintained w/ adequate shoulders.

## HOLLY

### Yogi Bear's Jellystone Park Camp-Resort

7072 East Grange Hall Rd., Holly 48442. T: (248) 634-8621; F: (248) 634-3177; www.michcampgrounds.com/jellystone-holly; lsyogi@megsinet.net.

🚐 ★★★★      ▲ ★★★

| | |
|---|---|
| Beauty: ★★★ | Site Privacy: ★★★★ |
| Spaciousness: ★★★★ | Quiet: ★★★★ |
| Security: ★★★★ | Cleanliness: ★★★★ |
| Insect Control: None | Facilities: ★★★★ |

Easy access off I-75 is a major draw for this campground, as is a long list of activities provided for campers. An activities director keeps fun times rolling with a creative list of activities for all ages. One unusual activity invites visitors to "fine tune" their campers by comparing notes on how to repair or fix up a camper and where to visit, when to camp, and what to see. Located three miles east of Holly, Yogi Bear's Jellystone Park of Holly offers shaded grassy sites with gravel parking spots. Laid out in a series of loops, the campground has 30 seasonal campers, 40 pull-through sites, and a typical site width of 30 feet. The campground is open all year but has limited winter facilities and would appeal to only the hardiest campers. One time it might be fun to brave the cold would be for the annual Dickens Olde Fashioned Christmas Festival in Holly during weekends in late Nov. and throughout Dec. But be prepared for frigid weather and possible snow. The speed limit is 7.5 mph and quiet times are 11 p.m. to 8 a.m.

## BASICS

**Operated by:** Leon & Sandy Sterling. **Open:** All year. **Site Assignment:** Reservations w/ 1-night deposit; refund (minus $5) w/ 7-day notice. **Registration:** At campground office. **Fee:** $33 (cash, check, credit cards). **Parking:** At site.

## FACILITIES

**Number of RV Sites:** 146. **Number of Tent-Only Sites:** 40. **Hookups:** Electric (20, 30 amps), water. **Each Site:** Picnic table, fire ring. **Dump Station:** Yes. **Laundry:** Yes. **Pay Phone:** Yes. **Rest Rooms and Showers:** Yes. **Fuel:** No. **Propane:** Yes. **Internal Roads:** Paved/gravel, in good condition. **RV Service:** No. **Market:** 3 mi. west in Holly. **Restaurant:** 3 mi. west in Holly. **General Store:** Yes. **Vending:** Yes. **Swimming Pool:** Yes. **Playground:** Yes. **Other:** Arcade, mini-golf, rental cabins, kiddie train, bumper boats, T-Rex, bounce house, power wheels, basketball, rental bikes, horseshoes, movies, activities director, adults room. **Activities:** Swimming, scheduled activities. **Nearby Attractions:** Children's Museum, Huckleberry Railroad, paddlewheeler, museums, Longway Planetarium, Flint River, antiques, golf, arts & crafts. **Additional Information:** Holly Chamber of Commerce, (248) 634-1900.

## RESTRICTIONS

**Pets:** Leash only. **Fires:** Fire ring only. **Alcoholic Beverages:** Permitted. **Vehicle Maximum Length:** None. **Other:** No check-ins after 9 p.m.

## TO GET THERE

From junction of I-75 and Grange Hall Rd., take Exit 101 and drive 100 yards east on Grange Hall Rd. Roads are wide and well maintained with broad shoulders.

## HOPKINS

### East Lake Camping

3091 Weick Dr., Hopkins 49328. T: (616) 793-7177

🚐 ★★★               ⛺ ★★★

| | |
|---|---|
| Beauty: ★★★★ | Site Privacy: ★★★ |
| Spaciousness: ★★★ | Quiet: ★★★★ |
| Security: ★★★★ | Cleanliness: ★★★★ |
| Insect Control: ★★★ | Facilities: ★★★ |

Located midway between Grand Rapids, Holland, and Kalamazoo, East Lake Camping offers family camping in the hills around East Lake. The quiet country setting outside Hopkins features camping sites from rustic to full hookups. The campground has open and shaded sites on a hilly terrain. The best sites are closest to the large lake. East Lake Camping has 59 seasonal campers, a typical site width of 30 feet, and seven pull-through sites. Chapel services are offered on Sunday. The lake has a nice sandy beach for swimmers and is a good place to fish and boat. Owners enforce basic regulations to keep the campground safe, quiet, and family-oriented, while still maintaining a friendly atmosphere.

## BASICS

**Operated by:** Greg & Catherine Miller. **Open:** May 1–Oct.1. **Site Assignment:** Reservations w/ 1-night deposit; refund (minus $5) w/ 7-day notice. **Registration:** At campground office. **Fee:** $23 (cash, check, credit cards). **Parking:** At site.

## FACILITIES

**Number of RV Sites:** 109. **Number of Tent-Only Sites:** 1. **Hookups:** Electric (20, 30, 50 amps), water, sewer. **Each Site:** Picnic table, fire ring. **Dump Station:** Yes. **Laundry:** Yes. **Pay Phone:** Yes. **Rest Rooms and Showers:** Yes. **Fuel:** No. **Propane:** No. **Internal Roads:** Gravel, in good condition. **RV Service:** No. **Market:** 1 mi. **Restaurant:** 1 mi. **General Store:** Yes. **Vending:** Yes. **Swimming Pool:** No. **Playground:** Yes. **Other:** East Lake, sandy beach, pavilion, coin games, rec room, basketball, shuffleboard, sports field, horseshoes, boat ramp, boat dock, volleyball, hiking trail, rental RVs, rental cabin. **Activities:** Swimming, hiking, fishing, boating (rental rowboats, kayaks, paddleboats available), scheduled weekend activities. **Nearby Attractions:** Gerald B. Ford Museum, Fredrick Meijer Gardens, zoo, Michigan Adventure Amusement Park, Roger B. Chaffee Planetarium, golf, tennis, rivers & lakes, antiques, Wooden Shoe Factory. **Additional Information:** Grand Rapids/ Kent County CVB, (800) 678-9859.

## RESTRICTIONS

**Pets:** Leash only. **Fires:** Fire ring only. **Alcoholic Beverages:** Permitted. **Vehicle Maximum Length:** 35 ft.

## TO GET THERE

From US 131, take Wayland Exit 64 and drive 3 mi. west on 135th Ave., then 2.5 mi. south on 18th St., then 2.5 mi. west on 130th Ave. to Weick Dr. Roads are mostly wide and well maintained w/ narrow shoulders in spots.

## HOUGHTON LAKE

### Houghton Lake Travel Park

370 Cloverleaf Ln., Houghton Lake 48629. T: (989) 422-3931; www.houghtonlaketravelpark.com.

🚐 ★★★                    🏕 ★★★

Beauty: ★★★                Site Privacy: ★★★
Spaciousness: ★★★          Quiet: ★★★★
Security: ★★★★             Cleanliness: ★★★★
Insect Control: None        Facilities: ★★★

Houghton Lake Travel Park offers easy access to Michigan's largest inland lake. Houghton Lake is ten miles long and six miles wide with a 31-mile shoreline. The campground offers open, level sites. All sites are pull-throughs and there are 21 seasonal campers. Tent sites are in a rustic section with more green space and privacy. A tradition of the travel park, located 12 miles south of Frederic, is the train ride. Sports enthusiasts and vacationers have replaced the loggers and commercial anglers who once were the vital elements of Houghton Lake. The village is the core of a year-round resort area that borders the lake. Summer brings boaters and water skiers. Winter attracts snow skiers. Fishing knows no season. The rural campground closes in Oct., so it is not available for the winter season of ice fishing and snowmobiling.

## BASICS

**Operated by:** Ron & Jo Seim. **Open:** Apr. 1–Oct. 15. **Site Assignment:** Reservations w/ 1-night deposit; refund w/ 7-day notice. **Registration:** At campground office. **Fee:** $23 (cash, check, credit cards). **Parking:** At site.

## FACILITIES

**Number of RV Sites:** 60. **Number of Tent-Only Sites:** 20. **Hookups:** Electric (20, 30 amps), water, sewer. **Each Site:** Picnic table, fire ring. **Dump Station:** Yes. **Laundry:** Yes. **Pay Phone:** Yes. **Rest Rooms and Showers:** Yes. **Fuel:** No. **Propane:** Yes. **Internal Roads:** Gravel, in good condition. **RV Service:** No. **Market:** 12 mi. north in Frederic. **Restaurant:** 12 mi. north in Frederic. **General Store:** Yes. **Vending:** Yes. **Swimming Pool:** Yes. **Playground:** Yes. **Other:** Rec room, rental cabins, sports field, horseshoes, volleyball. **Activities:** Swimming. **Nearby Attractions:** Houghton Lake, fishing, golf, amusement parks, mini-golf, Merritt Speedway, Firemans Memorial, antiques, arts & crafts. **Additional Information:** Houghton Lake Chamber of Commerce, (800) 248-5253.

## RESTRICTIONS

**Pets:** Leash only. **Fires:** Fire ring only. **Alcoholic Beverages:** Permitted. **Vehicle Maximum Length:** None.

## TO GET THERE

From the junction of US 27 and Hwy. 55, drive 220 yards east on Hwy. 55, then south on Cloverleaf Ln. Roads are wide and well maintained w/ broad shoulders.

## HOUGHTON LAKE

### Sandyoak RV Park

2757 Owens Rd., Houghton Lake 48629. T: (800) 323-0220

🚐 ★★★★                   🏕 n/a

Beauty: ★★★                Site Privacy: ★★★
Spaciousness: ★★★★         Quiet: ★★★★
Security: ★★★★             Cleanliness: ★★★★
Insect Control: None        Facilities: ★★★★

Located in the town of Houghton Lake, Sandyoak RV Park is a resort with camping lots for sale or rent. No tents are allowed. The campground has 183 seasonal campers and no pull-through sites. Laid out in a series of loops, the park has an indoor heated pool, two heated bathhouses, and two laundries. Sites are mostly grassy and shaded with a typical site width of 40 feet. A large clubhouse with kitchen facilities is available for gatherings. Speed limit is ten mph, a bit high especially in the playground areas. Most permanent sites are well maintained and decorated. To keep the RV park attractive, the association has a rule that the sales and rental agent has the right to refuse the registration of any trailer that would be "detrimental to the general appearance" of the park. They also have the right to instruct that such trailers must be removed from the park by the owner.

## BASICS

**Operated by:** Sandyoak Village Assoc. **Open:** All year. **Site Assignment:** Reservations w/ 1-night deposit; refund w/ 2-week notice. **Registration:** At campground office. **Fee:** $22 (cash, check). **Parking:** At site.

## FACILITIES

**Number of RV Sites:** 227. **Number of Tent-Only Sites:** 0. **Hookups:** Electric (30 amps), water, sewer, cable TV. **Each Site:** Picnic table, fire ring. **Dump Station:** No. **Laundry:** Yes. **Pay Phone:** Yes. **Rest Rooms and Showers:** Yes. **Fuel:** No. **Propane:** No. **Internal Roads:** Paved, in good condition. **RV Service:** No. **Market:** 1 block. **Restaurant:** 1 block. **General Store:** No. **Vending:** No. **Swimming Pool:** Yes. **Playground:** Yes. **Other:** Clubhouse, horseshoes, shuffleboard, basketball, sales office, spa, rec hall, game room, recreation field, hiking trails. **Activities:** Swimming, hiking, scheduled activities. **Nearby Attractions:** Houghton Lake, fishing, golf, amusement parks, minigolf, Merritt Speedway, Firemans Memorial, antiques, arts & crafts. **Additional Information:** Houghton Lake Chamber of Commerce, (800) 248-5253.

## RESTRICTIONS

**Pets:** Leash only; max. of 2 per site. **Fires:** Fire rings only; must be extinguished w/ water before retiring for night. **Alcoholic Beverages:** At sites only. **Vehicle Maximum Length:** None. **Other:** Children under 12 not permitted in hot tub.

## TO GET THERE

From the junction of US 27 and Hwy. 55, drive 6 mi. east on Hwy. 55 (West Houghton Lake Dr.), then 1 block south on Owens Dr. Roads are wide and well maintained w/ broad shoulders.

## HOUGHTON LAKE
### Wooded Acres Family Campground

997 Federal Ave., Houghton Lake 48629. T: (989) 422-3413; www.woodedacrescampground.net; ddietzel@freeway.net.

🚐 ★★★★                    ⛺ ★★★

| | |
|---|---|
| Beauty: ★★★ | Site Privacy: ★★★ |
| Spaciousness: ★★★ | Quiet: ★★★ |
| Security: ★★★★ | Cleanliness: ★★★★ |
| Insect Control: None | Facilities: ★★★★ |

Located in a large resort area in Houghton Lake, Wooded Acres Family Campground offers open and secluded sites in a wooded area. Laid out in a series of loops, the campground has 30 seasonal campers, 30 pull-through sites and a typical site width of 30 feet. The best RV sites are 77–88 because they offer full hookups. The best tent site is 14 because it is well shaded, large, and offers more privacy. Security measures include one entrance/exit, owners who live on site, and campground patrols. As the name indicates, Wooded Acres has a wealth of trees and enforces rules to keep them. Cutting any standing timber or vegetation is prohibited. If a tree branch is in the way of a camper, staff employees should be notified to deal with the problem. Violation of the regulation results in a $100 fine. For safety and quietness, snowmobiles, motorcycles, scooters, mopeds, and three- and four-wheelers are not allowed to be ridden in the park. Golf carts also are prohibited, except for use by elderly people or those with disabilities. The campground is well maintained and features an antique John Deere Tractor theme.

## BASICS

**Operated by:** Dave & Tina Dietzel. **Open:** All year. **Site Assignment:** Reservations w/ 1-night deposit; refund (minus $5) w/ 7-day notice. **Registration:** At campground office. **Registration:** At campground office. **Fee:** $28 (cash, check, credit cards). **Parking:** At site.

## FACILITIES

**Number of RV Sites:** 72. **Number of Tent-Only Sites:** 30. **Hookups:** Electric (30, 50 amps), water, sewer. **Each Site:** Picnic table, fire ring. **Dump Station:** Yes. **Laundry:** Yes. **Pay Phone:** No. **Rest Rooms and Showers:** Yes. **Fuel:** No. **Propane:** Yes. **Internal Roads:** Gravel, in good condition. **RV**

Service: No. Market: 2 mi. north in Houghton Lake. Restaurant: 2 mi. north in Houghton Lake. General Store: Yes, limited. Vending: No. Swimming Pool: Yes. Playground: Yes. Other: Pavilion, rental cabin, gameroom, basketball, volleyball, shuffleboard, horseshoes, fishing pond, sports field. Activities: Swimming, fishing. Nearby Attractions: Houghton Lake, fishing, amusement parks, mini-golf, Merritt Speedway, golf, Firemans Memorial, antiques, arts & crafts. Additional Information: Houghton Lake Chamber of Commerce, (800) 248-5253.

## RESTRICTIONS

Pets: Leash only. Fires: Fire ring only. Alcoholic Beverages: Permitted. Vehicle Maximum Length: 40 ft.

## TO GET THERE

From the junction of US 27 and Hwy. 55, drive 2 mi. east on Hwy. 55, then 1 mi. south on Loxley. Roads are wide and well maintained w/ broad shoulders.

## INDIAN RIVER

### Indian River RV Resort & Campground

561 North Straits Hwy., Indian River 49749. T: (888) 792-CAMP; www.michcampgrounds.com/indianriver; ircgrest@email.msn.com.

| 🚐 ★★★★ | ⛺ ★★★★ |
|---|---|
| Beauty: ★★★★ | Site Privacy: ★★★★ |
| Spaciousness: ★★★★ | Quiet: ★★★★ |
| Security: ★★★★ | Cleanliness: ★★★★★ |
| Insect Control: ★★★★★ | Facilities: ★★★★ |

Just minutes from I-75, Indian River RV Resort & Campground offers convenience in the heart of the Inland Waterways and the gateway to Mackinaw City. Located in Indian River, the campground offers shaded level sites with a typical site width of 45 feet. Sites are mostly gravel with 75 pull-throughs. Tent sites are in an area offering more green space and privacy. A large pavilion is handy for groups and family gatherings. Facilities are so sparkling-clean that they must be attended to more often than the customary once a day. Owners provide security and enforce simple regulations to keep the campground safe, quiet, and comfortable, while still being friendly.

## BASICS

Operated by: Don & Nancy Schlickau. Open: Apr. 15–Nov. 1. Site Assignment: Reservations w/ 1-night deposit; refund w/ 2-week notice. Registration: At campground office. Fee: $25 (cash, check, credit cards). Parking: At site.

## FACILITIES

Number of RV Sites: 120. Number of Tent-Only Sites: 17. Hookups: Electric (20, 30 amps), water, sewer, cable TV. Each Site: Picnic table, fire ring. Dump Station: Yes. Laundry: Yes. Pay Phone: Yes. Rest Rooms and Showers: Yes. Fuel: No. Propane: Yes. Internal Roads: Gravel, in good condition. RV Service: No. Market: Less than 1 mi. Restaurant: Less than 1 mi. General Store: Yes. Vending: Yes. Swimming Pool: Yes. Playground: Yes. Other: Pavilion, rental cabins, coin games, rec hall, horseshoes, basketball, volleyball, badminton, sports field, hiking trials. Activities: Swimming, hiking, scheduled weekend activities. Nearby Attractions: Mackinac Island, golf, casino, Cross in the Woods, Lake Michigan, beaches, dunes, ferry, Old Mill Creek State Historic Park, Fort Michilimackinac, antiques, scenic drives, arts & crafts, Mackinac Bridge, Mackinac Bridge Museum. Additional Information: Greater Mackinaw City Area Chamber of Commerce, (800) 814-0160.

## RESTRICTIONS

Pets: Leash only. Fires: Fire ring only. Alcoholic Beverages: Permitted. Vehicle Maximum Length: 45 ft.

## TO GET THERE

From the junction of I-75 North and Hwy. 27, take Exit 313 and drive 1.5 mi. north on Hwy. 27. Roads are wide and well maintained w/ broad shoulders.

## INDIAN RIVER

### Yogi Bear's Jellystone Park Camp-Resort

2201 E M-68, Indian River 49749. T: (231) 238-8259; www.gocampingamerica.com/yogiindianriver; jellystoneindianriver@gocampingamerica.com.

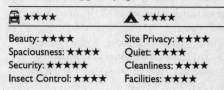

| 🚐 ★★★★ | ⛺ ★★★★ |
|---|---|
| Beauty: ★★★★ | Site Privacy: ★★★★ |
| Spaciousness: ★★★★ | Quiet: ★★★★ |
| Security: ★★★★★ | Cleanliness: ★★★★ |
| Insect Control: ★★★★ | Facilities: ★★★★ |

Campers usually know what they will find when they pull into a Yogi Bear's Jellystone Park. Facilities and security are top-notch. Activities are abundant and well organized. Rest rooms and showers are sparkling-clean, and the grounds are well maintained. But the Indian River Yogi Bear's has an extra surprise. The heated swimming pool is in the shape of Michigan with a road map on the bottom. That nice touch shows the attention to detail this campground goes to make a visit special. The campground offers level, wooded sites with a typical site width of 30 feet. There are 36 pull-through sites. Tent sites are in a rustic area with more green space and privacy. The campgrounds is in the heart of Northern Michigan with all its attractions and reservations are strongly recommended. Rangers are on hand for security and to answer questions or lend a helping hand to campers.

## BASICS

**Operated by:** Clark & Barbara Tallman & Fred Jana. **Open:** May 15–Sept. 15. **Site Assignment:** Reservations w/ 1-night deposit; refund (minus $5) w/ 7-day notice. **Registration:** At campground office. **Fee:** $35 (cash, check, credit cards). **Parking:** At site.

## FACILITIES

**Number of RV Sites:** 156. **Number of Tent-Only Sites:** 24. **Hookups:** Electric (20, 30, 50 amps), water, sewer. **Each Site:** Picnic table, fire ring. **Dump Station:** Yes. **Laundry:** Yes. **Pay Phone:** Yes. **Rest Rooms and Showers:** Yes. **Fuel:** No. **Propane:** Yes. **Internal Roads:** Paved/gravel, in good condition. **RV Service:** No. **Market:** 3 mi. west in Indian River. **Restaurant:** 3 mi. west in Indian River. **General Store:** Yes. **Vending:** Yes. **Swimming Pool:** Yes. **Playground:** Yes. **Other:** Mini-golf, nature trails, pavilion, outdoor theater, tetherball, horseshoes, bocce ball, volleyball, shuffleboard, game room, rental cabins, basketball, activities director, snack bar, coin games, sports field. **Activities:** Swimming, hiking, scheduled activities. **Nearby Attractions:** Mackinac Island, golf, casino, Cross in the Woods, Lake Michigan, beaches, dunes, ferry, Old Mill Creek State Historic Park, Fort Michilimackinac, antiques, scenic drives, arts & crafts, Mackinac Bridge, Mackinac Bridge Museum. **Additional Information:** Greater Mackinaw City Area Chamber of Commerce, (800) 814-0160.

## RESTRICTIONS

**Pets:** Leash only. **Fires:** Fire ring only. **Alcoholic Beverages:** Permitted. **Vehicle Maximum Length:** 40 ft.

## TO GET THERE

From I-75, take Indian River Exit 310, drive 4 mi. east on Hwy. 68. Roads are wide and well maintained w/ broad shoulders.

# INTERLOCHEN

## Interlochen State Park

M 137, Interlochen 49643. T: (231) 276-9511; www.michigandnr.com.

| 🚐 ★★★ | 🅰 ★★★★ |
|---|---|
| Beauty: ★★★★ | Site Privacy: ★★★ |
| Spaciousness: ★★★ | Quiet: ★★★★ |
| Security: ★★★★ | Cleanliness: ★★★ |
| Insect Control: ★★★ | Facilities: ★★ |

Established in 1919, Interlochen State Park was the first campground in Michigan's state park system. The campground, 14 miles southwest of Traverse City, is nestled among one of the state's few remaining stands of virgin pine. Located between two lakes, the park offers a rustic campground with 72 sites along Green Lake and a modern campground with 428 sites at Duck Lake. In addition to enjoying a natural setting, watersports, and recreation, campers can attend summer concerts given by premier entertainers next door at Interlochen National Music Camp. Walking trails lead from the campground to the cultural center. Modern campsites with electricity at Duck Lake have rest rooms with flush toilets. The Duck Lake campground offers two loops of campsites on each side of the day-use area with its park store, volleyball, video arcade, beach, and swimming area. But boat launch ramps are provided on both lakes. As usual, the rest rooms could be better maintained. The tree-lined shores of Green Lake offers rustic camping. Duck Lake sites are mostly gravel, with a typical site width of 30 feet and five pull-through sites. Security is great with a 24-hour attendant and regular campground patrols.

## BASICS

**Operated by:** State of Michigan. **Open:** Apr. 15–Nov. 1. **Site Assignment:** Reservations w/ 1-night deposit; refund (minus $5) w/ 1-week notice.

Call (800) 44-PARKS. **Registration:** At campground office. **Fee:** $17, plus $4 a day or $20 a season for state park sticker fee. **Parking:** At site.

FACILITIES

**Number of RV Sites:** 428. **Number of Tent-Only Sites:** 72. **Hookups:** Electric (30 amps). **Each Site:** Picnic table, fire ring. **Dump Station:** Yes. **Laundry:** No. **Pay Phone:** Yes. **Rest Rooms and Showers:** Yes. **Fuel:** No. **Propane:** No. **Internal Roads:** Paved/gravel, in good condition. **RV Service:** No. **Market:** 4 mi. **Restaurant:** 4 mi. **General Store:** Yes. **Vending:** Yes. **Swimming Pool:** No. **Playground:** Yes. **Other:** Duck Lake, Green Lake, coin games, swimming beach, boat ramp, horseshoes, game room, sports field, display of 1890s logging era. **Activities:** Swimming, fishing, boating (rental rowboats available). **Nearby Attractions:** Interlochen National Music Camp, canoe livery, Grand Traverse Bay, Sleeping Bear Sand Dunes, casino, golf, outlet mall, cherry orchards, winter sports, Old Mission, replica schooner, museums, wineries. **Additional Information:** Interlochen Chamber of Commerce, (231) 276-7141.

RESTRICTIONS

**Pets:** Leash only. **Fires:** Fire ring only. **Alcoholic Beverages:** Permitted. **Vehicle Maximum Length:** 30 ft. **Other:** 15-day stay limit.

TO GET THERE

From the junction of US 31 and M-137, drive 2 mi. south on M-137. Roads are wide and well maintained w/ adequate shoulders.

## ITHACA

### Just-In-Time Campgrounds

8421 Earl Pierce Rd., Ithaca 48847. T: (989) 875-2865; F: (989) 875-4464; www.justintimecampgrounds.com; cal@justintimecampgrounds.com.

🚐 ★★★          ⛺ ★★★

Beauty: ★★★          Site Privacy: ★★★
Spaciousness: ★★★     Quiet: ★★★
Security: ★★★         Cleanliness: ★★★
Insect Control: None   Facilities: ★★★

Just-In-Time Campgrounds is a beautiful little nook about seven miles east of Ithaca. An abundance of trees and a spring-fed lake add to the rural setting. But a sandpit across from the lake stands out like a sore thumb. The campground offers a choice of shaded or open sites, some backing up into the woods or situated right on the lake. Well-maintained grass adds to the beauty. The campground has 29 seasonal campers and no pull-through sites. No license is needed for fishing in Lake Earl. No outboard motors are permitted on the lake, and the campground has only a few boats to rent, so it is best to bring your own, including required life preservers. Be aware that the water outside the roped-in swimming area is very deep and dangerous. No swimming or wading is permitted outside the roped-in area. No lifeguard is on duty, and swimmers are urged to never swim alone. Children must always be accompanied by an adult when swimming. No pets are allowed at the campground.

BASICS

**Operated by:** Cal & Roxie Claxton. **Open:** May 1–Oct. 15. **Site Assignment:** Reservations w/ 1-night deposit; refunds w/ 7-day notice. **Registration:** At campground office. **Fee:** $25 (cash, check, credit cards). **Parking:** At site.

FACILITIES

**Number of RV Sites:** 50. **Number of Tent-Only Sites:** 0. **Hookups:** Electric (30 amps), water, sewer. **Each Site:** Picnic table, fire ring. **Dump Station:** Yes. **Laundry:** No. **Pay Phone:** Yes. **Rest Rooms and Showers:** Yes. **Fuel:** No. **Propane:** Yes. **Internal Roads:** Gravel, in good condition. **RV Service:** No. **Market:** 7 mi. west in Ithaca. **Restaurant:** 7 mi. west in Ithaca. **General Store:** Yes, limited. **Vending:** Yes. **Swimming Pool:** No. **Playground:** Yes. **Other:** Lake Earl, swimming beach, rental cabins. **Activities:** Swimming, fishing, boating (electric motors only, rental rowboats available). **Nearby Attractions:** Golf, hiking, horseback riding, charter boats, historic downtown, antiques, arts & crafts, museums. **Additional Information:** Travel Michigan, (888) 784-7328.

RESTRICTIONS

**Pets:** Not permitted. **Fires:** Fire ring only. **Alcoholic Beverages:** Permitted. **Vehicle Maximum Length:** 40 ft.

TO GET THERE

From the junction of US 27 and Washington Rd., drive 7 mi. east on Washington Rd., then 2 mi. south on Ransom, then 0.5 mi. east on Pierce Rd. Roads are wide and well maintained w/ broad shoulders, except for Pierce Rd. which is a rough gravel surface.

## LAKE LEELANAU

### Lake Leelanau RV Park

3101 Lake Shore Dr., Lake Leelanau 49653. T: (231) 256-7236; F: (231) 256-7238; www.lakeleelanau rvpark.com; donrrman@aol.com.

🚐 ★★★★          ⛺ ★★★

Beauty: ★★★★              Site Privacy: ★★★★
Spaciousness: ★★★★         Quiet: ★★★★
Security: ★★★★             Cleanliness: ★★★★
Insect Control: ★★★★       Facilities: ★★★★

Check out all the boats and fishing gear at Lake Leelanau RV Park and you'll know one of the main draws for this campground. Located on 700 feet of frontage on the shores of Lake Leelanau, the campground offers easy access to 21 miles of clear waters for boating, fishing, and other water activities. The campground also has a boat launch, gas pump, and 98 boat docks available for rent. A safe sandy beach with large shallow swimming area attracts big and little swimmers. Sites are mostly grassy and scattered among trees. Lakefront sites are mostly open and grassy with a concrete pad and patio. Laid out in a series of loops, the campground has a typical site width of 30 feet, 116 seasonal campers, and 15 pull-through sites. Paved roads make it easy to maneuver RVs and boat trailers in the campground. An extra is the free pipe organ concerts every Sunday evening, played on the 3,576-pipe, 62-rank pipe organ right in the office.

### BASICS

**Operated by:** Donald & Marilyn Wilson. **Open:** May 1–Oct. 15. **Site Assignment:** Reservations w/ 1-night deposit; refund (minus $5) w/ 7-day notice. **Registration:** At campground office. **Fee:** $35 (cash, check, credit cards). **Parking:** At site.

### FACILITIES

**Number of RV Sites:** 196. **Number of Tent-Only Sites:** 0. **Hookups:** Electric (20, 30, 50 amps), water, sewer, cable TV. **Each Site:** Picnic table, fire ring. **Dump Station:** Yes. **Laundry:** Yes. **Pay Phone:** Yes. **Rest Rooms and Showers:** Yes. **Fuel:** Yes. **Propane:** Yes. **Internal Roads:** Paved, in good condition. **RV Service:** No. **Market:** 3 mi. **Restaurant:** 3 mi. **General Store:** Yes. **Vending:** Yes. **Swimming Pool:** No. **Playground:** Yes. **Other:** Lake Leelanau, sandy beach, badminton, sports field, horseshoes, volleyball, boat dock, boat ramp, marina. **Activities:** Swimming, fishing, boating (rental motorboats, pontoons, canoes, paddleboats, seadoos available), scheduled activities. **Nearby Attractions:** Historic Fishtown, orchards, wineries, Manitou Island, excursion boats, Sleeping Bear Dunes, beaches, golf, casino, Interlochen Music Camp. **Additional Information:** Leelanau Peninsula Chamber of Commerce, (231) 256-9895.

### RESTRICTIONS

**Pets:** Leash only. **Fires:** Fire ring only. **Alcoholic Beverages:** Permitted. **Vehicle Maximum Length:** None.

### TO GET THERE

From the junction of Hwy. 204 and CR 643, drive 3.5 mi. south on CR 643. Roads are mostly wide and well maintained w/ adequate shoulders.

## LUDINGTON

### Crystal Lake Best Holiday Trav-L-Park

1884 West Hansen Rd., Scottville 49454. T: (231) 757-4510

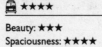

🚐 ★★★★          ⛺ ★★★

Beauty: ★★★              Site Privacy: ★★★★
Spaciousness: ★★★★        Quiet: ★★★★
Security: ★★★★            Cleanliness: ★★★★
Insect Control: ★★★★      Facilities: ★★★★

A rural lakeside campground near Ludington, Crystal Lake Best Holiday Trav-L-Park offers secluded sites with a choice of shade or open. The typical site width is 30 feet. There are 30 seasonal campers and no pull-through sites. A nice plus is that children camp free. The wooded campground also has a very clean, tiled bathroom which must see more than the usual once-a-day cleaning. The lake has a nice sandy walk-out beach, that is also kept very clean. The best sites, of course, are as close to the lake as possible. Security measures include owners who keep a close watch on the campground to make sure it stays a clean, quiet, family-oriented facility. Their efforts seem to be working.

### BASICS

**Operated by:** The Purcells. **Open:** Apr. 1–Nov. 1. **Site Assignment:** Reservations w/ 1-night deposit; refund (minus $5) w/ 7-day notice. **Regis-**

**tration:** At campground office. **Fee:** $26 (cash, check, credit cards). **Parking:** At site.

## FACILITIES

**Number of RV Sites:** 160. **Number of Tent-Only Sites:** 0. **Hookups:** Electric (20, 30 amps), water, sewer. **Each Site:** Picnic table, fire ring. **Dump Station:** Yes. **Laundry:** Yes. **Pay Phone:** Yes. **Rest Rooms and Showers:** Yes. **Fuel:** No. **Propane:** Yes. **Internal Roads:** Paved/gravel, in good condition. **RV Service:** No. **Market:** 3 mi. west. **Restaurant:** 3 mi. west. **General Store:** Yes. **Vending:** Yes. **Swimming Pool:** No. **Playground:** Yes. **Other:** Crystal Lake, sandy beach, rec hall, coin games, boat dock, fishing lake, mini-golf, basketball, badminton, sports field, horseshoes, hiking trails, volleyball, snack bar, ice cream parlor. **Activities:** Swimming, hiking, fishing, boating (rental rowboats, canoes, kayaks, paddleboats available), scheduled weekend activities. **Nearby Attractions:** Lake Michigan, Pere Marquette River, harbor, SS Badger cruises, illuminated cross, beaches, dunes, antiques, scenic drives, arts & crafts, White Pine Village, golf, tennis, charter fishing, lighthouse, seaplane rides. **Additional Information:** Ludington Area CVB, (800) 542-4600.

## RESTRICTIONS

**Pets:** Leash only. **Fires:** Fire ring only. **Alcoholic Beverages:** Permitted. **Vehicle Maximum Length:** Inquire ahead.

## TO GET THERE

From west junction of US 10 and US 31, drive 3 mi. east on US 10/31, then 1.5 mi. north on Stiles Rd. and 0.5 mi. east on Hansen Rd. Roads are generally wide and well maintained w/ narrow shoulders in spots.

## LUDINGTON

### Poncho's Pond

5335 West Wallace Rd., Ludington 49431. T: (888) 308-6602; F: (231) 845-5538; www.poncho.com.

🚐 ★★★★★                    ⛺ ★★★★

| | |
|---|---|
| Beauty: ★★★★ | Site Privacy: ★★★★★ |
| Spaciousness: ★★★★★ | Quiet: ★★★★ |
| Security: ★★★★★ | Cleanliness: ★★★★★ |
| Insect Control: ★★★★★ | Facilities: ★★★★★ |

Poncho's Pond has a well-deserved reputation for a quality place to stay. Located in Ludington, only two miles from Lake Michigan beaches, Poncho's isn't content to rest on its laurels. The friendly owners keep a close watch on maintenance and are always looking for ways to improve the campground. Cleanliness is tops as are the lighted, paved roads. The campground boasts two pools—one for children and families, the other for adults, along with an adult spa. Laid out in a series of loops, the campground has a typical site width of 35 feet, 55 seasonal campers, and 68 pull-through sites. Located in the center of the park is a pleasant three-acre pond stocked with fish to keep young anglers happy. Sites are mostly open and level, with the most popular ones being by the pond. Each lot has cable TV at no extra charge. For security measures, owners live on site and make sure the campground is secure. Even though the owners of Poncho's Pond and nearby Vacation Station RV Park have the same last name, they are not related. But they both have top-notch facilities.

## BASICS

**Operated by:** Robert Smith Jr. & Nancy Smith. **Open:** Apr. 1–Oct. 31. **Site Assignment:** Reservations w/ 1-night deposit; refund w/ 7-day notice. **Registration:** At campground office. **Fee:** $32 (cash, check, credit cards). **Parking:** At site.

## FACILITIES

**Number of RV Sites:** 202. **Number of Tent-Only Sites:** 8. **Hookups:** Electric (30, 50 amps), water, sewer, cable TV, phone. **Each Site:** Picnic table, fire ring. **Dump Station:** Yes. **Laundry:** Yes. **Pay Phone:** Yes. **Rest Rooms and Showers:** Yes. **Fuel:** No. **Propane:** Yes. **Internal Roads:** Paved, in good condition. **RV Service:** No. **Market:** 2 blocks. **Restaurant:** 2 blocks. **General Store:** Yes. **Vending:** Yes. **Swimming Pool:** Yes. **Playground:** Yes. **Other:** Pond, rec hall, pavilion, coin games, spa, basketball, movies, badminton, sports field, horseshoes, volleyball, club house. **Activities:** Swimming, fishing, boating (rental paddleboats available), scheduled activities. **Nearby Attractions:** Lake Michigan, Pere Marquette River, harbor, SS Badger cruises, illuminated cross, beaches, dunes, antiques, scenic drives, arts & crafts, White Pine Village, golf, tennis, charter fishing, lighthouse, seaplane rides. **Additional Information:** Ludington Area CVB, (800) 542-4600.

## RESTRICTIONS

**Pets:** Leash only. **Fires:** Fire ring only. **Alcoholic Beverages:** Permitted. **Vehicle Maximum Length:** None.

## TO GET THERE

From the junction of US 31 and US 10, drive 2 mi. west on US 10. Roads are wide and well maintained w/ broad shoulders.

# LUDINGTON

## Vacation Station RV Park

4895 West US 10, Ludington 49431. T: (877) 856-0390; F: (616) 843-8897; www.vacationstationrv-park.com; camp@vacationstationrvpark.com.

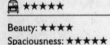 ★★★★★　　　▲ ★★★★

Beauty: ★★★★　　　　Site Privacy: ★★★★★
Spaciousness: ★★★★★　Quiet: ★★★★★
Security: ★★★★★　　　Cleanliness: ★★★★★
Insect Control: ★★★★★　Facilities: ★★★★★

Ask a camping family to create their dream campground, and this might be it. That's what the Smith family did in 1997. Vacation Station RV Park in Ludington offers the tops in convenience, clean facilities, and activities. Plus, the owners are friendly and want campers to enjoy their stay. Located on one of the state's most beautiful shorelines, the campground has a quiet, natural setting with a "neighborhood" feel. Adjacent to a family fun park, the campground is within walking distance of restaurants and shopping. Vacation Station has lighted paved roads, a choice of open or shaded sites, and exceptionally clean rest rooms and showers. A nice touch is flowers in the rest rooms and attention to detail that means more than a daily cleaning. The rural campground has a typical site width of 40 feet, 50 seasonal campers in a secluded area away from overnight campers, and 16 pull-through sites. A clubhouse overlooks a private pond with a fountain. Security includes an on-site resident manager and regular patrols of the campground.

## BASICS

**Operated by:** The Smith Family. **Open:** Apr. 1–Oct. 31. **Site Assignment:** Reservations w/ credit card; refund (minus $5) w/ 7-day notice. **Registration:** At campground office. **Fee:** $33 (cash, check, credit cards). **Parking:** At site.

## FACILITIES

**Number of RV Sites:** 150. **Number of Tent-Only Sites:** 0. **Hookups:** Electric (20, 30, 50 amps), water, sewer, phone, cable TV. **Each Site:** Picnic table, fire ring. **Dump Station:** Yes. **Laun-dry:** Yes. **Pay Phone:** Yes. **Rest Rooms and Showers:** Yes. **Fuel:** No. **Propane:** Yes. **Internal Roads:** Paved, in good condition. **RV Service:** No. **Market:** Across the street. **Restaurant:** Across the street. **General Store:** Yes. **Vending:** Yes. **Swimming Pool:** Yes. **Playground:** Yes. **Other:** Fishing pond, snack bar, game room, adult spa, rec hall, coin games, basketball, movies, badminton, sports field, horseshoes, volleyball. **Activities:** Swimming, boating, fishing, (rental paddleboats available), scheduled activities. **Nearby Attractions:** Lake Michigan, Pere Marquette River, harbor, SS Badger cruises, illuminated cross, beaches, dunes, antiques, scenic drives, arts & crafts, White Pine Village, golf, tennis, charter fishing, lighthouse, seaplane rides. **Additional Information:** Ludington Area CVB, (800) 542-4600.

## RESTRICTIONS

**Pets:** Leash only. **Fires:** Fire ring only. **Alcoholic Beverages:** At sites only. **Vehicle Maximum Length:** None.

## TO GET THERE

From west junction of US 31/10, drive 0.9 mi. west on US 10. Roads are wide and well maintained w/ broad shoulders.

# MACKINAW CITY

## Mackinaw Mill Creek Camping

P.O. Box 728, Mackinaw City 49701. T: (231) 436-5584; F: (208) 246-4350; www.campmackinaw.com; office@campmackinaw.com.

🚐 ★★★★　　　▲ ★★★★

Beauty: ★★★★　　　　Site Privacy: ★★★★
Spaciousness: ★★★★　Quiet: ★★★★
Security: ★★★★　　　Cleanliness: ★★★★
Insect Control: ★★★★　Facilities: ★★★★

The beautiful view of Mackinac Bridge is reason enough to try this campground. But there is so much more to make a camper happy. Located in Mackinaw City, Mackinaw Mill Creek Camping has more than one mile of shoreline, which means more campers get lakeside spots. Just five minutes from Mackinac Island ferry docks, the campground offers free shuttles to the ferries. Laid out in a series of loops, the campground has level, grassy sites. It offers a choice of shaded or open sites, with a typical site width of 25 feet. There are 20 seasonal campers and no pull-through sites. Reservations are recommended, especially on busy weekends. Quiet time from 10 p.m. to 9 a.m. is enforced, with no generators allowed at any time in the campground. No motorbikes of any kind are permitted. Speed limit is five mph. Security measures include a manager who lives on site and provides regular patrols of the campground.

## BASICS

**Operated by:** Richard & Rose Rogala. **Open:** May 1–Oct. 31. **Site Assignment:** Reservations w/ 1-night deposit; refund w/ 7-day notice. **Registration:** At campground office. **Fee:** $20 (cash, check, credit cards). **Parking:** At site.

## FACILITIES

**Number of RV Sites:** 525. **Number of Tent-Only Sites:** 75. **Hookups:** Electric (30 amps), water, sewer, Internet. **Each Site:** Picnic table, fire ring. **Dump Station:** Yes. **Laundry:** No. **Pay Phone:** Yes. **Rest Rooms and Showers:** Yes. **Fuel:** No. **Propane:** Yes. **Internal Roads:** Paved/gravel, in good condition. **RV Service:** No. **Market:** 2 mi. north in Mackinaw City. **Restaurant:** 2 mi. north in Mackinaw City. **General Store:** Yes. **Vending:** Yes. **Swimming Pool:** Yes. **Playground:** Yes. **Other:** Lake Huron, rental cabins, rec hall, basketball, boat pier, foor bridge, mini-golf, coin games, sports field, hiking trails, badminton. **Activities:** Swimming, fishing, boating, hiking, local tours. **Nearby Attractions:** Mackinac Island, golf, casino, Lake Michigan, beaches, Olde Mill State Historic Park, Fort Michilamackinac, antiques, scenic drives, arts & crafts, Mackinac Bridge, Mackinac Bridge Museum. **Additional Information:** Greater Mackinaw City Area Chamber of Commerce, (800) 814-0160.

## RESTRICTIONS

**Pets:** Leash only. **Fires:** Fire ring only. **Alcoholic Beverages:** At sites only. **Vehicle Maximum Length:** None. **Other:** No camping motorcyclists. Do not feed seagulls, Canadian geese or swans as their droppings may damage the finish on cars or campers.

## TO GET THERE

From I-75, take Exit 338 and drive 0.2 mi. south past Ramada Inn, then 2.5 mi. east and south on US 23. Roads are wide and well maintained w/ broad shoulders.

## MACKINAW CITY
## Tee Pee Campground

P.O. Box 10, Mackinaw City 49701. T: (231) 436-5391; www.teepeecampground.com; gjcooley@triton.net.

🚐 ★★★★          ⛺ ★★★★

Beauty: ★★★★          Site Privacy: ★★★★
Spaciousness: ★★★★    Quiet: ★★★★
Security: ★★★★         Cleanliness: ★★★★
Insect Control: ★★★     Facilities: ★★★

Location is everything, and Tee Pee Campground has a terrific location. On Lake Huron in Mackinaw City, the campground has an excellent view of Mackinac Bridge and Mackinac Island. Some lucky campers can be lulled to sleep by the sounds of the lake lapping the shore. Nightly beach campfires give a friendly atmosphere to the campground owned by the same family since 1969. Tee Pee is a ten-minute walk from downtown attractions. Laid out in a horseshoe, the campground offers level, mostly shaded sites, a typical site width of 35 feet, six pull-through sites, and eight seasonal campers. Another plus is free shuttle service to ferry boats and a casino. The most popular sites, of course, are as close to the lake as possible. Reservations are recommended, especially for busy weekends. Quiet hours starting at 10 p.m. are enforced, as is a five mph speed limit. Security includes a resident manager and regular patrols of the campground.

## BASICS

**Operated by:** Gene & Jo Cooley. **Open:** May 15–Oct. 15. **Site Assignment:** Reservations w/ 1-night deposit; refund (minus $5) w/ 48-hour notice. **Registration:** At campground office. **Fee:** $22 (cash, check, credit cards). **Parking:** At site.

## FACILITIES

**Number of RV Sites:** 100. **Number of Tent-Only Sites:** 0. **Hookups:** Electric (20, 30 amps), water. **Each Site:** Picnic table, fire ring. **Dump Station:** Yes. **Laundry:** No. **Pay Phone:** Yes. **Rest Rooms and Showers:** Yes. **Fuel:** No. **Propane:** No. **Internal Roads:** Gravel, in good condition. **RV Service:** No. **Market:** 0.5 mi. northwest in Mackinaw City. **Restaurant:** 0.5 mi. northwest in Mackinaw City. **General Store:** Yes, limited. **Vending:**

Yes. **Swimming Pool:** No. **Playground:** Yes.
**Other:** Lake Huron, swimming beach, rec room,
coin games, basketball, badminton, sports field, vol-
leyball, horseshoes, bonfire pit, boat dock. **Activi-
ties:** Swimming, fishing, boating, local tours. **Nearby
Attractions:** Mackinac Island, golf, casino, Lake
Michigan, beaches, dunes, ferry, Old Mill Creek State
Historic Park, Fort Michilimackinac, antiques, scenic
drives, arts & crafts, Mackinac Bridge, Mackinac
Bridge Museum. **Additional Information:** Greater
Mackinaw City Area Chamber of Commerce, (800)
814-0160.

RESTRICTIONS

**Pets:** Leash only. **Fires:** Fire ring only. **Alcoholic
Beverages:** Permitted. **Vehicle Maximum
Length:** 38 ft.

TO GET THERE

From the junction of I-75 and US 23, drive 1
mi. southeast on US 23. Roads are wide and
well maintained w/ broad shoulders.

## MANISTIQUE
### Indian Lake Travel Resort

HCO1 Box 3286, Manistique 49854. T: (906) 341-
2807

| 🚐 ★★★★ | ⛺ ★★★ |
|---|---|
| Beauty: ★★★★ | Site Privacy: ★★★★ |
| Spaciousness: ★★★★ | Quiet: ★★★★ |
| Security: ★★★★ | Cleanliness: ★★★★ |
| Insect Control: ★★★★ | Facilities: ★★★★ |

Located six miles west of Manistique, in the
heart of the Hiawatha National Forest, Indian
Lake Travel Resort is popular for its water attractions. Surrounded by trees, the campground is
also quiet and clean. Situated on the southwest
shore of Indian Lake, the campground has level,
mowed-grass sites with a choice of open or
shaded. A safe sandy beach is a nice spot for
swimming. The typical site width is 35 feet. The
campground has seven seasonal campers and
four pull-through sites. The campground charges
no fee to launch boats of registered guests. The
best sites are closest to Indian Lake. Rates at
about $15 are very reasonable for such a popular
tourism area.

BASICS

**Operated by:** Richard & Jeanette Ellis. **Open:** May
1–Oct. 15. **Site Assignment:** Reservations w/ 1-
night deposit; refund w/ 7-day notice. **Registra-**
tion: At campground office. **Fee:** $20 (cash, check).
**Parking:** At site.

FACILITIES

**Number of RV Sites:** 58. **Number of Tent-
Only Sites:** 0. **Hookups:** Electric (20, 30 amps),
water, sewer. **Each Site:** Picnic table, fire ring.
**Dump Station:** Yes. **Laundry:** Yes. **Pay Phone:**
Yes. **Rest Rooms and Showers:** Yes. **Fuel:** Yes.
**Propane:** Yes. **Internal Roads:** Gravel, in good
condition. **RV Service:** No. **Market:** 3 mi.
**Restaurant:** 3 mi. **General Store:** Yes, limited.
**Vending:** Yes. **Swimming Pool:** No. **Playground:**
Yes. **Other:** Indian Lake, rec hall, sandy beach, boat
ramp, badminton, sports field, horseshoes, hiking
trails, volleyball, boat dock. **Activities:** Swimming,
fishing, boating (rental rowboats available). **Nearby
Attractions:** Lake Michigan, lighthouse, maritime
museum, golf, fish hatchery, state parks, antiques,
Seney Wildlife Refuge, Big Spring, Siphon Bridge,
snowmobile trails, casino, scenic drive. **Additional
Information:** Schoolcraft County Chamber of
Commerce, (906) 341-5010.

RESTRICTIONS

**Pets:** Leash only. **Fires:** Fire ring only. **Alcoholic
Beverages:** Permitted. **Vehicle Maximum
Length:** None.

TO GET THERE

From the junction of US 2 and Hwy. 149, drive
3.75 mi. northwest on Hwy. 149, then 0.5 mi.
north on CR 455. Roads are mostly wide and
well maintained w/ adequate shoulders.

## MARSHALL
### Tri-Lakes Trails Campground

219 Perrett Rd., Marshall 49068. T: (616) 781-2297

| 🚐 ★★★ | ⛺ ★★★ |
|---|---|
| Beauty: ★★★★ | Site Privacy: ★★★ |
| Spaciousness: ★★★★ | Quiet: ★★★ |
| Security: ★★★★ | Cleanliness: ★★★★ |
| Insect Control: Yes | Facilities: ★★★ |

Tri-Lakes Trails Campground has the natural
beauty and economic price to make it a popular
place for campers who may prefer the tradeoffs
of amenities for price and more natural ambience. The public announcement service is a
noisy distraction on a quiet day. Located five
miles south of Marshall, Tri-Lake Trails has three
lakes and a nice nature trail through virgin timber. Sites are open, shaded, and grassy, with 160

seasonals and no pull-through sites. The typical site width is 40 feet, most popular spots are by the lake. Speed limit is six mph. The entrance to the campground is beautiful, like a state park with a good road and woods on both sides. A sign along the way does note that "if you don't like rules and common courtesy, pleasure turn around here."

## BASICS

**Operated by:** Jack & Jean Gladstone, Jack & Doris Sebring, Bob & Faye Sebring. **Open:** May 1–Oct. 1. **Site Assignment:** Reservations w/ 1-night deposit; refund w/ 7-day notice. **Registration:** At campground office. **Fee:** $18 (cash, check). **Parking:** At site.

## FACILITIES

**Number of RV Sites:** 300. **Number of Tent-Only Sites:** 22. **Hookups:** Electric (30 amps), water. **Each Site:** Picnic table, fire ring. **Dump Station:** Yes. **Laundry:** No. **Pay Phone:** Yes. **Rest Rooms and Showers:** Yes. **Fuel:** No. **Propane:** Yes. **Internal Roads:** Mostly paved, in great condition. **RV Service:** No. **Market:** 5 mi. north in Marshall. **Restaurant:** 5 mi. north in Marshall. **General Store:** Yes, limited. **Vending:** Yes. **Swimming Pool:** No. **Playground:** Yes. **Other:** Lake, pond, swimming beach, pavilion, activity barn, hiking trails, shuffleboard, mini golf, horseshoes, recreation field, boat dock, badminton, volleyball. **Activities:** Swimming, fishing, boating ( rental rowboats available), scheduled weekend activities. **Nearby Attractions:** Historic homes, golf, antiques, arts & crafts shops, museums. **Additional Information:** Marshall Area Chamber of Commerce, (800) 877-5163.

## RESTRICTIONS

**Pets:** Leash only. **Fires:** Fire ring only. **Alcoholic Beverages:** Permitted. **Vehicle Maximum Length:** None. **Other:** No scooters, skateboards or roller blades permitted. Small motors only on lake.

## TO GET THERE

From the junction of I-94 and I-69, drive 5.75 mi. south on I-69, take Exit 32, then 1.25 mi. east on F Dr. South, then 0.25 mi. south on Old US 27, then 0.75 mi. west on Perrett Rd. Roads are wide and well maintained w/ generally good shoulders, but entrance is through a residential neighborhood. Campground signs ask campers to limit trips through neighborhood and also to be aware of speed traps.

## MEARS

## Hide-A-Way Campground

9671 West Silver Lake Rd., Mears 49436. T: (231) 873-4428; F: (231) 873-0402; www.hideawaycampground.com; generalinfo@hideawaycampground.com.

| 🚐 ★★ | ⛺ ★★ |
|---|---|
| Beauty: ★★★ | Site Privacy: ★★★ |
| Spaciousness: ★★★ | Quiet: ★★★ |
| Security: ★★★ | Cleanliness: ★★ |
| Insect Control: ★★ | Facilities: ★★ |

Hide-A-Way Campground has so much going for it. Located in Mears, it is close to Lake Michigan, Silver Lake attractions, and sand dunes. There is enough natural beauty and outdoor activity to keep most campers happy. But the campground itself needs some work. The sand dunes about a quarter mile away make the campground a handy base for "duners," and the campground can get crowded when the sand dune meets are going on. Campsites are mostly shaded, with a typical site width of 30 feet. Some sites are level. A 340-foot water slide is a popular attraction. The water slide is open to the public and has discounts and some free time for Hide-A-Way campers.

## BASICS

**Operated by:** Dan & Laurie Kolosci. **Open:** May 1–Oct. 1. **Site Assignment:** Reservations w/ 1-night deposit; refund w/ 2-week notice. No 1-night reservations. **Registration:** At campground office. **Fee:** $28 (cash, check, credit cards). **Parking:** At site.

## FACILITIES

**Number of RV Sites:** 175. **Number of Tent-Only Sites:** 38. **Hookups:** Electric (20, 30 amps), water. **Each Site:** Picnic table, fire ring. **Dump Station:** Yes. **Laundry:** Yes. **Pay Phone:** Yes. **Rest Rooms and Showers:** Yes. **Fuel:** No. **Propane:** Yes. **Internal Roads:** Paved/gravel, in fair condition. **RV Service:** No. **Market:** 2 mi. **Restaurant:** 2 mi. **General Store:** Yes. **Vending:** Yes. **Swimming Pool:** Yes. **Playground:** Yes. **Other:** Game room, sports field, water slide, rental units. **Activities:** Swimming. **Nearby Attractions:** Lake Michigan, sand dune, state parks, golf, fruit farms, harbor, riverboats, lighthouse, antiques, gemstone factory, arts & crafts. **Additional Information:** Oceana County Tourism Bureau, (616) 873-3982.

## RESTRICTIONS

**Pets:** Leash only. **Fires:** Fire ring only. **Alcoholic Beverages:** Permitted. **Vehicle Maximum Length:** None.

## TO GET THERE

From the junction of US 31 and Shelby Rd., drive 5 mi. west on Shelby Rd., then 4.5 mi. north on Scenic Dr. Roads are mostly wide and well maintained w/ narrow shoulders in places.

## MEARS

### Sandy Shores Campground & Resort

8595 West Silver Lake, Mears 49436. T: (231) 873-3003; F: (231) 873-2142.

| 🚐 ★★★★ | 🏕 ★★★ |
|---|---|
| Beauty: ★★★★ | Site Privacy: ★★★★ |
| Spaciousness: ★★★★ | Quiet: ★★★★ |
| Security: ★★★★ | Cleanliness: ★★★★ |
| Insect Control: ★★★★ | Facilities: ★★★★ |

Located in a sand dune recreation area in Mears, Sandy Shores Campground & Resort is a wonderful spot to enjoy all the area activities. Right next to Silver Lake State Park, the campground is on a good fishing lake with a large sandy beach for swimming. Sites are level and grassy with a choice of open or shade. The typical site width is 40 feet. The campground has 140 seasonal campers and 11 pull-through sites. Rest rooms and showers are very clean and well maintained, which must be the result of more than once-a-day attention. Reservations are recommended since about two-thirds of the campground is filled with seasonal campers. Security measures are top-notch with owners who live on the premises. The campground's central location in the midst of such a popular resort area also means that local law enforcement officials will be patrolling.

## BASICS

**Operated by:** Jerry & Chris Klepper. **Open:** May 1–Oct. 1. **Site Assignment:** Reservations w/ 1-night deposit; refund (minus $5) w/ 7-day notice. **Registration:** At campground office. **Fee:** $30 (cash, check, credit cards). **Parking:** At site.

## FACILITIES

**Number of RV Sites:** 210. **Number of Tent-Only Sites:** 0. **Hookups:** Electric (30 amps), water, sewer. **Each Site:** Picnic table, fire ring. **Dump Station:** Yes. **Laundry:** Yes. **Pay Phone:** Yes. **Rest Rooms and Showers:** Yes. **Fuel:** No. **Propane:** Yes. **Internal Roads:** Paved/gravel, in good condition. **RV Service:** No. **Market:** Less than 1 mi. **Restaurant:** Less than 1 mi. **General Store:** Yes. **Vending:** Yes. **Swimming Pool:** Yes. **Playground:** Yes. **Other:** Silver Lake, badminton, volleyball, boat dock, marina, rental cottage. **Activities:** Swimming, fishing, boating (rental rowboats, canoes, sailboats, paddleboats available). **Nearby Attractions:** Lake Michigan, sand dunes, state parks, golf, fruit farms, harbor, riverboats, lighthouse, antiques, gemstone factory, arts & crafts. **Additional Information:** Oceana County Tourism Bureau, (616) 873-3982.

## RESTRICTIONS

**Pets:** Leash only. **Fires:** Fire ring only. **Alcoholic Beverages:** Permitted. **Vehicle Maximum Length:** None.

## TO GET THERE

From the junction of US 31 and Shelby Rd., drive 5 mi. west on Shelby Rd., then 4 mi. north on Scenic Dr., then 0.5 mi. east on Silver Lake Rd. Roads are generally wide and well maintained w/ adequate shoulders.

## MEARS

### Silver Lake Yogi Bear's Jellystone Park Camp-Resort

8239 West Hazel Rd., Mears 49436. T: (616) 873-4502; www.campjellystone.com; silveryogi@yahoo.com.

| 🚐 ★★★★ | 🏕 ★★★★ |
|---|---|
| Beauty: ★★★ | Site Privacy: ★★★★ |
| Spaciousness: ★★★★ | Quiet: ★★★ |
| Security: ★★★★ | Cleanliness: ★★★★ |
| Insect Control: ★★★★ | Facilities: ★★★★ |

Located near a large sand dune area and next door to an amusement center, Silver Lake Yogi Bear's Jellystone Park Camp-Resort has enough activities to keep anyone busy. The campground itself boasts a big slate of things to do. Just a quarter mile away is Silver Lake, one mile is the dunes, and two miles away is Lake Michigan Beach and a lighthouse. Next door are a slide, go-carts, adventure golf, bumper boats, an arcade, and dune buggy rentals. The campground offers open or shaded sites with a typical site width of 40 feet. There are 40 seasonal campers. Rest rooms and showers are cleaned often to keep up with all the children and sand lovers. The heated pool is a refreshing change from the cold Lake Michigan swimming beach. Security measures include regular campground patrols. Reservations are strongly recommended.

## BASICS

**Operated by:** Craig & Lorie Cihak. **Open:** Apr. 15–Oct. 15. **Site Assignment:** Reservations w/ 1-night deposit; refund w/ 2-week notice. **Registration:** At campground office. **Fee:** $34 (cash, check, credit cards). **Parking:** At site.

## FACILITIES

**Number of RV Sites:** 200. **Number of Tent-Only Sites:** 23. **Hookups:** Electric (20, 30 amps), water, sewer, phone. **Each Site:** Picnic table, fire ring. **Dump Station:** Yes. **Laundry:** Yes. **Pay Phone:** Yes. **Rest Rooms and Showers:** Yes. **Fuel:** No. **Propane:** No. **Internal Roads:** Paved/gravel, in good condition. **RV Service:** No. **Market:** 1 mi. **Restaurant:** 1 mi. **General Store:** Yes. **Vending:** Yes. **Swimming Pool:** Yes. **Playground:** Yes. **Other:** Rec hall, pavilion, coin games, fishing pond, mini-golf, basketball, shuffleboard, movies, horseshoes, volleyball, rental trailers, rental cabins, sports field. **Activities:** Swimming, fishing, scheduled activities. **Nearby Attractions:** Lake Michigan, sand dunes, state parks, golf, fruit farms, harbor, riverboats, lighthouse, antiques, gemstone factory, arts & crafts. **Additional Information:** Oceana County Tourism Bureau, (616) 873-3982.

## RESTRICTIONS

**Pets:** Leash only. **Fires:** Fire ring only. **Alcoholic Beverages:** Permitted. **Vehicle Maximum Length:** None.

## TO GET THERE

From US 31, take Hart Exit and drive 5.5 mi. west on Polk Rd./56th Ave./Fox Rd., then 0.5 mi. west on Hazel Rd. Roads are wide and well maintained w/ adequate shoulders.

# MIDLAND
## River Ridge Campground

1989 West Pine River Rd., Breckenridge 48615.
T: (800) 647-2267

🚐 ★★★★          ⛺ ★★★★

| | |
|---|---|
| Beauty: ★★★★ | Site Privacy: ★★★★ |
| Spaciousness: ★★★★ | Quiet: ★★★★ |
| Security: ★★★★ | Cleanliness: ★★★★ |
| Insect Control: ★★★★ | Facilities: ★★★★ |

A wooded campground with some open sites on Pine River, River Ridge Campground offers two important camping ingredients—quiet and cleanliness. Located in Breckenridge, the campground also has a scenic river and plenty of activities to keep campers happy. Good fishing can be found in the river or the spring-fed pond where no license is required. Campsites are level with a typical site width of 30 feet. There are 30 seasonal campers and ten pull-through sites. The best sites for RVs and tents are alongside the river. Swimmers have a choice between the heated pool, pond, or river. An added water plus is the spa. Security includes a traffic control gate and owners who keep a close watch on the campground.

## BASICS

**Operated by:** Dan & Louella Staley. **Open:** May 1–Oct. 15. **Site Assignment:** Reservations w/ 1-night deposit; refund w/ 7-day notice. **Registration:** At campground office. **Fee:** $20 (cash, check, credit cards). **Parking:** At site.

## FACILITIES

**Number of RV Sites:** 150. **Number of Tent-Only Sites:** 12. **Hookups:** Electric (20, 30, 50 amps), water, sewer, phone. **Each Site:** Picnic table, fire ring. **Dump Station:** Yes. **Laundry:** Yes. **Pay Phone:** Yes. **Rest Rooms and Showers:** Yes. **Fuel:** No. **Propane:** Yes. **Internal Roads:** Gravel, in good condition. **RV Service:** No. **Market:** 6 mi. north. **Restaurant:** 6 mi. north. **General Store:** Yes, limited. **Vending:** No. **Swimming Pool:** Yes. **Playground:** Yes. **Other:** Pine River, rec hall, pavilion, coin games, spa, basketball, badminton, sports field, horseshoes, volleyball, rental cabins. **Activities:** Swimming, fishing, boating (rental kayaks, paddleboats, tubes available). **Nearby Attractions:** Bowling, mini-golf, hiking trails, outdoor concert park, farmers' market,

Alden B. Down Home & Studio, Chippewa Nature Center, Dow Gardens, antiques, arts & crafts, golf, casino. **Additional Information:** Midland County CVB, (888) 464-3526.

## RESTRICTIONS

**Pets:** Leash only; indoor pets only. **Fires:** Fire ring only. **Alcoholic Beverages:** At sites only. **Vehicle Maximum Length:** None.

## TO GET THERE

From the junction of Hwy. 20 and Meridian Rd., drive 3 mi. south on Meridian Rd., then 4.5 mi. west on Pine River Rd. Roads are mostly wide and well maintained w/ narrow shoulders in spots.

## MIDLAND

## Valley Plaza RV Park

5221 Bay City Rd., Midland 48642. T: (517) 496-2159; www.valleyplazaresort.com.

| 🚐 ★★★ | ⛺ n/a |
|---|---|
| Beauty: ★★★ | Site Privacy: ★★★★ |
| Spaciousness: ★★★★ | Quiet: ★★★ |
| Security: ★★★★ | Cleanliness: ★★★★ |
| Insect Control: ★★★★ | Facilities: ★★★★ |

Campers can get spoiled at Valley Plaza RV Park with all the luxury features in the recreation complex. Located five miles south of Midland, the campground is behind a recreation complex that includes a motel, restaurant, theatre, bowling alley, health club, tanning beds, indoor mini-golf, arcade, and more. This is not an out-in-the-country kind of campground. It is more like an open space with trees that still have a bunch of growing to do to provide shade. Sites are mostly open with a typical site width of 30 feet. There are 12 seasonal campers and 55 pull-through sites. The campground has a three-acre lake with a sandy beach and seasonal water sports. Sites are within a well-illuminated and fenced area, ensuring privacy. Be aware that no tents are permitted. Many campers come to enjoy the facilities at the campground as well as those at the recreation complex. Security is tops with a security patrol that keeps a close eye on the area.

## BASICS

**Operated by:** Jason Raponis. **Open:** Mar. 1–Nov. 1. **Site Assignment:** Reservations w/ 1-night deposit; refund (minus $5) w/ 7-day notice. **Regis-**

tration: At campground office. **Fee:** $25 (cash, check, credit cards). **Parking:** At site.

## FACILITIES

**Number of RV Sites:** 96. **Number of Tent-Only Sites:** 0. **Hookups:** Electric (20, 30, 50 amps), water, sewer. **Each Site:** Picnic table, fire ring. **Dump Station:** Yes. **Laundry:** No. **Pay Phone:** Yes. **Rest Rooms and Showers:** Yes. **Fuel:** Yes. **Propane:** Yes. **Internal Roads:** Paved, in good condition. **RV Service:** No. **Market:** 5 mi. north in Midland. **Restaurant:** Walking distance. **General Store:** Yes. **Vending:** Yes. **Swimming Pool:** Yes. **Playground:** Yes. **Other:** Lake, rec hall, pavilion, coin games, wading pool, sauna, whirlpool, fishing pond, mini golf, basketball, badminton, horseshoes, volleyball, boat dock, adults room, sports field. **Activities:** Swimming, fishing, boating (rental paddleboats, kayaks available), scheduled activities. **Nearby Attractions:** Bowling, mini-golf, hiking trails, outdoor concert park, farmers' market, Alden B. Down Home & Studio, Chippewa Nature Center, Dow Gardens, antiques, arts & crafts, golf, casino. **Additional Information:** Midland County CVB, (888) 464-3526.

## RESTRICTIONS

**Pets:** Leash only. **Fires:** Fire ring only. **Alcoholic Beverages:** Permitted. **Vehicle Maximum Length:** None. **Other:** No tents allowed.

## TO GET THERE

From the junction of I-75 and US 10, take Exit 162B and drive 10 mi. west on US 10 to Bay City Rd. exit, then drive 0.1 mi. west on Bay City Rd. Roads are wide and well maintained w/ broad shoulders.

## MILAN

## KC Campground

14048 Sherman Rd., Milan 48160. T: (734) 439-1076

| 🚐 ★★★ | ⛺ ★★★ |
|---|---|
| Beauty: ★★★ | Site Privacy: ★★★ |
| Spaciousness: ★★★ | Quiet: ★★★ |
| Security: ★★★★ | Cleanliness: ★★★ |
| Insect Control: ★★★ | Facilities: ★★★ |

A rural campground with mostly shaded sites in a grassy meadow, KC Campground is located three miles east of Milan. The best sites are along a very small pond used for swimming. The campground has a typical site width of 30 feet, with 20 seasonal campers and 15 pull-through sites. Laid out in a series of loops, the campground has separate tent areas with more green space and privacy. Quiet time between 10 p.m. and 8 a.m. is enforced, and no motorcycles, minibikes, or ATVs are allowed. Reservations are recommended during the annual Milan Bluegrass Festival in Aug. The festival draws top names in Bluegrass entertainment. Security measures at the campground include an owner and manger who live on site, one entrance/exit road, and regular patrols of the campground.

## BASICS

**Operated by:** Mark & Peggy Ann Gaynier. **Open:** May 1–Oct. 31. **Site Assignment:** Reservations w/ 1-night deposit; refund w/ 72-hour notice. **Registration:** At campground office. **Fee:** $20 (cash, check, credit cards). **Parking:** At site.

## FACILITIES

**Number of RV Sites:** 100. **Number of Tent-Only Sites:** 50. **Hookups:** Electric (20, 30 amps), water. **Each Site:** Picnic table, fire ring. **Dump Station:** Yes. **Laundry:** No. **Pay Phone:** No. **Rest Rooms and Showers:** Yes. **Fuel:** No. **Propane:** Yes. **Internal Roads:** Gravel, in good condition. **RV Service:** No. **Market:** 3 mi. west in Milan. **Restaurant:** 3 mi. west in Milan. **General Store:** Yes, limited. **Vending:** No. **Swimming Pool:** No. **Playground:** Yes. **Other:** Swimming pond, rec hall, volleyball, basketball, horseshoes, sports field. **Activities:** Swimming. **Nearby Attractions:** Golf, Cabela's, Cedar Point, Toledo Center of Science & Industry, Greenfield Village, Monroe County Historical Museum, River Raisin Battlefield, Sauders Farm & Craft Village, Toledo Zoo, Yankee Air museum, antiques. **Additional Information:** Monroe County Convention & Tourism Bureau, (800) 252-3011.

## RESTRICTIONS

**Pets:** Leash only. **Fires:** Fire ring only. **Alcoholic Beverages:** At sites only. **Vehicle Maximum Length:** 54 ft.

## TO GET THERE

From the junction of US 23 and Plank Rd., take Exit 25 and drive 1.5 mi. southeast on Plank Rd., then 1 mi. east Sherman Rd. Roads are mostly wide and well maintained, but Plank Rd. has narrow shoulders, and the access road is bumpy and gravel.

## MONROE

### Harbortown RV Resort

14931 LaPlaisance Rd., Monroe 48161. T: (734) 384-4700; www.harbortownrv.com.

🚐 ★★★★　　　🅰 ★

| | |
|---|---|
| Beauty: ★★★ | Site Privacy: ★★★ |
| Spaciousness: ★★★ | Quiet: ★★ |
| Security: ★★★★★ | Cleanliness: ★★★★★ |
| Insect Control: ★★★★★ | Facilities: ★★★★★ |

Opened in spring of 2000, Harbortown RV Resort is a state-of-the-art facility in Monroe, that includes Time Out Family Recreation Center. Bring plenty of coins for the activities. Offering easy access from I-75, the campground is only one mile from Lake Erie and all its water sports. Laid out in a series of loops, the campground offers level, open, paved sites with a typical site width of 30 feet. There are 105 pull-throughs. Facilities are new and squeaky clean. A full-time staff must be at work constantly to keep the campground in such tip-top shape. Security is great; it doesn't seem likely anyone would enter or exit without being seen. Tents are permitted, but there is no separate section for them. Tent campers must pay the regular fee for an RV site. Harbortown seems like a campground of the future. There are several opportunities for improvement, however. One would be the addition of propane for sale; it's not easy to find nearby. Another would be the need for some shade trees; that will come with time when the landscaping has a chance to mature. The last is the installation of a hedge or other sound buffer next to the train tracks bordering one edge of the campground.

## BASICS

**Operated by:** Private Operator. **Open:** All year. **Site Assignment:** Reservations w/ 1-night deposit; refund w/ 2-week notice. **Registration:** At campground office. **Fee:** $32 (cash, check, credit cards). **Parking:** At site.

## FACILITIES

**Number of RV Sites:** 250. **Number of Tent-Only Sites:** 0. **Hookups:** Electric (20, 30, 50 amps), water, sewer, phone, cable TV. **Each Site:** Picnic table, fire ring. **Dump Station:** Yes. **Laundry:** Yes. **Pay Phone:** Yes. **Rest Rooms and**

**Showers:** Yes. **Fuel:** No. **Propane:** No. **Internal Roads:** Paved, in good condition. **RV Service:** No. **Market:** Next door. **Restaurant:** Next door. **General Store:** Yes. **Vending:** Yes. **Swimming Pool:** Yes. **Playground:** Yes. **Other:** Rec hall, coin games, mini-golf, movies, horseshoes, volleyball, go-karts, 18-hole golf course, sports field, rental cabins, batting cages. **Activities:** Swimming, scheduled activities. **Nearby Attractions:** Cabela's, outlet mall, Lake Erie, Vietnam War Memorial, Heck Park, historic tours, Monroe County Historical Museum, River Raisin Battlefield Visitor Center, antiques, arts & crafts, Navarre-Anderson Trading Post Complex. **Additional Information:** Monroe County Convention & Tourism Bureau, (800) 252-3011.

## RESTRICTIONS

**Pets:** Leash only. **Fires:** Fire ring only. **Alcoholic Beverages:** Permitted. **Vehicle Maximum Length:** None.

## TO GET THERE

From the junction of I-75 and Laplaisance Rd., take Exit 11 and drive 0.5 mi. west on Laplaisance Rd. Roads are wide and well maintained w/ broad shoulders.

## MONTAGUE

### Jerry's Campground

4540 Dowling St., Montague 49437. T: (231) 894-4903

🚐 ★★★★                   ⛺ ★★★★

| | |
|---|---|
| Beauty: ★★★ | Site Privacy: ★★★ |
| Spaciousness: ★★★ | Quiet: ★★★★ |
| Security: ★★★★ | Cleanliness: ★★★★ |
| Insect Control: ★★★★ | Facilities: ★★★ |

Why do most campers go to Jerry's Campground? Although the campground offers little activities of its own, it does provide a fish-cleaning hut and complimentary fish freezing. That tells you what the major draw is. Jerry's Campground in Montague, is across from beautiful White Lake and two blocks from the public boat launch. It is also at the south end of the Montague/Hart Bike Trail. Most people use Jerry's Campground as a base to enjoy area activities. Golf is nearby, and shops and dining are within walking distance. A campground in town, Jerry's has mostly open, flat, grassy sites with a typical site width of 30 feet. The campground has 25 seasonal campers and 21 pull-through sites. Quiet hours from 10 p.m. to 7 a.m. are enforced. Security measures are good with patrols and local police always close at hand.

## BASICS

**Operated by:** Jerry Woller. **Open:** Late Apr.–late Oct. **Site Assignment:** Reservations w/ 1-night deposit; refund w/ 7-day notice. **Registration:** At campground office. **Fee:** $20 (cash, check). **Parking:** At site.

## FACILITIES

**Number of RV Sites:** 51. **Number of Tent-Only Sites:** 4. **Hookups:** Electric (30 amps), water, sewer, cable TV. **Each Site:** Picnic table, grill. **Dump Station:** Yes. **Laundry:** No. **Pay Phone:** Yes. **Rest Rooms and Showers:** Yes. **Fuel:** No. **Propane:** No. **Internal Roads:** Gravel, in good condition. **RV Service:** No. **Market:** 1 mi. **Restaurant:** Walking distance. **General Store:** No. **Vending:** Yes. **Swimming Pool:** No. **Playground:** Yes. **Other:** Pavilion, horseshoes, fish-cleaning station. **Activities:** None. **Nearby Attractions:** Lake Michigan, White Lake, marinas, Michgan's Adventure Amusement Park, White River Lighthouse Museum, golf, bike trail, mini-golf, world's largest weather vane, bike trail. **Additional Information:** White Lake Area Chamber of Commerce, (800) 879-9702.

## RESTRICTIONS

**Pets:** Leash only. **Fires:** Grills only. **Alcoholic Beverages:** Permitted. **Vehicle Maximum Length:** None.

## TO GET THERE

From the junction of US 31 and Business 31, take Whitehall-Montague Exit and drive 2.25 mi. west on Business 31. Roads are wide and well maintained w/ broad shoulders.

## MT. PLEASANT

### Shardi's Hide-Away

340 North Loomis Rd., Mt. Pleasant 48858. T: (517) 773-4268

🚐 ★★★                   ⛺ ★★★

| | |
|---|---|
| Beauty: ★★★ | Site Privacy: ★★★ |
| Spaciousness: ★★★ | Quiet: ★★★ |
| Security: ★★★ | Cleanliness: ★★★ |
| Insect Control: None | Facilities: ★★★ |

A rural campground in a semi-wooded setting, Shardi's Hide-Away is located six miles east of Mt. Pleasant. Sites are level, mostly shaded and with a typical site width of 25 feet. There are no seasonal campers and the campground has eight pull-through sites. The campground is a popular place for deer hunters and campers who enjoy mushroom and berry picking. The playground features a big wooden boat and a jeep which are hits with youngsters. The ten mph speed limit is rather high, but traffic generally travels slower because of the gravel and dirt road. Reservations are highly recommended during festival times— Apr. for the Maple Syrup Festival, May for the Highland Scottish Festival, July for the Bluegrass Festival and Antique Engine Show, and Aug. for the Isabella County Fair.

## BASICS

**Operated by:** The Miller Family. **Open:** All year. **Site Assignment:** Reservations w/ 1-night deposit; no refunds**Registration:** At campground office. **Registration:** At campground office. **Fee:** $22 (cash, check, credit cards). **Parking:** At site.

## FACILITIES

**Number of RV Sites:** 102. **Number of Tent-Only Sites:** 10. **Hookups:** Electric (20, 30, 50 amps), water, sewer. **Each Site:** Picnic table, fire ring. **Dump Station:** Yes. **Laundry:** No. **Pay Phone:** No. **Rest Rooms and Showers:** Yes. **Fuel:** No. **Propane:** No. **Internal Roads:** Gravel/dirt, in fair condition. **RV Service:** No. **Market:** 6 mi. west in Mt. Pleasant. **Restaurant:** 6 mi. west in Mt. Pleasant. **General Store:** Yes. **Vending:** No. **Swimming Pool:** Yes. **Playground:** Yes. **Other:** Pavilion, rental cabins, hiking trails, shuffleboard, volleyball, horseshoes, sand hill, basketball, tetherball, fishing pond, badminton, recreation field. **Activities:** Swimming, fishing, hiking. **Nearby Attractions:** Gambling casino, horse & car race tracks, golf, canoeing, tubing, fishing, antiques, farmers market. **Additional Information:** Mt. Pleasant Area CVB, (800) 772-4433.

## RESTRICTIONS

**Pets:** Leash only. **Fires:** Fire ring only. **Alcoholic Beverages:** Permitted. **Vehicle Maximum Length:** None.

## TO GET THERE

From the junction of US 27 and Hwy. 20, drive 3.5 mi. east on Hwy. 20, then 2.5 mi. north on Loomis Rd. Roads are wide and well maintained w/ broad shoulders, except for Loomis Rd. which is a rough gravel surface.

# MUNISING
## Wandering Wheels Campground

P.O. Box 419, Munising 49862. T: (906) 387-3315; F: (906) 387-3315; www.wanderingwheels.com; vbragg@up.net.

🚐 ★★★★          ⛺ ★★★

| | |
|---|---|
| Beauty: ★★★★ | Site Privacy: ★★★★ |
| Spaciousness: ★★★★ | Quiet: ★★★★ |
| Security: ★★★★ | Cleanliness: ★★★★ |
| Insect Control: ★★★★ | Facilities: ★★★★ |

Wandering Wheels Campground, three-and-a-half miles east of Munising, is surrounded by scenic attractions and activities. The campground is quite nice in and of itself. Sites are level, secluded, and mostly wooded. About half are grassy and half are dirt. The typical site width is 40 feet and the campground has 44 pull-through sites. Free showers in the sparkling- clean facilities are a nice plus. Wandering Wheels also has camping cabins with gas fireplaces that cost about $40 for up to four persons, which is cheaper than most motels and far more pleasant. Reservations are recommended for the campsites and cabins. Security is good, with owners keeping a close eye on the campground.

## BASICS

**Operated by:** Dennis & Vickie Bragg. **Open:** May 1–Oct. 15. **Site Assignment:** Reservations w/ 1-night deposit; refund w/ 7-day notice. **Registration:** At campground office. **Fee:** $26 (cash, check, credit cards). **Parking:** At site.

## FACILITIES

**Number of RV Sites:** 88. **Number of Tent-Only Sites:** 12. **Hookups:** Electric (20, 30, 50 amps), water, sewer, phone, cable TV. **Each Site:** Picnic table, fire ring. **Dump Station:** Yes. **Laundry:** Yes. **Pay Phone:** Yes. **Rest Rooms and Showers:** Yes. **Fuel:** No. **Propane:** Yes. **Internal Roads:** Gravel, in good condition. **RV Service:** No. **Market:** Less than 1 mi. **Restaurant:** Next door. **General Store:** Yes. **Vending:** Yes. **Swimming Pool:** Yes. **Playground:** Yes. **Other:** Rec room, coin games, basketball, badminton, sports field, horseshoes, volleyball, rental ~ ties: Swimming. **Nearby Attrac**

Pictured Rocks National Lakeshore, golf, Alger Underwater Preserve, boat tours, shipwreck tours, glass bottom boat tours, snowmobiling. **Additional Information:** Munising Visitors Bureau, (906) 387-2138.

### RESTRICTIONS

**Pets:** Leash only. **Fires:** Fire ring only. **Alcoholic Beverages:** Permitted. **Vehicle Maximum Length:** None.

### TO GET THERE

From town, drive 3.5 mi. east on Hwy. 28. Roads are wide and well maintained w/ broad shoulders.

## NILES

### Spaulding Lake Campground

2305 Bell Rd., Niles 49120. T: (616) 684-1393; F: (616) 684-4065.

🚐 ★★★★          ▲ ★★★

Beauty: ★★★★          Site Privacy: ★★★★
Spaciousness: ★★★★     Quiet: ★★★★
Security: ★★★★         Cleanliness: ★★★★
Insect Control: ★★★★    Facilities: ★★★★

On the Indiana/Michigan border in Niles, Spaudling Lake Campground is a good base to cover a wide area, including Amish country in Northern Indiana. The campground has three man-made ponds, one for swimming and two for fishing. Just five miles north of South Bend, Spaulding Lake is the closest campground to Notre Dame. No fishing license is required at the spring-fed, stocked pond. Sites are level and grassy, with a typical site width of 30 feet. The campground has 15 seasonal campers and 44 pull-through sites. Be aware that the campground does not permit alcohol anywhere on the premises. The campground and facilities are clean and well maintained. Rules and security measures are enforced. The goal is a family-oriented campground where people feel comfortable camping. Spaulding Lake Campground doesn't lack for campers, so the owners must be achieving their goal.

### BASICS

**Operated by:** Nolan & Virginia Spaulding. **Open:** Apr. 1–Oct. 15. **Site Assignment:** Reservations w/ 1-night deposit; refund (minus $5) w/ 7-day notice. **Registration:** At campground office. **Fee:** $20 check). **Parking:** At site.

### FACILITIES

**Number of RV Sites:** 120. **Number of Tent-Only Sites:** 0. **Hookups:** Electric (20, 30, 50 amps), water, sewer, cable TV, phone. **Each Site:** Picnic table, fire ring. **Dump Station:** Yes. **Laundry:** Yes. **Pay Phone:** Yes. **Rest Rooms and Showers:** Yes. **Fuel:** No. **Propane:** Yes. **Internal Roads:** Gravel, in good condition. **RV Service:** No. **Market:** 3 mi. **Restaurant:** 3 mi. **General Store:** Yes. **Vending:** Yes. **Swimming Pool:** No. **Playground:** Yes. **Other:** Swimming lake, fishing lake, rec hall, coin games, trout stream, basketball, shuffleboard, bandminton, sports field, pavilion, horseshoes, volleyball, hiking trails. **Activities:** Swimming, fishing, hiking. **Nearby Attractions:** Amish Country, Fort St. Joseph Museum, historic homes, antiques, arts & crafts, Fernwood Botanic Garden & Nature Center, Notre Dame. **Additional Information:** Four Flags Area Council on Tourism, (616) 684-7444.

### RESTRICTIONS

**Pets:** Leash only. **Fires:** Fire ring only. **Alcoholic Beverages:** Not permitted. **Vehicle Maximum Length:** None. **Other:** No outside firewood permitted.

### TO GET THERE

From the junction of US 12 and Hwy. 51, drive 0.25 mi. south on Hwy. 51, then 2 mi. east on Bell Rd. Roads are generally wide and well maintained w/ adequate shoulders.

## ONTONAGON

### River Pines RV Park & Campground

600 River Rd., Ontonagon 49953. T: (800) 424-1520; www.ontonagonmi.com/riverpines; gladorp@up.net.

🚐 ★★★★          ▲ ★★★★

Beauty: ★★★★          Site Privacy: ★★★★
Spaciousness: ★★★★     Quiet: ★★★★
Security: ★★★★         Cleanliness: ★★★★
Insect Control: ★★★★    Facilities: ★★★★

A little gem along the Ontonagon River, River Pines RV Park & Campground offers great facilities with sparkling-clean rest rooms. Located outside Ontonagon, the campground has open or shaded level sites, with a typical site width of 35 feet. Laid out in a series of loops, the campground has 30 pull-through sites. A separate tent section in the woods allows more green space and privacy. A four-season campground, River

Pines features easy access to 500 miles of snowmobile trails and five major ski hills within a 60-mile radius. Winter group housing in available in the main building for those frigid, snowy Michigan winters. The best RV sites are in the pine tree section. Walleye and salmon fishing are popular in the river by the campground. With only 32 sites, reservations are strongly recommended from June through Sept. Security includes owners who live on the site and keep a close watch on the campground.

## BASICS

**Operated by:** Dot Phillips & Gladys Chamberlain. **Open:** All year. **Site Assignment:** Reservations w/ 1-night deposit; refund w/ 7-day notice. **Registration:** At campground office. **Fee:** $21 (cash, check, credit cards). **Parking:** At site.

## FACILITIES

**Number of RV Sites:** 30. **Number of Tent-Only Sites:** 2. **Hookups:** Electric (20, 30, 50 amps), water, sewer, phone, cable TV. **Each Site:** Picnic table, fire ring. **Dump Station:** Yes. **Laundry:** Yes. **Pay Phone:** Yes. **Rest Rooms and Showers:** Yes. **Fuel:** No. **Propane:** Yes. **Internal Roads:** Gravel, in good condition. **RV Service:** No. **Market:** 1 mi. east in Ontonagon. **Restaurant:** 1 mi. east in Ontonagon. **General Store:** Yes, limited. **Vending:** Yes. **Swimming Pool:** No. **Playground:** Yes. **Other:** Rec hall, coin games, boat dock, fishing river, basketball, bandminton, sports field, horseshoes, volleyball. **Activities:** Fishing, boating (rental canoe, rowboats, paddleboats, motorboats available). **Nearby Attractions:** Ontonagon River, 45 waterfalls, Porcupine Mountains State Park, sailing, backpacking, hiking, Presque Isle Falls, Lake of the Clouds, golf, antiques, arts & crafts, Ontonagon County Historical Museum. **Additional Information:** Ontonagon County Chamber of Commerce, (906) 884-4735.

## RESTRICTIONS

**Pets:** Leash only. **Fires:** Fire ring only. **Alcoholic Beverages:** Permitted. **Vehicle Maximum Length:** None.

## TO GET THERE

From the junction of US 45 and Hwy. 64, drive 0.25 mi. south on Hwy. 64, then 0.5 mi. east on River Rd. Roads are mostly wide and well maintained w/ adequate shoulders.

## ORTONVILLE
### Clearwater Campground

1140 South M-15, Ortonville 48462. T: (248) 627-3820

🚐 ★★★          ⛺ ★★★

| | |
|---|---|
| Beauty: ★★★ | Site Privacy: ★★★ |
| Spaciousness: ★★★ | Quiet: ★★★ |
| Security: ★★★★ | Cleanliness: ★★★ |
| Insect Control: ★★★ | Facilities: ★★★ |

A lakeside campground with open and shaded sites, Clearwater Campground is located in Ortonville. Laid out in a series of loops, the campground has a typical site width of 25 feet. It has 30 seasonal campers and eight pull-through sites. All sites have full hookup, and tents are not allowed on any of the full hookup sites. Tents are permitted only in the primitive area which offers more green space and privacy. Quiet time from 10 p.m. to 8 a.m. is enforced, as is a five mph speed limit. No mini-bikes, off-road bikes or similar vehicles are permitted in the park. The campground also has a rule that any RV that is detrimental to the appearance of the park may be refused registration. The campground manager decides what constitutes a detrimental appearance. Security measures include a manager who lives on site and a gate that requires a card pass to enter.

## BASICS

**Operated by:** Mike & Christie Neadow & Mark & Michaelanne Reis. **Open:** Apr. 15–Oct. 15. **Site Assignment:** Reservations w/ 1-night deposit; refund w/ 7-day notice. **Registration:** At campground office. **Fee:** $25 (cash, check). **Parking:** At site.

## FACILITIES

**Number of RV Sites:** 209. **Number of Tent-Only Sites:** 15. **Hookups:** Electric (30, 50 amps), water, sewer, cable TV, phone. **Each Site:** Picnic table, fire ring. **Dump Station:** Yes. **Laundry:** Yes. **Pay Phone:** Yes. **Rest Rooms and Showers:** Yes. **Fuel:** No. **Propane:** Yes. **Internal Roads:** Paved, in good condition. **RV Service:** No. **Market:** 0.25 mi. north in Ortonville. **Restaurant:** Across the street. **General Store:** Yes, limited. **Vending:** Yes. **Swimming Pool:** No. **Playground:** Yes. **Other:** Swimming lake, pavilion, mini tolf, sports field, horseshoes. **Activities:** Swimming, fishing, boating (electric motors only), scheduled weekend activities. **Nearby Attractions:** Children's Museum, Huckleberry Railroad, paddle-wheeler, museums, Longway Planetarium, Flint River, antiques, golf, arts & crafts. **Additional Information:** Holly Chamber of Commerce, (248) 634-1900.

## RESTRICTIONS

**Pets:** Leash only; 1 pet per site. **Fires:** Fire ring only. **Alcoholic Beverages:** Permitted. **Vehicle Maximum Length:** None. **Other:** Tents permitted only on primitive sites.

## TO GET THERE

From the junction of I-75 and Hwy. 15, take Exit 91 and drive 6.2 mi. north on Hwy. 15. Roads are wide and well maintained w/ broad shoulders.

## PENTWATER

## Whispering Surf Camping Resort

7070 South Lake Shore Dr., Pentwater 49449. T: (231) 869-5050; F: (231) 869-5935; www.denaliseed.com/wsurf; wsurf@denaliseed.com.

| 🚐 ★★★ | 🛖 ★★★★ |
|---|---|
| Beauty: ★★★★ | Site Privacy: ★★★★ |
| Spaciousness: ★★★★ | Quiet: ★★★★ |
| Security: ★★★★ | Cleanliness: ★★★★ |
| Insect Control: ★★★★ | Facilities: ★★★ |

One of Michigan's oldest continuously operating resorts, Whispering Surf Camping Resort got its start in 1913. But the campground is not outdated. Full hookups and modern facilities are available, along with free hot showers. Located four miles north of Pentwater, between Bass Lake and Lake Michigan, Whispering Surf is forested with oak, pine, and white birch trees. Tucked in the North Woods, the campground offers shaded sites and a private beach. Sites are mostly grassy with a typical site width of 35 feet. There are 20 seasonals that maintain their sites nicely. It's an eight-mile walk to Lake Michigan and its white "singing sands." The campground has a rustic tent area for more green space and privacy. A fishing license is required to fish in the lake. The turn-of-the-century pavilion is now used for recreation and as a meeting place for groups. It is one of the few such pavilions remaining in Michigan.

## BASICS

**Operated by:** Reginald Yaple. **Open:** May 15–Oct. 15. **Site Assignment:** Reservations w/ 1-night deposit; refund w/ 2-week notice. **Registration:** At campground office. **Fee:** $26 (cash, check, credit cards). **Parking:** At site.

## FACILITIES

**Number of RV Sites:** 65. **Number of Tent-Only Sites:** 20. **Hookups:** Electric (20, 30 amps), water, sewer. **Each Site:** Picnic table, fire ring. **Dump Station:** Yes. **Laundry:** No. **Pay Phone:** Yes. **Rest Rooms and Showers:** Yes. **Fuel:** No. **Propane:** No. **Internal Roads:** Gravel, in good condition. **RV Service:** No. **Market:** 1 mi. **Restaurant:** 1 mi. **General Store:** Yes, limited. **Vending:** Yes. **Swimming Pool:** No. **Playground:** Yes. **Other:** Bass Lake, boat dock, game room, rec hall, pavilion, coin games, swimming beach, horseshoes, boat ramp. **Activities:** Swimming, fishing, boating (rental canoe, paddleboats available) scheduled weekend activities. **Nearby Attractions:** Hart-Montague Bike Trail, state parks, White Pine Village, Rose Hawley Museum, lighthouses, Shrine of the Pines, English Double-Decker Bus Tour, historic homes, antiques, Lake Michigan Carferry. **Additional Information:** Pentwater Chamber of Commerce, (231) 869-4150.

## RESTRICTIONS

**Pets:** Leash only. **Fires:** Fire ring only. **Alcoholic Beverages:** Permitted. **Vehicle Maximum Length:** None.

## TO GET THERE

From north junction US 31 and Business US 31, drive 0.75 mi. west on Business US 31, then 1 mi. north on Lake Shore Dr. Roads are mostly wide and well maintained w/ adequate shoulders.

## PETERSBURG

## Monroe County KOA Kampground

US 23 at Exit 9, Petersburg 49270. T: (734) 856-4972; F: (734) 856-8224; www.koa.com.

| 🚐 ★★★★ | 🛖 ★★★★ |
|---|---|
| Beauty: ★★★★ | Site Privacy: ★★★★ |
| Spaciousness: ★★★★ | Quiet: ★★★★ |
| Security: ★★★★ | Cleanliness: ★★★★★ |
| Insect Control: Yes | Facilities: ★★★★ |

Nestled in maple, oak, and pine trees, Monroe County KOA Kampground is nine miles north of the Ohio line. Sites are grassy and mostly shaded. Laid out in a series of loops, the campground has a typical site width of 35 feet and 47 pull-through sites. There are no seasonal campers. A two-acre sandy-beach swimming lake is a popular draw. The beach is cleaned and dragged several times a week. The lake has two aerators putting oxygen in the lake year-round. Quiet hours are from 11 p.m. to 7 a.m., when no radio, TV or voices are to be heard beyond each camping site. No subwoofers on car stereos are allowed at any time. No golf carts or generators are allowed. Security includes traffic control gates and owners who live on the site and provide campground patrols.

## BASICS

**Operated by:** Ray & Donna Crots. **Open:** Apr. 13–Oct. 13. **Site Assignment:** Reservations w/ $50 deposit; refund (less half) w/ 48-hour notice. **Registration:** At campground office. **Fee:** $30 (cash, check, credit cards). **Parking:** At site.

## FACILITIES

**Number of RV Sites:** 230. **Number of Tent-Only Sites:** 50. **Hookups:** Electric (20, 30, 50 amps), water, sewer. **Each Site:** Picnic table, fire ring. **Dump Station:** Yes. **Laundry:** Yes. **Pay Phone:** Yes. **Rest Rooms and Showers:** Yes. **Fuel:** No. **Propane:** Yes. **Internal Roads:** Gravel, in good condition. **RV Service:** No. **Market:** 5 mi. south in Lambertville. **Restaurant:** 5 mi. south in Lambertville. **General Store:** Yes. **Vending:** Yes. **Swimming Pool:** No. **Playground:** Yes. **Other:** Rec hall, fishing lake, mini golf, shuffleboard, tetherball, basketball, horseshoes, baseball, trout pond, volleyball, club room, rental cabins, water slides, sandy beach, coin games, food wagon. **Activities:** Swimming, fishing, boating (rental rowboats, canoes, kayaks, paddleboats available), schedule weekend activities. **Nearby Attractions:** Golf, Cabela's, Cedar Point, Toledo Center of Science & Industry, Greenfield Village, Monroe Co. Historical Museum, River Raisin Battlefield, Sauders Farm & Craft Village, Toledo Zoo, Yankee Air Museum, antiques. **Additional Information:** Monroe County Convention & Tourism Bureau, (800) 252-3011.

## RESTRICTIONS

**Pets:** Leash only, $2 extra. **Fires:** Fire rings only; must be extinguished by 11 p.m. **Alcoholic Beverages:** At sites only. **Vehicle Maximum Length:** 40 ft.

## TO GET THERE

From the junction of US 23 and Hwy. 50, drive 9 mi. south on US 23, then 200 yards southeast on Summerfield Rd., then 10 yards east on Tunnicliffe Rd. Roads are wide and well maintained w/ broad shoulders.

# PETERSBURG

## Pirolli Park

6030 Sylvania-Petersburg Rd., Petersburg 49270. T: (734) 279-1487

🚐 ★★★                    ⛺ ★★★

| | |
|---|---|
| Beauty: ★★★ | Site Privacy: ★★★ |
| Spaciousness: ★★★ | Quiet: ★★★ |
| Security: ★★★★ | Cleanliness: ★★★ |
| Insect Control: Yes | Facilities: ★★★ |

When leaving Pirolli Park, visitors are not only bade farewell and asked to drive safely, they are also given directions to US 23. Every major stop also has signs directing travelers to the main road. More campgrounds should pick up on that useful idea. Laid out in a series of loops, the campground has 45 seasonal campers, 20 pull-through sites and a typical site width of 30 feet. Sites are level and mostly shaded. Located two miles south of Petersburg, the campground does not allow outside firewood to be brought into the area because of infectious tree diseases such as Dutch Elm Disease and because of gypsy moths. Firewood is for sale at the campground. Scheduled activities include such creative themes as cowboys-and-Indians weekend (where children make their own Native American headdress and get an Native American name), grandparents weekend, and law enforcement weekends. Security includes one entrance/exit road, owners who live on site, and regular campground patrols.

## BASICS

**Operated by:** James & Pat Pirolli. **Open:** All year. **Site Assignment:** Reservations w/ 1-night deposit; refund w/ 7-day notice. **Registration:** At campground office. **Fee:** $29 (cash, check, credit cards). **Parking:** At site.

## FACILITIES

**Number of RV Sites:** 200. **Number of Tent-Only Sites:** 50. **Hookups:** Electric (20, 30, 50 amps), water, sewer. **Each Site:** Picnic table, fire ring. **Dump Station:** Yes. **Laundry:** Yes. **Pay**

**Phone:** Yes. **Rest Rooms and Showers:** Yes. **Fuel:** No. **Propane:** Yes. **Internal Roads:** Paved/gravel, in good condition. **RV Service:** No. **Market:** 2 mi. north in Petersburg. **Restaurant:** 2 mi. north in Petersburg. **General Store:** Yes, well equipped, also sells beer, wine & liquor. **Vending:** Yes. **Swimming Pool:** No. **Playground:** Yes. **Other:** Swimming lake, fishing lake, sports field, horseshoes, volleyball, pavilion, rec hall, driving range, pavilion. **Activities:** Swimming, fishing, scheduled weekend activities. **Nearby Attractions:** Golf, Cabela's, Cedar Point, Toledo Center of Science & Industry, Greenfield Village, Monroe Co. Historical Museum, River Raisin Battlefield, Sauder Farm & Craft Village, Toledo Zoo, Yankee Air Museum, antiques. **Additional Information:** Monroe County Convention & Tourism Bureau, (800) 252-3011.

## RESTRICTIONS

**Pets:** Leash only, no rottweilers, chows, pitbulls, dobermans, German Shepherds are allowed. **Fires:** Fire ring only. **Alcoholic Beverages:** At sites only. **Vehicle Maximum Length:** 50 ft.

## TO GET THERE

From the junction of US 23 and Summerfield Rd., take Exit 9, drive 0.25 mi. north on Summerfield Rd., then 1.5 mi. west on Teal Rd., then 1.5 mi. southwest on Ida Center Rd., then 0.25 mi. south on Sylvania-Petersburg Rd. Roads are generally wide and well maintained w/ broad shoulders, sometimes becoming narrow shoulders.

## PETERSBURG

### Totem Pole Park

16333 Lulu Rd., Petersburg 49270. T: (800) 227-2110; F: (734) 279-2113; totem@cass.net.

| 🚐 ★★★ | 🅰 ★★★ |
|---|---|
| Beauty: ★★★ | Site Privacy: ★★★ |
| Spaciousness: ★★★ | Quiet: ★★★★ |
| Security: ★★★★ | Cleanliness: ★★★★ |
| Insect Control: None | Facilities: ★★★ |

A rural campground with open and shaded sites, Totem Pole Park is located three miles east of Petersburg. Laid out in a series of loops, the campground has 65 seasonal campers, 13 pull-through sites, and a typical site width of 35 feet. A nice playground features a wooden train and wooden fort. No motors are allowed on the lake, nor are metal, wooden or fiberglass boats. The lake area closes at dark. Most popular RV sites are the 13 pull-throughs. The best tent sites are 120–130 which are grassy and wooded, and offer more privacy. The speed limit is five mph, and no off-road vehicles such as motorcyles and ATVs are allowed. Quiet hours are 11 p.m. to 9 a.m. The campground adjoins state game land and offers a sandy bottom lake for swimming. Security includes one entrance/exit road and owners who live on site and offer patrols of the campground.

## BASICS

**Operated by:** Carl & Joyce Laming. **Open:** Apr. 15–Oct. 15. **Site Assignment:** Reservations w/ 1-night deposit; refund (minus $5) w/ 7-day notice. **Registration:** At campground office. **Fee:** $24 (cash, check, credit cards). **Parking:** At site.

## FACILITIES

**Number of RV Sites:** 119. **Number of Tent-Only Sites:** 11. **Hookups:** Electric (30, 50 amps), water, sewer. **Each Site:** Picnic table, fire ring. **Dump Station:** Yes. **Laundry:** No. **Pay Phone:** Yes. **Rest Rooms and Showers:** Yes. **Fuel:** No. **Propane:** No. **Internal Roads:** Gravel, in good condition. **RV Service:** No. **Market:** 10 mi. north in Dundee. **Restaurant:** 3 mi. west in Petersburg. **General Store:** Yes. **Vending:** Yes. **Swimming Pool:** No. **Playground:** Yes. **Other:** Swimming beach, pond fishing, basketball, horseshoes, sand volleyball, rental cabins, shuffleboard, pavilion, sports field. **Activities:** Swimming, fishing, scheduled weekend activities. **Nearby Attractions:** Golf, Cabela's, Cedar Point, Toledo Center of Science & Industry, Greenfield Village, Monroe Co. Historical Museum, River Raisin Battlefield, Sauders Farm & Craft Village, Toledo Zoo, Yankee Air Museum, antiques. **Additional Information:** Monroe County Convention & Tourism Bureau, (800) 252-3011.

## RESTRICTIONS

**Pets:** Leash only. **Fires:** Fire ring only. **Alcoholic Beverages:** Permitted. **Vehicle Maximum Length:** None.

## TO GET THERE

From the junction of US 23 and Summerfield Rd., take Exit 9, drive 2.5 mi. north on Summerfield Rd., then 0.25 mi. west on Lulu Rd. Summerfield Rd. is paved but bumpy; Lulu Rd. has a rough gravel surface.

## PETOSKEY
### Petoskey KOA

1800 North US 31, Petoskey 49770. T: (800) 933-1574; www.petoskeykoa.com; petkoa@msn.com.

🚐 ★★★★★          ▲ ★★★★

| | |
|---|---|
| Beauty: ★★★★★ | Site Privacy: ★★★★★ |
| Spaciousness: ★★★★★ | Quiet: ★★★★★ |
| Security: ★★★★★ | Cleanliness: ★★★★★ |
| Insect Control: ★★★★★ | Facilities: ★★★★★ |

In a vacation wonderland, Petoskey KOA is a camper's dream. Facilities are top-notch, cleanliness is A+, activities are varied and many, security and safety measures are excellent, and the folks who run the campground are friendly and hardworking. Campers return again and again to this Petoskey campground, and begin to feel part of the Rose family. Laid out in a series of loops, the campground offers level, open, and shaded sites in sloping and level terrain. There are 31 pull-through sites. Nice landscaping and attention to detail make Petoskey KOA a pleasure to see. No mats or carpets are permitted on grass or ground to keep the area nice. A recreation and activities director has a wealth of programs, including nature programs to educate as well as entertain. A gazebo kitchen with electric cooking burners, sinks, and picnic tables is a welcome facility for campers. A Fun Bus makes it easy to catch the shuttle and leave your car at home or parked with the camper. Security measures include a card-coded gate. A speed limit of five mph is enforced.

### BASICS
**Operated by:** The Rose Family. **Open:** Apr. 27–Oct. 15. **Site Assignment:** Reservations w/ 1-night deposit; refund w/ 2-week notice. **Registration:** At campground office. **Fee:** $30 (cash, check, credit cards). **Parking:** At site.

### FACILITIES
**Number of RV Sites:** 169. **Number of Tent-Only Sites:** 6. **Hookups:** Electric (20, 30, 50 amps), water, sewer, phone, cable TV. **Each Site:** Picnic table, fire ring. **Dump Station:** Yes. **Laundry:** Yes. **Pay Phone:** Yes. **Rest Rooms and Showers:** Yes. **Fuel:** No. **Propane:** Yes. **Internal Roads:** Paved/gravel, in good condition. **RV Service:** No. **Market:** 1 mi. **Restaurant:** 1 mi. **General Store:** Yes. **Vending:** Yes. **Swimming Pool:** Yes. **Playground:** Yes. **Other:** Hot tub, horseshoes, rec hall, sports field, rental cabins, game room, movies, rental cottages, coin games, volleyball, nature classes, recreation & activities director, local tours, rental cottages, shuttle bus, rental cars. **Activities:** Swimming, schedule activities. **Nearby Attractions:** Golf, marina, go-carts, bike trails, horseback riding, scenue drives, Lake Michigan Beach, Mackinac Island, casino, Tunnel of Trees Drive, Bay View historic community, Little Traverse Bay, antiques, Little Traverse Historical Museum. **Additional Information:** Petoskey/Harbor Springs/Boyne County Visitors Bureau, (800) 845-2828.

### RESTRICTIONS
**Pets:** Leash only. **Fires:** Fire ring only. **Alcoholic Beverages:** Permitted. **Vehicle Maximum Length:** None.

### TO GET THERE
From the junction of Hwy. 119 and US 31, drive 1 mi. north on US 31. Roads are wide and well maintained w/ broad shoulders.

## PORT HURON
### Fort Trodd Family Campground Resort

6350 Lapeer Rd., Clyde 48049. T: (810) 987-4889

🚐 ★★★★          ▲ n/a

| | |
|---|---|
| Beauty: ★★★★ | Site Privacy: ★★★★ |
| Spaciousness: ★★★★ | Quiet: ★★★★ |
| Security: ★★★★ | Cleanliness: ★★★★★ |
| Insect Control: ★★★★★ | Facilities: ★★★★ |

A campground can't get much more convenient than Fort Trodd Family Campground Resort, just a stone's throw from I-69. The grassy campground is nicely landscaped with a typical site width of 30 feet. Situated beside a 40-acre, spring-fed lake, the campground has three swimming beaches. The lake is stocked with largemouth bass and northern pike. Air-conditioned camping cabins for rent on an island are a nice addition. Located six miles west of Port Huron, the campground has 65 seasonal sites and 26 pull-throughs. Sites are a mix of paved, gravel, or grass with open or shade. Be aware that no tents are allowed. Facilities are sparkling-clean and well maintained. A group camping area is available with a pavilion. Security measures include a card-coded security gate.

## BASICS

**Operated by:** Tom & Kathy Hess. **Open:** May 1–Sept. 30. **Site Assignment:** Reservations w/ 1-night deposit; refund w/ 7-day notice. **Registration:** At campground office. **Fee:** $28 (cash, check, credit cards). **Parking:** At site.

## FACILITIES

**Number of RV Sites:** 185. **Number of Tent-Only Sites:** 0. **Hookups:** Electric (20, 30, 50 amps), water, sewer. **Each Site:** Picnic table, fire ring. **Dump Station:** Yes. **Laundry:** Yes. **Pay Phone:** Yes. **Rest Rooms and Showers:** Yes. **Fuel:** No. **Propane:** No. **Internal Roads:** Paved, in good condition. **RV Service:** No. **Market:** Two blocks. **Restaurant:** Two blocks. **General Store:** Yes. **Vending:** Yes. **Swimming Pool:** No. **Playground:** Yes. **Other:** Lake Tomka, 3 swimming beaches, rental cabin, pavilion, rec hall, coin games, basketball, shuffleboard, tennis, badminton, sports field, horseshoes, hiking trials, volleyball. **Activities:** Swimming, hiking, fishing, boating (rental canoes, kayaks, paddleboats available), scheduled weekend activities. **Nearby Attractions:** Parks, Fort Gratiot Lighthouse, Huron Lightship Museum, historic district, antiques, arts & crafts, golf, Port Huron Museum, Canadian International Border. **Additional Information:** Blue Water Area CVB, (800) 852-4242.

## RESTRICTIONS

**Pets:** Leash only. **Fires:** Fire ring only. **Alcoholic Beverages:** Permitted. **Vehicle Maximum Length:** None. **Other:** No tents allowed.

## TO GET THERE

From the junction of I-69 and Barth Rd., take Exit 194 and drive 500 feet north on Barth Rd. Roads are wide and well maintained w/ broad shoulders.

## PORT HURON

### Port Huron KOA

5111 Lapeer Rd., Kimball 48074. T: (810) 987-4070; www.koa.com/where/mi; phkoa@aol.com.

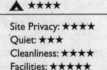

🚐 ★★★★                          ⛺ ★★★★

Beauty: ★★★★            Site Privacy: ★★★★
Spaciousness: ★★★★      Quiet: ★★★
Security: ★★★★★         Cleanliness: ★★★★
Insect Control: ★★★★    Facilities: ★★★★★

Just a stone's throw from the Canadian border, Port Huron KOA is a combination amusement park/campground. Located five miles west of Port Huron, the campground has enough activities to keep anyone hopping from morning into the night. Many of the activities like hayrides, train rides and movies are free but many others will need a ready supply of coins. Air conditioned rest rooms, a western town and two swimming pools are nice touches, as are the 1–6 passenger rental bikes. Sites are mostly level with a choice of open or heavily shaded. The campground has 56 pull-throughs and a typical site width of 42 feet. A separate area for tents allows for more privacy and green space. The best sites depend on what the goal of the camper is—if it's to enjoy all the activities with children, then sites close to the recreation are best; if it's to get some peace and commune with nature, then stay as far away from the recreation as possible. A traffic control gate helps with security.

## BASICS

**Operated by:** Private Operator. **Open:** Apr. 1–Oct. 31. **Site Assignment:** Reservations w/ 1-night deposit; refund w/ 2-week notice. **Registration:** At campground office. **Fee:** $28 (cash, check, credit cards). **Parking:** At site.

## FACILITIES

**Number of RV Sites:** 313. **Number of Tent-Only Sites:** 33. **Hookups:** Electric (20, 30, 50 amps), water, sewer, phone, cable TV. **Each Site:** Picnic table, fire ring. **Dump Station:** Yes. **Laundry:** Yes. **Pay Phone:** Yes. **Rest Rooms and Showers:** Yes. **Fuel:** No. **Propane:** No. **Internal Roads:** Paved/gravel, in good condition. **RV Service:** No. **Market:** 1 mi. **Restaurant:** 1 mi. **General Store:** Yes. **Vending:** Yes. **Swimming Pool:** Yes. **Playground:** Yes. **Other:** Adventure golf, batting cages, bumper boats, game room, Western Town, go-kart track, soccer, tennis, in-line skating rink, sports shop, Pursuit Park Paint Ball, rental cottages, train rides, pavilion, coin games, sports field, horseshoes, hiking trails, volleyball, basketball, baseball. **Activities:** Swimming, hiking, scheduled activities, movies. **Nearby Attractions:** Parks, Fort Gratiot Lighthouse, Huron Lightship Museum, historic district, antiques, arts & crafts, golf, Port Huron Museum, Canadian International. **Additional Information:** Blue River Area CVB, (800) 852-4242.

## RESTRICTIONS

**Pets:** Leash only. **Fires:** Fire ring only. **Alcoholic Beverages:** Permitted. **Vehicle Maximum Length:** None.

## TO GET THERE

From the junction of I-69 and Wadhams Rd., take Exit 196 and drive 0.5 mi. north on Wadhams Rd., then 0.25 mi. east on Lapeer Rd. Roads are mostly wide and well maintained w/ adequate shoulders.

## QUINCY

### Cottonwood Resort

801 West Wildwood Rd., Quincy 49082. T: (517) 639-4415

★★★★           ▲ ★★★★

| | |
|---|---|
| Beauty: ★★★★ | Site Privacy: ★★★ |
| Spaciousness: ★★★ | Quiet: ★★★★ |
| Security: ★★★ | Cleanliness: ★★★★ |
| Insect Control: None | Facilities: ★★★ |

Marble Lake is the centerpiece of Cottonwood Resort, located eight miles southeast of Coldwater. The lake leads into Branch County's Chain of Lakes, offering 2,500 acres of water in six lakes for fishing and water activities. A rural campground with shaded level sites, Cottonwood has 78 of its sites occupied by seasonal campers, leaving 15 for short-term campers. The typical site width is 25 feet, and the campground has four pull-throughs. Quiet time is 11 p.m. to 7 a.m., and the speed limit is five mph. The campground offers easy access from the interstate but, be sure to check that a site is available before planning to stop. Owners live on site to help with security measures.

### BASICS

**Operated by:** Barney & Eunice Pohl, Roy, Darla & Bailey Pohl. **Open:** May 1–Oct. 15. **Site Assignment:** Reservations w/ 1-night deposit; refund w/ 7-day notice. **Registration:** At campground office. **Fee:** $24 (cash, check). **Parking:** At site.

### FACILITIES

**Number of RV Sites:** 93. **Number of Tent-Only Sites:** 4. **Hookups:** Electric (30 amps), water, sewer. **Each Site:** Picnic table, fire ring. **Dump Station:** Yes. **Laundry:** No. **Pay Phone:** Yes. **Rest Rooms and Showers:** Yes. **Fuel:** No. **Propane:** Yes. **Internal Roads:** Gravel, in good condition. **RV Service:** No. **Market:** 8 mi. northwest in Coldwater. **Restaurant:** 8 mi. northwest in Coldwater. **General Store:** Yes, limited. **Vending:** Yes. **Swimming Pool:** No. **Playground:** Yes. **Other:** Marble Lake, swimming beach, rental cot-

tages, horseshoes, rec hall, video games, volleyball, boat ramp, sports field. **Activities:** Swimming, fishing, boating (rental fishing boats available). **Nearby Attractions:** Bowling, golf, summer theater, Branch County Historical Society, antiques, drive-in theaters, motor speedway, historic homes, museums, arts & crafts shops. **Additional Information:** Branch County Tourism Bureau, (800) 969-9333.

### RESTRICTIONS

**Pets:** Leash only. **Fires:** Fire ring only. **Alcoholic Beverages:** Permitted. **Vehicle Maximum Length:** None.

### TO GET THERE

From the junction of I-69 and US 12; drive 4.75 mi. east on US 12, then 2.25 mi. south on Main St. and Ray Quincy Rd., then 1 mi. west on Wildwood Rd. Roads are wide and well maintained w/ broad shoulders.

## RAPID RIVER

### Whitefish Hill Mobile Home & RV Park

8455 US 2, Rapid River 49878. T: (800) 476-6515; whtfish@up.net.

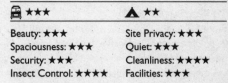

★★★           ▲ ★★

| | |
|---|---|
| Beauty: ★★★ | Site Privacy: ★★★ |
| Spaciousness: ★★★ | Quiet: ★★★ |
| Security: ★★★ | Cleanliness: ★★★★ |
| Insect Control: ★★★★ | Facilities: ★★★ |

An RV area in a mobile home park, Whitefish Hill Mobile Home & RV Park is just one-and-a-half miles from access waters to Little Bay De Noc. Located two miles east of Rapid River, the campground offers open, level, grassy sites with eight pull-throughs. The typical site width is 30 feet. A nice benefit is facilities that are open 24 hours a day. The focal point of the park is an old barn that houses an office, showers, small kitchen, and activity room. The campground is a popular base for fishing and hunting. Whitefish Hill opens earlier in the season and stays open later than many other campgrounds, which makes it handy for outdoor enthusiasts who want a home base that is modern rather than rustic. Security includes owners who live on site and keep an eye on the campground.

### BASICS

**Operated by:** Ed & Pat Violette. **Open:** Apr. 30–Nov. 30. **Site Assignment:** Reservations w/ 1-

night deposit; refund w/ 7-day notice. **Registration:** At campground office. **Fee:** $25 (cash, check, credit cards). **Parking:** At site.

## FACILITIES

**Number of RV Sites:** 23. **Number of Tent-Only Sites:** 2. **Hookups:** Electric (30, 50 amps), water, sewer, cable TV, phone. **Each Site:** Picnic table, fire ring. **Dump Station:** Yes. **Laundry:** Yes. **Pay Phone:** Yes. **Rest Rooms and Showers:** Yes. **Fuel:** No. **Propane:** No. **Internal Roads:** Paved/gravel, in good condition. **RV Service:** No. **Market:** 1 mi. **Restaurant:** 1 mi. **General Store:** No. **Vending:** Yes. **Swimming Pool:** No. **Playground:** Yes. **Other:** Game room, rental RVs, sports field, horseshoes, basketball, sauna, fish-cleaning station. **Activities:** None. **Nearby Attractions:** Little Bay De Noc, fishing, swimming, boating, scenic drives, Lake Michigan, Delta County Historical Museum, Sandpoint Lighthouse, antiques, arts & crafts. **Additional Information:** Delta County Area Chamber of Commerce, (888) 335-8264.

## RESTRICTIONS

**Pets:** Leash only. **Fires:** Fire ring only. **Alcoholic Beverages:** Permitted. **Vehicle Maximum Length:** None.

## TO GET THERE

From US 2 and US 41, drive 2.5 mi. east on US 2. Roads are wide and well maintained w/ adequate shoulders.

## ROSCOMMON

### Higgins Hills RV Park

3800 West Federal Hwy., Roscommon 48653. T: (800) 478-8151; www.michcampgrounds.com/ higginshills; snow@snowshoecenter.com.

| 🚐 ★★★★ | ⛺ ★★★★ |
|---|---|
| Beauty: ★★★★ | Site Privacy: ★★★★ |
| Spaciousness: ★★★★ | Quiet: ★★★★ |
| Security: ★★★★ | Cleanliness: ★★★★ |
| Insect Control: ★★★★ | Facilities: ★★★★ |

Location is everything, and Higgins Hills RV Park certainly has it. With easy access to I-75 and US 27, the campground is in a large lake resort area. Year-round activities abound, and Higgins Hills is open all year with limited facilities in the winter. One mile east of Higgins Hills, the campground offers level, shaded sites with a typical site width of 30 feet. There are 35 seasonal campers and 32 pull-through sites. The campground has abundant natural hardwoods and pine trees, deer, and other wildlife. It's only minutes to Higgins Lake and Au Sable River, and there are groomed snowmobile trails as well as cross-country and downhill skiing. The campground also is home to the Michigan Snowshoe Center, which offers a large selection of snowshoes and sporting equipment. Facilities are very clean, and owners provide on-site security.

## BASICS

**Operated by:** The Carr Family. **Open:** All year. **Site Assignment:** Reservations w/ 1-night deposit; refund w/ 7-day notice. **Registration:** At campground office. **Fee:** $25 (cash, check, credit cards). **Parking:** At site.

## FACILITIES

**Number of RV Sites:** 92. **Number of Tent-Only Sites:** 8. **Hookups:** Electric (20, 30 amps), water, sewer, phone. **Each Site:** Picnic table, fire ring. **Dump Station:** Yes. **Laundry:** Yes. **Pay Phone:** Yes. **Rest Rooms and Showers:** Yes. **Fuel:** No. **Propane:** Yes. **Internal Roads:** Gravel, in good condition. **RV Service:** No. **Market:** 1 mi. **Restaurant:** 1 mi. **General Store:** Yes. **Vending:** Yes. **Swimming Pool:** No. **Playground:** Yes. **Other:** Rec room, coin games, basketball, shuffleboard, badminton, sports field, volleyball, horseshoes, hiking trails, rental cabins, rental RVs. **Activities:** Hiking, scheduled weekend activities. **Nearby Attractions:** Higgins Lake, AuSable River, fishing, canoeing, hunting, Wellington Farm Park, state parks, golf, fish hatchery, bowling, antiques, arts & crafts. **Additional Information:** Higgins Lake-Roscommon Chamber of Commerce, (989) 275-8760.

## RESTRICTIONS

**Pets:** Leash only. **Fires:** Fire ring only. **Alcoholic Beverages:** Permitted. **Vehicle Maximum Length:** None.

## TO GET THERE

From the junction of I-75 and Old Hwy. 76, take Exit 244 and drive 1.25 mi. west on Old Hwy. 76. Roads are wide and well maintained w/ adequate shoulders.

## SAULT ST. MARIE
## Soo Locks Campground & RV Park

1001 East Portage Ave., Sault Ste. Marie 49783. T: (906) 632-3191

🚐 ★★★★          ⛺ ★★★

Beauty: ★★★
Spaciousness: ★★★
Security: ★★★★
Insect Control: ★★★★

Site Privacy: ★★★
Quiet: ★★★★
Cleanliness: ★★★★
Facilities: ★★★

Watch the freighters travel through Soo Locks from your campsite at Soo Locks Campground & RV Park in Sault Ste. Marie. With sites on St. Mary's River, the facility is the closest campground to the locks. Sites are mostly open and grassy, with a typical site width of 25 feet. Campers also can walk to the locks and watch ships pass through. Restaurants and other facilities are within one block. The campground has ten pull-through sites. Complimentary coffee is a nice welcoming touch. Facilities are very clean and well maintained, and owners provide good security. The best sites are closest to the river. Be aware that the area can be quite cold in May and in Oct. when the campground is open. The camping experience is definitely worth it, but be sure and bring plenty of warm blankets and clothing if camping during those times.

### BASICS

**Operated by:** Bob & Helen Collia. **Open:** May 1–Oct. 20. **Site Assignment:** Reservations w/ 1-night deposit; refund (minus $5) w/ 2-week notice. **Registration:** At campground office. **Fee:** $23 (cash, check, credit cards). **Parking:** At site.

### FACILITIES

**Number of RV Sites:** 100. **Number of Tent-Only Sites:** 0. **Hookups:** Electric (20, 30 amps), water. **Each Site:** Picnic table, fire ring. **Dump Station:** Yes. **Laundry:** Yes. **Pay Phone:** Yes. **Rest Rooms and Showers:** Yes. **Fuel:** No. **Propane:** No. **Internal Roads:** Paved/gravel, in good condition. **RV Service:** No. **Market:** 1 block. **Restaurant:** 1 block. **General Store:** Yes. **Vending:** Yes. **Swimming Pool:** No. **Playground:** Yes. **Other:** St. Mary's River, boat dock, rec room, coin games, adults room. **Activities:** Fishing, boating, boat tours. **Nearby Attractions:** Soo Locks, Locks Park Historic Walkway, Johnston Homestead, Museum Ship Valley Camp, River of History Museum, dinner cruises, boat tours, Tower of History, casino. **Additional Information:** Sault Area Chamber of Commerce & Convention & Bureau, (800) 647-2858.

### RESTRICTIONS

**Pets:** Leash only. **Fires:** Fire ring only. **Alcoholic Beverages:** Permitted. **Vehicle Maximum Length:** None.

### TO GET THERE

From the junction of I-75 and Easterday, take Exit 394 and drive 10.1 mi. west on Easterday, then 3 mi. north and east on Portage. Roads are wide and well maintained w/ adequate shoulders.

## SMYRNA
## Double R Ranch Camping Resort

4424 Whites Bridge Rd., Smyrna 48887. T: (800) 734-3575; www.doubleranch.com; rrranch@pathwaynet.com.

🚐 ★★★★          ⛺ ★★★★

Beauty: ★★★★
Spaciousness: ★★★★
Security: ★★★★
Insect Control: ★★★★

Site Privacy: ★★★★
Quiet: ★★★★
Cleanliness: ★★★★
Facilities: ★★★★

Double R Ranch Resort Campground is a ranch, resort, and campground with so much going for it, it's hard to know where to start. As a resort, it has a full slate of activities, like two heated swimming pools as well as a river and a variety of water sports. As a ranch, it has horses and one of West Michigan's best trail rides over hills, along forest paths, and fording streams, plus a bunkhouse where guests can enjoy the Wild West without roughing it. As a campground, it features camping by the river. Sites are mostly grassy and level, with a typical site width of 40 feet. The campground has ten seasonal sites and ten pull-throughs. Located 20 miles from Grand Rapids, the campground has a choice of open or shaded sites. The best sites are the wooded ones along Flat River. The Ironhorse golf course alone draws plenty of golfers with its 3,365-yard championship golf course.

### BASICS

**Operated by:** Richard & Mary Reeves. **Open:** May 1–Sept. 15. **Site Assignment:** Reservations w/ $25 deposit; refund w/ 2-week notice. **Registration:** At campground office. **Fee:** $25 (cash, check, credit cards). **Parking:** At site.

## FACILITIES

**Number of RV Sites:** 100. **Number of Tent-Only Sites:** 0. **Hookups:** Electric (20, 30 amps), water, sewer. **Each Site:** Picnic table, fire ring. **Dump Station:** Yes. **Laundry:** Yes. **Pay Phone:** Yes. **Rest Rooms and Showers:** Yes. **Fuel:** No. **Propane:** No. **Internal Roads:** Gravel, in good condition. **RV Service:** No. **Market:** 2 mi. **Restaurant:** 2 mi. **General Store:** Yes. **Vending:** Yes. **Swimming Pool:** Yes. **Playground:** Yes. **Other:** Flat River, rec hall, rec room, coin games, boat ramp, float trips, basketball, horseback riding trails, badminton, sports field, horseshoes, hiking trails, volleyball, snack bar, adult lounge, rental chalets, motel, 9-hole golf course. **Activities:** Swimming, fishing, golf, hiking, boating (rental canoes available), horseback riding (rental horses available), tubing, scheduled weekend activities. **Nearby Attractions:** Gerald B. Ford Museum, Fredrick Meijer Gardens, zoo, Michigan Adventure Amusement Park, Roger B. Chaffee Planetarium, golf, tennis, rivers & lakes, antiques, Wooden Shoe Factory. **Additional Information:** Grand Rapids/Kent County CVB, (800) 678-9859.

## RESTRICTIONS

**Pets:** Leash only. **Fires:** Fire ring only. **Alcoholic Beverages:** Permitted. **Vehicle Maximum Length:** None.

## TO GET THERE

From the junction of Hwy. 91 and Hwy. 44, drive 100 yards west on Hwy. 44, then 3 mi. south on White Bridge Rd. Roads are wide and well maintained w/ adequate shoulders.

## ST. IGNACE

## Castle Rock Mackinac Trail Campark

2811 Mackinac Tr., St. Ignace 49781. T: (800) 333-8754; www.stignace.com/lodging/castlecamp.

🚐 ★★★★          ⛺ ★★★★

Beauty: ★★★★          Site Privacy: ★★★★
Spaciousness: ★★★★     Quiet: ★★★★
Security: ★★★★         Cleanliness: ★★★★
Insect Control: ★★★★    Facilities: ★★★★

The sunsets alone are worth a night at Castle Rock Mackinac Trail Campark. Sites are nestled between landscaped trees on Lake Huron with half a mile of lake frontage in view of Mackinac Island. Campsites are available on or off the beach. Castle Rock provides the only beach camping on Lake Huron with a Mackinac Island view. The campground features 2,000 feet of sandy beach. Sites are level and grassy with a typical site width of 30 feet. There are six pull-throughs and a choice of open or shaded. Less than a mile from the St. Ignace city limits, the campground is next to a federal forest with trails and bird-watching. A nearby casino and a ferry service for Mackinac Island offer free shuttle service from the campground. The most popular sites are on the beach. Reservations are strongly recommended. Security includes careful watches of the campground, along with the assistance of local law officials, if necessary.

## BASICS

**Operated by:** Charles & Delores Muscott. **Open:** May 15–Oct. 10. **Site Assignment:** Reservations w/ $10 deposit; refund w/ 3-day notice. **Registration:** At campground office. **Fee:** $20 (cash, check, credit cards). **Parking:** At site.

## FACILITIES

**Number of RV Sites:** 65. **Number of Tent-Only Sites:** 15. **Hookups:** Electric (20, 30, 50 amps), water, sewer. **Each Site:** Picnic table, fire ring. **Dump Station:** Yes. **Laundry:** Yes. **Pay Phone:** Yes. **Rest Rooms and Showers:** Yes. **Fuel:** No. **Propane:** No. **Internal Roads:** Paved/gravel, in good condition. **RV Service:** No. **Market:** Two blocks. **Restaurant:** Two blocks. **General Store:** Yes. **Vending:** Yes. **Swimming Pool:** No. **Playground:** Yes. **Other:** Sandy beach, rec room, fishing pond, coin games, boat ramp, boat dock, badminton, sports field, horseshoes, volleyball, free casino shuttle, free ferry shuttle. **Activities:** Swimming, fishing, boating, local tours. **Nearby Attractions:** Castle Rock, Mackinac Bridge, Mackinac Island, Mackinaw City, Deer Ranch, ice arena, golf, casino, Fort De Baude Indian Museum, Marquette Mission Park & Museum of Ojibwa Culture, New France Discovery Center & Father Marquette National Memorial, Soo Locks, Ft. Michillimackinac, Tahqomenon Falls. **Additional Information:** St. Ignace Tourism Assoc., (800) 338-6660.

## RESTRICTIONS

**Pets:** Leash only. **Fires:** Fire ring only. **Alcoholic Beverages:** Permitted. **Vehicle Maximum Length:** None.

## TO GET THERE

From I-75, take Exit 348, drive 0.25 mi. south, then 0.25 mi. north on Mackinac Tr. Roads are wide and well maintained w/ broad shoulders.

## ST. IGNACE

### St. Ignace/Mackinac Island KOA

1242 US 2 West, St. Ignace 49781. T: (906) 643-9303; www.koa.com/where/mi; simikoa@sault.com.

🚐 ★★★★                    ⛺ ★★★★

Beauty: ★★★★          Site Privacy: ★★★★
Spaciousness: ★★★★    Quiet: ★★★★
Security: ★★★★         Cleanliness: ★★★★★
Insect Control: ★★★★   Facilities: ★★★★

Located in the heart of Michigan vacationland, St. Ignace-Mackinac Island KOA offers easy access to I-75 and quality facilities. Sites are grassy, wooded, and secluded, with a typical site width of 50 feet, and 82 pull-throughs. Campers are greeted with a travel info packet when they register, and the friendly staff is very helpful in recommending local attractions. The campground has its own attractions—a free Indian museum and a wildlife zoo featuring a live fox, bobcat, peacock, and deer. Campers are invited to hand-feed the deer and take photos. The campground also offers free shuttles to the island ferries and casino. A separate rustic tent area provides more green space and privacy. Campground facilities are very clean, and landscaping shows extra attention to detail.

## BASICS

**Operated by:** Private Operator. **Open:** May 1–Oct. 31. **Site Assignment:** Reservations w/ 1-night deposit; refund w/ 3-day notice. **Registration:** At campground office. **Fee:** $28 (cash, check, credit cards). **Parking:** At site.

## FACILITIES

**Number of RV Sites:** 140. **Number of Tent-Only Sites:** 60. **Hookups:** Electric (20, 30 amps), water, sewer, phone. **Each Site:** Picnic table, fire ring. **Dump Station:** Yes. **Laundry:** Yes. **Pay Phone:** Yes. **Rest Rooms and Showers:** Yes. **Fuel:** No. **Propane:** No. **Internal Roads:** Gravel, in good condition. **RV Service:** No. **Market:** 1 mi. **Restaurant:** 1 mi. **General Store:** Yes. **Vending:** Yes. **Swimming Pool:** Yes. **Playground:** Yes. **Other:** Rec room, coin games, rental cabins, mini golf, badminton, sports field, hiking trails. **Activities:** Swimming, hiking, local tours, free shuttle to ferry & casino. **Nearby Attractions:** Castle Rock, Mackinac Bridge, Mackinac Island, Mackinaw City, Deer Ranch, ice arena, golf, casino, Fort De Baude Indian Museum, Marquette Mission Park & Museum of Ojibwa Culture, New France Discovery Center & Father Marquette National Memorial, Soo Locks, Ft. Michillimackinac, Tahqomenon Falls. **Additional Information:** St. Ignace Tourism Assoc., (800) 338-6660.

## RESTRICTIONS

**Pets:** Leash only. **Fires:** Fire ring only. **Alcoholic Beverages:** Permitted. **Vehicle Maximum Length:** Inquire ahead.

## TO GET THERE

From the junction of I-75 and US 2, take Exit 344B and drive 2 mi. west on US 2. Roads are wide and well maintained w/ broad shoulders.

## THOMPSON

### Driftwood Shores Resort & RV Park

US 2, Thompson 49854. T: (800) 788-3111; www.wmallory.com; wmallory@up.net.

🚐 ★★★★                    ⛺ n/a

Beauty: ★★★★          Site Privacy: ★★★★
Spaciousness: ★★★★    Quiet: ★★★★
Security: ★★★★         Cleanliness: ★★★★★
Insect Control: ★★★★★  Facilities: ★★★

For the right kind of camper, Driftwood Shores Resort & RV Park is a sparkling gem. Located on Lake Michigan six miles west of Manistique, the campground offers 500 feet of shoreline and a sandy beach with complimentary float tubes. The campground caters to campers ages 55 and up but is open to anyone. What campers won't find are coin games, playgrounds, and activities aimed at children. What campers will find is peaceful surroundings, great fishing and birding, and benches, swings, and gliders overlooking the lake. Campers also are welcome to complimentary videos and all the free driftwood they can burn. The campground got its name from the wealth of driftwood that continues to wash up on its shores. The driftwood is the legacy of a sawmill that used to be nearby in the 1880s. It closed in the 1930s, but the driftwood keeps coming, enough for campers to take home as souvenirs, artists to gather up for painting and carving, and still enough left over for campfires. A huge stone fireplace is available for everyone to enjoy. Security measures include owners who live on site and offer regular patrols of the campground.

## BASICS

**Operated by:** Bill & Diane Mallory. **Open:** May 1–Oct. 31. **Site Assignment:** Reservations w/ full pay; refund w/ 2-week notice. **Registration:** At campground office. **Fee:** $18 (cash, check, credit cards). **Parking:** At site.

## FACILITIES

**Number of RV Sites:** 23. **Number of Tent-Only Sites:** 0. **Hookups:** Electric (30, 50 amps), water. **Each Site:** Picnic table, fire ring. **Dump Station:** Yes. **Laundry:** Yes. **Pay Phone:** Yes. **Rest Rooms and Showers:** Yes. **Fuel:** No. **Propane:** No. **Internal Roads:** Gravel, in good condition. **RV Service:** No. **Market:** 2 mi. **Restaurant:** 2 mi. **General Store:** No. **Vending:** No. **Swimming Pool:** No. **Playground:** No. **Other:** Lake Michigan, sandy beach, sports field, rental cabins, rental lodge rooms. **Activities:** Swimming, fishing, boating. **Nearby Attractions:** Lighthouse, maritime musem, golf, fish hatchery, state parks, antiques, Seney Wildlife Refuge, Big Spring, Siphon Bridge, snowmobile trails, casino, scenic drive. **Additional Information:** Schoolcraft County Chamber of Commerce, (906) 341-5010.

## RESTRICTIONS

**Pets:** Leash only. **Fires:** Fire ring only. **Alcoholic Beverages:** Permitted. **Vehicle Maximum Length:** None.

## TO GET THERE

From the junction of Hwy. 149 and US 2 and Little Harbor Rd., drive 0.5 mi. south on Thompson Rd. Roads are mainly wide and well maintained w/ adequate shoulders.

## TIPTON

### Ja Do Campground

5603 US 12, Tipton 49287. T: (517) 431-2111; F: (517) 431-2390; www.michcampgrounds.com/jado.

🚐 ★★★　　　🅰 ★★★

Beauty: ★★★
Spaciousness: ★★★★
Security: ★★★★
Insect Control: ★★★★

Site Privacy: ★★★★
Quiet: ★★★★
Cleanliness: ★★★★
Facilities: ★★★

Nestled in rolling hills in Tipton, Ja Do Campground offers open and shaded sites with a typical site width of 50 feet. Laid out in a series of loops, the campground has primitive sites with more green space and privacy for tent campers. The campground has 30 seasonal campers. A stocked fishing pond set in the woods has a nature trail leading to it. Quiet hours are 11 p.m. to 7 a.m., when all children must be at sites. No loud music is allowed at any time. Motorcycles, ATVs, minibikes, and scooters cannot be ridden in the campground. No bike riding is allowed after dark. Speed limit is ten mph, a bit high for such a family-friendly campground. Security is good, with owners keeping a close watch on the campground.

## BASICS

**Operated by:** Doug & Kay Miller. **Open:** May 1–Oct. 15. **Site Assignment:** Reservations w/ 1-night deposit; refund (minus $5) w/ 5-day notice. **Registration:** At campground office. **Fee:** $23 (cash, check, credit cards). **Parking:** At site.

## FACILITIES

**Number of RV Sites:** 100. **Number of Tent-Only Sites:** 30. **Hookups:** Electric (30, 50 amps), water, sewer, phone. **Each Site:** Picnic table, fire ring. **Dump Station:** Yes. **Laundry:** Yes. **Pay Phone:** Yes. **Rest Rooms and Showers:** Yes. **Fuel:** No. **Propane:** Yes. **Internal Roads:** Gravel, in good condition. **RV Service:** No. **Market:** 1 mi. **Restaurant:** 1 mi. **General Store:** Yes, limited. **Vending:** Yes. **Swimming Pool:** No. **Playground:** Yes. **Other:** Pond, basketball, horseshoes, hiking trails, volleyball. **Activities:** Fishing. **Nearby Attractions:** Michigan International Speedway, Irish Hills, golf, Mystery Hill, Adventure golf, waterskiing, Prehistoric Forest, Lenawee Historical Museum, Hudson Museum, St. Joseph's Shrine, Stagecoach Stop USA, Irish Hills Towers. **Additional Information:** Lenawee Conference & Visitors Bureau, (800) 682-6580.

## RESTRICTIONS

**Pets:** Leash only. **Fires:** Fire ring only. **Alcoholic Beverages:** Permitted. **Vehicle Maximum Length:** 40 ft.

## TO GET THERE

From the junction of US 12 and Hwy. 52, drive 4.5 mi. west on US 12. Roads are wide and well maintained w/ adequate shoulders.

## TRAVERSE CITY
### Holiday Park Campground

4860 US 31 South, Traverse City 49864. T: (231)
943-4410; www.michcampgrounds.com/holidaypark.

🚐 ★★★★          ⛺ ★★★★

| | |
|---|---|
| Beauty: ★★★★ | Site Privacy: ★★★★ |
| Spaciousness: ★★★★ | Quiet: ★★★★ |
| Security: ★★★★ | Cleanliness: ★★★★ |
| Insect Control: ★★★★ | Facilities: ★★★★ |

Nestled in a forest on the shores of Silver Lake, Holiday Park Campground offers quiet, level campsites with a choice of open or shade. Laid out in a loop, the campground has a typical site width of 35 feet, with 16 pull-throughs. Located seven miles south of Traverse City, the campground is open year-round with limited facilities in the winter. The best sites are on the lakefront—sites 66–75—which have full hookups. Other sites also are available on the lake, where campers can see some grand sunsets. A sandy beach offers nice swimming. Facilities are clean and well maintained and feature such landscaping touches as a split-rail fence and flower beds.

### BASICS
**Operated by:** Private Operator. **Open:** All year. **Site Assignment:** Reservations w/ 1-night deposit; refund w/ 7-day notice. **Registration:** At campground office. **Fee:** $35 (cash, check, credit cards). **Parking:** At site.

### FACILITIES
**Number of RV Sites:** 154. **Number of Tent-Only Sites:** 0. **Hookups:** Electric (20, 30 amps), water, sewer, phone. **Each Site:** Picnic table, fire ring. **Dump Station:** Yes. **Laundry:** Yes. **Pay Phone:** Yes. **Rest Rooms and Showers:** Yes. **Fuel:** No. **Propane:** Yes. **Internal Roads:** Paved/gravel, in good condition. **RV Service:** No. **Market:** 3 mi. **Restaurant:** 3 mi. **General Store:** Yes. **Vending:** Yes. **Swimming Pool:** No. **Playground:** Yes. **Other:** Silver Lake, sandy beach, boat ramp, boat dock, basketball, badminton, horseshoes, volleyball, sports field. **Activities:** Swimming, fishing, boating (rental rowboats, kayaks, paddleboats). **Nearby Attractions:** Grand Traverse Bay, Interlochen Music Camp, Sleeping Bear Sand Dunes, casinos, golf, outlet mall, cherry orchards, beaches, winter sports, Old Mission, parks, replica schooner, museums, wineries. **Additional Information:** Traverse City CVB, (800) 872-8377.

### RESTRICTIONS
**Pets:** Leash only. **Fires:** Fire ring only. **Alcoholic Beverages:** Permitted. **Vehicle Maximum Length:** None.

### TO GET THERE
From south junction Hwy. 37 and US 31, drive 1 mi. west on US 31. Roads are wide and well maintained w/ adequate shoulders.

## TRAVERSE CITY
### Timber Ridge Campground

4050 Hammond Rd., Traverse City 49686. T: (800)
909-2327; www.michcampgrounds.com/timberridge;
timberrg@traverse.net.

🚐 ★★★★          ⛺ ★★★★

| | |
|---|---|
| Beauty: ★★★★ | Site Privacy: ★★★★ |
| Spaciousness: ★★★★ | Quiet: ★★★★ |
| Security: ★★★★ | Cleanliness: ★★★★ |
| Insect Control: ★★★★ | Facilities: ★★★★ |

A secluded resort campground six miles east of Traverse City, Timber Ridge Campground offers gently rolling terrain. Sites are level and mostly shaded, with a typical site width of 30 feet. The campground has 43 pull-throughs and tent sites that have more green space and privacy. A lodge with a color TV, games, and fireplace is a nice amenity, especially in the winter when the area can get very cold and snow-covered. Open all year with limited facilities in the winter, the campground offers winter sports such as lighted ski trails. Timber Ridge also conducts learn-to-ski cross-country clinics throughout the season. The property borders over 60,000 acres of state land and trail systems for biking, hiking, and cross-country skiing. Reservations are recommended, particularly in July during the annual Traverse City Cherry Festival.

### BASICS
**Operated by:** Private Operator. **Open:** All year. **Site Assignment:** Reservations w/ 1-night deposit; refund (minus $10) w/ 5-day notice. **Registration:** At campground office. **Fee:** $38 (cash, check, credit cards). **Parking:** At site.

### FACILITIES
**Number of RV Sites:** 202. **Number of Tent-Only Sites:** 29. **Hookups:** Electric (20, 30 amps), water, sewer, phone. **Each Site:** Picnic table, fire ring. **Dump Station:** Yes. **Laundry:** Yes. **Pay

**Phone:** Yes. **Rest Rooms and Showers:** Yes. **Fuel:** No. **Propane:** Yes. **Internal Roads:** Paved/gravel, in good condition. **RV Service:** No. **Market:** 2 mi. **Restaurant:** 2 mi. **General Store:** Yes. **Vending:** Yes. **Swimming Pool:** Yes. **Playground:** Yes. **Other:** Wading pool, rec hall, pavilion, coin games, mini golf, basketball, shuffleball, movies, badminton, sports field, horseshoes, hiking trails, volleyball, rental cabins. **Activities:** Swimming, hiking, scheduled activities, winter sports. **Nearby Attractions:** Grand Traverse Bay, Interlochen Music Camp, Sleeping Bear Sand Dunes, casinos, golf, outlet mall, cherry orchards, beaches, winter sports, Old Mission, parks, replica schooner, museums, wineries. **Additional Information:** Traverse City CVB, (800) 872-8377.

<u>RESTRICTIONS</u>

**Pets:** Leash only. **Fires:** Fire ring only. **Alcoholic Beverages:** Not permitted. **Vehicle Maximum Length:** None.

<u>TO GET THERE</u>

From south junction US 31 and Hwy. 72, drive 5 mi. east on Hwy. 31/72, then 2 mi. south on Four Mile Rd., then 2 mi. east on Hammond Rd. Roads are mostly wide and well maintained w/ narrow shoulders in places.

## TRAVERSE CITY

### Traverse City South KOA

4050 Hammond Rd., Traverse City 49686. T: (800) 249-3203; F: (231) 947-5457; www.traversecitykoa.com; gtcamping@coslink.net.

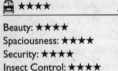 

| | |
|---|---|
| Beauty: ★★★★ | Site Privacy: ★★★★ |
| Spaciousness: ★★★★ | Quiet: ★★★★ |
| Security: ★★★★ | Cleanliness: ★★★★ |
| Insect Control: ★★★★ | Facilities: ★★★★ |

Located 15 miles south of Traverse City, the Traverse City South KOA is a family campground in a quiet country setting. Sites are level and grassy with a choice of open or shaded. The typical site width is 30 feet, and the campground has eight pull-throughs. Rest rooms are very clean; someone must check on them more than the usual once a day to keep them so spiffy. A wading pool is a popular spot with toddlers and their parents. The campground is a good base for Traverse City attractions, but it is also a destination campground for families. Owners keep a close watch on the campground for security and safety measures, but they are also friendly and helpful and seem to enjoy what they are doing.

<u>BASICS</u>

**Operated by:** Dave, Cathy, Stacy & Jamie Kuebler. **Open:** May 1–Oct. 15. **Site Assignment:** Reservations w/ 1-night deposit; refund w/ 2-week notice. **Registration:** At campground office. **Fee:** $30 (cash, check, credit cards). **Parking:** At site.

<u>FACILITIES</u>

**Number of RV Sites:** 110. **Number of Tent-Only Sites:** 8. **Hookups:** Electric (20, 30, 50 amps), water, sewer, phone. **Each Site:** Picnic table, fire ring. **Dump Station:** Yes. **Laundry:** Yes. **Pay Phone:** Yes. **Rest Rooms and Showers:** Yes. **Fuel:** No. **Propane:** Yes. **Internal Roads:** Gravel, in good condition. **RV Service:** No. **Market:** 3 mi. south in Buckley. **Restaurant:** 3 mi. south in Buckley. **General Store:** Yes. **Vending:** Yes. **Swimming Pool:** Yes. **Playground:** Yes. **Other:** Rec room, rental cabins, wading pool, coin games, basketball, movies, badminton, sports field, horseshoes, volleyball, snack bar, petting farm, hiking trails, snack bar. **Activities:** Swimming, hiking, scheduled activities. **Nearby Attractions:** Grand Traverse Bay, Interlochen Music Camp, Sleeping Bear Sand Dunes, casinos, golf, outlet mall, cherry orchards, beaches, winter sports, Old Mission, parks, replica schooner, museums, wineries. **Additional Information:** Traverse City CVB, (800) 872-8377.

<u>RESTRICTIONS</u>

**Pets:** Leash only. **Fires:** Fire ring only. **Alcoholic Beverages:** Permitted. **Vehicle Maximum Length:** None.

<u>TO GET THERE</u>

From the junction of US 31 and Hwy. 37, drive 10 mi. south on Hwy. 37. Roads are wide and well maintained w/ broad shoulders.

## VICKSBURG

### Oak Shores Resort Campground

13496 28th St., Vicksburg 49097. T: (800) 583-0662; oakshoresresort@aol.com.

| | |
|---|---|
| Beauty: ★★★ | Site Privacy: ★★★★ |
| Spaciousness: ★★★★ | Quiet: ★★★★ |
| Security: ★★★★ | Cleanliness: ★★★★ |
| Insect Control: ★★★★ | Facilities: ★★★★ |

Located halfway between Chicago and Detroit, Oak Shores Resort Campground in Vicksburg, is a popular stopping point as well as a destination in itself. Situated on Thrall Lake—a natural lake with a large sandy beach—Oak Shores is shaded by many beautiful mature oak trees. The rural campground has mostly grassy, level sites with a typical site width of 30 feet. There are 20 seasonal campers. Sites are modern or rustic with a group camping area. A heated rec hall is a nice option for groups. The best sites are closest to the lake. No motors are allowed on the lake. Facilities are clean and well maintained. Owners keep a close watch on the campground and provide security to keep it a family-oriented facility.

## BASICS

**Operated by:** Warren & Janet Wright. **Open:** May 1–Oct. 15. **Site Assignment:** Reservations w/ 1-night deposit; refund w/ 2-week notice. **Registration:** At campground office. **Fee:** $24 (cash, check, credit cards). **Parking:** At site.

## FACILITIES

**Number of RV Sites:** 117. **Number of Tent-Only Sites:** 20. **Hookups:** Electric (20, 30, 50 amps), water, sewer. **Each Site:** Picnic table, fire ring. **Dump Station:** Yes. **Laundry:** Yes. **Pay Phone:** Yes. **Rest Rooms and Showers:** Yes. **Fuel:** No. **Propane:** Yes. **Internal Roads:** Gravel, in fair condition. **RV Service:** No. **Market:** 5 mi. **Restaurant:** 5 mi. **General Store:** Yes. **Vending:** Yes. **Swimming Pool:** Yes. **Playground:** Yes. **Other:** Thrall Lake, sandy beach, rec hall, camping cabins, baseball, pavilion, hiking trails, game room, volleyball, basketball, badminton, horseshoes, boat ramp, boat dock. **Activities:** Swimming, fishing, boating (rental canoes, kayaks & paddleboats available). **Nearby Attractions:** Golf, antiques, Kalamazoo Aviation History Museum, Kalamazoo Institute of Arts, nature center, Kalamazoo Valley Museum, wineries. Gilmore Classic Car Museum, zoo. **Additional Information:** Kalamazoo County CVB, (800) 222-6363.

## RESTRICTIONS

**Pets:** Leash only. **Fires:** Fire ring only. **Alcoholic Beverages:** Permitted. **Vehicle Maximum Length:** None.

## TO GET THERE

From I-94, take Exit 80 and drive 9 mi. south on Sprinkle Rd., then 2 mi. east on V Ave. Roads are mostly wide and well maintained w/ adequate shoulders.

# WATERS

## Headwaters Camping & Cabins

11687 Headwaters Court, Waters 49797. T: (989) 705-2066

| 🚐 ★★★ | 🏕 ★★★ |
|---|---|
| Beauty: ★★★ | Site Privacy: ★★★★ |
| Spaciousness: ★★★★ | Quiet: ★★★★ |
| Security: ★★★★ | Cleanliness: ★★★★★ |
| Insect Control: None | Facilities: ★★★ |

Headwaters Court Camping & Cabins offers level, grassy sites with gravel parking spots on Bradford Lake. Located two miles south of Water, the campground also shows what a little creativity can do to brighten bathrooms. A "stone" floor and little critters painted on the walls make Headwaters' bathrooms more attractive and outdoorsy. Laid out in one big loop, the campground has five seasonals and seven pull-through sites. Sites are mostly open, with some situated right on a canal so boats can be left docked conveniently close to campsites. A welcoming extra is a free pancake breakfast every Sunday during the summer. Speed limit is five mph, and quiet hours are 10 p.m. to 9 a.m. Snowmobiling is a popular sport at the campground during winter. Security measures include one entrance/exit road, owners who live on site, and regular patrols of the campground.

## BASICS

**Operated by:** Steve & Kimi Kwapis. **Open:** All year. **Site Assignment:** Reservations w/ 1-night deposit; refund w/ 7 day notice. **Registration:** At campground office. **Fee:** $21 (cash, check, credit cards). **Parking:** At site.

## FACILITIES

**Number of RV Sites:** 76. **Number of Tent-Only Sites:** 4. **Hookups:** Electric (30, 50 amps), water, sewer. **Each Site:** Picnic table, fire ring. **Dump Station:** Yes. **Laundry:** No. **Pay Phone:** No. **Rest Rooms and Showers:** Yes. **Fuel:** No. **Propane:** No. **Internal Roads:** Gravel, in good condition. **RV Service:** No. **Market:** 2 mi. north in Waters. **Restaurant:** 2 mi. north in Waters. **General Store:** No. **Vending:** Yes. **Swimming Pool:** No. **Playground:** Yes. **Other:** Bradford Lake, swimming beach, boat ramp, volleyball, horseshoes, shuffleboard, boat dock, rental cabins, pavilion,. **Activities:** Swimming, fishing, boating, scheduled weekend activities. **Nearby Attractions:** Au Sable River, golf, bowling, ice skating, Bottle Cap Museum, canoeing, horseback riding, elk viewing, antiques, arts & crafts. **Additional Information:** Grayling Area Visitors Council, (800) 937-8837.

## RESTRICTIONS

**Pets:** Leash only, proof of immunizations required. **Fires:** Fire ring only. **Alcoholic Beverages:** Permitted. **Vehicle Maximum Length:** None. **Other:** No check in after 10 p.m.

## TO GET THERE

From I-75, take Exit 270, drive 0.25 mi. west on Marlett Rd., then 2 mi. south on Old 27, then 0.1 mi. west on Headwaters Court. Roads are wide and well maintained w/ broad shoulders.

## ZEELAND

### Dutch Treat Camping & Recreation

10300 Gordon, Zeeland 49464. T: (616) 772-4303

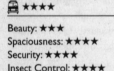

| | |
|---|---|
| Beauty: ★★★ | Site Privacy: ★★★★ |
| Spaciousness: ★★★★ | Quiet: ★★★★ |
| Security: ★★★★ | Cleanliness: ★★★★ |
| Insect Control: ★★★★ | Facilities: ★★★★ |

Right in the heart of vacationland, Dutch Treat Camping in Zeeland, offers level sites by a small pond. The campground has level sites with a choice of open or shaded sites and a typical site width of 35 feet. There are 15 seasonal campers and 44 pull-through sites. Rustic tent sites offer more green space and privacy. During May, millions of beautiful tulips provide a floral display in this western Michigan city settled by Dutch immigrants. Reservations are recommended during the annual tulip festival. Dutch Treat facilities are clean and well maintained. Most sites are grassy, but some gravel ones are available. A large deck around the heated pool is a nice bonus. A large recreation shelter is heated or air conditioned and provides a welcome spot during extreme weather. Church services are offered on Sundays. Owners make sure the campground is well monitored to maintain a friendly family atmosphere.

## BASICS

**Operated by:** Nelson Reimersma. **Open:** Apr. 1–Nov. 1. **Site Assignment:** Reservations w/ 1-night deposit; refund (minus $5) w/ 2-week notice. **Registration:** At campground office. **Fee:** $24 (cash, check, credit cards). **Parking:** At site.

## FACILITIES

**Number of RV Sites:** 105. **Number of Tent-Only Sites:** 15. **Hookups:** Electric (20, 30, 50 amps), water, sewer, phone. **Each Site:** Picnic table, fire ring. **Dump Station:** Yes. **Laundry:** Yes. **Pay Phone:** Yes. **Rest Rooms and Showers:** Yes. **Fuel:** No. **Propane:** No. **Internal Roads:** Paved, in good condition. **RV Service:** No. **Market:** Two blocks. **Restaurant:** Two blocks. **General Store:** Yes, limited. **Vending:** Yes. **Swimming Pool:** Yes. **Playground:** Yes. **Other:** Pond, horseshoes, rec hall, sports field, coin games, basketball, badminton, volleyball, game room. **Activities:** Swimming, fishing, boating (rental paddleboats available). **Nearby Attractions:** Lake Macatawa, Lake Michigan, bike trails, Cappon House Museum, De Klomp Wooden Shoe & Delftware Factory, Dutch Village, Holland Museum, tulip gardens, Windmill Island, antiques, arts & crafts. **Additional Information:** Holland Area CVB, (800) 506-1299.

## RESTRICTIONS

**Pets:** Leash only. **Fires:** Fire ring only. **Alcoholic Beverages:** Permitted. **Vehicle Maximum Length:** None.

## TO GET THERE

From the junction of Hwy. 31 and East/West Business I-196, drive 2.2 mi. east on I-96, then 0.25 mi. east on Gordon. Roads are wide and well maintained w/ broad shoulders.

# Minnesota

The "land of 10,000 lakes" isn't just bragging. In fact, Minnesota actually has more than 15,000 lakes and just about any known water-related activity. It also is the reputed home of Babe the Blue Ox, sidekick to that legendary lumberman, Paul Bunyan. Don't be surprised to see Babe and Paul statues along the roadsides.

Eastern timber wolves can be found at **Voyageurs National Park,** home of one of the last colonies of eastern timber wolves left in the continental United States. To appreciate hardships settlers faced, visit the **Walnut Grove** museum with memorabilia from resident Laura Ingalls Wilder, author of the "Little House on the Prairie" books. For history, towns like **New Ulm** have an unmistakable European accent in their shops, restaurants, festivals, and breweries. Shoppers flock from around the world for the huge **Mall of America** in **Bloomington.**

With such a wealth of outdoor activities, it's appropriate that America's first snowmobile was created in Minnesota. More than 15,000 miles of snowmobile trails in state recreation areas also make winter a popular outdoor time. Ice fishing, as highlighted in the movie "Grumpy Old Men," keeps away winter boredom for dedicated anglers. One of the first rivers in the nation to be granted the Wild and Scenic designation, the **St. Croix** has an outstandingly beautiful shoreline. To preserve the natuarl beauty of the area, the **Boundary Waters Canoe Area Wilderness,** part of Superior National Forest, has banned motorized boats on most of its more than 2,500 lakes. With a name meaning "lake with river flowing through," **Bemidji's Paul Bunyan Bike Trail** is a popular route for bicycling, skating, and snowmobiling.

Throughout Minnesota are cities with curious points of interest of their own. The **Runestone Museum** is located in **Alexandria** where mystery surounds the rock found in a Minnesota farmer's field in 1898. Carvings on the rock tell the tale of a Viking voyage that ended in tragedy in 1362. Known as Spam Town USA, **Austin** pays homage to its world famous meat product, and in **Duluth,** an unusual elevator bridge is 386 feet long and spans the canal entrance to Duluth Harbor. Located near the navigational headwaters of the Mississippi River, the city of **Grand Rapid** was the birthplace of Judy Garland and offers its own yellow brick road to her historic home. The **Mayo Clinic** in **Rochester** is known for its advanced technologies and pioneering discoveries in the world of medicine. The twin cities of **Minneapolis** and **St. Paul** have distinctive personalities and enough attractions to keep folks returning time after time.

**The following facilities accept payment in checks or cash only:**

Camp Waub-O-Jeeg, Taylors Falls

Forest Heights RV Park, Hibbing

Gull Lake Campground, Bemidji

Hidden Valley Campground, Preston

Money Creek Haven, Houston

Pioneer Campsite, Wabasha

Red Fox Campground & RV Park, Moose Lake

Sherwood Forest Campground, Gilbert

Silver Lake RV Park, Rochester

Vagabond Village, Park Rapids

**The following facilities have 20 or fewer sites:**

Charles A. Lindbergh State Park, Little Falls

Country Campground, Detroit Lakes

Doty's Riverview RV Park, Pine River

Forest Heights RV Park, Hibbing

Hidden Valley Campground, Preston

Interstate State Park, Taylors Falls

Nodak Lodge, Bena

Shores of Leech Lake Campground & Marina, Walker

Silver Rapids Lodge, Ely

Sugar Bay Campground/Resort, Grand Rapids

Sullivan's Resort & Campground, Brainerd

Upper Cullen Resort & Campground, Nisswa

# Campground Profiles

## ALBERT LEA
### Albert Lea- Austin KOA Kampground

Rte. 3, Box 15, Hayward 56043. T: (507) 373-5170

🚐 ★★★                    ⛺ ★★

| | |
|---|---|
| Beauty: ★★★ | Site Privacy: ★★★ |
| Spaciousness: ★★★★ | Quiet: ★★ |
| Security: ★★★★ | Cleanliness: ★★★★ |
| Insect Control: None | Facilities: ★★★★ |

Many a traveling camper must have breathed a sigh of relief to see the Albert Lea-Austin KOA Kampground from the interstate. In fact, the campground is so close to the highway that only a patch of grass and a barrier of trees separates the two. Convenience, cleanliness, and security attract repeat campers. Though it's not a particularly scenic place and there are almost no scheduled activities, the campground is a welcome overnight rest for weary travelers hoping to enjoy the area attractions. The campground offers large (45 × 60), open, gravel sites, at least half of which are pull-through. RVs would fare much better than tent campers. Though the campground is surrounded by serene farm fields and a golf course is next door, the noise of the interstate is inescapable.

**BASICS**

**Operated by:** Mike & Sharon Calow. **Open:** Apr. 20–Oct. 15. **Site Assignment:** Reservations w/ 1-night deposit; refund w/ notice by 4 p.m. the day before arrival. **Registration:** At campground office. **Fee:** $28 (cash, check, credit cards). **Parking:** At site.

**FACILITIES**

**Number of RV Sites:** 100. **Number of Tent-Only Sites:** 23. **Hookups:** Electric (30 amp), water, sewer. **Each Site:** Picnic table, fire ring. **Dump Station:** Yes. **Laundry:** Yes. **Pay Phone:** Yes. **Rest Rooms and Showers:** Yes. **Fuel:** No. **Propane:** Yes. **Internal Roads:** Gravel, in good condition. **RV Service:** No. **Market:** 3 mi. west in Hayward. **Restaurant:** 7 mi. west in Albert Lea. **General Store:** Yes. **Vending:** Yes. **Swimming Pool:** Yes. **Playground:** Yes. **Other:** Nature trail, volleyball, horseshoes, game room, recreation field. **Activities:** Swimming, scheduled activities on holiday weekends.

**Nearby Attractions:** Golf, Cabelo's, Mall of America, Story Lady Doll & Toy Museum, Freeborn County Museum & Historical Village, nature center, lake. **Additional Information:** Albert Lea—Freeborn County CVB, (800) 345-8414.

## RESTRICTIONS

**Pets:** Leash only. **Fires:** Fire ring only. **Alcoholic Beverages:** Permitted. **Vehicle Maximum Length:** None.

## TO GET THERE

From the junction of I-35 and I-90, take Exit 166 and drive 8 mi. east on I-90, then 0.5 mi. northeast on CR 46. Roads are wide and well maintained w/ broad shoulders.

## ALBERT LEA

### Hickory Hills Campground

Rte. 1, Box 166A, Albert Lea 56007. T: (866) 233-3680; F: (507) 852-2068; www.hickoryhillscampground.com; daveklug@smig.net.

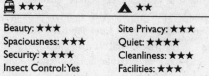

| 🚐 ★★★ | ▲ ★★ |
|---|---|
| Beauty: ★★★ | Site Privacy: ★★★ |
| Spaciousness: ★★★ | Quiet: ★★★★ |
| Security: ★★★★ | Cleanliness: ★★★ |
| Insect Control: Yes | Facilities: ★★★ |

In 1999, Hickory Hills Campground got new owners, and they've been working hard to fix it up. Showers and rest rooms have been fixed up, and the campground area has been regularly weeded and mowed. Located in a rural area with shaded, wooded sites, the campground is off the beaten path and has little outside noise. The only noise would be whatever the campers bring with them, and the owners try to keep that to a minimum. Sites are generally 30 × 60 with about 12 pull-through sites. At 35 × 84, the swimming pool is bigger than those at most campgrounds. Sites 1 and 10 are the most popular RV sites because they are the first in the park, located near the playground, and offer easy access to campground amenities. Tent sites are separated from RVs, but not enough to provide much privacy. With one entrance/exit and owners who live on site and patrol the area, security is very good. Also, it would be hard to imagine anyone driving all the way out to Hickory Hills on those gravel roads for any reason other than camping.

## BASICS

**Operated by:** Dave & Cheri Klug. **Open:** Apr. 15–Oct. 15. **Site Assignment:** Reservations accepted w/ no deposit; holiday weekends require $10 deposit. **Registration:** At campground office. **Fee:** $22 (cash, check, credit cards). **Parking:** At site.

## FACILITIES

**Number of RV Sites:** 94. **Number of Tent-Only Sites:** 5. **Hookups:** Electric (20, 30 amps), water. **Each Site:** Picnic table, fire ring. **Dump Station:** Yes. **Laundry:** Yes. **Pay Phone:** Yes. **Rest Rooms and Showers:** Yes. **Fuel:** No. **Propane:** No. **Internal Roads:** Gravel, rough in some spots. **RV Service:** No. **Market:** 7 mi. north in Albert Lea. **Restaurant:** 7 mi. north in Albert Lea. **General Store:** Yes. **Vending:** No. **Swimming Pool:** Yes. **Playground:** Yes. **Other:** Hiking trail, horseshoes, game room, recreation field, volleyball, mini-golf. **Activities:** Swimming, hiking, scheduled activities on weekends & holdiays such as karaoke, treasure hunt, sock hop dance, hog roast. **Nearby Attractions:** Lake, Freeborn County Museum & Historical Village, Story Lady Doll & Toy Museum, golf, aquatic center. **Additional Information:** Albert Lea-Freeborn County CVB, (900) 345-8414.

## RESTRICTIONS

**Pets:** Leash only. **Fires:** Fire ring only. **Alcoholic Beverages:** Permitted. **Vehicle Maximum Length:** None.

## TO GET THERE

From the junction of I-90 and Hwy. 13/69, take Exit 154 and drive 9.75 mi. south on Hwy. 69, then follow signs for 1.5 mi. on gravel roads. Gravel roads are wide but rough in spots.

## ALEXANDRIA

### Eden Acres Resort

5181 Fish Hook Dr. Southwest, Alexandria 56308. T: (320) 763-7434

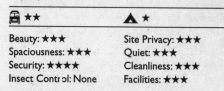

| 🚐 ★★ | ▲ ★ |
|---|---|
| Beauty: ★★★ | Site Privacy: ★★★ |
| Spaciousness: ★★★ | Quiet: ★★★ |
| Security: ★★★★ | Cleanliness: ★★★ |
| Insect Control: None | Facilities: ★★★ |

Located on the eastern shore of beautiful Lake Mary, Eden Acres Resort offers great fishing, fun swimming (when the lake water is warm enough), and other water activities. Many people come for the great fishing, and they usually aren't disappointed. Spring and fall are best for walleyes and crappies (running large at one to two pounds.). Sunfish are abundant from late June through early Aug. Northerns and bass are always waiting and put up a good fight. Unfortunately, only 7 of the 60 campground sites are not occupied by seasonals. Reservations are necessary and require a four-night minimum stay. Tents are allowed on the available sites—but it might not be much fun to be surrounded by RVs unless the tenter is really dedicated to fishing and lake activities.

## BASICS

**Operated by:** Ron & Pat Meyers. **Open:** Apr. 15–Oct. 15. **Site Assignment:** Reservations recommended w/ a 4-night min. stay. **Registration:** At campground office. **Fee:** $25 (cash, check, credit cards). **Parking:** At site.

## FACILITIES

**Number of RV Sites:** 60. **Number of Tent-Only Sites:** 0. **Hookups:** Electric (50 amp), water, sewer. **Each Site:** Some picnic tables. **Dump Station:** Yes. **Laundry:** Yes. **Pay Phone:** Yes. **Rest Rooms and Showers:** Yes. **Fuel:** Yes. **Propane:** No. **Internal Roads:** Gravel, in good condition. **RV Service:** No. **Market:** 5 mi. northeast in Alexandria. **Restaurant:** 5 mi. northeast in Alexandria. **General Store:** Yes. **Vending:** No. **Swimming Pool:** No. **Playground:** Yes. **Other:** Sandy beach on Lake Mary, swim area w/ raft, volleyball, horseshoes, paddleboat, lodge w/ TV, gameroom, video games, pinball, boats, motors, pntoon, boat lifts, boat launch. **Activities:** Fishing, swimming, boating (rentals available). **Nearby Attractions:** Golf, tennis, theater, shopping mall, antique stores, amusement park, Runestone Museum. **Additional Information:** Alexandria Lakes Area Chamber of Commerce, (800) 245-2539.

## RESTRICTIONS

**Pets:** Leash only. **Fires:** Fire ring only. **Alcoholic Beverages:** Permitted. **Vehicle Maximum Length:** 40 ft. **Other:** Must stay 4-night min.

## TO GET THERE

Take Exit 100 on I-94, drive 1.75 mi. west on Hwy. 27W, drive 1 mi. east on Lake Mary Rd. Lake Mary Rd. is gravel, in good condition.

## ALEXANDRIA
## Sun Valley Resort and Campground

10045 State Hwy. 27, Alexandria 56308. T: (320) 886-5417; F: (320) 886-5217; www.alexandriamn.com/sunvalley; sunvalley@rea-alp.com.

| 🚐 ★★★ | 🏕 ★★ |
|---|---|
| Beauty: ★★★ | Site Privacy: ★★★ |
| Spaciousness: ★★★ | Quiet: ★★★★ |
| Security: ★★★★ | Cleanliness: ★★★ |
| Insect Control: None | Facilities: ★★★ |

Located on Mill Lake, Sun Valley Resort and Campground has all but 30 of its sites occupied by seasonal campers, but the seasonals are generally located in clumps away from the unoccupied sites. And, 15 of the most requested lakeside sites have been reserved for non-seasonal campers. Tent campers are not separated from RV campers. The campground is typically used as a destination for campers rather than as an overnight spot for travelers. The rural campground—located away from the main resort—offers level, open, and shaded sites. A well stocked bait and tackle shop offers fishing licenses and freezer service. Swimmers use the heated pool or the lake for water recreation. Conveniently, the campground offers a babysitting service.

## BASICS

**Operated by:** Jeff & Lori Carstensen. **Open:** May 1–Oct. 1. **Site Assignment:** Reservations w/ $20 fee; no refund. **Registration:** At campground office. **Fee:** $22 (cash, check, credit card). **Parking:** At site.

## FACILITIES

**Number of RV Sites:** 74. **Number of Tent-Only Sites:** 0. **Hookups:** Electric (20, 30, 50 amps), water, sewer. **Each Site:** Picnic table, fire ring. **Dump Station:** Yes. **Laundry:** Yes. **Pay Phone:** Yes. **Rest Rooms and Showers:** Yes. **Fuel:** Yes. **Propane:** No. **Internal Roads:** Gravel, narrow in good condition. **RV Service:** No. **Market:** 7 mi. east in Alexandria. **Restaurant:** 7 mi. east in Alexandria. **General Store:** Yes. **Vending:** No. **Swimming Pool:** Yes. **Playground:** Yes. **Other:** Mill Lake, tennis court, mini-golf, bait & tackle shop, boat launch, piers, basketball, horseshoes, volleyball, shuffleboard, rec hall. **Activities:**

Fishing, swimming, boating (rental motorboats, canoes, rowboats & paddleboats available). **Nearby Attractions:** Golf, downhill & cross-country skiing, snowmobiling, ice fishing, Rune-stone Museum, Fort Alexandria Agricultural Exhibit. **Additional Information:** Alexandria Lakes Area Chamber of Commerce, (800) 245-2539.

<u>RESTRICTIONS</u>

**Pets:** Leash only, $2 daily fee or $10 per week. **Fires:** Fire ring only. **Alcoholic Beverages:** Permitted. **Vehicle Maximum Length:** 32 ft. **Other:** 3-day min. for holidays.

<u>TO GET THERE</u>

From the junction of I-94 and Hwy. 27, take Exit 100, drive 5 mi. west on Hwy. 27. Roads are wide and well maintained w/ broad shoulders.

## ALTURA

## Whitewater State Park

Rte. 1, Box 256, Altura 55910. T: (507) 932-3007; www.dnr.state.mn.us.

🚐 ★★          🏕 ★★★★

Beauty: ★★★★          Site Privacy: ★★★★
Spaciousness: ★★★★     Quiet: ★★★★
Security: ★★★★          Cleanliness: ★★★
Insect Control: None     Facilities: ★★

Established in 1919, Whitewater State Park is one of the most popular Minnesota state parks because of its dolomite cliffs, trout streams, hardwood forests, and noticeable lack of mosquitos. The absence of the pesky insects isn't because of vigilant spraying. Rather, it is the result of the fast-moving streams which don't give mosquitos a chance to breed. Located two miles south of Elba, the campground's screens of trees and plants keep it naturally quiet. Do note that the park gate is closed from 10 p.m. to 8 a.m., except to registered campers, and quiet time begins at 10 p.m. each night. The RV sites are mostly grassy and shady, with five pull-throughs. Size width varies from 15 to 30 feet. In addition to 55 tent camping sites, Whitewater also has four hike-in sites and a primitive area that can accommodate 100 tent campers. Tent campers have an edge at this wilderness campground: the tent sites outnumber the RV sites. Though rattlesnake sightings are rare, rep-tiles do live within the park. Hikers should report any sightings to the park office.

<u>BASICS</u>

**Operated by:** State of Minnesota. **Open:** All year. **Site Assignment:** Reservations w/ 1-night fee plus $7.25 non-refundable service charge; refunds (minus $5 & $7.25 service charge) w/ 3-day notice. **Registration:** At campground office. **Fee:** $15 (cash, check, credit cards). **Parking:** At site.

<u>FACILITIES</u>

**Number of RV Sites:** 47. **Number of Tent-Only Sites:** 59. **Hookups:** Electric (20, 30, 50 amps). **Each Site:** Picnic table, fire ring. **Dump Station:** Yes. **Laundry:** No. **Pay Phone:** Yes. **Rest Rooms and Showers:** Yes. **Fuel:** No. **Propane:** No. **Internal Roads:** Paved, gravel, in good condition. **RV Service:** No. **Market:** 2 mi. north in Elba. **Restaurant:** 2 mi. north in Elba. **General Store:** No. **Vending:** Yes. **Swimming Pool:** No. **Playground:** No. **Other:** Whitewater River, swimming beach, volleyball, horseshoes, hiking trails, ski touring trails, naturalist, interpretive center, visitor center, handicapped accessible fishing pier. **Activities:** Hiking, fishing, swimming, cross-country ski trails, interpretive programs. **Nearby Attractions:** Mayo Clinic, art center, Mayowood Mansion, golf, Olmsted County History Center, Root River State Trail, scenic drives. **Additional Information:** Rochester CVB, (800) 634-8277.

<u>RESTRICTIONS</u>

**Pets:** Leash only. **Fires:** Fire ring only. **Alcoholic Beverages:** Not permitted. **Vehicle Maximum Length:** 50 ft. **Other:** Vehicle permits of $20 per year or $4 per day are required to enter all Minnesota state parks; 14 day stay-limit.

<u>TO GET THERE</u>

From Elba, drive 2 mi. south on Hwy. 74. Roads are wide and well maintained w/ broad shoulders.

## AUSTIN

## Beaver Trails Campgrounds

21943 630th Ave. No. 1, Austin 55912. T: (507) 584-6611; F: (507) 584-6661; www.beavertrails.com; camping@beavertrails.com.

🚐 ★★★★          🏕 ★★★★

Beauty: ★★★          Site Privacy: ★★★★
Spaciousness: ★★★★     Quiet: ★★★★
Security: ★★★★          Cleanliness: ★★★
Insect Control: None     Facilities: ★★★★

Beaver Trails Campgrounds is four campgrounds in one. The Lodge Area is where the action is and is a favorite with families and children. As a result, it is a little noisier and crowded. The Quiet Area offers large sites (30 × 78), plenty of grass and trees, and some primitive sites. The Group Area can accommodte any size group and features pavilions for gatherings. The wooded Trails End Area has pack-in sites, chemical toilets, and plenty of solitude. It would be the best pick for tent campers. The campground is blessed with grassy, level sites each with its own tree. A big bonus for RV campers is that most of the sites are pull-throughs. It may have been unusual, but at the time of our visit, one of the campground's toilets was out of order and another wouldn't flush. With a campground this size, having two unusable toilets isn't pleasant.

## BASICS

**Operated by:** Bill & Carol Sheely. **Open:** Apr. 15–Oct. 15. **Site Assignment:** Reservations w/ $10 deposit; refund w/ 1-week notice, 2 week notice on holidays. **Registration:** At campground office. **Fee:** $26 (cash, check, credit cards). **Parking:** At site.

## FACILITIES

**Number of RV Sites:** 267. **Number of Tent-Only Sites:** 13. **Hookups:** Electric (20, 30, 50 amps), water, sewer. **Each Site:** Picnic table, fire ring. **Dump Station:** Yes. **Laundry:** Yes. **Pay Phone:** Yes. **Rest Rooms and Showers:** Yes. **Fuel:** No. **Propane:** Yes. **Internal Roads:** Gravel/paved in good condition. **RV Service:** No. **Market:** 8 mi. west in Austin. **Restaurant:** 8 mi. west in Austin. **General Store:** Yes. **Vending:** Yes. **Swimming Pool:** Yes. **Playground:** Yes. **Other:** Dance hall, shuffleboard, game room, ping-pong room, volleyball, meeting room, big screen TV, pavilion, hiking trails, badminton, horseshoes, snack bar, small animal zoo, outdoor stage, mini-golf, fish pond, coin games, wading pool. **Activities:** Swimming, fishing, canoeing (rental canoes & pedal boats available), movies, activities every weekend, such as karaoke, line dancing, Christmas inJuly, kid's crafts, train rides, story time. **Nearby Attractions:** Nature center, historical center, cave, Spam Museum, historic homes, skate park, golf, bowling, snowmobile trails, speedway, hockey rink. **Additional Information:** Austin CVB, (800) 444-5713.

## RESTRICTIONS

**Pets:** Leash only. **Fires:** Fire ring only. **Alcoholic Beverages:** Permitted. **Vehicle Maximum Length:** None.

## TO GET THERE

From the junction of US 218 and I-90, drive 7.5 mi. east on I-90, take Exit 187, drive 25 yards south on CR 20. Roads are wide and well maintained w/ broad shoulders.

## BEMIDJI
### Bemidji KOA

5705 Hwy. 2 West, Bemidji 56601. T: (218) 751-1792; bemidjikoa.com; kamp@bemidjikoa.com.

| 🚐 ★★★★ | ⛺ ★★★★ |
|---|---|
| Beauty: ★★★★ | Site Privacy: ★★★★ |
| Spaciousness: ★★★★ | Quiet: ★★★★ |
| Security: ★★★★ | Cleanliness: ★★★★ |
| Insect Control: Yes | Facilities: ★★★★ |

Located in the heart of the Northwoods county, two miles west of Bemidji, this KOA has five area lakes within four miles. Tall pine, spruce, fir, and white birch trees offer shade. The campground has 28 pull-throughs, and the typical site width is 20 feet. The RV sites have a gravel pad for parking. Laid out in a loop, the rural campground has a well-stocked store and a 24-hour laundry. Primitive tent sites are situated away from the RV sites in a wooded area. Summer temperatures are generally cool with daytime highs in the 70s and 80s. It can snow in May and Oct. The owner lives on site and offers regular patrols. As a friendly touch, the campground shows free movies every night and offers free popcorn in the pavilion. Every morning, free coffee is offered in the store.

## BASICS

**Operated by:** Keith & Mary Davidson. **Open:** May 1–Oct. 15. **Site Assignment:** Reservations w/ 1-night deposit; refund w/ 7-day notice. **Registration:** At campground office. **Fee:** $28 (cash, check, credit cards). **Parking:** At site.

## FACILITIES

**Number of RV Sites:** 100. **Number of Tent-Only Sites:** 11. **Hookups:** Electric (30, 50 amps), water, sewer, cable TV. **Each Site:** Picnic table, fire ring. **Dump Station:** Yes. **Laundry:** Yes. **Pay Phone:** Yes. **Rest Rooms and Showers:** Yes. **Fuel:** No. **Propane:** Yes. **Internal Roads:** Gravel, in good condition. **RV Service:** No. **Market:** 4 mi. east in Bemidji. **Restaurant:** 2 mi. east in Bemidji. **General Store:** Yes. **Vending:** No. **Swimming Pool:** Yes. **Playground:** Yes. **Other:** Mini-golf, video game room, book exchange, badminton, sports field, horseshoes, hiking trails, volleyball, rental cabins. **Activities:** Swimming, hiking, biking (rental bikes available), scheduled weekend activities. **Nearby Attractions:** Mississippi River, Paul Bunyan & Babe the Blue Ox statues, amusement parks, water slide, logging camp, fishing, golf. **Additional Information:** Bemidji Area Tourist Information, (800) 458-2223.

## RESTRICTIONS

**Pets:** Leash only. **Fires:** Fire ring only. **Alcoholic Beverages:** Permitted. **Vehicle Maximum Length:** None.

## TO GET THERE

From the junction of US 71 and US 2, drive 2.5 mi. west on US 2. Road is wide and well maintained w/ broad shoulders.

## BEMIDJI

### Gull Lake Campground

Rte. 1 Box 28, Tenstrike 56683. T: (218) 586-2842; www.resortwebonline.com/gulllakecampground.

| 🚌 ★★★★ | 🅰 ★★★★ |
|---|---|
| Beauty: ★★★★ | Site Privacy: ★★★★ |
| Spaciousness: ★★★★ | Quiet: ★★★★ |
| Security: ★★★★ | Cleanliness: ★★★★ |
| Insect Control: ★★★★ | Facilities: ★★★★ |

Overlooking Gull Lake just north of Bemidji, this campground offers 3,000 feet of lakeshore. Sites are grassy with a choice of open or shaded areas. The typical site width is a generous 45 feet, and the campground has six pull-throughs. Naturally, the best camping spots are closest to the water. Fishing is a popular pasttime here, and a clean, screened-in fish-cleaning house is located on site. Rest room and laundry facilities are very clean. Priding itself on being a quiet, family-oriented campground, Gull Lake takes measures to keep the facility safe and comfortable. The owners keep a close watch on the campground and set the mood for a friendly stay.

## BASICS

**Operated by:** Wes & Karen Nelson. **Open:** May 15–Oct. 1. **Site Assignment:** Reservations w/ 1-night deposit; refund w/ 7-day notice. **Registra-**

tion: At campground office. **Fee:** $20 (cash, check). **Parking:** At site.

## FACILITIES

**Number of RV Sites:** 71. **Number of Tent-Only Sites:** 21. **Hookups:** Electric (20, 30 amps), water, sewer. **Each Site:** Picnic table, fire ring. **Dump Station:** Yes. **Laundry:** Yes. **Pay Phone:** Yes. **Rest Rooms and Showers:** Yes. **Fuel:** Yes. **Propane:** Yes. **Internal Roads:** Gravel, in good condition. **RV Service:** No. **Market:** 5 mi. south. **Restaurant:** 5 mi. south. **General Store:** Yes. **Vending:** Yes. **Swimming Pool:** Yes. **Playground:** Yes. **Other:** Gull Lake, boat ramp, fish-cleaning house, rec room, coin games, horseshoes, shuffle-board, badminton, volleyball, sports field. **Activities:** Swimming, fishing, boating (rental fishing boats, canoes, paddleboats, rowboats available), scheduled weekend activities. **Nearby Attractions:** Mississippi River, Paul Bunyan & the Blue Ox statues, amusement parks, water slide, logging camp, fishing, golf, antiques, arts & crafts. **Additional Information:** Bemidji Area Tourist Information, (800) 458-2223.

## RESTRICTIONS

**Pets:** Leash only. **Fires:** Fire ring only. **Alcoholic Beverages:** Permitted. **Vehicle Maximum Length:** None.

## TO GET THERE

From West Junction US 2 and US 71, drive 10.5 mi. north on US 71, then 6 mi. north on CR 23. Roads are mostly wide and well maintained w/ narrow shoulders in spots.

## BENA

### Nodak Lodge

15080 Nodak Dr., Bena 56626. T: (800) 752-2758; www.nodaklodge.com; nodaks@means.net.

| 🚌 ★★★ | 🅰 ★★ |
|---|---|
| Beauty: ★★★ | Site Privacy: ★★★ |
| Spaciousness: ★★★ | Quiet: ★★★ |
| Security: ★★★ | Cleanliness: ★★★ |
| Insect Control: None | Facilities: ★★★ |

A lakeside RV area in a mobile home park, Nodak Lodge offers water recreation activities galore with fishing as a highlight. Charter boats and whole- or half-day launch fishing is available as are fishing guides. The marina features a large harbor with plenty of docking space and has boat rentals, a fish-cleaning house, gas, oil, and live bait. Dock boys are on hand to assist in the marina area and will clean and package a daily catch for a small fee. As often happens in a popular campground, all the full hookup sites are occupied by seasonals. The sites are grassy, level, and open with few trees, and the typical site width is 30 feet. There are no scheduled activities at this campground. The best RV site is B3 because it is bigger and has shade. Tent campers will like Nodak Lodge for its outdoor activities but might not like being clumped with RVs and mobile homes.

## BASICS

**Operated by:** Bob & Shirley Kline. **Open:** May 1–Oct. 1. **Site Assignment:** Reservations, no deposit necessary. **Registration:** At campground office. **Fee:** $20 (cash, check, credit cards). **Parking:** At site.

## FACILITIES

**Number of RV Sites:** 10. **Number of Tent-Only Sites:** 0. **Hookups:** Electric (30), water. **Each Site:** Picnic table, fire ring. **Dump Station:** Yes. **Laundry:** Yes. **Pay Phone:** Yes. **Rest Rooms and Showers:** Yes. **Fuel:** Yes. **Propane:** No. **Internal Roads:** Dirt, in fair condition. **RV Service:** No. **Market:** 20 mi. east in Deer River. **Restaurant:** 20 mi. east in Deer River. **General Store:** Yes. **Vending:** No. **Swimming Pool:** Yes. **Playground:** Yes. **Other:** Lake Winnibigoshish, tanning bed, marina, boat docks, fish-cleaning house, lodge, snack bar, game room, sports field, horseshoes, volleyball. **Activities:** Fishing, swimming, boating (rental motor boats, canoes & paddleboats available). **Nearby Attractions:** Hunting, hiking, mountain biking, fish-angling houses, fish-spearing houses, snowmobile trails, cross-country & downhill skiing. **Additional Information:** Grand Rapids CVB, (800) 472-6366.

## RESTRICTIONS

**Pets:** Leash only, $5 fee per day. **Fires:** Fire ring only. **Alcoholic Beverages:** Permitted. **Vehicle Maximum Length:** 40 ft.

## TO GET THERE

From the junction of CR 8 and US 2, drive 0.5 mi. west on US 2. Roads are wide and well maintained w/ broad shoulders.

## BIG LAKE
### Shady River Campground

21353 CR 5, Big Lake 55309. T: (612) 263-3705; www.shadyriver.com; shadyriver@hotmail.com.

🚐 ★★          ⛺ ★★

| | |
|---|---|
| Beauty: ★★★ | Site Privacy: ★★★ |
| Spaciousness: ★★★★ | Quiet: ★★★ |
| Security: ★★ | Cleanliness: ★★ |
| Insect Control: ★★★ | Facilities: ★★ |

Maple trees provide a cooling canopy at Shady River Campground located outside the town of Big Lake. The campground offers level, grassy sites with some open spots in a secluded rural location. The campground has a typical site width of 45 feet. Some sites are available on Elk River at a cost of $2 extra. Activities center around the river and include fishing, boating, and swimming. If you happen to drive through in Sept., you might be able to enjoy the annual pot-luck and pig roast. The cost is only $1, and if you bring your own utensils and something to drink, you can enjoy a festive dinner while making new friends with fellow campers.

## BASICS

**Operated by:** Dick & Arlyce Hewett. **Open:** May 1–Oct. 1. **Site Assignment:** Reservations w/ 1-night deposit; refund w/ 7-day notice. **Registration:** At campground office. **Fee:** $20 (cash, check, credit cards). **Parking:** At site.

## FACILITIES

**Number of RV Sites:** 75. **Number of Tent-Only Sites:** 0. **Hookups:** Electric (20, 30, 50 amps), water, sewer. **Each Site:** Picnic table, fire ring. **Dump Station:** Yes. **Laundry:** Yes. **Pay Phone:** Yes. **Rest Rooms and Showers:** Yes. **Fuel:** No. **Propane:** Yes. **Internal Roads:** Gravel, in fair condition. **RV Service:** No. **Market:** 2 mi. south. **Restaurant:** 2 mi. south. **General Store:** Yes, limited. **Vending:** Yes. **Swimming Pool:** No. **Playground:** Yes. **Other:** Elk River, rec room, horseshoes, volleyball. **Activities:** Swimming, fishing, boating (rental canoes, tubes & paddleboats available). **Nearby Attractions:** Sherburne National Wildlife Refuge, Sand Dunes State Forest, Munsinger & Clemens Gardens, Oliver H. Kelley living history farm, scenic drives, golf, horseback riding, antiques, arts & crafts. **Additional Information:** Big Lake Chamber of Commerce, (877) 363-0549.

## RESTRICTIONS

**Pets:** Leash only. **Fires:** Fire ring only. **Alcoholic Beverages:** Permitted. **Vehicle Maximum Length:** None.

## TO GET THERE

From the junction of Hwy. 25 and US 10, drive 2 blocks east on US 10, then 2 mi. north on CR 5. Roads are mostly wide and well maintained w/ adequate shoulders.

## BRAINERD

### Don and Mayva's Crow Wing Lake Campground

2393 Crow Wing Camp Rd., Brainerd 56401.
T: (218) 829-6468; www.brainerd.net/~cwcamp;
cwcamp@brainerd.net.

🚐 ★★★★        ▲ ★★★★

| | |
|---|---|
| Beauty: ★★★★ | Site Privacy: ★★★★ |
| Spaciousness: ★★★★ | Quiet: ★★★★ |
| Security: ★★★★ | Cleanliness: ★★★★ |
| Insect Control: None | Facilities: ★★★★ |

Nestled in 40 wooded acres on the shores of 400-acre Crow Wing Lake, Don and Mayva's Crow Wing Lake Campground offers plenty of mature oak tree shade, grassy sites, and RV locations with large concrete patios. The campstore is well stocked, including a snack bar and bait section. The campground has 40 seasonal sites, leaving 60 for visiting campers. The typical site width is 30 feet, and the campground has 16 pull-throughs. While tent campers are definitely in the minority, they are provided with separate grassy, wooded sites. Started in 1970 by the Kottke's, the campground is well organized and well maintained. Concrete patios and designated parking spots help keep the grass in good condition. The campground of the security is ensured with only one entrance road that passes the office, owners who live on site, and a regular area patrol. Quiet hours—which means no radios, generators or loud voices—are strictly enforced from 10 p.m. to 8 a.m., even on weekends. Reservations are strongly recommended as the campground fills up quickly on weekends and holidays. Weekday camping is recommended for those who like to avoid the crowds.

## BASICS

**Operated by:** Don & Mayva Kottke. **Open:** May 1–Oct. 1. **Site Assignment:** Reservations accepted w/ $30 deposit; refunds (minus $5) w/ 7-day notice. 2-night min. for weekends; 3-night min. for holidays. **Registration:** At campground office. **Fee:** $29 (cash, check, credit cards). **Parking:** At site.

## FACILITIES

**Number of RV Sites:** 90. **Number of Tent-Only Sites:** 10. **Hookups:** Electric (30, 50 amps), water, sewer. **Each Site:** Picnic table, fire ring. **Dump Station:** Yes. **Laundry:** Yes. **Pay Phone:** Yes. **Rest Rooms and Showers:** Yes. **Fuel:** Yes. **Propane:** No. **Internal Roads:** Gravel, in good condition. **RV Service:** No. **Market:** 10 mi. north in Brainerd. **Restaurant:** 5 mi. south in Port Ripley. **General Store:** Yes. **Vending:** Yes. **Swimming Pool:** Yes. **Playground:** Yes. **Other:** Crow Wing Lake, fish-cleaning house, boat launch, Frisbee golf, bankshot basketball, shuffleboard, badminton, softball, horseshoes, volleyball, nature trail, rec room, coin games,. **Activities:** Swimming, hiking, fishing, boating (rental motorboats, canoes, paddleboats, rowboats, pontoon boats available). **Nearby Attractions:** Raceway, casino, golf, Mille Lacs Indian Museum, Paul Bunyan Amusement Center, antique stores, art galleries, historic homes, Lindbergh State Park, Lindbergh Home & Interpretive Center. **Additional Information:** Brainerd Lakes Area Chamber of Commerce, (800) 450-2838.

## RESTRICTIONS

**Pets:** Leash only. **Fires:** Fire ring only. **Alcoholic Beverages:** Permitted. **Vehicle Maximum Length:** None.

## TO GET THERE

From the junction of Hwys 18, 371 and 210, drive 11.5 mi. south on Hwy. 371. Roads are wide and well maintained w/ broad shoulders.

## BRAINERD

### Sullivan's Resort and Campground

7685 CR 127, Brainerd 56401. T: (888) 829-5697; F: (218) 828-8785; www.sullivansresort.com; vacation@sullivansresort.com.

🚐 ★★★★        ▲ ★★★★

| | |
|---|---|
| Beauty: ★★★★ | Site Privacy: ★★★★ |
| Spaciousness: ★★★★ | Quiet: ★★★★ |
| Security: ★★★★ | Cleanliness: ★★★★ |
| Insect Control: ★★★★ | Facilities: ★★★★ |

Take a look at beautiful North Long Lake and the clean facilities at Sullivan's Resort and Campground, and you'll know why so many campers find their way to this spot located just three-and-a-half miles from the Paul Bunyan State Trail. The trail's first 50 miles are paved for bicycling, hiking, and skating. The campground's North Long Lake is seven miles long and three miles wide with 5,998 acres of clean, clear water. Shallow, sandy shores make the lake ideal for children and adults who like to play in the water. To accent the natural water attractions, Sullivan's also has a heated indoor-pool, a sauna, and a hot tub. Sullivan's has 16 seasonal campers, so reservations are recommended for those who wish to camp on the remaining sites. The campground has partly shaded sites on grassy, level ground along the lake. The typical site width is 30 feet, and there are no pull-throughs available.

## BASICS

**Operated by:** Lowell & Dee Sullivan. **Open:** May 1–Oct. 1. **Site Assignment:** Reservations w/ $50 non-refundable deposit. **Registration:** At campground office. **Fee:** $29 (cash, check, credit cards). **Parking:** At site. One car per site. Extra cars must be registered & parked in extra parking area.

## FACILITIES

**Number of RV Sites:** 50. **Number of Tent-Only Sites:** 0. **Hookups:** Electric (20, 30, 50 amps), water, sewer. **Each Site:** Picnic table, fire ring. **Dump Station:** Yes. **Laundry:** Yes. **Pay Phone:** Yes. **Rest Rooms and Showers:** Yes. **Fuel:** Yes. **Propane:** Yes. **Internal Roads:** Gravel, in good condition. **RV Service:** No. **Market:** 8 mi. east in Brainerd. **Restaurant:** 8 mi. east in Brainerd. **General Store:** Yes. **Vending:** Yes. **Swimming Pool:** Yes. **Playground:** Yes. **Other:** North Long Lake, hot tub, rec room, coin games, boat dock, boat ramp, fish-cleaning house, sandy beach, fish freezing service, shuffleboard, horseshoes, volleyball, recreation field, rental cabins, large retreat home. **Activities:** Fishing, swimming, boating (rental kayaks, pontoons, motor boats, canoes, paddleboats available). **Nearby Attractions:** Paul Bunyan Bike Trail, cross-county skiing, snowmobiling, Brainerd International Raceway, antiques, arts & crafts, Crow Wing County Historical Society Museum, golf, Paul Bunyan Amusement Center. **Additional Information:** Brainerd Lakes Area Chamber of Commerce, (800) 450-2838.

## RESTRICTIONS

**Pets:** No pets allowed. **Fires:** Fire ring only. **Alcoholic Beverages:** Permitted. **Vehicle Maximum Length:** None. **Other:** Tents & screen houses must be moved every 2–3 days on the same site; doormats & rugs not allowed on site.

## TO GET THERE

From the junction of Hwy. 210 and Hwy. 371, drive 7.5 mi. north on Hwy. 371, then 2.25 mi. northeast on CR 115, then 1 mi. east on CR 127. Roads are mostly wide and well maintained w/ adequate shoulders.

## BRANDON

## Kamp Kappy Family Resort and Campgrounds

13110 Devils Lake Rd. Northwest, Brandon 56315. T: (800) 845-2566; www.rea-alp.com/~bkampkap; bkampkap@rea-alp.com.

🚐 ★★★                          ⛺ ★★★★

| | |
|---|---|
| Beauty: ★★★★ | Site Privacy: ★★★ |
| Spaciousness: ★★★★ | Quiet: ★★★★ |
| Security: ★★★★ | Cleanliness: ★★★ |
| Insect Control: None | Facilities: ★★★ |

Third and fourth generations are now visiting the almost 100-year-old Kamp Kappy. Located on Devils Lake one-and-a-half miles north of Brandon, the campground has no highway or trains running by it to disturb the quiet. The only noise is what campers bring with them, and the owners work to keep that minimal. Part of a chain of lakes leading to the Minnesota River, Devils Lake is a 300-acre natural lake. Because the lake is small and stocked well, it is a relatively easy lake to fish, even in weather that would typically keep folks off most other lakes. The campground offers a fish-cleaning house with three sinks and plenty of freezer space for daily catches. The sandy swimming beach gradually slopes out to a swim dock, and the swimming area is marked with buoys. Sites are level, grassy, and shaded in this wooded lakeside campground. The typical site width is 40 feet, and the best RV sites are 1A and 2A because they provide slightly bigger pull-through spaces. Tent campers have a separate area overlooking the lake that is protected by an unobtrusive security light. With one dead-end access road, owners who live on the campground, and regular campground patrols, campers are likely to feel quite safe.

## BASICS

**Operated by:** Ray & Sharalyn Berndt. **Open:** May 1–Oct. 1. **Site Assignment:** Reservations w/ 1-night deposit; refunds (minus $15 fee) w/ 30-day notice. **Registration:** At campground office. **Fee:** $20 (cash, check, credit cards). **Parking:** At site.

## FACILITIES

**Number of RV Sites:** 50. **Number of Tent-Only Sites:** 14. **Hookups:** Electric (15, 20, 30 amps), water, sewer. **Each Site:** Picnic table, fire ring. **Dump Station:** Yes. **Laundry:** No. **Pay Phone:** Yes. **Rest Rooms and Showers:** Yes. **Fuel:** Yes. **Propane:** No. **Internal Roads:** Gravel, in good condition. **RV Service:** No. **Market:** 1.5 mi. south in Brandon. **Restaurant:** 1.5 mi. south in Brandon. **General Store:** Yes. **Vending:** Yes. **Swimming Pool:** No. **Playground:** Yes. **Other:** Devils Lake, sandy beach, Ray's R/C Land (radio control hobby shop), horseshoes, volleyball, badminton, basketball, rec room, fish-cleaning facility, pavilion, boat ramp, boat dock, sports field. **Activities:** Swimming, fishing, boating (rental motorboats, pontoons, canoes & paddleboats available). **Nearby Attractions:** Golf, tennis, Runestone Museum, Fort Alexandria Agricultural Exhibit. **Additional Information:** Alexandria Lakes Area Chamber of Commerce, (800) 245-2539.

## RESTRICTIONS

**Pets:** Leash only, $10 per pet per stay. **Fires:** Fire ring only. **Alcoholic Beverages:** Permitted. **Vehicle Maximum Length:** 35 ft.

## TO GET THERE

From the junction of I-94 and CR 7, take Exit 90 and drive 4 mi. north on CR 7, then 0.5 mi. west on access road. Roads are wide and well maintained w/ adequate shoulders.

## CASS LAKE

### Stony Point Resort Campground and RV Park

P.O. Box 518, Cass Lake 56633. T: (800) 332-6311; F: (218) 335-2680; www.stonyptresortcasslake.com; stonypt@paulbunyan.net.

 ★★★★ ▲ ★★★★

Beauty: ★★★★      Site Privacy: ★★★★
Spaciousness: ★★★★      Quiet: ★★★★

Security: ★★★★      Cleanliness: ★★★★
Insect Control: Yes      Facilities: ★★★★

Known as the "Little Venice of the North," Stony Point has a 2,000-foot winding boat canal. that keeps campers within close proximity to their boats. The campground is located two miles east of Cass Lake which is connected with seven other lakes. This is a nice stop for avid boaters. Located on the lake, the campsites are mostly shaded, level, and grassy with concrete patios. The typical site width is 35 feet, and there are 28 pull-throughs. The campground also has mobile homes and many seasonals. Tent sites are in a separate area for more privacy. The restaurant and lounge offers a complete menu and salad bar, as well as catering services for picnics and other events. The marina offers fish-cleaning, fish freezing, and fish packing. Security measures are good with owners who live on site, regular patrols, and surveillance cameras.

## BASICS

**Operated by:** Delbert & Kay Gangelhoff, Karen & Jim Bowley. **Open:** May 1–Oct. 15. **Site Assignment:** Reservations w/ 1-night deposit; refunds w/ 7-day notice. **Registration:** At campground office. **Fee:** $24 (cash, check, credit cards). **Parking:** At site.

## FACILITIES

**Number of RV Sites:** 165. **Number of Tent-Only Sites:** 10. **Hookups:** Electric (30, 50 amps), water, sewer. **Each Site:** Picnic table, fire ring. **Dump Station:** Yes. **Laundry:** Yes. **Pay Phone:** Yes. **Rest Rooms and Showers:** Yes. **Fuel:** Yes. **Propane:** Yes. **Internal Roads:** Gravel, in good condition. **RV Service:** No. **Market:** 2 mi. west in Cass Lake. **Restaurant:** On site. **General Store:** Yes. **Vending:** Yes. **Swimming Pool:** No. **Playground:** Yes. **Other:** Lake, boat canal, rec room, marina, concrete patios, restaurant & bar, video games, pavilion, recreation field, basketball, badminton, horseshoes, hiking trails, volleyball, fish-cleaning house. **Activities:** Swimming, boating (rental pontoon boats, kayaks, canoes, paddleboats, motor boats available), hiking, fishing, hunting. **Nearby Attractions:** Lakes, Native American burial grounds, logging museum, wildlife park, scenic drives, golf, tennis, bingo, casino, summer theater. **Additional Information:** Bemidji Area Tourist Information Center, (800) 458-2223, ext. 100.

## RESTRICTIONS

**Pets:** Leash only. **Fires:** Fire ring only. **Alcoholic Beverages:** Permitted. **Vehicle Maximum Length:** None.

## TO GET THERE

From the junction of Hwy. 371 and US 2, drive 2 mi. east on US 2. Roads are wide and well maintained w/ broad shoulders.

## CLOQUET

### Cloquet/Duluth KOA

1479 Old Carlton Rd., Cloquet 55720. T: (800) KOA-9506

🚐 ★★★★                    🏕 ★★★

Beauty: ★★                 Site Privacy: ★★★
Spaciousness: ★★★          Quiet: ★★★★
Security: ★★★★             Cleanliness: ★★★★
Insect Control: None       Facilities: ★★★★

Travelers on their way through the Cloquet and Duluth area are often pleased to find the Cloquet/Duluth KOA. It is very clean, offers good facilities, and is conveniently located near major roads. It is not much of a destination campground, however. Campers don't stop here planning to spend several days at the campground. The activities are rather skimpy, and it doesn't provide much in the way of natural beauty. Sites are level, open, and shaded, and 30 feet is the average site width. Most RV sites are gravel, and 27 are pull-throughs. The most requested RV sites are 1–10 because they offer full hookup and pull-through access. Tent sites are scattered throughout the campground. Security is provided by owners who live on the grounds providing regular patrols, and local police also keep an eye on the campground.

## BASICS

**Operated by:** Bill, Barbara, Bob, & Linde Higton. **Open:** May 1–Oct. 15. **Site Assignment:** Reservations w/ 1-night deposit; refunds w/ 5-day notice. **Registration:** At campground office. **Fee:** $25 (cash, check, credit cards). **Parking:** At site.

## FACILITIES

**Number of RV Sites:** 50. **Number of Tent-Only Sites:** 9. **Hookups:** Electric (30, 50 amps), water, sewer. **Each Site:** Picnic table, fire ring. **Dump Station:** Yes. **Laundry:** Yes. **Pay Phone:** Yes. **Rest Rooms and Showers:** Yes. **Fuel:** No.

**Propane:** Yes. **Internal Roads:** Gravel, in good condition. **RV Service:** No. **Market:** 1 mi. south in Cloquet. **Restaurant:** 3 mi. south in Cloquet. **General Store:** Yes. **Vending:** Yes. **Swimming Pool:** Yes. **Playground:** Yes. **Other:** Hot tub, horseshoes, volleyball, game room, badminton, basketball, rec hall, recreation field, TV room. **Activities:** Swimming, biking (rental bikes available), Saturday night hayride, weekly ice cream social. **Nearby Attractions:** Zoo, depot museum, harbor cruises, casino, paper mill tour, train rides, charter fishing, agate hounding, Congdon Mansion, canal park. **Additional Information:** Cloquet Area Chamber of Commerce, (800) 554-4350.

## RESTRICTIONS

**Pets:** Leash only. **Fires:** Fire ring only. **Alcoholic Beverages:** Permitted. **Vehicle Maximum Length:** 40 ft.

## TO GET THERE

From the junction of I-35 and Hwy. 45, take Exit 239 and drive 2 mi. south on Hwy. 45, then 0.25 mi. west on CR 3. Roads are wide and well maintained w/ broad shoulders

## COKATO LAKE

### Cokato Lake Campground

2945 CR 4 Southwest, Cokato 55321. T: (320) 286-5779

🚐 ★★★★                    🏕 ★★★★

Beauty: ★★★★              Site Privacy: ★★★★
Spaciousness: ★★★★        Quiet: ★★★★
Security: ★★★★            Cleanliness: ★★★★
Insect Control: None      Facilities: ★★★★

Located beside Cokato Lake on a hilly terrain, this campground offers mostly shaded, grassy sites with a typical site width of 25 feet. There are 12 pull-through sites, and some open spots for campers concerned about satellite TV reception. Laid out in a series of loops, the campground has 100 seasonal campers. Quiet hours are enforced from 11 p.m. to 8 a.m. when all children must remain at sites and radios must be off. Mini-bikes, ATVs, and gas golf carts are not allowed on the grounds. The swimming pool is closed on Mondays for maintenance. The speed limit is ten mph, rather high for a family campground, and campers are asked to limit driving after dark. Security includes owners who live on site and a security gate.

## BASICS

**Operated by:** Brent & Kathryn Helmke. **Open:**
May 1–Oct. 1. **Site Assignment:** Reservations w/ 1-
night deposit; refunds (minus $5) w/ 7-day notice.
**Registration:** At campground office. **Fee:** $25
(cash, check, credit cards). **Parking:** At site.

## FACILITIES

**Number of RV Sites:** 202. **Number of Tent-
Only Sites:** 23. **Hookups:** Electric (20, 30, 50
amps), water, sewer. **Each Site:** Picnic table, fire
ring. **Dump Station:** Yes. **Laundry:** Yes. **Pay
Phone:** Yes. **Rest Rooms and Showers:** Yes.
**Fuel:** No. **Propane:** Yes. **Internal Roads:** Gravel,
in good condition. **RV Service:** No. **Market:** 3 mi.
south in Cokato. **Restaurant:** 3 mi. south in
Cokato. **General Store:** Yes. **Vending:** Yes. **Swimming Pool:** Yes. **Playground:** Yes. **Other:** Rental
cabins & cottages, chapel, Cokato Lake, game room,
mini-golf, tennis, softball, volleyball, rec hall, pavilion,
boat ramp, boat dock. **Activities:** Swimming, fishing, boating (rental rowboats, canoes, paddleboats &
motorboats available, scheduled weekend activities.
**Nearby Attractions:** Charles A. Lindberg House
& History Center, Ellingson Car Museum, Minnesota
Baseball Hall of Fame, St. John's Benedictine Abbey,
golf, antiques, arts & crafts shops. **Additional
Information:** St. Cloud Area CVB, (800) 264-2940.

## RESTRICTIONS

**Pets:** Leash only. **Fires:** Fire ring only. **Alcoholic
Beverages:** Permitted. **Vehicle Maximum
Length:** 40 ft.

## TO GET THERE

From the junction of US 12 and CR 4, drive 3
mi. northeast on CR 4. Roads are wide and well
maintained w/ broad shoulders.

## DETROIT LAKES
## Country Campground

13639 260th Ave., Detroit Lakes 56501. T: (800)
898-7901; www.lakesnet.net/ccdl; ccdl@lakesnet.net.

🚐 ★★★★                   ⛺ ★★★★

Beauty: ★★★★            Site Privacy: ★★★★
Spaciousness: ★★★★       Quiet: ★★★★
Security: ★★★★           Cleanliness: ★★★★
Insect Control: ★★★★     Facilities: ★★★

Little touches are what make Country Campground such an inviting place to stay. The
entrance is welcoming with a trellis, old wagon-
wheel, flowers, and statues of friendly critters.

Other bits of landscaping around the campground are also pleasant. Located one mile south
of Detroit Lakes, which has a mile-long beach,
Country Campground offers level, grassy sites
along Glawe Lake. The typical site width is 40
feet, and there are 14 pull-through sites. A well-
organized gift shop with dolls, wood carvings,
ceramics, and hand-blown glass is a plus.
Another attraction is a fenced-in children's area
complete with swing sets, sandbox, and toys. A
dock with a love seat swing is a popular spot.
Security measures include owners who keep a
close watch on the campground.

## BASICS

**Operated by:** Elwood & Lois Orner. **Open:** May
1–Oct. 15. **Site Assignment:** Reservations w/ 1-
night deposit; refund w/ 7-day notice. **Registration:** At campground office. **Fee:** $20 (cash, check,
credit cards). **Parking:** At site.

## FACILITIES

**Number of RV Sites:** 30. **Number of Tent-
Only Sites:** 4. **Hookups:** Electric (30 amps),
water, sewer. **Each Site:** Picnic table, fire ring.
**Dump Station:** Yes. **Laundry:** No. **Pay Phone:**
Yes. **Rest Rooms and Showers:** Yes. **Fuel:** No.
**Propane:** Yes. **Internal Roads:** Gravel, in good
condition. **RV Service:** No. **Market:** 1 mi. north in
Detroit Lakes. **Restaurant:** 1 mi. north in Detroit
Lakes. **General Store:** Yes, limited. **Vending:** Yes.
**Swimming Pool:** No. **Playground:** Yes. **Other:**
Pavilion, fishing lake, recreation building, softball,
basketball, horseshoes, volleyball, lounge, gift shop,
croquet. **Activities:** Fishing, boating (paddleboats &
canoes available). **Nearby Attractions:** Swimming,
golf, two amusement parks, boating, snowmobiling,
cross-country skiing, downhill skiing, Becker County
Museum, 412 lakes, scenic drives, Tamarac National
Wildlife Refuge. **Additional Information:** Detroit
Lakes Regional Chamber of Commerce & Tourism
Bureau, (800) 542-3992.

## RESTRICTIONS

**Pets:** Leash only. **Fires:** Fire ring only. **Alcoholic
Beverages:** Permitted. **Vehicle Maximum
Length:** None.

## TO GET THERE

From the junction of US 10 and US 59., drive
south 2.2 mi. on US 50 to CR 22, then drive
south 0.5 mi. to West Lake Dr., then 1.2 mi. to
260th Ave., south 0.8 mi. Roads are mostly wide
and well maintained w/ adequate shoulders.

## ELY

### Silver Rapids Lodge

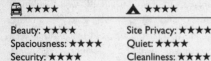

459 Kawishiwi Trail, Ely 55731. T: (800) 950-9425;
F: (218) 365-3540; wwwsilverrapidslodge.com;
rapids@northernet.com.

| 🚐 ★★★★ | 🏕 ★★★★ |
|---|---|
| Beauty: ★★★★ | Site Privacy: ★★★★ |
| Spaciousness: ★★★★ | Quiet: ★★★★ |
| Security: ★★★★ | Cleanliness: ★★★★ |
| Insect Control: ★★★★ | Facilities: ★★★★ |

At the gateway to the Boundary Waters, Silver Rapids Lodge has enough year-round outdoor activities to keep any sporting enthusiast happy. Silver Rapids has a nature and fishing guide on hand and rents a variety of boats for fishing, as well as equipment for winter sports (camping facilites are limited in the winter). Snowmobiles, skis, snowshoes, and portable ice-fishing houses are available for rent. Silver Rapids ski trails link into the Ely Hidden Valley and Mesabi ski trail system. One of the prettiest sights is the Friday and Saturday night lantern-skiing. The Tomahawk snowmobile trail system leads right to Silver Rapids' front door. The trail is groomed twice a week and offers some of the most picturesque scenery around. Camping sites are semi-wooded with pine trees and overlook a river and lake scenery. Sewer sites are on a hillside. The typical site width is 30 feet, and the campground has no pull-through sites. Security measures include owners who live on site and patrol the campground.

### BASICS

**Operated by:** Bryan & Pam Klubbin. **Open:** All year. **Site Assignment:** Reservations w/ 1-night deposit; refund w/ 60-day notice. **Registration:** At campground office. **Fee:** $30 (cash, check, credit cards). **Parking:** At site.

### FACILITIES

**Number of RV Sites:** 39. **Number of Tent-Only Sites:** 2. **Hookups:** Electric (20, 30 amps), water, sewer. **Each Site:** Picnic table, fire ring. **Dump Station:** Yes. **Laundry:** Yes. **Pay Phone:** Yes. **Rest Rooms and Showers:** Yes. **Fuel:** Yes. **Propane:** Yes. **Internal Roads:** Gravel, in good condition. **RV Service:** No. **Market:** 5 mi. southwest in Ely. **Restaurant:** Adjacent. **General Store:** Yes, limited. **Vending:** Yes. **Swimming Pool:** No. **Playground:**

Yes. **Other:** White Iron Lake, swimming beach, whirlpool, boat ramp, rec room, marina, coin games, basketball, shuffleboard, horseshoes, hiking trails, rental cabins, retreat house, suites. **Activities:** Swimming, fishing (rental portable ice-fishing house available), hiking, boating (rental pontoons, canoes, kayaks, paddleboats, motorboats available), scheduled activities. **Nearby Attractions:** Boundary Waters Canoe Area Wilderness, Ely/Winton History Museum, International Wolf Center, scenic drives, arts & crafts, antiques, snowmobiling, cross-country skiing, bowling, mini-golf, Dorothy Molter Museum. **Additional Information:** Ely Chamber of Commerce, (800) 777-7281.

### RESTRICTIONS

**Pets:** Leash only. **Fires:** Fire ring only. **Alcoholic Beverages:** Permitted. **Vehicle Maximum Length:** None.

### TO GET THERE

From the junction of Hwy. 1 and Hwy. 169, drive 1.75 mi. northeast on Hwy. 169, then 3 mi. east on CR 58 and CR 16. Roads are mostly wide and well maintained w/ narrow shoulders in spots.

## FARIBAULT

### Camp Faribo

21851 Bagley Ave., Faribault 55021. T: (800) 689-8453

| 🚐 ★★★★ | 🏕 ★★★ |
|---|---|
| Beauty: ★★★★ | Site Privacy: ★★★ |
| Spaciousness: ★★★ | Quiet: ★★★★ |
| Security: ★★★★ | Cleanliness: ★★★★ |
| Insect Control: ★★★★ | Facilities: ★★★★ |

An open, grassy campground with level sites, Camp Faribo is a handy camping spot if you plan to visit nearby attractions. Many campers come year after year to visit area attractions and to enjoy the activities at the campground. Camp Faribo is about 45 minutes from the Mall of America and the Minnesota Zoo and is close to ten lakes. The campground has a typical site width of 25 feet and has 20 pull-throughs. With only nine seasonal campers, the campground has plenty of room for visitors. The most popular sites are close to the heated swimming pool and the facilities. The owners keep a close watch on the campground to keep it quiet and family oriented.

## BASICS

**Operated by:** Chuck & Fern Kubalsky. **Open:** Apr. 15–May 15. **Site Assignment:** Reservations w/ 1-night deposit; refund (minus $5) w/ 15-day notice. **Registration:** At campground office. **Fee:** $22 (cash, check, credit cards). **Parking:** At site.

## FACILITIES

**Number of RV Sites:** 71. **Number of Tent-Only Sites:** 0. **Hookups:** Electric (20, 30, 50 amps), water, sewer. **Each Site:** Picnic table, fire ring. **Dump Station:** Yes. **Laundry:** Yes. **Pay Phone:** Yes. **Rest Rooms and Showers:** Yes. **Fuel:** No. **Propane:** Yes. **Internal Roads:** Gravel, in good condition. **RV Service:** No. **Market:** 2 mi. north. **Restaurant:** 2 mi. north. **General Store:** Yes. **Vending:** Yes. **Swimming Pool:** Yes. **Playground:** Yes. **Other:** Rec hall, coin games, shuffleboard, sports field, horseshoes, volleyball. **Activities:** Swimming. **Nearby Attractions:** Historic walking tours, Alexander Faribault House, Episcopal Cathedral, Faribault Woolen Mill, Ivan Whillock Studio, Rice County Museum of History, Mall of America, Minnesota Zoo, 10 lakes. **Additional Information:** Faribault Area Chamber of Commerce, (800) 658-2354.

## RESTRICTIONS

**Pets:** Leash only. **Fires:** Fire ring only. **Alcoholic Beverages:** Permitted. **Vehicle Maximum Length:** None.

## TO GET THERE

From the junction of I-35 and Hwy. 60, take Exit 56, drive 500 ft. east on Hwy. 60, then 1.5 mi. south on Western Ave. Roads are wide and well maintained w/ adequate shoulders.

## GILBERT

### Sherwood Forest Campground

Box 548, Gilbert 55741. T: (800) 403-1803

🚐 ★★★            ⛺ ★★★

Beauty: ★★★            Site Privacy: ★★
Spaciousness: ★★            Quiet: ★★★
Security: ★★★★            Cleanliness: ★★★
Insect Control: None            Facilities: ★★

Because it is located a couple of blocks from the main street of Gilbert, the Sherwood Forest Campground offers easy access on good paved roads. The campground is on a hill with the beach and Lake Ore-Be-Gone spread out below.

It is a good walk downhill from the campsites to the beach. Wooden plank steps have been built to make scaling down the hill easier for campers. The 140-acre lake is a huge mine pit lake resulting from the natural flooding of three iron-ore mines. The lake is popular for waterskiing, fishing, boating, and swimming. The Mesabi Trail runs directly past the campground. Laid out in a series of loops, the campground offers mostly grassy, open sites with an average width of 30 feet. The nine pull-through sites measure 24 × 100. Security is good—the campground is two blocks from the police station and city police patrol every hour. Showers and rest rooms have a code number given only to campers, so non-campers can't use the facilities.

## BASICS

**Operated by:** City of Gilbert. **Open:** May 1–Oct. 31. **Site Assignment:** Reservations accepted w/ $10 deposit; no refund but deposit can be applied to later visit. **Registration:** At campground office. **Fee:** $15 (cash, check). **Parking:** At site.

## FACILITIES

**Number of RV Sites:** 43. **Number of Tent-Only Sites:** 8. **Hookups:** Electric (30 amp), water, sewer. **Each Site:** Picnic table, fire ring. **Dump Station:** Yes. **Laundry:** No. **Pay Phone:** Yes. **Rest Rooms and Showers:** Yes. **Fuel:** No. **Propane:** No. **Internal Roads:** Paved, in good condition. **RV Service:** No. **Market:** 4 mi. north in Virginia. **Restaurant:** 3 blocks in Gilbert. **General Store:** No. **Vending:** No. **Swimming Pool:** No. **Playground:** Yes. **Other:** Lake Ore-Be-Gone, boat ramp, dock, swimming beach, volleyball, baseball field, hiking trail, picnic shelters. **Activities:** Swimming, fishing, boating, hiking. **Nearby Attractions:** Hockey Hall of Fame, water skiing, golf, skiing, Mesabi Trail, shops, Iron Range Historical Society, Iron World USA, Giant's Ridge ski & summer recreation area. **Additional Information:** City of Gilbert, (218) 749-3837.

## RESTRICTIONS

**Pets:** Leash only. **Fires:** Fire ring only. **Alcoholic Beverages:** At sites only. **Vehicle Maximum Length:** None.

## TO GET THERE

From the junction of US 53 and SR 37 East, drive 3 mi. east on SR 37 to Wisconsin Ave. (in town,) then drive 0.5 mi. southeast on Wisconsin Ave.

## GRAND RAPIDS
## Sugar Bay Campground/Resort

21812 Moose Point Rd., Cohasset 55721. T: (218) 326-8493

 ★★★           ★★

| | |
|---|---|
| Beauty: ★★★★ | Site Privacy: ★★★ |
| Spaciousness: ★★★★ | Quiet: ★★★★ |
| Security: ★★★★ | Cleanliness: ★★★★ |
| Insect Control: None | Facilities: ★★★ |

Campers who have seen the campground exit sign on the highway often pull in to Sugar Bay frustrated and tired. Since the state won't post a mileage sign for the campground, many campers who have turned off hoping to find a convenient night's rest are often a bit angry. It is almost a 14 mile trip from the highway to the campground. But it is worth it for a quiet night's sleep. The campground is small, well maintained, and clean. Sites are level, grassy, and some are shady with three pull-throughs and a typical site width of 40 feet. Baby trees are planted around the site. The Pokegama Lake campground features water activities and many repeat customers because of them. Bait and groceries are not sold at Sugar Bay, so be sure to take what you need, or you might have to drive 20 miles round trip to get it.

### BASICS
**Operated by:** Jim & Sandy Holasek. **Open:** May 11–Oct. 31. **Site Assignment:** Reservations w/ 1-night deposit; refunds w/ 7-day notice. **Registration:** At campground office. **Fee:** $17 (cash, check, credit cards). **Parking:** At site.

### FACILITIES
**Number of RV Sites:** 23. **Number of Tent-Only Sites:** 0. **Hookups:** Electric (20, 30, 50 amps), water, sewer. **Each Site:** Picnic table, fire ring. **Dump Station:** Yes. **Laundry:** No. **Pay Phone:** No. **Rest Rooms and Showers:** Yes. **Fuel:** Yes. **Propane:** No. **Internal Roads:** Gravel, in good condition. **RV Service:** No. **Market:** 10 mi. east in Grand Rapids. **Restaurant:** 8 mi east in Grand Rapids. **General Store:** Yes. **Vending:** No. **Swimming Pool:** No. **Playground:** No. **Other:** Pokegama Lake, boat ramp, boat dock, horseshoes, cement patios, marina. **Activities:** Swimming, fishing, boating (rental motor boats, paddleboats & pontoons available). **Nearby Attractions:** Golf, Forest History Center, Otasca Heritage Center,

Judy Garland Birthplace, Children's Discovery Museum. **Additional Information:** Grand Rapids Convention & Visitors Center, (800) 472-6366.

### RESTRICTIONS
**Pets:** Leash only, restricted to campsite. **Fires:** Fire ring only. **Alcoholic Beverages:** Permitted. **Vehicle Maximum Length:** 40 ft.

### TO GET THERE
From the junction of US 2 and US 169S, drive 7.5 mi. south on US 169, then 6 mi. west and north on CR 17, then 0.25 mi. east on CR 239. Roads are wide and well maintained w/ broad shoulders.

## HIBBING
## Forest Heights RV Park

2240 East 25th St., Hibbing 55746. T: (218) 263-5782

★★          ★

| | |
|---|---|
| Beauty: ★★ | Site Privacy: ★★ |
| Spaciousness: ★★ | Quiet: ★★ |
| Security: ★★★ | Cleanliness: ★★★ |
| Insect Control: Yes | Facilities: ★★ |

An urban campground located behind a mobile home park, Forest Heights RV Park would be a good place for travelers who are passing through or staying for a brief time to enjoy local attractions. The campground is not, however, a destination that most would consider for a camping experience. The campground has better infrastructure than most campgrounds—paved streets, curbs, and gutters, and sidewalks leading up to camping sites. Most of the sites are level, open, and grassy with six pull-throughs and a typical width of 35 feet. For RVs, it would be like staying in a mobile home park. For tents, it would be more like camping out in someone's backyard. The price, convenience, and city amenities are attractive. On-site activities are lacking, but Forest Heights does not pretend to be a camping resort.

### BASICS
**Operated by:** Alvin & Allayne Glover. **Open:** May 1–Oct. 31. **Site Assignment:** Reservation w/ 1-night deposit; no refund. **Registration:** At campground office. **Fee:** $18 (cash, check). **Parking:** At site.

## FACILITIES

**Number of RV Sites:** 44. **Number of Tent-Only Sites:** 6. **Hookups:** Electric (20, 30, 50 amps), water, sewer. **Each Site:** Picnic table, grill. **Dump Station:** Yes. **Laundry:** Yes. **Pay Phone:** No. **Rest Rooms and Showers:** Yes. **Fuel:** No. **Propane:** No. **Internal Roads:** Paved, in good condition. **RV Service:** No. **Market:** 1 mi. south in Hibbing. **Restaurant:** 1 mi. south in Hibbing. **General Store:** No. **Vending:** No. **Swimming Pool:** No. **Playground:** No. **Other:** Rec hall, sports field. **Activities:** None. **Nearby Attractions:** Swimming lake & park, First Settlers Museum, Hull Ruse Mahoning Mine, Greyhound Bus Origin Center, Paulucci Space Theatre. **Additional Information:** Hibbing Area Chamber of Commerce, (900) 444-2246.

## RESTRICTIONS

**Pets:** Leash only. **Fires:** Grills only. **Alcoholic Beverages:** Permitted. **Vehicle Maximum Length:** None.

## TO GET THERE

From the junction of Hwy. 37 and US 169/Hwy. 73, drive 1 mi. north on US 169/Hwy. 73, then 1 mi. east on 25th St.

# HINCKLEY

## Grand Casino Hinckley RV Resort

Rte. 3, Box 14, Hinckley 55037. T: (800) 995-GRAND; F: (952) 449-7785; www.grandcasinosminnesota.com.

🚐 ★★★★★          ▲ n/a

| | |
|---|---|
| Beauty: ★★★ | Site Privacy: ★★★ |
| Spaciousness: ★★★ | Quiet: ★★★★ |
| Security: ★★★★★ | Cleanliness: ★★★★★ |
| Insect Control: None | Facilities: ★★★★★ |

Grand Casino RV Resort is the best money can buy. A full-time cleaning staff keeps the rest rooms, showers, grounds, and other facilities spotless. The interior roads are better than you find in some towns. The grass is manicured like a golf course. The recreation options are excellent and suited to all ages. The security is outstanding—the campground office is open 24 hours a day, the campgrounds are well-lit and patrolled, and access is through a manned locked gate where visitors need an access code to enter. If you want to gamble and enjoy the pool and other amenities, it is well worth a visit. The Grand

Casino Hinckley is open 24 hours a day with blackjack tables and more than 2,000 slot machines, big-name entertainment acts from Las Vegas to Nashville, four restaurants, and an all-you-can-eat buffet. But, if you want to sit under a shade tree and commune with nature, this is not the place. Laid out in a series of loops, the campground is basically a big paved field with baby trees. The typical site width is 35 feet. All 222 sites have full hookup, and all sites are back-ins. Tent campers are out of luck. Tents are allowed only as an auxiliary unit.

## BASICS

**Operated by:** The Mille Lacs Band of Ojibwe. **Open:** All year. **Site Assignment:** Reservation w/ 1-night deposit; refund w/ 7-day notice. **Registration:** At campground office. **Fee:** $16 (cash, check, credit cards). **Parking:** At site.

## FACILITIES

**Number of RV Sites:** 222. **Number of Tent-Only Sites:** 0. **Hookups:** Electric (30, 50 amps), water, sewer, cable TV. **Each Site:** Picnic table, fire ring, light, patio. **Dump Station:** Yes. **Laundry:** Yes. **Pay Phone:** Yes. **Rest Rooms and Showers:** Yes. **Fuel:** No. **Propane:** No. **Internal Roads:** Paved, in excellent condition. **RV Service:** No. **Market:** 2 mi. west in Hinckley. **Restaurant:** Next door. **General Store:** Yes. **Vending:** Yes. **Swimming Pool:** Yes. **Playground:** Yes. **Other:** Casino, free shuttle to casino, lodge, performers in outdoor amphitheater & Silver Sevens Lounge, volleyball, horseshoes, game room, Kids Quest Activity Center, rec room, whirlpool, golf, badminton, video games, shuffleboard, basketball, recreation field, adults room. **Activities:** Gambling, swimming, golf. **Nearby Attractions:** Fire Museum, state trails, scenic drives, flea market, antique shops, historical sites. **Additional Information:** Hinckley CVB, (800) 996-4566.

## RESTRICTIONS

**Pets:** Leash only. **Fires:** Fire ring only. **Alcoholic Beverages:** Permitted. **Vehicle Maximum Length:** 60 ft. **Other:** Tents are permitted as an auxiliary unit only.

## TO GET THERE

From the junction of I-35 and Hwy. 48, drive 1 mi. east on Hwy. 48. Roads are wide and well maintained w/ broad shoulders.

## HINCKLEY
## St. Croix Haven Campground

Rte. 3 Box 385, Hinckley 55037. T: (320) 655-7989; www.worman.com/haven.

| 🚐 ★★★★ | ⛺ ★★★★ |
|---|---|
| Beauty: ★★★★ | Site Privacy: ★★★★ |
| Spaciousness: ★★★★ | Quiet: ★★★★ |
| Security: ★★★★ | Cleanliness: ★★★★ |
| Insect Control: No | Facilities: ★★★★ |

St. Croix Haven Campground has a major advantage over other campgrounds—it is laid out in a series of cul de sac patterns each with six sites. This arrangement provides for more spacious, private sites, particularly with several trees spaced between the sites. Located five miles west of Danbury, the campground offers a natural setting with level, grassy, and gravel sites, but no pull-throughs. Tent sites are in a special grassy section. The most popular RV sites are 27–44 because they are close to the pool and the bathroom. The heated indoor pool offers three seasons of swimming. A well-stocked campstore and a deluxe, all-carpeted adult lounge with a split rock fireplace, sundeck, and color TV add to the facilities. Security measures are good with one entrance past the office, owners who live on site, adequate lights, and campground patrol. Now, if the campground just had sewer hookups and some pull-throughs, it would be even better.

### BASICS
**Operated by:** Jerry & Joy Holt. **Open:** May 1–Oct. 22. **Site Assignment:** Reservations w/ 2-night deposit, refunds w/ 7-day notice. **Registration:** At campground office. **Fee:** $23 (cash, check, credit cards). **Parking:** At site.

### FACILITIES
**Number of RV Sites:** 92. **Number of Tent-Only Sites:** 20. **Hookups:** Electric (20, 30, 50 amps), water. **Each Site:** Picnic table, fire ring. **Dump Station:** Yes. **Laundry:** Yes. **Pay Phone:** Yes. **Rest Rooms and Showers:** Yes. **Fuel:** No. **Propane:** No. **Internal Roads:** Gravel, in good condition. **RV Service:** No. **Market:** 5 mi. east in Danbury. **Restaurant:** 5 mi. east in Danbury. **General Store:** Yes. **Vending:** No. **Swimming Pool:** Yes. **Playground:** Yes. **Other:** St. Croix River, game room, horseshoes, badminton, volleyball, covered pavilion, adult lounge, sundeck, private card rooms, sports field, hiking trail. **Activities:** Swimming, fishing, free firetruck rides, canoeing (rental canoes available), innertube floats (rental intertubes available, biking (rental bikes available), scheduled weekend activities. **Nearby Attractions:** Casino, Fire Museum, golf, state trails, scenic drives, flea market, antique shops, historical sites. **Additional Information:** Hinckley CVB, (800) 996-4566.

### RESTRICTIONS
**Pets:** Leash only. **Fires:** Fire ring only. **Alcoholic Beverages:** Permitted. **Vehicle Maximum Length:** None. **Other:** Friends & visitors must register at the campground office & pay a $3 fee.

### TO GET THERE
From the junction of I-35 and Hwy. 48, drive 23.5 mi. est on Hwy. 48, then 1 mi. north on CR 173. Roads are wide and well maintained w/ broad shoulders.

## HINCKLEY
## St. Croix State Park

Rte. 3, Box 450, Hinckley 55037. T: (320) 384-6591; www.dnr.state.mn.us.

| 🚐 ★★ | ⛺ ★★★★ |
|---|---|
| Beauty: ★★★★ | Site Privacy: ★★★★ |
| Spaciousness: ★★★★ | Quiet: ★★★★ |
| Security: ★★★★ | Cleanliness: ★★★ |
| Insect Control: None | Facilities: ★★ |

Located 15 miles east of Hinckley, St. Croix State Park is Minnesota's largest state park. Situated along the St. Croix River, the park covers over 33,000 acres of forests, meadows, marshes, and streams. The park was established in 1943 after being developed by the National Park Service as a demonstration area. It lives up to its reputation as a popular recreational spot. The park offers 127 miles of hiking trails, 75 miles of horse trails, 6 miles of paved trails, 80 miles of groomed snowmobile trails, and 6 miles of ski trails. The RV sites are gravel and rather small at 15 × 60. They are mostly shaded with no pull-through sites available. Tent sites include two pack-in sites, ten primitive canoe campsites, and a primitive group camp for up to 200 campers. Tent campers have more room and privacy in their wilderness setting.

## BASICS

**Operated by:** State of Minnesota. **Open:** All year. **Site Assignment:** Reservations w/ 1-night fee plus $7.25 non-refundable service charge. Refunds (minus $5 fee & $7.25 service charge ) w/ 3-day notice. **Registration:** At campground office. **Fee:** $15 (Cash, check, credit cards). **Parking:** At site.

## FACILITIES

**Number of RV Sites:** 42. **Number of Tent-Only Sites:** 170. **Hookups:** Electric (30 amps). **Each Site:** Picnic table, fire ring. **Dump Station:** Yes. **Laundry:** No. **Pay Phone:** Yes. **Rest Rooms and Showers:** Yes. **Fuel:** No. **Propane:** No. **Internal Roads:** Paved/gravel, in good condition. **RV Service:** No. **Market:** 22 mi. north in Hinckley. **Restaurant:** 22 mi. north in Hinckley. **General Store:** Yes. **Vending:** Yes. **Swimming Pool:** No. **Playground:** Yes. **Other:** Lake w/ sandy beach, hiking trail, bike trail, interpretive center, horse camp area, enclosed picnic shelter, canoe landings. **Activities:** Swimming, fishing, hiking, boating (rental canoes available), biking (rental bikes available), year-round interpretive programs. **Nearby Attractions:** Casino, Fire Museum, golf, state trails, scenic drives, flea market, antique shops, historical sites. **Additional Information:** Hinckley CVB, (800) 996-4566.

## RESTRICTIONS

**Pets:** Leash only. **Fires:** Fire ring only. **Alcoholic Beverages:** Not permitted. **Vehicle Maximum Length:** 66 ft. **Other:** Vehicle permits of $20 per year or $4 per day are required to enter all Minnesota state parks; 14-day stay limit.

## TO GET THERE

From the junction of I-35 and Hwy. 48, take the Hinckley exit, drive 15 mi. east on Hwy. 48, then 5 mi. south on CR 22. Roads are wide and well maintained w/ broad shoulders.

## HOUSTON

## Money Creek Haven

18502 County 26, Houston 55943. T: (507) 896-3544

🚐 ★★★                    ⛺ ★★★

Beauty: ★★★            Site Privacy: ★★★
Spaciousness: ★★★★     Quiet: ★★★
Security: ★★★          Cleanliness: ★★★
Insect Control: None   Facilities: ★★★

The campsite's 40th birthday will be celebrated in 2002 by the same man who started it. About half the sites at Money Creek Haven are occupied by seasonals. The on-site restaurant serves several hundred people every morning with a big country breakfast. The restaurant offers mostly fast-food the rest of the day. The campground offers primarily shaded, grassy sites in a rural setting. The typical site size is 50 × 50 with a mix of back-in and pull-through sites. The best sites for RVs are in the B section, which offers full hookups, easy access, lots of shade, and a location by the pool. Tents are not well screened for privacy from RV campers. Be aware that no one is allowed in the swimming pool after dark.

## BASICS

**Operated by:** Allen Fitting. **Open:** Apr. 15–Oct. 15. **Site Assignment:** Reservations w/ 1-night deposit; refunds w/ 5-day notice. **Registration:** At campground office. **Fee:** $20 (cash, check). **Parking:** At site.

## FACILITIES

**Number of RV Sites:** 185. **Number of Tent-Only Sites:** 12. **Hookups:** Electric (20, 30 amps), water, sewer. **Each Site:** Picnic table, fire ring. **Dump Station:** Yes. **Laundry:** Yes. **Pay Phone:** Yes. **Rest Rooms and Showers:** Yes. **Fuel:** No. **Propane:** No. **Internal Roads:** Paved/gravel, in good condition. **RV Service:** No. **Market:** 6 mi. south in Houston. **Restaurant:** On site. **General Store:** Yes. **Vending:** Yes. **Swimming Pool:** Yes. **Playground:** Yes. **Other:** Game room w/ video & pool tables, horseshoes, volleyball, fishing pond, badminton, hiking trails, recreation field. **Activities:** Swimming, fishing, hiking, no scheduled activities. **Nearby Attractions:** Golf, snowmobile, farm tours, art & antique shops, scenic drives, nature center. **Additional Information:** Bluff Country Regional CVB, (800) 428-2030.

## RESTRICTIONS

**Pets:** Leash only. **Fires:** Fire ring only. **Alcoholic Beverages:** Permitted. **Vehicle Maximum Length:** None.

## TO GET THERE

From the junction of I-90 and Hwy. 76, drive 8 mi. south on Hwy. 76, then 0.25 mi. west on Hwy. 26. Roads are wide and well maintained w/ broad shoulders.

## ISLE
### South Isle Family Campground

39002 Hwy. 47, Isle 56342. T: (320) 676-8538;
www.ecenet.com/~sifcamp; sifcamp@ecenet.com.

🚐 ★★★          ⛺ ★★★

Beauty: ★★★          Site Privacy: ★★★
Spaciousness: ★★★     Quiet: ★★★
Security: ★★★         Cleanliness: ★★★
Insect Control: None  Facilities: ★★★

Family owned and operated since 1991, South
Isle Family Campground is located two miles
south of Isle. The rural campground is surrounded by woods, marsh land, and prairie grass
areas. The typical campsite width is 40 feet, and
the campground has 30 pull-throughs. However,
all the full hookup sites are occupied by seasonals. Sites are grassy and shaded to semi shaded. A
separate area for tent campers offers privacy and
more natural amenities. The campground is
known for its R/C airplane airstrip where hobby-
ists can fly their remote control airplanes and
curious bystanders can watch.

### BASICS
**Operated by:** Wally & Sue Heise. **Open:** May
1–Oct. 1. **Site Assignment:** Reservations w/ $25
deposit, $50 deposit on holiday weekends; refund
(minus $3 fee) w/ 7-day notice. **Registration:** At
campground office. **Fee:** $22 (cash, credit cards).
**Parking:** At site.

### FACILITIES
**Number of RV Sites:** 120. **Number of Tent-
Only Sites:** 9. **Hookups:** Electric (20, 30, 50
amps), water. **Each Site:** Picnic table, fire ring.
**Dump Station:** Yes. **Laundry:** Yes. **Pay Phone:**
Yes. **Rest Rooms and Showers:** Yes. **Fuel:** No.
**Propane:** No. **Internal Roads:** Gravel, in good
condition. **RV Service:** No. **Market:** Yes. **Restaurant:** 2 mi. north in Isle. **General Store:** 2 mi.
north in Isle. **Vending:** Yes. **Swimming Pool:** Yes.
**Playground:** Yes. **Other:** Kids fishing pond w/ free
paddleboat to use, horshoes, Frisbee golf course,
shuffleboard, nature trails, basketball, volleyball, softball, tetherball, badminton, TV lounge & video game
area. **Activities:** Swimming. hiking, scheduled weekend activities. **Nearby Attractions:** Golf, Mille
Lacs Lake, Soo Line Bicycle Trail, Mille Lacs Grand
Casino, craft & antique shops, museums, Father
Hennepin State Park. **Additional Information:**
Mille Lacs Area Tourism Council, (888) 350-2692.

### RESTRICTIONS
**Pets:** Leash only, $3 a day if more than 1 dog.
**Fires:** Fire ring only. **Alcoholic Beverages:** Permitted. **Vehicle Maximum Length:** None.
**Other:** Daily rates are based on 2 people; children
under age 4 are free; additional children are $1.50
per day; additional adults are $2.50 per day; visitors
are $2.50 per day.

### TO GET THERE
From town, drive 2 mi. south on Hwy. 47.
Road is in good shape.

## KELLIHER
### Rogers' Campground & RV Park

HC78 Box 20, Kelliher 56650. T: (800) 678-1871;
www.rogerscg.net; funn@rogerscg.net.

🚐 ★★★          ⛺ ★★★

Beauty: ★★★          Site Privacy: ★★★
Spaciousness: ★★★     Quiet: ★★★
Security: ★★★         Cleanliness: ★★★
Insect Control: ★★★   Facilities: ★★★

Located on the Upper Red Lake in Kelliher,
Rogers' Campground provides lakeside access.
The remote campground offers mostly open
campsites that enjoy the lakeside breeze. More
shaded sites are offered in the back. The typical
site width is 25 feet. Laid out in a series of loops,
the campground has four pull-through sites and
20 seasonal campers. Shotley Brook winds its way
through the center of the campground, making
many on-the-water campsites. Over 800 feet of
sandy beach is available on Upper Red Lake, a
very shallow lake with no drop-off making it a
nice swimming beach. A private concrete boat
ramp and protected harbor add to the boating
activities. To protect the peace and quiet, as well
as the abundant wildlife—including an active
eagle's nest on the property—no ATVs are
allowed in the campground. Though only the
most hearty would want to camp in northern
Minnesota during the winter, the campground
provides some wintertime amenities. Available
for rent are several cabins and ice-fishing shacks.
Owners also have three snowplows to make the
campground passable for winter campers.

### BASICS
**Operated by:** Jerry & Joani Barthel. **Open:** All
year. **Site Assignment:** Reservations w/ 1-night

deposit; refund (minus $5) w/ 2-week notice. **Registration:** At campground office. **Fee:** $18 (cash, check, credit cards). **Parking:** At site.

### FACILITIES

**Number of RV Sites:** 74. **Number of Tent-Only Sites:** 0. **Hookups:** Electric (20, 30 amps), water, sewer. **Each Site:** Picnic table, fire ring. **Dump Station:** Yes. **Laundry:** Yes. **Pay Phone:** Yes. **Rest Rooms and Showers:** Yes. **Fuel:** No. **Propane:** No. **Internal Roads:** Gravel, in good condition. **RV Service:** No. **Market:** 14 mi. southeast in Kelliher. **Restaurant:** 14 mi. southeast in Kelliher. **General Store:** Yes, limited. **Vending:** Yes. **Swimming Pool:** No. **Playground:** Yes. **Other:** Upper Red Lake, swimming beach, hiking trails, fish-cleaning house, sports field, croquet, pavilion, tetherball, volleyball, basketball, horseshoes, rec room, boat dock, boat ramp, badminton, rental houses. **Activities:** Swimming, fishing, hiking, boating (rental tubes, paddleboats & kayaks available), scheduled weekend activities. **Nearby Attractions:** Mississippi River, Paul Bunyan & Babe the Blue Ox statues, water parks, water slide, logging camp, fishing, golf, antiques, arts & crafts. **Additional Information:** Bemidji Area Tourist Information, (800) 458-2223.

### RESTRICTIONS

**Pets:** Leash only. **Fires:** Fire ring only. **Alcoholic Beverages:** Permitted. **Vehicle Maximum Length:** None.

### TO GET THERE

From the junction of CR 36 and Hwy. 72, drive 9 mi. north on Hwy. 72, then 5 mi. west on CR 23, then 0.75 mi. north on access road. Roads are mostly wide and well maintained w/ adequate shoulders.

## LAKE ITASCA
### Itasca State Park

HC 05 Box 4, Lake Itasca 56470. T: (218) 266-2100; www.dnr.state.mn.us.

🚐 ★★★          ⛺ ★★★★

Beauty: ★★★★          Site Privacy: ★★★★
Spaciousness: ★★★          Quiet: ★★★★
Security: ★★★★          Cleanliness: ★★★
Insect Control: None          Facilities: ★★★

Itasca State Park really offers two campgrounds—Bear Paw Campground along the shores of Lake Itasca and Pine Ridge Campground, originally the 1930s Civilian Conservation Corps Camp. Both campgrounds have shady, back-in sites with a typical site size of 15 × 60 feet. Some sites have 40-foot widths. During the off season, Pine Ridge Campground is open for rustic winter camping with pit toilets; water is available at the park headquarters. For those looking for solitude, 11 year-round back country campsites are accessible via one- to five-mile hikes. These sites offer fire rings and pit toilets but no water supply, and campers must carry out their garbage. Itasca also offers group camps with a staff cabin, dining hall with kitchen, modern toilet facility, and a tent area for up to 75 people. What Itasca State Park lacks in camping amenities, it makes up for in beauty and recreational opportunities.

### BASICS

**Operated by:** State of Minnesota. **Open:** May 15–Oct. 15. **Site Assignment:** Reservations w/ 1-night deposit; refund (minus $5 fee) w/ 3-day notice. A non-refundable $7.25 reservation fee is charged per camping reservation. **Registration:** At campground office. **Fee:** $15 (cash, check, credit cards), plus $4 day park fee or $20 for season permit. **Parking:** At site.

### FACILITIES

**Number of RV Sites:** 100. **Number of Tent-Only Sites:** 135. **Hookups:** Electric (20, 30 amps). **Each Site:** Picnic table, fire ring. **Dump Station:** Yes. **Laundry:** No. **Pay Phone:** Yes. **Rest Rooms and Showers:** Yes. **Fuel:** No. **Propane:** No. **Internal Roads:** Paved/gravel, in good condition. **RV Service:** No. **Market:** 3 mi. north to Lake Itasca. **Restaurant:** Douglas Lodge at park. **General Store:** No. **Vending:** Yes. **Swimming Pool:** No. **Playground:** Yes. **Other:** Hiking trails, hostel, sandy beach, bike trail, several lakes, lodges, cabins, tour boat, gift shop, visitor center, lodge, amphitheatre, boat landing, fire tower, interpretive center. **Activities:** Swimming, fishing, hiking, biking, (rental bikes available), boating (rental pontoons, paddleboat, canoe & fishing boats available), naturalist programs, workshops. **Nearby Attractions:** Scenic drives, historic sites. **Additional Information:** Minnesota Office of Tourism, (800) 657-3700.

### RESTRICTIONS

**Pets:** Leash only. **Fires:** Fire ring only. **Alcoholic Beverages:** Not permitted. **Vehicle Maximum Length:** 60 ft. **Other:** 14-day stay limit.

## To Get There

From Park Rapids, drive 20 mi. north on US 71. Road is fair condition w/ often narrow shoulders.

## LANESBORO

## Eagle Cliff Campground and Lodging

Rte. 1, Box 344, Lanesboro 55949. T: (507) 467-2598

🚐 ★★★              ⛺ ★★★★

Beauty: ★★★★              Site Privacy: ★★★
Spaciousness: ★★★        Quiet: ★★★★
Security: ★★★★            Cleanliness: ★★★★★
Insect Control: None       Facilities: ★★★

Located in a valley with bluffs rising on one side and the Root River running on another, Eagle Cliff Campground and Lodging is a great place for river activities. It has a useful rinse area to keep the river water and dirt out of spotless showers and bathroom facilities. The wilderness campground has no scheduled activities or swimming pool, thereby allowing the river to be the center of recreation. All sites are grassy and level, and there are no gravel or paved sites. Many RV sites are open with young trees too little to provide shade. The typical site width is 45 feet with a dozen pull-throughs. A special section by the river has been set aside for tent campers, and, unlike many campgrounds, Eagle Cliff has more tent sites than RV sites. Visiting during the week would be best because the campground quickly fills on weekends. Reservations are recommended.

## BASICS

**Operated by:** Naber family. **Open:** Apr. 1–Dec. 1. **Site Assignment:** Reservations w/ 1-night deposit; refunds w/ 2-weeks notice. **Registration:** At campground office. **Fee:** $19 (cash, check, credit cards). **Parking:** At site.

## FACILITIES

**Number of RV Sites:** 62. **Number of Tent-Only Sites:** 88. **Hookups:** Electric (20, 30, 50), water, sewer. **Each Site:** Picnic table, fire ring. **Dump Station:** Yes. **Laundry:** Yes. **Pay Phone:** Yes. **Rest Rooms and Showers:** Yes. **Fuel:** No. **Propane:** No. **Internal Roads:** Gravel, in good condition. **RV Service:** No. **Market:** 3 mi. west in Lanesboro. **Restaurant:** 3 mi. west in Lanesboro.

**General Store:** Yes. **Vending:** Yes. **Swimming Pool:** No. **Playground:** Yes. **Other:** River rinse-off area, game room, horseshoes, volleyball, canoe landing, recreation field. **Activities:** Hunting, fishing, boating (rental kayaks, canoes & tubes available), biking (rental bikes available), hiking. **Nearby Attractions:** Golf, scenic drives, petting zoo, Amish tours. **Additional Information:** Lanesboro Office of Visitor Information, (800) 944-2670.

## RESTRICTIONS

**Pets:** Leash only. **Fires:** Fire ring only. **Alcoholic Beverages:** Permitted. **Vehicle Maximum Length:** 40 ft. **Other:** No check-in after 11 p.m. You will be charged if your dog digs holes.

## To Get There

From the junction of US 52 and Hwy. 16, drive 9 mi. east on Hwy. 16.

## LITTLE FALLS

## Charles A. Lindbergh State Park

P.O. Box 364, Little Falls 56345. T: (320) 616-2525; www.dnr.state.mn.us.

🚐 ★★              ⛺ ★★★★

Beauty: ★★★★              Site Privacy: ★★★★
Spaciousness: ★★★★        Quiet: ★★★★
Security: ★★★★            Cleanliness: ★★★
Insect Control: None       Facilities: ★★

This state park was established in 1931 when 110 acres were donated to the state in memory of Charles A. Lindbergh, Sr. World renowned for his trans-Atlantic solo flight in 1927, Lindbergh lived his boyhood years in the house by the park overlooking the Mississippi River. Water and woodland activities are a major attraction in the state park. The Pike Creek meanders through and empties into the Mississippi River in the southern part of the park. Located one-and-a-half miles south of Little Falls, the campground's sites are mostly shaded and level with back-ins and no pull-throughs. The most popular RV sites are 1, 3, 7, 9, 10, 11, and 12 because they offer electricity and are next to Pike Creek. Tent sites are in a separate loop. Also, there is one hike-in site and one site available by canoe. Security is great with one access road, a security gate which is closed from 10 p.m. to 8 a.m. except to registered campers, and regular patrols by park rangers and city police.

## BASICS

**Operated by:** State of Minnesota. **Open:** All year. **Site Assignment:** First come, first served; no reservations accepted. **Registration:** At campground office. **Fee:** $15 (cash, check, credit cards). **Parking:** At site.

## FACILITIES

**Number of RV Sites:** 15. **Number of Tent-Only Sites:** 23. **Hookups:** Electric (30 amps). **Each Site:** Picnic table, fire ring. **Dump Station:** Yes. **Laundry:** No. **Pay Phone:** No. **Rest Rooms and Showers:** Yes. **Fuel:** No. **Propane:** No. **Internal Roads:** Paved, in good condition. **RV Service:** No. **Market:** No. **Restaurant:** 1.5 mi. north in Little Falls. **General Store:** 1.5 mi. north in Little Falls. **Vending:** No. **Swimming Pool:** No. **Playground:** Yes. **Other:** Picnic area, enclosed shelters, hiking & skiing trails, boat ramp, ranger station. **Activities:** Fishing, hiking, boating (rental canoes available). **Nearby Attractions:** Charles A. Lindbergh House State Historic Site, Weyerhaeuser Museum, Minnesota Military Museum, Pine Grove Park & Zoo, bowling, golf, horseback riding, tennis. **Additional Information:** Little Falls CVB, (800) 325-5916.

## RESTRICTIONS

**Pets:** Leash only. **Fires:** Fire ring only. **Alcoholic Beverages:** "3.2" beer only. **Vehicle Maximum Length:** 50 ft. **Other:** Vehicle permits of $20 per year or $4 per day are required to enter all Minnesota state parks; 14-day stay limit.

## TO GET THERE

From the junction of Hwy. 27 and CR 52, drive 1.5 mi. southwest on CR 52. Roads are wide and well maintained w/ broad shoulders.

## LITTLE FALLS

### Fletcher Creek Campground

20771 Hwy. 371, Little Falls 56345. T: (800) 337-9636

🚐 ★★                    ▲ ★★★

| | |
|---|---|
| Beauty: ★★★ | Site Privacy: ★★ |
| Spaciousness: ★★ | Quiet: ★★★ |
| Security: ★★★★★ | Cleanliness: ★★ |
| Insect Control: None | Facilities: ★★ |

Mississippi River canoe trips set Fletcher Creek Campground apart from other camping experiences. The campground provides shuttle service, a canoe, paddles, and life jackets for an eight-mile river trip for $15 per person. It usually takes people two to three hours to make the entire trip. If that isn't long enough, the campground also offers 16 mile trips for $25. Those trips usually take five to six hours. The shuttle service takes campers up the river where they paddle canoes back down to the campground landing. Canoe rental is available at $3.50 per hour with a maximum cost of $25 per day. The campground offers semi-wooded and open sites with 15 pull-throughs. The typical site width is 25 feet. The most popular RV sites are 1–7 by the creek, and the sites in Bunny Hollow are most attractive to tent campers because of the privacy and shade. Security is tops at the campground—there is one entrance and the campground is patrolled by the owner who is a former policeman.

## BASICS

**Operated by:** Dennis Heise. **Open:** May 1–Oct. 31. **Site Assignment:** Reservations; no deposit required except for holiday weekends ($10); refund w/ 30-day notice. **Registration:** At campground office. **Fee:** $20 (cash, check, credit cards). **Parking:** Fire rings only.

## FACILITIES

**Number of RV Sites:** 35. **Number of Tent-Only Sites:** 20. **Hookups:** Electric (20, 30, 50 amps), water, sewer. **Each Site:** Picnic table, fire ring. **Dump Station:** Yes. **Laundry:** Yes. **Pay Phone:** No. **Rest Rooms and Showers:** Yes. **Fuel:** No. **Propane:** No. **Internal Roads:** Gravel, in good condition. **RV Service:** No. **Market:** 6 mi. south in Little Falls. **Restaurant:** 3 mi. south in Little Falls. **General Store:** Yes. **Vending:** No. **Swimming Pool:** Yes. **Playground:** Yes. **Other:** Fletcher Creek, mini-golf, volleyball, badminton, horseshoes, sports field, rec room. **Activities:** Fishing, swimming, canoeing (rental canoes available). **Nearby Attractions:** Charles A. Lindbergh House State Historic Site, Weyerhaeuser Museum, Minnesota Military Museum, Pine Grove Park & Zoo, bowling, golf, horseback riding, tennis. **Additional Information:** Little Falls CVB, (800) 325-5916.

## RESTRICTIONS

**Pets:** Leash only. **Fires:** Fire ring only. **Alcoholic Beverages:** Permitted. **Vehicle Maximum Length:** 40 ft.

## TO GET THERE

From the junction of US 10 and Hwy. 371, drive 6 mi. south on Hwy. 371. Roads are wide and well maintained w/ broad shoulders.

## MOOSE LAKE

### Red Fox Campground and RV Park

P.O. Box 356, Moose Lake 55767. T: (800) 569-4181

🚐 ★★★                    🏕 ★★★

Beauty: ★★★              Site Privacy: ★★★
Spaciousness: ★★★        Quiet: ★★★
Security: ★★★★           Cleanliness: ★★★
Insect Control: None      Facilities: ★★★

Red Fox Campground and RV Park offers easy access from I-35, two miles south of Moose Lake. But it also is easy to drive past it. The campground is located behind a Conoco gas station, which serves as a convenience and fast-food store for campers. The campground features a typical site width of 30 feet but the sites are long. Site 34 is 100 feet long, and sites 19 and 20 are 90 feet long. The shortest site length is 45 feet. Sites are level, shady, and grassy with 11 pull-throughs. A separate tent site sets tent campers off from RVs for more privacy. The campground has very good security measures—a manager lives on site, visitors must leave by 10 p.m., and city police patrol the grounds regularly.

### BASICS

**Operated by:** Bob & Bena Adamczak. **Open:** May 15–Oct. 15. **Site Assignment:** Reservations accepted w/ $15 deposit; refund (minus a $3 fee) w/ week notice. **Registration:** At campground office. **Fee:** $23.50 (cash, check). **Parking:** At site.

### FACILITIES

**Number of RV Sites:** 36. **Number of Tent-Only Sites:** 50. **Hookups:** Electric (30, 50 amps), water. **Each Site:** Picnic table, fire ring. **Dump Station:** Yes. **Laundry:** Yes. **Pay Phone:** No. **Rest Rooms and Showers:** Yes. **Fuel:** No. **Propane:** No. **Internal Roads:** Gravel, narrow but good condition. **RV Service:** No. **Market:** 2 mi. north in Moose Lake. **Restaurant:** 2 mi. north in Moose Lake. **General Store:** No. **Vending:** No. **Swimming Pool:** No. **Playground:** Yes. **Other:** Pond w/ sandy beach, basketball, recreation building, putting green, horseshoes, group picnic area, hiking trails, volleyball, mini-golf. **Activities:** Swimming, fishing, hiking. **Nearby Attractions:** Casinos, state park, whitewater rafting, bike trails, golf, bowling, State Agate Center. **Additional Information:** Duluth Convention & Visitors Center, (800) 438-5884.

### RESTRICTIONS

**Pets:** Leash only. **Fires:** Fire ring only. **Alcoholic Beverages:** At sites only. **Vehicle Maximum Length:** None.

### TO GET THERE

From the junction of I-35 and Hwy. 73, take Exit 214, drive 500 ft. west behind Conoco gas station. Road is wide and well maintained w/ broad shoulders.

## NISSWA

### Fritz's Resort and Campground

P.O. Box 803, Nisswa 56468. T: (218) 568-8988; www.fritzresort.com; fritzrst@uslink.net.

🚐 ★★★★                   🏕 ★★

Beauty: ★★★★            Site Privacy: ★★★
Spaciousness: ★★★        Quiet: ★★★
Security: ★★★★           Cleanliness: ★★★★
Insect Control: None      Facilities: ★★★★

Fritz's Resort and Campground offers easy access and a nice roster of activities, as many campers have already discovered. All but 25 RV sites are occupied by seasonal campers. Call ahead to be sure a site is open before pulling in. Also be aware that pets are not allowed from Memorial Day to Labor Day. The rural campground is well organized in a series of loops with level, shaded sites, cement patios, and 15 pull-throughs. The typical site width is 25 feet. Tent campers are sort of left out with only three sites available, but they are well shaded. Being so close to the highway, two-and-a-half miles north of Nisswa, it's inevitable that traffic noise would creep in a bit. Lake Edna is a beautiful attraction, and the beach is groomed every morning by a maintenance team to keep it that way. The best RV sites are 1–4 around the rec hall because they are pull-throughs and roomy at 60 × 100. Security is good with owners who live on site, a regular campground patrol, and city police driving through the area.

### BASICS

**Operated by:** Richard & Jane Geike. **Open:** May 1–Oct. 1. **Site Assignment:** Reservations w/ $30 deposit; refund (minus $10) w/ 21 day notice. **Registration:** At campground office. **Fee:** $24 (cash, check, credit cards). **Parking:** At site.

## FACILITIES

**Number of RV Sites:** 70. **Number of Tent-Only Sites:** 3. **Hookups:** Electric (30, 50 amps), water, sewer. **Each Site:** Picnic table, fire ring. **Dump Station:** Yes. **Laundry:** Yes. **Pay Phone:** Yes. **Rest Rooms and Showers:** Yes. **Fuel:** Yes. **Propane:** Yes. **Internal Roads:** Paved, in good condition. **RV Service:** No. **Market:** 2.5 mi. south in Nisswa. **Restaurant:** 2.5 mi. south in Nisswa. **General Store:** Yes. **Vending:** No. **Swimming Pool:** No. **Playground:** Yes. **Other:** Lake Edna, sandy beach, rec hall, pool tables, ping pong, shuffleboard, 9-hole golf course, snack bar, adult room, fish-cleaning house, tennis court. **Activities:** Swimming, fishing, boating (rental motorboats, pontoons, canoes, paddleboats available). **Nearby Attractions:** Cross-country skiing, snowmobiling, raceway, Crow Wing County Historical Society, Paul Bunyan Amusement Center, Paul Bunyan Trail. **Additional Information:** Brainerd Lakes Area Chamber of Commerce, (800) 450-2838.

## RESTRICTIONS

**Pets:** Pets will be allowed in campgrounds only before Memorial weekend & after Labor Day; $3 per day for each pet. **Fires:** Fire ring only. **Alcoholic Beverages:** Permitted. **Vehicle Maximum Length:** None.

## TO GET THERE

From Nisswa, drive 1.5 mi. north on Hwy. 371

# NISSWA

## Upper Cullen Resort and Campground

P.O. Box 72, Nisswa 56468. T: (218) 963-2249; www.uppercullen.com; lakefun@uslink.net.

| 🚐 ★★★ | 🛖 ★★★ |
|---|---|
| Beauty: ★★★ | Site Privacy: ★★★ |
| Spaciousness: ★★★ | Quiet: ★★★★ |
| Security: ★★★★ | Cleanliness: ★★★ |
| Insect Control: None | Facilities: ★★★ |

A rural lakeside facility, Upper Cullen Resort and Campground is a peaceful family place. Located on the eastern shore of the Upper Cullen Lake, five miles east of Nisswa, the secluded, heavily wooded campground features nature in abundance. Arranged in a series of loops, the campground has well-shaded level sites but no pull-throughs. The quiet surroundings and outdoor activities would probably appeal to tent campers. But there is no area set off for tents; tent sites are interspersed among RVs. Security is good with only one entrance to the campground, owners who live on site, and regular patrols. Reservations are recommended as the campground is very popular in June, July, and Aug.

## BASICS

**Operated by:** Bruce & Donna Galles. **Open:** May 1–Oct. 1. **Site Assignment:** Reservations w/ 2-night deposit; refund if site re-rented. **Registration:** At campground office. **Fee:** $24 (cash, check, credit cards). **Parking:** At site.

## FACILITIES

**Number of RV Sites:** 43. **Number of Tent-Only Sites:** 7. **Hookups:** Electric (20, 30 amps), water, sewer. **Each Site:** Picnic table, fire ring. **Dump Station:** Yes. **Laundry:** Yes. **Pay Phone:** Yes. **Rest Rooms and Showers:** Yes. **Fuel:** Yes. **Propane:** No. **Internal Roads:** Gravel, narrow but in good condition. **RV Service:** No. **Market:** 5 mi. west in Nisswa. **Restaurant:** 5 mi. west in Nisswa. **General Store:** Yes. **Vending:** No. **Swimming Pool:** No. **Playground:** Yes. **Other:** Upper Cullen Lake, sandy beach, horseshoes, shuffleboard, badminton, volleyball, basketball, tetherball, boat ramp, game room, nature trails, boat ramp, boat dock. **Activities:** Swimming, fishing, boating (rental motorboats, canoes, paddleboats & pontoons), hayrides, scheduled activities. **Nearby Attractions:** Cross-country skiing, snowmobiling, raceway, Crow Wing County Historical Society Museum, Paul Bunyan Amusement Center, Paul Bunyan Trail. **Additional Information:** Brainerd Lakes Area Chamber of Commerce, (800) 450-2838.

## RESTRICTIONS

**Pets:** Leash only. **Fires:** Fire ring only. **Alcoholic Beverages:** Permitted. **Vehicle Maximum Length:** 40 ft.

## TO GET THERE

From downtown Nisswa, drive 2.25 mi. east on CR 18, then 2.5 mi. north on Old Hwy. 18. Roads are wide and well maintained w/ broad shoulders.

## OGILVIE

### Hilltop Family Campground

2186 Empire St., Ogilvie 56358. T: (320) 272-4300;
www.hilltopcampground.com; hilltop@ncis.

 ★★★            ▲ ★★★

| | |
|---|---|
| Beauty: ★★★ | Site Privacy: ★★★ |
| Spaciousness: ★★★★ | Quiet: ★★★★ |
| Security: ★★★ | Cleanliness: ★★★ |
| Insect Control: None | Facilities: ★★★ |

Located six miles south of Ogilvie, Hilltop Family Campground offers spacious, wooded sites near a lake. The typical site width is 40 feet. Tent campers can use any sites, but there is no primitive area. The general store has limited stock, and all of the full hookup sites are occupied by the 80 seasonals. Laid out in a series of loops, the campground has grassy sites—there are no concrete RV pads—and shade from Norway pines and other hardwood trees. The rural campground has 12 pull-through sites. Day visitors pay a $3 fee and must leave by 10 p.m. Quiet hours, including no radio playing, are between 11 p.m. and 8 a.m. No one under age 16 is allowed in the spa pool or spa area. Also, children under 14 must be accompanied by an adult at the swimming pool. Although the campground speed limit is ten mph, the owners ask that campers walk instead of drive around the campground because of children playing.

**BASICS**

**Operated by:** John & Dot Forrest. **Open:** May 1–Oct. 1. **Site Assignment:** Reservations w/ 1-night deposit; refunds w/ 10-day notice. **Registration:** At campground office. **Fee:** $26 (cash, check, credit cards). **Parking:** At site.

**FACILITIES**

**Number of RV Sites:** 123. **Number of Tent-Only Sites:** 0. **Hookups:** Electric (20, 30, 50 amps), water. **Each Site:** Picnic table, fire ring. **Dump Station:** Yes. **Laundry:** Yes. **Pay Phone:** Yes. **Rest Rooms and Showers:** Yes. **Fuel:** No. **Propane:** No. **Internal Roads:** Gravel, in fair condition. **RV Service:** No. **Market:** 6 mi. south to Ogilvie. **Restaurant:** 6 mi. south to Ogilvie. **General Store:** Yes. **Vending:** No. **Swimming Pool:** Yes. **Playground:** Yes. **Other:** Fish-cleaning house, boat parking, rec hall, library, snack area, electronic games, pool table, spa tub, volleyball, basketball, soft-ball, horseshoes, hiking trails. **Activities:** Swimming, hiking. **Nearby Attractions:** Fishing & boating across road on Ann Lake, golf,. **Additional Information:** St. Cloud Area CVB, (800) 264-2940.

**RESTRICTIONS**

**Pets:** Leash only, $3 per pet per day. **Fires:** Fire ring only. **Alcoholic Beverages:** Permitted. **Vehicle Maximum Length:** None.

**TO GET THERE**

From the junction of Hwy. 23 and Hwy. 47, drive 5 mi. north on Hwy. 47, then 0.75 mi. east on CR 90, then 0.25 mi. south on Empire St. Roads are narrow and in fair condition w/ narrow shoulders.

## ORTONVILLE

### Lakeshore RV Park & Fruit Farm

Rte. 1 Box 95, Ortonville 56278. T: (800) 9FOR-FUN; F: (320) 839-3701; www.lakeshorervpark.com; mrddragt@maxminn.com.

🚐 ★★★★            ▲ ★★★★

| | |
|---|---|
| Beauty: ★★★★ | Site Privacy: ★★★★ |
| Spaciousness: ★★★★ | Quiet: ★★★★ |
| Security: ★★★★ | Cleanliness: ★★★★★ |
| Insect Control: ★★★★ | Facilities: ★★★★ |

A winning combination for campers is at Lakeshore RV Park and Fruit Farm. Located three miles north of Ortonville, the campground on the shores of Big Stone Lake offers level, prepared sites in a working apple orchard. The campground has a typical site width of 30 feet and 30 pull-through sites with a choice of open or shaded. Cleanliness is tops and it's a pleasure to see such sparkling rest room facilities. Apples are available to be picked starting in Sept. A separate primitive area for tents allows more green space and privacy. The mini-golf course is an unusually challenging one, with such toughies as Adam's Rib and the Apple and the Worm in the Dutchman's Rock Garden. Security measures are good with owners who keep a close eye on the campground to make sure it is quiet, clean, and family-oriented.

**BASICS**

**Operated by:** Dennis, Carol, Steve & Colette Dragt. **Open:** Apr. 15–Oct. 15. **Site Assignment:** Reservations w/ 1-night deposit; refund w/ 7-day notice. **Registration:** At campground office. **Fee:** $22 (cash, check, credit cards). **Parking:** At site.

## FACILITIES

**Number of RV Sites:** 40. **Number of Tent-Only Sites:** 15. **Hookups:** Electric (30, 50 amps), water, sewer. **Each Site:** Picnic table, fire ring. **Dump Station:** Yes. **Laundry:** Yes. **Pay Phone:** Yes. **Rest Rooms and Showers:** Yes. **Fuel:** No. **Propane:** Yes. **Internal Roads:** Gravel, in good condition. **RV Service:** No. **Market:** 3 mi. south in Ortonville. **Restaurant:** 3 mi. south in Ortonville. **General Store:** Yes, limited. **Vending:** Yes. **Swimming Pool:** Yes. **Playground:** Yes. **Other:** Big Stone Lake, arcade, hot tub, boat ramp, train rides, rec room, mini-golf, pavilion, sports field, volleyball, boat dock. **Activities:** Swimming, fishing, boating (rental excursion boat, bumper boats, pontoons, charter fishing, paddleboats available). **Nearby Attractions:** Golf, excursion boats, scenic drives, antiques, arts & crafts, wildlife refuge, mahogany granite quarries. **Additional Information:** Big Stone Lake Area Chamber of Commerce, (800) 568-5722.

## RESTRICTIONS

**Pets:** Leash only. **Fires:** Fire ring only. **Alcoholic Beverages:** Permitted. **Vehicle Maximum Length:** None.

## TO GET THERE

From the junction of US 12 and Hwy. 7, drive 3 mi. north on Hwy. 7. Roads are wide and well maintained w/ broad shoulders.

## PARK RAPIDS
### Spruce Hill Campgrounds

17404 Driftwood Ln., Park Rapids 56470. T: (218) 732-3292

| 🚐 ★★★ | ⛺ ★★★ |
|---|---|
| Beauty: ★★★ | Site Privacy: ★★★ |
| Spaciousness: ★★★ | Quiet: ★★★★ |
| Security: ★★★ | Cleanliness: ★★★ |
| Insect Control: None | Facilities: ★★★ |

Tall evergreen, poplar, and oak trees offer abundant shade at this wilderness campground overlooking Long Lake. Located two miles east of Park Rapids, Spruce Hill Campground is primarily a destination. Campers come here for the lake fishing, swimming, and boating. There are 25 seasonal sites, five pull-throughs, and the typical site width is 35 feet. Laid out in a series of loops, the campground has grassy sites with patios for RVs. The best RV sites are 11–14

because they are all pull-throughs, they are the biggest, and they overlook the lake. The best tent sites are the ones backing up to the woods away from RVs with more shade and privacy. Quiet time is enforced between 10 p.m. and 8 a.m. The owners live on site, keeping an eye on security and safety. The posted speed limit is five mph and the owners mean it.

## BASICS

**Operated by:** John & Judi Nelson. **Open:** May 1–Oct. 1. **Site Assignment:** Reservations w/ 1-night deposit; refund w/ 14-day notice. **Registration:** At campground office. **Fee:** $25 (cash, check, credit cards). **Parking:** At site.

## FACILITIES

**Number of RV Sites:** 50. **Number of Tent-Only Sites:** 7. **Hookups:** Electric (30 amps), water, sewer. **Each Site:** Picnic table, fire ring. **Dump Station:** Yes. **Laundry:** No. **Pay Phone:** Yes. **Rest Rooms and Showers:** Yes. **Fuel:** No. **Propane:** No. **Internal Roads:** Gravel, in good condition. **RV Service:** No. **Market:** 2 mi. west in Park Rapids. **Restaurant:** 2 mi. west in Park Rapids. **General Store:** Yes. **Vending:** No. **Swimming Pool:** No. **Playground:** Yes. **Other:** Long Lake, volleyball, basketball, game room, boat ramp, sports field. **Activities:** Swimming, fishing, boating (rental motorboats, pontoons, canoes, paddleboats available). **Nearby Attractions:** Itasca State Park, historic sites, antiques, arts & crafts shops, golf, tennis, horseback riding, go carts, Heartland Trail. **Additional Information:** Park Rapids Area Chamber of Commerce, (800) 247-0054.

## RESTRICTIONS

**Pets:** Leash only. **Fires:** Fire ring only. **Alcoholic Beverages:** Permitted. **Vehicle Maximum Length:** None.

## TO GET THERE

From the junction of US 71 and Hwy. 34, drive 2 mi. east on Hwy. 34, then 1 mi. south on West Long Lake Rd., then 0.5 mi. east on access road. Roads are wide and well maintained w/ broad shoulders.

## PARK RAPIDS
### Vagabond Village

HC06, Box 381A, Park Rapids 56470. T: (218) 732-5234; www.vagabondvillage.com; gocamping@vagabondvillage.com.

🚐 ★★★★　　　　　　🏕 ★★★★

Beauty: ★★★★　　　　Site Privacy: ★★★★
Spaciousness: ★★★★　　Quiet: ★★★★
Security: ★★★★　　　　Cleanliness: ★★★★
Insect Control: Yes　　　Facilities: none

Surrounded by birch and pine trees, Vagabond Village Campground overlooks Potato Lake with views of hills and water. Located eight miles north of Park Rapids, the campground has level, mostly open sites with a typical site width of 50 feet. Laid out in a series of loops, Vagabond Village has ten pull-through sites and 35 seasonal campers. Most RVs prefer the bigger sites near the facilities. Tents usually like F section best, because it is more private with green space and separated from RVs. Several outside shelters are popular for group gatherings and family reunions. A nice soda fountain serves old-fashioned ice cream and other treats. Security measures include owners who live on site, regular campground patrols, a gate, and surveillance cameras.

## BASICS

**Operated by:** The Nelson Family. **Open:** May 15–Oct. 1. **Site Assignment:** Reservation w/ $30 deposit; refund (minus $5) w/ 15-day notice. **Registration:** At campground office. **Fee:** $28 (cash, check). **Parking:** At site.

## FACILITIES

**Number of RV Sites:** 125. **Number of Tent-Only Sites:** 3. **Hookups:** Electric (20, 30, 50 amps), water, sewer. **Each Site:** Picnic table, fire ring. **Dump Station:** Yes. **Laundry:** Yes. **Pay Phone:** Yes. **Rest Rooms and Showers:** Yes. **Fuel:** No. **Propane:** Yes. **Internal Roads:** Gravel/dirt, in good condition. **RV Service:** No. **Market:** 8 mi. south in Park Rapids. **Restaurant:** 8 mi. south in Park Rapids. **General Store:** Yes, limited. **Vending:** Yes. **Swimming Pool:** Yes. **Playground:** Yes. **Other:** Potato Lake, volleyball, hiking trails, horseshoes, sports field, bandminton, tennis, rec hall, pavilion, boat ramp, boat dock, croquet, game room, soda fountain, pavilions. **Activities:** Swimming, fishing, boating (rental motorboats, pontoons, paddleboats, canoes available), hiking, scheduled weekend activities. **Nearby Attractions:** Itasca State Park, tennis, horseback riding, golf, go-carts, Heartland Trail, antiques, historic sites, arts & crafts shops. **Additional Information:** Park

Rapids Area Chamber of Commerce, (800) 247-0054.

## RESTRICTIONS

**Pets:** Leash only. **Fires:** Fire ring only. **Alcoholic Beverages:** Permitted. **Vehicle Maximum Length:** 50 ft.

## TO GET THERE

From the junction of Hwy. 34 and US 71, drive 7.25 mi. north on US 71, then 6 mi. east on CR 40, then 0.5 mi. on access road. Roads are wide and well maintained w/ broad shoulders.

# PINE CITY

# Pokegama Lake RV Park and Golf Course

Rte. 4, Box 54, Pine City 55063. T: (800) 248-6552; F: (320) 629-5400.

🚐 ★★★　　　　　　🏕 ★★★

Beauty: ★★★　　　　　Site Privacy: ★★★
Spaciousness: ★★★　　　Quiet: ★★★
Security: ★★★★　　　　Cleanliness: ★★★★
Insect Control: None　　　Facilities: ★★★

Pokegama Lake RV Park and Golf Course is a nice family place with many activities. In fact, it is so popular that 97 of the full-hookup sites are taken by seasonals. That leaves 15 full hookup sites and 26 with water and electric for visiting RVs. Reservations are strongly recommended for the campground six miles north of Pine City. Most people come for the golfing, swimming, fishing, and boating. The fish-cleaning house is located away from campers—but yet is convenient- and is kept very clean with a garbage disposal at the bottom of the fish-cleaning counter. Campsites are both open and wooded with 30 pull-throughs. The typical site width is 25 feet with the campground laid out in a series of loops. A welcome respite for adults is a modular adult recreation center that does not allow anyone under age 18.

## BASICS

**Operated by:** Bill & Shirl Woischke. **Open:** May 1–Oct. 1. **Site Assignment:** Reservations w/ $10 deposit; refund w/ 7-day notice; 3-night min. on holiday weekends w/ $40 deposit; refund w/ 14-day notice. **Registration:** At campground office. **Fee:** $21 (cash, check, credit cards). **Parking:** At site.

## FACILITIES

**Number of RV Sites:** 138. **Number of Tent-Only Sites:** 30. **Hookups:** Electric (20, 30 amps), water, sewer. **Each Site:** Picnic table, fire ring. **Dump Station:** Yes. **Laundry:** No. **Pay Phone:** No. **Rest Rooms and Showers:** Yes. **Fuel:** No. **Propane:** No. **Internal Roads:** Paved, in good condition. **RV Service:** No. **Market:** 6 mi. south in Pine City. **Restaurant:** 0.5 mi. south in Pokegama Lake. **General Store:** Yes. **Vending:** No. **Swimming Pool:** Yes. **Playground:** Yes. **Other:** Pokegama Lake, lounge area w/ color TV, rec room, video games, pool tables, screened picnic shelter, adult recreation center, horseshoes, volleyball, basketball, fish-cleaning house, boat harbor, boat ramps, boat docks, 9-hole golf. **Activities:** Golfing, swimming, fishing, boating skiing, scheduled activities on holiday weekends. **Nearby Attractions:** North West Company Fur Post, supper club in walking distance, antique shops, scenic drives, museum. **Additional Information:** Pine City Area Chamber of Commerce, (320) 629-3861.

## RESTRICTIONS

**Pets:** Leash only. **Fires:** Fire ring only. **Alcoholic Beverages:** At sites only. **Vehicle Maximum Length:** 40 ft.

## TO GET THERE

From the junction of I-35 and CR 11, take Exit 171 and drive 4 mi. west on CR 11, then 1 block south on access road. Roads are wide and well maintained w/ broad shoulders

## PINE RIVER

### Doty's Riverview RV Park

3040 16th Ave. Southwest, Pine River 56474.
T: (218) 587-4112

🚐 ★★★            ⛺ ★★★

Beauty: ★★★              Site Privacy: ★★★
Spaciousness: ★★★        Quiet: ★★★★
Security: ★★★★           Cleanliness: ★★★★
Insect Control: None       Facilities: ★★

Doty's Riverview RV Park has two big natural attractions going for it—the Pine River and the Paul Bunyan Trail. Doty's is the closest campground—right across the street—to the 100-mile-long trail that runs from Brainerd to Bemidji. The trail is popular for biking, rollerblading, jogging, walking, and snowmobiling. Located two miles south of Pine River, the campground also offers easy access to the river. Canoes can be rented at the campground, for a trip that starts in the Arvig Creek that flows through the campground and leads into the Pine River and then into White Fish Lake. As avid campers, the Dotys opened the campground next to their home in 1990. RV sites are grassy with cement patios and mostly shady by pine, oak, and elm trees. The typical site width is 30 feet and the campground has three pull-throughs. Tent sites are separate from RVs and provide more privacy and shade. The best RV sites are 1–9 because they are on the east side and get better satellite TV reception, and sites 11, 19, and 20 because they are on the west side and get more shade in the afternoon. Firewood is provided free. Think maybe a small washer and dryer could be squeezed in somewhere?

## BASICS

**Operated by:** Bob & Twyla Doty. **Open:** May 1–Oct. 1. **Site Assignment:** Reservations w/ no deposit. **Registration:** At campground office. **Fee:** $16. **Parking:** At site.

## FACILITIES

**Number of RV Sites:** 26. **Number of Tent-Only Sites:** 4. **Hookups:** Electric (30 amps), water, sewer. **Each Site:** Picnic table, fire ring. **Dump Station:** Yes. **Laundry:** No. **Pay Phone:** No. **Rest Rooms and Showers:** Yes. **Fuel:** No. **Propane:** No. **Internal Roads:** Gravel, in fair condition. **RV Service:** No. **Market:** 2 mi. north in Pine River. **Restaurant:** 2 mi. north in Pine River. **General Store:** No. **Vending:** No. **Swimming Pool:** No. **Playground:** Yes. **Other:** Rec hall, ping pong, pool table, horseshoes, volleyball, badminton,. **Activities:** Fishing, canoeing (rental canoes available), biking. **Nearby Attractions:** Paul Bunyan Trail, Paul Bunyan Amusement Center, raceway, Crow Wing County Historical Society, cross-country skiing, snow. **Additional Information:** Pine River Area Chamber of Commerce, (800) BUNYAN..

## RESTRICTIONS

**Pets:** Leash only. **Fires:** Fire ring only. **Alcoholic Beverages:** Permitted. **Vehicle Maximum Length:** None.

## TO GET THERE

From the junction of Hwy. 371 and CR 44, drive 0.25 mi. east on CR 44. Roads are wide and well maintained w/ broad shoulders.

## PIPESTONE

### Pipestone RV Campground

919 North Hiawatha Ave., Pipestone 56164. T: (507) 825-2455; rvcmpgrd@rconnect.com.

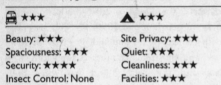

Beauty: ★★★
Spaciousness: ★★★
Security: ★★★★
Insect Control: None

Site Privacy: ★★★
Quiet: ★★★
Cleanliness: ★★★
Facilities: ★★★

Pipestone RV Campground offers level, grassy sites with crushed stone for RV pads. The typical site width is 35 feet and the rural campground has 24 pull-throughs. A fully stocked campstore also features complimentary morning coffee and a good selection of souvenirs and crafts. Most of the sites are shaded with tall oak trees. The most popular RV sites are 1–24 because they offer full service. Tenters favor sites in the back where it is more rustic and away from RVs. Located in Pipestone, the campground doesn't have any seasonal campers. It does offer large camping teepees for rent that kids seem to love to sleep in with their parents. Security is good with owners who live on the premises and regular patrols by city police.

**BASICS**

**Operated by:** Carl & Nancy Cowan. **Open:** May–Oct. **Site Assignment:** Reservations w/ $10 fee; refunds w/ 24-hour notice. **Registration:** At campground office. **Fee:** $24 (cash, check, credit cards). **Parking:** At site.

**FACILITIES**

**Number of RV Sites:** 53. **Number of Tent-Only Sites:** 13. **Hookups:** Electric (20, 30 amps), water, sewer. **Each Site:** Picnic table, fire ring. **Dump Station:** Yes. **Laundry:** Yes. **Pay Phone:** Yes. **Rest Rooms and Showers:** Yes. **Fuel:** No. **Propane:** No. **Internal Roads:** Gravel, in good condition. **RV Service:** No. **Market:** 7 blocks south in Pipestone. **Restaurant:** 7 blocks south in Pipestone. **General Store:** Yes. **Vending:** No. **Swimming Pool:** Yes. **Playground:** Yes. **Other:** Horseshoes, rental teepees, volleyball, tetherball, enclosed pavilion, rec hall, sports field. **Activities:** Swimming. **Nearby Attractions:** Across the street from Pipestone National Monument & Hiawatha Pageant Grounds, antiques, crafts. **Additional Information:** Pipestone Area CVB, (800) 336-6125.

**RESTRICTIONS**

**Pets:** Leash only. **Fires:** Fire ring only. **Alcoholic Beverages:** Permitted. **Vehicle Maximum Length:** None.

**TO GET THERE**

From the junction of Hwy. 23 and Hwy. 30, drive 0.25 mi. west on Hwy. 30, then 1.25 mi. north on Hiawatha Ave. Roads are wide and well maintained w/ broad shoulders.

## PRESTON

### Hidden Valley Campground

Rte. 1, Box 56, Preston 55965. T: (507) 765-2467; www.hiddenvalleycampground.com; info@hiddenvalleycampground.com.

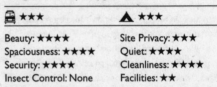

Beauty: ★★★★
Spaciousness: ★★★★
Security: ★★★★
Insect Control: None

Site Privacy: ★★★
Quiet: ★★★★
Cleanliness: ★★★★
Facilities: ★★

Located on the edge of Preston, Hidden Valley Campground has two major recreation attractions going for it—the Root River and the 65-mile-long Root River Bike Trail. Nestled in a valley of willows, oaks, and pines, the campground is bordered by a well-stocked trout stream. In the same family since 1968, the campground is kept wooded and shady by a tree-planting program which sees about 50–100 trees planted every year. Laid out in a series of loops, the campground has mostly grassy, shady, large sites with no pull-through sites. The typical site width is 50 feet. The most popular RV sites are the 16 along the river. Tent sites are separate from RVs, in a more wooded, primitive area that offers more privacy. About three-and-a-half miles of hiking trails take hikers through the pine woods and ravines to the bluff. Quiet and security measures are good with a 10 p.m. quiet time, an owner who lives on site, regular patrols, plus swing-throughs from city police and county sheriff deputies. Changes are being implemented that should improve campground facilities, including a central building, more services, and more sites.

**BASICS**

**Operated by:** Tim & Stef Bestor. **Open:** Apr. 15–Oct. 15. **Site Assignment:** Reservations w/ no deposit. **Registration:** At campground office. **Fee:** $15 (cash, check). **Parking:** At site.

## FACILITIES

**Number of RV Sites:** 37. **Number of Tent-Only Sites:** 8. **Hookups:** Electric (30 amps), water. **Each Site:** Picnic table, fire ring. **Dump Station:** Yes. **Laundry:** No. **Pay Phone:** No. **Rest Rooms and Showers:** Yes. **Fuel:** No. **Propane:** No. **Internal Roads:** Gravel, in good condition. **RV Service:** No. **Market:** 0.5 mi. west in Preston. **Restaurant:** 0.5 mi. west in Preston. **General Store:** No. **Vending:** No. **Swimming Pool:** No. **Playground:** Yes. **Other:** Root River, swimming beach, sports field, horseshoes, volleyball, hiking trails, basketball. tetherball, softball. **Activities:** Swimming, fishing, canoeing (rental canoes available), hiking. **Nearby Attractions:** State park, Amish community, scenic drives, historic sites, antique & craft shops. **Additional Information:** Preston Area Tourism Assoc., (888) 845-2100.

## RESTRICTIONS

**Pets:** Leash only. **Fires:** Fire pits only. **Alcoholic Beverages:** Permitted. **Vehicle Maximum Length:** None.

## TO GET THERE

From north junction of Hwy. 16 and US 52, drive 2 mi. south on Hwy. 16/US 52 to bridge, then 0.25 mi. north on gravel road. Roads are wide and well maintained w/ good shoulders.

# PRESTON

## Old Barn Resort

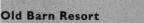

Rte. 3 Box 57, Preston 55965. T: (800) 552-2512; F: (507) 467-2382; www.bluffcountry.com.

 ★★★★      ★★★★

Beauty: ★★★★          Site Privacy: ★★★★
Spaciousness: ★★★      Quiet: ★★★★
Security: ★★★★         Cleanliness: ★★★★
Insect Control: None    Facilities: ★★★★

A big four-story white barn is the hub for the Old Barn Resort. Built in 1884 by Edward Allis of Allis-Chalmers, the barn was restored in 1988 to house a bar and grill, banquet rooms, and a 44-bed hostel. The campground is located in a scenic valley in Historic Bluff County, right on the Root River State Trail. The campsites are mostly open and level with a typical site width of 30 feet. A few pull-through sites are available. Favorite sites

for RVs are A4 and A19 because they are on the ends and quieter. Tent campers like F1 and G1 because they offer more shade. The heated pool is a nice combination of indoor/outdoor, with a roof that lets the sunshine in and sides that can be opened for an outdoor feeling. The Old Barn books up quickly and recommends reservations be made three to four months in advance for holidays and two nights in advance for summer weekends.

## BASICS

**Operated by:** Doug & Shirley Brenner. **Open:** Apr. 1–Nov. 1. **Site Assignment:** Reservations accepted w/ 1-night deposit; refund w/ 2-week notice; reservations require 2-night min. for weekends & 3-night min. for holidays. **Registration:** At campground office. **Fee:** $25.50 (cash, check, credit cards). **Parking:** At site.

## FACILITIES

**Number of RV Sites:** 130. **Number of Tent-Only Sites:** 40. **Hookups:** Electric (30, 50 amps), water, sewer. **Each Site:** Picnic table, fire ring. **Dump Station:** Yes. **Laundry:** Yes. **Pay Phone:** Yes. **Rest Rooms and Showers:** Yes. **Fuel:** No. **Propane:** No. **Internal Roads:** Gravel, in fair condition. **RV Service:** No. **Market:** 3 mi. southwest in Preston. **Restaurant:** On site. **General Store:** Yes. **Vending:** Yes. **Swimming Pool:** Yes. **Playground:** Yes. **Other:** Golf course, Root River, hiking trail, game room, horseshoe, volleyball, basketball, sports field. **Activities:** Hiking, golf, swimming, fishing, biking (rental bikes available), boating (rental canoes & inner tubes available). **Nearby Attractions:** State park, Amish community, scenic drives, historic sites, antique & craft shops. **Additional Information:** Preston Area Tourism Assoc., (888) 845-2100.

## RESTRICTIONS

**Pets:** Leash only. **Fires:** Fire ring only. **Alcoholic Beverages:** Permitted. **Vehicle Maximum Length:** None.

## TO GET THERE

From the junction of US 52 and CR 17 (Apple Orchard Rd.) at west edge of town, drive 3 mi. east on CR 17, then 1 mi north on gravel road. Gravel road is bumpy, in fair condition.

## RICHMOND

### El Rancho Manana

27302B Ranch Rd., Richmond 56368. T: (320) 597-2740; F: (320) 597-2740.

🚐 ★★★★                    ⛺ ★★★★

Beauty: ★★★★          Site Privacy: ★★★★
Spaciousness: ★★★★   Quiet: ★★★★
Security: ★★★★★        Cleanliness: ★★★★
Insect Control: None     Facilities: ★★★★

Campers don't have to go out West to experience a ranch setting. El Rancho Manana, ten miles north of Cold Springs, offers 1,208 acres of campground, riding stable, pastures, lake, pond and riding trails on a working ranch. The rural, rolling, lakeside campground is out in the middle of nowhere, no houses around. Seasonal campers have reserved 28 of the campsites. The wilderness setting offers mostly shady, grassy sites but there are some gravel and open RV sites available. The typical site width is 45 feet and the campground has 60 pull-throughs. Secluded tent sites are available in the woods and by the lake. The quiet family campground has rules that are enforced to preserve the peace and security. A gate has been installed and all campers are asked for a $20 deposit or drivers license in return for a security card, which will be returned at time of departure. Visitors must leave the campground by 10 p.m. Quiet hours are from 11 p.m. to 10 a.m. and all radios must be turned off between 10 p.m. and 10 a.m. The speed limit is five mph. The owners live on the campground and provide regular patrols. But it is hard to imagine that anyone would want to drive all that way back those rough, dusty gravel roads unless they want to camp and enjoy the recreation.

### BASICS

**Operated by:** Ward family. **Open:** May 15–Sept. 30. **Site Assignment:** Reservations w/ 2-night deposit; refunds w/ 2-week notice. **Registration:** At campground office. **Fee:** $28 (cash, check, credit cards). **Parking:** At site.

### FACILITIES

**Number of RV Sites:** 115. **Number of Tent-Only Sites:** 30. **Hookups:** Electric (20, 30, 50 amps), water, sewer. **Each Site:** Picnic table, fire ring. **Dump Station:** Yes. **Laundry:** Yes. **Pay Phone:** Yes. **Rest Rooms and Showers:** Yes.

**Fuel:** Yes. **Propane:** Yes. **Internal Roads:** Gravel/dirt, in good condition. **RV Service:** No. **Market:** 10 mi. south in Cold Springs. **Restaurant:** 10 mi. south in Cold Springs. **General Store:** Yes. **Vending:** Yes. **Swimming Pool:** No. **Playground:** Yes. **Other:** Rec hall, horse stables, game room, hiking trails, horse trails, horseshoes, volleyball, baseball, sandy swimming beach, Long Lake, shelter, boat landing, boat docks, mountain biking trails, badminton. **Activities:** Swimming, fishing, boating (rental rowboats, pontoons, canoes, paddleboats available), hayrides, hiking, mountain biking, horseback riding (rental horses available), planned activities. **Nearby Attractions:** Golf, historic sites, museums, Minnesota Baseball Hall of Fame, antique shops, art galleries. **Additional Information:** St. Cloud Area CVB, (800) 264-2940.

### RESTRICTIONS

**Pets:** Leash only. **Fires:** Fire ring only. **Alcoholic Beverages:** At sites only. **Vehicle Maximum Length:** None. **Other:** A $20 deposit or drivers license in return for a security card to operate security gate; deposit or license will be returned at time of departure.

### TO GET THERE

From the junction of I-94 and CR 9, take Exit 153 and drive 8.5 mi. south on CR 9, then 0.5 mi. east on Manana Rd., then 2 mi. north on Ranch Rd. Roads are wide and well maintained w/ good shoulders. Ranch Rd. is rough gravel and can stir up a lot of dust.

## ROCHESTER

### Rochester KOA

5232 65th Ave Southeast, Rochester 55904. T: (507) 288-0785

🚐 ★★★★                    ⛺ ★★

Beauty: ★★★          Site Privacy: ★★★★
Spaciousness: ★★★★   Quiet: ★★★★
Security: ★★★★        Cleanliness: ★★★★★
Insect Control: None     Facilities: ★★★★

Rochester KOA is a nice, clean, well-run, friendly, safe place to stay. It is not particularly pretty but that is not the owners' fault. They have done what they could to make it attractive, including having exceptionally clean bathrooms. But the natural beauty just isn't there. The open, rural campground is conveniently located just a quarter mile from I-90 and features level sites mostly 30 feet wide. The most popular sites are 4–16 with full hookup. A separate grassy tent site offers privacy, but tents must be moved daily by noon to protect the grass. The campground is mostly used for overnight stays by RVs on their way to or from somewhere. For that, it fits the need perfectly.

## BASICS

**Operated by:** Roger & Barb Philip. **Open:** Mar. 15–Oct. 31. **Site Assignment:** Reservations accepted w/ 1-night deposit; refund (minus $5 fee) w/ 2-day notice, 1-week notice on holidays. **Registration:** At campground office. **Fee:** $28 (cash, credit cards). **Parking:** At site.

## FACILITIES

**Number of RV Sites:** 73. **Number of Tent-Only Sites:** 20. **Hookups:** Electric (30 amp), water, sewer. **Each Site:** Picnic table, fire ring. **Dump Station:** Yes. **Laundry:** Yes. **Pay Phone:** Yes. **Rest Rooms and Showers:** Yes. **Fuel:** No. **Propane:** Yes. **Internal Roads:** Gravel, in good condition. **RV Service:** No. **Market:** 6 mi. north in Rochester. **Restaurant:** 6 mi. north in Rochester. **General Store:** Yes. **Vending:** Yes. **Swimming Pool:** Yes. **Playground:** Yes. **Other:** Volleyball, basketball, badminton, game room, horseshoes, rec hall, recreation field. **Activities:** Swimming, no scheduled activities except an ice cream social on Sat. nights from Memorial Day to Labor Day. **Nearby Attractions:** Mayo Clinic, park, art center, Mayowood Mansion, Olmsted County History Center, Root River State Trail, scenic drive, shopping center. **Additional Information:** Rochester CVB, (800) 634-8277.

## RESTRICTIONS

**Pets:** Leash only. **Fires:** Fire ring only. **Alcoholic Beverages:** Permitted. **Vehicle Maximum Length:** None. **Other:** Camper visitors may stay only 1 hour & may not use any facilities including pool, playground, or rest rooms.

## TO GET THERE

From the junction of I-90 and US 52, take Exit 218, drive 0.25 mi. south on US 52, then 500 ft. east on 54th St. Southeast, then 100 ft. north on 65th Ave. Roads are wide and well maintained w/ broad shoulders.

## ROCHESTER

### Silver Lake RV Park

1409 North Broadway, Rochester 55906. T: (507) 289-6412

| 🚐 ★★★ | 🏕 n/a |
|---|---|
| Beauty: ★★ | Site Privacy: ★★★ |
| Spaciousness: ★★★ | Quiet: ★★★★ |
| Security: ★★★★★ | Cleanliness: ★★★★★ |
| Insect Control: None | Facilities: ★★ |

Silver Lake RV Park is a metro facility used mainly by family and patients at the Mayo Clinic and other medical facilities. The Rochester City Bus Lines picks up passengers less than a block from the campground entrance and arrives at the Mayo Clinic in seven to nine minutes. Each campground guest receives a complimentary round-trip bus ticket and additonal tickets may be purchased at the campground at a discounted price of $1.60 per round trip. Taxi and wheelchair van services also are available. Cleanliness and security are tops. The campground is surrounded by a privacy fence and chain-link fence, there is only one entrance, and city police patrol the area. Rest rooms and showers have combination locks with the combination given to guests when they check in. Private phones may be available upon request and the campground office takes messages and delivers them to guests as soon as possible. The campground is surprisingly quiet to be the midst of a city. It also is easy to miss the turn in on a busy street.

## BASICS

**Operated by:** Silver Lake RV Park Inc. **Open:** Apr. 1–Nov. 1. **Site Assignment:** Reservations recommended, no deposit required. **Registration:** At campground office. **Fee:** $29 (cash, check). **Parking:** At site.

## FACILITIES

**Number of RV Sites:** 58. **Number of Tent-Only Sites:** 0. **Hookups:** Electric (30, 50 amps), water, sewer, cable TV. **Each Site:** Picnic table. **Dump Station:** No. **Laundry:** Yes. **Pay Phone:** Yes. **Rest Rooms and Showers:** Yes. **Fuel:** No. **Propane:** No. **Internal Roads:** Paved, in good condition. **RV Service:** No. **Market:** Across the street. **Restaurant:** Next door. **General Store:** No. **Vending:** No. **Swimming Pool:** No. **Playground:** No.

**Other:** River, horseshoes. **Activities:** Fishing. **Nearby Attractions:** Mayo Clinic, walking & bike trail, movie theaters, shopping center, restaurants, historic homes, museums, park. **Additional Information:** Rochester CVB, (800) 634-8277.

<u>RESTRICTIONS</u>

**Pets:** Leash only. **Fires:** Not permitted in city limits. **Alcoholic Beverages:** Permitted. **Vehicle Maximum Length:** None. **Other:** No tents allowed.

<u>TO GET THERE</u>

From the junction of Hwy. 14 and US 63, drive 2.3 mi. north on US 63. Roads are wide and well maintained w/ broad shoulders.

## ROYALTON

## Two Rivers Park

P.O. Box 137, Royalton 56373. T: (320) 584-5125

| 🚐 ★★★★ | ⛺ ★★★★ |
|---|---|
| Beauty: ★★★★ | Site Privacy: ★★★★ |
| Spaciousness: ★★★★ | Quiet: ★★★★ |
| Security: ★★★★ | Cleanliness: ★★★★ |
| Insect Control: None | Facilities: ★★★ |

Two Rivers Park is located three miles south of Royalton, on a peninsula formed by the waters of the Mississippi and Platte Rivers. Not surprisingly, the campground is popular for water activities, especially its inner tube float trips. Starting with a shuttle bus trip to the beginning point, you can lean back in a huge inner tube and float three-and-a-half miles back to the park through the beautiful Platte River Valley. The relaxing trip takes about two hours and costs $7 a person, children age five and under are free. Laid out in a series of loops, the landscaped campground offers grassy shaded sites with 20 pull-throughs. The typical site width is among the largest in any campground—60 feet. From water front to high bluff and whispering pine sites, tent campers have a wonderful choice of places. Security and safety measures are good—the campground has one access road and owners live on site and provide regular patrols. Quiet time is from 11 p.m. to 8 a.m., visitors must leave by 10 p.m., the playground closes at dusk, no bike riding after dark, and children must be on site by 10 p.m. The posted speed limit is "as fast as a child can walk." With all it has going for it, the campground has one pesky flaw—no laundry facilities for all those wet and dirty clothes from river activities.

BASICS

**Operated by:** Bernie & Pat Palmer. **Open:** May 15–Sept. 15. **Site Assignment:** Reservations w/ full payment; 3-night min. on holiday weekends; refunds (minus $5 fee) w/ 7-day notice. **Registration:** At campground office. **Fee:** $20 (cash, check, credit cards). **Parking:** At site.

FACILITIES

**Number of RV Sites:** 60. **Number of Tent-Only Sites:** 20. **Hookups:** Electric (20, 30 amps), water. **Each Site:** Picnic table, fire ring. **Dump Station:** Yes. **Laundry:** No. **Pay Phone:** No. **Rest Rooms and Showers:** Yes. **Fuel:** No. **Propane:** Yes. **Internal Roads:** Paved/gravel, in good condition. **RV Service:** No. **Market:** 3 mi. north in Royalton. **Restaurant:** 3 mi. north in Royalton. **General Store:** Yes. **Vending:** Yes. **Swimming Pool:** No. **Playground:** Yes. **Other:** Game room, tubing shuttle bus, volleyball, mini-golf, badminton, basketball, croquet, chucker golf, boat launch, recreation field, shelter building, boat ramp, horseshoes, hiking trails. **Activities:** Fishing, river swimming, boating, agate hunting, inner tube float trips, planned activities. **Nearby Attractions:** Golf, zoo, bowling, roller skating, water slide, museums, tennis, skeet shoot, game farm, go-cart tracks. **Additional Information:** Little Falls CVB, (800) 325-5916.

RESTRICTIONS

**Pets:** Leash only. **Fires:** Fire ring only. **Alcoholic Beverages:** Permitted. **Vehicle Maximum Length:** None. **Other:** No jet skis, personal watercraft allowed.

TO GET THERE

From the junction of US 10 and CR 40, drive 100 ft. southwest on CR 40, then 1 mi. south on CR 73, then 0.5 mi. west on 145th St. Roads are wide and well maintained w/ good shoulders.

## SAVAGE

## Town & Country Campground

12630 Boone Ave. South, Savage 55378. T: (612) 445-1756; www.townandcountrycampground.com.

| 🚐 ★★★★ | ⛺ ★★★★ |
|---|---|
| Beauty: ★★★★ | Site Privacy: ★★★★ |
| Spaciousness: ★★★★ | Quiet: ★★★★ |
| Security: ★★★★ | Cleanliness: ★★★★ |
| Insect Control: ★★★★ | Facilities: ★★★★ |

Town & County Campground in Savage, has done a good job of providing "city close and country quiet." Conveniently located 18 miles southwest of Minneapolis, Town & Country is surprisingly quiet and homey for being so close to a metro area. Attractive landscaping, including bushes and flowers, adds to the welcoming atmosphere. There's even Eagle Creek for quiet walks and a big shade tree on the playground—a nice change from campgrounds whose playgrounds are sitting right out in the broiling sun. Sites are level, grassy, shaded, or open with a typical site width of 35 feet. Laid out in a series of loops, the campground has 15 pull-through sites and five seasonal campers. Security is great with owners who keep a close eye on the site. A speed limit of five mph is enforced, as is quiet time from 10 p.m. to 7 a.m. Be aware that campfires are not permitted on individual sites, but there is a community fire ring available with wood provided.

## BASICS

**Operated by:** David & Jill Olmstead. **Open:** Apr. 1–Nov. 1. **Site Assignment:** Reservations w/ $25 deposit; refund w/ 48-hour notice. **Registration:** At campground office. **Fee:** $28 (cash, check, credit cards). **Parking:** At site; 1 car per site only.

## FACILITIES

**Number of RV Sites:** 82. **Number of Tent-Only Sites:** 10. **Hookups:** Electric (20, 30, 50 amps), water, sewer, phone, cable TV. **Each Site:** Picnic table. **Dump Station:** Yes. **Laundry:** Yes. **Pay Phone:** Yes. **Rest Rooms and Showers:** Yes. **Fuel:** No. **Propane:** No. **Internal Roads:** Paved, in good condition. **RV Service:** No. **Market:** Couple of blocks. **Restaurant:** Couple of blocks. **General Store:** Yes, limited. **Vending:** Yes. **Swimming Pool:** Yes. **Playground:** Yes. **Other:** Spa, game room, storm shelter, sports field, stream, coin games, basketball. **Activities:** Swimming. **Nearby Attractions:** Mall of America, Minnesota Zoo, Mississippi River cruises, casino, Minnesota Children's Zoo, Murphy's Landing Historic Village, Fort Snelling State Park, horse racing, auto racing, antiques, gold, horseback riding. **Additional Information:** Greater Minneapolis Convention & Visitors Assoc., (800) 445-7412.

## RESTRICTIONS

**Pets:** Leash only; extra fee of $1 per pet. **Fires:** In community fire ring only; not at individual sites. **Alcoholic Beverages:** Permitted. **Vehicle Maxi-** **mum Length:** None. **Other:** Motorcycles & motorbikes not to be ridden, except to & from site.

## TO GET THERE

From the junction of I-35W and Hwy. 13S, take Exit 38 and drive 4.5 mi. west on Hwy. 13S, then 500 ft. south on Hwy. 13, then 0.5 mi. west on 126th St. to Boone Ave. Roads are mostly wide and well maintained w/ adequate shoulders.

## ST. CHARLES

### Lazy D Campground

R. R. 1, Box 252, Altura 55910. T: (507) 932-3098; www.lazyd-camping-trailrides.com.

| 🚐 ★★★ | 🏕 ★★★★ |
|---|---|
| Beauty: ★★★★ | Site Privacy: ★★★★ |
| Spaciousness: ★★★★ | Quiet: ★★★★ |
| Security: ★★★ | Cleanliness: ★★★ |
| Insect Control: None | Facilities: ★★★ |

A river runs through Lazy D Campground. And it's filled with trout. That's one reason the campground is popular. Another is that is offers horseback rides and other equestrian treats and the horses are on site. Located in the wilderness bluff country on the Middle Branch of the Whitewater River, the campground has spacious (40 × 50 the smallest) level, grassy sites. RV and tent sites are both available alongside the stream. The campground is mowed and the spring-fed water flows fast so mosquitos aren't a problem. What is a problem for some is the lack of a laundry and no pull-through sites.

## BASICS

**Operated by:** Mark & Betty Thoreson. **Open:** Apr. 1–Dec. 1. **Site Assignment:** Reservations w/ 1-night deposit; refunds w/ 7-day notice. **Registration:** At campground office. **Fee:** $17 (cash, check, credit cards). **Parking:** At site.

## FACILITIES

**Number of RV Sites:** 65. **Number of Tent-Only Sites:** 25. **Hookups:** Electric (20, 30, 50 amps), water, sewer. **Each Site:** Picnic table, fire ring. **Dump Station:** Yes. **Laundry:** No. **Pay Phone:** Yes. **Rest Rooms and Showers:** Yes. **Fuel:** No. **Propane:** No. **Internal Roads:** Gravel, in good condition. **RV Service:** No. **Market:** 8 mi. south in St. Charles. **Restaurant:** 2 mi. north in Elba. **General Store:** Yes. **Vending:** Yes. **Swimming Pool:**

Yes. **Playground:** Yes. **Other:** Game room, volleyball, basketball, tether ball, horseshoes, antique carriage museum, trout stream, recreation field.
**Activities:** Fishing, swimming, horseback riding (horses on site), pony rides, hay rides, trail rides, inner tubing, covered wagon rides, sleigh rides.
**Nearby Attractions:** Aquatic center, golf, fire tower, hiking trails, beach, Historic Marnach House.
**Additional Information:** Rochester CVB, (800) 634-8277.

## RESTRICTIONS

**Pets:** Leash only. **Fires:** Fire ring only. **Alcoholic Beverages:** Permitted. **Vehicle Maximum Length:** None.

## TO GET THERE

From the junction of I-90 and Hwy. 74, take Exit 233, drive 8.5 mi. north on Hwy. 74, then 150 yards west on CR 139.

## ST. CLOUD

## St. Cloud Campground and RV Park

2491 2nd St. Southeast, St. Cloud 56304. T: (800) 690-7045; F: (320) 202-8990; stcloudcampgrd@aol.com.

🚐 ★★★★            ⛺ ★★★★

| | |
|---|---|
| Beauty: ★★★★ | Site Privacy: ★★★★ |
| Spaciousness: ★★★★ | Quiet: ★★★★ |
| Security: ★★★★★ | Cleanliness: ★★★★★ |
| Insect Control: Yes | Facilities: ★★★★ |

St. Cloud Campground and RV Park plays host to many camping club rallys. That's one indication of what a well run, popular facility it is. Another indication is to visit, drive through, stay, and see why it is one of the best in the state. Laid out in a series of loops, the campground offers a mix of gravel and grassy, shaded and open RV sites with a typical site width of 30 feet and 40 pull-throughs at 35 × 70. As campers check in, a guide escorts them to their site, shows them where the hookup is, and makes sure the sewer site is correctly attached to the RV. Just a little over a mile outside St. Cloud, the campground is in a quiet country setting. Tent campers have several different sites separated from RVs, as well as a primitive area offering more room and privacy. Security is tops with an owner who lives on site, regular patrols, Workkampers who live in each row of campsites and keep an eye on their

area, and county sheriff patrols coming through for rounds.

## BASICS

**Operated by:** Jim & Dana Reed. **Open:** May 1–Oct. 15. **Site Assignment:** Reservations w/ no deposit. **Registration:** At campground office. **Fee:** $23.50 (cash, check, credit cards). **Parking:** At site.

## FACILITIES

**Number of RV Sites:** 88. **Number of Tent-Only Sites:** 17. **Hookups:** Electric (30, 50 amps), water, sewer. **Each Site:** Picnic table, fire ring. **Dump Station:** Yes. **Laundry:** Yes. **Pay Phone:** Yes. **Rest Rooms and Showers:** Yes. **Fuel:** No. **Propane:** Yes. **Internal Roads:** Gravel, in good condition. **RV Service:** No. **Market:** 2 mi. west in St. Cloud. **Restaurant:** 2 mi. west in St. Cloud. **General Store:** Yes. **Vending:** No. **Swimming Pool:** Yes. **Playground:** Yes. **Other:** Hiking trails, volleyball, basketball, badminton, croquet, lodge, book exchange, pool table, electronic games, heated rally center building w/ kitchenette, game room. **Activities:** Swimming, hiking. **Nearby Attractions:** Charles A. Lindberg House & History Center, Ellingson Car Museum, Minnesota Baseball Hall of Fame, Munsinger Gardens & Clemens Gardens, Stearn's County Heritage Center, St. John's Benedictine Abbey. **Additional Information:** St. Cloud Area CVB, (800) 264-2940.

## RESTRICTIONS

**Pets:** Leash only. **Fires:** Fire ring only. **Alcoholic Beverages:** Permitted. **Vehicle Maximum Length:** None.

## TO GET THERE

From the junction of US 10 and Hwy. 23, drive 1 block east on Hwy. 23 to lights at 14th Ave., drive south 1 block, then east 1 mi. Roads are wide and well maintained w/ broad shoulders.

## STURGEON LAKE

## Timberline Campground

9152 Timberline Rd., Sturgeon Lake 55783. T: (218) 372-3272

🚐 ★★★★            ⛺ ★★★★

| | |
|---|---|
| Beauty: ★★★★ | Site Privacy: ★★★★ |
| Spaciousness: ★★★★ | Quiet: ★★★★ |
| Security: ★★★★ | Cleanliness: ★★★★★ |
| Insect Control: None | Facilities: ★★★★ |

Set in a rural river valley six miles south of Moose Lake, Timberline Campground offers RV sites in a variety of sizes, from 28 × 50 to 50 × 100. The grounds are well maintained and guests are welcome to hunt for agates and pick wild berries in the campground and surrounding area. Sites are generally shaded and often covered with pine needles. More than half the sites are occupied by seasonals, many of whom have landscaped their sites and added personal touches. RV sites 165–168 and 181–184 are most desirable. They are larger, more private sites. The campground is quiet with a natural buffer of pine trees and noise-softening pine needle carpet. Tents have a separate section with some privacy from RV campers. Security is tops—the campground has one access road which is monitored, the owners live on site, and the grounds are patrolled.

## BASICS

**Operated by:** Jeff & Sue Floding. **Open:** May 1–Sept. 30. **Site Assignment:** Reservations accepted w/ $20 deposit; refund (minus $4) w/ 5-day notice. **Registration:** At campground office. **Fee:** $25 (cash, check, credit cards). **Parking:** At site.

## FACILITIES

**Number of RV Sites:** 76. **Number of Tent-Only Sites:** 19. **Hookups:** Electric (20, 30, 50 amps), water, sewer. **Each Site:** Picnic table, fire ring. **Dump Station:** Yes. **Laundry:** Yes. **Pay Phone:** Yes. **Rest Rooms and Showers:** Yes. **Fuel:** No. **Propane:** No. **Internal Roads:** Paved/gravel, in good condition. **RV Service:** No. **Market:** 6 mi. north in Moose Lake. **Restaurant:** 4 mi. east in Sturgeon Lake. **General Store:** Yes. **Vending:** Yes. **Swimming Pool:** Yes. **Playground:** Yes. **Other:** Screened shelter pavilion, bike path, hiking path, snack bar, video game room, 3-hole golf course, Moose River, horseshoe, basketball, volleyball, rec room, sports field, river beach, innertube launch. **Activities:** Swimming, fishing, hiking, shuttle canoe service, boating (rental paddleboats available), berry picking, agate hunting, biking (rental bikes available), tubing (rental tubes available), Saturday night movies, scheduled activities. **Nearby Attractions:** Casinos, museums, golf, state trails, scenic drives, flea market, antique shops, historical sites. **Additional Information:** Hinckley CVB, (800) 996-4566.

## RESTRICTIONS

**Pets:** Leash only. **Fires:** Fire ring only. **Alcoholic Beverages:** Permitted. **Vehicle Maximum**

**Length:** None. **Other:** Visitors are charged $5 per person per day.

## TO GET THERE

From the junction of I-35 and CR 46, take Exit 209, drive 2.25 mi. west on CR 46 (through business district) to Timberlane Rd., drive north 0.75 mi. on Timberlane. Roads are wide and well maintained w/ broad shoulders.

# TAYLORS FALLS

## Camp Waub-O-Jeeg

2185 Chisago St., Taylors Falls 55084. T: (651) 465-5721; www.taylorsfalls.com/waubojeeg.

🚐 ★★★  　　　　🅰 ★★★★

| | |
|---|---|
| Beauty: ★★★ | Site Privacy: ★★★★ |
| Spaciousness: ★★★★ | Quiet: ★★★★ |
| Security: ★★★★ | Cleanliness: ★★★ |
| Insect Control: None | Facilities: ★★ |

Once you get there, Camp Waub-O-Jeeg is a nice quiet place to stay. But driving an RV on some of those roads is a bit tricky. CR 16 is wide and well maintained with mostly broad shoulders, but it is a curvy scenic road. The real test is the steep narrow hill leading from the campground office into the campground. Since the campground is atop a hill, the main access road is paved but it is steep, narrow, and winding with a pull-off lane in case a vehicle is coming down while another is going up. Very narrow, rough, gravel roads lead into the campsites. But it really feels like camping once you arrive. Sites are secluded on wooded, rolling terrain with level, prepared shaded spots. The typical site width is 20 feet with no pull-throughs. The sites seem bigger and more private because of all the trees surrounding them. Tent campers in particular will appreciate the privacy and wilderness setting. Security measures are good with a gate that is closed at night, owners who live on site and patrol, and regular patrols by local police. Located five miles west of Taylors Falls, the campground got its unusual name from a brave Chippewa war leader born about 1747.

## BASICS

**Operated by:** Ron & Beth Egge. **Open:** Apr. 15–Oct. 15. **Site Assignment:** Reservations w/ 1-night deposit; refund w/ 48-hour notice. **Registration:** At campground office. **Fee:** $21 (cash, check). **Parking:** At site.

## FACILITIES

**Number of RV Sites:** 25. **Number of Tent-Only Sites:** 45. **Hookups:** Electric (30 amps), water. **Each Site:** Picnic table, fire ring. **Dump Station:** Yes. **Laundry:** No. **Pay Phone:** No. **Rest Rooms and Showers:** Yes. **Fuel:** No. **Propane:** No. **Internal Roads:** Gravel, in fair condition. **RV Service:** No. **Market:** 5 mi. east in Taylors Falls. **Restaurant:** 5 mi. east in Taylors Falls. **General Store:** Yes. **Vending:** No. **Swimming Pool:** No. **Playground:** Yes. **Other:** St. Croix River, pavilion, shuffleboard, badminton, horseshoes, hiking trail, volleyball. **Activities:** Swimming, fishing, hiking. **Nearby Attractions:** Scenic drives, Wild Mountain, art shops, antique stores, historic homes, skiing, snowboarding, Wildlife Educational Center, golf, rock climbing. **Additional Information:** Taylors Falls Chamber of Commerce, (80) 447-4958.

## RESTRICTIONS

**Pets:** Leash only. **Fires:** Fire ring only. **Alcoholic Beverages:** At sites only. **Vehicle Maximum Length:** 30 ft.

## TO GET THERE

From the junction of Hwy. 95 and CR 16, drive 2 mi. north on CR 16.

## TAYLORS FALLS
### Interstate State Park

P.O. Box 254, Taylors Falls 55084. T: (651) 465-5711; www.dnr.state.mn.us.

| 🚐 ★★ | ▲ ★★★★ |
|---|---|
| Beauty: ★★★★★ | Site Privacy: ★★ |
| Spaciousness: ★★ | Quiet: ★★★ |
| Security: ★★★★ | Cleanliness: ★★★ |
| Insect Control: None | Facilities: ★★ |

Few private campgrounds can compete with the natural beauty of city, state, and national parks. Interstate State Park is one of the most beautiful in Minnesota. However, few public parks can compete with the facilities offered at private campgrounds—such as water and sewer hookups, laundry, general store, and heated swimming pool. That's the case with Interstate State Park. And enough campers must find the beauty and recreational activities more important than the comfort amenities because this campground is often packed. Folks know a good thing when they see it. Establihsed in 1895, it is the oldest state park in both Wisconsin and Minnesota, and is located on the border of Taylors Falls in Minnesota and St. Croix Falls in Wisconsin. The park is best known for the towering rocky gorge which forms the dalles of the river and for the glacial potholes that are the deepest in the world. Laid out in a loop, the campground offers shady, level, back-in sites—no pull-throughs. Both RV and tent sites are right on the river, with sites 5–23 offering the best view. Swimming is prohibited because of the drop-offs, deep channel, and strong current.

## BASICS

**Operated by:** State of Minnesota. **Open:** Mar. 1–Dec. 1. **Site Assignment:** Reservations w/ 1-night fee plus $7.25 non-refundable service charge; refunds (minus $5 fee & $7.25 service charge) w/ 3-day notice. **Registration:** At campground office. **Fee:** $15 (cash, check, credit cards). **Parking:** At site.

## FACILITIES

**Number of RV Sites:** 22. **Number of Tent-Only Sites:** 15. **Hookups:** Electric (30, 50 amps). **Each Site:** Picnic table, fire ring. **Dump Station:** Yes. **Laundry:** No. **Pay Phone:** Yes. **Rest Rooms and Showers:** Yes. **Fuel:** No. **Propane:** No. **Internal Roads:** Paved, in good condition. **RV Service:** No. **Market:** 2 mi. north in Taylors Falls. **Restaurant:** 2 mi. north in Taylors Falls. **General Store:** No. **Vending:** Yes. **Swimming Pool:** No. **Playground:** No. **Other:** St. Croix River, nature store, picnic shelters, hiking trail, visitor center, volleyball. **Activities:** Fishing, hiking, boating (rental canoes available). **Nearby Attractions:** Scenic drives, Wild Mountain, art shops, antique stores, historic homes, skiing, snowboarding, Wildlife Educational Center, golf, rock climbing,. **Additional Information:** Taylors Falls Chamber of Commerce, (800) 447-4958.

## RESTRICTIONS

**Pets:** Leash only. **Fires:** Fire ring only. **Alcoholic Beverages:** "3.2" beer only. **Vehicle Maximum Length:** 50 ft. **Other:** Vehicle permits of $20 per year or $4 per day are required to enter all Minnesota state parks; 14-day stay limit.

## TO GET THERE

From Taylors Falls, drive 1.5 mi. south on US 8. Road is wide and well maintained w/ broad shoulders.

## TAYLORS FALLS
### Wildwood RV Park and Campground

P.O. Box 235, Taylors Falls 55084. T: (800) 447-4958; www.wildmountain.com; camp@wildmountain.com.

🚐 ★★★          ▲ ★★

Beauty: ★★                Site Privacy: ★★
Spaciousness: ★★★          Quiet: ★★★
Security: ★★★★            Cleanliness: ★★
Insect Control: No          Facilities: ★★★

Location is everything. Wildwood RV Park and Campground, three miles east of Taylors Falls, is expensive for what it offers but it is located in a favorite tourist area. With easy access to Hwy. 95, the campground has level, mostly shaded sites with a mix of gravel and grassy areas and 30 pull-throughs. The typical site width is 30 feet. The campground has 33 seasonal campers. Many overnight campers stop by for the convenience after seeing the campground signs on the highway. Security is good with a manager that lives on site, a gate that is closed at night, and regular patrols. The $20 fee for tent sites is rather steep for what a tent camper gets—little privacy or distance from RV campers.

### BASICS
**Operated by:** Raedeke family. **Open:** May 1–Oct. 15. **Site Assignment:** Weekend reservations require a 2-night stay & $35 deposit; refund w/ 14-day notice. **Registration:** At campground office. **Fee:** $25 (cash, check, credit cards). **Parking:** At site.

### FACILITIES
**Number of RV Sites:** 78. **Number of Tent-Only Sites:** 60. **Hookups:** Electric (20, 30, 50 amps), water, sewer. **Each Site:** Picnic table, fire ring. **Dump Station:** Yes. **Laundry:** No. **Pay Phone:** Yes. **Rest Rooms and Showers:** Yes. **Fuel:** No. **Propane:** No. **Internal Roads:** Gravel, in fair condition. **RV Service:** No. **Market:** 8 mi. east in St. Croix. **Restaurant:** 3 mi. west in Taylors Falls. **General Store:** Yes. **Vending:** Yes. **Swimming Pool:** Yes. **Playground:** Yes. **Other:** Mini-golf, wading pool, mountain bike trails, game room, basketball, horseshoes, free shuttles to Taylors Falls Canoe Rental 7 days a week. **Activities:** Swimming. **Nearby Attractions:** Scenic drives, Wild Mountain, art shops, antique stores, historic homes, skiing,

snowboarding, Wildlife Educational Center, golf, rock climbing. **Additional Information:** Taylors Falls Chamber of Commerce, (800) 447-4958.

### RESTRICTIONS
**Pets:** Leash only, plus $4.70 fee. **Fires:** Fire ring only. **Alcoholic Beverages:** Permitted. **Vehicle Maximum Length:** 40 ft.

### TO GET THERE
From the junction of Hwy. 95 and US 8, drive 3 mi. west on US 8 and 95. Road is wide and well maintained w/ broad shoulders.

## WABASHA
### Pioneer Campsite

130 Pioneer Dr., Wabasha 55981. T: (651) 565-2242

🚐 ★★★          ▲ ★★★

Beauty: ★★★              Site Privacy: ★★★
Spaciousness: ★★★          Quiet: ★★★
Security: ★★★            Cleanliness: ★★★
Insect Control: None        Facilities: ★★★

A rural campground with access to the Mississippi River, Pioneer Campsite is four-and-a-half miles east of Wabasha. The campground offers a choice of shaded or open, grassy or sandy sites, with a typical site width of 35 feet. There are 20 pull-through sites and 183 seasonal campers. The grounds are somewhat hilly with plenty of trees, lots of birds, and bird feeders. "Behold the beauty of the Lord," a campground sign says. Church services are offered on Sundays. Laid out in a series of loops, Pioneer Campsites has a separate area for tent campers for more green space and privacy. Security measures include owners who live on site and provide patrols of the campgrounds.

### BASICS
**Operated by:** Ray & Lorraine Logan. **Open:** April 15–Oct. 15. **Site Assignment:** Reservations w/ 1-night deposit; refund w/ 7-day notice. **Registration:** At campground office. **Fee:** $24 (cash, check). **Parking:** At site.

### FACILITIES
**Number of RV Sites:** 240. **Number of Tent-Only Sites:** 7. **Hookups:** Electric (20, 30, 50 amps), water, sewer. **Each Site:** Picnic table, fire ring. **Dump Station:** Yes. **Laundry:** Yes. **Pay Phone:** Yes. **Rest Rooms and Showers:** Yes. **Fuel:** No. **Propane:** No. **Internal Roads:**

Paved/gravel, in good condition. **RV Service:** No. **Market:** 4.5 mi. west in Wabasha. **Restaurant:** 4.5 mi. west in Wabasha. **General Store:** Yes, limited. **Vending:** Yes. **Swimming Pool:** Yes. **Playground:** Yes. **Other:** Rec hall, recreation game, coin games, river, mini-golf, basketball, sports field, horseshoes, hiking trails, volleyball, boat ramp. **Activities:** Swimming, hiking, fishing, boating (rental canoes, rowboats available). **Nearby Attractions:** Mississippi River, toy museum, golf, Arrowhead Bluffs Museum, antiques, historic sites, arts & crafts shops. **Additional Information:** Wabasha Area Chamber of Commerce, (800) 565-4158.

## RESTRICTIONS

**Pets:** Leash only. **Fires:** Fire ring only. **Alcoholic Beverages:** Permitted. **Vehicle Maximum Length:** 40 ft.

## TO GET THERE

From the junction of Hwy. 60 and US 61, drive 4 mi. south on US 61, then 0.75 mi. north on CR 30, then 2.5 mi. east on CR 24, then 0.25 mi. east on Prairie Ln. Roads are wide and well maintained w/ broad shoulders but you have to go through a residential area to get to the campground.

## WALKER

### Moonlight Bay Resort and Campground on Leech Lake

6409 Wedgewood Rd., Northwest, Walker 56484.
T: (888) 973-7078; F: (218) 547-3047;
www.fishandgame.com/moonlight.

| 🚐 ★★★ | 🛖 ★★ |
|---|---|
| Beauty: ★★★★ | Site Privacy: ★★ |
| Spaciousness: ★★ | Quiet: ★★★ |
| Security: ★★★ | Cleanliness: ★★★ |
| Insect Control: None | Facilities: ★★★ |

First off, all but 20 of the campground sites at Moonlight Bay Resort and Campground on Leech Lake are occupied by seasonals. That's what happens when a campground has a pretty setting, a nice restaurant with an eating deck overlooking the lake, good access, and a lot of water activities. The campground is built on a hill that runs down to the lake, so most campers have a nice view of the lake. Sites are level with concrete pads to park on. But some of the tiered sites have to be backed onto down a bit of a

grade and that might not be a pleasant experience for some squeamish drivers—particularly if the ground is wet. Located five miles north of Walker, the campground's typical site width is 25 feet and most of the area is wooded with giant pine trees. Leech Lake is a famous fishing spot with its walleye, northern, perch, and muskie. Campers can bring a boat and launch it at the concrete ramp or have the campground launch it. The resort also has ample space to dock a boat after a day of fishing. Live bait and other fishing necessities are sold at the tackle shop. A golf course and driving range are right across the street. The best RV sites are 57 and 65 because they offer easy access and are bigger at 50 × 75. Tent sites are mingled among RVs.

## BASICS

**Operated by:** Al & Diane Sproessig. **Open:** May 1–Oct. 1. **Site Assignment:** Reservations w/ $15 deposit; no refunds; credit will be given for following year if 60-day notice given. **Registration:** At campground office. **Fee:** $20 (cash, check, credit cards). **Parking:** At site.

## FACILITIES

**Number of RV Sites:** 107. **Number of Tent-Only Sites:** 10. **Hookups:** Electric (30, 50 amps), water, sewer, cable TV. **Each Site:** Picnic table, fire ring. **Dump Station:** Yes. **Laundry:** No. **Pay Phone:** Yes. **Rest Rooms and Showers:** Yes. **Fuel:** Yes. **Propane:** Yes. **Internal Roads:** Paved, in good condition. **RV Service:** No. **Market:** 5 mi. south in Walker. **Restaurant:** On site. **General Store:** Yes. **Vending:** No. **Swimming Pool:** Yes. **Playground:** Yes. **Other:** rec room, boat dock, boat ramp, marina, horseshoes, hiking trails, volleyball, video game room, croquet, shuffleboard. **Activities:** Fishing, swimming, boating (rental motor boats, canoes, paddleboats, kayaks available), scheduled weekend activities. **Nearby Attractions:** Golf, hunting, birdwatching, snowmobiling, skiing, horseback riding, antique & craft shops, Museum of Natural History, Sugar Point Battle Monument, Itasca State Park. **Additional Information:** Leech Lake Area Chamber of Commerce, (800) 833-1118.

## RESTRICTIONS

**Pets:** Leash only, $6 fee per day. **Fires:** Fire ring only. **Alcoholic Beverages:** Permitted. **Vehicle Maximum Length:** 40 ft. **Other:** 3-day min. stay on holidays.

## To Get There

From the junction of Hwy. 34, Hwy. 200 and
Hwy. 371, drive 5.5 mi. north on Hwy. 371,
then 0.5 mi. east on access road. Roads are wide
and well maintained w/ broad shoulders.

## WALKER

## Shores of Leech Lake Campground and Marina

Box 327, Walker 56484. T: (218) 547-1819;
www.shoresofleechlake.com.

🚐 ★★★★          ▲ ★

Beauty: ★★★★          Site Privacy: ★★★
Spaciousness: ★★★          Quiet: ★★★★
Security: ★★★★          Cleanliness: ★★★
Insect Control: Yes          Facilities: ★★★★

The best sites in Shores of Leech Lake Campground and Marina are on the water—not just
the shoreline but on the actual lake itself. Covered boat slips with water and electric hookups
make this a wonderful place for people who want
to camp on their boats. Some of the 20- to 30-
foot floating bungalows have homesteaded this
harbor for more than a decade. Nestled deep in
the Chippewa National Forest, Leech Lake is the
third largest lake in Minnesota. Except for the
eagles, mosquitoes, deer, bear, and fireflies who
make their home here, midweek sailors often
have this 20-mile-wide, 23-mile-long body of
water to themselves. Many lakefront campground sites are occupied by seasonal campers.
Sites have a typical width of 30 feet, are shaded
and level with eight pull-throughs. Only one site
is set aside for tent campers. The campground
located three miles north of Walker, has a full
service marina with gas, bait, ice, marine power,
pump-out station, boat, and motor rentals. A
comfortable lodge offers sandwiches, pizza, beer,
wine, and free coffee.

## Basics

**Operated by:** Mitch & Mara Loomis. **Open:** May
1–Oct. 15. **Site Assignment:** Reservations for 3-
night min. w/ 1-night deposit; refund w/ 14-day
notice. **Registration:** At campground office. **Fee:**
$24 (cash, check, credit cards). **Parking:** At site.

## Facilities

**Number of RV Sites:** 47. **Number of Tent-
Only Sites:** 1. **Hookups:** Electric (30 amp), water,

sewer, cable TV, phone. **Each Site:** Picnic table, fire
ring. **Dump Station:** Yes. **Laundry:** Yes. **Pay
Phone:** Yes. **Rest Rooms and Showers:** Yes.
**Fuel:** Yes. **Propane:** No. **Internal Roads:** Dirt,
rough & narrow. **RV Service:** No. **Market:** 2.5 mi.
south in Walker. **Restaurant:** 2.5 mi. south in
Walker. **General Store:** Yes. **Vending:** Yes. **Swimming Pool:** No. **Playground:** Yes. **Other:** Leech
Lake, fish-cleaning house, sandy beach, basketball
court, hiking trails, boat ramp, boat dock, rec room,
lodge. **Activities:** Swimming, fishing, boating, hiking,
(rental canoes, sailboats, paddleboats, motor boats
available). **Nearby Attractions:** Golf, hunting, bird-
watching, snowmobiling, skiing, horseback rides,
antique & craft stores, Museum of Natural History,
Sugar Point Battle Monument, Itasca State Park.
**Additional Information:** Leech Lake Area Chamber of Commerce, (800) 833-1118.

## Restrictions

**Pets:** Leash only, $10 fee per night. **Fires:** Fire ring
only. **Alcoholic Beverages:** Permitted. **Vehicle
Maximum Length:** None.

## To Get There

From the junction of Hwy. 34 and Hwy.
200/371, drive 2.5 mi. north on Hwy. 371,
then 0.5 mi. east on access road. Roads are wide
and well maintained w/ good shoulders.

## WASECA

## Kiesler's Campground

Box 503B, Waseca 56093. T: (800) 533-4642, ext. 5;
www.kieslers.com; camp@kieslers.com.

🚐 ★★★★          ▲ ★★★★

Beauty: ★★★★          Site Privacy: ★★★★
Spaciousness: ★★★★          Quiet: ★★★★
Security: ★★★★          Cleanliness: ★★★★
Insect Control: None          Facilities: ★★★★

If you played from sunup to sundown, you probably wouldn't run out of things to do at Kiesler's
Campground. Recreation choices are everywhere, including a 2,000-square-foot heated
swimming pool with a gigantic enclosed slide
and a heated wading pool, along with a nice lake
for fishing and swimming. A wood chip base on
the playground makes it both cleaner for children and less painful if they fall. Laid out in a
series of loops, the rural campground offers a tree
on every site, gravel pads for RVs, and a typical
site width of 40 feet. Not surprisingly, Kiesler's

has 80 seasonal campers. Surprisingly, it has only ten pull-throughs. Although tents can be put on any site, most tenters seem to prefer the east area of the park which is more wooded and away from RVs. Security measures are good with owners who live on site, regular patrols, and a traffic control gate that requires a pass to enter.

## BASICS

**Operated by:** Steve Kiesler. **Open:** Apr. 15–Oct. 1. **Site Assignment:** Reservations accepted w/ $30 deposit, $50 on holidays; refund (minus $5 fee) w/ 7-day notice. **Registration:** At campground office. **Fee:** $33 (cash, check, credit cards). **Parking:** At site.

## FACILITIES

**Number of RV Sites:** 280. **Number of Tent-Only Sites:** 17. **Hookups:** Electric (30, 50 amps), water, sewer, cable TV. **Each Site:** Picnic table, fire ring. **Dump Station:** Yes. **Laundry:** Yes. **Pay Phone:** Yes. **Rest Rooms and Showers:** Yes. **Fuel:** No. **Propane:** Yes. **Internal Roads:** Gravel, in good condition. **RV Service:** No. **Market:** 1.5 mi. west in Waseca. **Restaurant:** Within walking distance. **General Store:** Yes. **Vending:** Yes. **Swimming Pool:** Yes. **Playground:** Yes. **Other:** Volleyball, shuffleboard, horseshoes, mini-golf, game room, basketball, wading pool, hiking trails, recreation building, boat docks, lake. **Activities:** Swimming, fishing, hiking, boating (rental motorboats available), scheduled weekend activities. **Nearby Attractions:** Cabela's, Heritage Halls Museum, golf, antique & craft shops, Mall of America, Farmamerica. **Additional Information:** Owatonna Area Convention & Tourism, (800) 423-6466.

## RESTRICTIONS

**Pets:** Leash only but encourage campers to leave pets at home. **Fires:** Fire ring only. **Alcoholic Beverages:** Permitted. **Vehicle Maximum Length:** 40 ft. **Other:** All visitors must register as day campers at $4 per person per day.

## TO GET THERE

From the junction of US 14 and Hwy. 13, drive east 1.5 mi. Roads are wide and well maintained w/ broad shoulders.

# WINONA
## Prairie Island Campground

1120 Prairie Island Rd., Winona 55987. T: (507) 452-4501

🚐 ★★　　　▲ ★★★

Beauty: ★★★　　　Site Privacy: ★★★
Spaciousness: ★★★　　Quiet: ★★★
Security: ★★★★　　Cleanliness: ★★★
Insect Control: None　　Facilities: ★★

Located on the banks of the Mississippi River, one-and-a-half miles north of Winona, Missouri, Prairie Island Campground is surrounded by city park land including hiking trails and a deer park. Five golf courses are located within a 25-mile radius. Arranged in a series of loops, the sites are level, grassy, and mostly shaded with 20 pull-throughs. The typical site width is 40 feet. Tent sites have some privacy away from RV sites. Security is great—resident managers live on site, the entrance gate is closed at night, and the campground is patrolled. Like all riverfront campgrounds, however, the site sometimes floods. It doesn't happen every year, but it is best to check for flood conditions before planning an overnight stay.

## BASICS

**Operated by:** City of Winona. **Open:** Apr. 1–Nov. 1. **Site Assignment:** Reservations accepted; no deposit. **Registration:** At campground office. **Fee:** $15 (cash, check, credit cards). **Parking:** At site.

## FACILITIES

**Number of RV Sites:** 86. **Number of Tent-Only Sites:** 90. **Hookups:** Electric (20, 30, 50 amps). **Each Site:** Picnic table, fire ring. **Dump Station:** Yes. **Laundry:** No. **Pay Phone:** Yes. **Rest Rooms and Showers:** Yes. **Fuel:** No. **Propane:** No. **Internal Roads:** Paved, in good condition. **RV Service:** No. **Market:** 1.5 mi. south in Winona. **Restaurant:** 1.5 mi. south in Winona. **General Store:** Yes. **Vending:** No. **Swimming Pool:** No. **Playground:** Yes. **Other:** Mississippi River, sandy beach, boat launch, game room, walking trails, putting green, video/paperback library, recreation field, fish-cleaning station. **Activities:** Fishing, swimming, hiking, boating (rental canoes available), planned weekend activities. **Nearby Attractions:** River boat cruises, aquatic park, 208-ft. water slide, Steamboat Center, ice arena, golf, Winona County Historical Museum, antique & art shops. **Additional Information:** Winona Area Chamber of Commerce CVB, (800) 657-4972.

RESTRICTIONS

**Pets:** Leash only. **Fires:** Fire ring only. **Alcoholic Beverages:** Permitted. **Vehicle Maximum Length:** None.

TO GET THERE

From the junction of US 61 and Pelzer St., drive northeast 1.5 mi. on Pelzer to Prairie Island Rd., drive 1 mi. east on Prairie Island Rd. Roads are wide and well maintained w/ broad shoulders.

## WINONA
### Winona KOA

Rte. 6, Box 181, Winona 55987. T: (877) 454-2267

🚐 ★★★          ⛺ ★★★

Beauty: ★★★          Site Privacy: ★★★
Spaciousness: ★★★    Quiet: ★★★
Security: ★★★        Cleanliness: ★★★
Insect Control: None  Facilities: ★★★

Located in hilly country eight miles south of Winona, the Winona KOA is a rural campground with sites on three levels of the hillside. A metal staircase leads up to the office and playroom. The third tier of campsites has a steep hill going up to it. The different levels of campground allow for more privacy and a better view. The campground attracts a lot of local campers —there are 27 seasonal campers—as well as travelers on their way to the Wisconsin Dells. Campsites are generally shady with mature oak trees, level, and grassy. The typical site width is 30 feet and the campground has 12 pull-throughs. Most sites have gravel pads for RVs. Tent sites have more trees, grass, and greenery. For security, the owner lives on site and patrols the campground.

BASICS

**Operated by:** Gordie & Ann Rasmussen. **Open:** Apr. 15–Oct. 15. **Site Assignment:** Reservations w/ no deposit. **Registration:** At campground office. **Fee:** $24 (cash, check, credit cards). **Parking:** At site.

FACILITIES

**Number of RV Sites:** 60. **Number of Tent-Only Sites:** 12. **Hookups:** Electric (20, 30, 50 amps), water. **Each Site:** Picnic table, fire ring. **Dump Station:** Yes. **Laundry:** Yes. **Pay Phone:** Yes. **Rest Rooms and Showers:** Yes. **Fuel:** No. **Propane:** Yes. **Internal Roads:** Paved/gravel, in good condition. **RV Service:** No. **Market:** 8 mi. north in Winona. **Restaurant:** 4 mi. south in Pickwick. **General Store:** Yes. **Vending:** Yes. **Swimming Pool:** Yes. **Playground:** Yes. **Other:** Mississippi River, rec room, pavilion, boat ramp, boat dock, sports field, hiking trails, horseshoes, volleyball, marina. **Activities:** Swimming, fishing, hiking, boating (rental canoes available), planned weekend activities. **Nearby Attractions:** Museums, Polish Cultural Institute, golf, boating, aquatic center, antique shops, art galleries, ice arena. **Additional Information:** Winona CVB, (800) 657-4972.

RESTRICTIONS

**Pets:** Leash only. **Fires:** Fire ring only. **Alcoholic Beverages:** Permitted. **Vehicle Maximum Length:** None.

TO GET THERE

From the junction of Hwy. 43 and US 61/14, drive 6 mi. south and east on US 61/14. Roads are wide and well maintained w/ broad shoulders.

# Ohio

With a name meaning "great" in Iroquois, Ohio has a big reputation to live up to. And it does that quite easily. From Lake Erie on its northern border to the Ohio River on its southern, the Buckeye State offers a treasure trove of water recreation. But wait, there's a lot more than water sports! **Hocking State Forest** and **Hocking Hills State Park** in southern Ohio, for example, add climbing and rappelling on 99 acres of sheer rock faces and challenging cliffs, including climbs from 20 to 120 feet.

Ohio's 72 state parks offer 57 campgrounds and recreation galore. At **Mohican State Park** near **Mansfield,** Clear Fork River is stocked with more than 100,000 brown trout for a fishing fantasy. **Cleveland** has one of the nation's largest park systems with its 100-mile chain of city parks, known as the "Emerald Necklace." For an unusual adventure, try scuba diving adjacent to downtown Cleveland where a **freshwater reef** has been created by the remains of the demolished Cleveland Municipal Stadium. In **Sandusky,** the 364-acre **Cedar Point Amusement Park** features 60 rides, including 13 spine-tingling roller coasters. See the stars at **Akron's Civil Theatre,** where the blinking stars and floating clouds are simulated on the ceiling. At the **Hale Farm and Village,** travel back in time to the mid-1800s as craftsmen and village residents portray life as it was in Ohio's Western Reserve. Historic **Sauder Village** in **Archbold** and **Roscoe Village** in **Coshocton** likewise celebrate the past.

Called "the most beautiful of America's inland cities" by Winston Churchill, **Cincinnati** saved its famed railroad station, **Union Terminal,** and turned it into several museums and an OMNIMAX theater. Nearby **Lebanon** evokes an unusual Colonial atmosphere, and **Waynesville** is renowned for its antique shops. In its 100 acres, **Fort Ancient** contains a prehistoric earthwork built by the Hopewell Indians. Stop in **Columbus** to see one of the nation's largest collections of reptiles at the **Columbus Zoo,** as well as the first gorilla born in captivity. In **Dayton,** check out where Orville and Wilbur Wright first dreamed of flying in and visit the **United States Air Force Museum.**

**Hinckley** has the dubious honor every March 15th of welcoming home squadron after squadron of buzzards returning from winter in the Smoky Mountains. If you prefer more variety, about 110 kinds of birds are known to nest in Hocking Hills State Park in **Logan.** **Put-In-Bay** on **South Bass Island** is known for its fish hatcheries, wineries, and caves, while **COSI Toledo** is a hands-on center that makes learning science fun.

*The following facilities accept payment in checks or cash only:*

Carthage Gap Campground, Athens

Scenic Hills RV Park, Berlin

Pin-Oak Acres, Leavittsburg

The Landings Family Campground, Marietta

Poor Farmer's Campground, Piqua

Chippewa Valley Campground, Seville

Camp Qtokee, Sidney

Hidden Acres Campground, West Salem

Town & Country Camp Resort, West Salem

Shady Lake Campground, Findlay

*The following facility features 50 or fewer sites:*

Blue Lagoon Campground, Butler

# Campground Profiles

## ASHLAND
## Hickory Lakes Campground

23 Township Rd. 1300 Meyers Rd., West Salem 44287. T: (419) 869-7587; F: (419) 869-5007; www.gocampingamerica.com/hickorylakesoh; hickory lake@bright.net.

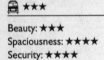

Beauty: ★★★
Spaciousness: ★★★★
Security: ★★★★
Insect Control: None

Site Privacy: ★★★★
Quiet: ★★★★
Cleanliness: ★★★
Facilities: ★★★

Hickory Lakes Campground is pleasant and serene with ponds, trees, meadows, and a sandy bottom swimming lake, although some of the seasonal campers need to repair and tidy up their sites. Owners should understand that as a rule, seasonal RVs must be 1982 or newer. However, it is not the age but the level of disrepair and poor maintenance of some of the seasonal sites that mar the campground's beauty. Located 15 miles east of Ashland, Hickory Lakes offers shaded or open sites surrounding a lake. There are 100 seasonal campers and 14 pull-through sites. Camping areas are grassy with gravel parking spots, and most sites are shaded by a tree. The best RV sites are C17–19 and C21–23, all overlooking the pond. Speed limit is five mph, and children 17 and younger must be on their sites by 10 p.m. Security measures are tops, with one entrance/ exit road, a security gate requiring a coded card,

surveillance cameras, owners who live on site, and regular campground patrols.

**BASICS**

**Operated by:** Randy & Karen Burkhead. **Open:** May 1–Oct. 15. **Site Assignment:** Reservations w/ 1-night deposit; refund w/ 7-day notice. **Registration:** At campground office. **Fee:** $22 ( cash, check, credit cards). **Parking:** At site.

**FACILITIES**

**Number of RV Sites:** 200. **Number of Tent-Only Sites:** 0. **Hookups:** Electric (20, 30, 50 amps), water. **Each Site:** Picnic table, fire ring. **Dump Station:** Yes. **Laundry:** Yes. **Pay Phone:** Yes. **Rest Rooms and Showers:** Yes. **Fuel:** No. **Propane:** Yes. **Internal Roads:** Gravel, in good condition. **RV Service:** No. **Market:** 15 mi. west in Ashland. **Restaurant:** 15 mi. west in Ashland. **General Store:** Yes. **Vending:** Yes. **Swimming Pool:** No. **Playground:** Yes. **Other:** Swimming lake, 3 fishing lakes, horseshoes, pavilion, recreation barn, rental cabins, coin games, hiking trail, volleyball, basketball, sports field. **Activities:** Swimming, fishing, hiking, scheduled weekend activities. **Nearby Attractions:** Golf, Ashland College, canoeing, Sea World, antiques, reservoir, Amish country, Cedar Point, outlet mall, Carousel Park, Living Bible Museum. **Additional Information:** Ashland Area Chamber of Commerce, (419) 281-4584.

**RESTRICTIONS**

**Pets:** Leash only. **Fires:** Fire ring only. **Alcoholic Beverages:** Permitted. **Vehicle Maximum Length:** None. **Other:** No working caravans.

## TO GET THERE

From the junction of I-71 and US 250, take Exit 186 and drive 6 mi. east on US 250, then 1 mi. north on Township Rd. 63, then 0.5 mi. east on Township Rd. 1300. US 250 is wide and well maintained w/ broad shoulders. Township Rds. 63 and 1300 are well maintained but narrow and winding w/ narrow shoulders. The campground entrance is over a dam between two ponds.

## ATHENS
### Carthage Gap Campground

22575 Brimstone Rd., Coolville 45723. T: (740) 667-3072

🚐 ★★★★          ▲ ★★★

| | |
|---|---|
| Beauty: ★★★★ | Site Privacy: ★★★★ |
| Spaciousness: ★★★★ | Quiet: ★★★★ |
| Security: ★★★★ | Cleanliness: ★★★★ |
| Insect Control: None | Facilities: ★★★★ |

A rural campground by a lake, Carthage Gap Campground has the little touches that make camping a pleasure, including friendly owners. The campground is well maintained, right down to such niceties as a clean, pleasantly decorated laundry room. Sites are level, with a choice of open or shaded. Located ten miles west of Athens, the campground has 100 seasonal campers and 30 pull-through sites. The typical site width is 40 feet. No license or fee is required for campers to use the fishing lake. Many weekends feature campground-wide meals, such as a corn roast, bean soup supper, pancake breakfast and ice cream and dessert social. Security measures include one entrance/exit road, owners who live on site, and the presence of four local policemen as seasonal campers.

### BASICS

**Operated by:** Gloyd & Nina McDermott. **Open:** Apr. 15–Nov. 1. **Site Assignment:** Reservations w/ 1-night deposit; no refunds but will honor the deposit for a year. **Registration:** At campground office. **Fee:** $22 (cash, check). **Parking:** At site.

### FACILITIES

**Number of RV Sites:** 135. **Number of Tent-Only Sites:** 0. **Hookups:** Electric (20, 30, 50 amps), water, sewer. **Each Site:** Picnic table, fire ring. **Dump Station:** Yes. **Laundry:** Yes. **Pay Phone:** Yes. **Rest Rooms and Showers:** Yes. **Fuel:** No.

**Propane:** Yes. **Internal Roads:** Gravel, in good condition. **RV Service:** No. **Market:** 10 mi. east in Athens. **Restaurant:** 10 mi. east in Athens. **General Store:** No. **Vending:** Yes. **Swimming Pool:** No. **Playground:** Yes. **Other:** Swimming lake, fishing lake, basketball, volleyball, horseshoes, pavilion, hiking trails. **Activities:** Swimming, fishing, hiking, scheduled weekend activities. **Nearby Attractions:** Cave, golf, Ohio University, museums, historic homes, Fenton Glass Factory, antiques, arts & crafts. **Additional Information:** Athens Area Chamber of Commerce, (740) 594-2251.

### RESTRICTIONS

**Pets:** Leash only. **Fires:** Fire ring only. **Alcoholic Beverages:** Permitted. **Vehicle Maximum Length:** None.

### TO GET THERE

From the junction of Hwy. 7 and US 50, drive 3.5 mi. west on US 50, then 0.5 mi. north on CR 56. US 50 is wide and well maintained w/ broad shoulders. CR 56 is wide and well maintained w/ narrow shoulders. A steep, narrow, gravel hill leads into the campground.

## AURORA
### Yogi Bear's Jellystone Park Camp-Resort

3392 State Rte. 82, Mantua 44255. T: (800) 344-YOGI; www.jellystoneohio.com.

🚐 ★★★★          ▲ ★★★★

| | |
|---|---|
| Beauty: ★★★ | Site Privacy: ★★★★ |
| Spaciousness: ★★★★ | Quiet: ★★★★ |
| Security: ★★★★★ | Cleanliness: ★★★★★ |
| Insect Control: None | Facilities: ★★★★ |

Pull into a Yogi Bear's Jellystone Park Camp-Resort and you know what to expect—clean facilities, good security, a family atmosphere, and plenty of activities. That's what the Yogi Bear four miles east of Aurora offers. The campground also has a great location—ten minutes from Sea World and Six Flags Ohio, ten minutes from the Ohio Turnpike, and a half hour from Cleveland. Situated on a 50-acre spring-fed lake, Yogi Bear's has 110 seasonal campers, an activities director, and a typical site width of 33 feet. Most popular RV sites are the 40 pull-throughs with full hookups. Although tents can be placed on any site, tent campers seem to prefer the rustic area with no hookups and more privacy. Laid out in a series of loops, the campground has mostly grassy, open sites, and trees are scarace. Security is tops, with an entrance gate manned 24 hours a day, along with regular patrols of the campground.

## BASICS

**Operated by:** Yogi Bear's Jellystone Park Camp-Resorts. **Open:** May 1–Oct. 15. **Site Assignment:** Reservations w/ 1-night deposit; refunds w/ 7-day notice. **Registration:** At campground office. **Fee:** $44 (cash, credit cards). **Parking:** At site.

## FACILITIES

**Number of RV Sites:** 310. **Number of Tent-Only Sites:** 115. **Hookups:** Electric (30, 50 amps), water, sewer. **Each Site:** Picnic table, fire ring. **Dump Station:** Yes. **Laundry:** Yes. **Pay Phone:** Yes. **Rest Rooms and Showers:** Yes. **Fuel:** No. **Propane:** Yes. **Internal Roads:** Paved/gravel, in good condition. **RV Service:** No. **Market:** 4 mi. west in Aurora. **Restaurant:** 4 mi. west in Aurora. **General Store:** Yes. **Vending:** Yes. **Swimming Pool:** Yes. **Playground:** Yes. **Other:** Lake, swimming beach, game room, snack bar, rental cottages & cabins, mini-golf, pavilion, coin games, wading pool, boat ramp, boat dock, basketball, shuffleboard, sports field, volleyball, hiking trails. **Activities:** Swimming, fishing, electric motors only boating (rental rowboats, paddlebaots, canoes, kayaks available), hiking, scheduled activities. **Nearby Attractions:** Sea World, Six Flags, golf, museums, antiques, historic homes, arts & crafts shops, outlet stores. **Additional Information:** Portage County Visitor & Convention Bureau, (800) 648-6342.

## RESTRICTIONS

**Pets:** Leash only. **Fires:** Fire ring only. **Alcoholic Beverages:** At sites only. **Vehicle Maximum Length:** 40 ft.

## TO GET THERE

From the junction of Hwy. 306 and Hwy. 82, drive 4 mi. east on Hwy. 82. Roads are wide and well maintained w/ broad shoulders.

## BATAVIA

### East Fork State Park

P.O. Box 119, Bethel 45106. T: (513) 724-6521; www.dnr.state.oh.us/odnr/parks.

 ★★★              ▲ ★★★

Beauty: ★★★★          Site Privacy: ★★
Spaciousness: ★★       Quiet: ★★★★

Security: ★★★★          Cleanliness: ★★★
Insect Control: None     Facilities: ★★★

One of the largest camping areas in the state, East Fork State Park offers 416 sites for either RVs or tents. Thirty-one seasonal sites are also available, as is a 17-site equestrian camp. Located 15 miles southwest of Williamsburg and 25 mi. from Cincinnati, the park's terrain includes both rugged hills and open meadows. There are 2,160 acres of water and unlimited-horsepower boating, with access available at five launch ramps. For sport fishing, East Fork is stocked with hybrid striper and as well as largemouth and smallmouth bass, bluegill, and crappie. East Fork has a 1,200-foot swimming beach. Campsites are 18 × 30, with most under a canopy of mature beech, sugar maple, and white oak. There are no pull-through sites. Park rangers provide security with regular patrols from a nearby ranger station.

## BASICS

**Operated by:** State of Ohio. **Open:** All year. **Site Assignment:** First come, first served. No reservations. **Registration:** At campground office. **Fee:** $17 (cash, check, credit cards). **Parking:** At site.

## FACILITIES

**Number of RV Sites:** 416. **Number of Tent-Only Sites:** 0. **Hookups:** Electric (30 amps). **Each Site:** Picnic table, fire ring. **Dump Station:** Yes. **Laundry:** No. **Pay Phone:** Yes. **Rest Rooms and Showers:** Yes. **Fuel:** No. **Propane:** No. **Internal Roads:** Paved, in good condition. **RV Service:** No. **Market:** 15 mi. northeast in Williamsburg. **Restaurant:** 15 mi. northeast in Williamsburg. **General Store:** Yes. **Vending:** Yes. **Swimming Pool:** No. **Playground:** Yes. **Other:** William H. Harsha Lake, swimming beach, boat ramp, amphitheater, horseshoes, pavilion, horseback riding trails, hiking trails, rental camps, rental RVs. **Activities:** Swimming, boating, fishing, hiking, scheduled activities. **Nearby Attractions:** Golf, museums, historic homes, zoo, Kings Island amusement park, conservatory, antiques. **Additional Information:** Clermont County CVB, (800) 796-4282.

## RESTRICTIONS

**Pets:** Leash only, pet camping area; $1 per pet a day, max. 2 pets. **Fires:** Fire ring only. **Alcoholic Beverages:** Not permitted. **Vehicle Maximum Length:** 35 ft. **Other:** 14-day stay limit.

## TO GET THERE

From the junction of I-275 and Hwy. 32, drive

10 mi. east on Hwy. 32, then 0.25 mi. south on Half Acre Rd., then 500 feet east on access road. Roads are wide and well maintained w/ broad shoulders.

## BELLVILLE
### Honeycreek Valley Campground

1219 Honeycreek Rd. West, Bellville 44813. T: (419) 886-2777

🚐 ★★★                  ⛺ ★★★

Beauty: ★★★                Site Privacy: ★★★
Spaciousness: ★★★          Quiet: ★★★★
Security: ★★★★             Cleanliness: ★★★
Insect Control: Yes         Facilities: ★★★

A county campground on a lake, Honeycreek Valley Campground offers level ground with a choice of open or shaded sites. Located in a valley with forests rising around it, the quiet campground is graced with vibrant autumn foliage and flowering dogwoods in the spring. Three miles west of Bellville, the campground has a typical site width of 30 feet, 30 seasonal campers, and 25 pull-through sites. Laid out in tiers, the campground has a five mph speed limit and enforces quiet hours between 11 p.m. and 9 a.m. Fishing is catch and release only. Security includes a one-road loop, an owner who lives on site, and regular campground patrols.

### BASICS
**Operated by:** Mike Romano. **Open:** May 1–Oct. 15. **Site Assignment:** Reservations w/ 1-night deposit; refund w/ 7-day notice. **Registration:** At campground office. **Fee:** $20 (cash, check, credit cards). **Parking:** At site.

### FACILITIES
**Number of RV Sites:** 50. **Number of Tent-Only Sites:** 35. **Hookups:** Electric (30 amps), water, sewer. **Each Site:** Picnic table, fire ring. **Dump Station:** Yes. **Laundry:** Yes. **Pay Phone:** Yes. **Rest Rooms and Showers:** Yes. **Fuel:** No. **Propane:** No. **Internal Roads:** Gravel, in fair condition. **RV Service:** Yes. **Market:** 3 mi. east in Bellville. **Restaurant:** 3 mi. east in Bellville. **General Store:** Yes. **Vending:** Yes. **Swimming Pool:** No. **Playground:** Yes. **Other:** Swimming lake, pavilion, fishing lake, nature trails, horseshoes, volleyball, softball, coin games, sports field. **Activities:** Swimming, fishing, hiking, boating (rental paddleboats available), scheduled weekend activities. **Nearby Attractions:** Living Bible Museum, Johnny Appleseed Monument, Richland Carousel Park, state forest, covered bridge, Amish country, Mid Ohio Sports Car Course, golf, antiques, arts & crafts, Kingwood Center, B & O Bike Trail. **Additional Information:** Mansfield-Richland Area Chamber of Commerce, (419) 522-3211.

### RESTRICTIONS
**Pets:** Leash only. **Fires:** Fire ring only. **Alcoholic Beverages:** At sites only. **Vehicle Maximum Length:** None.

### TO GET THERE
From the junction of I-71 and Hwy. 97, drive 3 mi. east on Hwy. 97, then 1.5 mi. south on Hwy. 13, then 2 mi. west on Honey Creek Rd. Hwy. 97 and Hwy. 13 are wide and well maintained w/ broad shoulders. Honey Creek Rd. is a country road, mainly gravel, winding, and narrow w/ narrow shoulders.

## BELLVILLE
### Yogi Bear's Jellystone Park Camp-Resort

SR 546 at Black Rd., Bellville 44813. T: (419) 886-CAMP

🚐 ★★★                  ⛺ ★★★

Beauty: ★★★                Site Privacy: ★★★★
Spaciousness: ★★★★         Quiet: ★★★★
Security: ★★★              Cleanliness: ★★★★
Insect Control: Yes         Facilities: ★★★

Yogi Bear's Jellystone Park Mansfield, located eight miles south of Bellville, features rolling terrain along a lake. Laid out in a series of loops, the campground has 80 seasonal campers (some sites in not very good shape), three pull-through sites, and an average site width of 45 feet. Sites are level and grassy, with a choice of shaded or open. The entrance is a nice welcome to the campground with a fence, flowers, and ivy climbing a trellis. Security is provided by owners who live on site. Speed limit is 10.5 mph, high for a Yogi Bear facility. Quiet hours are 11 p.m. to 8 a.m. and minors age 18 and under are not permitted on the park grounds after 7:30 p.m. without adult supervision. Best RV sites are by the lake. Best tent sites are in a rustic area by the woods that affords more green space and privacy.

### BASICS
**Operated by:** Bill Bings. **Open:** Apr. 15–Oct. 28. **Site Assignment:** Reservations w/ 1-night

deposit; refund w/ 7-day notice. **Registration:** At campground office. **Fee:** $27 (cash, check, credit cards). **Parking:** At site.

## FACILITIES

**Number of RV Sites:** 175. **Number of Tent-Only Sites:** 30. **Hookups:** Electric (30, 50 amps), water, sewer. **Each Site:** Picnic table, fire ring. **Dump Station:** Yes. **Laundry:** Yes. **Pay Phone:** Yes. **Rest Rooms and Showers:** Yes. **Fuel:** No. **Propane:** Yes. **Internal Roads:** Gravel, in good condition. **RV Service:** None. **Market:** 8 mi. north in Bellville. **Restaurant:** 8 mi. north in Bellville. **General Store:** Yes. **Vending:** Yes. **Swimming Pool:** No. **Playground:** Yes. **Other:** Swimming beach, pavilion, rental cabins, volleyball, game room, outdoor theater, horseshoes, stocking fishing lake, boat ramp, boat dock, recreation field. **Activities:** Swimming, fishing, boating (rental rowboats, canoes & paddleboats available), scheduled activities. **Nearby Attractions:** Amish Country, Mid-Ohio Race Track, golf, Mohican Forest, canoeing, plant tours, Malabar Farm State Park, Living Bible Museum, Richland Carousel Park, ski resorts, Ohio State Reformatory. **Additional Information:** Mansfield-Richland Area Chamber of Commerce, (419) 522-3211.

## RESTRICTIONS

**Pets:** Leash only. **Fires:** Fire ring only. **Alcoholic Beverages:** At sites only. **Vehicle Maximum Length:** None. **Other:** Bass & catfish under 15 inches must be returned to the lake immediately.

## TO GET THERE

From the junction of I-71 and Hwy. 97, take Exit 165 and drive 1.5 mi. southeast on Hwy. 97, then 3 mi. west on Mock Rd., then 4 mi. south on Hwy. 546, then 0.25 mi. southwest on Black Rd. Roads are wide and well maintained but have narrow shoulders in spots.

## BERLIN

### Scenic Hills RV Park

4483 TR 367, Millersburg 44654. T: (330) 893-3258

🚐 ★★★★                          ▲ n/a

| | |
|---|---|
| Beauty: ★★★ | Site Privacy: ★★★★ |
| Spaciousness: ★★★★ | Quiet: ★★★★ |
| Security: ★★★★ | Cleanliness: ★★★★ |
| Insect Control: None | Facilities: ★★★ |

Because there are so many nearby attractions here in the heart of Amish country, Scenic Hills

RV Park offers little on-site recreation. Located one mile east of Berlin, the campground accepts full-hookup units only. No tents are allowed. The campground offers open sites on a grassy hilltop with sunrise and sunset views. Scenic Hills has 12 seasonal campers and 40 pull-through sites, with a typical site width of 40 feet. The campground has no rest rooms. A craft shop and store are located on the grounds. Sites are laser leveled to assure easier parking for RVs and easy access for big rigs. Security and safety measures include a five-mph speed limit and owners who live nearby and keep a close eye on the campground.

## BASICS

**Operated by:** Sam & Mary Hershberger. **Open:** Apr. 1–Nov. 1. **Site Assignment:** Reservations w/ 1-night deposit; refund w/ 7-day notice. **Registration:** At campground office. **Fee:** $20 (cash, check). **Parking:** At site.

## FACILITIES

**Number of RV Sites:** 88. **Number of Tent-Only Sites:** 0. **Hookups:** Electric (20, 30, 50 amps), water, sewer, phone. **Each Site:** Picnic table, fire ring. **Dump Station:** Yes. **Laundry:** No. **Pay Phone:** Yes. **Rest Rooms and Showers:** No. **Fuel:** No. **Propane:** Yes. **Internal Roads:** Gravel, in good condition. **RV Service:** No. **Market:** 1 mi. west in Berlin. **Restaurant:** 1 mi. west in Berlin. **General Store:** Yes. **Vending:** No. **Swimming Pool:** No. **Playground:** No. **Other:** Sports field, horseshoes. **Activities:** None. **Nearby Attractions:** Amish country, Wendell August Forge, arts & crafts, antiques, Behalt cyclorama, Rolling Ridge Ranch, Schrock's Amish Farm, scenic drives. **Additional Information:** Holmes County Chamber of Commerce & Tourism Bureau, (330) 674-3975.

## RESTRICTIONS

**Pets:** Leash only. **Fires:** Fire ring only. **Alcoholic Beverages:** At sites only. **Vehicle Maximum Length:** None.

## TO GET THERE

From the junction of US 62 and Hwy. 39, drive 1 mi. east on Hwy. 39, then 0.25 mi. south on TR 367. Roads are wide and well maintained w/ mostly broad shoulders.

## BLANCHESTER
### Stonelick State Park

2895 Lake Dr., Pleasant Plain 45162. T: (513) 625-7544; F: (513) 625-7526; www.dnr.state.oh.us/odnr/parks; stonelick.parks@dnr.state.oh.us.

🚐 ★★★          ▲ ★★★★

Beauty: ★★★★          Site Privacy: ★★★
Spaciousness: ★★★          Quiet: ★★★★
Security: ★★★★          Cleanliness: ★★★
Insect Control: None          Facilities: ★★★

Tucked away in the rolling highlands six miles southwest of Blanchester, Stonelick State Park was originally created in 1950 as a wildlife area for local sporting enthusiasts. Now the area is operated by the state and offers a variety of outdoor recreational activities centered around a 200-acre lake. The woodland campground setting offers mostly grassy, shady sites. The typical site size is 15 × 40 feet with no pull-throughs. Laid out in a series of loops, Stonelick offers six non-electric sites for tent campers, although tents and RVs are permitted on any of the sites. Four Rent-A-Camp units consisting of a tent, dining canopy, cooler, cook stove and other equipment can be rented during the summer months by reservation. The lake is well known for catches of bass, bluegill, crappie and catfish. A valid Ohio hunting and/or fishing license is required. There is a laundry facility. Campground security is great, with a ranger-controlled access station and regular patrols.

#### BASICS
**Operated by:** State of Ohio. **Open:** All year. **Site Assignment:** First come, first served. No reservations. **Registration:** At campground office. **Fee:** $15 (cash, check, credit cards). **Parking:** At site.

#### FACILITIES
**Number of RV Sites:** 109. **Number of Tent-Only Sites:** 6. **Hookups:** Electric (50 amps). **Each Site:** Picnic table, fire ring. **Dump Station:** Yes. **Laundry:** Yes. **Pay Phone:** Yes. **Rest Rooms and Showers:** Yes. **Fuel:** No. **Propane:** Yes. **Internal Roads:** Paved, in good condition. **RV Service:** No. **Market:** 6 mi. northeast in Blanchester. **Restaurant:** 6 mi. northeast in Blanchester. **General Store:** Yes. **Vending:** Yes. **Swimming Pool:** No. **Playground:** Yes. **Other:** Stonelick lake, beach, boat launch, amphitheater, hiking trail, rental camper units. **Activities:** Swimming, fishing, boating (electric

motors only), hiking, schedule activities. **Nearby Attractions:** Kings Island Amusement Park, Blue Jacket outdoor drama, Wilmington College, antqiues, museums. **Additional Information:** Clinton County CVB, (877) 4-A-VISIT.

#### RESTRICTIONS
**Pets:** Leash only, pet camping area; $1 per night per pet, max. of 2 pets. **Fires:** Fire pits only. **Alcoholic Beverages:** Not permitted. **Vehicle Maximum Length:** 35 ft. **Other:** 14-day stay limit.

#### TO GET THERE
From the junction of Hwy. 28 and Hwy. 133, drive 6 mi. southwest on Hwy. 133, then 1.5 mi. south on Hwy. 727. Roads are wide and well maintained w/ good shoulders.

## BLUFFTON
### Twin Lakes Park

3506 Township Rd. 34, Bluffton 45817. T: (419) 477-5255; twinlakes@turbosurf.net.

🚐 ★★★          ▲ ★★★

Beauty: ★★★          Site Privacy: ★★★
Spaciousness: ★★★          Quiet: ★★★
Security: ★★★          Cleanliness: ★★★
Insect Control: Yes          Facilities: ★★★

A grassy campground on two lakes, Twin Lakes Park offers level, wooded, and open sites. Located five miles north of Bluffton, the campground's typical site has a width of 30 feet. There are 50 seasonals and three pull-through sites. Situated near I-75, the campground is subject to some noise from vehicles whizzing past. The best RV sites are by the lake or near the facilities. Tent sites are in a separate area with more greenery and privacy. A flea market, where campers set-up is free, is a popular event that takes place the last Saturday of each month, May through Aug. Safety measures include a 5.5-mph speed limit and speed bumps. Security includes one entrance/exit through a card-coded gate, owners who live on site, and regular patrols.

#### BASICS
**Operated by:** Bob & Elaine Harris. **Open:** All year. **Site Assignment:** Reservations w/ 1-night deposit; refunds "if you name appears in the Findlay Courier obituary columns.". **Registration:** At campground office. **Fee:** $30 (cash, check, credit cards). **Parking:** At site.

## FACILITIES

**Number of RV Sites:** 85. **Number of Tent-Only Sites:** 10. **Hookups:** Electric (30, 50 amps), water, sewer. **Each Site:** Picnic table, fire ring. **Dump Station:** Yes. **Laundry:** No. **Pay Phone:** Yes. **Rest Rooms and Showers:** Yes. **Fuel:** No. **Propane:** Yes. **Internal Roads:** Paved, in good condition. **RV Service:** No. **Market:** 5 mi. south in Bluffton. **Restaurant:** 5 mi. south in Bluffton. **General Store:** Yes, limited. **Vending:** Yes. **Swimming Pool:** No. **Playground:** Yes. **Other:** Swimming lake, fishing lake, volleyball, horseshoes, shuffleboard, basketball, shelter house, game room, volleyball, sandy beach, sports field. **Activities:** Swimming, fishing, boating (rental rental rowboats, canoe, paddleboats available), scheduled weekend activities. **Nearby Attractions:** Golf, antiques, museums, historic homes, arts & crafts shops, motorsports park, Children's Garden, skating arena, Neil Armstrong Air & Space Museum, Indian Lake. **Additional Information:** Lima/Allen County CVB, (888) 222-6075.

## RESTRICTIONS

**Pets:** Leash only; $2 for first pet, $3 for additional. Must provide proof current vaccinations for pets. **Fires:** Fire ring only. **Alcoholic Beverages:** Permitted. **Vehicle Maximum Length:** None. **Other:** No hunting of frogs or turtles, limit of 2 bass.

## TO GET THERE

From the junction of I-75 and Hwy. 235, take Exit 145 and drive 0.1 mi. south on Hwy. 235, then 0.5 mi. east on Township Rd. 34. The roads are wide and well maintained w/ broad shoulders.

## BOWLING GREEN

### Fire Lake Camper Park

13630 West Kramer Rd., Bowling Green 43402. T: (419) 352-1185; www.gocampingamerica.com.

| 🚐 ★★★ | 🛆 ★★★ |
|---|---|
| Beauty: ★★★ | Site Privacy: ★★★ |
| Spaciousness: ★★★ | Quiet: ★★★ |
| Security: ★★★★ | Cleanliness: ★★★★ |
| Insect Control: Yes | Facilities: ★★★ |

A rural campground by an eight-acre lake, Fire Lake Camper Park offers open and shaded sites with easy access to the interstate. Some highway traffic noise can be heard at the far end of the campground. Sites are grassy with gravel pads for parking. The campground has 45 seasonal campers and five pull-through sites. Many sites are right on the lake, and most offer a lake view. A design flaw affecting a number of sites is the positioning of vehicle parking between the lake and the campsites. Typical site width is 30 feet. The campground is adjacent to the Slippery Elm Trail, a 23-mile trail that is free and open to the public for biking, walking, running, skating, horseback riding, and rollerblading. The trail, which is also wheelchair accesible, is a beautiful natural corridor converted from an unused railroad track. Bikes are available for rent at the campground. Security measures include owners who live on site, one entrance/exit road (with an enforced five-mph speed limit), and regular campground patrols.

## BASICS

**Operated by:** Martin & Jennifer Gladieux. **Open:** Apr. 15–Oct. 15. **Site Assignment:** Reservations w/ 1-night deposit; refunds w/ 7-day notice. **Registration:** At campground office. **Fee:** $22 (cash, check, credit cards). **Parking:** At site.

## FACILITIES

**Number of RV Sites:** 96. **Number of Tent-Only Sites:** 20. **Hookups:** Electric (30 amps), water. **Each Site:** Picnic table, fire ring. **Dump Station:** Yes. **Laundry:** Yes. **Pay Phone:** Yes. **Rest Rooms and Showers:** Yes. **Fuel:** No. **Propane:** Yes. **Internal Roads:** Paved/gravel, in good condition. **RV Service:** No. **Market:** 3 mi. north in Bowling Green. **Restaurant:** 3 mi. north in Bowling Green. **General Store:** Yes. **Vending:** Yes. **Swimming Pool:** No. **Playground:** Yes. **Other:** Lake, swimming beach, rental cabins, basketball, volleyball, pavilion, rec room, boat dock, sports field, rental bikes. **Activities:** Swimming, catch-&-release fishing, boating (rental kayaks & paddleboats available), scheduled weekend activities. **Nearby Attractions:** Bowling Green State University, Slippery Elm Trail, museum, Sauder Historic village, golf, antiques, mill, canal boat, passenger train, Toledo Zoo. **Additional Information:** Greater Toledo CVB, (800) 243-4667.

## RESTRICTIONS

**Pets:** Leash only. **Fires:** Fire ring only. **Alcoholic Beverages:** At sites only. **Vehicle Maximum Length:** None.

## TO GET THERE

From the junction of I-75 and US 6, take Exit 179 and drive 1.5 mi. west on US 6, then 0.5 mi. south on Hwy. 25, then 0.5 mi. west on

Kramer Rd. Roads are wide and well maintained w/ broad shoulders.

## BROOKVILLE
### Dayton Tall Timbers KOA Resort

7796 Wellbaum Rd., Brookville 45309. T: (937) 833-3888; daytonkoa@aol.com.

🚐 ★★★★                     ⛺ ★★★

Beauty: ★★★★                Site Privacy: ★★★★
Spaciousness: ★★★★          Quiet: ★★★★
Security: ★★★★★             Cleanliness: ★★★★★
Insect Control: None         Facilities: ★★★★★

Dayton Tall Timbers Resort KOA has all the large and small touches that make camping a pleasure. Laid out in a series of loops, the campground is grassy with gravel parking spots and concrete patios. The semi-wooded facility offers a choice of open or shaded sites. The typical site width is 30 feet, and the campground has 20 seasonal campers and 150 pull-through sites. Little ponds, gazebos, flowers, brick walkways, benches, and a covered bridge add to the beauty. A well-stocked general store also features craft and souvenir items. A spring-fed fishing lake has bass, bluegill, perch, crappie, and catfish. No mini-bikes, mopeds or golf carts are allowed. Modest swimwear is required, i.e., no revealing bikinis or thongs. Alcoholic beverages are permitted at campsites, but tables should be kept free of open containers. Speed limit is five mph. Security measures include owners who live on site, one entrance/exit road, and regular campground patrols.

### BASICS
**Operated by:** Jim & Jane Rose. **Open:** Apr. 1–Nov. 1. **Site Assignment:** Reservations w/ 1-night deposit; refund (minus $5) w/ 7-day notice. **Registration:** At campground office. **Fee:** $32 (cash, check, credit cards). **Parking:** At site.

### FACILITIES
**Number of RV Sites:** 235. **Number of Tent-Only Sites:** 0. **Hookups:** Electric (20, 30, 50 amps), water, sewer, modem. **Each Site:** Picnic table, fire ring. **Dump Station:** Yes. **Laundry:** Yes. **Pay Phone:** Yes. **Rest Rooms and Showers:** Yes. **Fuel:** No. **Propane:** Yes. **Internal Roads:** Paved/gravel, in good condition. **RV Service:** No. **Market:** 3 mi. west in Brookville. **Restaurant:** 3 mi. west in Brookville. **General Store:** Yes. **Vending:** Yes. **Swimming Pool:** Yes. **Playground:** Yes.

**Other:** Petting zoo, basketball, horseshoes, mini golf, game room, picnic shelter, hiking trail, volleyball, rental cabins, badminton, fishing lake, coin games, pavilion, sports field. **Activities:** Swimming, boating (rental paddleboats available), fishing, hiking, scheduled activities. **Nearby Attractions:** Golf, US Air Force Museum, Sunwatch Indian Village, Wright Cycle Company Shop, Dayton Art Institute, Packard Museum, historic homes, musuems, outdoor drama, Paramount Kings Island Theme Park, Museum of Discovery. **Additional Information:** Dayton & Montgomery County CVB, (800) 221-8235.

### RESTRICTIONS
**Pets:** Leash only. **Fires:** Fire ring only. **Alcoholic Beverages:** At sites only. **Vehicle Maximum Length:** None.

### TO GET THERE
From the junction of I-70 and Hwy. 49N, take Exit 24 and drive 0.5 mi. north on Hwy. 49, then 0.5 mi. west on Pleasant Plains Rd., then 0.25 mi. south on Wellbaum Rd. Roads are wide and well maintained w/ broad shoulders.

## BUCKEYE LAKE
### Buckeye Lake KOA

P.O. Box 972, Buckeye Lake 43008. T: (740) 928-0706; buckeyekoa@aol.com.

🚐 ★★★★                     ⛺ ★★★★

Beauty: ★★★★                Site Privacy: ★★★★
Spaciousness: ★★★★          Quiet: ★★★★
Security: ★★★★              Cleanliness: ★★★★
Insect Control: Yes          Facilities: ★★★★

Located 23 miles east of Columbus, Buckeye Lake KOA offers shady, level sites. The campground has ten seasonals, 102 pull-through sites, and a typical site width of 35 feet. Our favorite RV sites are the full-hookup ones. The best tent sites are in the primitive area at the rear of the campground, with more trees and privacy. Some tenters prefer the sites with full hookup or water and electric, but the tradeoff is a little less privacy and green space. Because it is convenient to the interstate and offers easy access, the campground is popular with campers visiting Columbus attractions. No outside firewood is permitted in the campground in order to prevent tree diseases. Firewood is for sale at the campground. A small gift shop also is a nice touch. The campground provides on-site security 24 hours a day.

## BASICS

**Operated by:** Preble Family. **Open:** Apr. 2, Oct. 31. **Site Assignment:** Reservations w/ 1-night deposit; refund w/ 7-day notice. **Registration:** At campground office. **Fee:** $38 (cash, check, credit cards). **Parking:** At site.

## FACILITIES

**Number of RV Sites:** 177. **Number of Tent-Only Sites:** 28. **Hookups:** Electric (20, 30, 50 amps), water, sewer, phone, cable TV. **Each Site:** Picnic table, fire ring. **Dump Station:** Yes. **Laundry:** Yes. **Pay Phone:** Yes. **Rest Rooms and Showers:** Yes. **Fuel:** No. **Propane:** Yes. **Internal Roads:** Gravel, in good condition. **RV Service:** No. **Market:** 2 mi. south. **Restaurant:** 2 mi. south. **General Store:** Yes. **Vending:** Yes. **Swimming Pool:** Yes. **Playground:** Yes. **Other:** Rec hall, pavilion, coin games, mini-golf, basketball, shuffleboard, movies, badminton, sports field, horseshoes, hiking trails, volleyball, rental cabins. **Activities:** Swimming, hiking, scheduled weekend activities. **Nearby Attractions:** Golf, art musuem, Columbus Zoo, botanical garden & conservatory, German Village, Ohio Statehouse, COSI Columbus, antiques, arts & crafts, Ohio State University, museums, historic homes. **Additional Information:** Greater Columbus CVB, (800) 345-4386.

## RESTRICTIONS

**Pets:** Leash only. **Fires:** Fire rings only, no outside wood can be brought in. **Alcoholic Beverages:** At sites only. **Vehicle Maximum Length:** None.

## TO GET THERE

From the junction of I-70 and Hwy. 79, take Exit 129A, then drive 1.5 mi. south on Hwy. 79. Roads are wide and well maintained w/ broad shoulders.

## BUTLER

### Blue Lagoon Campground

1597 SR 97 East, Butler 44822. T: (419) 883-3888; bluelagooncg@aol.com.

 ★★★                    ▲ ★★★

Beauty: ★★★              Site Privacy: ★★★★
Spaciousness: ★★★★        Quiet: ★★★★
Security: ★★★★            Cleanliness: ★★★★
Insect Control: None       Facilities: ★★★

Nestled in the foothills of the Appalachian Mountains along Clear Fork River, Blue Lagoon Campground offers level, open sites with a typical site width of 50 feet. Located three miles west of Butler, the campground has one seasonal camper and two pull-through areas. A five-mph speed limit and quiet hours between 11 p.m. and 8 a.m. are enforced. The river is stocked by the Ohio Division of Natural Resources with trout and 26 other species of fish. The property is the only full-facility campground with direct access to the Richland B & O Bike Trail, an 18-mile paved multi-use trail. Open year-round during daylight hours and accessible to people with disabilities, the trail is off-limits to motorized vehicles and horseback riding. Security measures at the campground include owners who live on site and locked bathroom facilities. Campers pay a $5 deposit to obtain a bathroom key.

## BASICS

**Operated by:** David & Linda Chalut. **Open:** May 1–Oct. 15. **Site Assignment:** Reservations w/ 1-night deposit; refund (minus $4) w/ 7-day notice. **Registration:** At campground office. **Fee:** $22 (cash, credit cards). **Parking:** At site.

## FACILITIES

**Number of RV Sites:** 27. **Number of Tent-Only Sites:** 17. **Hookups:** Electric (20, 30 amps), water, sewer. **Each Site:** Picnic table, fire ring. **Dump Station:** Yes. **Laundry:** Yes. **Pay Phone:** No. **Rest Rooms and Showers:** Yes. **Fuel:** No. **Propane:** Yes. **Internal Roads:** Paved, in good condition. **RV Service:** No. **Market:** 3 mi. east in Butler. **Restaurant:** 3 mi. east in Butler. **General Store:** Yes. **Vending:** No. **Swimming Pool:** No. **Playground:** Yes. **Other:** Swimming pond, fishing river, volleyball, rental cabin, tetherball, horseshoes, basketball. **Activities:** Swimming, fishing. **Nearby Attractions:** Living Bible Museum, Johnny Appleseed Monument, Richland Carousel Park, state forest, covered bridge, Amish country, Mid-Ohio Sports Car Course, golf, antiques, arts & crafts, Kingwood Center. **Additional Information:** Mansfield-Richland Area Chamber of Commerce, (419) 522-3211.

## RESTRICTIONS

**Pets:** Leash only, $1 per pet. **Fires:** Fire rings only; fires must be extinguished before retiring for night. **Alcoholic Beverages:** Permitted. **Vehicle Maximum Length:** None. **Other:** RV outdoor mats larger than 2 × 3 ft. are not permitted.

## TO GET THERE

From the junction of I-71 and Hwy. 97, take Exit 165 and drive 7.7 mi. east on Hwy. 97.

Roads are wide and well maintained w/ broad shoulders.

## BUTLER
### Butler Mohican KOA

6918 Bunker Hill Rd. South, Butler 44822. T: (419) 883-3314; F: (419) 883-3149; www.koa.com/ where/oh/35134.htm; ButlerMohicanKOA@aol.com.

🚐 ★★★                    ⛺ ★★★

| | |
|---|---|
| Beauty: ★★★ | Site Privacy: ★★★★ |
| Spaciousness: ★★★★ | Quiet: ★★★★ |
| Security: ★★★★ | Cleanliness: ★★ |
| Insect Control: None | Facilities: ★★★ |

A quiet country campground, Butler Mohican KOA is semi wooded with a choice of open or shaded sites. The rental cabins look new, but the rest of the campground could use some cleaning and fixing up. Located eight miles east of Butler, the campground has five seasonal campers, 15 pull-through sites, and a typical site width of 35 feet. Quiet time from 10:30 p.m. to 8:30 a.m. is enforced. No generators or loud music are allowed at any time. Speed limit is ten mph. Fishing in Broken Arrow Lake is from dawn to dusk only, and all fish must be released when caught. Swimming and wading are not permitted in the lake. Security measures include one entrance/exit road, surveillance cameras, and owners who live on the site.

### BASICS
**Operated by:** Kevin & Cathy Wies. **Open:** Apr. 1–Nov. 1. **Site Assignment:** Reservations w/ $25 deposit; refund (minus $5) w/ 3-day notice. **Registration:** At campground office. **Fee:** $25 (cash, check, credit cards). **Parking:** At site.

### FACILITIES
**Number of RV Sites:** 57. **Number of Tent-Only Sites:** 33. **Hookups:** Electric (20, 30, 50 amps), water, sewer. **Each Site:** Picnic table, fire ring. **Dump Station:** Yes. **Laundry:** Yes. **Pay Phone:** Yes. **Rest Rooms and Showers:** Yes. **Fuel:** No. **Propane:** No. **Internal Roads:** Gravel, in good condition. **RV Service:** No. **Market:** 8 mi. west in Butler. **Restaurant:** 8 mi. west in Butler. **General Store:** Yes. **Vending:** No. **Swimming Pool:** Yes. **Playground:** Yes. **Other:** Broken Arrow Lake, rental cabins, pavilion, game room, basketball, horseshoes, coin games, hiking trails. **Activities:** Swimming, fishing, hiking, scheduled weekend activities. **Nearby**

**Attractions:** Living Bible Museum, Johnny Appleseed Monument, Richland Carousel Park, state forest, covered bridge, Amish country, Mid Ohio Sports Car Course, golf, antiques, arts & crafts, Kingwood Center, B & O Bike Trail. **Additional Information:** Mansfield-Richland Area Chamber of Commerce, (419) 522-3211.

### RESTRICTIONS
**Pets:** Leash only. **Fires:** Fire ring only. **Alcoholic Beverages:** Permitted. **Vehicle Maximum Length:** None.

### TO GET THERE
From the junction of Hwy. 95 and Hwy. 97, drive 3.5 mi. east on Hwy. 97, then 2 mi. south on Bunkerhill Rd. Hwy. 97 is wide and well maintained with generally broad shoulders. Bunkerhill Rd. is a winding country road with narrow shoulders.

## CAMBRIDGE
### Hillview Acres Campground

66271 Wolfs Den Rd., Cambridge 43725. T: (740) 439-3348

🚐 ★★★                    ⛺ ★★★

| | |
|---|---|
| Beauty: ★★★★ | Site Privacy: ★★★★ |
| Spaciousness: ★★★★ | Quiet: ★★★★ |
| Security: ★★★★ | Cleanliness: ★★ |
| Insect Control: None | Facilities: ★★★ |

Hillview Acres Campground looks like a state park except the roads aren't paved. Located one mile east of Cambridge, the campground has a wealth of natural beauty—rolling hillsides, old forests, and ponds. The campground itself is clean and well maintained but needs a new shower and bathroom facility. The ten-mph speed limit also could be cut in half because the campground has such steep narrow hills and so many youngsters playing outdoors. Sitting atop a hill, the campground is quiet with no highway noise. Campers have a choice of shaded or open sites; the hills are beautiful in autumn foliage. Laid out in a series of loops well separated from each other, the campground has a typical site width of 33 feet. There are 70 seasonal campers and seven pull-through sites. Quiet time is from 11 p.m. to 7 a.m., and no "foul" music is permitted at any time. Security measures here include one entrance/exit road, owners who live on site, and regular patrols of the campground.

## BASICS

**Operated by:** John & Nancy Walker. **Open:** Apr. 15–Oct. 31. **Site Assignment:** Reservations w/ 1-night deposit; refunds w/ 48-hour notice. **Registration:** At campground office. **Fee:** $20 (cash, check, credit cards). **Parking:** At site.

## FACILITIES

**Number of RV Sites:** 145. **Number of Tent-Only Sites:** 25. **Hookups:** Electric (30 amps), water. **Each Site:** Picnic table, fire ring. **Dump Station:** Yes. **Laundry:** No. **Pay Phone:** Yes. **Rest Rooms and Showers:** Yes. **Fuel:** No. **Propane:** No. **Internal Roads:** Gravel, in good condition. **RV Service:** No. **Market:** 1 mi. west in Cambridge. **Restaurant:** 1 mi. west in Cambridge. **General Store:** Yes. **Vending:** No. **Swimming Pool:** Yes. **Playground:** Yes. **Other:** Rec room, pavilion, coin games, catch-&-release fishing pond, basketball, badminton, sports field, horseshoes, hiking trails, volleyball. **Activities:** Swimming, fishing, hiking, scheduled weekend activities. **Nearby Attractions:** State parks, golf, antiques, art glass factories & museums, Living Word outdoor drama, museums, Hopalong Cassidy Museum, riding stable, Amish country. **Additional Information:** Cambridge Visitors & Convention Bureau, (800) 933-5480.

## RESTRICTIONS

**Pets:** Leash only. **Fires:** Fire ring only. **Alcoholic Beverages:** Permitted. **Vehicle Maximum Length:** None.

## TO GET THERE

From the junction of I-77 and US 22, drive 4 mi. east on US 22, then 0.25 mi. south on Wolf's Den Rd. US 22 is wide and well maintained w/ mostly broad shoulders. Wolf's Den Rd. is narrow and winding w/ steep hills.

## CAMBRIDGE
### Spring Valley Campground

8000 Dozer Rd., Cambridge 43725. T: (740) 439-9291

|  ★★★★ | 🅰 ★★★★ |
|---|---|
| Beauty: ★★★★ | Site Privacy: ★★★★ |
| Spaciousness: ★★★★ | Quiet: ★★★★ |
| Security: ★★★★ | Cleanliness: ★★★★ |
| Insect Control: None | Facilities: ★★★ |

With easy access off the interstate, Spring Valley Campground is surprisingly quiet. The grassy campground is cushioned by beautiful hills and woods. Level sites include 21 pull-throughs and a typical site width of 35 feet. Most sites have trees, but there are some open sites. There are also 65 seasonal campers. The well-maintained campground has a five-mph speed limit and quiet time beginning at 11 p.m. Sunday through Friday and at midnight on Saturday. The 3.5-acre lake is stocked with bass, crappie, and bluegill. It also has a beach area, slides, and diving boards, as well as a separate swimming pool. Security includes one entrance/exit road and owners who live on site.

## BASICS

**Operated by:** Hlads family. **Open:** Apr. 1–Nov. 1. **Site Assignment:** Reservations w/ $10 deposit, not refundable or transferable. **Registration:** At campground office. **Fee:** $23 (cash, check, credit cards). **Parking:** At site.

## FACILITIES

**Number of RV Sites:** 180. **Number of Tent-Only Sites:** 50. **Hookups:** Electric (30, 50 amps), water, sewer, cable TV. **Each Site:** Picnic table, fire ring. **Dump Station:** Yes. **Laundry:** No. **Pay Phone:** Yes. **Rest Rooms and Showers:** Yes. **Fuel:** No. **Propane:** Yes. **Internal Roads:** Gravel, in good condition. **RV Service:** No. **Market:** 1 mi. in any direction. **Restaurant:** 1 mi. in any direction. **General Store:** Yes. **Vending:** Yes. **Swimming Pool:** Yes. **Playground:** Yes. **Other:** Lake, pavilion, rental cabins, basketball, rec room, coin games, badminton, sports field, horseshoes, hiking trails, volleyball. **Activities:** Swimming, fishing, hiking, scheduled weekend activities. **Nearby Attractions:** State parks, golf, antiques, art glass factories & museums, Living Word outdoor drams, museums, Hopalong Cassidy Museum, riding stable, Amish country. **Additional Information:** Cambridge Visitors & Convention Bureau, (800) 933-5480.

## RESTRICTIONS

**Pets:** Leash only. **Fires:** Fire ring only. **Alcoholic Beverages:** Not permitted. **Vehicle Maximum Length:** None.

## TO GET THERE

From the junction of I-77 and I-70, drive 1 mi. west on I-70. Take Exit 178, then 50 yards south on Hwy. 209, then 1 mi. west on Dozer Rd. Roads are wide and well maintained w/ broad shoulders.

## CANTON

### Bear Creek Resort Ranch KOA

3232 Downing St. Southwest, East Sparta 44626. T: (330) 484-3901

🚐 ★★★★          ⛺ ★★★★

Beauty: ★★★★              Site Privacy: ★★★★
Spaciousness: ★★★★         Quiet: ★★★★
Security: ★★★★              Cleanliness: ★★★★★
Insect Control: None         Facilities: ★★★★

A hilly campground with level sites, Bear Creek Ranch Resort offers a western flair. Horses and ponies are available, and the campground provides miles of wooded horse trails. Located three miles south of Canton, the campground has grassy sites with gravel parking spots, along with a choice of open or shaded sites. The campground has 12 seasonal campers, 42 pull-through sites, and a typical site width of 35 feet. The facility is very clean and well maintained, including such touches as a live ivy plant, curtains, and wallpaper border in the bathroom. The most popular sites for tents and RVs both are alongside the lake and in the woods. No generators or loud radios are permitted, and quiet times are between 11 p.m. and 8 a.m. Speed limit is ten mph—rather high for such a child-pleasing campground. Security includes owners who live on site and provide regular patrols.

#### BASICS

**Operated by:** Lee & Carol Soehnlen. **Open:** All year. **Site Assignment:** Reservations w/ 1-night deposit; refund w/ 1-day notice. **Registration:** At campground office. **Fee:** $28 (cash, credit cards). **Parking:** At site.

#### FACILITIES

**Number of RV Sites:** 782. **Number of Tent-Only Sites:** 30. **Hookups:** Electric (50 amps), water, sewer. **Each Site:** Picnic table, fire ring. **Dump Station:** Yes. **Laundry:** Yes. **Pay Phone:** Yes. **Rest Rooms and Showers:** Yes. **Fuel:** No. **Propane:** Yes. **Internal Roads:** Paved/gravel, in good condition. **RV Service:** No. **Market:** 3 mi. north in Canton. **Restaurant:** 3 mi. north in Canton. **General Store:** Yes. **Vending:** Yes. **Swimming Pool:** Yes. **Playground:** Yes. **Other:** Catch-&-release fishing pond, rental cabins, pavilion, mini golf, activities field, basketball, volleyball, badminton, tetherball, horseshoes, game room, coin games, horseback riding trails. **Activities:** Swimming, fishing, horseback riding (rental horses available), boating (rental paddleboat available), scheduled weekend activities. **Nearby Attractions:** Pro Football Hall of Fame, golf, Canton Classic Car Museum, antiques, arts & crafts, McKinley Museum of History, Science & Industry, McKinley National Memorial, historic homes, Amish community. **Additional Information:** Canton/Stark County CVB.

#### RESTRICTIONS

**Pets:** Leash only. **Fires:** Fire ring only. **Alcoholic Beverages:** At sites only. **Vehicle Maximum Length:** None.

#### TO GET THERE

From the junction of 1-77 and Fohl Rd., take Exit 99, drive 3 mi. south on Sherman Church Rd., then 1 mi. east on Haut Rd. Roads are wide and well maintained w/ mostly broad shoulders.

## DELAWARE

### Alum Creek State Park Campground

3615 South Old State Rd., Delaware 43015. T: (740) 548-4039

🚐 ★★★★          ⛺ ★★★★

Beauty: ★★★★              Site Privacy: ★★★★
Spaciousness: ★★★★         Quiet: ★★★★
Security: ★★★★              Cleanliness: ★★★★
Insect Control: None         Facilities: ★★★

For beauty, it is hard to beat most state parks. At Alum Creek State Park Campground, the surroundings include mature forests of maple, oak, elm, and locust trees, along with a huge inland beach, lovely lake and pond, and a variety of hiking trails. Sites are mostly shaded and level with no pull-throughs. There are also no seasonal campers. RVs or tents have access to any site. The most popular areas are on G road because of its proximity to the beach, and the ends of B, G, L, and K roads because they are premium sites near the lake. Security includes a gatehouse, campground office, and regular patrols by campground officers.

#### BASICS

**Operated by:** State of Ohio. **Open:** All year. **Site Assignment:** First come, first served. No reservations. **Registration:** At campground office. **Fee:** $17 (cash, check, credit cards). **Parking:** At site.

## FACILITIES

**Number of RV Sites:** 297. **Number of Tent-Only Sites:** 0. **Hookups:** Electric (15 amps). **Each Site:** Picnic table, fire ring. **Dump Station:** Yes. **Laundry:** No. **Pay Phone:** Yes. **Rest Rooms and Showers:** Yes. **Fuel:** No. **Propane:** No. **Internal Roads:** Paved, in good condition. **RV Service:** No. **Market:** 6 mi. east in Delaware. **Restaurant:** 6 mi. east in Delaware. **General Store:** Yes. **Vending:** Yes. **Swimming Pool:** No. **Playground:** Yes. **Other:** Swimming lake, beach, nature trails, fishing lake, amphitheater, pond, basketball, volleyball, horseshoes, boat dock, boat ramp, horse trails, sports field. **Activities:** Swimming, fishing, hiking, boating (rental boats available), scheduled activities. **Nearby Attractions:** Golf, Ohio Statehouse, Ohio State University, science museum, Columbus Zoo, German Village, museums, historic homes, antiques, arts & crafts, tennis, baseball, horse racing. **Additional Information:** Greater Columbus CVB, (800) 800) 345-4386.

## RESTRICTIONS

**Pets:** Leash only, pet camping area, $1 fee per pet per day. **Fires:** Fire ring only. **Alcoholic Beverages:** Not permitted. **Vehicle Maximum Length:** 35 ft. **Other:** 14-day stay limit.

## TO GET THERE

From the junction of I-71 and Hwy. 36/37, drive 1 mi. west on Hwy. 36/37. Road is wide and well maintained w/ broad shoulders.

## DELAWARE

### Cross Creek Camping Resort

3190 South Old State Rd., Delaware 43015. T: (740) 549-2267; www.alumcreek.com.

🚐 ★★★★        ▲ ★★★★

Beauty: ★★★★        Site Privacy: ★★★★
Spaciousness: ★★★★        Quiet: ★★★★
Security: ★★★★        Cleanliness: ★★★★★
Insect Control: Yes        Facilities: ★★★★

Ringed by woods, Cross Creek Camping Resort offers shaded or open spots on level sites. The campground is grassy with gravel parking spaces. Located five miles southeast of Delaware, the campground has 30 seasonal campers, 11 pull-through sites, and a typical site width of 35 feet. The facility is well maintained, with sparkling restrooms, that have curtains on both the shower the dressing room. A whimsical touch is a fire hydrant painted like a dog. Security and safety measures include a five-mph speed limit, speed bumps, a traffic control gate, and a manager who lives on site and patrols the campground. Open year-round, Cross Creek Camping Resort is a popular winter stopover for campers because of its proximity to Columbus and because water hookups are available at the campground in the winter.

## BASICS

**Operated by:** Steve Cross. **Open:** All year. **Site Assignment:** Reservations w/ 1-night deposit; refund w/ 7-day notice. **Registration:** At campground office. **Fee:** $28 (cash, check, credit cards). **Parking:** At site.

## FACILITIES

**Number of RV Sites:** 179. **Number of Tent-Only Sites:** 21. **Hookups:** Electric (30, 50 amps), water, sewer. **Each Site:** Picnic table, fire ring. **Dump Station:** Yes. **Laundry:** Yes. **Pay Phone:** Yes. **Rest Rooms and Showers:** Yes. **Fuel:** No. **Propane:** Yes. **Internal Roads:** Paved, in good condition. **RV Service:** No. **Market:** 5 mi. northwest in Delaware. **Restaurant:** 5 mi. northwest in Delaware. **General Store:** Yes. **Vending:** Yes. **Swimming Pool:** Yes. **Playground:** Yes. **Other:** Pavilion, shuffleboard, basketball, tennis, horseshoes, club house, game room, fishing pond, billiards, coin games, movies, volleyball, badminton. **Activities:** Swimming, fishing, hiking, scheduled activities. **Nearby Attractions:** Golf, Ohio Statehouse, Ohio State University, science museum, Columbus Zoo, German Village, museums, historic homes, antiques, arts & crafts, tennis, baseball, horse racing. **Additional Information:** Greater Columbus CVB, (800) 345-4386.

## RESTRICTIONS

**Pets:** Leash only. **Fires:** Fire ring only. **Alcoholic Beverages:** At sites only. **Vehicle Maximum Length:** None.

## TO GET THERE

From the junction of I-71, US 36, and Hwy. 37, take Exit 131 and drive 3 mi. west on US 36/Hwy. 37, then 3 mi. south on Lackey Rd. Roads are wide and well maintained w/ broad shoulders.

# FINDLAY

## Shady Lake Campground

11506 Township Rd. 101, Findlay 45840. T: (419) 423-3490

🚐 ★★★          ⛺ ★★★

Beauty: ★★               Site Privacy: ★★★
Spaciousness: ★★★        Quiet: ★★★
Security: ★★★            Cleanliness: ★★
Insect Control: Yes       Facilities: ★★★

A rural lakeside campground with open and shaded sites, Shady Lake Campground offers easy access from the interstate. Located three miles north of Findlay, the campground has 70 seasonal campers and five pull-through sites. The typical site width is 35 feet. Quiet hours are from 10 p.m. to 8 a.m. and children under 18 years of age are to be at their campsite at sundown, unless accompanied by an adult. A maximum of two sets of lights is permitted per campsite, and they must be turned off upon retiring for the night. Security lights and Christmas lights are not permitted. All fish are catch and release except bluegill. Speed limit is five mph and includes bicycles. A railroad track runs along one side of the campground, detracting somewhat from the camping experience.

### BASICS

**Operated by:** Terry & Claudia Rowland. **Open:** Apr. 15–Oct. 15. **Site Assignment:** Reservations w/ 1-night deposit; refunds w/ 7-day notice. **Registration:** At campground office. **Fee:** $17 (cash, check). **Parking:** At site.

### FACILITIES

**Number of RV Sites:** 130. **Number of Tent-Only Sites:** 20. **Hookups:** Electric (30 amps), water. **Each Site:** Picnic table, fire ring. **Dump Station:** Yes. **Laundry:** No. **Pay Phone:** Yes. **Rest Rooms and Showers:** Yes. **Fuel:** No. **Propane:** Yes. **Internal Roads:** Gravel, in good condition. **RV Service:** No. **Market:** 3 mi. south in Findlay. **Restaurant:** 3 mi. south in Findlay. **General Store:** Yes, limited. **Vending:** Yes. **Swimming Pool:** No. **Playground:** Yes. **Other:** Lake, pavilion, swimming beach, shuffleboard, sports field, horseshoes, volleyball. **Activities:** Swimming, fishing, boating (rental rowboats, canoes & paddleboats available). **Nearby Attractions:** Golf, museums, canal boat, passenger train, antiques, Toledo Zoo, boaucms, antiques, arts & crafts shops. **Additional Information:** Greater Toledo CVB, (800) 243-4667.

### RESTRICTIONS

**Pets:** Leash only. **Fires:** Fire ring only. **Alcoholic Beverages:** Permitted. **Vehicle Maximum Length:** None.

### TO GET THERE

From the junction of US 224 and I-75, drive 2 mi. north on I-75, take Exit 161, drive 0.5 mi. east on Township Rd 99, then 1.5 mi. north on CR 220, then 0.5 mi. west on Township Rd 101. Roads are wide and well maintained w/ broad shoulders.

# GALENA

## Berkshire Lake Campground

1848 Alexander Rd., Galena 43021. T: (740) 965-2321

🚐 ★★★          ⛺ n/a

Beauty: ★★★             Site Privacy: ★★★
Spaciousness: ★★★       Quiet: ★★★★
Security: ★★★★          Cleanliness: ★★★
Insect Control: None     Facilities: ★★★

A tradition since 1966, Berkshire Lake Campgrounds is still run by its original owner and now attracts the grandchildren of some old-time campers. The campground also has an action committee composed of veteran Berkshire campers to coordinate and oversee activities and help support campground improvements. Sites are mostly grassy and shaded, with 175 seasonal campers and eight pull-throughs. No tents are allowed. Laid out in a series of loops, the campground has a fishging-only lake (no swimming or boating). A ten-mph speed limit is enforced, as are quiet hours from midnight until 8 a.m. Security measures here include a gate, an owner who lives on site, and regular patrols of the campground.

### BASICS

**Operated by:** Bill Davis. **Open:** All year. **Site Assignment:** Reservations w/ 1-night deposit; refund w/ 7-day notice. **Registration:** At campground office. **Fee:** $21 (cash, check, credit cards). **Parking:** At site.

### FACILITIES

**Number of RV Sites:** 350. **Number of Tent-Only Sites:** 0. **Hookups:** Electric (30 amps), water, sewer. **Each Site:** Picnic table, fire ring.

**Dump Station:** No. **Laundry:** Yes. **Pay Phone:** Yes. **Rest Rooms and Showers:** Yes. **Fuel:** No. **Propane:** Yes. **Internal Roads:** Gravel, in fair condition. **RV Service:** Yes. **Market:** 6 mi. northeast in Sunbury. **Restaurant:** 6 mi. northeast in Sunbury. **General Store:** Yes. **Vending:** No. **Swimming Pool:** Yes. **Playground:** Yes. **Other:** Mini golf, basketball, horseshoes, volleyball, game room, meeting room, lake, sports field, coin games. **Activities:** Swimming, fishing, scheduled weekend activities. **Nearby Attractions:** Golf, Ohio Statehouse, Ohio State University, science museum, Columbus Zoo, German Village, museums, historic homes, antiques, arts & crafts, tennis, baseball, horse racing. **Additional Information:** Greater Columbus CVB, (800) 345-4386.

## RESTRICTIONS

**Pets:** Leash only. **Fires:** Fire ring only. **Alcoholic Beverages:** Not permitted. **Vehicle Maximum Length:** 40 ft. **Other:** No tents allowed.

## TO GET THERE

From the junction of I-71 and Hwy. 36/37, drive 0.25 mi. east on Hwy. 36/37, then 3 mi. south on South Galena Rd. (CR 34), then 0.5 mi. southwest on Alexander. Bear left at the 5-way stop. Roads are wide and well maintained w/ broad shoulders, except for some narrow shoulders on South Galena Rd.

## GENEVA-ON-THE-LAKE

### Indian Creek Camping Resort

4710 Lake Rd. East, Geneva-on-the Lake 44041. T: (440) 466-8191; F: (440) 466-6900; www.indian-creekresort.com.

| 🚐 ★★★★★ | ▲ ★★★★★ |
|---|---|
| Beauty: ★★★★★ | Site Privacy: ★★★★★ |
| Spaciousness: ★★★★★ | Quiet: ★★★★★ |
| Security: ★★★★★ | Cleanliness: ★★★★★ |
| Insect Control: None | Facilities: ★★★★★ |

Make up a list of what the ideal campground would have. Then drive to Geneva-on-the-Lake ; chances are that dream facility would be waiting at the Indian Creek Camping Resort. In addition to the beautiful non-denominational chapel (services every Sunday), there's also an "automatic external defibrillator" to save a life in the event of cardiac arrest. Then there's the two heated swimming pools—one for adults only and one for families. The tiled bathrooms are so clean they gleam. The grass is well manicured, and the folks are friendly. Sites are level and grassy, shaded or open, and with a typical site width of a generous 45 feet. A full-service restaurant, Farone's, and the Step Above Lounge offer a good choice of food and drink. Security includes a traffic control gate and owners who live on site and don't miss much that goes on in the campground. Not surprisingly, about half the camping sites are taken by seasonal campers, which means it is a good idea to book a reservation.

## BASICS

**Operated by:** The Andrus family. **Open:** All year, limited facilities in the winter. **Site Assignment:** Reservations w/ 1-night deposit; refund w/ 7-day notice. **Registration:** At campground office. **Fee:** $34 (cash, check, credit cards). **Parking:** At site.

## FACILITIES

**Number of RV Sites:** 553. **Number of Tent-Only Sites:** 30. **Hookups:** Electric (20, 30, 50 amps), water, sewer, phone, cable TV. **Each Site:** Picnic table, fire ring. **Dump Station:** Yes. **Laundry:** Yes. **Pay Phone:** Yes. **Rest Rooms and Showers:** Yes. **Fuel:** Yes. **Propane:** Yes. **Internal Roads:** Paved/gravel, in good condition. **RV Service:** No. **Market:** 4 mi. east in Geneva-On-The-Lake. **Restaurant:** On site. **General Store:** Yes. **Vending:** Yes. **Swimming Pool:** Yes. **Playground:** Yes. **Other:** Chapel, baseball, volleyball, shuffleboard, game room, horseshoes, pavilions, fishing lake, coin games, sports field, hiking trails, restaurant & lounge. **Activities:** Swimming, fishing, hiking, scheduled activities, local tours. **Nearby Attractions:** Lake Erie, boat races, roller skating, Lake Farmpark, golf, summer concerts, antiques, state parks, historic homes, scenic drives, covered bridges. **Additional Information:** Ashtabula County CVB, (800) 337-6746.

## RESTRICTIONS

**Pets:** Leash only. **Fires:** Fire ring only. **Alcoholic Beverages:** Permitted. **Vehicle Maximum Length:** None.

## TO GET THERE

From the junction of I-90 and Hwy. 45, take Exit 223 and drive 6 mi. north on Hwy. 45, then 4 mi. west on Hwy. 531. Roads are wide and well maintained w/ broad shoulders.

## HILLSBORO
### Rocky Fork State Park

9800 North Shore Dr., Hillsboro 45133. T: (937) 393-3210; www.dnr.state.oh.us/odnr/parks.

🚐 ★★★★          ⛺ ★★★★

Beauty: ★★★★          Site Privacy: ★★★
Spaciousness: ★★★     Quiet: ★★★★
Security: ★★★★         Cleanliness: ★★★★
Insect Control: None    Facilities: ★★★★

At last, a state campground with full hookups. But you have to be fast to get one of those sites. Rocky Fork State Park has only 20 full hookups (sites 301–320), and folks are waiting in line for those precious spots. Located four miles east of Hillsboro, Rocky Fork State Park is a paradise for outdoor recreation enthusiasts. Unlimited horsepower boating allows for excellent skiing on the lake, which also provides catches of bass, muskellunge, and walleye. A scenic gorge, dolomite caves, and natural wetlands add to the beauty. Two large public beaches with changing booths and bathhouses are located on the north and south sides of the lake. A short hiking trail near the campground takes nature lovers to an observation station where excellent birdwatching can be enjoyed. Laid out in a series of loops, the grassy campground offers shaded and open sites with an average size of 12 × 35 feet. There are no pull-through sites. Park rangers provide security and regular patrols.

### BASICS
**Operated by:** State of Ohio. **Open:** All year. **Site Assignment:** First come, first served. No reservations. **Registration:** At campground office. **Fee:** $20 (cash, check, credit cards). **Parking:** At site.

### FACILITIES
**Number of RV Sites:** 148. **Number of Tent-Only Sites:** 82. **Hookups:** Electric (30 amps), water, sewer. **Each Site:** Picnic table, fire ring. **Dump Station:** Yes. **Laundry:** Yes. **Pay Phone:** Yes. **Rest Rooms and Showers:** Yes. **Fuel:** No. **Propane:** Yes. **Internal Roads:** Paved, in good condition. **RV Service:** No. **Market:** 4 mi. west in Hillsboro. **Restaurant:** Restaurant on site. **General Store:** Yes. **Vending:** No. **Swimming Pool:** No. **Playground:** Yes. **Other:** Rocky Fork Lake, swimming beach, boat launch, hiking trails, marinas, amphitheater, basketball, volleyball, horseshoes, mini-golf, boat dock. **Activities:** Swimming, fishing, boating (rental fishing boats & pontoons available), hiking, scheduled activities. **Nearby Attractions:** Nature sanctuary, Fort Hill Indian mounds, museums, Serpent Mound, golf, Kings Island amusement park. **Additional Information:** Highland County CVB, (937) 393-4883.

### RESTRICTIONS
**Pets:** Leash only, in pet camping areas; $1 per night per pet, maxiumum of 2 pets. **Fires:** Fire ring only. **Alcoholic Beverages:** Not permitted. **Vehicle Maximum Length:** 35 ft. **Other:** 14-day stay limit.

### TO GET THERE
From Hillsboro, drive 3.5 mi. east on SR 124 to North Shore Dr., then 1 mi. northeast. Roads are wide and well maintained w/ broad shoulders.

## JACKSON
### Deerland Resort

974 Standpipe Rd., Jackson 45640. T: (740) 286-6422; F: (740) 286-1995.

🚐 ★★★★          ⛺ ★★★★

Beauty: ★★★★          Site Privacy: ★★★★
Spaciousness: ★★★★    Quiet: ★★★★
Security: ★★★★         Cleanliness: ★★★★
Insect Control: Yes     Facilities: ★★★

Deerland Resort offers a country setting with rolling hills and a beautiful lake. But the resort lacks one popular recreation that campers often seek—there is no swimming. Located two miles south of Jackson, the campground is arranged in tiers overlooking the lake. The campground has 35 seasonals, and all the sites are pull-throughs. Sites are open or shaded, with the best tent sites by the water and dam. A fee is charged for fishing. The resort has four pages of rules and regulations, including notice that children under the age of 18 must be at their sites during curfew from 11 p.m. to 8 a.m. unless accompanied by an adult. Curfew violators will be escorted back to their sites, a report will be filed with the resort manager, and second-time offenders will be required to leave Deerland Resort. A five-mph speed limit also is enforced. Security measures include a one-way road and traffic control gate.

### BASICS
**Operated by:** Marge & Bill Parks. **Open:** Apr. 1–Nov. 1. **Site Assignment:** Reservations w/ 1-

night deposit; refund w/ 7-day notice. **Registration:** At campground office. **Fee:** $24 (cash, check, credit cards). **Parking:** At site.

## FACILITIES

**Number of RV Sites:** 79. **Number of Tent-Only Sites:** 15. **Hookups:** Electric (30, 50 amps), water, sewer. **Each Site:** Picnic table, fire ring. Dump Station: Yes. **Laundry:** Yes. **Pay Phone:** Yes. **Rest Rooms and Showers:** Yes. **Fuel:** No. **Propane:** No. **Internal Roads:** Gravel, in fair condition. RV Service: No. Market: 2 mi. north in Jackson. **Restaurant:** 2 mi. north in Jackson. **General Store:** No. **Vending:** Yes. **Swimming Pool:** No. **Playground:** Yes. **Other:** Fishing lake, rec room, coin games, mini golf, basketball, shuffleboard, horseshoes, hiking trails, volleyball, rental paddleboats, rental cabins, banquet facilities. **Activities:** Fishing, hiking. **Nearby Attractions:** Noah's Ark Animal Farm, antiques, arts & crafts, gold, Bob Evans Original Farm, Splash Down Water Park, wildlife area. Additional Information: Jackson Area Chamber of Commerce, (740) 286-2722.

## RESTRICTIONS

**Pets:** Leash only. **Fires:** Fire ring only. **Alcoholic Beverages:** Permitted. **Vehicle Maximum Length:** None.

## TO GET THERE

From the junction of Hwy. 32 and US 35, drive 3 mi. southeast on US 35, then 1 mi. west on CR 55. Hwy. 32 is wide and well maintained w/ broad shoulders. CR 55 is wide and well maintained w/ narrow shoulders.

## JACKSON

### Yogi Bear's Jellystone Park Camp-Resort

1527 McGiffins Rd., Jackson 45640. T: (800) 282-2167; www.placesohio.com/yogibear.

| 🚐 ★★★ | ▲ ★ |
|---|---|
| Beauty: ★★★ | Site Privacy: ★★★ |
| Spaciousness: ★★★ | Quiet: ★★★ |
| Security: ★★★★ | Cleanliness: ★★★★ |
| Insect Control: None | Facilities: ★★★ |

Yogi Bear's Jellystone Park Camp-Resort offers level, gravel sites along a fishing lake with very few trees. Most sites are open, and some have concrete patios. Arranged in a loop around the four-acre lake, the campground has 30 seasonal campers, 25 pull-through sites, and a typical site width of 25 feet. Located five miles east of Jackson and adjacent to Noah's Ark Animal Farm, the campground is right next to the main highway. Fishing is not included in the camping rate; it costs $9 per adult (age 13 and up) to fish for 12 hours with two poles. Children ages 4–12 cost $6 for one pole for 12 hours. The fishing ticket is void if you leave the lake. There is a limit of four catfish under ten pounds per trip. All fish ten pounds and over must be returned back to the lake. A 5.5-mph speed limit and quiet times from 11 p.m. to 8 a.m. are enforced. Security measures include one-way roads, owners who live on site, and regular patrols of the campground.

## BASICS

**Operated by:** Dan & Edna Byler. **Open:** All year. **Site Assignment:** Reservations w/ 1-night deposit; refund w/ 14-day notice. **Registration:** At campground office. **Fee:** $22 (cash, check, credit cards). **Parking:** At site.

## FACILITIES

**Number of RV Sites:** 79. **Number of Tent-Only Sites:** 0. **Hookups:** Electric (30, 50 amps), water, sewer. **Each Site:** Picnic table, fire ring. **Dump Station:** Yes. **Laundry:** Yes. **Pay Phone:** Yes. **Rest Rooms and Showers:** Yes. **Fuel:** No. **Propane:** Yes. **Internal Roads:** Paved/gravel, in good condition. **RV Service:** No. **Market:** 5 mi. west in Jackson. **Restaurant:** 5 mi. west in Jackson. **General Store:** Yes. **Vending:** Yes. **Swimming Pool:** Yes. **Playground:** Yes. **Other:** Fast food restaurant, pay lake, rental cabins, horseshoes, basketball, volleyball, tetherball, shuffleboard, pavilion, mini golf. **Activities:** Swimming, fishing, scheduled weekend activities. **Nearby Attractions:** Noah's Ark Animal Farm, antiques, arts & crafts, golf, Bob Evans Original Farm, Splash Down Water Park, wildlife area. **Additional Information:** Jackson Area Chamber of Commerce, (740) 286-2722.

## RESTRICTIONS

**Pets:** Leash only. **Fires:** Fire ring only. **Alcoholic Beverages:** Not permitted. **Vehicle Maximum Length:** None. **Other:** Rental cabins are non-smoking & require a $50 deposit.

## TO GET THERE

From the junction of US 35 and Hwy. 32, drive 5 mi. east on Hwy. 32. Roads are wide and well maintained w/ broad shoulders.

## LATHAM
### Long's Retreat Family Resort

50 Bell Hollow Rd., Latham 45646. T: (937) 588-3725; www.longsretreat.com.

🚐 ★★★          ⛺ ★★★

Beauty: ★★★           Site Privacy: ★★★
Spaciousness: ★★★★    Quiet: ★★★★
Security: ★★★★         Cleanliness: ★★★
Insect Control: None    Facilities: ★★★

Long's Retreat Family Resort is built around a lake and offers a wide array of water activities and other recreation. Two giant 300- and 350-foot water slides, a hydrotube slide, raindrop, diving boards, and sandy beach make the lake a popular place. Located five miles west of Latham, Ohio, Long's Retreat has open and shaded sites on rolling terrain. Most of the shade is from woods on the perimeter of the campground. Sites are level, with 300 seasonal campers, 75 pull-throughs, and a typical site width of 40 feet. The best RV sites are in area B because of the pine trees, proximity to facilities, and scenic views. Although those sites lack water hookups, many RV campers choose the benefits over that disadvantage. The best tent sites are in areas A or E because they are located on a peninsula on the lake where campers can fish almost from their campsite. Security includes an owner who lives on site and patrols by the local deputy sheriffs department.

### BASICS
**Operated by:** Eric Long. **Open:** All year. **Site Assignment:** No reservations; first come, first served. **Registration:** At campground office. **Fee:** $16 (cash, check, credit cards). **Parking:** At site.

### FACILITIES
**Number of RV Sites:** 350. **Number of Tent-Only Sites:** 100. **Hookups:** Electric (30 amps), water, sewer. **Each Site:** Picnic table, fire ring. **Dump Station:** Yes. **Laundry:** Yes. **Pay Phone:** Yes. **Rest Rooms and Showers:** Yes. **Fuel:** No. **Propane:** Yes. **Internal Roads:** Paved, in good condition. **RV Service:** No. **Market:** 3 mi. east in Latham. **Restaurant:** 3 mi. east in Latham. **General Store:** Yes. **Vending:** Yes. **Swimming Pool:** No. **Playground:** Yes. **Other:** Swimming lake, sandy beach, giant waterslide, go-carts, mini-golf, arcade, rental cabins, basketball, fishing lake, go-kart track, mini golf, tennis, game room, recreation field,

badminton, hiking trails, volleyball. **Activities:** Swimming, fishing, hiking, boating (electric motors only, rental canoes, paddleboats available), scheduled weekend activities. **Nearby Attractions:** Fort Hill State Memorial & Nature Preserve, Indian mounds, museums, golf, Serpent Mound, Kings Island amusement park, Octagonal Schoolhouse, antiques. **Additional Information:** Highland County CVB, (937) 393-4883.

### RESTRICTIONS
**Pets:** Leash only. **Fires:** Fire ring only. **Alcoholic Beverages:** Permitted. **Vehicle Maximum Length:** None.

### TO GET THERE
From the junction of Hwy. 41 and Hwy. 124, drive 5.25 mi. east on Hwy. 124, then 0.1 mi. northwest on Bell Hollow Rd. Roads are wide and well maintained w/ broad shoulders.

## LEAVITTSBURG
### Pin-Oak Acres

4063 Eagle Creek Rd., Leavittsburg 44430. T: (216) 898-8559

🚐 ★★★          ⛺ ★★★

Beauty: ★★★        Site Privacy: ★★★
Spaciousness: ★★★   Quiet: ★★★
Security: ★★★       Cleanliness: ★★★
Insect Control: Yes  Facilities: ★★★

A rural campground in a semi-wooded area, Pin-Oak Acres Family Camping offers level sites laid out in a series of loops. Located five miles east of Leavittsburg, the campground has 12 pull-through sites and a typical site width of 35 feet. The swimming lake is chemically treated, so it is almost like a swimming pool separate from the fishing lake. Sites are grassy, with a choice of open or shaded. The best RV sites are 69–78 in the rear of the campground, where it is quieter, has full hookups, and backs into the woods. Sites 1–17 also are favorites because they are on a creek. The primitive area has the best tent sites because it is more wooded and offers privacy. Security measures include one-way roads and owners who live on site and keep an eye on the campground.

### BASICS
**Operated by:** Ray & Ele Price. **Open:** May 1–Oct. 15. **Site Assignment:** Reservations w/ 1-night deposit; no refunds. **Registration:** At campground office. **Fee:** $13 (cash). **Parking:** At site.

## FACILITIES

**Number of RV Sites:** 81. **Number of Tent-Only Sites:** 40. **Hookups:** Electric (30 amps), water, sewer. **Each Site:** Picnic table, fire ring. **Dump Station:** Yes. **Laundry:** Yes. **Pay Phone:** No. **Rest Rooms and Showers:** Yes. **Fuel:** No. **Propane:** No. **Internal Roads:** Gravel, in fair condition. **RV Service:** No. **Market:** 5 mi. east in Leavittsburg. **Restaurant:** 5 mi. east in Leavittsburg. **General Store:** No. **Vending:** No. **Swimming Pool:** No. **Playground:** Yes. **Other:** Swimming lake, fishing pond, horseshoes, pavilion, game room, coin games, basketball, volleyball, hiking trails, sports field, jogging area. **Activities:** Swimming, fishing, hiking, schedule weekend activities. **Nearby Attractions:** Golf, covered bridge, Geauga Lake, coliseum, reservoir, Sea World, cheese factory, water mill, Hale Farm, Packard Music Hall, antiques, arts & crafts. **Additional Information:** Youngstown CVB, (800) 447-8201.

## RESTRICTIONS

**Pets:** Leash only. **Fires:** Fire ring only. **Alcoholic Beverages:** At sites only. **Vehicle Maximum Length:** 38 ft.

## TO GET THERE

From the junction of Ohio Turnpike and Hwy. 5, take Exit 14/209, drive 0.2 mi. west on Hwy. 5, then 3.5 mi. north on Newton Falls-Braceville Rd., then 0.5 mi. east on Eagle Creek Rd. Roads are generally wide and well maintained but have narrow shoulders in spots.

## LIMA

### Sun Valley Family Campgrounds

9779 Faulkner Rd., Harrod 45850. T: (419) 648-2235

🚐 ★★★          ⛺ ★★★

| | |
|---|---|
| Beauty: ★★ | Site Privacy: ★★★ |
| Spaciousness: ★★★ | Quiet: ★★★ |
| Security: ★★★★ | Cleanliness: ★★★ |
| Insect Control: Yes | Facilities: ★★★ |

A rural campground with level, shaded sites, Sun Valley Campgrounds has only 31 sites available for overnight campers, so reservations are required. The rest of the RV sites are used by 211 seasonal campers. Laid out in a series of loops, the campground, located five miles northeast of Westminster, offers a typical site width of 30 feet and one pull-through. Speed limit is five mph, and quiet time is from 11 p.m. to 8 a.m. A life-guard is on duty in the swimming area, and children ages 12 and under must have a parent to sign them in. Only two-person tents may be set up on lots with campers and must be approved by the office first. Tent-camping sites are located in the primitive area, which offers more green space and privacy. Security measures include one entrance/exit road, a coded traffic gate, and regular campground patrols.

## BASICS

**Operated by:** Richard Williams & Darrel Reed. **Open:** Apr.–Oct. **Site Assignment:** Reservations required w/ non-refundable $15 fee. **Registration:** At campground office. **Fee:** $19 (cash, check, credit cards). **Parking:** At site.

## FACILITIES

**Number of RV Sites:** 242. **Number of Tent-Only Sites:** 50. **Hookups:** Electric (20, 30, 50 amps), water, sewer. **Each Site:** Picnic table, fire ring. **Dump Station:** Yes. **Laundry:** Yes. **Pay Phone:** Yes. **Rest Rooms and Showers:** Yes. **Fuel:** No. **Propane:** Yes. **Internal Roads:** Gravel, in good condition. **RV Service:** No. **Market:** 5 mi. southwest in Westminster. **Restaurant:** 5 mi. southwest in Westminster. **General Store:** Yes, limited. **Vending:** Yes. **Swimming Pool:** No. **Playground:** Yes. **Other:** Volleyball, shuffleboard, horseshoes, game room, pavilion, video games, fishing lake, outdoor stage & dance floor, biking trails, sports field. **Activities:** Swimming, fishing, boating (electric motors only), scheduled weekend activities. **Nearby Attractions:** Golf, antiques, museums, historic homes, arts & crafts, motorsports park, Children's Garden, skating arena, Neil Armstrong Air & Space Museum, Indian Lake. **Additional Information:** Lima/Allen County CVB, (888) 222-6075.

## RESTRICTIONS

**Pets:** Leash only. **Fires:** Fire ring only. **Alcoholic Beverages:** Permitted. **Vehicle Maximum Length:** None.

## TO GET THERE

From the junction of Hwy. 309 and Hwy. 117, drive 9 mi. southeast on Hwy. 117, then 2 mi. north on Phillips Rd., then 0.75 mi. east on Faulkner Rd. Roads are wide and well maintained; Phillips Rd. has mostly good shoulders; Faulkner Rd. has narrow shoulders. Be careful not to miss the turnoff on Faulker Rd.; it is in the middle of a cemetery.

## LOUDONVILLE

## Camp Toodik Family Campground, Cabins, & Canoe Livery

770 TR 462, Loudonville 44842. T: (419) 994-3835; F: (419) 994-4093; www.camptoodik.org; mrtoodik@aol.com.

🚐 ★★★★                    ▲ ★★★★

Beauty: ★★★★          Site Privacy: ★★★★
Spaciousness: ★★★★    Quiet: ★★★★
Security: ★★★★         Cleanliness: ★★★★
Insect Control: ★★★★   Facilities: ★★★★

Located in the foothills of the Appalachian Mountains, four miles north of Loudonville, Camp Toodik Family Campground, Cabins, & Canoe Livery offers beautiful, rolling, grassy terrain overlooking a river valley. Sites are level and mostly shaded, with three pull-through sites and a typical site width of 45 feet. The campground is convenient to the interstate and to the largest Amish settlement in the Midwest. A big plus at the campground is its convenience for canoeing and kayaking. Campground personnel will take canoers or kayakers upstream for a quiet scenic float back to the campground. Campground restrooms are not only very clean but also have the added luxury touch of matted floors. For tenters, the campground offers great, shaded sites right on the river. Security and safety measures include a traffic control gate and owners who keep a close eye on the campground.

### BASICS

**Operated by:** Britt & Nancy Young. **Open:** Apr. 1–Nov. 1. **Site Assignment:** Reservations w/ 1-night deposit; refund w/ 7-day notice. **Registration:** At campground office. **Fee:** $40 (cash, check, credit cards). **Parking:** At site.

### FACILITIES

**Number of RV Sites:** 172. **Number of Tent-Only Sites:** 16. **Hookups:** Electric (20, 30, 50 amps), water, sewer, phone. **Each Site:** Picnic table, fire ring. **Dump Station:** Yes. **Laundry:** Yes. **Pay Phone:** Yes. **Rest Rooms and Showers:** Yes. **Fuel:** No. **Propane:** Yes. **Internal Roads:** Gravel, in good condition. **RV Service:** No. **Market:** 4 mi. south in Loudonville. **Restaurant:** 4 mi. south in Loudonville. **General Store:** Yes. **Vending:** Yes. **Swimming Pool:** Yes. **Playground:** Yes. **Other:** Rec hall, pavilion, coin games, river/pond fishing, mini-golf, basketball, shuffleboard, movies, badminton, sports field, horseshoes, hiking trails, volleyball, rental cabins, rental tent trailers. **Activities:** Swimming, hiking, fishing, canoeing, kayaking (rental canoes, kayaks available), scheduled activities. **Nearby Attractions:** Amish Country, Mid-Ohio Race Track, golf, Mohican Forest, plant tours, Malabar Farm State Park, Living Bible Museum, Richland Carousel Park, ski resorts, Ohio State Reformatory. **Additional Information:** Mansfield-Richland Area Chamber of Commerce, (419) 522-3211.

### RESTRICTIONS

**Pets:** Leash only. **Fires:** Fire ring only. **Alcoholic Beverages:** Permitted. **Vehicle Maximum Length:** None.

### TO GET THERE

From the junction of Hwy. 3 and Hwy. 39/60, drive 2.5 mi. southeast on Hwy. 39/60, then 0.75 mi. north on Township Rd. 462. Roads are wide and well maintained w/ broad shoulders.

## MARIETTA

## The Landings Family Campground

P.O. Box 220, Reno 45773. T: (740) 373-6180

🚐 ★★★                    ▲ ★★★

Beauty: ★★★           Site Privacy: ★★★
Spaciousness: ★★★     Quiet: ★★★★
Security: ★★★★        Cleanliness: ★★★
Insect Control: None   Facilities: ★★★

Don't even consider dropping by the Landings and finding an open campsite. Reservations are a must. With 103 seasonal campers, the campground has only five sites available for short-term visitors. And that number seems to dwindle with each passing year. Located five miles north of Marietta, the campground has over 1,200 feet of Ohio River frontage. Look at all the boat trailers and big boats, and you'll know what the main draw is for this campground. Campers by the river have a beautiful view; campers back in the field are not so lucky. Sites are mostly open, but some shade is available. The speed limit is ten mph, and quiet time starts at 11 p.m. each night. Security includes a one-way road, an owner who lives on site, and regular patrols of the campgrounds.

### BASICS

**Operated by:** David Cook. **Open:** Apr. 1–Nov. 1. **Site Assignment:** Reservations w/ 1-night deposit; refunds w/ 7-day notice. **Registration:** At campground office. **Fee:** $21 (cash, check). **Parking:** At site.

## FACILITIES

**Number of RV Sites:** 108. **Number of Tent-Only Sites:** 75. **Hookups:** Electric (20, 30 amps), water, sewer. **Each Site:** Picnic table, fire ring. **Dump Station:** Yes. **Laundry:** No. **Pay Phone:** Yes. **Rest Rooms and Showers:** Yes. **Fuel:** No. **Propane:** No. **Internal Roads:** Gravel, in good condition. **RV Service:** No. **Market:** 5 mi. south in Marietta. **Restaurant:** 5 mi. south in Marietta. **General Store:** No. **Vending:** No. **Swimming Pool:** Yes. **Playground:** Yes. **Other:** Ohio River, boat ramp, horseshoes. **Activities:** Swimming, fishing, boating, waterskiing. **Nearby Attractions:** Showboat, Museum of the Northwest Territory, Ohio River museum, historic homes, Harmar Village, Mound Cemetery, trolley tours, stern-wheeler cruises, golf, antiques. **Additional Information:** Marietta/Washington County CVB, (800) 288-2577.

## RESTRICTIONS

**Pets:** Leash only. **Fires:** Fire ring only. **Alcoholic Beverages:** Permitted. **Vehicle Maximum Length:** 40 ft.

## TO GET THERE

From the junction of I-77 and SR 7, take Exit 1 and drive 3 mi. north on SR 7. Roads are wide and well maintained w/ broad shoulders.

## MT. GILEAD
## Mt. Gilead Campground

SR 95, Mt. Gilead 43338. T: (419) 768-3428

| 🚐 ★★★ | 🏕 ★★★ |
|---|---|
| Beauty: ★★★ | Site Privacy: ★★★ |
| Spaciousness: ★★★ | Quiet: ★★★ |
| Security: ★★★★ | Cleanliness: ★★★ |
| Insect Control: Yes | Facilities: ★★★ |

Located three miles west of Chesterville, Mt Gilead Campground offers open or shaded sites, most of them grassy with gravel parking spots. Arranged in a series of loops, the campground has 40 seasonal campers, 154 pull-through sites, and a typical site width of 27 feet. No generators are permitted, and quiet hours are from 10 p.m. to 8 a.m. The best sites for tents are 21 and 141–147 because they are more level and are located in the back of the campground with more green space and privacy. The best RV sites

are 32–35 and 125–31 because they are bigger and closer to the facilities. Security measures include an entrance past the office, an owner who lives on site, and regular patrols of the campground.

## BASICS

**Operated by:** Chris Hansen. **Open:** Apr. 1–Oct. 31. **Site Assignment:** First come, first served; no reservations. **Registration:** At campground office. **Fee:** $26 (cash, check, credit cards). **Parking:** At site.

## FACILITIES

**Number of RV Sites:** 154. **Number of Tent-Only Sites:** 40. **Hookups:** Electric (30, 50 amps), water, sewer. **Each Site:** Picnic table, fire ring. **Dump Station:** Yes. **Laundry:** Yes. **Pay Phone:** Yes. **Rest Rooms and Showers:** Yes. **Fuel:** No. **Propane:** Yes. **Internal Roads:** Gravel, in fair condition. **RV Service:** No. **Market:** 3 mi. east in Chesterville. **Restaurant:** 0.5 mi. east toward Chesterville. **General Store:** Yes. **Vending:** No. **Swimming Pool:** Yes. **Playground:** Yes. **Other:** Fishing pond, game room, pavilion, horseshoes, volleyball, recreation field. **Activities:** Swimming, fishing, boating (rental paddleboats available), scheduled weekend activities. **Nearby Attractions:** Golf, flea markets, antiques, Living Bible Museum, carousel park, Amish village, state forest, covered bridge. **Additional Information:** Mansfield-Richland Area Chamber of Commerce, (419) 522-3211.

## RESTRICTIONS

**Pets:** Leash only. **Fires:** Fire ring only. **Alcoholic Beverages:** Permitted. **Vehicle Maximum Length:** None.

## TO GET THERE

From the junction of I-71 and US 95, take Exit 151 and drive 0.5 mi. west on US 95. Roads are wide and well maintained w/ broad shoulders.

## PEEBLES
## Mineral Springs Lake Resort

162 Bluegill Rd., Peebles 45660. T: (937) 587-3132

| 🚐 ★★★ | 🏕 ★★★★ |
|---|---|
| Beauty: ★★★★ | Site Privacy: ★★★ |
| Spaciousness: ★★★★ | Quiet: ★★★ |
| Security: ★★★★ | Cleanliness: ★★★ |
| Insect Control: None | Facilities: ★★★ |

A rural campground adjoining a pretty lake, Mineral Springs Lake Resort has natural beauty but could fix up its entranceway. It's a shame one of the first things a visitor sees on entering is a clump of dumpsters and recycling bins. Located two miles southeast of Peebles, the campground has 240 seasonal campers, 12 pull-through sites, and a typical site width of 50 feet. The wooded campground offers mostly shaded sites on its rolling terrain. The best sites are by the lake. The speed limit is ten mph, rather high especially with so many golf carts in use. Security measures include owners who live on site, surveillance cameras, and a gate. Rates are very reasonable for such a nice campground with a good array of activities.

## BASICS

**Operated by:** Robin Waddell. **Open:** Apr. 1–Nov. 1. **Site Assignment:** Reservations w/ 1-night deposit; refund w/ 7-day notice. **Registration:** At campground office. **Fee:** $18 (cash, check, credit cards). **Parking:** At site.

## FACILITIES

**Number of RV Sites:** 280. **Number of Tent-Only Sites:** 100. **Hookups:** Electric (20, 30 amps), water, sewer. **Each Site:** Picnic table, fire ring. **Dump Station:** Yes. **Laundry:** Yes. **Pay Phone:** Yes. **Rest Rooms and Showers:** Yes. **Fuel:** No. **Propane:** Yes. **Internal Roads:** Paved/gravel, in good condition. **RV Service:** No. **Market:** 2 mi. northwest in Peebles. **Restaurant:** 2 mi. northwest in Peebles. **General Store:** Yes. **Vending:** Yes. **Swimming Pool:** No. **Playground:** Yes. **Other:** Swimming lake, basketball, mini golf, volleyball, crazy cars, surf bikes, mountain bikes, horseshoes, fishing lake, rec room, pavilion, coin games, boat ramp, boat dock, hiking trails. **Activities:** Swimming, fishing, hiking, boating (electric motors only; rental paddleboats, canoes, rowboats available). **Nearby Attractions:** Diving quarry, Serpent Mound, Davis Memorial, Amish community, caves, Tecumseh outdoor drama, golf, historic homes, antiques, arts & crafts. **Additional Information:** Adams County Travel & Visitors Bureau, (877) 687-7446.

## RESTRICTIONS

**Pets:** Leash only. **Fires:** Fire ring only. **Alcoholic Beverages:** At sites only. **Vehicle Maximum Length:** None.

## TO GET THERE

From the junction of Hwy. 41 and Hwy. 32 at the south edge of town, drive 1.25 mi. east on Hwy. 32, then 2 mi. south on Steam Furnace Rd., then 2 mi east on Mineral Springs Rd. Hwy. 32 is wide and well maintained w/ broad shoulders. Steam Furnace Rd. is winding w/ some narrow shoulders at points. Mineral Springs Rd. is generally well maintained w/ narrow shoulders.

## PIQUA
### Poor Farmer's Campground

7211 North Lostcreek-Shelby Rd., Fletcher 45326. T: (937) 368-2449; poorfarmersrv.com.

★★  ▲ ★★

Beauty: ★★★ Site Privacy: ★★★
Spaciousness: ★★★ Quiet: ★★★★
Security: ★★★ Cleanliness: ★★★
Insect Control: None Facilities: ★★

A rural campground associated with RV sales and service, Poor Farmer's Campground is located nine miles east of Piqua. Sites are grassy, open, and shaded with a typical site width of 35 feet. Arranged in a series of loops, the campground has 120 seasonal sites and 16 pull-throughs. Speed limit is five mph; violators will be warned once, then they will have to park at the camp office and walk to and from their site. To help provide quiet, safety, and a better camping experience, seasonals are not allowed to mow their lots on Friday evening, Saturday, or Sunday. Nor are campers allowed to hang out laundry on Fridays, Saturdays, or Sundays.

## BASICS

**Operated by:** Steve & Patty Springer. **Open:** All year. **Site Assignment:** Reservations w/ no deposit. **Registration:** At campground office. **Fee:** $15 (cash, check). **Parking:** At site.

## FACILITIES

**Number of RV Sites:** 500. **Number of Tent-Only Sites:** 0. **Hookups:** Electric (20, 30 amps), water. **Each Site:** Picnic table, fire ring. **Dump Station:** Yes. **Laundry:** No. **Pay Phone:** Yes. **Rest Rooms and Showers:** Yes. **Fuel:** No. **Propane:** Yes. **Internal Roads:** Gravel, in good condition. **RV Service:** Yes. **Market:** 9 mi. west in Piqua. **Restaurant:** 9 mi. west in Piqua. **General Store:** No. **Vending:** Yes. **Swimming Pool:** No. **Playground:** Yes. **Other:** Shelter, pond, wildlife area, creek, basketball, horseshoes, volleyball, museum of antique tractors & farm machinery, hiking trails. **Activities:** Hiking, fishing, scheduled weekend activities. **Nearby Attractions:** Woods reserve & sanctuary, golf, historic farmstead, Piatt Castles, Kiser Lake, Air Force Museum, antiques, arts & crafts. **Additional Information:** Miami County Visitors & Convention Bureau, (800) 348-8993.

### RESTRICTIONS

**Pets:** Leash only but no large dogs permitted "at management discretion.". **Fires:** Fire ring only. **Alcoholic Beverages:** Not permitted. **Vehicle Maximum Length:** None.

### TO GET THERE

From the junction of I-75 and US 36, take Exit 82 and drive 6 mi. east on US 36, then 0.75 mi. south on Lost Creek-Shelby Rd. US 36 is wide and well maintained w/ broad shoulders. Lost Creek-Shelby Rd. is well maintained w/ narrow shoulders.

## PORT CLINTON
### East Harbor State Park

1169 North Buck Rd., Lakeside-Marblehead 43440. T: (419) 734-5857; F: (419) 734-1473; www.dnr.state.oh.us/odnr/parks; east.harbor.parks@dnr.state.oh.us.

🚐 ★★★          ⛺ ★★★★

| | |
|---|---|
| Beauty: ★★★★ | Site Privacy: ★★★ |
| Spaciousness: ★★★ | Quiet: ★★★★ |
| Security: ★★★★ | Cleanliness: ★★★ |
| Insect Control: None | Facilities: ★★★ |

Situated on a peninsula stretching into the waters of Lake Erie, East Harbor State Park has the largest campground in the Ohio State Park system. Laid out in a series of loops, the campground offers level sites with a choice of open or shaded. Located eight miles west of Port Clinton, Ohio, the campground is part of the 1,152-acre state park. A 1,500-foot sand beach is popular with swimmers. East Harbor lies on the fringe of Ohio's prairie marsh zone, home of more wildlife than any other type of habitat in the state. Hundreds of migrating songbirds rest here before winging north across the lake. The campground has 142 pull-through sites and welcomes big rigs. Lake Erie offers unlimited-horsepower boating opportunities, including a full-time boat mechanic, boat supplies, boat storage, and a restaurant. East Harbor's seven-mile hiking trail system leads through the many different habitats within the park. Park rangers provide security patrols and check on entering motorists.

### BASICS

**Operated by:** State of Ohio. **Open:** All year. **Site Assignment:** First come, first served. No reservations. **Registration:** At campground office. **Fee:** $17 (cash, check, credit cards). **Parking:** At site.

### FACILITIES

**Number of RV Sites:** 366. **Number of Tent-Only Sites:** 204. **Hookups:** Electric (20, 30, 50 amps). **Each Site:** Picnic table, fire ring. **Dump Station:** Yes. **Laundry:** Yes. **Pay Phone:** Yes. **Rest Rooms and Showers:** Yes. **Fuel:** No. **Propane:** No. **Internal Roads:** Paved, in good condition. **RV Service:** No. **Market:** 8 mi. east in Port Clinton. **Restaurant:** 8 mi. east in Port Clinton. **General Store:** Yes, limited. **Vending:** Yes. **Swimming Pool:** No. **Playground:** Yes. **Other:** Swimming lake, fishing lake, pavilion, rec room, boat ramp, boat dock, sports field, hiking trails, volleyball, rental RVs, rental tents, nature center. **Activities:** Swimming, boating (rental boats available), hiking, fishing, scheduled activities. **Nearby Attractions:** Lake Erie, ferry, Put-in-Bay, Kelley's Island, lighthouse, winery, golf, Cedar Point Amusement Park, antiques, boating. **Additional Information:** Ottawa County Visitors Bureau, (800) 441-1271.

### RESTRICTIONS

**Pets:** Leash only; $1 fee per pet per day. **Fires:** Fire ring only. **Alcoholic Beverages:** Not permitted. **Vehicle Maximum Length:** None. **Other:** 14-day stay limit.

### TO GET THERE

From the junction of Hwy. 2 and Hwy. 269, drive 4 mi. north on Hwy. 269. Roads are wide and well maintained w/ broad shoulders.

## PORT CLINTON
### Tall Timbers Campground Resort

340 Christy Chapel Rd., Port Clinton 43452. T: (419) 732-3938; www.OnLakeErie.com/TallTimbers.

🚐 ★★★          ⛺ ★★★

| | |
|---|---|
| Beauty: ★★★ | Site Privacy: ★★★ |
| Spaciousness: ★★★ | Quiet: ★★★ |
| Security: ★★★★ | Cleanliness: ★★★ |
| Insect Control: None | Facilities: ★★★ |

Nestled in a woods near the shores of Lake Erie, Tall Timbers Campground Resort is in the heart of a popular recreation area and is the walleye fishing capital of the world. Not surprisingly, many of the campers who visit Tall Timbers come for all the area attractions. But the campground has a goodly number of recreation opportunities itself. Located in Port Clinton, the campground has 300 seasonal campers, five pull-through sites, and a typical site width of 30 feet. Laid out in a series of loops, the campground offers grassy, shaded, and open sites. The best RV sites are the pull-throughs; the best tent sites are 1–39, which offer water and electric hookups in an area by a pond. The primitive camping area is also a favorite with tenters because it is separated from RVs and has more grass and trees. Security and safety measures include a five-mph speed limit, one entrance/exit road, a manager who lives on site, and patrols of the campground.

## BASICS

**Operated by:** Dave & Cindy Young. **Open:** May 1–Oct. 31. **Site Assignment:** Reservations w/ 1-night deposit; refund w/ 7-day notice. **Registration:** At campground office. **Fee:** $25 (cash, check, credit cards). **Parking:** At site.

## FACILITIES

**Number of RV Sites:** 409. **Number of Tent-Only Sites:** 24. **Hookups:** Electric (30 amps), water. **Each Site:** Picnic table, fire ring. **Dump Station:** Yes. **Laundry:** Yes. **Pay Phone:** Yes. **Rest Rooms and Showers:** Yes. **Fuel:** No. **Propane:** No. **Internal Roads:** Gravel, in fair condition. **RV Service:** No. **Market:** 1 mi. east. **Restaurant:** 1 mi. east. **General Store:** Yes. **Vending:** Yes. **Swimming Pool:** No. **Playground:** Yes. **Other:** Swimming pond, game room, fishing pond, fish cleaning facility, sports field, volleyball, basketball, horseshoes, pavilion, activity director. **Activities:** Swimming, fishing, weekend activities. **Nearby Attractions:** Lake Erie, ferry, Put-in-Bay, Kelley's Island, lighthouse, winery, golf, Cedar Point Amusement Park, antiques, boating, museums, historic homes. **Additional Information:** Ottawa County Visitors Bureau, (800) 441-1271.

## RESTRICTIONS

**Pets:** Leash only. **Fires:** Fire ring only. **Alcoholic Beverages:** At sites only. **Vehicle Maximum Length:** 40 ft.

## TO GET THERE

From the junction of Hwy. 2 and Hwy. 53, drive 1.25 mi. north on Hwy. 53, then 1.5 mi. west on Hwy. 163, then 0.25 mi. south on Christy Chapel Rd. Roads are wide and well maintained w/ generally broad shoulders.

# PORTSMOUTH
## Shawnee State Park

4404 State Rte. 125, Portsmouth 45663. T: (740) 858-4561; www.dnr.state.oh.us/odnr/parks.

🚐 ★★★★                     ⛺ ★★★★

Beauty: ★★★★              Site Privacy: ★★★
Spaciousness: ★★★          Quiet: ★★★★
Security: ★★★★             Cleanliness: ★★★
Insect Control: None        Facilities: ★★★

Located in the Applachian foothills near the banks of the Ohio River 15 miles east of Portsmouth, Shawnee State Park is nestled in the 63,000-acre Shawnee State Forest. Once the hunting grounds of the Shawnee Indians, the region is one of the most picturesque in the state, featuring erosion-carved valleys and wooded hills. The rugged beauty of the area has earned it the nickname "The Little Smokies." Shawnee State Forest is the largest of Ohio's 19 state forests and contains impressive stands of oak, hickory, sassafras, buckeye, black gum, pitch pine, and Virginia pine. It also includes a 42-mile backpack trail with primitive campsites, over 70 miles of bridle trails, a horse campground, an 8,000-acre wilderness area, and five small fishing lakes. Laid out in a series of loops, the campground offers paved pads for RVs with back-in site sizes of 25 × 40 feet. Sites are a mix of shaded and open. A ranger station and regular campground patrols provide security.

## BASICS

**Operated by:** State of Ohio. **Open:** All year. **Site Assignment:** First come, first served. No reservations. **Registration:** At campground office. **Fee:** $17 (cash, check, credit cards). **Parking:** At site.

## FACILITIES

**Number of RV Sites:** 104. **Number of Tent-Only Sites:** 3. **Hookups:** Electric (20, 30, 50 amps). **Each Site:** Picnic table, fire ring. **Dump Station:** Yes. **Laundry:** Yes. **Pay Phone:** Yes. **Rest Rooms and Showers:** Yes. **Fuel:** No. **Propane:** No. **Internal Roads:** Paved, in good condition. **RV Service:** No. **Market:** 15 mi. west in Portsmouth. **Restaurant:** At lodge on site. **General Store:** Yes. **Vending:** Yes. **Swimming Pool:** No. **Playground:** Yes. **Other:** Roosevelt Lake, Turkey Creek Lake, Bear Lake, swimming beach, pavilion, golf, horseback riding trails, hiking trails, horseshoes, volleyball, boat ramp, rental cottages, lodge, mini-golf, tennis, shuffleboard.

**Activities:** Swimming, fishing, electric motorboating (rental rowboats & canoes available), biking (rental bikes available), scheduled activities. **Nearby Attractions:** Serpent Mound, antiques, floodwall murals, Ohio River, museums, historic homes, raceway. **Additional Information:** Portsmouth Area CVB, (740) 353-1116.

## RESTRICTIONS

**Pets:** Leash only, in pet camping area. Fee $1 per day per pet, max. 2 pets. **Fires:** Fire ring only. **Alcoholic Beverages:** Not permitted. **Vehicle Maximum Length:** 35 ft. **Other:** 14-day stay limit.

## TO GET THERE

From the junction of US 52 and State Rd. 125, drive 6 mi. north on SR 125. Roads are wide and well maintained w/ usually good shoulders. SR 125 is very hilly and curving.

## SEVILLE
### Chippewa Valley Campground

8809 Lake Rd., Seville 44273. T: (330) 769-2090

| | |
|---|---|
| Beauty: ★★ | Site Privacy: ★★ |
| Spaciousness: ★★ | Quiet: ★★★ |
| Security: ★★★ | Cleanliness: ★ |
| Insect Control: Yes | Facilities: ★ |

Chippewa Valley Campgrounds has a handy location, right off the interstate, five miles northest of Seville. It also has the nice trees and grass that make a good campground, though when we visited, the entrance road was poorly tended and passed by some unsightly buildings. Laid out in a series of loops, the campground has 25 seasonal campers, 40 pull-through sites, and a 13-acre stocked lake. Sites are mostly grassy and shaded. Traffic from the interstate is audible in front parts of the campground. The speed limit is ten mph—"three strikes and you are removed from the park with no refund," rules state. Quiet hours are from 11 p.m. to 8 a.m. Children are not to be permitted on other sites unless invited. Security measures include an entrance gate that is locked from 10 p.m. to 8 a.m. Seasonal campers have a card to open the gate, but overnight campers don't. To enter, overnight campers have to park their vehicles by the gate and get the manager to let them in. A manager lives on site and patrols the campground.

## BASICS

**Operated by:** Guillermo Carrasco. **Open:** May 1–Oct. 31. **Site Assignment:** Reservations w/ 1-night deposit; refund w/ 7-day notice. **Registration:** At campground office. **Fee:** $21 (cash, check). **Parking:** At site.

## FACILITIES

**Number of RV Sites:** 160. **Number of Tent-Only Sites:** 40. **Hookups:** Electric (30, 50 amps), water, sewer. **Each Site:** Picnic table, fire ring. **Dump Station:** No. **Laundry:** No. **Pay Phone:** Yes. **Rest Rooms and Showers:** Yes. **Fuel:** No. **Propane:** No. **Internal Roads:** Paved/gravel, in poor condition. **RV Service:** No. **Market:** 5 mi. southeast in Seville. **Restaurant:** 5 mi. southeast in Seville. **General Store:** No. **Vending:** Yes. **Swimming Pool:** No. **Playground:** Yes. **Other:** Pavilion, rec room, basketball, tennis, baseball, shuffleboard, horseshoes, lake. **Activities:** Fishing, swimming. **Nearby Attractions:** Amish country, golf, Pro Football Hall of Fame, Rock & Roll Hall of Fame, Sea World, Cleveland Zoo, antiques, arts & crafts, museums, historic homes. **Additional Information:** Medina County CVB, (800) 860-2943.

## RESTRICTIONS

**Pets:** Leash only. No pitbulls, dobermans or rottweillers permitted. **Fires:** Fire ring only. **Alcoholic Beverages:** Permitted. **Vehicle Maximum Length:** None.

## TO GET THERE

From the junction of I-76 and I-71, take Exit 209, drive west 0.2 mi. on US 224 to CR 19, then north 0.2 mi. Roads are wide and well maintained w/ broad shoulders.

## SEVILLE
### Maple Lakes Recreational Park

4275 Blake Rd., Seville 44273. T: (330) 336-2251; F: (330) 334-8042; www.maplelakes.com; maplelk@gte.net.

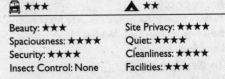

| | |
|---|---|
| Beauty: ★★★ | Site Privacy: ★★★★ |
| Spaciousness: ★★★★ | Quiet: ★★★★ |
| Security: ★★★★ | Cleanliness: ★★★★ |
| Insect Control: None | Facilities: ★★★ |

A grassy campground on hilly terrain, Maple Lakes Recreational Park offers both open and shaded spots. A steep hill leads into the campground. The speed limit is ten mph, but speed bumps slow it down even more. Arranged in a series of loops, the campground has 150 seasonal campers, ten pull-through sites, and a typical site width of 35 feet. Level campsites are grassy with gravel parking spots. Be aware that pets must be kept on campsites; no dog-walking is allowed. Quiet hours are enforced between 11 p.m. and 8:30 a.m. With the woods surrounding it, autumn would be a peak time to view the changing foliage—but the campground closes Oct. 1, just as the leaves are showing their colors. Security includes a gate, owners who live on site, and regular patrols of the campground.

**BASICS**

**Operated by:** Romeyn family. **Open:** Apr. 1–Oct. 1. **Site Assignment:** Reservations w/ 1-night deposit; refund w/ 7-day notice. **Registration:** At campground office. **Fee:** $25 (cash, check, credit cards). **Parking:** At site.

**FACILITIES**

**Number of RV Sites:** 225. **Number of Tent-Only Sites:** 0. **Hookups:** Electric (30, 50 amps), water, sewer. **Each Site:** Picnic table, fire ring. **Dump Station:** Yes. **Laundry:** Yes. **Pay Phone:** Yes. **Rest Rooms and Showers:** Yes. **Fuel:** No. **Propane:** Yes. **Internal Roads:** Paved/gravel, in good condition. **RV Service:** No. **Market:** 3 mi. south in Seville. **Restaurant:** 3 mi. south in Seville. **General Store:** Yes. **Vending:** Yes. **Swimming Pool:** Yes. **Playground:** Yes. **Other:** Game room, pavilion, fishing lake, badminton, coin games, horseshoes, volleyball, basketball, ball field. **Activities:** Swimming, fishing, scheduled weekend activities. **Nearby Attractions:** Amish country, golf, Pro Football Hall of Fame, Rock & Roll Hall of Fame, Sea World, Cleveland Zoo, antiques, arts & crafts, museums, historic homes. **Additional Information:** Medina County CVB, (800) 860-2943.

**RESTRICTIONS**

**Pets:** Leash only. Pets cannot be walked in campground, have to be transported to pet area. **Fires:** Fire ring only. **Alcoholic Beverages:** At sites only. **Vehicle Maximum Length:** None. **Other:** No working transient caravans.

**TO GET THERE**

From the junction of I-76 and Hwy. 3, drive 1 mi. northeast on Hwy. 3, then 1 mi. east on CR 118 (Blake Rd.). Roads are wide and well maintained but have narrow shoulders in spots.

## SHREVE

### Whispering Hills Recreation

P.O. Box 607, Shreve 44676. T: (800) 992-2435; F: (330) 567-3299; www.whisperinghillsrvpark.com; WHRI@bright.net.

RV ★★★★ Tent ★★★★

| | |
|---|---|
| Beauty: ★★★ | Site Privacy: ★★★ |
| Spaciousness: ★★★ | Quiet: ★★★★ |
| Security: ★★★★ | Cleanliness: ★★★★ |
| Insect Control: None | Facilities: ★★★★ |

Located on rolling hills deep in the heart of Amish country, three miles south of Shreve, Whispering Hills Recreation is a destination campground. Most folks come here for vacations or brief getaways to enjoy the large array of recreational opportunities. Two big draws are the olympic-sized swimming pool and the Ol' Smokehaus Restaurant (serving homecooked food, Amish baked goods, and Ruth's famous apple dumplings). The country campground has 85 seasonals, an average site size of 25 × 45, ten pull-throughs, and a tree on almost every site. Laid out in a series of loops, the campground is mostly grassy and quiet with natural tree buffers. The most popular RV sites are the six with pull-throughs and sewer hookups. A separate tent section allows for more privacy away from RVs. Security measures include owners who live on site, regular patrols, and random patrols from the local sheriff's department.

**BASICS**

**Operated by:** Ruth Murray Saurer. **Open:** Apr. 15–Oct. 15. **Site Assignment:** Reservations w/ $25 deposit; refund (minus $5) w/ 48-hour notice. **Registration:** At campground office. **Fee:** $29 (cash, check, credit cards). **Parking:** At site.

**FACILITIES**

**Number of RV Sites:** 300. **Number of Tent-Only Sites:** 40. **Hookups:** Electric (30, 50 amps), water, sewer. **Each Site:** Picnic table, fire ring. **Dump Station:** Yes. **Laundry:** Yes. **Pay Phone:** Yes. **Rest Rooms and Showers:** Yes. **Fuel:** No. **Propane:** Yes. **Internal Roads:** Paved/gravel, in good condition. **RV Service:** No. **Market:** 3 mi. north in Shreve. **Restaurant:** on site. **General Store:** Yes. **Vending:** Yes. **Swimming Pool:** Yes. **Playground:** Yes. **Other:** Fishing lake, mini-golf, volleyball, hiking trails, basketball, rec room, pavilion, coin games, boat dock, sports field, RV rentals, cabin rentals. **Activities:** Swimming, fishing, boating (electric motors only), church services, free entertainment, scheduled weekend activities. **Nearby Attractions:** Golf, antiques, arts & crafts shops, nature preserve, railroad museum, Toy & Hobby Museum, wildlife area. **Additional Information:** Wayne County CVB (800) 362-6474.

## RESTRICTIONS

**Pets:** Leash only. **Fires:** Fire ring only. **Alcoholic Beverages:** Permitted. **Vehicle Maximum Length:** None.

## To Get There

From the junction of US 30 and SR 3, drive 1.8 mi. southwest on SR 3 to SR 226, then 8.2 mi. south to SR 514, then 2 mi. south. The roads are generally in good condition w/ adequate shoulders.

## SIDNEY

### Camp Qtokee

2686 St. Rte. 29, Sidney 45365. T: (937) 492-7324

🚐 ★      🏕 ★

| | |
|---|---|
| Beauty: ★★ | Site Privacy: ★★ |
| Spaciousness: ★★ | Quiet: ★★ |
| Security: ★★★ | Cleanliness: ★★ |
| Insect Control: None | Facilities: ★★ |

Camp Otokee has two major things going for it—easy access from the interstate and signs pointing the way. Maintained as a camping getaway and recreation spot for the local Eagles organization, Camp Otkoee welcomes nonmember campers and would be a handy place to stay. Built on a lake on the north edge of Sidney, the campground has 90 seasonal campers, leaving 30 sites for visiting campers. Sites are mostly shaded and grassy, with 36 pull-throughs. No gas motors are allowed on the lake, and all game fish are to be released. A separate primitive tent area is set off from RVs, with no vehicles driving in or out of the area after dark unless it is an emergency. Also, all vehicles on campground property must be licensed and driveable at all times. Quiet hours are 11 p.m. to 8 a.m., and the speed limit is five mph. Security measures include one entrance/exit, a manager who lives on site, and regular campground patrols.

## BASICS

**Operated by:** Sidney Eagles FOE 1403. **Open:** All year. **Site Assignment:** Reservations w/ 1-night deposit; refund w/ 7-day notice. **Registration:** At campground office. **Fee:** $19 (cash, check). **Parking:** At site.

## FACILITIES

**Number of RV Sites:** 120. **Number of Tent-Only Sites:** 7. **Hookups:** Electric (30, 50 amps), water. **Each Site:** Picnic table, fire ring. **Dump Station:** Yes. **Laundry:** No. **Pay Phone:** No. **Rest Rooms and Showers:** Yes. **Fuel:** No. **Propane:** No. **Internal Roads:** Gravel, in good condition. **RV Service:** No. **Market:** 2 mi. south in Sidney. **Restaurant:** 2 mi. south in Sidney. **General Store:** No. **Vending:** Yes. **Swimming Pool:** No. **Playground:** Yes. **Other:** Swimming beach, rec hall, video games, basketball, volleyball, horseshoes, ping pong. **Activities:** Swimming, fishing, boating (rental rowboats, paddleboats, canoes available). **Nearby Attractions:** Woods reserve & sanctuary, golf, historic farmstead, museums, antiques, Piatt Castles, Air Force Museum, arts & crafts shops. **Additional Information:** Miami County Visitors & Convention Bureau, (800) 348-8993.

## RESTRICTIONS

**Pets:** Leash only. **Fires:** Fire ring only. **Alcoholic Beverages:** Permitted. **Vehicle Maximum Length:** None.

## To Get There

From the junction of I-75 and SR 29, take Exit 93 and drive 0.4 mi. northwest on SR 29. Roads are wide and well maintained w/ broad shoulders. Gravel road leading into campground is narrow.

## VAN BUREN

### Pleasant View Recreation

12611 Township Rd. 218, Van Buren 45889. T: (419) 299-3897

🚐 ★★★★      🏕 ★★★★

| | |
|---|---|
| Beauty: ★★★ | Site Privacy: ★★★★ |
| Spaciousness: ★★★★ | Quiet: ★★★★ |
| Security: ★★★★ | Cleanliness: ★★★★ |
| Insect Control: None | Facilities: ★★★★ |

The name of this campground lets campers know what to expect—enough recreation possibilities to keep children and adults happy. A rural campground one mile off I-75 in Van Buren, Pleasant View Recreation offers both open and wooded sites with 40 pull-throughs. As often happens, seasonals have 230 of the campground sites, leaving 70 for overnight campers. Sites are level, with a typical site width of 32 feet. The speed limit is five mph with speed bumps. The best RV sites are in Campers Loop because they offer full hookups and are near the pond. Tent sites are in a separate area by the pond with more green space and privacy. Laid out in a series of loops, the campground is a bargain with rates running from $15 to $22 for a family of two adults, two children, and one vehicle. Additional children are $1, adults are $2, and vehicles are $1. Security measures include a card-coded traffic gate, owners who live on site, and occasional campground patrols.

## BASICS

**Operated by:** Dan & Kathy Gant. **Open:** All year. **Site Assignment:** Reservations w/ 1-night deposit; refunds w/ 7-day notice. **Registration:** At campground office. **Fee:** $22 (cash, check, credit cards). **Parking:** At site.

## FACILITIES

**Number of RV Sites:** 300. **Number of Tent-Only Sites:** 45. **Hookups:** Electric (30, 50 amps), water, sewer. **Each Site:** Picnic table, fire ring. **Dump Station:** Yes. **Laundry:** Yes. **Pay Phone:** Yes. **Rest Rooms and Showers:** Yes. **Fuel:** No. **Propane:** Yes. **Internal Roads:** Paved/gravel, in good condition. **RV Service:** No. **Market:** 5 mi. northwest in North Baltimore. **Restaurant:** 5 mi. northwest in North Baltimore. **General Store:** Yes. **Vending:** Yes. **Swimming Pool:** Yes. **Playground:** Yes. **Other:** Fishing pond, adult card room, mini golf, dance hall, game room, restaurant, horseshoes, baseball, sports field, volleyball, basketball, shuffleboard, coin games, tennis, badminton. **Activities:** Swimming, fishing, boating (rental paddleboats available), scheduled weekend activities. **Nearby Attractions:** Historic courthouse, golf, nature preserve, equestrian farm, motor sports park, Ghost Town, museums, Little Red Schoolhouse, planetarium, Riverside Train. **Additional Information:** Findlay CVB, (419) 423-3315.

## RESTRICTIONS

**Pets:** Leash only. **Fires:** Fire ring only. **Alcoholic Beverages:** Permitted. **Vehicle Maximum Length:** None.

## TO GET THERE

From the junction of I-75 and Hwy. 613, take Exit 164, drive 0.75 mi. east on Hwy. 613, then 0.25 mi. southeast on Township 218. Roads are wide and well maintained w/ broad shoulders.

# WAPAKONETA

## Glacier Hill Lakes

11675 Wapak-Freyburg Rd., Wapakoneta 45895. T: (419) 738-3005

| 🚐 ★★★ | 🅰 ★★ |
|---|---|
| Beauty: ★★★ | Site Privacy: ★★★ |
| Spaciousness: ★★★ | Quiet: ★★ |
| Security: ★★★★ | Cleanliness: ★★★★ |
| Insect Control: None | Facilities: ★★★ |

A rural campground on hilly terrain, Glacier Hill Lakes is centered around its two lakes. With 180 seasonal campers, the campground accepts no reservations for its remaining 50 RV sites, so be sure to have a back-up plan ready. Sites are open or shaded, with 24 pull-throughs and a typical site width of 40 feet. Some major utility lines and towers run through the campground, and in some areas campers can hear the lines buzzing. A ten-mph speed limit seems a bit high with so many children around, but the speed is lessened by speed bumps. Security measures include an owner who lives on site, regular patrols, and a card-coded traffic gate.

## BASICS

**Operated by:** Earl Wuebbenhorst. **Open:** All year. **Site Assignment:** First come, first served; no reservations. **Registration:** At campground office. **Fee:** $21 (cash, check, credit cards). **Parking:** At site.

## FACILITIES

**Number of RV Sites:** 230. **Number of Tent-Only Sites:** 15. **Hookups:** Electric (30, 50 amps), water, sewer. **Each Site:** Picnic table, fire ring. **Dump Station:** Yes. **Laundry:** No. **Pay Phone:** Yes. **Rest Rooms and Showers:** Yes. **Fuel:** No. **Propane:** Yes. **Internal Roads:** Gravel, in good condition. **RV Service:** Yes. **Market:** 3 mi. northwest in Wapakoneta. **Restaurant:** 3 mi. northwest in Wapakoneta. **General Store:** Yes. **Vending:** Yes. **Swimming Pool:** No. **Playground:** Yes. **Other:** Swimming lake, shelter house, horseshoes, volleyball, fishing lake, pavilion, sports field, boating lake (no motors allowed). **Activities:** Swimming, fishing, some scheduled activities, boating (rental canoes, rowboats, paddleboats available). **Nearby Attractions:** Neil Armstrong Air & Space Museum, Ohio Caverns, Piatt Castle, train displays, bicycle museum, antiques, US Air Force Museum, Indian Lake, golf. **Additional Information:** Wapakoneta Area Chamber of Commerce (419) 738-2911.

## RESTRICTIONS

**Pets:** Leash only. **Fires:** Fire ring only. **Alcoholic Beverages:** Permitted. **Vehicle Maximum Length:** None.

## TO GET THERE

From the junction of I-75 and US 33, take Exit 110 and drive 0.5 mi. east on US 33, then 0.75 mi. southeast on Wapak-Fisher Rd. (CR 33A), then 2 mi. south on Wapak-Freyburg Rd. The roads are wide and well maintained w/ broad shoulders

## WAPAKONETA
### Wapakoneta/Lima South KOA

14719 Cemetery Rd., Wapakoneta 45895. T: (419) 738-6016; www.koa.com; wapakkoa@bright.net.

| 🚐 ★★★★ | 🏕 ★★★★ |
|---|---|
| Beauty: ★★★★ | Site Privacy: ★★★★ |
| Spaciousness: ★★★★ | Quiet: ★★★ |
| Security: ★★★★ | Cleanliness: ★★★★ |
| Insect Control: Yes | Facilities: ★★★★ |

Wapakoneta/Lima East KOA offers easy interstate access, clean facilities, and comfortable amenities. Located close to I-75 one mile east of Wapakoneta, the campground has to contend with some traffic noise. Under new ownership since 2001, the campground has level grassy sites with gravel for parking. The typical site width is 27 feet, with a typical site length of 70 feet. There are 50 pull-through sites and no seasonal campers. The speed limit is eight mph, quiet hours are 10:30 p.m. to 8 a.m., and generators are not permitted at any time. The best RV sites are 1, 3, and 5 because they are bigger and have more grass. The best tent site is 44 because it has more trees and shade. Security includes owners who live on site, regular patrols, and a coded gate. Security gates are closed between 11 p.m. and 6 a.m.

## BASICS

**Operated by:** John & Debbie Schuettler. **Open:** Feb. 30–Dec. 3. **Site Assignment:** Reservations w/ 1-night deposit; refund w/ 7-day notice. **Registration:** At campground office. **Fee:** $33 (cash, credit cards). **Parking:** At site.

## FACILITIES

**Number of RV Sites:** 68. **Number of Tent-Only Sites:** 6. **Hookups:** Electric (30, 50 amps), water, cable TV. **Each Site:** Picnic table, fire ring. **Dump Station:** Yes. **Laundry:** Yes. **Pay Phone:** Yes. **Rest Rooms and Showers:** Yes. **Fuel:** No. **Propane:** Yes. **Internal Roads:** Gravel, in good condition. **RV Service:** No. **Market:** 1 mi. west in Wapakoneta. **Restaurant:** 1 mi. west in Wapakoneta. **General Store:** Yes. **Vending:** Yes. **Swimming Pool:** Yes. **Playground:** Yes. **Other:** Club room, basketball, volleyball, horseshoes, pavilion, rental cabins, coin games, sports field, rental bikes. **Activities:** Swimming. **Nearby Attractions:** Neil Armstrong Air & Space Museum, Ohio Caverns, Piatt Castle, train displays, bicycle museum, antiques, US Air Force Museum, Indian Lake, golf. **Additional Information:** Wapakoneta Area Chamber of Commerce, (419) 738-2911.

## RESTRICTIONS

**Pets:** Leash only. **Fires:** Fire ring only. **Alcoholic Beverages:** Permitted. **Vehicle Maximum Length:** None.

## TO GET THERE

From I-75, take northbound Exit 110 or southbound Exit 111, drive east to first intersection, then 0.75 mi. north on Cemetery Rd., past membership resort. Roads are wide and well maintained w/ broad shoulders.

## WAYNESVILLE
### Caesar Creek State Park

8570 East State Rte. 73, Waynesville 45068. T: (513) 897-3055; www.ohiostateparks.org.

| 🚐 ★★★ | 🏕 ★★★ |
|---|---|
| Beauty: ★★★★ | Site Privacy: ★★★ |
| Spaciousness: ★★★ | Quiet: ★★★ |
| Security: ★★★★ | Cleanliness: ★★★ |
| Insect Control: None | Facilities: ★★★ |

For beauty, natural amenities, naturalist programs, roads, and maintenance, it's usually hard to beat a state park. But for facilities like water hookups and laundries, state parks are often at the bottom of the scale. Caesar Creek State Park has all the pluses you would expect, as well as the minuses often found at a state-run park. The

2,830-acre Caesar Creek Lake was created in 1978 when Caesar's Creek, which empties into the Little Miami River, was dammed by the Army Corps of Engineers for flood control and as a water resource. Legend has it that the creek was named for a runaway slave called Cezar who camped on its banks and lived with a local Native American tribe. Popular for waterskiing, pleasure boating, swimming, and fishing, Caesar Creek Lake offers a huge beach and four boat ramps. A pioneer village, visitors center, and a wealth of nature center programs are also big draws. Located ten miles east of Waynesville, Caesar Creek State Park Campground offers sites with electricity which can be used by either tents or RVs. An equestrian camp with 25 sites is available for overnight trail rides. The typical site size is 12 × 35 feet. Guests have a choice of shaded or open sites, but no pull-throughs are available. Park rangers provide security patrols and check on entering motorists.

## BASICS

**Operated by:** State of Ohio. **Open:** All year. **Site Assignment:** First come, first served. No reservations. **Registration:** At campground office. **Fee:** $17 (cash, check, credit cards). **Parking:** At site.

## FACILITIES

**Number of RV Sites:** 287. **Number of Tent-Only Sites:** 0. **Hookups:** Electric (30 amps). **Each Site:** Picnic table, fire ring. **Dump Station:** Yes. **Laundry:** No. **Pay Phone:** Yes. **Rest Rooms and Showers:** Yes. **Fuel:** No. **Propane:** Yes. **Internal Roads:** Paved, in good condition. **RV Service:** No. **Market:** 10 mi. west in Waynesville. **Restaurant:** 10 mi. west in Waynesville. **General Store:** Yes. **Vending:** Yes. **Swimming Pool:** No. **Playground:** Yes. **Other:** Caesar Creek lake, swimming beach, boat ramp, pavilion, horseback riding trails, horseshoes, hiking trails, nature center, wildlife area, rental RVs. **Activities:** Swimming, fishing, boating, hiking, scheduled activities. **Nearby Attractions:** Antiques, arts & crafts shops, skydiving, Kings Island amusement park, bike trails, pioneer village, golf, Quaker meeting house, Blue Jacket outdoor drama. **Additional Information:** Warren County CVB, (800) 433-1072.

## RESTRICTIONS

**Pets:** Leash only, pet camping area; $1 fee extra per pet per day, max. of 2 pets. **Fires:** Fire ring only. **Alcoholic Beverages:** Not permitted. **Vehicle**

**Maximum Length:** 35 ft. **Other:** 14-day stay limit.

## TO GET THERE

From Waynesville, drive 8 mi. east on SR 73 to SR 380, then drive 3 mi. north to Center Rd., then 1 mi. west. Roads are wide and well maintained w/ broad shoulders.

# WAYNESVILLE

## Spring Valley Frontier Campground

9580 Collett Rd., Waynesville 45068. T: (937) 862-4510; www.gocampingamerica.com; nlineen@aol.com.

🚐 ★★★          ⛺ ★★

Beauty: ★★                     Site Privacy: ★★
Spaciousness: ★★★          Quiet: ★★★
Security: ★★★★              Cleanliness: ★★★
Insect Control: None         Facilities: ★★★

Located off the beaten path eight miles north of Waynesville, Spring Valley Frontier Campground is a wooded, rural property with 45 seasonal campers in the back half. Typical site width is 30 feet, with three pull-through sites. Laid out in a series of loops, the campground is mostly shaded by mature sycamore, ash, and walnut trees. Sites are grassy, with crushed limestone for RV pads. Tent sites are separated from RVs, offering more privacy and natural surroundings. Campsites tend to fill up quickly, particularly with RV clubs, so it is advisable to call ahead. Security measures include one access road that goes past the office and owners who live on the premises. A five-mph speed limit is enforced, and the campground has speed bumps to slow down traffic.

## BASICS

**Operated by:** Paul & Nancy Lineen. **Open:** All year. **Site Assignment:** Reservations w/ no deposit. **Registration:** At campground office. **Fee:** $22 (cash, credit cards). **Parking:** At site.

## FACILITIES

**Number of RV Sites:** 75. **Number of Tent-Only Sites:** 22. **Hookups:** Electric (30, 50 amps), water, sewer. **Each Site:** Picnic table, fire ring. **Dump Station:** Yes. **Laundry:** Yes. **Pay Phone:** Yes. **Rest Rooms and Showers:** Yes. **Fuel:** No. **Propane:** Yes. **Internal Roads:** Paved/gravel, in fair condition. **RV Service:** No. **Market:** 8 mi. south in

Waynesville. **Restaurant:** 8 mi. south in Waynesville. **General Store:** Yes. **Vending:** Yes. **Swimming Pool:** Yes. **Playground:** Yes. **Other:** Mini-golf, shelter house, rec hall, basketball, rental cabins, rental mobile homes. **Activities:** Swimming. **Nearby Attractions:** Antiques, arts & crafts shops, skydiving, Kings Island amusement park, bike trail, pioneer village, Caesar Creek State Park, canoe livery, wildlife area, golf, Blue Jacket outdoor drama. **Additional Information:** Warren County CVB, (800) 433-1072.

### RESTRICTIONS

**Pets:** Leash only. **Fires:** Fire ring only. **Alcoholic Beverages:** Permitted. **Vehicle Maximum Length:** None.

### TO GET THERE

From the junction of I-75 and US35E, take exit 52B, drive 16 mi. east on US 35 Bypass, then 7 mi. south on US 42, then 1.75 mi. east on Roxanna, New Burlington Rd., then 0.75 mi. south on Pence Jones Rd., then 0.2 mi. west on Collett Rd. Roads are often narrow and twisty w/ poor shoulders.

## WEST SALEM
### Hidden Acres Campground

P.O. Box 40, West Salem 44287. T: (419) 853-4687

| 🚐 ★★★ | ⛺ ★★★ |
|---|---|
| Beauty: ★★★★ | Site Privacy: ★★★★ |
| Spaciousness: ★★★★ | Quiet: ★★★★ |
| Security: ★★★ | Cleanliness: ★★★★ |
| Insect Control: None | Facilities: ★★★ |

Located two-and-a-half miles south of West Salem, Hidden Acres Campground offers level, grassy sites, mostly shaded by mature trees. Some open sites are available right on a lake. Laid out in a series of loops, the campground has 110 seasonal campers, two pull-through sites, and a typical site width of 35 feet. Attractive touches include a gazebo, water fountain, and wooden fishing pier. The camp store offers fast food; on weekends, the also serve special dishes such as chili or sauerkraut and kielbasa. A five-mph speed limit and quiet time from 11 p.m. to 9 a.m. are enforced. An unusual rule forbids perming or coloring of hair in the restrooms. An extra fee of $2 per pole is charged for fishing in the stocked lake, but there is a small pond where fishing is free. Hidden Acres is in back of a small mobile home park.

### BASICS

**Operated by:** Jim & Ginger Kovacich, Jim & Sandy Whittlesey. **Open:** Apr. 15–Oct. 15. **Site Assignment:** Reservations w/ 1-night deposit; refund w/ 7-day notice. **Registration:** At campground office. **Fee:** $24 (cash, check). **Parking:** At site.

### FACILITIES

**Number of RV Sites:** 180. **Number of Tent-Only Sites:** 0. **Hookups:** Electric (30, 50 amps), water, sewer. **Each Site:** Picnic table, fire ring. **Dump Station:** Yes. **Laundry:** No. **Pay Phone:** No. **Rest Rooms and Showers:** Yes. **Fuel:** No. **Propane:** Yes. **Internal Roads:** Paved/gravel, in good condition. **RV Service:** No. **Market:** 2.5 mi. north in West Salem. **Restaurant:** 1.5 mi. north in West Salem. **General Store:** Yes. **Vending:** No. **Swimming Pool:** Yes. **Playground:** Yes. **Other:** Fishing lake, shuffleboard, basketball, game room, horseshoes, shelter house, sports field, volleyball. **Activities:** Fishing, swimming, boating (rental paddleboats available). **Nearby Attractions:** State Parks, antiques, golf, museums, historic homes, arts & crafts. **Additional Information:** Ashland Area Chamber of Commerce (419) 281-4584.

### RESTRICTIONS

**Pets:** Leash only, proof immunization required. **Fires:** Fire ring only. **Alcoholic Beverages:** At sites only. **Vehicle Maximum Length:** None. **Other:** No working caravans permitted. Max. stay for tents is 7 days. Electric heaters are prohibited.

### TO GET THERE

From the junction of Hwy. 301 and US 42, drive 3 mi. west on US 42, then 200 yards south on Township Rd 810. Roads are wide and well maintained w/ broad shoulders.

## WEST SALEM
### Town & Country Camp Resort

7555 Shilling Rd., West Salem 44287. T: (419) 853-4550

| 🚐 ★★★★ | ⛺ ★★★★ |
|---|---|
| Beauty: ★★★★ | Site Privacy: ★★★★ |
| Spaciousness: ★★★★ | Quiet: ★★★★ |
| Security: ★★★★ | Cleanliness: ★★★★ |
| Insect Control: None | Facilities: ★★★★ |

Town & Country Camp Resort is only two miles south of West Salem, but it has a definite country feel. Sites are grassy with gravel parking spots, and campers have a choice of shaded or open sites. Several lakes and a woods add to the country atmosphere. Laid out in a series of loops, the campground has 120 seasonal campers and ten pull-through sites. All sites have sewer connections so there is no dump station. A five-mph speed limit is enforced, as is quiet time from 11 p.m. to 8 a.m. No license is required for fishing in the campground lakes, and there is no limit on bluegills. Bass must be at least 12 inches with a limit of four per day, and catfish must be returned to the lake. Security measures include owners who live on site, a security gate, and regular patrols of the campgrounds.

## BASICS

**Operated by:** Don & Linda Castella. **Open:** Apr. 1–Oct. 31. **Site Assignment:** Reservations accepted without deposit, except on holidays. Holiday reservations w/ 1-night deposit; refunds w/ 7-day notice. **Registration:** At campground office. **Fee:** $25 (cash, check). **Parking:** At site.

## FACILITIES

**Number of RV Sites:** 200. **Number of Tent-Only Sites:** 25. **Hookups:** Electric (30 amps), water, sewer. **Each Site:** Picnic table, fire ring. **Dump Station:** No. **Laundry:** Yes. **Pay Phone:** Yes. **Rest Rooms and Showers:** Yes. **Fuel:** No. **Propane:** Yes. **Internal Roads:** Gravel, in good condition. **RV Service:** No. **Market:** 2 mi. north in West Salem. **Restaurant:** 2 mi. north in West Salem. **General Store:** Yes, limited. **Vending:** Yes. **Swimming Pool:** Yes. **Playground:** Yes. **Other:** Fishing lake, game room, pavilion, softball, horseshoes, basketball, volleyball. **Activities:** Swimming, fishing, scheduled activities. **Nearby Attractions:** State parks, antiques, golf, museums, historic homes, arts & crafts. **Additional Information:** Ashland Area Chamber of Commerce, (419) 281-4584.

## RESTRICTIONS

**Pets:** Leash only. **Fires:** Fire ring only. **Alcoholic Beverages:** Must be kept in covered containers. **Vehicle Maximum Length:** 40 ft. **Other:** No working caravans are permitted.

## TO GET THERE

From the junction of I-71 and SR 539, take Exit 198, drive 1 mi. northwest on SR 539 to Shilling Rd., drive 1 mi. north. SR 539 is a good road, well maintained w/ broad shoulders. The entry road is paved, but it's also narrow, hilly, and twisting w/ a narrow squeeze past a farm silo.

## WILMINGTON
### Cowan Lake State Park

729 Beechwood Rd., Wilmington 45177. T: (937) 289-2105; www.dnr.state.oh.us/odnr/parks.

🚐 ★★★                          ⛺ ★★★

Beauty: ★★★★          Site Privacy: ★★★
Spaciousness: ★★★      Quiet: ★★★★
Security: ★★★★         Cleanliness: ★★★
Insect Control: None      Facilities: ★★★

Located five miles west of Wilmington, Cowan Lake State Park has a 700-acre lake as a centerpiece. The lake is very popular for sailboats and pontoon boats. The lake has a ten-horsepower limit on motors. The Cowan Lake region was once a stronghold of the Miami and Shawnee Indians. Cowan Creek was named for the area's first surveyor, John Cowan. A dam was completed across Cowan Creek in 1950, and in 1968, Cowan Lake was dedicated as a state park. Campground sites are suitable for tents or RVs. Four sites are wheelchair accessible. Pet camping is offered on designated sites. Unlike many state campgrounds, Cowan Lake offers laundry facilities. Most sites are shaded by a beech and maple forest, and the average site size is 14 × 40 feet. There are no pull-through sites. Security is good, with park rangers who patrol and monitor motorists at a park gate.

## BASICS

**Operated by:** State of Ohio. **Open:** All year. **Site Assignment:** First come, first served. No reservations. **Registration:** At campground office. **Fee:** $17 (cash, check, credit cards). **Parking:** At site.

## FACILITIES

**Number of RV Sites:** 237. **Number of Tent-Only Sites:** 18. **Hookups:** Electric (50 amps). **Each Site:** Picnic table, fire ring. **Dump Station:** Yes. **Laundry:** Yes. **Pay Phone:** Yes. **Rest Rooms and Showers:** Yes. **Fuel:** No. **Propane:** No. **Internal Roads:** Paved, in good condition. **RV Service:** No. **Market:** 5 mi. east in Wilmington. **Restaurant:** 5 mi. east in Wilmington. **General Store:** Yes. **Vending:** Yes. **Swimming Pool:** No. **Playground:** Yes. **Other:** Cowan Lake, beach, boat dock, boat ramp, hiking trails, pavilion, horseshoes, game room, mini-golf, mountain bike trail, rental cabins. **Activities:** Swimming, fishing, hiking, low-speed boating (rental canoes, motorboats available), scheduled activities. **Nearby Attractions:** Kings Island amusement park, Blue Jacket outdoor drama, antiques, covered bridge, pottery, pheasant farm, Wilmington College, rails-to-trails recreational trail. **Additional Information:** Clinton County CVB, (877) 4-A-VISIT.

## RESTRICTIONS

**Pets:** Leash only. Pet camping area, $1 fee per pet per day. **Fires:** Fire ring only. **Alcoholic Beverages:** Not permitted. **Vehicle Maximum Length:** 35 ft. **Other:** 14-day stay limit.

## TO GET THERE

From Wilmington, drive 3 mi. south on US 68 to Dalton Rd., then 1.5 mi. Roads are wide and well maintained w/ broad shoulders.

## WILMINGTON

### Thousand Trails-Wilmington

1786 State Rd. 380, Wilmington 45177. T: (800) 334-9103; F: (937) 655-8065; www.1000trails.com.

| 🚐 ★★★★ | ⛺ ★★★★ |
|---|---|
| Beauty: ★★★ | Site Privacy: ★★★★ |
| Spaciousness: ★★★★ | Quiet: ★★★★ |
| Security: ★★★★★ | Cleanliness: ★★★★★ |
| Insect Control: None | Facilities: ★★★★ |

Thousand Trails—Wilmington is part of a nationwide network of 57 campground resorts for members of a private camping club. Membership options with annual dues allow members to camp at every preserve in the system or choose only a favorite region. Non-members are allowed a get-acquainted visit. Located seven miles west of Wilmington, the campground is on a preserve of gently rolling land surrounding a lake. The typical site width is 40 feet, and the campground has two pull-throughs. Sites are mostly shaded by mature oak, maple, and ash trees. Members have access to such extras as an iron and ironing board in the laundry and canoes and paddleboats on the small lake. The campground has 40 rally sites and ten tent sites in a wooded area with water hookups. Three stocked ponds are for catch-and-release fishing only. Quiet time is enforced from 11 p.m. to 8 a.m., as is a five-mph speed limit. Security is excellent, with a gate that requires a code to get in, a manager on site, and regular patrols.

## BASICS

**Operated by:** Thousand Trails Inc. **Open:** May 1–Oct. 31. **Site Assignment:** Reservations w/ 1-night deposit; refund w/ 24-hour notice. **Registration:** At campground office. **Fee:** $25 (cash, check, credit cards). **Parking:** At site.

## FACILITIES

**Number of RV Sites:** 164. **Number of Tent-Only Sites:** 10. **Hookups:** Electric (30 amps), water, sewer. **Each Site:** Picnic table, fire ring. **Dump Station:** Yes. **Laundry:** Yes. **Pay Phone:** Yes. **Rest Rooms and Showers:** Yes. **Fuel:** No. **Propane:** Yes. **Internal Roads:** Paved/gravel, in good condition. **RV Service:** No. **Market:** 10 mi. east in Wilmington. **Restaurant:** 7 mi. east in Wilmington. **General Store:** Yes. **Vending:** Yes. **Swimming Pool:** No. **Playground:** Yes. **Other:** Adult lodge, basketball, campfire circle, family lodge, horseshoe, meeting room, mini-golf, shuffleboard, wading pool, whirlpool, tennis, volleyball, hiking trail, fishing pond, rental trailers. **Activities:** Swimming, fishing, hiking, electric motorboating (free canoes, paddleboats available), scheduled weekend activities. **Nearby Attractions:** Kings Island amusement park, pottery, Blue Jacket outdoor drama, pheasant farm, Wilmington College, antiques, covered bridge, rails-to-trails recreational trail. **Additional Information:** Clinton County CVB, (877) 4-A-VISIT.

## RESTRICTIONS

**Pets:** Leash only. **Fires:** Fire ring only. **Alcoholic Beverages:** Permitted. **Vehicle Maximum Length:** None. **Other:** 14-day stay limit.

## TO GET THERE

From the junction of I-71 and Hwy. 73, take Exit 45, drive 0.25 mi. east on Hwy. 73, then 1.5 mi. south on Hwy. 380. Roads are wide and well maintained w/ broad shoulders.

# Wisconsin

Along with its famed cheese and cherries, Wisconsin offers a vacationer's paradise. From its rugged Door County peninsula to the state's biggest city of Milwaukee and on to the scenic Dells, America's Dairyland provides a variety of attractions.

The St. Croix River shares gorgeous gorges, rock formations, and waterfalls, while the national lakeshore has more lighthouses than any other national park. With 15,000 inland lakes and 25,000 miles of waterways—along with borders on Lakes Michigan and Superior, the St. Croix, Menomonie, and Brule Rivers, and the mighty Mississippi—Wisconsin is a water wonderland. Scuba divers explore shipwrecks waiting at "death's door," the watery passage between **Door County** and **Washington Island.** Navigable its entire length, the winding **Kickapoo** is called "the crookedest river in the world." For heights, head to **Devil's Lake State Park** near **Baraboo** for the 500-foot bluffs or to **Granddad Bluff** which towers 600 feet above **La Crosse.** Stretches of Class V rapids make the **Montreal River** a popular spot for expert kayakers. For exploration, the rugged sea caves dotting the bases of sandstone cliffs are a great choice.

To turn back the clock, visit the living history village in **New Glarus,** often called "Little Switzerland." The great architecture of Frank Lloyd Wright is preserved in **Madison** and **Spring Green,** as is circus memorabilia in **Baraboo.** Climb aboard the "Lumberjack Special" steam-powered train, puffing from the Laona historic depot to **Camp Five Museum Complex,** to learn about logging.

As Wisconsin's oldest state park, **Interstate State Park** in **St. Croix Falls** is home to an unusual rock outcropping known as the Old Man of the Dalles. Climb aboard a boat in the **Wisconsin Dells** for a cruise past rock formations, canyons, islands, and sandstone cliffs. In **Green Bay,** the Packers (founded in 1919) lay claim to being the oldest professional football team in the National Football League.

Anglers will enjoy seeing the **National Fresh Water Fishing Hall of Fame** in **Hayward.** Housed in a building designed to resemble a muskellunge, the facility is complete with an observation deck in the mouth of the giant fish. **Horicon** offers boat tours of a wetland inhabited by more than 260 species of birds.

True to its name, the lovely village of **Land O' Lakes** is surrounded by about 135 lakes. Stroll the tree-shaded streets of **Madison** where the impressive **1917 State Capitol** offers free tours showcasing state history and artwork.

## The following facilities accept payment in checks or cash only:

Big Lake Campground, Algoma

Timber Trail Campground, Algoma

Turtle Creek Campsite, Beloit

Benson's Century Camping Resort,
Campbellsport

Chetek River Campground, Chetek

Mississippi Sports and Recreation, De Soto

Elmer's RV Park and Campgrounds, Eau
Claire

Hickory Hills Campground, Edgerton

Hy-Land Court, Ellison Bay

Lake Hilbert Campground, Goodman

Tomorrow Wood Campground, Hancock

Lake Chippewa Campground, Hayward

Wildwood Campground, Iron River

Edgewater Acres Campground, Menomonie

Lakeview Campground, Milton

Wolf River Trips and Campgrounds,
New London

Maple View Campground, Norman

Coon's Deep Lake Campground, Oxford

Aqualand Camp Resort, Sister Bay

Scenic View Campground, Spooner

Monument Point Camping, Sturgeon Bay

Timber Trail Campground, West Bend

Veterans Memorial Campground, West
Salem

Red Barn Campground, Shell Lake

Rivers Edge Campground, Stevens Point

The Out-Post Campground, Tomahawk

## The following facilities feature 20 or fewer sites:

Lost Falls Resort and Campground, Black
River Falls

Mississippi Sports and Recreation, De Soto

Elmer's RV Park and Campgrounds,
Eau Claire

Creekview Campground, Edgerton

Hy-Land Court, Ellison Bay

Wildwood Campground, Iron River

Ham Lake Campground, Laona

Granger's Campground, Oakdale

Coon's Deep Lake Campground, Oxford

Scenic View Campground, Spooner

Raft 'N Rest Campground and Rafting ,
White Lake

Wolf River-Nicolet Forest Campground and
Outdoor Center, White Lake

Holiday Lodge Golf Resort, Wyeville

## ALGOMA
### Big Lake Campground

2427 Lake St., Algoma 54201. T: (920) 487-2726;
mlthomas@itol.com.

🚐 ★★★          ⛺ ★★★

Beauty: ★★              Site Privacy: ★★
Spaciousness: ★★★       Quiet: ★★★
Security: ★★★           Cleanliness: ★★★★
Insect Control: None    Facilities: ★★★

Located in Algoma, Big Lake Campground is surrounded by vacation land. It is only minutes from Northeast Wisconsin's many attractions—Lake Michigan and Door County, in particular. Campground sites are level, with a typical site width of 30 feet. Some sites are open, but most are shaded and back up into the woods. Laid out in a series of loops, the campground has one pull-through site. Boats also are allowed in the campground. Arrangements can be made ahead of time for charter fishing and for tee times at the local 18-hole golf course. For snowmobiling and ice-fishing enthusiasts, the campground is open from Jan. through Mar., with reservations. Tent sites are in a separate wooded area with more green space and privacy. Security measures include owners who live on site year-round and regular patrols by city police.

### BASICS
**Operated by:** Mike & Linda Thomas. **Open:** Apr. 15–Oct. 15; Jan.–Mar. w/ reservations. **Site Assignment:** Reservations w/ no deposit. **Registration:** At campground office. **Fee:** $20 (cash & check). **Parking:** At site.

### FACILITIES
**Number of RV Sites:** 72. **Number of Tent-Only Sites:** 12. **Hookups:** Electric (20, 30, 50 amps), water, sewer. **Each Site:** Picnic table, fire ring. **Dump Station:** Yes. **Laundry:** Yes. **Pay Phone:** No. **Rest Rooms and Showers:** Yes. **Fuel:** No. **Propane:** No. **Internal Roads:** Gravel/dirt, in good condition. **RV Service:** No. **Market:** 0.25 mi. north in Algoma. **Restaurant:** 0.25 mi. north in Algoma. **General Store:** No. **Vending:** No. **Swimming Pool:** No. **Playground:** Yes. **Other:** Recreation field, volleyball, horseshoes, lighted fish-cleaning station, fish freezing, game room, badminton, adults room. **Activities:** None. **Nearby Attractions:** Lake Michigan, boat launch,

fishing piers, beaches, golf, Door County, antiques, museums, charter fishing, cheese factories, harbor, winery, snowmobiling, ice fishing, zoo, jail museum. **Additional Information:** Algoma Area Chamber of Commerce, (920) 487-2041.

### RESTRICTIONS
**Pets:** Leash only. **Fires:** Fire ring only. **Alcoholic Beverages:** Permitted. **Vehicle Maximum Length:** None.

### TO GET THERE
From the junction of Hwy. 54 and Hwy. 42, drive 1 mi. south on Hwy. 41. Roads are wide and well maintained w/ broad shoulders.

## ALGOMA
### Timber Trail Campground

N 8326 CR M, Algoma 54201. T: (920) 487-3707; timbertrail@itol.com.

🚐 ★★★          ⛺ ★★

Beauty: ★★              Site Privacy: ★★
Spaciousness: ★★★★     Quiet: ★★★
Security: ★★★★          Cleanliness: ★★★★
Insect Control: None    Facilities: ★★★

Located near Algoma, Timber Trail Campground offers grassy, shaded sites close to Door County. The campground has 35 seasonal campers, four pull-through sites, and a typical site width of 40 feet. Tent sites are in a separate area with privacy from RVs and more green space. The best RV sites are 48, 49, and 50 because they are larger and more secluded in the woods. Security and safety measures include a five-mph speed limit and owners who live on site and provide regular patrols of the campground. Although part of the campground's major draw is its proximity to Door County, there are also several activities at the property. Another plus is clean bathrooms. Prices are very reasonable for being located in such a popular vacation area.

### BASICS
**Operated by:** Mike & Alisa Herrick. **Open:** Apr. 15–Oct. 15. **Site Assignment:** Reservations w/ 1-night deposit; refund w/ 2-week notice. **Registration:** At campground office. **Fee:** $20 (cash, check). **Parking:** At site.

### FACILITIES
**Number of RV Sites:** 62. **Number of Tent-Only Sites:** 8. **Hookups:** Electric (20, 30, 50

amps), water. **Each Site:** Picnic table, fire ring.
**Dump Station:** Yes. **Laundry:** Yes. **Pay Phone:**
Yes. **Rest Rooms and Showers:** Yes. **Fuel:** No.
**Propane:** Yes. **Internal Roads:** Gravel, in good
condition. **RV Service:** No. **Market:** 1 mi. south-
east in Algoma. **Restaurant:** 1 mi. southeast in
Algoma. **General Store:** Yes. **Vending:** No.
**Swimming Pool:** Yes. **Playground:** Yes. **Other:**
Rec room, fishing lake/river, badminton, sports field,
horseshoes, hiking trails, volleyball, riverboat launch.
**Activities:** Swimming, fishing, boating (rental canoe
available), hiking, scheduled weekend activities.
**Nearby Attractions:** Lake Michigan, boat launch,
fishing piers, beaches, golf, Door County, antiques,
museums, charter fishing, cheese factories, harbor,
winery, snowmobiling, ice fishing, zoo, jail museum.
**Additional Information:** Algoma Area Chamber
of Commerce (920) 487-2041.

## RESTRICTIONS

**Pets:** Leash only. **Fires:** Fire ring only. **Alcoholic
Beverages:** Permitted. **Vehicle Maximum
Length:** None.

## TO GET THERE

From the junction of Hwy. 54 and Hwy. 42,
drive 0.5 mi. north on Hwy. 42, then 1 mi. west
on CR S, then 0.75 mi. north on CR M. The
roads are wide and well maintained w/ broad
shoulders.

## BAGLEY
## River of Lakes Campground and Resort

132A Packer Dr., Bagley 53801. T: (608) 996-2275

🚐 ★★          ⛺ ★★★

Beauty: ★★★          Site Privacy: ★★
Spaciousness: ★★          Quiet: ★★★
Security: ★★★          Cleanliness: ★★★
Insect Control: None          Facilities: ★★★

Family owned and operated for over 40 years,
River of Lakes Resort and Campground is
located in the heart of the upper Mississippi
bluff country in an area of lakes and backwater
sloughs. That means plenty of water activities,
including good fishing for bass, pike, catfish, and
other panfish. However, it also means the Mississippi River sometimes leaves its banks and floods
this campground one mile south of Bagley. Be
sure the area is not in the midst of a flood or
soon will be before you make camping plans.

The entrance to the campground is over a railroad track and through an area of about 100
summer cottages and mobile homes. The campground has 75 seasonal lots in addition to the
ones available for visitors. Many regulars return
and bring their boats. Sites 57–59 are the most
popular because they are on the riverfront.

## BASICS

**Operated by:** Rob & Gary Irish. **Open:** Apr.
15–Oct. 15. **Site Assignment:** First come, first
served. **Registration:** At campground office. **Fee:**
$17 (cash, check, credit cards). **Parking:** At site.

## FACILITIES

**Number of RV Sites:** 120. **Number of Tent-
Only Sites:** 0. **Hookups:** Electric (20, 30 amps,)
water, sewer. **Each Site:** Picnic table, fire ring.
**Dump Station:** Yes. **Laundry:** No. **Pay Phone:**
Yes. **Rest Rooms and Showers:** Yes. **Fuel:** Yes.
**Propane:** Yes. **Internal Roads:** Blacktop, in good
condition. **RV Service:** No. **Market:** 17 mi. north
to Prairie du Chien. **Restaurant:** 1 mi. north to
Bagley. **General Store:** Yes. **Vending:** No. **Swimming Pool:** No. **Playground:** Yes. **Other:** Rec
hall, pavilion, river, pond, shuffleboard, horseshoes,
badminton, sports field, fish-cleaning facility, boat
ramp, basketball, sandy beach & swim area. **Activities:** Swimming, fishing, boating (rental rowboats,
canoes, paddleboats, motor boats available).
**Nearby Attractions:** Casino, Villa Louis historical
site, Kickapoo Indian Caverns, Native American
Museum, car ferry, Museum of Agricultural History
& Village Life. **Additional Information:** Prairie du
Chien Chamber of Commerce, (800) 732-1673.

## RESTRICTIONS

**Pets:** Leash only. **Fires:** Fire pits only. **Alcoholic
Beverages:** Permitted. **Vehicle Maximum
Length:** None.

## TO GET THERE

From the junction of CR X and CR A, drive 1
mi. south on CR A, then 0.75 mi. west on Willow Ln. Roads are wide and well maintained w/
broad shoulders.

## BAGLEY
## Syalusing State Park

13081 State Park Ln., Bagley 53801. T: (608) 996-2261

🚐 ★★          ⛺ ★★★★

Beauty: ★★★★          Site Privacy: ★★★★
Spaciousness: ★★★★          Quiet: ★★★★

Security: ★★★★     Cleanliness: ★★★
Insect Control: None     Facilities: ★★

The 2,674-acre Wyalusing State Park got its name from the Munsee-Delaware Native American word meaning "home of the warrior." As with most state park campgrounds, Wyalusing is short on amenities and long on beauty and recreational opportunities. Although the park doesn't offer swimming, the Wyalusing Recreation Area two miles south of the park entrance is a county operated beach, boat ladning, and picnic area on the Mississippi River. No fees are required. Located five miles north of Bagley, the wilderness campground is covered by mature maple, cedar, oak, black walnut, and white pine trees. The best sites are atop a 500-foot bluff overlooking the Wisconsin River. Although the sites have no hookups, they are popular with both tents and RVs. Activity at Wyalusing slows during the winter but doesn't stop. Winter camping, ice fishing, cross-country skiing, sledding, snowshoeing, hiking, and wildlife observation draw campers to the park as the temperature plunges. Sevral campsites, including some with electricity, are kept plowed open all winter. Water is available near the group tent area. Winter camping here is only for the very hardy, but those numbers seem to increase each year.

## BASICS

**Operated by:** State of Wisconsin. **Open:** All year. **Site Assignment:** Reservations w/ entire stay deposit; refund (minus $9.50) w/ 4-day notice. **Registration:** At campground office. **Fee:** $13 (cash, check, credit cards), plus $5 daily park fee of $18 annual fee if Wisconsin resident; $7 daily fee or $25 annual fee if not Wisconsin resident. **Parking:** At site.

## FACILITIES

**Number of RV Sites:** 34. **Number of Tent-Only Sites:** 76. **Hookups:** Electric (30 amps). **Each Site:** Picnic table, fire ring. **Dump Station:** Yes. **Laundry:** No. **Pay Phone:** Yes. **Rest Rooms and Showers:** Yes. **Fuel:** No. **Propane:** No. **Internal Roads:** Paved, in good condition. **RV Service:** No. **Market:** 12 m. west in Prairie du Chien. **Restaurant:** 5 mi. south in Bagley. **General Store:** Yes. **Vending:** Yes. **Swimming Pool:** No. **Playground:** Yes. **Other:** Backwaters of the Mississippi & Wisconsin rivers, tennis, canoe trail, boat ramp, hiking trail, shelter, nature center, bike trail.

**Activities:** Fishing, boating, hiking, biking, nature education programs. **Nearby Attractions:** Casino, Villa Louis historical site, Kickapoo Indian Caverns, Native American Museum. **Additional Information:** Prairie du Chien Chamber of Commerce, (800) 732-1673.

## RESTRICTIONS

**Pets:** Leash only. **Fires:** Fire ring only. **Alcoholic Beverages:** Permitted. **Vehicle Maximum Length:** None. **Other:** 14-day stay limit.

## TO GET THERE

From Bagley, drive 7 mi. north on CR X, then 1 mi. on CR C. Roads are in average condition w/ often narrow shoulders.

## BAGLEY

## Yogi Bear's Jellystone Park Camp-Resort

11354 CR X, Bagley 53801. T: (608) 996-2201; www.jellystonebagley.com; yogibagley@mailtds.net.

🚐 ★★★★     ⛺ ★★★

Beauty: ★★★     Site Privacy: ★★★
Spaciousness: ★★★     Quiet: ★★★
Security: ★★★★     Cleanliness: ★★★★
Insect Control: No     Facilities: ★★★★

Campers know what to expect when they go to a Yogi Bear's Jellystone Park-Resort: clean facilities, a quiet, secure campground, and plenty of activities for children. The Bagley campground offers all that, plus a valley site with hills on both sides and the Mississippi River across the road. A railroad track also runs right by the campground. Laid out in a series of loops, the campground has sites that are flat, grassy, and mostly open. Many of the trees were wiped out by a 1998 tornado. Site sizes vary, with some as large as 40 feet wide and 100 feet deep. The campground has seven pull-throughs and 62 seasonal campers. Non-campers are allowed to use the recreational facilities for $3 per day per person, Sunday through Thursday, holidays excluded. Located one mile north of Bagley, the campground enforces quiet time from 10:30 p.m. to 8 a.m., and no mini-bikes, dirt bikes, three- or four-wheelers, or ATVs are allowed in the park at any time. Motorcycles are permitted only to and from the campsite. A five-mph speed limit includes bicycles, too. Security measures include a campground gate that is closed after 10 p.m. as well as "rangers" who patrol the park regularly.

## BASICS

**Operated by:** Mike & Kim Esler. **Open:** May 1–Oct. 15. **Site Assignment:** Reservations w/ 1-night deposit; refunds w/ 14-day notice. **Registration:** At campground office. **Fee:** $32 (cash, check, credit cards). **Parking:** At site.

## FACILITIES

**Number of RV Sites:** 206. **Number of Tent-Only Sites:** 11. **Hookups:** Electric (30 amps), water, sewer. **Each Site:** Picnic table, fire ring. **Dump Station:** Yes. **Laundry:** Yes. **Pay Phone:** Yes. **Rest Rooms and Showers:** Yes. **Fuel:** No. **Propane:** Yes. **Internal Roads:** Paved/gravel, in good condition. **RV Service:** No. **Market:** 15 mi. north in Prairie du Chien. **Restaurant:** 1 mi. south in Bagley. **General Store:** Yes. **Vending:** Yes. **Swimming Pool:** Yes. **Playground:** Yes. **Other:** Pavilion, mini-golf, Yogi cartoons at outdoor the-atreamphitheatre, ranger station w/ fireplace & lounge, game room, snack bar, shuffleboard, horseshoes, ping-pong, basketball, volleyball, walking trails, rental cabins. **Activities:** Swimming, activity director, scheduled activities. **Nearby Attractions:** House on the Rock, Villa Louis, Mississippi River boat rides, antiques, state parks, golf, caves, minies, locks & dams, fishing, water sports. **Additional Information:** Prairie du Chien Chamber of Commerce, (800) 732-1673.

## RESTRICTIONS

**Pets:** Leash only. **Fires:** Fire ring only. **Alcoholic Beverages:** At sites only. **Vehicle Maximum Length:** None.

## TO GET THERE

From the junction of CR A and CR X in Bagley, drive 1 mi. north on on CR X. Roads are wide and well maintained w/ good shoulders.

## BAILEYS HARBOR

### Baileys Bluff Campground and RV Park

2701 CR EE, Baileys Harbor 54202. T: (920) 839-2109

🚐 ★★★        ▲ ★★★

Beauty: ★★              Site Privacy: ★★★★
Spaciousness: ★★★★      Quiet: ★★★

Security: ★★★★          Cleanliness: ★★
Insect Control: None     Facilities: ★★★

Baileys Bluff Campground and RV Park really is up on a bluff, about one mile west of Baileys Harbor. Drive slowly up the entrance and look back at the view. In the right spots, you have a 20-mile vista. The campground itself is very wooded and not suitable for satellite TV. The wilderness sites have a typical site width of 30 feet; there are 16 seasonal sites and two pull-throughs. Laid out in a series of loops, most sites have plenty of natural screening with trees, bushes, and other greenery. As one of Wisconsin's finest fishing areas, Baileys Bluff provides a fish-cleaning station and free freezer space for catches. A five-mph speed limit is enforced, and campers should be extra cautious driving up and down the bluff entrance. For security measures, the campground has one entrance/exit,, and owners who live on site and provide regular campground patrols.

## BASICS

**Operated by:** Bob & Cheryl Hook. **Open:** Apr. 15–Oct. 20. **Site Assignment:** Reservations w/ 1-night deposit; refund w/ 2-week notice. **Registration:** At campground office. **Fee:** $24 (cash, check, credit cards). **Parking:** At site.

## FACILITIES

**Number of RV Sites:** 52. **Number of Tent-Only Sites:** 33. **Hookups:** Electric (30 amps), water. **Each Site:** Picnic table, fire ring. **Dump Station:** Yes. **Laundry:** Yes. **Pay Phone:** Yes. **Rest Rooms and Showers:** Yes. **Fuel:** No. **Propane:** No. **Internal Roads:** Gravel, in good condition. **RV Service:** No. **Market:** 1 mi. east in Baileys Harbor. **Restaurant:** 1 mi. east in Baileys Harbor. **General Store:** Yes, limited. **Vending:** Yes. **Swimming Pool:** No. **Playground:** Yes. **Other:** Fish cleaning & freezing, badminton, horseshoes, hiking trails, volleyball, game room, recreation field, rental trailers. **Activities:** Hiking. **Nearby Attractions:** Golf, Door County, nature sanctuary, Lake Michigan, fishing, swimming, beaches, bike routes, Moonlight & North bays, sport fishing, antiques, arts & crafts, cherry orchards, cheese. **Additional Information:** Baileys Harbor Visitor Information Center, (920) 839-2366.

## RESTRICTIONS

**Pets:** Leash only. **Fires:** Fire ring only. **Alcoholic Beverages:** Permitted. **Vehicle Maximum**

**Length:** 36 ft. **Other:** No arrivals after 10 p.m. without advance approval.

## To Get There

From the junction of Hwy. 57 and CR F/EE, drive 0.75 mi. west on CR F/EE, then 0.25 mi. west on CR EE. Roads are wide and well maintained w/ broad shoulders.

## BAILEYS HARBOR
### Baileys Grove Travel Park and Campground

2552 CR F & EE, Baileys Harbor 54202. T: (866) 839-2559; F: (920) 839-1339; campnowwi@yahoo.com.

🚐 ★★★              ⛺ ★★★

| | |
|---|---|
| Beauty: ★★ | Site Privacy: ★★ |
| Spaciousness: ★★★ | Quiet: ★★★ |
| Security: ★★★★ | Cleanliness: ★★★★ |
| Insect Control: None | Facilities: ★★★ |

Baileys Grove Travel Park and Campground offers convenience and easy access to northern Door County and Lake Michigan. Less than a mile from Baileys Grove, the campground is right off the country road, next to a small private airport. Campsites are level and grassy with a shade tree on every site for a wooded (not wilderness) setting. A tree buffer around the campground helps provide quiet and privacy. Baileys Grove has 16 seasonal campers and 25 pull-throughs, with a typical site width of 40 feet. As a popular destination for fishing, the campground offers a fish-cleaning station and freezing facilities. A five-mph speed limit is enforced, as are quiet hours from 10 p.m. to 7 a.m. Security measures include one entrance/exit road and an owner who lives on site and provides regular patrols.

## Basics

**Operated by:** Elwyn & Leann Kropuenske. **Open:** May 1–Oct. 15. **Site Assignment:** Reservations w/ 1-night deposit; refund w/ 7-day notice. **Registration:** At campground office. **Fee:** $24 (cash, check, credit cards). **Parking:** At site.

## Facilities

**Number of RV Sites:** 59. **Number of Tent-Only Sites:** 12. **Hookups:** Electric (30 amps), water, sewer. **Each Site:** Picnic table, fire ring. **Dump Station:** Yes. **Laundry:** Yes. **Pay Phone:** Yes. **Rest Rooms and Showers:** Yes. **Fuel:** No.

**Propane:** No. **Internal Roads:** Gravel, in good condition. **RV Service:** No. **Market:** 1 mi. north in Baileys Harbor. **Restaurant:** 1 mi. north in Baileys Harbor. **General Store:** Yes, limited. **Vending:** Yes. **Swimming Pool:** Yes. **Playground:** Yes. **Other:** Fish-cleaning station & freezing, game room, adults room, horseshoes, badminton, volleyball. **Activities:** Swimming. **Nearby Attractions:** Golf, Door County, nature sanctuary, Lake Michigan, fishing, beaches, bike routes, Moonlight & North bays, sport fishing, antiques, arts & crafts, cherry orchards, cheese. **Additional Information:** Baileys Harbor Visitor Information Center, (920) 839-2366.

## Restrictions

**Pets:** Leash only. **Fires:** Fire rings only, must be extinguished by 11 p.m. **Alcoholic Beverages:** Permitted. **Vehicle Maximum Length:** None.

## To Get There

From the junction of Hwy. 57 and CR F/EE, drive 0.7 mi. west on CR F/EE. Roads are wide and well maintained w/ broad shoulders.

## BANCROFT
### Vista Royalle Campground

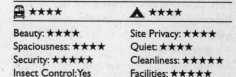

8025 Isherwod Rd., Bancroft 54921. T: (715) 335-6860

🚐 ★★★★              ⛺ ★★★★

| | |
|---|---|
| Beauty: ★★★★ | Site Privacy: ★★★★ |
| Spaciousness: ★★★★ | Quiet: ★★★★ |
| Security: ★★★★★ | Cleanliness: ★★★★★ |
| Insect Control: Yes | Facilities: ★★★★★ |

As avid campers, Jim and Judy Kollock decided 26 years ago to open a campground with the amenities they looked for when camping. To be sure they got off on the right foot, the Kollocks worked with a landscape architect to create the initial layout. It shows. Tall pine trees, spacious (40 × 60 feet) sites and a man-made lake with a sandy bottom and big sandy beach set Vista Royalle Campground apart from others. The lake is aerated and treated to keep it clean. Favorite RV campsites for families are sites 1–10 along the beach. A lodge with a fireplace, video games, movies, and a television welcome children (wholesome, non-"raunchy" movies and games only). Security is also tops, as the campground has one video-monitored access road and owners who live on site and patrol.

## BASICS

**Operated by:** Jim & Judy Kollock. **Open:** Apr. 20–Oct. 20. **Site Assignment:** Reservations w/ 1-night deposit. Refund w/ 3-day notice or 7-day notice on holidays. **Registration:** At campground office. **Fee:** $26 (cash, check, credit cards). **Parking:** At site.

## FACILITIES

**Number of RV Sites:** 200. **Number of Tent-Only Sites:** 0. **Hookups:** Electric (20, 30, 50 amps), water, sewer. **Each Site:** Picnic table, fire ring. **Dump Station:** Yes. **Laundry:** Yes. **Pay Phone:** Yes. **Rest Rooms and Showers:** Yes. **Fuel:** No. **Propane:** Yes. **Internal Roads:** Gravel, in good condition. **RV Service:** No. **Market:** 1 mi. south to Bancroft. **Restaurant:** 1 mi. south to Bancroft. **General Store:** Yes. **Vending:** Yes. **Swimming Pool:** No. **Playground:** Yes. **Other:** Swimming pond w/ sandy beach, mini-golf, snack shack, fishing pond, rec hall, shuffleboard, horseshoes, shelter house, video games, basketball. **Activities:** Swimming, fishing, planned activities. **Nearby Attractions:** Chain of lakes, several golf courses, water park, tours of vegetable farming & paper mills. **Additional Information:** Stevens Point Area CVB, (715) 344-2556.

## RESTRICTIONS

**Pets:** Leash only. **Fires:** Fire ring only. **Alcoholic Beverages:** Permitted. **Vehicle Maximum Length:** 50 ft.

## TO GET THERE

From Exit 143 at the junction of US 51 and CR W, drive east 0.75 mi. to Isherwood Rd., drive north 1 mi. Roads are wide and well maintained w/ broad shoulders.

## BELOIT

### Turtle Creek Campsite

3513 East CR S, Beloit 53511. T: (608) 362-7768

🚐 ★★★          ⛺ ★★★

| | |
|---|---|
| Beauty: ★★★ | Site Privacy: ★★★ |
| Spaciousness: ★★★ | Quiet: ★★★ |
| Security: ★★★★ | Cleanliness: ★★★★ |
| Insect Control: None | Facilities: ★★★ |

Located 500 feet off I-90 in Beloit, Turtle Creek Campsite is a good stopping-off point, as well as a destination for campers seeking activities along the creek. With such a convenient highway location, however, the sounds of traffic do float over the campground. The facility has 75 pull-through sites and a typical site width of 30 feet. Spots are level, grassy, and semi-wooded. An open field is popular with big rigs and campers with satellite TV. Laid out in a series of loops, the campground offers sites right along Turtle Creek and in a beautiful oak grove. Paddlers can access the creek here for a leisurely canoe trip (no motors allowed). Safety and security measures include quiet time enforced at 10:30 p.m., one entrance/exit road, and owners who live on site and provide regular patrols. Visitors must register and pay $2 per adult and child but are not allowed to use the swimming facilities and must leave at dark.

## BASICS

**Operated by:** The George Denu family. **Open:** May 15–Oct. 1. **Site Assignment:** Reservations w/ 1-night deposit; no refunds. **Registration:** At campground office. **Fee:** $18 (cash). **Parking:** At site.

## FACILITIES

**Number of RV Sites:** 48. **Number of Tent-Only Sites:** 52. **Hookups:** Electric (20, 30 amps), water. **Each Site:** Picnic table, fire ring. **Dump Station:** Yes. **Laundry:** No. **Pay Phone:** Yes. **Rest Rooms and Showers:** Yes. **Fuel:** No. **Propane:** No. **Internal Roads:** Gravel, in good condition. **RV Service:** No. **Market:** 3 mi. west in Beloit. **Restaurant:** 3 mi. west in Beloit. **General Store:** No. **Vending:** No. **Swimming Pool:** Yes. **Playground:** Yes. **Other:** Turtle Creek, air-conditioned rec hall, pavilion, coin games, fishing river, basketball, sports field, horseshoes, hiking trails, volleyball. **Activities:** Swimming, hiking, fishing, boating (no motors). **Nearby Attractions:** Golf, the Angel Museum, Beloit College, historic districts, Logan Museum of Anthropology, Pohlman Field, self-guided walking tours, antiques, arts & crafts. **Additional Information:** Beloit Convention & Visitor Bureau, (800) 423-5648.

## RESTRICTIONS

**Pets:** Leash only; 1 pet to a site. **Fires:** Fire ring only. **Alcoholic Beverages:** Permitted. **Vehicle Maximum Length:** None. **Other:** 3-day stay limit for tents.

## TO GET THERE

From the junction of I-43 and I-90, take Exit 183 (Shopiere Rd.), drive 2 mi. north on I-90, then 500 feet east on CR S. Roads are wide and well maintained w/ broad shoulders.

## BLACK RIVER FALLS
### Lost Falls Resort and Campground

N2974 Sunnyvale Rd., Black River Falls 54615.
T: (800) 329-3911

🚐 ★★          ⛺ ★★★

Beauty: ★★★               Site Privacy: ★★★
Spaciousness: ★★★          Quiet: ★★★★
Security: ★★★★             Cleanliness: ★★★
Insect Control: None       Facilities: ★★★

Lost Falls Resort and Campground, ten miles west of Black River Falls, is a destination in itself. It may be too far from the interstate for some campers, and the gravel road leading down to the campground is quite narrow (as are the interior roads). The Black River is the center of activities for Lost Falls Resort and Campground, and outdoor activities abound. RV sites are generally grassy, shaded, and spacious (50 × 50), but the campground offers only one pull-through site. The best spots for tent campers are in the woods and along the river. However, RVs are not allowed by the river. Be sure and bring all the food and supplies you need, as the campstore sells mostly candy, ice cream, and snacks.

### BASICS
**Operated by:** Ed & Rose Schaper. **Open:** May 1–Oct. 1. **Site Assignment:** Reservations w/ 1-night deposit; full refund if vacancy is filled. No refund on holiday weekends. **Registration:** At campground office. **Fee:** $22 (cash, check, credit cards). **Parking:** At site.

### FACILITIES
**Number of RV Sites:** 20. **Number of Tent-Only Sites:** 10. **Hookups:** Electric (20, 30 amps), water, sewer. **Each Site:** Picnic table, fire ring. **Dump Station:** No. **Laundry:** No. **Pay Phone:** No. **Rest Rooms and Showers:** Yes. **Fuel:** No. **Propane:** No. **Internal Roads:** Gravel, in fair condition. **RV Service:** No. **Market:** 10 mi. east in Black River Falls. **Restaurant:** 6 mi. west in Melrose. **General Store:** Yes. **Vending:** Yes. **Swimming Pool:** No. **Playground:** Yes. **Other:** River, hiking trails, badminton, horseshoes, basketball, canoe landing. **Activities:** Fishing, swimming, boating (rental canoes, kayaks & tubes available), hiking, storytelling every Saturday night by Rose Schaper. **Nearby Attractions:** State forest, bike/ATV trails, water park. **Additional Information:** Black River Falls Area Chamber of Commerce, (800) 404-4008.

### RESTRICTIONS
**Pets:** Leash only. **Fires:** Fire ring only. **Alcoholic Beverages:** Permitted. **Vehicle Maximum Length:** None.

### TO GET THERE
From the junction of I-94 and Hwy. 54, take Exit 116, drive 10.5 mi. west and south on Hwy. 54, then 0.25 mi. south on Sunnyvale Rd. Roads are wide and well maintained w/ good shoulders.

## BLACK RIVER FALLS
### Parkland Village Campground

N6150 Julianna Rd., Black River Falls 54615. T: (715) 284-9700

🚐 ★★          ⛺ ★★★

Beauty: ★★★               Site Privacy: ★★★★
Spaciousness: ★★★★         Quiet: ★★★
Security: ★★★              Cleanliness: ★★★★
Insect Control: None       Facilities: ★★★

Located halfway between the Madison/Milwaukee metro area and Minneapolis/St. Paul, Parkland Village Campground must be a welcome sight for snowbirds heading south for the winter or back home in the summer. The campground is a short distance from the interstate, yet its tree buffer makes it quiet enough to get some rest. The entrance is through a mobile home park. Twenty large (65 × 60 feet) pull-through sites offer easy in-and-out for overnight campers. Although a dump station is located nearby, it would be handy to have one in the campground. An important note is that Parkland Village is open all year. Water is shut off in the campground, but campers still have access to showers, rest rooms and other campground facilities. Most winter campers are late-traveling snowbirds or outdoor enthusiasts wanting to hunt, snowmobile, and cross-country ski. Parkland Village doesn't offer scheduled activities, preferring to let campers devise their own entertainment.

### BASICS
**Operated by:** Dan & Barb Potkonak. **Open:** All year. **Site Assignment:** Reservation w/ 1-night deposit; no refund. **Registration:** At campground office. **Fee:** $23 (cash, check, credit cards). **Parking:** At site.

## FACILITIES

**Number of RV Sites:** 80. **Number of Tent-Only Sites:** 0. **Hookups:** Electric (20, 30, 50 amps), water, sewer. **Each Site:** Picnic table, fire ring. **Dump Station:** No. **Laundry:** Yes. **Pay Phone:** Yes. **Rest Rooms and Showers:** Yes. **Fuel:** No. **Propane:** No. **Internal Roads:** Gravel, in good condition. **RV Service:** No. **Market:** 0.5 mi. north in Black River Falls. **Restaurant:** Next door. **General Store:** No. **Vending:** Yes. **Swimming Pool:** Yes. **Playground:** Yes. **Other:** TV & game room, pond, patio, ATV & snowmobile trails. **Activities:** Swimming, hiking, fishing, snowmobiling & ATV riding. **Nearby Attractions:** Cross-country ski trails, scuba diving, casino, golf, roller skating, Tufts Museum, water sports, shopping, cranberry marshes. **Additional Information:** Warrens Area Business Assoc., (608) 378-4200.

## RESTRICTIONS

**Pets:** Leash only. **Fires:** Fire pits only. **Alcoholic Beverages:** Permitted. **Vehicle Maximum Length:** None.

## TO GET THERE

From the junction of I-94 and Hwy. 54, take Exit 116 and drive 300 yards east on Hwy. 54, then 0.25 mi. south on Oasis Rd. Roads are wide and well maintained w/ broad shoulders.

# BOULDER JUNCTION
## Camp Holiday

P.O. Box 67, Boulder Junction 54512. T: (715) 385-2264; F: (715) 385-2966; www.campholiday.com; campholiday@centurytel.net.

🚐 ★★★★    ▲ ★★★

| | |
|---|---|
| Beauty: ★★★ | Site Privacy: ★★★ |
| Spaciousness: ★★★ | Quiet: ★★★ |
| Security: ★★★★ | Cleanliness: ★★★ |
| Insect Control: None | Facilities: ★★★★ |

Set in the heart of the Northern Highland-American Legion State Forest, Camp Holiday has nearly 200 lakes within a ten-mile radius. The campground, four miles southwest of Boulder Junction, offers a choice of shaded or open sites alongside Rudolph Lake. Camp Holiday has 100 seasonal campers, 21 pull-through sites, and a typical site width of 40 feet. The lake offers excellent fishing for largemouth bass and panfish and the area is known as the musky capital of the world. Laid out in a series of loops, the facility's most popular sites are by the lake. Sightings of eagles, nesting loons, and beaver are common in the area. Security and safety measures include a ten-mph speed limit (rather high with all the activities going on), a ban on motors on the lake, quiet time from 10:30 p.m. to 7:30 a.m., and owners who live on site and offer regular patrols of the campground. Since it is open until Nov. 1, Camp Holiday is a good place to enjoy the fall foliage.

## BASICS

**Operated by:** Al & Lila Vehrs. **Open:** May 1–Nov. 1. **Site Assignment:** Reservations held w/ 1-night deposit on credit card; no fee w/ 7-day notice of cancellation. **Registration:** At campground office. **Fee:** $25 (cash, check, credit cards). **Parking:** At site.

## FACILITIES

**Number of RV Sites:** 159. **Number of Tent-Only Sites:** 2. **Hookups:** Electric (30, 50 amps), water, sewer, phone. **Each Site:** Picnic table, fire ring. **Dump Station:** Yes. **Laundry:** Yes. **Pay Phone:** Yes. **Rest Rooms and Showers:** Yes. **Fuel:** No. **Propane:** Yes. **Internal Roads:** Paved/gravel, in good condition. **RV Service:** No. **Market:** 4 mi. northeast in Boulder Junction. **Restaurant:** 4 mi. northeast in Boulder Junction. **General Store:** Yes, limited. **Vending:** No. **Swimming Pool:** No. **Playground:** Yes. **Other:** Rudolph Lake, swimming beach, horseshoes, volleyball, basketball, shuffleboard, rec hall, game room, trails, boat launch, fishing lake. **Activities:** Swimming, fishing, boating (rental rowboats, canoes, kayaks available), scheduled weekend activities, hiking. **Nearby Attractions:** Lakes, forest, antiques, hiking, boating, cross-county skiing, bicycling, arts & crafts, scenic drive. **Additional Information:** Boulder Junction Chamber of Commerce, (800) 466-8579.

## RESTRICTIONS

**Pets:** Leash only. **Fires:** Fire ring only. **Alcoholic Beverages:** Permitted. **Vehicle Maximum Length:** 45 ft.

## TO GET THERE

From the junction of US 51 and CR H, drive 3 mi. northeast on CR H, then 500 feet east on Rudolph Lake Ln. Roads are generally wide and well maintained w/ narrow shoulders in some areas.

## BRISTOL

### Happy Acres Kampground

22230 45th St., Bristol 53104. T: (262) 857-7373; www.happyacres.com; info@happyacres.com.

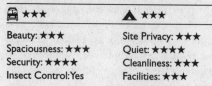

🚐 ★★★                          ⛺ ★★★

| | |
|---|---|
| Beauty: ★★★ | Site Privacy: ★★★ |
| Spaciousness: ★★★ | Quiet: ★★★★ |
| Security: ★★★★ | Cleanliness: ★★★ |
| Insect Control: Yes | Facilities: ★★★ |

Established by veteran campers in 1970, Happy Acres Kampground is a popular place with families. Reservations are recommended for all weekends between Memorial Day and Labor Day. Reservations are mandatory and must be finalized at least two weeks prior to a holiday weekend. Located halfway between Chicago and Milwaukee about nine miles off I-94, Happy Acres offers convenient access for travelers. Laid out in a series of loops, the campground has 46 seasonal campers and 13 pull-through sites. A rolling grassy campground, Happy Acres has open and wooded sites. The best sites are 61, 62, and 64 because they are by the lake and offer more green space. A separate tenting area allows privacy from RVs and more trees and greenery. The campground has 25 acres of walking trails. The speed limit is ten mph, and rules note that the facility "is not a drivers education training site." Mini-bikes, dirt bikes, mopeds, go-carts, and golf carts are not allowed. Quiet time from 10 p.m. to 9 a.m. is strictly enforced. The owners live on site and provide 24-hour security protection for the campground.

#### BASICS

**Operated by:** Bill & Irene Davis. **Open:** May 1–Sept. 30. **Site Assignment:** Reservations w/ 1-night deposit; refund (minus $5) w/ 7-day notice. **Registration:** At campground office. **Fee:** $30 (cash, check, credit cards). **Parking:** At site.

#### FACILITIES

**Number of RV Sites:** 150. **Number of Tent-Only Sites:** 18. **Hookups:** Electric (20, 30 amps), water. **Each Site:** Picnic table, fire ring. **Dump Station:** Yes. **Laundry:** Yes. **Pay Phone:** Yes. **Rest Rooms and Showers:** Yes. **Fuel:** No. **Propane:** Yes. **Internal Roads:** Gravel, in good condition. **RV Service:** No. **Market:** 3 mi. south in Padlock Lake. **Restaurant:** 1 mi. east. **General Store:** Yes.

**Vending:** Yes. **Swimming Pool:** Yes. **Playground:** Yes. **Other:** Mini zoo, pond, hiking trails, pavilion, swimming beach, mini golf, horseshoes, volleyball, basketball, lounge, game room, boat dock, rental cabins, rental trailers. **Activities:** Swimming, fishing, hiking, boating (rental rowboats, paddleboats available), scheduled weekend activities. **Nearby Attractions:** Six Flags Great America, Milwaukee Zoo, Dairyland Dog Track, Lake Geneva, Lake Michigan, outlet malls, antiques, arts & crafts, golf, scenic drive. **Additional Information:** Kenosha Area Chamber of Commerce, (800) 654-7309.

#### RESTRICTIONS

**Pets:** Leash only, "leave nervous watch dogs home". **Fires:** Fire ring only. **Alcoholic Beverages:** Permitted. **Vehicle Maximum Length:** None.

#### TO GET THERE

From the junction of Hwy. 50 and US 45, drive 2 mi. north on US 45, then 1.5 mi. west on CR NN. Roads are wide and well maintained w/ sometimes narrow shoulders.

## BRUSSELS

### Quietwoods South Camping Resort

9245 Lovers Ln., Brussels 54204. T: (888) 378-2005

🚐 ★★★                          ⛺ ★★★

| | |
|---|---|
| Beauty: ★★★ | Site Privacy: ★★★ |
| Spaciousness: ★★★ | Quiet: ★★★ |
| Security: ★★★★ | Cleanliness: ★★★★ |
| Insect Control: Yes | Facilities: ★★★ |

Quietwoods South Camping Resort, located four miles north of Brussels, is the first campground as you enter Door County. Many of its campers are returnees, along with 65 seasonals. The campground offers secluded, wooded sites in a rural area. The typical site width is 36 feet, with eight pull-throughs. Tents are in a separate area with more green space and privacy. Security measures include one-way roads and an owner who lives on site and provides regular patrols of the campground.

#### BASICS

**Operated by:** Michael & Christine Mar.ant. **Open:** May 1–Oct. 15. **Site Assignment:** Reservations w/ $20 deposit; refund w/ 1-week notice. **Registration:** At campground office. **Fee:** $23 (cash, check, credit cards). **Parking:** At site.

## FACILITIES

**Number of RV Sites:** 150. **Number of Tent-Only Sites:** 10. **Hookups:** Electric (30 amps), water. **Each Site:** Picnic table, fire ring. **Dump Station:** Yes. **Laundry:** Yes. **Pay Phone:** Yes. **Rest Rooms and Showers:** Yes. **Fuel:** No. **Propane:** No. **Internal Roads:** Paved/gravel, in good condition. **RV Service:** No. **Market:** 4 mi. south in Brussels. **Restaurant:** 4 mi. south in Brussels. **General Store:** Yes. **Vending:** Yes. **Swimming Pool:** Yes. **Playground:** Yes. **Other:** Game room, pavilion, mini-golf, volleyball, game room, adult lounge, horseshoes, baseball, fishing pond, rental trailers & pop-ups, small bar. **Activities:** Swimming, fishing, scheduled weekend activities. **Nearby Attractions:** Door County, cherry & apple orchards, fishing, golf, hiking, boating, Lake Michigan, Green Bay, historic sites, antiques, arts & crafts shops, summer stock theatre, parks, bike trails. **Additional Information:** Door County Chamber of Commerce, (800) 527-3529.

## RESTRICTIONS

**Pets:** Leash only. **Fires:** Fire ring only. **Alcoholic Beverages:** Permitted. **Vehicle Maximum Length:** None.

## TO GET THERE

From the junction of Hwy. 57 and CR C, drive 2.5 mi. north on CR C, then 1.5 mi. east on CR K, then 0.5 mi. north on Lovers Ln. The roads are wide and well maintained w/ broad shoulders.

## CALEDONIA

## Yogi Bear's Jellystone Park Camp-Resort

8425 WI 38, Caledonia 53108. T: (262) 835-2565; www.jellystone-caledonia.com; yogipark@aol.com.

| 🚐 ★★★★ | 🛖 ★★★ |
|---|---|
| Beauty: ★★★ | Site Privacy: ★★★ |
| Spaciousness: ★★★ | Quiet: ★★★ |
| Security: ★★★★ | Cleanliness: ★★★ |
| Insect Control: None | Facilities: ★★★★ |

Located one mile south of Oak Creek, Yogi Bear's Jellystone Camp-Resort is a popular destination in itself as well as a camping spot for Milwaukee visitors. Most sites are level and shaded with gravel spots for RVs. The campground has no seasonal campers and offers 22 pull-throughs. Tent campers have a separate area with more green space and privacy. The best sites for RVs are on Jellystone Ave. because they are bigger and located near the pool and other facilities. A five-mph speed limit is enforced, as is quiet time from 11 p.m. to 8 a.m. Ill-mannered conduct is not tolerated, nor is the use of foul language. Security measures include one entrance/exit to the campground, security guards, and a park manager who lives on site.

## BASICS

**Operated by:** Jim & Ellen Votaw. **Open:** Apr. 15–Oct. 15. **Site Assignment:** Reservations w/ $50 deposit, $75 for holidays; refund (minus $5 fee) w/ 7-day notice. **Registration:** At campground office. **Fee:** $38 (cash, check, credit cards). **Parking:** At site.

## FACILITIES

**Number of RV Sites:** 222. **Number of Tent-Only Sites:** 25. **Hookups:** Electric (30, 50 amps), water, sewer. **Each Site:** Picnic table, fire ring. **Dump Station:** Yes. **Laundry:** Yes. **Pay Phone:** Yes. **Rest Rooms and Showers:** Yes. **Fuel:** No. **Propane:** Yes. **Internal Roads:** Paved/gravel, in good condition. **RV Service:** No. **Market:** 1 mi. north in Oak Creek. **Restaurant:** 1 mi. north in Oak Creek. **General Store:** Yes. **Vending:** Yes. **Swimming Pool:** Yes. **Playground:** Yes. **Other:** Adult lounge, cafe, mini golf, volleyball, basketball, game room, fishing pond, rental cabins, kiddie pool, recreation field, cartoon theatre. **Activities:** Swimming, kiddie fishing, scheduled activities. **Nearby Attractions:** Zoo, brewery tours, golf, antiques, arts & crafts, museum, historic homes, nature center, baseball. **Additional Information:** Greater Milwaukee CVB, (800) 554-1448.

## RESTRICTIONS

**Pets:** Leash only. **Fires:** Fire ring only. **Alcoholic Beverages:** At sites only. **Vehicle Maximum Length:** 40 ft.

## TO GET THERE

From I-94, take Exit 326 and drive 2 mi. east on Seven Mile Rd., then 0.25 mi. north on Hwy. 38. Roads are wide and well maintained w/ broad shoulders.

## CAMPBELLSPORT

### Benson's Century Camping Resort

N3845 Hwy. 67, Campbellsport 53010. T: (920) 533-8597

🚐 ★★                    ⛺ ★★★

Beauty: ★★★              Site Privacy: ★★★
Spaciousness: ★★★        Quiet: ★★★★
Security: ★★★★           Cleanliness: ★★★★
Insect Control: None      Facilities: ★★

Long Lake forms the centerpiece of Benson's Century Camping Resort, located nine miles east of Campbellsport. Arranged in a series of loops, the campground offers mostly shaded, grassy sites, with three pull-throughs and 100 seasonal campers. The typical site width is 35 feet. Safety measures include a five-mph speed limit, no mini-bikes allowed, and no parking on roadway. Throwing stones in the campground or lake is also prohibited. Tent sites are in a separate area away from RVs with more trees and green space. Security includes one entrance/exit past the office, owners who live on site providing regular campground patrols, and police officers who keep an eye on the campground.

### BASICS

**Operated by:** Nancy Benson. **Open:** May 15–Oct. 15. **Site Assignment:** Reservations w/ 1-night deposit; no refund. **Registration:** At campground office. **Fee:** $20 (cash, check). **Parking:** At site.

### FACILITIES

**Number of RV Sites:** 168. **Number of Tent-Only Sites:** 82. **Hookups:** Electric (50 amps), water. **Each Site:** Picnic table, fire ring. **Dump Station:** Yes. **Laundry:** No. **Pay Phone:** Yes. **Rest Rooms and Showers:** Yes. **Fuel:** No. **Propane:** Yes. **Internal Roads:** Paved, in good condition. **RV Service:** No. **Market:** 9 mi. west in Campbellsport. **Restaurant:** Next door. **General Store:** Yes, limited. **Vending:** Yes. **Swimming Pool:** No. **Playground:** Yes. **Other:** Long Lake, boat launch, pier, beach, rec room, snack bar, horseshoes, volleyball, game room, sports field. **Activities:** Swimming, fishing, boating (rental fishing boats, canoes, paddleboats available). **Nearby Attractions:** Riding stables, golf, hiking trails, trout ponds, Kettle Moraine, historic homes, museums, antiques, arts & crafts. **Additional Information:** Fond du Lac Area CVB, (800) 937-9123.

### RESTRICTIONS

**Pets:** Leash only. **Fires:** Fire ring only. **Alcoholic Beverages:** Permitted. **Vehicle Maximum Length:** 38 ft.

### TO GET THERE

From the junction of US 45 and Hwy. 67, drive 6 mi. northeast on Hwy. 67

## CHETEK

### Chetek River Campground

590 24th St., Chetek 54728. T: (715) 924-2440; www.chetekriver.com; camp@chetekriver.com.

🚐 ★★★★                  ⛺ ★★★

Beauty: ★★★              Site Privacy: ★★★★
Spaciousness: ★★★★       Quiet: ★★★★
Security: ★★★★           Cleanliness: ★★★★
Insect Control: None      Facilities: ★★★

Chetek River Campground does so many little things right, and that all adds up to a very pleasant campground. Some of the extras: guests may visit campers free of charge (there is a $2 charge to swim), and free "doggie bags" for cleaning up after pets are available at the office. The campground is chock full of activities for children, including a local high school basketball coach who offers clinics and games every Saturday. Located less than a mile west of Chetek, the campground is situated on the Chetek River, where you can take a tubing trip or rent a canoe. The rural campground has 50 seasonals and is booked up almost every weekend, so reservations are strongly recommended. Laid out in a series of loops, the campground has a typical site width of 36 feet, with back-in, grassy, open sites. A popular spot for family reunions, the campground has a giant grill that can hold 50 pieces of chicken. Quiet hours from 10 p.m. to 8 a.m. are enforced, as is a five-mph speed limit. Owners live on site and provide 24-hour security. With all those children enjoying river activities and other outdoors play, it sure would be nice to have laundry facilities at such a top-notch family campground.

### BASICS

**Operated by:** Jan Gebhardt & Christine Gay. **Open:** May 1–Sept. 30. **Site Assignment:** Reservations w/ 1-night deposit; refund w/ 7-day notice. **Registration:** At campground office. **Fee:** $22 (cash, check). **Parking:** At site.

## FACILITIES

**Number of RV Sites:** 100. **Number of Tent-Only Sites:** 0. **Hookups:** Electric (20, 30 amps), water. **Each Site:** Picnic table, fire ring. **Dump Station:** Yes. **Laundry:** No. **Pay Phone:** Yes. **Rest Rooms and Showers:** yes. **Fuel:** No. **Propane:** No. **Internal Roads:** Paved/gravel, in good condition. **RV Service:** No. **Market:** 1 mi. east in Chetek. **Restaurant:** 1 mi. east in Chetek. **General Store:** No. **Vending:** Yes. **Swimming Pool:** Yes. **Playground:** Yes. **Other:** Red Cedar River, basketball, volleyball, shuffleboard, horseshoes, mini-golf, pool table, ping pong, air hockey, video games, TV room, badminton, recreation field, scheduled weekend activities. **Activities:** Swimming, fishing, tubing trips, boating (rental canoes available), biking, (rental pedal karts available). **Nearby Attractions:** Museums, golf, fishing lakes, antiques. **Additional Information:** Chippewa Valley CVB, (888) 523-3866.

## RESTRICTIONS

**Pets:** Leash only. **Fires:** Fire ring only. **Alcoholic Beverages:** Permitted. **Vehicle Maximum Length:** 40 ft. **Other:** Bury fish guts in a designated area. Shovels are provided.

## TO GET THERE

From the junction of US 53 and Hwy. 1, take Exit 126, drive 0.25 mi. south on Hwy. 1 to River Rd., then 0.75 mi. south on River Rd. Roads are wide and well maintained w/ good shoulders.

## CHIPPEWA FALLS

### O'Neil Creek Campground & RV Park

14956 105th Ave., Chippewa Falls 54729. T: (715) 723-6581; www.discover-net.net/~oneilcreek; oneilcreek@discover-net.net.

🚐 ★★★★          ⛺ ★★★★

| | |
|---|---|
| Beauty: ★★★★ | Site Privacy: ★★★ |
| Spaciousness: ★★★ | Quiet: ★★★★ |
| Security: ★★★★ | Cleanliness: ★★★★ |
| Insect Control: None | Facilities: ★★★★ |

Located four miles north of Chippewa Falls, O'Neil Creek Campground & RV Park has level, shaded, wooded sites, some along a gently flowing creek. The campground has 200 seasonal campers, 16 pull-through sites, and a typical site width of 28 feet. Be aware that all full hookups are occupied by seasonals. Campers have direct access to Lake Wissota and the Chippewa River system. Motor downstream from the campground on O'Neil Creek to Lake Wissota (15 miles long and three miles wide) and the Chippewa River system. Tent sites are in a separate area with privacy from RVs and more green space. Showers and rest rooms are tiled and very clean. A nice benefit is no visitor fee. However, all visitors must leave the campground by 11 p.m., or they will be charged as an overnight guest.

## BASICS

**Operated by:** Mike & Judy Rabska. **Open:** Apr. 15–Oct. 15. **Site Assignment:** Reservations w/ 1-night deposit; refund (minus $5) w/ 7-day notice. **Registration:** At campground office. **Fee:** $30 (cash, check, credit cards). **Parking:** At site.

## FACILITIES

**Number of RV Sites:** 390. **Number of Tent-Only Sites:** 35. **Hookups:** Electric (20, 30, 50 amps), water, sewer, phone. **Each Site:** Picnic table, fire ring. **Dump Station:** Yes. **Laundry:** Yes. **Pay Phone:** Yes. **Rest Rooms and Showers:** Yes. **Fuel:** No. **Propane:** Yes. **Internal Roads:** Paved/gravel, in good condition. **RV Service:** No. **Market:** 4 mi. south in Chippewa Falls. **Restaurant:** 4 mi. south in Chippewa Falls. **General Store:** Yes. **Vending:** Yes. **Swimming Pool:** No. **Playground:** Yes. **Other:** O'Neil Creek, nature trails, boat ramp, rec room, horseshoes, volleyball, mini golf, boat dock, rental cabins, pavilion, coin games, basketball, sports field. **Activities:** Swimming, hiking, boating (rental paddleboats, rowboats & canoes available), fishing, float trips, scheduled activities. **Nearby Attractions:** Golf, Lake Wissota, Chippewa Rose Society Garden, Irvine Park, zoo, swimming pool, tennis, Glen Loch Dam aned Overlook, museum, Leinenkugel Brewery, antiques, arts & crafts. **Additional Information:** Chippewa Falls Area Chamber of Commerce, (888) 723-0024.

## RESTRICTIONS

**Pets:** Leash only. **Fires:** Fire ring only. **Alcoholic Beverages:** Permitted. **Vehicle Maximum Length:** None.

## TO GET THERE

From the junction of Hwy. 124 and US 53, drive 5 mi. north on US 53, then 2 mi. east on County Trunk S, then 2 mi. north on Hwy. 124, then 0.75 mi. east on 105th Ave. Roads are generally wide and well maintained w/ broad shoulders, though there is one bad curve down to campground.

## COLOMA

### Coloma Camperland

N 1130 5th Rd., Coloma 54930. T: (715) 228-3611; www.colomacamperland.com; colomarv@uniontel.net.

🚐 ★★★                    ⛺ ★★★

Beauty: ★★★              Site Privacy: ★★★
Spaciousness: ★★★        Quiet: ★★★★
Security: ★★★★           Cleanliness: ★★★★
Insect Control: None     Facilities: ★★★

It's not a pleasant subject to mention, but if an RV had to break down, this would be the place to do it. Coloma Camperland offers camper sales, RV parts, supplies and services—along with being a nice place to stay. Located off Hwy. 39 and 21 in Coloma, Camperland has six large (40 × 50 feet), grassy pull-through sites, the most requested ones in the campground. Laid out in a series of loops, the campground offers both wooded and open sites. A family campground and a comfortable spot for overnight travelers, Camperland has good security with only one way into the facility, owners who live on site, and patrols by night personnel. For safety, bike riding is not allowed in the campground after dark.

**BASICS**

**Operated by:** Chris & Carole Johnson. **Open:** Apr. 1–Dec. 1. **Site Assignment:** Reservations w/ $20 deposit, refund w/ 2-week notice. **Registration:** At campground office. **Fee:** $20. **Parking:** At site.

**FACILITIES**

**Number of RV Sites:** 85. **Number of Tent-Only Sites:** 10. **Hookups:** Electric (30 amps), water, sewer. **Each Site:** Picnic table, fire ring. **Dump Station:** Yes. **Laundry:** Yes. **Pay Phone:** Yes. **Rest Rooms and Showers:** Yes. **Fuel:** No. **Propane:** Yes. **Internal Roads:** Gravel, in fair condition. **RV Service:** Yes. **Market:** 0.5 mi. north in Coloma. **Restaurant:** 0.5 mi. north in Coloma. **General Store:** Yes. **Vending:** Yes. **Swimming Pool:** Yes. **Playground:** Yes. **Other:** Game room, shelter, volleyball, shuffleboard, horseshoes, sports field. **Activities:** Swimming, planned weekend activities. **Nearby Attractions:** Fishing, hunting, snowmobile trail, golf, biking, horseback riding, scenic drive, 35 minutes to casino, Wisconsin Dells. **Additional Information:** Wisconsin Dells Visitor & Convention Bureau, (800) 223-3557.

**RESTRICTIONS**

**Pets:** Leash only. **Fires:** Fire pits only. **Alcoholic Beverages:** At sites only. **Vehicle Maximum Length:** None.

**TO GET THERE**

From the junction of Hwy. 51 and 21, drive 0.25 mi. east on Hwy. 21, then 1 mi. south on CR CH. Roads are wide and well maintained w/ good shoulders.

## CRIVITZ

### High Falls Family Camping

W11594 Archer Ln., Crivitz 54114. T: (715) 757-3399; www.exploringthenorth.com/highfalls/campground.html; hffc@cybrzn.com.

🚐 ★                        ⛺ ★★

Beauty: ★★★              Site Privacy: ★★
Spaciousness: ★★         Quiet: ★★
Security: ★★★            Cleanliness: ★★
Insect Control: None     Facilities: ★★

Located 13 miles west of Crivitz, High Falls Family Campground is starting an expansion project to provide new bathrooms and showers, a laundry and new store. The result should be a more user-friendly campground. The campground offers wooded and open sites in a rural setting. Laid out in a series of loops, the grassy campground has one pull-through site and 39 seasonal campers. A primitive tent camping area also includes walk-in sites for a more secluded spot. Security measures include a five-mph speed limit and one-way roads. Quiet hours are 10 p.m. to 8 a.m. Paths leading to the lake are on property owned by Wisconsin Public Service Corporation, and visitors must respect the land and avoid littering. Boats must be moored at public landings and not along the shoreline. Security includes owners who live on site and provide regular campground patrols.

**BASICS**

**Operated by:** Ed & Cheryl Wruk & Leonard & Cindy Wahl. **Open:** May 1–Oct. 15. **Site Assignment:** Reservations w/ 50 percent deposit, 100 percent on holidays; refund (less $4 fee) w/ 10-day notice. **Registration:** At campground office. **Fee:** $15 (cash, check, credit cards). **Parking:** At site.

**FACILITIES**

**Number of RV Sites:** 88. **Number of Tent-Only Sites:** 8. **Hookups:** Electric (20, 30, 50 amps), water. **Each Site:** Picnic table, fire ring. **Dump Station:** Yes. **Laundry:** No. **Pay Phone:** Yes. **Rest Rooms and Showers:** No. **Fuel:** No. **Propane:** No. **Internal Roads:** Gravel, in fair condition. **RV Service:** No. **Market:** 13 mi. east in Crivitz. **Restaurant:** 1 mi. northwest. **General Store:** Yes, limited. **Vending:** Yes. **Swimming Pool:** No. **Playground:** Yes. **Other:** Nature trails, volleyball, horseshoes, basketball, lake. **Activities:** Swimming, hiking, fishing, boating (rental hydrobikes & canoes available), scheduled weekend activities. **Nearby Attractions:** Golf, tennis, water ski shows, river & lake fishing, white water rafting, horseback riding, flea markets, antiques, museums, waterfalls. **Additional Information:** Marinette County Area Chamber of Commerce, (800) 236-6681.

## RESTRICTIONS

**Pets:** Leash only. **Fires:** Fire ring only. **Alcoholic Beverages:** Permitted. **Vehicle Maximum Length:** 36 ft.

## TO GET THERE

From the junction of US 141 and CR W, drive 0.5 mi. west on CR W, then 8 mi. northwest on CR A, then 3.5 mi. west on CR X, then 0.25 mi. south on Boat Landing Rd. 3, then 0.25 mi. west on Archer Ln. Roads are wide and well maintained w/ broad shoulders.

## CRIVITZ

### Peshtigo River Campground

W7948 Airport Rd., Crivitz 54114. T: (715) 854-2986; F: (715) 854-3120; peshti@cybrzn.com.

| 🚐 ★★★ | ⛺ ★★★★ |
|---|---|
| Beauty: ★★★ | Site Privacy: ★★★ |
| Spaciousness: ★★★★ | Quiet: ★★★ |
| Security: ★★★★ | Cleanliness: ★★★★ |
| Insect Control: Yes | Facilities: ★★★ |

The Peshtigo River Campground calls it "stress reduction therapy"—floating down the historic Pestigo River in a big innertube, stopping along the way for a sandbar picnic, if you want. After the two- to six-hour trip, all pressure (except that in the tubes) should be gone, they say. The campground offers free shuttles to the put-in. Camping sites are level and shaded, with most backing up into the woods. To ensure future shade, small trees have been planted, and campers are welcome to "adopt" a tree and water it during their stay. The typical site width is 50 feet, with eight pull-throughs and 40 seasonal campers. A separate area for tent campers provides more green space and privacy. Some open sites for RVs are located near the front of the campground, which is one mile south of Crivitz. Quiet time between 11 p.m. and 7 a.m. is enforced Safety measures include one-way roads and a ten-mph speed limit, rather high for such a child-friendly campground. Security is provided by one entrance and exit, regular patrols, and an owner (a retired police officer) who lives on site.

## BASICS

**Operated by:** Rick Greene. **Open:** May 1–Dec. 1. **Site Assignment:** Reservations w/ $20 deposit; refund (minus 20 percent service charge) w/ 2-week notice. **Registration:** At campground office. **Fee:** $20 (cash, check, credit cards). **Parking:** At site.

## FACILITIES

**Number of RV Sites:** 100. **Number of Tent-Only Sites:** 10. **Hookups:** Electric (20, 30 amps), water. **Each Site:** Picnic table, fire ring. **Dump Station:** Yes. **Laundry:** Yes. **Pay Phone:** Yes. **Rest Rooms and Showers:** Yes. **Fuel:** No. **Propane:** No. **Internal Roads:** Gravel, in good condition. **RV Service:** Yes. **Market:** 1 mi. north in Crivitz. **Restaurant:** 1 mi. north in Crivitz. **General Store:** Yes. **Vending:** Yes. **Swimming Pool:** No. **Playground:** Yes. **Other:** Peshtigo River, swimming area, horseshoes, volleyball, nature trails, fish freezer, rental cabins, rec room, pavilion, sports field. **Activities:** Swimming, river tubing (rental tubes available), boating (rental canoes available), fishing, hiking, scheduled activities. **Nearby Attractions:** Golf, tennis, water ski shows, river & lake fishing, white water rafting, riding stables, flea markets, antiques, museums, waterfalls. **Additional Information:** Marinette County Area Chamber of Commerce, (800) 236-6681.

## RESTRICTIONS

**Pets:** Leash only. **Fires:** Fire ring only. **Alcoholic Beverages:** Permitted. **Vehicle Maximum Length:** None.

## TO GET THERE

From the junction of US 141 and CR W, drive 2 mi. south on US 141, then 500 feet west on Airport Rd. Roads are wide and well maintained w/ broad shoulders.

## DE SOTO

### Mississippi Sports and Recreation

E870 Hwy. 35, De Sota 54624. T: (608) 648-3630;
tghelf@aol.com.

🚐 ★★                              ⛺ ★★★

Beauty: ★★                  Site Privacy: ★★
Spaciousness: ★★★      Quiet: ★★★
Security: ★★★★          Cleanliness: ★★★
Insect Control: None      Facilities: ★★★

Mississippi Sports and Recreation is a work in
progress. Started in 1999 by an energetic young
man, the campground has three important things
going for it—convenience, price, and access to
the Mississippi River. An easy pull-in off Hwy.
35, the campground is near the Mississippi River
and offers campsites with electric hookups for a
low $10. With river activities as its primary draw,
the campground offers a very well-stocked tackle
shop along with a marina and boat rentals. The
idea is for a camper to be able to put a boat in the
river, moor it in a boat slip, and leave it for a
weekend or full week of water activities. Not just
a summer resort, this campground two miles
north of De Soto attracts RV campers in the winter for ice fishing and snowmobiling. Laid out in
a series of loops, the campground offers back-in
and pull-through sites, but the sites are rather
small and not well screened by greenery yet.

### BASICS

**Operated by:** Thomas L. Ghelf. **Open:** All year.
**Site Assignment:** Reservations w/ no deposit.
**Registration:** At campground office. **Fee:** $10
(cash, check). **Parking:** At site.

### FACILITIES

**Number of RV Sites:** 25. **Number of Tent-
Only Sites:** 20. **Hookups:** Electric (30 amps),
water. **Each Site:** Picnic table, fire ring. **Dump
Station:** No. **Laundry:** Yes. **Pay Phone:** Yes. **Rest
Rooms and Showers:** Yes. **Fuel:** No. **Propane:**
No. **Internal Roads:** Gravel, in good condition. **RV
Service:** No. **Market:** 7 mi. south in Lansing.
**Restaurant:** 2 mi. south in DeSoto. **General
Store:** Yes. **Vending:** No. **Swimming Pool:** No.
**Playground:** Yes. **Other:** Bait & tackle store, full-
service marina repair, walking trails, fish-cleaning
facility, pond, boat dock, marina. **Activities:** Fishing,
boating (rental motor boats available), hiking, fishing
tournaments, live music twice a month. **Nearby**

**Attractions:** State parks, museums, historic
homes, golf, scenic drives. **Additional Information:** Prairie du Chien Chamber of Commerce,
(800) 732-1673.

### RESTRICTIONS

**Pets:** Yes. **Fires:** Fire pits only. **Alcoholic Beverages:** Permitted. **Vehicle Maximum Length:**
None.

### TO GET THERE

Take Hwy. 35 and drive 2 mi. north of De Soto.
Roads are wide and well maintained w/ good
shoulders.

## EAGLE RIVER

### Pine Aire Resort & Campground

4443 Chain O' Lakes Rd., Eagle River 54521.
T: (800) 597-6777; F: (715) 479-2658;
www.pine-aire.com; vacation@pine-aire.com.

🚐 ★★★★                         ⛺ ★★★★

Beauty: ★★★★            Site Privacy: ★★★
Spaciousness: ★★★      Quiet: ★★★★
Security: ★★★★          Cleanliness: ★★★★
Insect Control: ★★★     Facilities: ★★★★

Located in the beautiful Northwoods lakes region
two miles north of Eagle River, Pine Aire Resort
and Campground seems an unlikely place to find
a gourmet restaurant. But the Logging Camp
Kitchen & Still features surprising dining
choices, such as veal Chardonnay with wild
mushrooms and barley risotto, plus special cranberry applesauce and chutney made in the
kitchen. Craft workshops at the Calico Cottage
also let you know this is not an ordinary campground. Laid out in a series of loops, the campground has a choice of open or shaded sites. It has
19 seasonal campers, 13 pull-through sites, and a
typical site width of 20 feet. Some lakeside campsites are available. The campground is a popular
spot because of the wealth of recreational activities available and because of its quiet, natural surroundings. Regular night security keeps a close
eye on the campground.

### BASICS

**Operated by:** Ron & Cindy Meinholz. **Open:** All
year. **Site Assignment:** Reservations w/ $25
deposit; refund w/ 2-week notice. **Registration:** At
campground office. **Fee:** $42 (cash, check, credit
cards). **Parking:** At site.

## FACILITIES

**Number of RV Sites:** 121. **Number of Tent-Only Sites:** 15. **Hookups:** Electric (15, 20, 30 amps), water, sewer. **Each Site:** Picnic table, fire ring. **Dump Station:** Yes. **Laundry:** Yes. **Pay Phone:** Yes. **Rest Rooms and Showers:** Yes. **Fuel:** No. **Propane:** Yes. **Internal Roads:** Paved/gravel, in good condition. **RV Service:** No. **Market:** 2 mi. south in Eagle River. **Restaurant:** On site. **General Store:** Yes, limited. **Vending:** Yes. **Swimming Pool:** No. **Playground:** Yes. **Other:** Swimming lake, rec room, restaurant, volleyball, basketball, lounge, game room, tennis, marina, snack bar, bar, pavilion, trails, boat launch, rental cottages,. **Activities:** Swimming, fishing, hiking, boating (rental motor boats, canoes, paddleboats, rowboats, pontoons, ski boats, wave runners, acqua cycles available), scheduled activities. **Nearby Attractions:** Casinos, golf, historic boathouses, Nicolet National Forest, Ottawa National Forest, scenic drives, antiques, arts & crafts, ski trails, Trees For Tomorrow Environmental Education Center. **Additional Information:** Eagle River Area Chamber of Commerce, (800) 359-6315.

## RESTRICTIONS

**Pets:** Leash only. **Fires:** Fire ring only. **Alcoholic Beverages:** Permitted. **Vehicle Maximum Length:** None.

## TO GET THERE

From the junction of Hwy. 70 and Northbound US 45, drive 3 mi. north on US 45, then 0.1 mi. east on Chain-O-Lakes road. Roads are mostly wide and well maintained w/ narrow shoulders in spots.

## EAU CLAIRE

## Elmer's RV Park and Campgrounds

8027 Hwy. 12, Fall Creek 54742. T: (715) 832-6277

🚐 ★★          ▲ ★★

| | |
|---|---|
| Beauty: ★★ | Site Privacy: ★★ |
| Spaciousness: ★★ | Quiet: ★★★ |
| Security: ★★★ | Cleanliness: ★★★ |
| Insect Control: None | Facilities: ★★ |

Elmer Backstrom went broke growing beans on this property, so 35 years ago he turned it into a campground. He knows most every birch, pine, and poplar tree on the site because he planted them himself. The major pluses for the campground are the convenience it offers, easy access from US 53, and eight pull-through sites, in addition to a very reasonable price. The major minuses are small sites (some 22 × 50 feet) located too close together and no general store or swimming pool. Sites are generally grassy and shady. Most campers who stay at Elmer's are either overnight travelers or people who are visiting the area for family and friends. Elmer lives on the site and keeps a close eye on the comings and goings.

## BASICS

**Operated by:** Elmer Backstrom. **Open:** Apr. 15–Oct. 15. **Site Assignment:** First come, first served. **Registration:** At campground office. **Fee:** $14 (cash, check). **Parking:** At site.

## FACILITIES

**Number of RV Sites:** 30. **Number of Tent-Only Sites:** 5. **Hookups:** Electric (30 amps), water, sewer. **Each Site:** Picnic table, fire ring. **Dump Station:** No. **Laundry:** Yes. **Pay Phone:** Yes. **Rest Rooms and Showers:** Yes. **Fuel:** No. **Propane:** No. **Internal Roads:** Gravel, in good condition. **RV Service:** No. **Market:** 4 mi. west in Eau Claire. **Restaurant:** 4 mi. west in Eau Claire. **General Store:** No. **Vending:** Yes. **Swimming Pool:** No. **Playground:** Yes. **Activities:** None. **Nearby Attractions:** Park, Chippewa Valley Museum, Paul Bunyan Logging Camp & Interpretive Center. **Additional Information:** Chippewa Valley CVB, (888) 523-3866.

## RESTRICTIONS

**Pets:** Leash only. **Fires:** Fire ring only. **Alcoholic Beverages:** Permitted. **Vehicle Maximum Length:** None.

## TO GET THERE

From the junction of US 53 and Hwy. 12, drive east 4.5 mi. on Hwy. 12. Roads are wide and well maintained w/ broad shoulders

## EDGERTON

## Creekview Campground

748 Albion Rd., Edgerton 53534. T: (608) 884-3288

🚐 ★★          ▲ ★★

| | |
|---|---|
| Beauty: ★★ | Site Privacy: ★★ |
| Spaciousness: ★★ | Quiet: ★★★★ |
| Security: ★★★★ | Cleanliness: ★★★ |
| Insect Control: None | Facilities: ★★ |

Creekview Campground is so low-key it doesn't even have a brochure. It did at one time, but most folks who stay at Creekview have either stayed there before or were told about the place by someone who did. With its easy access to a major interstate, it wouldn't be a bad place to spend the night while going or coming from someplace else. Located in a quiet country setting beside a creek, the campground caters to senior citizens. Eight of its sites are taken by seasonals who like the peaceful area. The level sites are grassy, shady, and there are a couple of pull-throughs. There are no planned activities, but there is a golf course within walking distance. Tent campers don't have a separate place set aside for them but are welcome to any of the sites. The favorite campsites are the eight by the creek. Security is good, since the owners live in a house in front of the campground; there is only one access road, and the grounds are patrolled. It also helps that the campground doesn't seem to attract campers who want to make noise.

## BASICS

**Operated by:** Howard & Jeanne Richardson. **Open:** Apr. 15–Oct. 31. **Site Assignment:** Reservations w/ no deposit. **Registration:** At campground office. **Fee:** $15. **Parking:** At site.

## FACILITIES

**Number of RV Sites:** 25. **Number of Tent-Only Sites:** 0. **Hookups:** Electric (20, 30, 50 amps), water. **Each Site:** Picnic table, fire ring. **Dump Station:** Yes. **Laundry:** No. **Pay Phone:** No. **Rest Rooms and Showers:** Yes. **Fuel:** No. **Propane:** No. **Internal Roads:** Gravel, in fair condition. **RV Service:** No. **Market:** 4 mi. south in Edgerton. **Restaurant:** 2 mi. northeast in Stoughton. **General Store:** No. **Vending:** No. **Swimming Pool:** No. **Playground:** No. **Other:** Rec room, pavilion, sports field, horseshoes, hiking trail. **Activities:** None. **Nearby Attractions:** Golf, swimming, boating, horseback riding, historic Milton House, Lake Koshkonong. **Additional Information:** Milton Area Chamber of Commerce, (608) 868-6222.

## RESTRICTIONS

**Pets:** Leash only. **Fires:** Fire ring only. **Alcoholic Beverages:** Permitted. **Vehicle Maximum Length:** None.

## TO GET THERE

From the junction of I-90 and Hwy. 51-73, take Exit 160 N, then drive 300 feet west and 1.5 mi. north on Albion Rd. Roads are in good condition w/ good shoulders.

## EDGERTON
## Hickory Hills Campground

856 Hillside Rd., Edgerton 53534. T: (608) 884-6327

🚐 ★★★★  ⛺ ★★★★

Beauty: ★★★★  Site Privacy: ★★★★★
Spaciousness: ★★★★★  Quiet: ★★★★★
Security: ★★★★★  Cleanliness: ★★★★★
Insect Control: None  Facilities: ★★★★

Hickory Hills Campground, located four miles north of Edgerton, certainly has personality. It's not all neatly laid out with same-size, same-look sites. Most sites are spacious, ranging from 40 × 60 to 30 × 45 feet. About evenly split between grassy and gravel sites, the wilderness setting offers mostly shady spots sheltered by mature hickory and oak trees. The campground store is not a jumble of odds and ends but an attractive arrangement of light groceries, ice cream, snacks, pop, camping supplies, toiletries, and bait, along with souvenirs and gift items. About half the camping sites are occupied by seasonals. All campers probably wish that Hickory Hills offered laundry facilities.

## BASICS

**Operated by:** Richard & Cynthia Poff. **Open:** May 1–Oct. 15. **Site Assignment:** Reservations for 2 nights or more w/ 1-night deposit; no refund but a camping credit if notified 48 hours in advance. **Registration:** At campground office. **Fee:** $28 (cash, check). **Parking:** At site.

## FACILITIES

**Number of RV Sites:** 300. **Number of Tent-Only Sites:** 0. **Hookups:** Electric (20, 30, 50 amps), water, sewer. **Each Site:** Picnic table. **Dump Station:** Yes. **Laundry:** No. **Pay Phone:** Yes. **Rest Rooms and Showers:** Yes. **Fuel:** No. **Propane:** Yes. **Internal Roads:** Gravel/paved, in good condition. **RV Service:** No. **Market:** 4 mi. south in Edgerton. **Restaurant:** 4 mi. south in Edgerton. **General Store:** Yes. **Vending:** Yes. **Swimming Pool:** Yes. **Playground:** Yes. **Other:** Mini-golf, shuffleboard, gameroom, snack bar, spring fed lake, juke box, lodge, horseshoes. **Activities:** Swimming, biking (rental bikes available) fishing, boating (rental boats available), planned weekend activities. **Nearby Attractions:** Horseback riding, golf, Lake Koshkonong, historic Milton House. **Additional Information:** Milton Area Chamber of Commerce, (608) 868-6222.

## RESTRICTIONS

**Pets:** Leash only. **Fires:** Fire ring only. **Alcoholic Beverages:** Permitted. **Vehicle Maximum Length:** None.

## TO GET THERE

From the junction of I-90 and Hwy. 73, take Exit 160, drive 0.5 mi. north on Hwy. 73, then 0.75 mi. east on Hwy. 106, then 0.75 mi. north on Hillside Rd. Roads are wide and well maintained w/ broad shoulders.

## EGG HARBOR
### Camp-Tel Family Campground

8164 Hwy. 42, Egg Harbor 54209. T: (920) 868-3278; FamilyCampground.homestead.com/Camptel.html; camptel@dcemail.com.

🚐 ★★                          🏕 ★★★

Beauty: ★★★                  Site Privacy: ★★
Spaciousness: ★★             Quiet: ★★★
Security: ★★★★              Cleanliness: ★★★★
Insect Control: None         Facilities: ★★★

Located in the heart of the Door County Peninsula, Camp-Tel Family Campground is one mile north of Egg Harbor, right off Hwy. 42. Sites are mostly shaded and gravel with two pull-throughs and 39 seasonal campers. The typical site width is 25 feet. Laid out in a series of loops, Camp-Tel offers a separate area for tent campers with more green space and privacy. For safety, a five-mph speed limit is enforced, and mini-bikes and skateboards are not permitted. Quiet time is from 10:30 p.m. to 7 a.m., and all children and teenagers are required to be at their sites during those hours. Be aware that running electric heaters and air conditioners is not allowed. Security includes one entrance/exit, owners who live on site, and a campground patrol. The owners also offer a reward for information leading to the arrest, conviction, and restitution in connection with damage to Camp-Tel property.

## BASICS

**Operated by:** Rich & Marian Irmens. **Open:** May 15–Oct. 15. **Site Assignment:** Reservations w/ 1-night deposit; refund (minus $5 service fee) w/ 7-day notice. **Registration:** At campground office. **Fee:** $19 (cash, check, credit cards). **Parking:** At site.

## FACILITIES

**Number of RV Sites:** 104. **Number of Tent-Only Sites:** 17. **Hookups:** Electric (20 amps), water. **Each Site:** Picnic table, fire ring. **Dump Station:** Yes. **Laundry:** Yes. **Pay Phone:** Yes. **Rest Rooms and Showers:** Yes. **Fuel:** No. **Propane:** No. **Internal Roads:** Paved/gravel, in good condition. **RV Service:** No. **Market:** 1 mi. south in Egg Harbor. **Restaurant:** 1 mi. south in Egg Harbor. **General Store:** Yes. **Vending:** Yes. **Swimming Pool:** Yes. **Playground:** Yes. **Other:** Rec room, TV room, volleyball, badminton, basketball, horseshoes, rental A frames, recreation field. **Activities:** Swimming. **Nearby Attractions:** Door County, cherry & apple orchards, fishing, golf, bird-watching, hiking, boating, Lake Michigan, Green Bay, historic sites, antiques, arts & crafts shops, stock theatre, parks, bike trails. **Additional Information:** Door County Chamber of Commerce, (800) 527-3529.

## RESTRICTIONS

**Pets:** Leash only. **Fires:** Fire ring only. **Alcoholic Beverages:** Permitted. **Vehicle Maximum Length:** None. **Other:** No air conditioners or heaters.

## TO GET THERE

From the junction of CR E and Hwy. 42, drive 1.5 mi. north on Hwy. 42. Roads are wide and well maintained w/ broad shoulders.

## EGG HARBOR
### Door County Camping Retreat

4906 Court Rd., Egg Harbor 54209. T: (866) 830-5145; www.doorcountrycamp.com; office@doorcountrycamp.com.

🚐 ★★★★                      🏕 ★★★

Beauty: ★★★★               Site Privacy: ★★★★
Spaciousness: ★★★★         Quiet: ★★★★
Security: ★★★★              Cleanliness: ★★★★
Insect Control: None         Facilities: ★★★★

Door County Camping Retreat, located three miles south of Egg Harbor, offers wooded campsites and a grassy, open meadow. Average site width is 30 feet, with 12 pull-throughs and 30 seasonal campers. Sites generally have a nice buffer of trees and bushes for privacy. Tent sites are separate from RV area with more green space. Speed limit is five mph, and quiet hours are 10 p.m. to 8 a.m. All radios, TVs, and stereos must be off by 10 p.m., and children must be on sites by 10:30 p.m. Only one warning for noise will be given, and then violators will be evicted without refund. Profanity also is not tolerated, and violators will be evicted without refund. Security measures include one entrance/exit, one-way roads, and regular patrols of the campground.

## BASICS

**Operated by:** John Moravec. **Open:** May 1–Oct. 20. **Site Assignment:** Reservations w/ $25 deposit; no refund but will put it on account for next stay. **Registration:** At campground office. **Fee:** $25 (cash, check, credit cards). **Parking:** At site.

## FACILITIES

**Number of RV Sites:** 160. **Number of Tent-Only Sites:** 50. **Hookups:** Electric (30, 50 amps), water, sewer. **Each Site:** Picnic table, fire ring. **Dump Station:** Yes. **Laundry:** Yes. **Pay Phone:** Yes. **Rest Rooms and Showers:** Yes. **Fuel:** No. **Propane:** Yes. **Internal Roads:** Gravel, in good condition. **RV Service:** No. **Market:** 3 mi. north in Egg Harbor. **Restaurant:** 3 mi. north in Egg Harbor. **General Store:** Yes. **Vending:** Yes. **Swimming Pool:** Yes. **Playground:** Yes. **Other:** Nature trails, pavilion, game room, arcade games, pool table, pop-up rentals, camping cabins, volleyball, basketball, horseshoes, badminton, sports field. **Activities:** Swimming, hiking, biking (rental bikes available), scheduled weekend activities. **Nearby Attractions:** Door County, cherry & apple orchards, fishing, golf, hiking, boating, Lake Michigan, historic sites, antiques, arts & crafts, parks, bike trails, museums. **Additional Information:** Door County Chamber of Commerce, (800) 527-3529.

## RESTRICTIONS

**Pets:** Leash only. **Fires:** Fire ring only. **Alcoholic Beverages:** Permitted. **Vehicle Maximum Length:** 40 ft. **Other:** No bug lights allowed.

## TO GET THERE

From the junction of CR E and Hwy. 42, drive 3.75 mi. south on Hwy. 42, then 0.25 mi. east on Sunny Point Rd., then 0.5 mi. north on Court Rd. Roads are wide and well maintained w/ broad shoulders.

## EGG HARBOR
### Frontier Wilderness Campground

4375 Hillside Rd., Egg Harbor 54209. T: (920) 868-3349

| 🚐 ★★★★★ | ⛺ ★★★★ |
|---|---|
| Beauty: ★★★★ | Site Privacy: ★★★★ |
| Spaciousness: ★★★★ | Quiet: ★★★★ |
| Security: ★★★★ | Cleanliness: ★★★★★ |
| Insect Control: Yes | Facilities: ★★★★★ |

Nope, it was no hallucination. The voice of Clint Black was actually singing in the women's outhouse at Frontier Wilderness Campground. The campground, located 2.5 miles south of Egg Harbor, has the distinction of providing music in its outhouses. Ask the owners how they do it. That is just one indication that this is no run-of-the-mill camping spot. Other special touches are a big indoor pool, complete with sauna and exercise site; a dumpster station inside a fancy little wooden enclosure; toilet rooms with real slate floors and blue fixtures; and private washrooms with mirrors. Instead of shower stalls with concrete floors and peek-a-boo curtains, Frontier Wilderness offers individual private shower rooms. An adult center has TV, carpet, reading chairs, sofas, tables, and other quality furnishings, instead of just a couple of rickety old chairs and worn-out furniture often found in some facilities. The campground has a typical site width of 36 feet, seven pull-throughs, and 180 seasonal campers. Laid out in a series of loops, the campground offers gravel sites for RVs and sand-bed sites for tents—either a drive-up site or a short walk-in site. A five-mph speed limit is enforced, as are quiet hours from 10 p.m. to 8 a.m. Security measures include surveillance cameras, one entrance/exit, owners who live on site, and regular patrols. Although Frontier Wilderness Campground lacks some amenities, such as sewer and 50-amp electric hookups, it more than makes up for those deficits with an abundance of other features, including top-notch cleanliness, beautiful landscaping with real flowers, and hanging baskets even at the outhouses.

## BASICS

**Operated by:** Ray & Carla Kempen. **Open:** May 1–Oct. 31. **Site Assignment:** Reservations w/ 1-

night deposit; refund w/ 7-day notice. **Registration:** At campground office. **Fee:** $23 (cash, check, credit cards). **Parking:** At site.

## FACILITIES

**Number of RV Sites:** 250. **Number of Tent-Only Sites:** 0. **Hookups:** Electric (20, 30 amps), water. **Each Site:** Picnic table, fire ring. **Dump Station:** Yes. **Laundry:** Yes. **Pay Phone:** Yes. **Rest Rooms and Showers:** Yes. **Fuel:** No. **Propane:** No. **Internal Roads:** Paved/gravel, in good condition. **RV Service:** No. **Market:** 2.5 mi. north in Egg Harbor. **Restaurant:** 2.5 mi. north in Egg Harbor. **General Store:** Yes. **Vending:** Yes. **Swimming Pool:** Yes. **Playground:** Yes. **Other:** Cedar-lined sauna, exercise dome, mini golf, game room, pavilion, activity center, adult lounge, badminton, sports field, volleyball, recreation field. **Activities:** Swimming, live music on holiday weekends. **Nearby Attractions:** Door County, Lake Michigan, cherry & apple orchards, golf, fishing, hiking, boating, historic sites, antiques, arts & crafts, bike trails, Green Bay, parks. **Additional Information:** Door County Chamber of Commerce, (800) 527-3529.

## RESTRICTIONS

**Pets:** Leash only. **Fires:** Fire ring only. **Alcoholic Beverages:** Permitted. **Vehicle Maximum Length:** None. **Other:** No smoking in any public buildings.

## TO GET THERE

From the junction of CR E and Hwy. 42, drive 2.5 mi. south on Hwy. 42, then 1.5 mi. east on Hillside Rd. Roads are wide and well maintained w/ broad shoulders.

## ELLISON BAY
### Hy-Land Court

11563 Hwy. 42, Ellison Bay 54210. T: (920) 854-4850

🚐 ★★                        ▲ ★

| | |
|---|---|
| Beauty: ★★ | Site Privacy: ★★ |
| Spaciousness: ★★ | Quiet: ★★★ |
| Security: ★★★ | Cleanliness: ★★★★ |
| Insect Control: None | Facilities: ★★ |

Located two miles south of Ellison Bay, Hy-Land Court is part of a mobile home park. Many of the campers are repeat business, so it is best to make reservations well in advance. The wooded campground features shaded, level sites with grass and gravel pads for RVs. The typical site width is 20 feet, and the campground has six

pull-throughs and two seasonal campers. Speed limit is five mph. Quiet hours are in constant effect and "absolute silence" is required after 10 p.m., according to campground rules. Pets are not encouraged, but "if you must have a pet," it must be leashed at all times and not walked anywhere in the park. The campground has two entrance/exit roads. Security measures include an owner who lives on site and regular patrols of the campground.

## BASICS

**Operated by:** Dale Hilander. **Open:** May 1–Nov. 1. **Site Assignment:** Reservations w/ 1-night deposit; refund w/ 7-day notice. **Registration:** At campground office. **Fee:** $23 (cash, check). **Parking:** At site.

## FACILITIES

**Number of RV Sites:** 28. **Number of Tent-Only Sites:** 0. **Hookups:** Electric (20, 30, 50 amps), water, sewer. **Each Site:** Picnic table, fire ring. **Dump Station:** Yes. **Laundry:** No. **Pay Phone:** No. **Rest Rooms and Showers:** Yes. **Fuel:** No. **Propane:** No. **Internal Roads:** Paved/gravel, in good condition. **RV Service:** No. **Market:** 2 mi. north in Ellison Bay. **Restaurant:** 2 mi. north in Ellison Bay. **General Store:** No. **Vending:** No. **Swimming Pool:** No. **Playground:** No. **Activities:** None. **Nearby Attractions:** Door County, cherry & apple orchards, fishing, golf, hiking, boating, Lake Michigan, historic sites, antiques, arts & crafts, parks, bike trails. **Additional Information:** Door County Chamber of Commerce, (800) 527-3529.

## RESTRICTIONS

**Pets:** Leash only but pets are not encouraged. **Fires:** Fire ring only. **Alcoholic Beverages:** At sites only. **Vehicle Maximum Length:** None.

## TO GET THERE

From the junction of Hwy. 57 and Hwy. 42 (Sister Bay), drive 3.5 mi. north on Hwy. 42. Roads are wide and well maintained w/ broad shoulders.

## ELLISON BAY
### Wagon Trail Campground

1190 Hwy. ZZ, Ellison Bay 54210. T: (920) 854-4818; www.wagontrailcampground.com; wtc@dcwis.com.

🚐 ★★★★                   ▲ ★★★★

| | |
|---|---|
| Beauty: ★★★★ | Site Privacy: ★★★★ |
| Spaciousness: ★★★★ | Quiet: ★★★★ |

Security: ★★★★  Cleanliness: ★★★★★
Insect Control: None  Facilities: ★★★★

Think of the things you want in a campground, and Wagon Trail probably has most of them. Secluded and wooded with an average site width of 30 feet, Wagon Trail is the northernmost campground on the Door County peninsula. Most sites are sandy, with some grassy ones for tents. Laid out in a series of loops, Wagon Trail has four pull-throughs and 26 seasonals in a separate area. Located three-and-a-half miles northwest of Ellison Bay, Wagon Trail is one of the few campgrounds with direct access to the water (trails lead right to the lake). With a name like Wagon Trail, it's no surprise the campground features a western motif, including tree branches for curtain rods, branch-trim bed frames, and mirrors in the rest rooms. Other nice touches include a heated bathroom and rec room. Fresh-brewed coffee is served mornings in the well-stocked camp store, and the bathroom features free hot showers with plenty of electric outlets. The best RV sites are on Lady Slipper Ln., which is more secluded. The best tent sites are the three hideaways that have their own driveway for more privacy. Quiet time is from 10 p.m. to 8 a.m., with no radios allowed during those hours. Owners and the manager walk the grounds at night to be sure it is quiet and safe. Campfires must be out by midnight. Dogs are not allowed to sleep outside the camping unit at night.

### BASICS

**Operated by:** Dick Bartlett & Cheri Ault. **Open:** May 5–Oct. 15. **Site Assignment:** Reservations w/ 1-night deposit; refund (minus $8) w/ 7-day notice. **Registration:** At campground office. **Fee:** $36 (cash, check, credit cards). **Parking:** At site.

### FACILITIES

**Number of RV Sites:** 88. **Number of Tent-Only Sites:** 28. **Hookups:** Electric (30, 50 amps), water, sewer. **Each Site:** Picnic table, fire ring. **Dump Station:** Yes. **Laundry:** Yes. **Pay Phone:** Yes. **Rest Rooms and Showers:** Yes. **Fuel:** No. **Propane:** Yes. **Internal Roads:** Paved/gravel, in good condition. **RV Service:** No. **Market:** 3.5 mi. northwest in Ellison Bay. **Restaurant:** Walking distance. **General Store:** Yes. **Vending:** Yes. **Swimming Pool:** No. **Playground:** Yes. **Other:** Lake, swimming beach, rec room, hiking trails, volleyball, recreation field, rental cabins, badminton, horse-

shoes, adults room. **Activities:** Swimming, fishing, hiking. **Nearby Attractions:** Door County, Lake Michigan, cherry & apple orchards, fishing, boating, golf, historic sites, antiques, arts & crafts, parks, bike trails, nature conservancy. **Additional Information:** Door County Chamber of Commerce, (800) 527-3529.

### RESTRICTIONS

**Pets:** Leash only. **Fires:** Fire ring only. **Alcoholic Beverages:** Permitted. **Vehicle Maximum Length:** 45 ft.

### TO GET THERE

From the junction of Hwy. 42 and CR ZZ in Sister Bay, drive 6 mi. northeast on CR ZZ. Roads are wide and well maintained w/ broad shoulders.

## FISH CREEK
## Path O' Pines Campground

3709 CR F, Fish Creek 54212. T: (800) 868-7802; doorcountycampgrounds.com; crimp@dcwis.com.

🚐 ★★★  ⛺ ★★★

Beauty: ★★★  Site Privacy: ★★★
Spaciousness: ★★★  Quiet: ★★★
Security: ★★★  Cleanliness: ★★★
Insect Control: None  Facilities: ★★★

Located in the heart of Wisconsin vacationland, Path O' Pines Campground offers level, mostly shaded spots near a good access road. About a mile east of Fish Creek, the campground has 20 seasonal campers, 40 pull-through sites, and a typical site width of 30 feet. Laid out in a series of loops, the campground has gravel sites for RVs to park on. Security and safety measures include a five-mph speed limit and owners who live on site. The office staff is very good about sharing information oncerning activities in Door County. Although the campground doesn't offer swimming, it is located near three beaches within a one- to three-mile area. Quiet hours beginning at 10 p.m. are enforced. Violators receive one warning, then are asked to leave if the disturbance continues.

### BASICS

**Operated by:** Tim & Janet Johnson. **Open:** May 15–Oct. 10. **Site Assignment:** Reservations w/ $25 deposit (2-night min.); refund (minus $5) w/ 5-day notice. **Registration:** At campground office. **Fee:** $30 (cash, check, credit cards). **Parking:** At site.

## FACILITIES

**Number of RV Sites:** 85. **Number of Tent-Only Sites:** 10. **Hookups:** Electric (30 amps), water. **Each Site:** Picnic table, fire ring. **Dump Station:** Yes. **Laundry:** Yes. **Pay Phone:** Yes. **Rest Rooms and Showers:** Yes. **Fuel:** No. **Propane:** Yes. **Internal Roads:** Paved/gravel, in good condition. **RV Service:** No. **Market:** 1 mi. west in Fish Creek. **Restaurant:** 1 mi. west in Fish Creek. **General Store:** Yes. **Vending:** Yes. **Swimming Pool:** No. **Playground:** Yes. **Other:** Fish Creek, rec room, TV & game room, adults room, recreation field. **Activities:** None. **Nearby Attractions:** Door County, cherry & apple orchards, fishing, swimming, hiking, golf, boating, Lake Michigan, historic sites, antiques, arts & crafts, parks, bike trails. **Additional Information:** Fish Creek Information Center (800) 577-1880.

## RESTRICTIONS

**Pets:** Leash only. **Fires:** Fire ring only. **Alcoholic Beverages:** Permitted. **Vehicle Maximum Length:** None.

## TO GET THERE

From the junction of Hwy. 42 and CR F, drive 0.5 mi. east on CR F. Road is wide and well maintained w/ broad shoulders.

## FOND DU LAC

### Westward Ho Camp Resort

N5456 Division Rd., Glenbeulah 53023. T: (920) 526-3407

🚐 ★★★★          ⛺ ★★★★

Beauty: ★★★★          Site Privacy: ★★★★
Spaciousness: ★★★★     Quiet: ★★★★
Security: ★★★★         Cleanliness: ★★★★
Insect Control: None   Facilities: ★★★★

The first all-western theme park in Wisconsin and nestled in the North Kettle Moraine, Westward Ho Camp Resort is only minutes away from the historic Wade House—the old stagecoach stop for the early settlers going west or east. The rolling grassy campground offers a choice of wooded, semi-wooded, or open sites, and enough activities to wear out any child or parent. The typical site width is 40 feet, and there are no pull-throughs. Laid out in a series of loops, the campground has a five-mph speed limit and permits no skateboards. Rollerblades and bikes are not allowed

after dark. Quiet time is 10:30 to 8 a.m., with no radios after 10:30 p.m. The Trading Post offers a pool table and color TV, plus a well-stocked general store and souvenir shop. Security includes one entrance/exit with a gate that is locked from 11 p.m. to 8 a.m., owners who live on site, and a sheriff's patrol of the campgrounds.

## BASICS

**Operated by:** James & Linda Schott. **Open:** May 15–Sept. 30. **Site Assignment:** Reservations w/ full deposit; refunds (minus $15) w/ 14-day notice. **Registration:** At campground office. **Fee:** $38 (cash, check, credit cards). **Parking:** At site.

## FACILITIES

**Number of RV Sites:** 234. **Number of Tent-Only Sites:** 66. **Hookups:** Electric (30, 50 amps), water, sewer. **Each Site:** Picnic table, fire ring. **Dump Station:** Yes. **Laundry:** Yes. **Pay Phone:** Yes. **Rest Rooms and Showers:** Yes. **Fuel:** No. **Propane:** No. **Internal Roads:** Paved, in good condition. **RV Service:** No. **Market:** 12 mi. east in Plymouth. **Restaurant:** 5 mi. north in St. Cloud. **General Store:** Yes. **Vending:** Yes. **Swimming Pool:** Yes. **Playground:** Yes. **Other:** Frontier Theater, live petting farm, chuck wagon, music hall, game room, children's fishing ond, 10-station exercise trail, mini golf, movie, tetherball, baseball, basketball, volleyball, shuffleboard, horseshoes, hiking trail, wading pool, coin games. **Activities:** Swimming, fishing, hiking, movies, scheduled activities. **Nearby Attractions:** Wildlife refuge, trout & coho fishing, museums, horseback riding, Lake Michigan, sailing, summer stock theatre, antiques, arts & crafts, historic site. **Additional Information:** Fond du Lac Area CVB, (800) 937-9123.

## RESTRICTIONS

**Pets:** Leash only. **Fires:** Fire rings only; fires not permitted past midnight (township ordinance). **Alcoholic Beverages:** Permitted. **Vehicle Maximum Length:** 40 ft.

## TO GET THERE

From the junction of US 41 and Hwy. 23, drive 16 mi. east on Hwy. 23, then 3 mi. south on CR G, then 0.5 mi. east on CR T. Roads are wide and well maintained w/ broad shoulders.

# FORT ATKINSON

## Jellystone Park at Fort Atkinson

N551 Wishing Well Dr., Fort Atkinson 53538.
T: (920) 568-4100; www.bearsatfort.com.

🚐 ★★★★          ⛺ ★★★★

| | |
|---|---|
| Beauty: ★★★★ | Site Privacy: ★★★★ |
| Spaciousness: ★★★★ | Quiet: ★★★★ |
| Security: ★★★★ | Cleanliness: ★★★★ |
| Insect Control: None | Facilities: ★★★★ |

Check out the facilities and the activities, and you'll see why so many seasonal campers (380) chose to stay at Jellystone Park of Fort Atkinson. With a full-time activities director, the campground has enough going on to keep anyone busy. The grassy hilltop campground is pleasant enough just to sit around and do nothing. The campground has back-in sites and a typical site width of 35 feet. Laid out in a series of loops, the campground has level sites with a choice of shaded or open. Security and safety measures include a ban on motorcycles and scooters, proof of license and insurance for golf cart drivers, and a nightly quiet time. All guests/visitors must wear wristbands, and all vehicles must display a vehicle pass. Rangers patrol the campground.

### BASICS

**Operated by:** Steve Cline. **Open:** May 15–Sept. 15. **Site Assignment:** Reservations w/ 1-night deposit; refund (minus $5) w/ 10-day notice. **Registration:** At campground office. **Fee:** $26 (cash, check, credit cards). **Parking:** At site.

### FACILITIES

**Number of RV Sites:** 569. **Number of Tent-Only Sites:** 20. **Hookups:** Electric (30, 50 amps), water. **Each Site:** Picnic table, fire ring. **Dump Station:** Yes. **Laundry:** Yes. **Pay Phone:** Yes. **Rest Rooms and Showers:** Yes. **Fuel:** No. **Propane:** Yes. **Internal Roads:** Paved/gravel, in good condition. **RV Service:** No. **Market:** 4 mi. north in Fort Atkinson. **Restaurant:** 4 mi. north in Fort Atkinson. **General Store:** Yes. **Vending:** Yes. **Swimming Pool:** Yes. **Playground:** Yes. **Other:** Pond, snack bar, baseball, full-time activities director, mini golf, tennis, horseshoes, volleyball, basketball, shuffleboard, lounge, game room, pavilion, trails, kids/ fishing pond, rangers kitchen, wading pool, coin games. **Activities:** Swimming, hiking, fishing, movies, scheduled activities. **Nearby Attractions:** Aquatic park, boat launch, horseback riding, Lake Koshkonong, Fireside Dinner Theatre, golf, bicycle trails, roller skating, bowling, hang gliding, archery range, Hoard Historical Museum, National Dairy Shrine & Jones Dairy Farm, Dwight Foster House, Milton House Museum, Hexagon Stagecoach Inn, Replica of Old Fort Koshkonong. **Additional Information:** Fort Atkinson Area Chamber of Commerce, (888) 733-3678.

### RESTRICTIONS

**Pets:** Leash only. **Fires:** Fire ring only. **Alcoholic Beverages:** At sites only. **Vehicle Maximum Length:** None.

### TO GET THERE

From the junction of US 12 and Hwy. 26, drive 5.25 mi. southwest on Hwy. 26, then 0.75 mi. west on Koshkonong Lake Rd., then 0.25 mi. south on Wishing Well Dr. Roads are wide and well maintained w/ broad shoulders.

# FREMONT

## Yogi Bear's Jellystone Park Camp-Resort

P.O. Box 497, Fremont 54940. T: (800) 258-3315; F: (920) 446-3450; www.fremontjellystone.com.

🚐 ★★★★          ⛺ ★★★★

| | |
|---|---|
| Beauty: ★★★★ | Site Privacy: ★★★★ |
| Spaciousness: ★★★★ | Quiet: ★★★★ |
| Security: ★★★★ | Cleanliness: ★★★★ |
| Insect Control: ★★★★ | Facilities: ★★★★ |

Campers can usually count on a wealth of activities at Yogi Bear campgrounds. The Yogi Bear Jellystone Park Camp-Resort at Fremont has a huge bonus by being located on the shores of Partridge Lake. The 990-acre lake is part of the Wolf River Flowage. From the Yogi Bear boat ramp, there is more than 125 miles of navigable waterways. Not surprisingly, the most popular sites are the ones on the lake with private docks. Laid out in a series of loops, the campground has 50 seasonal campers, 28 pull-through sites, and a typical site width of 50 feet. Sites are level, with a choice of open or shaded. To accompany its water wonderland, the campground has a bait and tackle shop and an array of rental boats with enough good fishing to keep big and little kids happy. Quiet hours from 11 p.m. to 7 a.m. are enforced. Security is tops, with rangers who keep a close eye on the campground.

## BASICS

**Operated by:** John & Alyssa Harlan. **Open:** Apr. 15–Oct. 15. **Site Assignment:** Reservations w/ 50 percent deposit of total reservation; refund (minus $7) w/ 7-day notice. If less than 7-day notice given, full refund less 1 night will be returned. Reservations w/ 2-night min. on weekends; 3-night min. on holidays. **Registration:** At campground office. **Fee:** $45 (cash, check, credit cards). **Parking:** At site.

## FACILITIES

**Number of RV Sites:** 251. **Number of Tent-Only Sites:** 31. **Hookups:** Electric (20, 30, 50 amps), water, sewer. **Each Site:** Picnic table, fire ring. **Dump Station:** Yes. **Laundry:** Yes. **Pay Phone:** Yes. **Rest Rooms and Showers:** Yes. **Fuel:** No. **Propane:** Yes. **Internal Roads:** Paved/gravel, in good condition. **RV Service:** No. **Market:** 2 mi. east in Fremont. **Restaurant:** 2 mi. east in Fremont. **General Store:** Yes. **Vending:** Yes. **Swimming Pool:** Yes. **Playground:** Yes. **Other:** Partridge Lake, arcade, mini golf, horseshoes, volleyball, basketball, shuffleboard, rec hall, game room, pavilion, nature trails, boat launch, gift shop, rental cabins, rental cottages, bait & tackle shop, boat ramp, badminton, sports field. **Activities:** Swimming, fishing (fishing guides available), hiking, boating (rental pontoons, rowboats, canoes, kayaks, jon boats available), scheduled activities. **Nearby Attractions:** Golf, horseback riding, waterslide, go-karts, cheese factories, bowling, canoeing, tubing, outlet mall, biking trails, Amish arts & crafts, antiques, harbor boat rides, Green Bay Packer Hall of Fame, zoo. **Additional Information:** Fremont Chamber of Commerce, (920) 446-3838.

## RESTRICTIONS

**Pets:** Leash only; $2 per night. **Fires:** Fire ring only. **Alcoholic Beverages:** Permitted. **Vehicle Maximum Length:** None.

## TO GET THERE

From the junction of CR H & US 10, drive 1.5 mi. west on US 10. Roads are wide and well maintained w/ broad shoulders.

## GALESVILLE

### Rivers Edge Campground & Resort

W16751 Pow Wow Ln., Galesville 54630. T: (608) 582-2995

 ★★           ★★

Beauty: ★★
Spaciousness: ★★★
Security: ★★★★
Insect Control: None

Site Privacy: ★★★
Quiet: ★★★
Cleanliness: ★★
Facilities: ★★

Located three miles south of Galesville, Rivers Edge Campground & Resort is a wooded campground with mostly grassy, shaded sites. Seasonals occupy 34 sites. The typical site width is 24 feet, with tall pine trees providing buffers between sites in many areas. Arranged in a series of loops, the campground offers nine pull-throughs and the Rivers Edge Bar, which is open all year to serve fast food and drinks. Most of the campers at Rivers Edge are local people and families who have been going there for years. Security measures include owners who live on site, regular patrols, and a gate that is locked from 11 p.m. to 8 a.m.

## BASICS

**Operated by:** Tom & Yvette Sulser. **Open:** May 15–Sept. 15. **Site Assignment:** Reservations accepted w/ no deposit. **Registration:** At campground office. **Fee:** $19 (cash, check, credit cards). **Parking:** At site.

## FACILITIES

**Number of RV Sites:** 54. **Number of Tent-Only Sites:** 40. **Hookups:** Electric (20, 30 amps), water. **Each Site:** Picnic table, fire ring. **Dump Station:** Yes. **Laundry:** No. **Pay Phone:** Yes. **Rest Rooms and Showers:** Yes. **Fuel:** No. **Propane:** No. **Internal Roads:** Paved, in good condition. **RV Service:** No. **Market:** 3 mi. north in Galesville. **Restaurant:** 3 mi. north in Galesville. **General Store:** No. **Vending:** Yes. **Swimming Pool:** Yes. **Playground:** Yes. **Other:** Black River, beach, game room, rec hall, adults room, horseshoes, sports field, hiking trails, mini-golf, badminton, volleyball, basketball. **Activities:** Fishing, swimming, boating (rental canoes available). **Nearby Attractions:** Museums, antiques, zoo, paddlewheel boat. **Additional Information:** La Crosse Area CVB, (800) 658-9424.

## RESTRICTIONS

**Pets:** Leash only. **Fires:** Fire ring only. **Alcoholic Beverages:** Permitted. **Vehicle Maximum Length:** None.

## TO GET THERE

From the junction of Hwys 54, 35, and 53, drive 3 mi. southeast on Hwy. 53. Roads are wide and well maintained w/ broad shoulders.

## GOODMAN
## Lake Hilbert Campground

N20470 Town Pike Rd., Fence 54541. T: (715) 336-3013

🚐 ★★                    ▲ ★★

Beauty: ★★               Site Privacy: ★★
Spaciousness: ★★         Quiet: ★★★
Security: ★★             Cleanliness: ★★★
Insect Control: None     Facilities: ★★

Located four miles north of Armstrong Creek, Lake Hilbert Campground offers mostly shady, grassy sites. Laid out in a series of loops, the campground has ten pull-throughs and 22 seasonal campers. The best thing the campground has going for it is Lake Hilbert, which has a large park, boat landing, recreational area, fishing, and waterskiing. Quiet hours are from 10 p.m. to 6 a.m., and no loud music is allowed at any time. A ten-mph speed limit seems a bit high for a campground with children. Picnic tables may not be moved from other sites, unless you want to pay a $5 fee for the extra table. For security measures, the owner lives on site, and the campground has one entrance/exit road. Campground regulations also require that no personal belongings be left outside when the campsite is not in use.

### BASICS

**Operated by:** Mike Kocken. **Open:** Apr. 1–Nov. 31. **Site Assignment:** Reservations w/ 1-night deposit; refund w/ 14-day notice. **Registration:** At campground office. **Fee:** $16 (cash, check). **Parking:** At site.

### FACILITIES

**Number of RV Sites:** 50. **Number of Tent-Only Sites:** 20. **Hookups:** Electric (30, 50 amps), water. **Each Site:** Picnic table, fire ring. **Dump Station:** Yes. **Laundry:** No. **Pay Phone:** Yes. **Rest Rooms and Showers:** Yes. **Fuel:** No. **Propane:** No. **Internal Roads:** Paved/gravel, in good condition. **RV Service:** No. **Market:** 4 mi. south in Armstrong. **Restaurant:** Next door. **General Store:** No. **Vending:** Yes. **Swimming Pool:** No. **Playground:** Yes. **Other:** Lake Hilbert, swimming beach, game room, rental cabins. **Activities:** Swimming, fishing, boating. **Nearby Attractions:** Train rides, logging museum, gambling casinos, nature center, bird refuge, Chequamegon-Nicolet National Forest. **Additional Information:** Laona Chamber

of Commerce, (715) 674-3007.

### RESTRICTIONS

**Pets:** Leash only. **Fires:** Fire ring only. **Alcoholic Beverages:** Permitted. **Vehicle Maximum Length:** None.

### TO GET THERE

Take Hwy. 141 to Pembine, drive 20 mi. west on Hwy. 8 to Goodman, and drive 3 mi. north on CR H. Roads are wide and well maintained w/ broad shoulders.

## HANCOCK
## Tomorrow Wood Campground

N 3845 7th Dr., Hancock 54943. T: (715) 249-5954

🚐 ★★                    ▲ ★★

Beauty: ★★               Site Privacy: ★★★
Spaciousness: ★★★        Quiet: ★★★
Security: ★★★            Cleanliness: ★★★★
Insect Control: None     Facilities: ★★

A rustic rural campground on Fish Lake four miles southwest of Hancock, Tomorrow Wood Campground is popular as a fishing destination. The lake has bass, crappie, and lots of other pan fish. All the sewer sites are taken by seasonals. Laid out in a series of loops, the campground offers tall pine, oak, and other hardwood trees. All sites are wooded, with a typical width of 40 feet and no pull-throughs. Quiet hours from 11 p.m. to 8 a.m. are enforced, as is a five-mph speed limit. Owners live on the site and provide regular patrols, as well as seasonals who keep an eye on the campground. The best RV sites are 312 and 410 because they are bigger and offer more space. The best tent sites are P423 and 427 because they are more secluded and located away from RVs.

### BASICS

**Operated by:** Edward & Bonnie Zdroik. **Open:** May 1–Oct. 1. **Site Assignment:** Reservations w/ 1-night deposit; refund w/ 7-day notice. **Registration:** At campground office. **Fee:** $19 (cash, check). **Parking:** At site.

### FACILITIES

**Number of RV Sites:** 115. **Number of Tent-Only Sites:** 30. **Hookups:** Electric (30, 50 amps), water, sewer. **Each Site:** Picnic table, fire ring. **Dump Station:** Yes. **Laundry:** Yes. **Pay Phone:** Yes. **Rest Rooms and Showers:** Yes. **Fuel:** No. **Propane:** Yes. **Internal Roads:** Gravel, in good condition. **RV Service:** No. **Market:** 4 mi. northeast in Hancock. **Restaurant:** 4 mi. northeast in Hancock. **General Store:** Yes. **Vending:** No. **Swimming Pool:** No. **Playground:** Yes. **Other:** Fish Lake, basketball, horseshoes, volleyball, pavilion, sandy beach, pavilion, sports field. **Activities:** Swimming, fishing, boating (rental rowboats available), scheduled weekend activities. **Nearby Attractions:** Rainbow Falls Water Park, golf, Mead Wildlife Refuge, Grotto Shrine, manufacturers mall. **Additional Information:** Stevens Point Area CVB, (800) 236-4626.

### RESTRICTIONS

**Pets:** Leash only. **Fires:** Fire ring only. **Alcoholic Beverages:** Permitted. **Vehicle Maximum Length:** None.

### TO GET THERE

At the junction of Hwy. 51 and CR V, drive 1.25 mi. east on CR V, then 2 mi. southeast on CR GG, then 0.5 mi. south on 7th Dr. Roads are wide and well maintained w/ adequate shoulders.

## HAYWARD

## Lake Chippewa Campground

8380 North CTH CC, Hayward 54843. T: (715) 462-3672; www.lakechip.com; lakechip@pctcnet.net.

| 🚐 ★★★★ | 🏕 ★★★★ |
|---|---|
| Beauty: ★★★★ | Site Privacy: ★★★★ |
| Spaciousness: ★★★★ | Quiet: ★★★★ |
| Security: ★★★★ | Cleanliness: ★★★★ |
| Insect Control: None | Facilities: ★★★★ |

Lake Chippewa Campground is located on an island in the heart of Lake Chippewa. Connected by a bridge and a causeway to the mainland, the campground offers great water activities. The 17,000-acre Chippewa Flowage is Wisconsin's largest wilderness lake, with most of its lakeshore undeveloped, wild, and scenic. The campground offers level, shaded, wooded sites, with 16 seasonal campers, 20 pull-through sites, and a typical site width of 30 feet. Campers can beach their boat or canoe right outside their RV door. Unobstructed views of water and seasonal foliage are also available. Reservations are recommended, especially for weekends and holidays.

Since the campground stays open until Nov. 1, campers can enjoy the great fall foliage. Muskie is king here, but other popular fish are walleye, crappie, bluegill, and perch. The best sites, of course, are by the lake.

### BASICS

**Operated by:** Don & Judy Robinson. **Open:** May 1–Nov. 1. **Site Assignment:** Reservations w/ 1-night deposit; refund (minus $5) w/ 7-day notice. **Registration:** At campground office. **Fee:** $25 (cash, check). **Parking:** At site.

### FACILITIES

**Number of RV Sites:** 170. **Number of Tent-Only Sites:** 10. **Hookups:** Electric (20, 30, 50 amps), water, sewer. **Each Site:** Picnic table, fire ring. **Dump Station:** Yes. **Laundry:** Yes. **Pay Phone:** Yes. **Rest Rooms and Showers:** Yes. **Fuel:** No. **Propane:** No. **Internal Roads:** Paved/gravel, in good condition. **RV Service:** No. **Market:** 7 mi. south. **Restaurant:** 2 mi. **General Store:** Yes, limited. **Vending:** Yes. **Swimming Pool:** No. **Playground:** Yes. **Other:** Chippewa Flowage, snack shop, sandy beach, baseball, mini golf, horseshoes, volleyball, basketball, rec hall, game room, trails, fish-cleaning station, rental RVs, rental cabins, boat landing, boat dock. **Activities:** Swimming, fishing, boating (rental motorboats, canoes, paddleboats available), scheduled activities. **Nearby Attractions:** National Freshwater Fishing Hall of Fame, lumberjack shows, zoo, golf, horseback riding, national forest, fishing, casinos, antiques, arts & crafts, Sawyer County Historical Society & Museum. **Additional Information:** Hayward Area Chamber of Commerce, (715) 634-8662.

### RESTRICTIONS

**Pets:** Leash only. **Fires:** Fire ring only. **Alcoholic Beverages:** Permitted. **Vehicle Maximum Length:** None.

### TO GET THERE

From the junction of US 63 and Hwy. 27, drive 0.5 mi. south on Hwy. 27, then 13 mi. east on CR B, then 5 mi. south on CR CC. Roads are mostly wide and well maintained w/ narrow shoulders in spots.

## HIXTON

### Hixton-Alma Center KOA

N9657 State Rd. 95, Alma Center 54611. T: (800) 562-2680

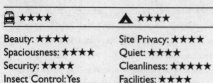

🚐 ★★★★     ▲ ★★★★

Beauty: ★★★★    Site Privacy: ★★★★
Spaciousness: ★★★★    Quiet: ★★★★
Security: ★★★★    Cleanliness: ★★★★★
Insect Control: Yes    Facilities: ★★★★

This is not a "party" campground. The Hixton-Alma Center KOA, 12 miles east of Black River Falls, is where families and campers come to enjoy a peaceful country setting with plenty of birds and flowers. The campground owner has an iron fist when it comes to rowdiness, but she also has a green thumb and spends a good number of hours tending her tulips and lilacs. She feeds birds year-round and uses a garlic spray to control mosquitos without harming wildlife. A small spring-fed pond provides catch-and-release fishing for youngsters. An immaculate bathroom not only has shiny waxed floors, but also features bouquets of fresh flowers. Each large (40 × 50 feet) campsite has a tree, grass, and a gravel pad for RVs; most are pull-throughs. Secluded wilderness sites are available for tent campers.

### BASICS

**Operated by:** Jim & Donna Rankin. **Open:** Apr. 1–Nov. 30. **Site Assignment:** Reservations w/ 1-night deposit; refund w/ 24-hour notice. **Registration:** At campground office. **Fee:** $24 (cash, check, credit cards). **Parking:** At site.

### FACILITIES

**Number of RV Sites:** 50. **Number of Tent-Only Sites:** 16. **Hookups:** Electric (30, 50 amps), water, sewer. **Each Site:** Picnic table, fire ring. **Dump Station:** Yes. **Laundry:** Yes. **Pay Phone:** Yes. **Rest Rooms and Showers:** Yes. **Fuel:** No. **Propane:** No. **Internal Roads:** Gravel, in good condition. **RV Service:** No. **Market:** 12 mi. west in Black River Falls. **Restaurant:** 12 mi. west in Black River Falls. **General Store:** Yes. **Vending:** No. **Swimming Pool:** Yes. **Playground:** Yes. **Other:** Hiking trails, small fishing pond for children, volleyball, horseshoes, pavilion w/ juke box, videos, pool table. **Activities:** Hiking, swimming, fishing, birdwatching, biking (rental bikes available). **Nearby Attractions:** Golf, diving, canoeing, orchard, casino, Thunderbird Museum, antique & craft shops. **Additional Information:** Black River Falls Area Chamber of Commerce, (800) 404-4008.

### RESTRICTIONS

**Pets:** Leash only. **Fires:** Fire ring only. **Alcoholic Beverages:** At sites only. **Vehicle Maximum Length:** None.

### TO GET THERE

From the junction of I-94 and Hwy. 95, take Exit 105, drive 3.5 mi. east on Hwy. 95. The roads are wide and well maintained w/ broad shoulders.

## IRON RIVER

### Wildwood Campground

9505 Wildwood Rd., Iron River 54847. T: (715) 372-4072; wildcamp@win.bright.net.

🚐 ★★     ▲ ★★

Beauty: ★★★    Site Privacy: ★★★
Spaciousness: ★★★    Quiet: ★★★
Security: ★★★    Cleanliness: ★★★
Insect Control: ★★★    Facilities: ★★

Located two miles outside Iron River, Wildwood Campground has a beautiful spot on 18-acre Peterson Lake. There is no highway noise, and no jet skis or power boats are permitted on the lake. That means the campground is peaceful and quiet—except when ATVs roar off. Local ATV trails are accessible directly from the campgrounds. The closer to the lake, the better for most campers. Sites are level with plenty of shade, and typical site width of 30 feet.

### BASICS

**Operated by:** Carl & Sandra Westlund. **Open:** May 1–Oct. 15. **Site Assignment:** Reservations w/ 1-night deposit; refund (minus $5) w/ 7-day notice. **Registration:** At campground office. **Fee:** $14 (cash). **Parking:** At site.

### FACILITIES

**Number of RV Sites:** 23. **Number of Tent-Only Sites:** 2. **Hookups:** Electric (20, 30 amps), water, sewer. **Each Site:** Picnic table, fire ring. **Dump Station:** Yes. **Laundry:** No. **Pay Phone:** Yes. **Rest Rooms and Showers:** Yes. **Fuel:** No. **Propane:** No. **Internal Roads:** Gravel, in good condition. **RV Service:** No. **Market:** 2 mi. west in Iron River. **Restaurant:** 2 mi. west in Iron River. **General Store:** Yes, limited. **Vending:** Yes. **Swim-**

ming Pool: No. Playground: Yes. Other: Peterson Lake, swim beach, pavilion, ATV trails, hiking trails, rental camper bus. Activities: Swimming, fishing, boating (rental paddleboats, rowboats, canoes available). Nearby Attractions: Apostle Islands, Brule River, waterfalls, ferry boats, musuems, Big Top Chautauqua, fish hatcheries, scenic drives, antiques. Additional Information: Iron River Area Chamber of Commerce, (715) 372-8558.

## RESTRICTIONS

Pets: Leash only. Fires: Fire ring only. Alcoholic Beverages: Permitted. Vehicle Maximum Length: None.

## TO GET THERE

From the junction of Hwy. 2 and Wayside Rd., drive 2.75 mi. south on Wayside Rd., then 0.5 mi. east on Wildwood Dr. Roads are mostly wide and well maintained w/ narrow shoulders in spots.

## KEWAUNEE

## Cedar Valley Campground

5098 Cedar Valley Rd., Kewaunee 54216. T: (920) 388-4983

🚐 ★★★                    ⛺ ★★★

| | |
|---|---|
| Beauty: ★★ | Site Privacy: ★★★ |
| Spaciousness: ★★★ | Quiet: ★★★ |
| Security: ★★★★ | Cleanliness: ★★★ |
| Insect Control: None | Facilities: ★★★ |

A rural campground along the Kewaunee River, Cedar Valley Campground offers level, grassy, mostly shaded sites. Located six miles west of Kewaunee, the campground has 64 seasonal campers, 30 pull-through sites, and a typical site width of 30 feet. The river serves as the campground's focal point and provides fishing and swimming; there's also a swimming pool. The most popular campsites for both tents and RVs are along the river, where spots are more secluded and offer more green space. The campground is in the heart of Wisconsin vacationland, but it also offers a fair amount of activities on site. Safety and security measures include a five-mph speed limit, speed bumps, a manager who lives on site, a traffic-control gate, and regular patrols of the campground.

## BASICS

Operated by: John Pagel. Open: Apr. 25–Oct. 15. Site Assignment: Reservations w/ 1-night

deposit; refund w/ 7-day notice. Registration: At campground office. Fee: $20 (cash, check, credit cards). Parking: At site.

## FACILITIES

Number of RV Sites: 115. Number of Tent-Only Sites: 25. Hookups: Electric (30 amps), water. Each Site: Picnic table, fire ring. Dump Station: Yes. Laundry: Yes. Pay Phone: Yes. Rest Rooms and Showers: Yes. Fuel: No. Propane: Yes. Internal Roads: Gravel/sand, in good condition. RV Service: No. Market: 6 mi. east in Kewaunee. Restaurant: 6 mi. east in Kewaunee. General Store: Yes, limited. Vending: No. Swimming Pool: Yes. Playground: Yes. Other: Kewaunee River, mini golf, badminton, sports field, horseshoes, hiking trails, volleyball, basketball. Activities: Swimming, fishing, hiking, scheduled weekend activities. Nearby Attractions: Lake Michigan, boating, charter fishing, harbor, boat launch, cheese factories, antiques, arts & crafts, Door County, zoo, jail museum, golf, nautical museum, nature walk. Additional Information: Kewaunee Chamber of Commerce, (800) 666-8214.

## RESTRICTIONS

Pets: Leash only. Fires: Fire ring only. Alcoholic Beverages: Permitted. Vehicle Maximum Length: None.

## TO GET THERE

From the junction of Hwy. 42 and Hwy. 29, drive 0.75 mi. west on Hwy. 29, then 5 mi. northwest on CR C, then 0.75 mi. north on Cedar Valley Rd. (CR B). Roads are wide and well maintained w/ mostly broad shoulders.

## KEWAUNEE

## Kewaunee Village RV Park

333 Terraqua Dr., Kewaunee 54216. T: (800) 274-9684; F: (920) 388-4853; www.kewauneevillage.com; info@kewauneevillage.com.

🚐 ★★★★                    ⛺ ★★★

| | |
|---|---|
| Beauty: ★★★ | Site Privacy: ★★ |
| Spaciousness: ★★ | Quiet: ★★★ |
| Security: ★★★★ | Cleanliness: ★★★★ |
| Insect Control: None | Facilities: ★★★★ |

Location is everything, and Kewaunee Village RV Park certainly has a prime spot. Situated just over one mile north of downtown Kewaunee, the campground is right off the main road of Hwy. 42. It also is next to Lake Michigan on a beautiful harbor with a boat launch, charter fishing, and marina facilities. There is even a fish-cleaning house at the harbor and fish-freezing services for campers at the campground. Camp sites are level and mostly open, with a typical site width of 40 feet. Kewaunee Village RV Park has 64 pull-through sites, 24 seasonal campers, and city water and sewer. The campground has some shade trees, but it is not a wooded facility. RVs must be parked only on gravel pad areas, not on the grass. A ten-mph speed limit is enforced (a lower one might be better with so many children on site), as is quiet time from 11 p.m. to 7 a.m. Young adults and children must be on their sites by 10 p.m. Security measures include one entrance/exit, a regular patrol, and owners who live on site.

## BASICS

**Operated by:** Dean, Nanette & Katie Kulm; Warren & Kathy Clark. **Open:** May 15–Oct. 15. **Site Assignment:** Reservations w/ 1-night deposit; refund w/ 3-day notice. **Registration:** At campground office. **Fee:** $27 (cash, check, credit card). **Parking:** At site.

## FACILITIES

**Number of RV Sites:** 74. **Number of Tent-Only Sites:** 15. **Hookups:** Electric (20, 30, 50 amps), water, sewer. **Each Site:** Picnic table, fire ring. **Dump Station:** Yes. **Laundry:** Yes. **Pay Phone:** Yes. **Rest Rooms and Showers:** Yes. **Fuel:** No. **Propane:** Yes. **Internal Roads:** Paved/gravel, in good condition. **RV Service:** No. **Market:** 1.5 mi. south in Kewaunee. **Restaurant:** 1.5 mi. south in Kewaunee. **General Store:** Yes. **Vending:** No. **Swimming Pool:** Yes. **Playground:** Yes. **Other:** Pavilion, game & video room, mini golf, recreation field, horseshoes, fish freezing, shuffleboard. **Activities:** Swimming, sheduled weekend activities. **Nearby Attractions:** Lake Michigan, boating, charter fishing, harbor, boat launch, cheese factories, antiques, arts & crafts shops, Door County, zoo, jail museum, golf, art galleries, nautical museum, nature walk. **Additional Information:** Kewaunee Chamber of Commerce, (800) 666-8214.

## RESTRICTIONS

**Pets:** Leash only, max. of 2 pets per site. **Fires:** Fire rings only. All fires must be extinguished by 11 p.m. Must be put out w/ water & no glowing embers remain. **Alcoholic Beverages:** Permitted. **Vehicle Maximum Length:** None. **Other:** Generators may not be used in the campground.

## TO GET THERE

From the junction of Hwy. 29 and Hwy. 42, drive 0.75 mi. north on Hwy. 42. Roads are wide and well maintained w/ broad shoulders.

## LAKEWOOD

### Heaven's Up North Family Campground

18344 Lake John Rd., Lakewood 54138. T: (715) 276-6556; www.heavensupnorth.com; heavnsupno@ez.net.com.

 ★★★★       ★★★★

Beauty: ★★★★       Site Privacy: ★★★★
Spaciousness: ★★★★   Quiet: ★★★★
Security: ★★★★       Cleanliness: ★★★★★
Insect Control: No    Facilities: ★★★★

Located three miles west of Lakewood, Heaven's Up North Family Campground is a wooded, rolling facility with some steep hills leading to some of the campsites. But that hilly terrain also adds to the beauty. Quiet is maintained at the wilderness campground by having plenty of trees and other green space as buffers between sites and by enforcing 10 p.m. to 7 a.m. quiet times. No loud or amplified music is allowed at any time. Group-camping sites are not available in order to cut down on noise. The typical site width is 50 feet, and the campground has four pull-through sites and 76 seasonal campers. Laid out in a series of loops, the campground has a five-mph speed limit and one-way roads. Security measures include one entrance/exit, owners who live on site, and regular campground patrols. Open year-round, the campground is kept plowed in the winter for campers who want to hunt or go snowmobiling or ice fishing.

## BASICS

**Operated by:** Marlene Sauriol. **Open:** All year. **Site Assignment:** Reservations w/ 2-night deposit; no refunds. **Registration:** At campground office. **Fee:** $23 (cash, check, credit cards). **Parking:** At site.

## FACILITIES

**Number of RV Sites:** 110. **Number of Tent-Only Sites:** 5. **Hookups:** Electric (20, 30 amps), water. **Each Site:** Picnic table, fire ring. **Dump Station:** Yes. **Laundry:** Yes. **Pay Phone:** Yes. **Rest**

**Rooms and Showers:** Yes. **Fuel:** No. **Propane:** No. **Internal Roads:** Gravel, in good condition. **RV Service:** No. **Market:** 3 mi. east in Lakewood. **Restaurant:** 3 mi. east in Lakewood. **General Store:** Yes, limited. **Vending:** Yes. **Swimming Pool:** Yes. **Playground:** Yes. **Other:** Game room, coin games, mini golf, horseshoes, recreation field, volleyball. **Activities:** Swimming. **Nearby Attractions:** Casino, bingo, gingerbread houses, fish hatchery, logging camp, golf, fishing & boating lakes, winery, art studio. **Additional Information:** Lakewood Area Chamber of Commerce, (715) 276-6500.

## RESTRICTIONS

**Pets:** Leash only. **Fires:** Fire ring only. **Alcoholic Beverages:** Permitted. **Vehicle Maximum Length:** 36 ft.

## TO GET THERE

From the junction of Hwy. 32 and CR F in Lakewood, drive 2 mi. northeast on CR F, then 3 mi. north on Lake John Rd. Roads are wide and well maintained w/ broad shoulders.

## LAKEWOOD

## Maple Heights Campground

P.O. Box 130, Lakewood 54138. T: (715) 276-6441

&#128649; ★★★              &#9650; ★★★

| | |
|---|---|
| Beauty: ★★★ | Site Privacy: ★★★ |
| Spaciousness: ★★★ | Quiet: ★★★★ |
| Security: ★★★★ | Cleanliness: ★★★★ |
| Insect Control: None | Facilities: ★★★ |

Maple Heights Campground, located 1.5 miles north of Lakewood, has two notable landmarks—a canopy of huge maple, beech, and hemlock trees, and a giant statue of Paul Bunyan's Babe the Blue Ox, a favorite photo op. The campground borders the Nicolet National Forest and offers a wealth of nearby water activities. Over 60 lakes are within ten miles. The McCas-lin Brook trout stream meanders around the campground, and it is located between two popular rafting rivers, the Wolf and Peshtigo. The campground's 50-foot heated pool is also hard to ignore. Laid out in a series of loops, Maple Heights offers a typical site width of 30 feet, 85 pull-throughs, and 50 seasonal campers. Sites in the secluded, wooded campground are level and mostly shady. Seasonal campers are mostly clumped in sections. The best RV site is LB because it is larger, has water and electricity, and is close to the pool and other facil-

ities. The best tent site is B13 because it is large and backs up into the national forest. Speed limit is five mph, and quiet time between 11 p.m. and 7:30 a.m. means music must be turned off and voices kept low. Security includes one entrance/exit road, owners who live on site, and regular patrols of the campground.

## BASICS

**Operated by:** Mike & Carolyn Kubitz. **Open:** Apr. 1–Dec. 1. **Site Assignment:** Reservations w/ $20 deposit; refund w/ 7-day notice. **Registration:** At campground office. **Fee:** $20 (cash, check, credit cards). **Parking:** At site.

## FACILITIES

**Number of RV Sites:** 93. **Number of Tent-Only Sites:** 7. **Hookups:** Electric (20, 30, 50 amps), water. **Each Site:** Picnic table, fire ring. **Dump Station:** Yes. **Laundry:** Yes. **Pay Phone:** Yes. **Rest Rooms and Showers:** Yes. **Fuel:** No. **Propane:** No. **Internal Roads:** Gravel, in good condition. **RV Service:** No. **Market:** 1.5 mi. south in Lakewood. **Restaurant:** 1.5 mi. south in Lakewood. **General Store:** Yes. **Vending:** Yes. **Swimming Pool:** Yes. **Playground:** Yes. **Other:** McCaslin Brook trout stream, rec room, snack bar, mini golf, volleyball, horseshoes, ping pong, pavilion, hiking trail, sports field. **Activities:** Swimming, fishing, hiking. **Nearby Attractions:** Casino, bingo, gingerbread houses, fish hatchery, logging camp, golf, fishing & boating lakes, winery, art studio. **Additional Information:** Lakewood Area Chamber of Commerce, (715) 276-6500.

## RESTRICTIONS

**Pets:** Leash only. **Fires:** Fire ring only. **Alcoholic Beverages:** Permitted. **Vehicle Maximum Length:** None.

## TO GET THERE

From the junction of CR F and Hwy. 32, drive 2 mi. north on Hwy. 32. Roads are wide and well maintained w/ broad shoulders.

## LAONA

## Ham Lake Campground

RR 1 Box 434, Wabeno 54566. T: (715) 674-2201; F: (715) 674-5028; hamlake@newnorth.net.

&#128649; ★★★              &#9650; ★★★

| | |
|---|---|
| Beauty: ★★ | Site Privacy: ★★★ |
| Spaciousness: ★★★ | Quiet: ★★★ |

Security: ★★★★          Cleanliness: ★★★
Insect Control: None      Facilities: ★★★

With easy access off Hwy. 32, Ham Lake Campground is a rural facility four miles south of Laona. Located on Ham Lake, the campground offers level, grassy sites with a choice of shade or open. The campground has 22 seasonal campers, 11 pull-through sites, and a typical site width of 30 feet. The mini golf set up could definitely use some work. The road going to sites R, T, K, and S has a steep, narrow hill that requires slow, careful maneuvering. The best RV site is B5 because it is a pull-through near the lake. The campground is a popular place to stay because it is conveniently near a wealth of recreational opportunities, as well as offering many on site. Security includes owners who live on site and keep a close watch on the campground.

## BASICS

**Operated by:** Terry & Judy Collins. **Open:** May 1–Oct. 15. **Site Assignment:** Reservations w/ $25 deposit; refund w/ 7-day notice. **Registration:** At campground office. **Fee:** $20 (cash, check, credit cards). **Parking:** At site.

## FACILITIES

**Number of RV Sites:** 44. **Number of Tent-Only Sites:** 1. **Hookups:** Electric (30 amps), water, sewer. **Each Site:** Picnic table, fire ring. **Dump Station:** Yes. **Laundry:** Yes. **Pay Phone:** Yes. **Rest Rooms and Showers:** Yes. **Fuel:** No. **Propane:** Yes. **Internal Roads:** Paved/gravel, in good condition. **RV Service:** No. **Market:** 4 mi. north in Laona. **Restaurant:** 4 mi. north in Laona. **General Store:** Yes, limited. **Vending:** No. **Swimming Pool:** No. **Playground:** Yes. **Other:** Ham Lake, swimming beach, rec room, pavilion, mini golf, badminton, sports field, horseshoes, hiking trail, rental cabin & cottages, volleyball, fishing lake, boat dock. **Activities:** Swimming, fishing, hiking, boating (rental rowboats, canoes & paddleboats available). **Nearby Attractions:** Chequamegon-Nicolet National Forest, steam-powered train, lumberjack museum, bird refuge, casino, golf, snowmobile & cross-country ski trails, fishing, hunting, canoeing, antiques, arts & crafts, scenic drive, trout fishing. **Additional Information:** Laona Chamber of Commerce, (715) 674-3007.

## RESTRICTIONS

**Pets:** Leash only. **Fires:** Fire ring only. **Alcoholic Beverages:** Permitted. **Vehicle Maximum Length:** None.

## TO GET THERE

From the junction of US 8 and Hwy. 32, drive 4 mi. south on Hwy. 32. Road is wide and well maintained w/ broad shoulders.

## MENOMONIE

### Edgewater Acres Campground

E5468 670th Ave., Menomonie 54751. T: (715) 235-3291; www.mycampground.com; info@mycampground.com.

🚐 ★★★                    ⛺ ★★★★

Beauty: ★★★★              Site Privacy: ★★★
Spaciousness: ★★★          Quiet: ★★★
Security: ★★★              Cleanliness: ★★★
Insect Control: ★★★         Facilities: ★★★

Located an hour from the Twin Cities and a half hour from Eau Claire, Edgewater Acres Campground is a handy stopping point. Many campers also choose Edgewater Acres because of its water activities. Secluded sites are available on the Red Cedar River. The campground is seven miles from the start of the Red Cedar Bike Trail. Laid out in a series of loops, the campground has 38 seasonal campers and a typical site width of 30 feet. A separate tent area offers more greenery and privacy. A separate group area also allows group campers to have adjoining sites. The campground offers great fishing and a nice shoreline for children to fish from. Sites are level with a choice of shade or sun. The best sites are located on the shoreline.

## BASICS

**Operated by:** Tina King. **Open:** May 1–Oct. 1. **Site Assignment:** Reservations w/ 1-night deposit; refund w/ 7-day notice. **Registration:** At campground office. **Fee:** $22 (cash). **Parking:** At site.

## FACILITIES

**Number of RV Sites:** 55. **Number of Tent-Only Sites:** 17. **Hookups:** Electric (15, 20 amps), water. **Each Site:** Picnic table, fire ring. **Dump Station:** Yes. **Laundry:** No. **Pay Phone:** Yes. **Rest Rooms and Showers:** Yes. **Fuel:** No. **Propane:** No. **Internal Roads:** Gravel, in good condition. **RV Service:** No. **Market:** 3 mi. north in Menomonie. **Restaurant:** 3 mi. north in Menomonie. **General Store:** Yes, limited. **Vending:** Yes. **Swimming Pool:** Yes. **Playground:** Yes. **Other:** Fish-cleaning house, boat launch, horseshoes, volleyball, basketball, rec hall, game room, fishing lake, fishing river, sports field.

**Activities:** Fishing, swimming, boating (rental canoes, paddleboats, rowboats available). **Nearby Attractions:** Golf, antiques, Empire in Pine Lumber Museum, Wakanda Water Park, go-cart races, stock car races, Crystal Cave, Wilson Place Museum, Caddie Woodlawn Historic Park, Mabel Tainter Theater, state park. **Additional Information:** Menomonie Area Local Tourism, (800) 283-1862.

## RESTRICTIONS

**Pets:** Leash only. **Fires:** Fire ring only. **Alcoholic Beverages:** Permitted. **Vehicle Maximum Length:** None.

## TO GET THERE

From the junction of I-94 and Hwy. 25, take Exit 41, drive 2 mi. north on Hwy. 25, then 1.5 mi. east on CR BB, then 0.75 mi. south on Cedar Falls Rd. (530th St.), then 0.5 mi. east on gravel road. Roads are mostly wide and well maintained w/ good shoulders.

## MILTON

### Hidden Valley RV Resort and Campground

872 East Hwy. 59, Milton 53563. T: (800) 469-5515; www.hiddenvalleyrvresort.com.

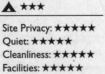

| 🚐 ★★★★ | ▲ ★★★ |
|---|---|
| Beauty: ★★★★ | Site Privacy: ★★★★★ |
| Spaciousness: ★★★★★ | Quiet: ★★★★★ |
| Security: ★★★★★ | Cleanliness: ★★★★★ |
| Insect Control: None | Facilities: ★★★★★ |

Hidden Valley RV Resort and Campground, two miles east of Edgerton, makes a wonderful first impression with its stone waterfall at the entrance. And the rural campground lives up that impression. Grounds are manicured almost like a golf course; sites are spacious (40 feet wide), mostly grassy with gravel pads, and adjoin a grassy park area. The campground opened in 1993, and most of the trees are still rather small to provide much shade. Exceptionally clean, modern facilities along with a large, three-level clubhouse add luxury touches. Tent campers are permitted to use RV sites, but the campground may be a bit too organized for many tent enthusiasts. The campground has a manager who lives on site, regular patrols, and one-way roads throughout the facility for security.

## BASICS

**Operated by:** Jim & Marcia Kersten. **Open:** Apr. 15–Oct. 15. **Site Assignment:** Reservations accepted w/ 1-night deposit; refund (minus $10 fee) w/ 7-day notice. **Registration:** At campground office. **Fee:** $29 (cash, check, credit cards). **Parking:** At site.

## FACILITIES

**Number of RV Sites:** 175. **Number of Tent-Only Sites:** 0. **Hookups:** Electric (20, 30, 50 amps), water, sewer. **Each Site:** Picnic table, fire ring. **Dump Station:** Yes. **Laundry:** Yes. **Pay Phone:** Yes. **Rest Rooms and Showers:** Yes. **Fuel:** No. **Propane:** Yes. **Internal Roads:** Gravel, in good condition. **RV Service:** No. **Market:** 2 mi. west in Edgerton. **Restaurant:** 0.1 mi. any direction. **General Store:** Yes. **Vending:** No. **Swimming Pool:** Yes. **Playground:** Yes. **Other:** Hot tub, video game room, lounge areas, meeting room, deck, TV room, 4-acre recreations area including softball, volleyball, horseshoes. **Activities:** Swimming, biking (rental bikes available), planned weekly activities. **Nearby Attractions:** Waterskiing, boating, fishing, swimming on Lake Koshkonong, golf, Milton House Museum. **Additional Information:** Milton Area Chamber of Commerce, (608) 868-6222.

## RESTRICTIONS

**Pets:** Leash only. **Fires:** Fire ring only. **Alcoholic Beverages:** Permitted. **Vehicle Maximum Length:** None.

## TO GET THERE

From the junction of I-90 and Hwy. 59, take Exit 163 and drive 0.75 mi. east on Hwy. 59. Roads are wide and well maintained w/ broad shoulders.

## MILTON

### Lakeland Camping Resort

1948 West Hwy. 59, Milton 53563. T: (608) 868-4700

| 🚐 ★★★ | ▲ n/a |
|---|---|
| Beauty: ★★★ | Site Privacy: ★★★ |
| Spaciousness: ★★★ | Quiet: ★★★★ |
| Security: ★★★★ | Cleanliness: ★★★★ |
| Insect Control: None | Facilities: ★★★★ |

The statistics are impressive: about 575 total campground sites on beautiful Lake Kosh-konong (the state's second largest lake), a well-stocked campground store, and wealth of recreational activities. But Lakeland Camping Resort is filled mostly with seasonal campers. Only 30 overnight sites are available, so reservations are strongly recommended. The sites are mostly shaded, with nine pull-throughs (30 × 60 feet) and eight with sewer. Laid out in a series of loops, the campground offers a pleasant wilderness/rural setting with over a mile of lakeshore. Tents are not permitted. The complex, 2.5 miles north of Edgerton, includes Lakeland Custom Coach RV Sales and Service Center.

## BASICS

**Operated by:** Lakeland Leisure Corp. **Open:** May 1–Nov. 1. **Site Assignment:** Reservations w/ 1-night deposit, 3-night deposit for holidays; refund w/ week notice. **Registration:** At campground office. **Fee:** $33.15 (cash, check, credit cards). **Parking:** At site.

## FACILITIES

**Number of RV Sites:** 500. **Number of Tent-Only Sites:** 0. **Hookups:** Electric (20, 30, 50 amps), water, sewer. **Each Site:** Picnic table, fire ring. **Dump Station:** Yes. **Laundry:** Yes. **Pay Phone:** Yes. **Rest Rooms and Showers:** Yes. **Fuel:** No. **Propane:** Yes. **Internal Roads:** Paved, in good condition. **RV Service:** Yes. **Market:** 2.5 mi. west in Edgerton. **Restaurant:** 2.5 mi. west in Edgerton. **General Store:** Yes. **Vending:** Yes. **Swimming Pool:** Yes. **Playground:** Yes. **Other:** Lake, sandy beach, tennis courts, recreation center, boat launch, game room, nature trails, cross-country & snowmobile trails, bait shop. **Activities:** Swimming, fishing, boating (rental boats available), hiking, planned. **Nearby Attractions:** Golf, Milton House Museum, hunting preserve, horseback riding, antique shops, county fairs & festivals, 35 mi. to Madison. **Additional Information:** Greater Madison CVB, (800) 373-6376.

## RESTRICTIONS

**Pets:** Leash only. **Fires:** Fire pits only. **Alcoholic Beverages:** Permitted. **Vehicle Maximum Length:** None. **Other:** No tents. Limit of 2 trout per day, per person in pond. Pets must be on 7-ft. leash.

## TO GET THERE

From the junction of I-90 and East State Rd 59, drive 2 mi. east on 59. Roads are wide and well-maintained w/ broad shoulders

## MILTON

### Lakeview Campground

1901 East WI 59, Milton 53563. T: (608) 868-7899

🚐 ★★        ▲ ★★

Beauty: ★★★          Site Privacy: ★★
Spaciousness: ★★       Quiet: ★★★
Security: ★★★          Cleanliness: ★★★
Insect Control: None    Facilities: ★★

Located on the shore of Lake Koshkonong, Lakeview Campground offers mooring facilities a short walk from campsite. Docks are provided for easy entry and exit from the boats. RV sites are level, mostly grassy, and shaded, with two pull-throughs. Both primitive and improved sites are available for tent campers. Tent sites on the shore are most popular with tent campers. Lakeview's 800 feet of shoreline boasts two beaches. The main beach, located directly in front of the lodge, is best for swimming and picnics on provided picnic benches. The smaller secluded beach to the northwest of the camp is a rustic retreat used mostly for tanning or quiet times. Check out the "window wall" of the lodge offering a panoramic view that stretches up to ten miles

## BASICS

**Operated by:** Dorothy Zaccari. **Open:** Apr. 1–Oct. 31. **Site Assignment:** Reservations w/ 1-night fee; refunds w/ 7-day notice. **Registration:** At campground office. **Fee:** $26 (cash). **Parking:** At site.

## FACILITIES

**Number of RV Sites:** 75. **Number of Tent-Only Sites:** 30. **Hookups:** Electric (30, 50 amps). **Each Site:** Picnic table, fire ring. **Dump Station:** Yes. **Laundry:** No. **Pay Phone:** No. **Rest Rooms and Showers:** Yes. **Fuel:** Yes. **Propane:** No. **Internal Roads:** Gravel, in good condition. **RV Service:** No. **Market:** 4 mi. west in Milton. **Restaurant:** 4 mi. west in Milton. **General Store:** No. **Vending:** No. **Swimming Pool:** No. **Playground:** Yes. **Other:** Lake Koshkonong, rec room, boat dock, gameroom, lodge, snack bar. **Activities:** Swimming, fishing, boating, lodge. **Nearby Attractions:** Waterskiing, golf, Milton House Museum, horseback riding, skeet shooting. **Additional Information:** Milton Area Chamber of Commerce, (800) 868-6222.

## RESTRICTIONS

**Pets:** Leash only. **Fires:** Fire ring only. **Alcoholic Beverages:** Permitted. **Vehicle Maximum Length:** None.

## TO GET THERE

From the junction of I-90 and Hwy. 59, take Exit 163, then drive 1.5 mi. east on Hwy. 59. Roads are wide and well maintained w/ broad shoulders.

## MINOCQUA

### Patricia Lake Campground

8505 Camp Pinemere Rd., Minocqua 54548. T: (715) 356-3198; F: (715) 358-3149; patlake@newnorth.net.

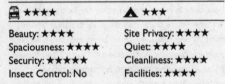

🚐 ★★★                      ▲ ★★★

| | |
|---|---|
| Beauty: ★★★ | Site Privacy: ★★★ |
| Spaciousness: ★★★ | Quiet: ★★★ |
| Security: ★★★ | Cleanliness: ★★★★ |
| Insect Control: ★★★ | Facilities: ★★★★ |

Situated on the Oneida/Vilas County border near Chequamegon National Forest in Minocqua, Patricia Lake Campground features wooded sites on Patricia Lake. A small, deep, spring-fed lake with no wake, Patricia Lake has good fishing for bass, northern pike and crappies. Nearby is the famous Minocqua Chain of Lakes for excellent fishing. Sites are level and mostly wooded. A separate tenting area offers tenters more green space and privacy. The campground has four pull-through sites, 69 seasonal campers, and a typical site width of 30 feet. The campground is conveniently located one mile from an 18-hole golf course and petting zoo and three miles from downtown shops. Most popular sites are closest to the lake. Campground owners provide security and make sure the campground is kept quiet and family oriented.

## BASICS

**Operated by:** David & Joy Taber. **Open:** May 1–Oct. 15. **Site Assignment:** Reservations w/ 1-night deposit; refund w/ 2-week notice. **Registration:** At campground office. **Fee:** $23 (cash, check, credit cards). **Parking:** At site.

## FACILITIES

**Number of RV Sites:** 97. **Number of Tent-Only Sites:** 3. **Hookups:** Electric (20, 30 amps), water, sewer. **Each Site:** Picnic table, fire ring. **Dump Station:** Yes. **Laundry:** Yes. **Pay Phone:** Yes. **Rest Rooms and Showers:** Yes. **Fuel:** Yes. **Propane:** Yes. **Internal Roads:** Gravel, in fair condition. **RV Service:** No. **Market:** 3 mi. south. **Restaurant:** 3 mi. south. **General Store:** Yes.

**Vending:** Yes. **Swimming Pool:** No. **Playground:** Yes. **Other:** Patricia Lake, swimming beach, horseshoes, volleyball, basketball, game room, pavilion, boat launch, recreation field, hiking trails. **Activities:** Swimming, fishing, hiking, boating (rental canoes, paddleboats, rowboats available). **Nearby Attractions:** Golf, Peck's Wildwood Wildlife Park & Nature Center, casino, antiques, arts & crafts, cross-country skiing, snowmobiling, professional repertory theater, Circle M Corral amusement park. **Additional Information:** Minocqua-Arbor Vitae-Woodrull Area Chamber of Commerce, (800) 446-6784.

## RESTRICTIONS

**Pets:** Leash only; small pets only. **Fires:** Fire ring only. **Alcoholic Beverages:** Permitted. **Vehicle Maximum Length:** None.

## TO GET THERE

From south junction US 51 and Hwy. 70, drive 2.5 mi. west on Hwy. 70, then 0.5 mi. south on Camp Pinemere Rd. Roads are mostly wide and well maintained w/ borad shoulders.

## MONTELLO

### Buffalo Lake Camping Resort

555 Lake Ave., Montello 53949. T: (888) 297-2915; F: (608) 297-9072; buffalolakecamping.com; lake@maqs.net.

🚐 ★★★★                     ▲ ★★★

| | |
|---|---|
| Beauty: ★★★★ | Site Privacy: ★★★★ |
| Spaciousness: ★★★★ | Quiet: ★★★★ |
| Security: ★★★★★ | Cleanliness: ★★★★ |
| Insect Control: No | Facilities: ★★★★ |

Buffalo Lake Camping Resort has the benefits of being located within the town of Montello, without the drawbacks of city noise and traffic. With a barrier of trees and large grassy areas, the campground is secluded and quiet. The campground is situated on 2,200-acre Buffalo Lake, the largest in Marquette County (called a "Sportsman's Paradise"), and the lake is well known for its northern pike, bass, crappie, bluegill, and perch. A well-stocked campground store carries groceries, beer, ice, firewood, camping supplies, snacks, clothing, souvenirs, fishing licenses, live bait, tackle, and boat rentals. A new laundry, rest rooms, and showers are kept clean, and rules about cleanliness and quiet are enforced. Recycling is mandatory, with recycling areas located throughout the campground. Quiet hours are 11 p.m. to 7 p.m. and children under 18 years old must remain in their campsite with adult supervision after 10 p.m. Owners live next door, the back gate to the campground is locked at night, and city police patrol the campground for security.

## BASICS

**Operated by:** Linda & Gary Doudna. **Open:** Apr. 12–Oct. 14. **Site Assignment:** Reservations w/ 2-night deposit; refund (minus $5 fee) w/ 14-day notice. **Registration:** At campground office. **Fee:** $28 (cash, check, credit cards). **Parking:** At site.

## FACILITIES

**Number of RV Sites:** 111. **Number of Tent-Only Sites:** 0. **Hookups:** Electric (20, 30, 50 amps), water, sewer. **Each Site:** Picnic table, fire ring. **Dump Station:** Yes. **Laundry:** Yes. **Pay Phone:** Yes. **Rest Rooms and Showers:** Yes. **Fuel:** No. **Propane:** Yes. **Internal Roads:** Gravel, in good condition. **RV Service:** No. **Market:** 1 mi. south in Montello. **Restaurant:** Across the road. **General Store:** Yes. **Vending:** Yes. **Swimming Pool:** Yes. **Playground:** Yes. **Other:** Arcade, bait & tackle, horseshoes, covered pavilion, basketball, volleyball, lake boat dock, 4 piers, boat ramp, fish-cleaning house. **Activities:** Swimming, fishing, boating (rental canoes, kayaks & rowboats available), planned activities. **Nearby Attractions:** Rivers & trout streams, scenic country roads, 30 mi. to Wisconsin Dells. **Additional Information:** Wisconsin Dells Visitor & Convention Bureau, (800) 223-3557.

## RESTRICTIONS

**Pets:** Leash only. **Fires:** Fire pits only. **Alcoholic Beverages:** Permitted. **Vehicle Maximum Length:** None.

## TO GET THERE

From Madison, take I-90/94 to Exit 108B to WI 23 East, drive 8 mi. to CR C (Lake Ave.), 0.75 mi. to entrance. Roads are wide and well maintained w/ broad shoulders.

## MONTELLO
### Kilby Lake Campground

N4492 Fern Ave., Montello 53949. T: (877) 497-2344; www.kilbylake.com; klcg@yahoo.com.

 ★★★★          ▲ ★★★★

Beauty: ★★★★          Site Privacy: ★★★★
Spaciousness: ★★★★     Quiet: ★★★★

Security: ★★★★★          Cleanliness: ★★★★★
Insect Control: None     Facilities: ★★★★★

Since opening their campground in 1993, Jim and Sharon Caulfield have tried to add a little something every year for campers. The results are obvious. Located two miles west of Montello, Kilby Lake Campground has the wilderness beauty of a state park with extras usually not found at such facilities. Rustic sites are generally spacious (some 30 × 60 feet) and separated by mature oak trees. The 50-acre Kilby Lake is restricted to no wake to ensure cleanliness and great fishing. Known as a family campground, Kilby Lake Campground also sets aside and enforces "adult times." Friday and Saturday from 8 p.m. to 10 p.m., the heated swimming pool is reserved for adults only. Children may not be in the pool area during that time. Children under 16 also are not allowed in the whirlpool at any time. The 2001 addition was a bird sanctuary located just off the hiking trail behind the petting zoo. The campground offers scheduled birding tours and owl calling evenings. With all it has going for it, Kilby Lake Campground suffers from the results of popularity—66 of the full-hookup sites are occupied by seasonals, leaving only seven for visiting campers. Reservations are definitely recommended.

## BASICS

**Operated by:** Jim & Sharon Caulfield. **Open:** Apr. 15–Dec. 1. **Site Assignment:** Reservations w/ 50 percent deposit, special event & holiday weekend 100 percent deposit; refunds (minus $5 fee) w/ 7-day notice or 14 days prior to holiday & special events. **Registration:** At campground office. **Fee:** $28 (cash, check, credit cards). **Parking:** At site.

## FACILITIES

**Number of RV Sites:** 122. **Number of Tent-Only Sites:** 0. **Hookups:** Electric (20, 30, 50 amps), water, sewer. **Each Site:** Picnic table, fire ring. **Dump Station:** Yes. **Laundry:** Yes. **Pay Phone:** Yes. **Rest Rooms and Showers:** Yes. **Fuel:** No. **Propane:** Yes. **Internal Roads:** Gravel, in good condition. **RV Service:** No. **Market:** 2 mi. east in Montello. **Restaurant:** 2 mi. east in Montello. **General Store:** Yes. **Vending:** Yes. **Swimming Pool:** Yes. **Playground:** Yes. **Other:** Farm animal petting zoo, whirlpool, lake, bird sanctuary, mini-golf, game room, shelter, horseshoes, hiking trail, beach house, beach, piers. **Activities:** Swimming, fishing, boating (rental rowboats, canoes & paddle-boats available), bird-watching, hiking, scheduled activities. **Nearby Attractions:** Rivers & trout streams, scenic country roads, 30 mi. to Wisconsin Dells. **Additional Information:** Wisconsin Dells CVB, (800) 223-3557.

### RESTRICTIONS

**Pets:** Leash only. **Fires:** Fire ring only. **Alcoholic Beverages:** Permitted. **Vehicle Maximum Length:** 40 ft. **Other:** 3-night min. on Memorial Day, Raspberry Fest & Labor Day, 4-night min. on 4th of July.

### TO GET THERE

From the junction of Hwy. 23 and Hwy. 50/49, drive 6 mi. east on Hwy. 23 to Fern Ave. Drive north on Fern 0.4 mi. Roads are wide and well maintained w/ broad shoulders.

## MONTELLO
### Wilderness Campground

N 1499 State Hwy. 22, Montello 53949. T: (608) 297-2002; www.wildernesscampground.com; wildrnes@palacenet.net.

🚐 ★★★★　　　　🏕 ★★★★

| | |
|---|---|
| Beauty: ★★★★ | Site Privacy: ★★★★ |
| Spaciousness: ★★★★ | Quiet: ★★★★ |
| Security: ★★★★ | Cleanliness: ★★★★ |
| Insect Control: None | Facilities: ★★★★ |

Under the same ownership for more than three decades, Wilderness Campground offers easy access and a quiet facility away from highway noise. Located seven miles south of Montello, in the heart of Wisconsin's vacation land, the campground is on the shores of beautiful Bonnie and Hidden Lakes. The three private lakes provide plenty of water recreation, along with a large heated swimming pool. Laid out in a series of loops, the campground has 100 seasonal campers, 75 pull-through sites, and a typical site width of 45 feet. Sites are grassy, level, and mostly shaded in a rambling oak woodland. A separate tent area provides privacy from RVs and more green space. The best sites for tents and RVs are along the lakes. Tons of turtles and frogs keep down the mosquito population without insecticides. Security and safety measures include a 10 p.m. curfew for youngsters, a ban on bicycles on the roads after 8 p.m., quiet time starting 11 p.m., and owners who live on site and provide regular campground patrols.

### BASICS

**Operated by:** Bea Weiss. **Open:** Apr. 15–Oct. 15. **Site Assignment:** Reservations w/ 50 percent deposit; refund (minus $5) w/ 14-day notice. **Registration:** At campground office. **Fee:** $30 (cash, check, credit cards). **Parking:** At site.

### FACILITIES

**Number of RV Sites:** 290. **Number of Tent-Only Sites:** 10. **Hookups:** Electric (15, 20, 30, 50 amps), water, sewer, phone. **Each Site:** Picnic table, fire ring. **Dump Station:** Yes. **Laundry:** Yes. **Pay Phone:** Yes. **Rest Rooms and Showers:** Yes. **Fuel:** No. **Propane:** Yes. **Internal Roads:** Paved/gravel, in good condition. **RV Service:** No. **Market:** 6 mi. north in Montello. **Restaurant:** 6 mi. north in Montello. **General Store:** Yes. **Vending:** Yes. **Swimming Pool:** Yes. **Playground:** Yes. **Other:** Three private lakes, dance hall, petting zoo, hiking trails, rental cabins, rental RVs, mini golf, rec hall, mini farm, pavilion, coin games, snack bar, boat ramp, badminton, sports field, volleyball, sandy beach. **Activities:** Hiking, swimming, fishing, boating (no motors allowed, rental rowboats, canoes & paddleboats available), scheduled activities. **Nearby Attractions:** Wisconsin Dells, golf, horseback riding, wildlife refuge, granite quarries, historic homes, museums, fish hatchery, Circus World museum, Devil's Lake, casino, stock car racing, antiques, arts & crafts. **Additional Information:** Wisconsin Dells Visitor & Convention Bureau, (800) 223-3557.

### RESTRICTIONS

**Pets:** Leash only. **Fires:** Fire ring only. **Alcoholic Beverages:** Permitted. **Vehicle Maximum Length:** None.

### TO GET THERE

From the junction of Hwy. 23 and Hwy. 22 southbound, drive 7 mi. south on Hwy. 22. Roads are wide and well maintained w/ mostly broad shoulders.

## NEW LONDON
### Wolf River Trips and Campgrounds

E8041 County Hwy. X, New London 54961. T: (920) 982-2458; F: (920) 982-6122; rivertrips@yahoo.com.

🚐 ★★★　　　　🏕 ★★★

| | |
|---|---|
| Beauty: ★★★ | Site Privacy: ★★★ |
| Spaciousness: ★★★ | Quiet: ★★★ |

Security: ★★★★  Cleanliness: ★★★★
Insect Control: None  Facilities: ★★★

Located five miles southwest of New London, Little Wolf Trips and Campground offers wooded sites along Little Wolf River and rustic sites on Big Wolf River. Tubing trips start at the campground, where a shuttle bus takes tubers to the put-in point on the Wolf River. From there, the river takes tubers through rocks, rapids and quiet drifting areas back to the campground. The typical site width is 24 feet, and the campground has ten pull-throughs and 20 seasonal campers. The most desirable sites for both RVs and tents are along the river. All sites are either grassy or sand. An on-site lounge serves fast food and drinks. Security measures include one entrance/ exit road, owners who live on site, regular patrols, and a 24-hour staffed security phone.

## BASICS

**Operated by:** Mark & Gary Flease & Janet Koplien. **Open:** May 1–Oct. 1. **Site Assignment:** Reservations w/ 1-night deposit; refund w/ 10-day notice. **Registration:** At campground office. **Fee:** $20 (cash, check). **Parking:** At site.

## FACILITIES

**Number of RV Sites:** 105. **Number of Tent-Only Sites:** 30. **Hookups:** Electric (15, 30, 50 amps), water, sewer. **Each Site:** Picnic table, fire ring. **Dump Station:** Yes. **Laundry:** Yes. **Pay Phone:** Yes. **Rest Rooms and Showers:** Yes. **Fuel:** No. **Propane:** No. **Internal Roads:** Paved/gravel, in good condition. **RV Service:** No. **Market:** 5 mi. northeast in New London. **Restaurant:** 5 mi. northeast in New London. **General Store:** Yes, limited. **Vending:** Yes. **Swimming Pool:** No. **Playground:** Yes. **Other:** Wolf River, tennis, ball diamond, volleyball, rec hall, lounge, horseshoes, shuffleboard, pavilion, hiking trails. **Activities:** Swimming, fishing, canoeing (rental canoes available), tubing, boat ramp, boat dock,. **Nearby Attractions:** Chapel in the Woods, covered bridges, snowmobile trails, Red Mill, sternwheeler cruises, golf, museums, historic sites, antiques, Wisconsin Veterans Museum. **Additional Information:** Waupaca Area Chamber of Commerce, (888) 417-4040.

## RESTRICTIONS

**Pets:** Leash only. **Fires:** Fire ring only. **Alcoholic Beverages:** Permitted. **Vehicle Maximum Length:** None.

## TO GET THERE

From the junction of US 45 and Hwy. 54, drive 4 mi. west on Hwy. 54, then 1 mi. south on Larry Rd., then 2 blocks west on CR X. The roads are wide and well maintained w/ broad shoulders.

# NORMAN

## Maple View Campground

N1460 Hwy. B, Kewaunee 54216. T: (920) 776-1588

🚐 ★★★  ⛺ ★★★

Beauty: ★★★  Site Privacy: ★★★★
Spaciousness: ★★★★  Quiet: ★★★★
Security: ★★★  Cleanliness: ★★★
Insect Control: None  Facilities: ★★★

Perched on a high ridge, Maple View Campground is wooded with maple trees, of course. It may be the only campground that makes its own maple syrup from its own maple trees. The syrup is for sale in the camp store. Located eight miles south of Kewaunee, Maple View has level sites; mostl are shaded, but some open ones are available for those who worry about satellite TV reception. Laid out in a series of loops, the campground offers four pull-throughs, 35 seasonals, and a typical site width of 36 feet. Most sites have a green buffer of trees and bushes for privacy and quietness. The best RV site is 22, known as the "honeymoon suite," offering a bigger spot and closeness to facilities. But you don't have to be a newlywed to stay there. The best tent sites are in a separate area down by the lake where they offer privacy away from RVs. Facilities are smoke-free. You don't need a license to fish in the private lake, which is stocked with perch, bluegill, and largemouth bass. Quiet time is 11 p.m. to 8 a.m., the speed limit is five mph, and the owners live on site to ensure safety and quietness.

## BASICS

**Operated by:** Joyce LaCrosse. **Open:** May 1–Oct. 15. **Site Assignment:** Reservations w/ 1-night deposit; refund w/ 7-day notice. **Registration:** At campground office. **Fee:** $18 (cash & check). **Parking:** At site.

## FACILITIES

**Number of RV Sites:** 65. **Number of Tent-Only Sites:** 10. **Hookups:** Electric (20, 30, 50 amps), water. **Each Site:** Picnic table, fire ring. **Dump Station:** Yes. **Laundry:** Yes. **Pay Phone:**

Yes. **Rest Rooms and Showers:** Yes. **Fuel:** No. **Propane:** No. **Internal Roads:** Gravel, in good condition. **RV Service:** No. **Market:** 8 mi. north in Kewaunee. **Restaurant:** 8 mi. north in Kewaunee. **General Store:** Yes, limited. **Vending:** Yes. **Swimming Pool:** No. **Playground:** Yes. **Other:** Lake, swimming beach, pavilion, ball diamond, horseshoes, volleyball, basketball, rental cabins, hiking trails, badminton. **Activities:** Swimming, fishing, hiking, boating (no motors), scheduled weekend activities. **Nearby Attractions:** Lake Michigan, boating, charter fishing, harbor, boat launch, cheese factories, antiques, arts & crafts, Door County, zoo, jail museum, golf, nautical museum, nature walk. **Additional Information:** Kewaunee Chamber of Commerce, (800) 666-8214.

### RESTRICTIONS

**Pets:** Leash only. **Fires:** Fire ring only. **Alcoholic Beverages:** Permitted. **Vehicle Maximum Length:** None.

### TO GET THERE

From the junction of Hwy. 42 and CR G, drive 3 mi. west on CR G, then 500 feet south on Norman Rd. Roads are wide and well maintained w/ broad shoulders.

## OAKDALE
### Granger's Campground

Rte. 3, Tomah 54660. T: (608) 372-4511

| 🚐 ★★ | ▲ ★★ |
|---|---|
| Beauty: ★★ | Site Privacy: ★★ |
| Spaciousness: ★★ | Quiet: ★★★ |
| Security: ★★★ | Cleanliness: ★★ |
| Insect Control: None | Facilities: ★★★ |

Level grassy sites in a rural location with handy interstate access make this a good spot for travelers looking for an overnight stay. Granger's Campground also offers RV repair service and is located next to Granger's outdoor power equipment business. But don't count on Dwayne Granger being able to quickly work in a last-minute repair—the shop has a waiting list. Thirty-five large (50 × 80 feet) pull-through sites arranged in a series of loops provide easy in-and-out for RVs. Located six miles east of Tomah, the campground features few recreational outlets or activities and doesn't offer much privacy for tent campers. Security is good, with lights on the premises and an owner who

lives on site and patrols the facilities. Noise can be a bit bothersome, depending on the interstate traffic and vehicles driving down the county road by the campground.

### BASICS

**Operated by:** Grangers LLC. **Open:** Apr. 1–Dec. 1. **Site Assignment:** Reservation w/ one-night deposit, refund w/ 7-day notice. **Registration:** At campground office. **Fee:** $13.66 (cash, check, credit cards). **Parking:** At site.

### FACILITIES

**Number of RV Sites:** 45. **Number of Tent-Only Sites:** 3. **Hookups:** Electric (30 amps), water, sewer. **Each Site:** Picnic table, fire ring. **Dump Station:** Yes. **Laundry:** Yes. **Pay Phone:** Yes. **Rest Rooms and Showers:** Yes. **Fuel:** No. **Propane:** Yes. **Internal Roads:** Gravel, in good condition. **RV Service:** Yes. **Market:** 6 mi. west in Tomah. **Restaurant:** 6 mi. west in Tomah. **General Store:** Yes. **Vending:** No. **Swimming Pool:** No. **Playground:** Yes. **Other:** Pavilion, horseshoes, basketball, volleyball, badminton. **Activities:** Pancake breakfast on holidays, hayrides on holidays & weekends. **Nearby Attractions:** Bike trail, cranberry museum, golf, roller rink, cranberry festival, 45 min. drive to Wisconsin Dells. **Additional Information:** Warrens Area Business Assoc., (608) 378-4878.

### RESTRICTIONS

**Pets:** Leash only. **Fires:** Fire ring only. **Alcoholic Beverages:** At sites only. **Vehicle Maximum Length:** 55 ft.

### TO GET THERE

From the junction of I-90/94 and CR PP, take Exit 48, drive 0.4 mi. north on CR PP. The roads are wide and well maintained w/ good shoulders.

## OAKDALE
### Oakdale KOA

P.O. Box 150, Oakdale 54649. T: (800) KOA-1737

| 🚐 ★★★★ | ▲ ★★ |
|---|---|
| Beauty: ★★★ | Site Privacy: ★★★ |
| Spaciousness: ★★★ | Quiet: ★★ |
| Security: ★★★★ | Cleanliness: ★★★★ |
| Insect Control: None | Facilities: ★★★★ |

It's inevitable: Access this convenient (just one block) to the interstate also means a noisy campground with the rumbling of trucks and cars passing by. This is probably more of a distraction for tent campers than RVs. But convenience is what Oakdale KOA has in abundance. Located in the heart of cranberry country, six miles southeast of Tomah, the campground is a popular site during the annual Cranberry Festival in Sept., as well as for bike riders on the nearby state bike trails. The pluses are mature pine and oak trees (with beautiful fall foliage) and mostly pull-through, level sites with new water and electric hookups. Shade is abundant, but some trees have been newly cut for those RVs with satellite dishes. New tent sites with concrete curbing outlining tent placement areas offer dependability for campers.

## BASICS

**Operated by:** William Rood. **Open:** May 11–Oct. 15. **Site Assignment:** Reservations w/ 1-night deposit; refunds w/ 24-hour notice. **Registration:** At campground office. **Fee:** $24 (cash, check, credit cards). **Parking:** At site.

## FACILITIES

**Number of RV Sites:** 47. **Number of Tent-Only Sites:** 6. **Hookups:** Electric (20, 30, 50 amps), water, sewer, cable TV, phone. **Each Site:** Picnic table, fire ring. **Dump Station:** Yes. **Laundry:** Yes. **Pay Phone:** Yes. **Rest Rooms and Showers:** Yes. **Fuel:** No. **Propane:** Yes. **Internal Roads:** Gravel, in good condition. **RV Service:** No. **Market:** 6 mi. northwest in Tomah. **Restaurant:** 6 mi. northwest in Tomah. **General Store:** Yes. **Vending:** No. **Swimming Pool:** Yes. **Playground:** Yes. **Other:** Game room, heated & air-conditioned pavilion, horseshoes, volleyball. **Activities:** Swimming, biking. **Nearby Attractions:** State bike trails, cranberry festival & tours, Tomah tractor pull, golf, roller skating. **Additional Information:** Warrens Area Business Assoc. (608) 378-4878.

## RESTRICTIONS

**Pets:** Leash only. **Fires:** Fire pits only. **Alcoholic Beverages:** At sites only. **Vehicle Maximum Length:** None.

## TO GET THERE

From the junction of I-90/94 and CR PP, take Exit 48, drive 1 block n on CR PP, then 2 blocks east on Woody Dr., 1 block south on Jay Street. Roads are well maintained w/ broad shoulders.

## ONTARIO

## Brush Creek Campground

S190 Opal Rd., Ontario 54651. T: (608) 337-4344

🚐 ★★      ⛺ ★★★★

Beauty: ★★★      Site Privacy: ★★★★
Spaciousness: ★★★★      Quiet: ★★★★
Security: ★★★★      Cleanliness: ★★★
Insect Control: None      Facilities: ★★★

A self-described "Mom and Pop" operation, Brush Creek Campground caters to tent campers. Campers can choose between terraced sites on a hill or more level sites by a creek. Located in the Kickapoo Valley, 24 miles east of Sparta, the wilderness campground has spring-fed creeks, wooded hills, and rolling meadows, with plenty of room to breathe and enjoy the peace and quiet. Special tent sites are reserved in the woods and along the creek. Campers are not permitted to carry in firewood because the owner says they often bring in too much wood and leave it dumped on site, or bring in wood that won't burn. Plentiful stacks of firewood can be bought at the campground for a couple of dollars. Security is good, as the campground is located on a dead-end country road, and the owners live on site and patrol the area.

## BASICS

**Operated by:** Bud & Sis Kalb. **Open:** May 1–Oct. 31. **Site Assignment:** Reservations w/ $20, refund w/ 7-day notice. **Registration:** At campground office. **Fee:** $16. **Parking:** At site.

## FACILITIES

**Number of RV Sites:** 35. **Number of Tent-Only Sites:** 70. **Hookups:** Electric (20, 30, 50 amps), water, sewer. **Each Site:** Many picnic table, fire ring. **Dump Station:** Yes. **Laundry:** Yes. **Pay Phone:** Yes. **Rest Rooms and Showers:** Yes. **Fuel:** No. **Propane:** No. **Internal Roads:** Gravel, in rough condition. **RV Service:** No. **Market:** 24 mi. west in Sparta. **Restaurant:** 2 mi. east in Ontario. **General Store:** Yes. **Vending:** Yes. **Swimming Pool:** No. **Playground:** Yes. **Other:** Pond, creeks, rec room, snack bar, hiking trails, horseshoes, volleyball, cable swing on lake. **Activities:** Swimming, fishing, hiking, kayak rentals, biking, scheduled weekend activities. **Nearby Attractions:** Golf, horseback riding, boating (rental kayaks available), Amish community, scenic drives. **Additional Information:** La Crosse Area CVB, (800) 658-9424.

## RESTRICTIONS

**Pets:** Leash only. **Fires:** Fire pits only. **Alcoholic Beverages:** Permitted. **Vehicle Maximum Length:** 33 ft. **Other:** 2-night min. on all reservations, 3-night min. on holidays. No firewood can be brought in, must be bought on premises.

## TO GET THERE

From the junction of Hwy. 131 and 33, drive 3 mi. west on Hwy. 33, then 0.5 mi. south on Opal Rd. Hwy. 33 is good road but watch out for Amish buggies sharing the roadway

# OSHKOSH

## Kalbus' Country Harbor

5309 Lake Rd., Oshkosh 54902. T: (920) 426-0062; F: (920) 426-4162.

| 🚐 ★★★ | ▲ ★★★ |
|---|---|
| Beauty: ★★★ | Site Privacy: ★★ |
| Spaciousness: ★★★ | Quiet: ★★★★ |
| Security: ★★★ | Cleanliness: ★★★★ |
| Insect Control: None | Facilities: ★★★ |

Seeing the lines of empty boat trailers sitting at the entrance to Kalbus' County Harbor lets you know one of the main attractions of this campground. Located seven miles south of Oshkosh, Country Harbor is the only campground on the west side of Lake Winnebago. Owned by the Kalbus family since the 1940s, the campground offers lake views from every site. Easy-access boat launching and docking is located in the center of the campground on a man-made channel. The beach area has a sandy shore and sand bottom, making it popular with snorkelers. The typical site width is 35 feet, and the campground has eight pull-through sites and 22 seasonal campers. All sites seem about equally good. Security measures include an owner who lives on site and provides regular patrols of the campground.

## BASICS

**Operated by:** Jerry Kalbus. **Open:** May 1–Oct. 31. **Site Assignment:** Reservations w/ 1-night deposit plus $5; refund (minus $5) w/ 7-day notice. **Registration:** At campground office. **Fee:** $25 (cash, check, credit cards). **Parking:** At site.

## FACILITIES

**Number of RV Sites:** 49. **Number of Tent-Only Sites:** 8. **Hookups:** Electric (20, 30, 50 amps), water, sewer. **Each Site:** Picnic table, fire ring. **Dump Station:** Yes. **Laundry:** Yes. **Pay Phone:** Yes. **Rest Rooms and Showers:** Yes. **Fuel:** Yes. **Propane:** Yes. **Internal Roads:** Gravel, in good condition. **RV Service:** No. **Market:** 6 mi. north in Oshkosh. **Restaurant:** 6 mi. north in Oshkosh. **General Store:** No. **Vending:** Yes. **Swimming Pool:** No. **Playground:** No. **Other:** Lake Winnebago, beach, boat launch, dock, fish-cleaning facilities. **Activities:** Swimming, fishing, boating (rental boats available). **Nearby Attractions:** Golf, The Morgan House, Grand Opera House, art center, arboretum, park, antiques, zoo, Military Veterans Museum, arts & crafts, EAA Air Adventure Museum. **Additional Information:** Oshkosh CVB, (877) 303-9200.

## RESTRICTIONS

**Pets:** Leash only. **Fires:** Fire ring only. **Alcoholic Beverages:** Permitted. **Vehicle Maximum Length:** 40 ft.

## TO GET THERE

From the junction of US 41/Hwy. 26/CR N, drive 3 mi. east on CR N (becomes Fisk Rd.), then 1.5 mi. south on US 45, then 0.5 mi. east on Nekimi Ave., then 0.25 mi. north on Lake Rd. Roads are wide and well maintained w/ broad shoulders.

# OSSEO

## Osseo Camping Resort

50483 Oak Grove Rd., Osseo 54758. T: (715) 597-2102

| 🚐 ★★★ | ▲ ★★★ |
|---|---|
| Beauty: ★★★★ | Site Privacy: ★★★ |
| Spaciousness: ★★★ | Quiet: ★★★★ |
| Security: ★★★★ | Cleanliness: ★★★ |
| Insect Control: Yes | Facilities: ★★★ |

Osseo Camping Resort already has the basis for a good campground, and the new owners are embarking on major projects to make it even better. In 2001, they started adding new camping sections, a new office, new pool, and other improvements. Then they plan to start on the existing campground area. With a typical site size of 40 × 60 feet, the campground features mostly shaded, level, grassy sites. With one entrance, owners who live on site, and a night patrol, the campground boasts a good safety record. Remote wooded sites also are available for tent campers. The campground is conveniently located near I-90, one mile east of Osseo. It is 90 miles from the Wisconsin Dells, 156 miles from Madison, 88 miles from the Minnesota state line, and 125 miles from the Mall of America.

## BASICS

**Operated by:** Tom & Joy Levake. **Open:** Apr. 15–Oct. 31. **Site Assignment:** Reservations w/ 1-night deposit; refunds w/ 1-week notice. **Registration:** At campground office. **Fee:** $22 (cash, check, credit cards). **Parking:** At site.

## FACILITIES

**Number of RV Sites:** 104. **Number of Tent-Only Sites:** 20. **Hookups:** Electric (20, 30 amps), water, sewer. **Each Site:** Picnic table, fire ring. **Dump Station:** Yes. **Laundry:** Yes. **Pay Phone:** Yes. **Rest Rooms and Showers:** Yes. **Fuel:** No. **Propane:** Yes. **Internal Roads:** Gravel, in good condition. **RV Service:** No. **Market:** 1 mi. west in Osseo. **Restaurant:** 1 mi. west in Osseo. **General Store:** Yes. **Vending:** No. **Swimming Pool:** Yes. **Playground:** Yes. **Other:** Video & TV game room, basketball, volleyball, horseshoes, outdoor stage, community fire ring, mini-golf, nature trails. **Activities:** Swimming, hiking, Saturday hayrides & dances, theme weekends. **Nearby Attractions:** Lakes, Northland Fishing Museum, golf, buffalo farm, hunting, Amish shops & farm tours, casino, antique & craft shops. **Additional Information:** Chippewa Valley CVB, (999) 523-3866.

## RESTRICTIONS

**Pets:** Leash only. **Fires:** Fire ring only. **Alcoholic Beverages:** Permitted. **Vehicle Maximum Length:** None. **Other:** Other.

## TO GET THERE

From the junction of I-94 and US 10, take Exit 88, drive 0.25 mi. east on US 10, then 0.25 mi. south on Oak Grove Rd. Roads are wide and well maintained w/ broad shoulders.

# OXFORD

## Coon's Deep Lake Campground

348 Fish Ln., Oxford 53952. T: (608) 586-5644

🚐 ★★★                    ⛺ ★★★

Beauty: ★★★             Site Privacy: ★★★
Spaciousness: ★★★      Quiet: ★★★★

Security: ★★★★          Cleanliness: ★★★★
Insect Control: None     Facilities: ★★★

First off, Coon's Deep Lake Campground has 30 seasonal campers, which leaves only ten sites for other RVs. The place is popular because of its lake for fishing and swimming. Arranged in three layers of terraces, the campground overlooks the lake which is down the hillside. Sites are grassy, shaded, and level. The campground is surrouned by farm fields and woods, which gives it a quiet setting. Quiet hours are between 10 p.m. and 7 a.m. The best tent sites are in the woods away from RVs. The best available RV sites are 17-22 because they are larger and offer a nice view. There are no pull-through sites. A family-owned campground three miles west of Oxford, Coon's Deep Lake Campground is about 15 minutes from the Wisconsin Dells. But given the scarcity of overnight sites, it is recommended that you call ahead for reservations.

## BASICS

**Operated by:** George & Delores Benish. **Open:** May 1–Sept. 10. **Site Assignment:** Reservation w/ 2-night deposit; refund w/ 7-day notice. **Registration:** At campground office. **Fee:** $18 (cash, check). **Parking:** At site.

## FACILITIES

**Number of RV Sites:** 40. **Number of Tent-Only Sites:** 10. **Hookups:** Electric (30, 50 amps), water. **Each Site:** Picnic table, fire ring. **Dump Station:** Yes. **Laundry:** Yes. **Pay Phone:** No. **Rest Rooms and Showers:** Yes. **Fuel:** No. **Propane:** No. **Internal Roads:** Gravel, in good condition. **RV Service:** No. **Market:** 3 mi. east in Oxford. **Restaurant:** 3 mi. east in Oxford. **General Store:** No. **Vending:** Yes. **Swimming Pool:** No. **Playground:** Yes. **Other:** Deep Lake, swimming beach, rec room, sports field, horseshoes. **Activities:** Swimming, fishing, boating (rental rowboats, canoe, paddleboats available). **Nearby Attractions:** Wisconsin Dells, scenic drives, golf. **Additional Information:** Wisconsin Dells Visitor & Convention Bureau, (800) 223-3557.

## RESTRICTIONS

**Pets:** Leash only. **Fires:** Fire ring only. **Alcoholic Beverages:** Permitted. **Vehicle Maximum Length:** None.

## TO GET THERE

From the junction of CR A and Hwy. 82, drive 4 mi. west on Hwy. 82, then 1,000 feet north on paved access road. Roads are wide and well maintained w/ adequate shoulders.

## PITTSVILLE
### Dexter Park

400 Market St., Wisconsin Rapids 54495. T: (715) 421-8422; co.wood.wi.us.

🚐 ★★★                          ⛺ ★★★★

Beauty: ★★★★                Site Privacy: ★★★★
Spaciousness: ★★★★         Quiet: ★★★★
Security: ★★★★              Cleanliness: ★★★
Insect Control: None         Facilities: ★★★

Dexter Park is long on scenic beauty and short on man-made amenities. But that is exactly what some campers are seeking. Others should be forewarned that there is no handy laundry for those wet and dirty clothes, no well-stocked campstore for forgotten or used-up items, and no heated swimming pool for when it is too cold to set foot in the lake. Water and sewer hookups for RVs are non-existent, the electricity is 30 amps, and the rest room/shower facilities are adequate and passably clean. The beauty, however, is top-rate. The park is located on 1,235 acres around the 298-acre Lake Dexter, five miles south of Pittsville, and it offers over over 1,000 acres of wild or undeveloped land with abundant wildlife and game fish. Internal roads are paved and in excellent condition, and blacktop camp pads are provided on all campsites, most of which are wooded and secluded.

### BASICS

**Operated by:** Wood County. **Open:** May 1–Nov. 30. **Site Assignment:** Reservations w/ 1-night fee plus $5. Reservations cannot be made at campgrounds, must be made by telephone (715) 421-8422 or in person at county office Monday through Friday 9 a.m. to 3 p.m. Refund (minus the $5 fee) w/ 7-day notice. **Registration:** At park rangers station. **Fee:** $13 (cash, Wisconsin check) credit cards accepted only for reservation. **Parking:** At site.

### FACILITIES

**Number of RV Sites:** 69. **Number of Tent-Only Sites:** 28. **Hookups:** Electric (30 amp). **Each Site:** Some picnic table, fire ring. **Dump Station:** Yes. **Laundry:** No. **Pay Phone:** Yes. **Rest Rooms and Showers:** Yes. **Fuel:** No. **Propane:** No. **Internal Roads:** Paved, in excellent condition. **RV**

**Service:** No. **Market:** 5 mi. north in Pittsville. **Restaurant:** 1 mi. north in Lakeside. **General Store:** No. **Vending:** Yes. **Swimming Pool:** No. **Playground:** Yes. **Other:** Dexter Lake, beach, enclosed shelter, tennis courts, hiking trail, volleyball court, fish-cleaning house, basketball court, boat launch. **Activities:** Swimming, fishing, hiking, boating. **Nearby Attractions:** Hunting, berry picking, all-terrain vehicle areas, speedway, snowmobiling, golf, zoo. **Additional Information:** Wisconsin Rapids Area CVB, (800) 554-4484.

### RESTRICTIONS

**Pets:** Leash only. **Fires:** Fire pits only. **Alcoholic Beverages:** Permitted. **Vehicle Maximum Length:** None. **Other:** 2-night min. for weekends, 3-night for holidays.

### TO GET THERE

From the junction of Hwy. 80 and 54, drive 0.5 mi. west on 54. Roads are wide and well-maintained w/ broad shoulders.

## RICE LAKE
### Rice Lake-Haugen KOA

1876 29 3/4 Ave., Rice Lake 54868. T: (715) 234-2360; www.koa.com; ricelakekoa@aol.com.

🚐 ★★★★                         ⛺ ★★★★

Beauty: ★★★★                Site Privacy: ★★★★
Spaciousness: ★★★★         Quiet: ★★★★
Security: ★★★★              Cleanliness: ★★★★
Insect Control: ★★★★        Facilities: ★★★★

Rice Lake-Haugen KOA, located ten miles north of Rice Lake, offers relief from highway noise. Situated on Upper Devil's Lake, the campground has a nice beach and a dock where campers can fish. There is no charge to fish—a welcome break from campgrounds that charge that extra fee. The most popular camping spots are as close to the lake as possible. The campground has ten seasonal campers, eight pull-through sites, and a typical site width of 30 feet. The semi-wooded campground offers level, open, or shaded sites. Security is good—owners keep an eye on the facility and ensure that it is a quiet, family spot.

### BASICS

**Operated by:** Dave & Mary Jo Nelson. **Open:** Apr. 15–Oct. 15. **Site Assignment:** Reservations w/ 1-night deposit; refund w/ 7-day notice. **Registration:** At campground office. **Fee:** $28 (cash, check, credit cards). **Parking:** At site.

## FACILITIES

**Number of RV Sites:** 99. **Number of Tent-Only Sites:** 11. **Hookups:** Electric (20, 30, 50 amps), water, sewer. **Each Site:** Picnic table, fire ring. **Dump Station:** Yes. **Laundry:** Yes. **Pay Phone:** Yes. **Rest Rooms and Showers:** Yes. **Fuel:** No. **Propane:** Yes. **Internal Roads:** Gravel, in good condition. **RV Service:** No. **Market:** 10 mi. south in Rice Lake. **Restaurant:** 10 mi. south in Rice Lake. **General Store:** Yes, limited. **Vending:** Yes. **Swimming Pool:** Yes. **Playground:** Yes. **Other:** Upper Devil's Lake, beach, horseshoes, volleyball, basketball, game room, hiking trails, biking trails, boat launch, rental cabins, rental cottages, snack bar, sports field. **Activities:** Swimming, fishing, hiking, boating (rental rowboats, canoes, paddleboats available), scheduled activities. **Nearby Attractions:** Golf, stock car racing, nature preserve, horseback riding, Museum of Woodcarving, Barron County Historical Society Pioneer Village Museum, amusement center, casinos, antiques, cheese factories. **Additional Information:** Rice Lake Area Chamber of Commerce, (800) 523-6318.

## RESTRICTIONS

**Pets:** Leash only. **Fires:** Fire ring only. **Alcoholic Beverages:** Permitted. **Vehicle Maximum Length:** None.

## TO GET THERE

From the junction of US 53 and Hwy. 48, drive 10 mi. north on Hwy. 53, then 1 mi. east on the campground driveway. Roads are mostly wide and well maintained w/ broad shoulders.

## SHAWANO

### Kellogg's Kampsites

N1840 Airport Rd., Shawano 54166. T: (715) 526-2824

🚐 ★★          ▲ ★★

Beauty: ★★★          Site Privacy: ★★
Spaciousness: ★★          Quiet: ★★★
Security: ★★★★          Cleanliness: ★★
Insect Control: None          Facilities: ★★

Located one mile south of Shawano, Kellogg's Kampsites offers level sites on Shawano Lake. Over 65% of the sites are located on the water, either on the 500-plus feet of lakefront or the 0.1-mile channel. Campers can park their boats a few feet behind the camper. For those who camp in the center grove area, there's full acess to the lake only 100 feet away. Kellogg's also provides a boat launch to campers and free boat docking. At more than 6,000 acres, Shawano Lake is a great fishing spot and is big enough to handle boaters without feeling crowded. All sites come with a moveable metal "burning pad" for campfires. The typical site width is 24 feet, with no pull-throughs and 45 seasonal campers. Laid out in a series of loops, the campground has a five-mph speed limit. Security includes one entrance/exit road, owners who live on site, and regular patrols by city police.

## BASICS

**Operated by:** Klayton Kellogg. **Open:** Apr. 15–Oct. 15. **Site Assignment:** Reservations w/ 1-night deposit; refunds w/ 7-day notice. **Registration:** At campground office. **Fee:** $22 (cash, check, credit cards). **Parking:** At site.

## FACILITIES

**Number of RV Sites:** 75. **Number of Tent-Only Sites:** 6. **Hookups:** Electric (30 amps), water, sewer. **Each Site:** Picnic table, fire ring. **Dump Station:** Yes. **Laundry:** No. **Pay Phone:** No. **Rest Rooms and Showers:** Yes. **Fuel:** No. **Propane:** No. **Internal Roads:** Gravel, in fair condition. **RV Service:** No. **Market:** 1 mi. north in Shawano. **Restaurant:** 1 mi. north in Shawano. **General Store:** Yes. **Vending:** No. **Swimming Pool:** No. **Playground:** Yes. **Other:** Shawano Lake, beach, game room, fishing pier, horseshoes, rec hall, boat ramp, boat dock, sports field, volleyball, video games, fish-cleaning facilities. **Activities:** Swimming, boating (rental paddleboats available), some scheduled weekend activities. **Nearby Attractions:** Casino, go-karts, white water rafting, Wolf River, flea market, stock car races, farmers market, golf, hunting, fishing, museums, ATV trails. **Additional Information:** Shawano County Tourism Council, (800) 235-8528.

## RESTRICTIONS

**Pets:** Leash only. **Fires:** Fire ring only. **Alcoholic Beverages:** At sites only. **Vehicle Maximum Length:** 35 ft. **Other:** Air conditioners are not allowed.

## TO GET THERE

From the junction of Hwy. Bus 29 and CR H and CR HHH (Aiport Rd.), drive 1 mi. north on CR HHH. Roads are wide and well maintained w/ broad shoulders.

## SHELL LAKE
### Red Barn Campground

W6820 CR B, Shell Lake 54871. T: (715) 468-2575;
www.redbarncampground.com.

🚐 ★★★          ⛺ ★★★

Beauty: ★★★              Site Privacy: ★★★
Spaciousness: ★★★★       Quiet: ★★★★
Security: ★★★★           Cleanliness: ★★★
Insect Control: ★★★       Facilities: ★★★

Many youngsters don't have a grandma and
grandpa to visit on the farm. The Red Barn
Campground gives them a taste of that farm life.
Located two miles east of Shell Lake, the Red
Barn has rabbits, goats, chickens, horses, and
other animals to pet. A rooster's crow greets the
break of dawn, and children can gather their own
egg for breakfast. Campers also can pick strawberries in season (late June through early July) in
the U-Pick Patch. The campground has 15 seasonal campers, ten pull-through sites, and a typical site width of 30 feet. A grassy, semi-wooded
facility, the Red Barn offers a choice of open or
shaded sites. A separate tent area allows for more
green space and privacy. Lake access is available,
as are nature trails through the woods and fields.

### BASICS

**Operated by:** Lee & Dotty Swan. **Open:** May
15–Sept. 15. **Site Assignment:** Reservations w/ 1-
night deposit; refund w/ 7-day notice. **Registration:** At campground office. **Fee:** $23 (cash, check).
**Parking:** At site.

### FACILITIES

**Number of RV Sites:** 45. **Number of Tent-
Only Sites:** 25. **Hookups:** Electric (15, 20, 30, 50
amps), water. **Each Site:** Picnic table, fire ring.
**Dump Station:** Yes. **Laundry:** No. **Pay Phone:**
Yes. **Rest Rooms and Showers:** Yes. **Fuel:** No.
**Propane:** No. **Internal Roads:** Gravel, in good
condition. **RV Service:** No. **Market:** 2 mi. west in
Shell Lake. **Restaurant:** 2 mi. west in Shell Lake.
**General Store:** No. **Vending:** No. **Swimming
Pool:** No. **Playground:** Yes. **Other:** Petting zoo,
mini golf, horseshoes, volleyball, basketball, sports
field, hiking trails. **Activities:** Hiking, schedule activ-
ities. **Nearby Attractions:** Shell Lake beach, golf,
walking tour, historic sites, Railroad Memories
Museum, float trip, Wisconsin Great Northern Railroad, Museum of Woodcarving, Indianhead Art Cen-

ter, fish hatchery. **Additional Information:** Wash-
burn County Tourism Information Center, (800)
367-3306.

### RESTRICTIONS

**Pets:** Leash only. **Fires:** Fire ring only. **Alcoholic
Beverages:** Permitted. **Vehicle Maximum
Length:** None.

### TO GET THERE

From center of town, drive 0.5 mi. north on US
63, then 2 mi. east on CR B. Roads are wide
and well maintained w/ mostly broad shoulders.

## SISTER BAY
### Aqualand Camp Resort

Box 538, Sister Bay 54234. T: (920) 854-4573

🚐 ★★★          ⛺ ★★

Beauty: ★★★★            Site Privacy: ★★★
Spaciousness: ★★★        Quiet: ★★★★
Security: ★★★★           Cleanliness: ★★★★
Insect Control: None       Facilities: ★★★

In the heart of scenic Door County, Aqualand
Camp Resort is a semi-wooded campground with
level, gravel sites. The campground is occupied by
almost all seasonals. Only ten sites are left for
overnighters, so reservations are recommended.
The typical site width is 40 feet, and the campground has seven pull-throughs. Seasonal
campers take good care of their sites, including
landscaping and other knick-knacks, which adds
to the beauty of the campground. The speed limit
is five mph, and quiet times are enforced between
10 p.m. to 8 a.m., requiring "absolute quiet,"
according to campground rules. Just in time to
provide supper, rainbow trout fishing is allowed,
(with no license required) between the hours of
2–4 p.m. The campground furnishes the poles
and bait and even cleans the fish. You only pay for
what you catch at $4 a fish—but you must keep
all the fish you catch. Security includes one
entrance/exit road, owners who live on site, and
regular patrols of the campground.

### BASICS

**Operated by:** Mike & Karen McAndrews. **Open:**
May 25–Oct. 15. **Site Assignment:** Reservations
w/ 2-night deposit; refund w/ 1-week notice. **Registration:** At campground office. **Fee:** $26 (cash,
check). **Parking:** At site.

## FACILITIES

**Number of RV Sites:** 150. **Number of Tent-Only Sites:** 0. **Hookups:** Electric (30, 50 amps), water. **Each Site:** Picnic table, fire ring. **Dump Station:** Yes. **Laundry:** No. **Pay Phone:** Yes. **Rest Rooms and Showers:** Yes. **Fuel:** No. **Propane:** No. **Internal Roads:** Gravel, in good condition. **RV Service:** No. **Market:** 2 mi. north in Sister Bay. **Restaurant:** 2 mi. north in Sister Bay. **General Store:** No. **Vending:** No. **Swimming Pool:** Yes. **Playground:** Yes. **Other:** Fish-cleaning station, fish freezer, trout ponds, shuffleboard, sports field, volleyball. **Activities:** Swimming, fishing. **Nearby Attractions:** Door County, cherry & apple orchards, fishing, golf, hiking, boating, Lake Michigan, historic sites, antiques, arts & crafts, parks, bike trails. **Additional Information:** Door County Chamber of Commerce, (800) 527-3529.

## RESTRICTIONS

**Pets:** Leash only. **Fires:** Fire rings only; fires must be extinguished by midnight. **Alcoholic Beverages:** Permitted. **Vehicle Maximum Length:** None.

## TO GET THERE

From the junction of Hwy. 42 and Hwy. 57, drive 2.25 mi. south on Hwy. 57, then 0.25 mi. east on CR Q. Roads are wide and well maintained w/ broad shoulders.

## SPARTA

## Leon Valley Campground

9050 Jancing Ave., Sparta 54656. T: (608) 269-6400; www.campleonvalley.com.

🚐 ★★★          ⛺ ★★★★

| | |
|---|---|
| Beauty: ★★★★ | Site Privacy: ★★★★ |
| Spaciousness: ★★★ | Quiet: ★★★★ |
| Security: ★★★★ | Cleanliness: ★★★★★ |
| Insect Control: None | Facilities: ★★★ |

Leon Valley is out in the middle of nowhere, a valley surrounded by trees and hills. It's a great location for a peaceful, scenic campground. An attractive entranceway has an old wagon wheel, shrubs, and bushes. Thirty of the 105 RV sites are taken by seasonals. Sites are grassy with gravel pads for RVs, mostly shady, and level. Laid out in a series of loops, the campground offers a wilderness setting with 12 pull-through sites and an average site of 27 × 50 feet. The best RV sites

are in the A 40 section near the playground and bathrooms. Tent sites are spread out in the campground, including some secluded areas. The best tent sites are B 1–37 because they are more wooded and away from people. Security measures are good since the owners live on site, have a regular patrol, and lock up the entrance gate at midnight.

## BASICS

**Operated by:** Bernard & JoAnn Waege. **Open:** Apr. 1–Nov. 30. **Site Assignment:** Reservations w/ 1-night deposit; refund w/ 7-day notice, 14-day notice for holidays. **Registration:** At campground office. **Fee:** $22 (cash, check, credit cards). **Parking:** At site.

## FACILITIES

**Number of RV Sites:** 105. **Number of Tent-Only Sites:** 20. **Hookups:** Electric (30, 50 amps), water. **Each Site:** Picnic table, fire ring. **Dump Station:** Yes. **Laundry:** No. **Pay Phone:** Yes. **Rest Rooms and Showers:** Yes. **Fuel:** No. **Propane:** No. **Internal Roads:** Gravel, in good condition. **RV Service:** No. **Market:** 4 mi. north in Sparta. **Restaurant:** 4 mi. north in Sparta. **General Store:** Yes. **Vending:** Yes. **Swimming Pool:** Yes. **Playground:** Yes. **Other:** Basketball, volleyball, pavilion, horseshoes, snack bar, game room, hiking trail, sports field. **Activities:** Swimming, hiking. **Nearby Attractions:** Fort McCoy, 32-mi. bike trail, fishing, boating, hunting, horseback riding, canoeing, specialty shops, museums, craft mall, tennis, trap shooting, two self-guided historical walking tours. **Additional Information:** Sparta Tourism Bureau, (800) 354-BIKE.

## RESTRICTIONS

**Pets:** Leash only. **Fires:** Fire ring only. **Alcoholic Beverages:** Permitted. **Vehicle Maximum Length:** None.

## TO GET THERE

From the junction of I-90 and Hwy. 27, drive 4 mi. south on Hwy. 27, then 1.25 mi. east on Jancing Ave. Roads are wide and well maintained w/ broad shoulders (except for the paved access road, which has little shoulder room). The road also takes a couple of whopping big turns on the way in.

## SPOONER
### Scenic View Campground

24560 Scenic View Ln., Spooner 54801. T: (715) 468-2510; www.scenicviewcampground.com; cline@spacestar.net.

🚐 ★★★                     ⛺ ★★★★

Beauty: ★★★★            Site Privacy: ★★★
Spaciousness: ★★★        Quiet: ★★★
Security: ★★★            Cleanliness: ★★★
Insect Control: ★★★      Facilities: ★★★

Activities revolve around Poquette Lake at Scenic View Campground, located nine miles west of Spooner. Laid out in a series of loops, the campground has 20 seasonal campers and two pull-through sites. The best sites for tent campers are Areas 5 and 6, which offer more privacy and green space. Sites 5 and 6 offer no water or electric hookups, but water is handy nearby. The best RV sites are in Area 1, which features shaded, level spots overlooking the beautiful 100-acre lake. The sites are also near the beach and the main building which houses the bar and bathrooms. RVers that are camping with friends and might want several sites together would probably prefer Area 2 which is west of the main building and has sites with greater depth. Fed with clean, sparkling water, Poquette Lake is ideal for swimming and water sports. It has a sandy beach, swimming raft, and roped-off area for small children. The lake is brimming with bass, walleye, northern pike, and panfish. Check out the 11-pound pike caught in the lake and now hanging on a wall in the bar. Security measures include one way in and out past the owners' home.

### BASICS

**Operated by:** Tom & Carol Haseltine. **Open:** May 1–Oct. 10. **Site Assignment:** Reservations w/ 1-night deposit; refund (minus $5) w/ 2-week notice. **Registration:** At campground office. **Fee:** $22 (cash). **Parking:** At site.

### FACILITIES

**Number of RV Sites:** 40. **Number of Tent-Only Sites:** 5. **Hookups:** Electric (30 amps), water. **Each Site:** Picnic table, fire ring. **Dump Station:** Yes. **Laundry:** No. **Pay Phone:** Yes. **Rest Rooms and Showers:** Yes. **Fuel:** No. **Propane:** Yes. **Internal Roads:** Gravel, in good condition. **RV Service:** No. **Market:** 9 mi. east in Spooner. **Restaurant:** 9 mi. east in Spooner. **General**

**Store:** Yes, limited. **Vending:** Yes. **Swimming Pool:** No. **Playground:** Yes. **Other:** Swimming beach, pavilion, lounge, boat ramp, boat dock, horseshoes, volleyball, basketball, rec hall, game room rental campers, fishing lake, badminton, hiking trails. **Activities:** Swimming, fishing, hiking, boating (rental rowboats, paddleboats, motorboats available). **Nearby Attractions:** Golf, casinos, supper clubs, walking tour, historic sites, Wisconsin Great Northern Railroad, Railroad Memories Museum, fish hatchery, Indianhead Art Center, snowmobile trails, horseback riding. **Additional Information:** Burnett County Tourism Office, (800) 788-3164.

### RESTRICTIONS

**Pets:** Leash only. **Fires:** Fire ring only. **Alcoholic Beverages:** Permitted. **Vehicle Maximum Length:** None.

### TO GET THERE

From the junction of US 63 and Hwy. 70, drive 9.25 mi. west on Hwy. 70, then 0.5 mi. south on Scenic View Ln. Hwy. 70 is mostly wide and well maintained w/ broad shoulders. Scenic View Ln. has narrow shoulders in spots.

## ST. GERMAIN
### Lynn Ann's Campground

P.O. Box 8, St. Germain 54558. T: (715) 542-3456; F: (715) 542-2317; www.Lynnannscampground.com; heather@lynnannscampground.com.

🚐 ★★★                     ⛺ ★★★

Beauty: ★★★             Site Privacy: ★★★
Spaciousness: ★★★        Quiet: ★★★
Security: ★★★            Cleanliness: ★★★★
Insect Control: ★★★      Facilities: ★★★★

Located on Big St. Germain Lake in St. Germain, Lynn Ann's Campground offers open and wooded sites. The facility has ten seasonal campers, one pull-through site, and a typical site width of 36 feet. Laid out in a series of loops, camp sites are level and grassy. The campground offers a variety of water activities and rents boats and other water equipment. The lake is a popular fishing spot for muskies, walleye, bass, northerns, and panfish. No glass, bottles, or cans are permitted near the beach or water. To ensure a neat appearance, the campground requires that campsites be cleaned daily. Ceramic-tiled showers are a nice touch, but the showers are coin-operated. Owners keep a close watch on the campground for security measures.

## BASICS

**Operated by:** Mike & Heather Davidson. **Open:** May 5–Oct. 10. **Site Assignment:** Reservations w/ 1-night deposit; refund w/ 10-day notice. **Registration:** At campground office. **Fee:** $25 (cash, check, credit cards). **Parking:** At site.

## FACILITIES

**Number of RV Sites:** 90. **Number of Tent-Only Sites:** 0. **Hookups:** Electric (30 amps), water, sewer, Internet, cable TV. **Each Site:** Picnic table, fire ring. **Dump Station:** Yes. **Laundry:** Yes. **Pay Phone:** Yes. **Rest Rooms and Showers:** Yes. **Fuel:** Yes. **Propane:** Yes. **Internal Roads:** Gravel, in good condition. **RV Service:** No. **Market:** 3 mi. south. **Restaurant:** 3 mi. south. **General Store:** Yes. **Vending:** Yes. **Swimming Pool:** No. **Playground:** Yes. **Other:** Sandy beach, game room, hiking trails, horseshoes, volleyball, basketball, shuffleboard, boat launch, boat harbor, marina, rental trailers. **Activities:** Swimming, fishing, hiking, boating (rental pontoons, kayaks, wave runners, tubes, motor boats, sailboats, waterskis, canoes available). **Nearby Attractions:** Golf, casino, tennis, historic sites, national forest, museums, snowmobile trails, antiques, arts & crafts. **Additional Information:** St. Germain Chamber of Commerce, (800) 727-7203.

## RESTRICTIONS

**Pets:** Leash only. **Fires:** Fire ring only. **Alcoholic Beverages:** Permitted. **Vehicle Maximum Length:** None. **Other:** No oversized tents, trailers must provide drain containers.

## TO GET THERE

From the junction of Hwy. 70 and Hwy. 155, drive 2 mi. west on Hwy. 70, then 0.5 mi. north on Normandy Court, then 0.25 mi. east on South Shore Dr. Roads are mostly wide and well maintained w/ broad shoulders.

## STEVENS POINT

### Rivers Edge Campground

3368 Campsite Dr., Stevens Point 54481. T: (715) 344-8058

🚐 ★★★                    ▲ ★★★

Beauty: ★★★★          Site Privacy: ★★★
Spaciousness: ★★★      Quiet: ★★★
Security: ★★★★          Cleanliness: ★★★★
Insect Control: None     Facilities: ★★

With 12 miles of frontage on the beautiful Wisconsin River, Rivers Edge Campground has a head start on appealing to campers. The river is known for its good fishing and boating. The campground, located seven miles north of Stevens Point, offers waterfront or wooded campsites featuring a tree buffer to muffle highway noise. Easy access off I-51 and well-maintained connecting roads also give the campground an edge. Rivers Edge could really use a laundry and general store for the convenience of its campers and seasonal residents. Security gets high marks because the campground has one entrance, the manager lives on site, access to the fenced swimming pool is only through the office, and the grounds are patrolled. In addition, there are two rules that are strictly enforced: a speed limit of five mph (or violators will be asked to leave), and a 10 p.m. quiet time on weekdays (11 p.m. on Fridays and Saturdays).

## BASICS

**Operated by:** Jerry Fahrner. **Open:** May 1–Oct. 7. **Site Assignment:** Reservations w/ $20 deposit; refund w/ 48-hour notice. Full deposit in advance for holiday weekends. **Registration:** At campground office. **Fee:** $21 (cash, check). **Parking:** At site.

## FACILITIES

**Number of RV Sites:** 108. **Number of Tent-Only Sites:** 6. **Hookups:** Electric (20, 30, 50 amps), water. **Each Site:** Picnic table, fire ring. **Dump Station:** Yes. **Laundry:** No. **Pay Phone:** Yes. **Rest Rooms and Showers:** Yes. **Fuel:** No. **Propane:** Yes. **Internal Roads:** Gravel, in good condition. **RV Service:** No. **Market:** 7 mi. south in Stevens Point. **Restaurant:** Next door. **General Store:** No. **Vending:** Yes. **Swimming Pool:** Yes. **Playground:** Yes. **Other:** Boat launch, boat docks, rec hall w/ game room, sandy beach, volleyball courts, horseshoes. **Activities:** Swimming, fishing, boating, waterskiing, planned weekend activities. **Nearby Attractions:** 4 public golf courses within 25-mi. radius, Cedar Creek Manufacturer's Direct Mall, Rainbow Falls Water Park, Rib Mountain, Grotto Shrine, Mead Wildlife Refuge. **Additional Information:** Stevens Point Area CVB, (800) 236-4626.

## RESTRICTIONS

**Pets:** Leash only. **Fires:** Fire pits only. **Alcoholic Beverages:** Permitted. **Vehicle Maximum Length:** 30 ft. **Other:** 3-day min. on holiday weekends.

## TO GET THERE

From Exit 165 on US 51 northbound, drive 0.4 mi. east on CR X, 20.5 mi. north on Sunset Drive, 0.5 mi. west on Maple Dr., 0.25 mi. north on Campsite Dr. Roads are wide and well maintained w/ good shoulders.

## STURGEON BAY

### Monument Point Camping

5718 West Monument Point Rd., Sturgeon Bay 54235. T: (920) 743-9411

🚐 ★★★                    ⛺ ★★★★

Beauty: ★★★                Site Privacy: ★★★★
Spaciousness: ★★★★         Quiet: ★★★★
Security: ★★★★             Cleanliness: ★★★★
Insect Control: None       Facilities: ★★★

Located five miles south of Egg Harbor, Monument Point Camping offers secluded, wooded spots in the Door County area. Sites are level and surrounded by green space for little private nooks. Tall trees, shrubs, and other greenery help buffer noise and add to privacy. Laid out in a series of loops, the campground features gravel RV pads and dirt tent pads. The typical site width is 50 feet, with five pull-throughs and 24 seasonal campers. The biggest drawbacks include no water hookups, pool, or laundry, but the tradeoff might be worth it for the serenity of the camping site. The speed limit is five mph, with quiet hours from 10:30 p.m. to 8 a.m. Recycling is a state law in Wisconsin. Security measures include one entrance/exit, one-way roads, owners who live on site, and regular patrols of the campground.

## BASICS

**Operated by:** Doug & Debbie Krauel. **Open:** May 1–Oct. 20. **Site Assignment:** Reservations w/ $10 deposit; refunds (minus $5) w/ 7-day notice. **Registration:** At campground office. **Fee:** $22 (cash, check). **Parking:** At site.

## FACILITIES

**Number of RV Sites:** 76. **Number of Tent-Only Sites:** 9. **Hookups:** Electric (30 amps). **Each Site:** Picnic table, fire ring. **Dump Station:** Yes. **Laundry:** No. **Pay Phone:** No. **Rest Rooms and Showers:** Yes. **Fuel:** No. **Propane:** No. **Internal Roads:** Gravel, in good condition. **RV Service:** No. **Market:** 5 mi. north in Egg Harbor. **Restaurant:** 5 mi. north in Egg Harbor. **General Store:** Yes, limited. **Vending:** Yes. **Swimming Pool:** No.

**Playground:** Yes. **Other:** Game room, volleyball, horseshoes, recreation field, badminton, hiking trails. **Activities:** Hiking. **Nearby Attractions:** Door County, cherry & apple orchards, fishing, golf, hiking, boating, swimming, Lake Michigan, historic sites, antiques, arts & crafts, parks, Green Bay. **Additional Information:** Door County Chamber of Commerce (800) 527-3529.

## RESTRICTIONS

**Pets:** Leash only. **Fires:** Fire ring only. **Alcoholic Beverages:** Permitted. **Vehicle Maximum Length:** 40 ft.

## TO GET THERE

From north junction of Hwy. 42 and Hwy. 57 near Sturgeon Bay, drive 8 mi. north on Hwy. 42, then 1.25 mi. northwest on Monument Point Rd. Roads are wide and well maintained w/ broad shoulders.

## STURGEON BAY

### Potawatomi State Park Daisy Field Campground

3740 CR PD, Sturgeon Bay 54235. T: (920) 746-2890

🚐 ★★★★                   ⛺ ★★★★

Beauty: ★★★★              Site Privacy: ★★★
Spaciousness: ★★★          Quiet: ★★★★
Security: ★★★★             Cleanliness: ★★★★
Insect Control: None       Facilities: ★★★

Natural beauty is the basic asset of Potawatomi State Park. Located only a few miles from Sturgeon Bay on the Wisconsin Door County peninsula, the park consists of 1,200 acres of flat to gently rolling upland terrain bordered by steep slopes and rugged limestone cliffs along Sturgeon Bay. Laid out in a series of loops, campsites are level and mostly shaded, with two pull-through sites. The park also offers two camping options for people with accessibility limitations. Two accessible campsites are located in the south campground adjacent to the toilet/shower building. In addition, the Cabin by the Bay is a fully accessible indoor facility which can be reserved by people who are unable to use the more traditional campsites. The biggest drawback of the park and campground is lack of swimming facilities. Since there is not a sandy beach, swimming is not recommended. However, park staff will direct campers to the nearest public beach. The rest room facilities are cleaner than most state facilities, and the campground has excellent security, including one entrance/exit road past the ranger station, along with regular campground patrols by rangers.

## BASICS

**Operated by:** State of Wisconsin. **Open:** All year. **Site Assignment:** Reservations w/ entire stay deposit (2-night min.); refund (minus $9.50) w/ 2-day notice. **Registration:** At campground office. **Fee:** $13 (cash, check, credit cards), plus $5 daily park fee or $18 annual fee if Wisconsin resident; $7 daily fee or $25 annual fee if not Wisconsin resident. **Parking:** At site.

## FACILITIES

**Number of RV Sites:** 25. **Number of Tent-Only Sites:** 98. **Hookups:** Electric (20, 30 amps). **Each Site:** Picnic table, fire ring. **Dump Station:** Yes. **Laundry:** No. **Pay Phone:** Yes. **Rest Rooms and Showers:** Yes. **Fuel:** No. **Propane:** No. **Internal Roads:** Paved, in good condition. **RV Service:** No. **Market:** 3 mi. northeast in Sturgeon Bay. **Restaurant:** 3 mi. northeast in Sturgeon Bay. **General Store:** Yes, limited. **Vending:** No. **Swimming Pool:** No. **Playground:** Yes. **Other:** Sturgeon Bay, fishing lake, hiking trails, boat launch, observation tower, nature center, bike trails, pavilion, boat dock. **Activities:** Fishing, hiking, biking, boating, scheduled activities. **Nearby Attractions:** Lake Michigan, hiking trails, biking trails, fishing, Door County, golf, antiques, arts & crafts, historic sites, swimming. **Additional Information:** Door County Chamber of Commerce, (800) 527-3526.

## RESTRICTIONS

**Pets:** Leash only, some areas are pet free. **Fires:** Fire ring only. **Alcoholic Beverages:** Permitted. **Vehicle Maximum Length:** None. **Other:** 21-day stay limit.

## TO GET THERE

From Sturgeon Bay, drive 1.5 mi. west on CR C, then 2 mi. north on park road. Roads are wide and well maintained w/ mostly broad shoulders.

## STURGEON BAY

### Quietwoods North Camping Resort

3668 Grondin Rd., Sturgeon Bay 54235. T: (800) 986-2267; www.quietwoodsnorth.com.

 ★★★     ★★★

**Beauty:** ★★★
**Spaciousness:** ★★★
**Security:** ★★★★
**Insect Control:** None
**Site Privacy:** ★★
**Quiet:** ★★★★
**Cleanliness:** ★★★★
**Facilities:** ★★★

Located in the heart of Door County overlooking Sturgeon Bay waters, Quietwoods North Camping Resort offers a satisfaction guarantee. Within one hour of check-in, if campers are not satisfied with their site, campground services, or facilities, the problems will be corrected to the campers satisfaction or a refund will be given. Located two miles west of Sturgeon Bay, Quietwoods North offers a choice of full-sun or wooded sites and grassy or gravel spots. The typical site width is 30 feet, with five pull-throughs and 105 seasonal campers. Although Quietwoods North and Quietwoods South used to have the same owners, the two campgrounds are no longer affiliated. The best tent site is 420 because of its lush green setting and view of the bluff. The best RV site is S24 because it is bigger, offers full hookups, and borders on Potawatomi State Park. Quiet hours are 11 p.m. to 8 a.m., and the speed limit is ten mph—but motorists are encouraged to drive slower in the campground, according to the campground brochure. Security is provided by one entrance/exit that is locked at night and owners who live on site and perform regular patrols.

## BASICS

**Operated by:** The McClelland family. **Open:** May 1–Oct. 15. **Site Assignment:** Reservations w/ $25 deposit; refund (minus $5) w/ 7-day notice. **Registration:** At campground office. **Fee:** $30 (cash, check, credit cards). **Parking:** At site.

## FACILITIES

**Number of RV Sites:** 275. **Number of Tent-Only Sites:** 31. **Hookups:** Electric (20, 30, 50 amps), water, sewer. **Each Site:** Picnic table, fire ring. **Dump Station:** Yes. **Laundry:** Yes. **Pay Phone:** Yes. **Rest Rooms and Showers:** Yes. **Fuel:** No. **Propane:** No. **Internal Roads:** Paved/gravel, in good condition. **RV Service:** No. **Market:** 2 mi. east in Sturgeon Bay. **Restaurant:** 2 mi. east in Sturgeon Bay. **General Store:** Yes. **Vending:** Yes. **Swimming Pool:** Yes. **Playground:** Yes. **Other:** Game room, wading pool, snack bar, pavilion, mini golf, horseshoes, volleyball, basketball, tetherball, coin games, rental cabins, trailers & park models. **Activities:** Swimming, biking (rental bikes available), scheduled weekend activities. **Nearby Attractions:** Potawatomi State Park, hiking trails, biking trails, fishing, boat launch, Door County, golf, Sturgeon Bay, Lake Michigan, antiques, arts & crafts, historic sites. **Additional Information:** Door County Chamber of Commerce, (800) 527-3529.

## RESTRICTIONS

**Pets:** Leash only; large breeds, such as pitbulls, dobermans & rottweilers, require prior management approval. **Fires:** Fire rings only; fires must be extinguished by 1 a.m. **Alcoholic Beverages:** Permitted. **Vehicle Maximum Length:** 45 ft.

## TO GET THERE

From the junction of Hwy. 42/57 and CR PD, drive 1.25 mi. north on CR PD, then 1 mi. east on CR C, then 0.75 mi. north on Grondin Rd. Roads are wide and well maintained w/ broad shoulders.

## STURGEON BAY

### Yogi Bear's Jellystone Park Camp-Resort

3677 May Rd., Sturgeon Bay 54235. T: (920) 743-9001; www.campdoorcounty.com/yogibear.

| 🚐 ★★★ | 🔺 ★★ |
|---|---|
| Beauty: ★★★ | Site Privacy: ★★ |
| Spaciousness: ★★ | Quiet: ★★★ |
| Security: ★★★★ | Cleanliness: ★★★ |
| Insect Control: None | Facilities: ★★★ |

Yogi Bear's Jellystone Park Camp-Resort has enough activities to wear out any parent or child. It also is located in Door County, eight miles south of Sturgeon Bay, which means even more choices for recreation. The campground is semi-wooded, with some nicely shaded sites and some sitting right out in an open field. Laid out in a series of loops, the campground has two pull-through sites and 100 seasonal campers. The typical site width is 40 feet. The best RV site is 91 because it is in the woods and offers more space and privacy. Tent campers can use any site, but it is hard to pick unless you look to see what is beside it at the moment. Quiet hours are from 10:30 p.m. to 7 a.m.; campfires are to be extinguished by 1 a.m., and all activities ceased by the 1 a.m. curfew. Mopeds, mini-bikes, ATVs, skateboards, and golf carts are prohibited at all times. Security measures include one entrance/exit

road, and owners who live on site provide regular campground patrols.

## BASICS

**Operated by:** Dick & Sylvia Himes. **Open:** May 15–Oct. 15. **Site Assignment:** Reservations w/ $25 deposit; refund w/ 8-day notice. **Registration:** At campground office. **Fee:** $28 (cash, check, credit cards). **Parking:** At site.

## FACILITIES

**Number of RV Sites:** 289. **Number of Tent-Only Sites:** 0. **Hookups:** Electric (30, 50 amps), water, sewer. **Each Site:** Picnic talbe, fire ring. **Dump Station:** Yes. **Laundry:** Yes. **Pay Phone:** Yes. **Rest Rooms and Showers:** Yes. **Fuel:** No. **Propane:** No. **Internal Roads:** Paved/gravel, in good condition. **RV Service:** No. **Market:** 8 mi. north in Sturgeon Bay. **Restaurant:** 8 mi. north in Sturgeon Bay. **General Store:** Yes. **Vending:** Yes. **Swimming Pool:** Yes. **Playground:** Yes. **Other:** Goodie Shoppe, Yogi's theater, mini-golf, horseshoes, funnelball, tetherball, ping pong, football, hiking trails, softball, shuffleboard, volleyball, game room, kiddie pool, pavilion. **Activities:** Swimming, hiking, scheduled activities. **Nearby Attractions:** Door County, Lake Michian, historic sites, cherry & apple orchards, boating, fishing, golf, hiking, historic sites, antiques, arts & crafts shops, parks, summer stock theater, bike trails, Green Bay. **Additional Information:** Door County Chamber of Commerce, (800) 527-3529.

## RESTRICTIONS

**Pets:** Leash only. **Fires:** Fire ring only. **Alcoholic Beverages:** Permitted. **Vehicle Maximum Length:** None.

## TO GET THERE

From the junction of Hwy. 42/57 and CR C, drive 1 mi. north and 3 mi. west on CR C, then 1 mi. north on CR M, then 2 mi. west on Sand Bay Rd., then 500 feet south on May Rd. The roads are wide and well maintained w/ broad shoulders.

## TOMAHAWK

### The Out-Post Campground

9507 Hwy. N, Tomahawk 54497. T: (715) 453-3468

| 🚐 ★★★ | 🔺 ★★★ |
|---|---|
| Beauty: ★★★ | Site Privacy: ★★★ |
| Spaciousness: ★★★ | Quiet: ★★★ |

Security: ★★★   Cleanliness: ★★★
Insect Control: ★★★   Facilities: ★★★

Located on Deer Lake and Lake Nokomis three miles west of Tomahawk, the Out-Post Campground features a wide array of water activities. Sites are level and mostly shaded. The campground has 30 seasonal campers, 31 pull-through sites, and a typical site width of 30 feet. A separate area for tents offers more green space and privacy. The wooded campground offers plenty of hot water in its free showers. A rental housekeeping cottage is available year-round for winter enthusiasts. A concrete launching pad offers easy access to the water. Folks say fishing is good in the area, and swimmers like the sandy beach. The most popular sites are closest to the water. Security measures include a traffic-control gate.

## BASICS

**Operated by:** Lou & Kitty Miller. **Open:** Apr. 15–Oct. 15. **Site Assignment:** Reservations w/ 1-night deposit; refund w/ 2- week notice. **Registration:** At campground office. **Fee:** $33 (cash & check). **Parking:** At site.

## FACILITIES

**Number of RV Sites:** 230. **Number of Tent-Only Sites:** 40. **Hookups:** Electric (20, 30, 50 amps), water, sewer. **Each Site:** Picnic table, fire ring. **Dump Station:** Yes. **Laundry:** Yes. **Pay Phone:** Yes. **Rest Rooms and Showers:** Yes. **Fuel:** No. **Propane:** Yes. **Internal Roads:** Gravel, in fair condition. **RV Service:** No. **Market:** 3 mi. east in Tomahawk. **Restaurant:** 3 mi. east in Tomahawk. **General Store:** Yes, limited. **Vending:** Yes. **Swimming Pool:** No. **Playground:** Yes. **Other:** Snack bar, swimming beach, Lake Nokomis, Deer Lake, restaurant, marina, horseshoes, volleyball, basketball, shuffleboard, rec hall, lounge, game room, boat launch, hiking trail, bar. **Activities:** Swimming, fishing, boating (rental paddleboats, canoes, motorboats, rowboats available). **Nearby Attractions:** Golf, local park, Hiawatha Bike Trail, snowmobiling, antiques, arts & crafts, water ski shows, cross-country skiing, ice fishing. **Additional Information:** Tomahawk Regional Chamber of Commerce, (800) 569-2160.

## RESTRICTIONS

**Pets:** Leash only. **Fires:** Fire ring only. **Alcoholic Beverages:** Permitted. **Vehicle Maximum Length:** None.

## TO GET THERE

From the junction of US 51 and US 8 West, drive 3 mi. west on US 8, then 0.25 mi. north on CR L, then 1 mi. east on CR N. Roads are mostly wide and well maintained w/ adequate shoulders.

## TURTLE LAKE
### Turtle Lake RV Park

P.O. Box 526, Turtle Lake 54889. T: (715) 986-4140; speedys@chibardun.net.

🚐 ★★★          ▲ ★

Beauty: ★★          Site Privacy: ★★
Spaciousness: ★★★   Quiet: ★★★
Security: ★★★★      Cleanliness: ★★★★
Insect Control: Yes  Facilities: ★★★

Turtle Lake RV Park is a campground with an amusement center attached—Speedy's Family Fun Center. Many of the amusements require additional money. Laid out in a series of loops, the campground is mostly a flat, open field with gravel RV pads on grassy lots and a few trees. The typical site width is 30 feet, and the campground has 30 pull-throughs. Tents are allowed on any site, but there are few natural amenities to make it pleasant for tent campers. Located two blocks west of Turtle Lake, the campground offers excellent access from main roads. The St. Croix Casino is nearby, which may account for the campground rule that children under the age of 14 are not to be left unattended. Children under 14 also must be accompanied by an adult in the pool area. Quiet hours are enforced from 10 p.m. to 8 a.m. A ten-mph speed limit might be better reduced to half that since children probably spend much time going back and forth from the campground to the family fun center.

## BASICS

**Operated by:** Richard & Linda Phillips. **Open:** Apr. 15–Oct. 15. **Site Assignment:** Reservations w/ 1-night deposit; no refunds. **Registration:** At campground office. **Fee:** $18 (cash, credit cards). **Parking:** At site.

## FACILITIES

**Number of RV Sites:** 102. **Number of Tent-Only Sites:** 0. **Hookups:** Electric (30, 50 amps), water, sewer. **Each Site:** Picnic table, fire ring. **Dump Station:** Yes. **Laundry:** No. **Pay Phone:**

Yes. **Rest Rooms and Showers:** Yes. **Fuel:** No. **Propane:** No. **Internal Roads:** Gravel, in good condition. **RV Service:** No. **Market:** 2 blocks east in Turtle Lake. **Restaurant:** Next door. **General Store:** Yes. **Vending:** No. **Swimming Pool:** Yes. **Playground:** No. **Other:** Recreation field, pavilion, coin games, mini-golf, driving range, basketball, go-karts, bumper boats, bumper cars, ATV mud track, water games. **Activities:** Swimming. **Nearby Attractions:** Lakes, boating, fishing, winter sports, art galleries, ATV & snowmobile trails, Polk County Museum, antiques, Pioneer Village Museum, St. Croix Casino & Hotel. **Additional Information:** Turtle Lake Village Hall, (715) 986-2241.

## RESTRICTIONS

**Pets:** Leash only. **Fires:** Fire ring only. **Alcoholic Beverages:** At sites only. **Vehicle Maximum Length:** None. **Other:** Must shower w/ soap & water before entering pool.

## TO GET THERE

At the junction of US 63 and US 8, drive 500 feet east on US 8. Roads are wide and well maintained w/ broad shoulders.

## WARRENS

## Yogi Bear's Jellystone Park Camp-Resort

CR EW Box 67, Warrens 54666. T: (888) FUN-YOGI; www.jellystonewarrens.com.

| 🚐 ★★★★★ | 🏕 ★★★★ |
|---|---|
| Beauty: ★★★★ | Site Privacy: ★★★★ |
| Spaciousness: ★★★★ | Quiet: ★★★★ |
| Security: ★★★★★ | Cleanliness: ★★★★★ |
| Insect Control: None | Facilities: ★★★★★ |

Ask a child to design the perfect campground, and this might be the result. Yogi Bear's Jellystone Park Camp Resort is a children's wonderland. With a full-time summer activity director, the campground offers a huge smorgasbord of activities, handy snack bars, heated swimming pools, and a lake with a big sandy beach. Fifty pull-through sites (35 × 65 feet) and back ins (40 × 50 feet) offer easy access and a fair amount of privacy. Arranged in a series of loops, the nicely landscaped campground features mostly shady, grassy sites. One entrance to the campground and a security patrol help keep the campground safe and quiet. For such a popular family facility with

a large number of children, the campground is surprisingly peaceful, mainly because most of the play areas are located in a clump away from the campsites.

## BASICS

**Operated by:** Ed Van Der Molen. **Open:** All year. **Site Assignment:** Reservations w/ 1-night fee; refunds (minus $10 charge) w/ 14-day notice. Reservations require a 2-night min., 3-nights on holidays. **Registration:** At campground office. **Fee:** $33 (cash, check, credit cards). **Parking:** At site.

## FACILITIES

**Number of RV Sites:** 490. **Number of Tent-Only Sites:** 100. **Hookups:** Electric (30, 50 amps), water, sewer. **Each Site:** Picnic table, fire ring. **Dump Station:** Yes. **Laundry:** Yes. **Pay Phone:** Yes. **Rest Rooms and Showers:** Yes. **Fuel:** No. **Propane:** Yes. **Internal Roads:** 98 percent paved, rest gravel, in good condition. **RV Service:** No. **Market:** 8 mi. south in Tomah. **Restaurant:** In campground. **General Store:** Yes. **Vending:** Yes. **Swimming Pool:** Yes. **Playground:** Yes. **Other:** 400-ft. waterslide, adventure golf, mini-golf, game room, Yogi's playroom, sand volleyball court, shuffleboard, horseshoes, pavilions, basketball, tennis, baseball, bandstand. **Activities:** Swimming, paddleboat rental, a full-time activity director w/ over 100 activities offered weekly. **Nearby Attractions:** Cranberry festival, cranberry bog tours, Amish country, antique shops, art galleries, golf, casino. **Additional Information:** Tomah CVB, (800) 04-TOMAH.

## RESTRICTIONS

**Pets:** Leash only. **Fires:** Fire pits only. **Alcoholic Beverages:** Permitted. **Vehicle Maximum Length:** 45 ft.

## TO GET THERE

From the junction of I-94 and CR E, take Exit 135 and drive 0.5 mi. east on CR EW.

## WEST BEND

## Lake Lenwood Beach and Campground

7053 Lenwood Dr., West Bend 53090. T: (262) 334-1335; www.lakelenwood.com.

| 🚐 ★★★★ | 🏕 ★★★★ |
|---|---|
| Beauty: ★★★★ | Site Privacy: ★★★★ |
| Spaciousness: ★★★★ | Quiet: ★★★★ |
| Security: ★★★★ | Cleanliness: ★★★★ |
| Insect Control: None | Facilities: ★★★★ |

Want to know if a campground is well maintained? Check out the bathrooms. At Lake Lenwood Beach and Campground, the rest rooms are clean and nicely decorated. and so is the rest of the campground. Located 1.5 miles southwest of West Bend, the campground offers shaded and open sites around a beautiful lake. Almost every site has a tree or a shrub, the typical site width is 45 feet, there are gravel pads for RVs, and the campground has ten pull-throughs and 55 seasonal campers. An unusual 25-foot-high enclosed tower with a spiral slide is a thriller for children. The best RV sites are on the lakefront; the best tent sites are on the lakeshore in a isolated area. Quiet time is enforced between 9:30 p.m. and 8 a.m., with no radios allowed. Children must be at their campsite after dark. Owners are serious about no barking dogs allowed. Security includes one entrance/exit road, owners who live on site, and regular patrols of the campground.

## BASICS

**Operated by:** Mike & Mary Dricken. **Open:** Apr. 20–Oct. 12. **Site Assignment:** Reservations w/ 2-day min. & 2-day deposit; refunds (minus 15 percent charge) w/ 2-week notice. **Registration:** At campground office. **Fee:** $28 (cash, check, credit cards). **Parking:** At site.

## FACILITIES

**Number of RV Sites:** 125. **Number of Tent-Only Sites:** 30. **Hookups:** Electric (30, 50 amps), water, sewer, cable TV, phone. **Each Site:** Picnic table, fire ring. **Dump Station:** Yes. **Laundry:** Yes. **Pay Phone:** Yes. **Rest Rooms and Showers:** Yes. **Fuel:** No. **Propane:** No. **Internal Roads:** Gravel, in good condition. **RV Service:** No. **Market:** 1.5 mi. northwest in West Bend. **Restaurant:** 1 block. **General Store:** Yes, limited. **Vending:** Yes. **Swimming Pool:** No. **Playground:** Yes. **Other:** Lake Lenwood, beach, pier, basketball, horseshoes, hiking trails, volleyball, pavilion, sports field. **Activities:** Swimming, fishing, hiking, boating (rental fishing boats, canoes, kayaks, paddleboats, hydro-bikes & innertubes available). **Nearby Attractions:** Parks, Old Courthouse Square Museum, art museum, golf, indoor go karts, historic homes, antiques, arts & crafts, bike trail, hiking trail, outlet shops, nature areas. **Additional Information:** West Bend Chamber of Commerce, (888) 338-8666.

## RESTRICTIONS

**Pets:** Leash only, non-barking only. **Fires:** Fire ring only. **Alcoholic Beverages:** Permitted. **Vehicle Maximum Length:** None.

## TO GET THERE

From the junction of US 45 and CR D, drive 1 mi. east on CR D, then 1 mi. north on Hwy. 144, then 1 block east on Wallace Lake Rd. Roads are wide and well maintained w/ broad shoulders.

## WEST BEND

### Lazy Days Campground

1475 Lakeview Rd., West Bend 53090. T: (262) 675-6511; F: (262) 675-9133; www.wisvacations.com/lazydays; lazydays@ticon.net.

| 🚐 ★★★ | 🏕 ★★★ |
|---|---|
| Beauty: ★★★ | Site Privacy: ★★★★ |
| Spaciousness: ★★★★ | Quiet: ★★★★ |
| Security: ★★★★ | Cleanliness: ★★ |
| Insect Control: None | Facilities: ★★★ |

Located on a beautiful lake five miles south of West Bend, Lazy Days Campground offers grassy open or wooded sites in a wilderness setting. The gently rolling terrain has a typical site width of 50 feet, 40 pull-throughs, and 194 seasonal campers. Laid out in a series of loops, the campground has a separate section for tents with more green space and privacy. A few tent sites are spread out in other sections. Almost four decades in the same family, Lazy Days tries to ensure a tranquil campground by enforcing quiet time between 10 p.m. to 8 a.m., when no radios, TV, voices, or sounds should carry beyond the site. A nine-mph speed limit seems a bit high for a family-friendly campground, but the rutted roads may discourage anyone from driving over a crawl. Security measures include a guard shack, video surveillance cameras, and regular campground patrols, including drive-throughs by the local sheriff's department. Plus, the owner is a big fella who doesn't put up with any nonsense.

## BASICS

**Operated by:** Eric Waters. **Open:** Apr. 1–Oct. 31. **Site Assignment:** Reservations w/ no deposit; holiday reservations require 3-night deposit; refund w/ 7-day notice. **Registration:** At campground office. **Fee:** $27 (cash, check, credit cards). **Parking:** At site.

## FACILITIES

**Number of RV Sites:** 300. **Number of Tent-Only Sites:** 42. **Hookups:** Electric (30 amps), water, sewer. **Each Site:** Picnic table, fire ring. **Dump Station:** Yes. **Laundry:** Yes. **Pay Phone:** Yes. **Rest Rooms and Showers:** Yes. **Fuel:** Yes. **Propane:** Yes. **Internal Roads:** Gravel, in poor condition. **RV Service:** Yes. **Market:** 5 mi. north in West Bend. **Restaurant:** 2.5 mi. north towards West Bend. **General Store:** Yes. **Vending:** Yes. **Swimming Pool:** No. **Playground:** Yes. **Other:** Green Lake, sandy beach, game room, pavilion, dock, mini golf, volleyball, sports field, hiking trails. **Activities:** Swimming, fishing, hiking, boating (rental rowboats & paddleboats available), biking (rental bikes available), scheduled weekend activities. **Nearby Attractions:** Parks, Old Courthouse Square Museum, art museum, golf, indoor go karts, historic homes, antiques, arts & crafts, bike trail, hiking trail, outlet shops, nature areas. **Additional Information:** West Bend Area Chmber of Commerce, (888) 338-8666.

## RESTRICTIONS

**Pets:** Leash only. **Fires:** Fire ring only. **Alcoholic Beverages:** Permitted. **Vehicle Maximum Length:** None. **Other:** No electric heaters in the campground.

## TO GET THERE

From the junction of US 45 and eastbound Hwy. 144, drive 2.75 mi. northeast on Hwy. 144, then 2 mi. east on CR A, then 0.5 mi. south on Lakeview Rd. Roads are wide and well maintained w/ mostly good shoulders.

## WEST BEND
### Timber Trail Campground

7590 Good Luck Ln., West Bend 53090. T: (262) 338-8561

🚐 ★★★          ⛺ ★★★

Beauty: ★★★              Site Privacy: ★★★★
Spaciousness: ★★★★       Quiet: ★★★★
Security: ★★★★           Cleanliness: ★★★★
Insect Control: None      Facilities: ★★★

Timber Trail Campground is like camping under a canopy of maple and beechwood trees, except that 100 seasonal campers are there too. Located adjacent to Kettle Moraine Ice Age Trail four miles northwest of West Bend, Timber Trail offers mostly wooded gravel sites. If you're looking for an open spot for that satellite dish, this is not the place for you. But it is a very secluded, woodsy campground. Laid out in a series of loops, the rural campground has two pull-throughs and a typical site width of 45 feet. The best RV site is 216 because it offers full hookups and is close to facilities. The best tent site is 42 because it is very wooded and private, with a sandy spot for the tent. Tent-only sites are available in two separate areas. Security measures include owners who live on site and provide regular patrols of the campground.

## BASICS

**Operated by:** Brent & Judy Lange. **Open:** May 15–Oct. 15. **Site Assignment:** Reservations w/ 1-night deposit; refund w/ 7-day notice. **Registration:** At campground office. **Fee:** $22 (cash, check). **Parking:** At site.

## FACILITIES

**Number of RV Sites:** 130. **Number of Tent-Only Sites:** 5. **Hookups:** Electric (30 amps), water, sewer. **Each Site:** Picnic table, fire ring. **Dump Station:** Yes. **Laundry:** Yes. **Pay Phone:** Yes. **Rest Rooms and Showers:** Yes. **Fuel:** No. **Propane:** Yes. **Internal Roads:** Paved/gravel, in good condition. **RV Service:** No. **Market:** 5 mi. southeast in West Bend. **Restaurant:** 5 mi. southeast in West Bend. **General Store:** Yes, limited. **Vending:** Yes. **Swimming Pool:** Yes. **Playground:** Yes. **Other:** Whirlpool, recreation building, snack bar, ball field, tennis court, basketball, volleyball, hiking trails, horseshoes, fishing pond. **Activities:** Swimming, hiking, fishing, boating (no motors), scheduled weekend activities. **Nearby Attractions:** Parks, Old Courthouse Square Museum, art museum, golf, indoor go-karts, historic homes, antiques, arts & crafts, bike trail, hiking trail, outlet shops, nature areas, Kettle Moraine Ice Age Trail. **Additional Information:** West Bend Chamber of Commerce, (888) 338-8666.

## RESTRICTIONS

**Pets:** Leash only. **Fires:** Fire ring only. **Alcoholic Beverages:** Permitted. **Vehicle Maximum Length:** None.

## TO GET THERE

From the junction of US 45 and CR D, drive 1.5 mi. west on CR D, then 0.75 mi. north on Good Luck Ln. Roads are wide and well maintained w/ broad shoulders, but they are winding in spots.

## WEST SALEM
### Neshonoc Lakeside Campground

N5334 Neshonoc Rd., West Salem 54669. T: (888) 783-0035; neshcamp@aol.com.

🚐 ★★★★★          ⛺ ★★★★

Beauty: ★★★★★          Site Privacy: ★★★★★
Spaciousness: ★★★★★     Quiet: ★★★★★
Security: ★★★★★         Cleanliness: ★★★★★
Insect Control: None     Facilities: ★★★★★

Neshonoc Lakeside Camp has natural beauty galore, along with some great touches added by the owners over their 30 years. Located on Lake Neshonoc one mile east of West Salem, the campground offers beautiful views of the water and bluffs on the other shore. Not surprisingly, the most popular sites are 168–205 up on the hillside, where campers can see spectacular sunsets over the 600-acre lake. Also, not surprisingly, the most desirable lakeside spots have been snapped up by seasonal campers. Tent campers might yearn for a more wilderness section that affords some privacy away from RV campers. Exceptionally manicured grounds, mighty clean bathrooms, and color-coordinated reddish-brown paint on campground facilities adds to the visual appeal. Lighted wooden stairs with railings on both sides provide safe passage from the hillside to the heated pool and well-stocked camp store, which features cappuccino every day and sweet rolls from a local bakery on every weekend.

### BASICS
**Operated by:** Bob & Paula Martell. **Open:** Apr. 15–Oct. 15. **Site Assignment:** Reservations w/ 1-night deposit, refund w/ 72-hour notice. **Registration:** At campground office. **Fee:** $26 (cash, check, credit cards). **Parking:** At site.

### FACILITIES
**Number of RV Sites:** 240. **Number of Tent-Only Sites:** 0. **Hookups:** Electric (20, 30, 50 amps), water, sewer. **Each Site:** Picnic table, fire ring. **Dump Station:** Yes. **Laundry:** Yes. **Pay Phone:** Yes. **Rest Rooms and Showers:** Yes. **Fuel:** No. **Propane:** Yes. **Internal Roads:** Paved, in good condition. **RV Service:** No. **Market:** 1 mi. west in West Salem. **Restaurant:** 2.5 mi. west in West Salem. **General Store:** Yes. **Vending:** Yes. **Swimming Pool:** Yes. **Playground:** Yes. **Other:** Sandy beach, boat dock, video game room, sand volleyball court, horseshoes, basketball, croquet, softball. **Activities:** Swimming, boating (rental rowboats, paddleboats, kayaks & canoes available), haywagon rides, scheduled activities. **Nearby Attractions:** Bike trails, shopping center, golf, speedway, zoo, boat tours, historic homes, La Crosse's Riverfest & Oktoberfest. **Additional Information:** Onalaska Center for Commerce & Tourism, (800) 873-1901.

### RESTRICTIONS
**Pets:** Leash only. **Fires:** Fire pits only. **Alcoholic Beverages:** Permitted. **Vehicle Maximum Length:** None.

### TO GET THERE
From the junction of I-90 and CR 3, take Exit 12, drive 1.5 mi. north on CR C through village, then 1.5 mi. east on Hwy. 16, then 1,000 feet south on paved road. Roads are wide and well maintained w/ broad shoulders

## WEST SALEM
### Veterans Memorial Campground

N4668 CR VP, West Salem 54669. T: (608) 786-4011

🚐 ★★★          ⛺ ★★★★

Beauty: ★★★★          Site Privacy: ★★★★
Spaciousness: ★★★       Quiet: ★★★★
Security: ★★★★          Cleanliness: ★★★★
Insect Control: Yes      Facilities: ★★★

At Veterans Memorial Campground, visitors can camp so close to the La Crosse River that they can almost fish from their RV or tent. The La Crosse County park, located in West Salem, lacks many of the amenities campers often want—a laundry, swimming pool, general store, games, and activities—but it has that beautiful river. Wonderful views and unfettered access to the river more than compensate for the shortage of amenities. Located less than three miles from I-90, the campground offers easy access for travelers, including 50 pull-through sites. The most popular sites, of course, are on the river, and tenters have private areas of their own. Security is tops, as a manager lives on site and city police patrol every night. As a friendly touch, the campground provides free firewood—and a little wagon to haul it to the campsite.

### BASICS
**Operated by:** La Crosse County. **Open:** Apr. 15–Oct. 15. **Site Assignment:** First come, first served. **Registration:** At campground office. **Fee:** $16 (cash, check). **Parking:** At site.

## FACILITIES

**Number of RV Sites:** 90. **Number of Tent-Only Sites:** 10. **Hookups:** Electric (20, 30, 50 amps). **Each Site:** Picnic table, fire ring. **Dump Station:** Yes. **Laundry:** No. **Pay Phone:** Yes. **Rest Rooms and Showers:** Yes. **Fuel:** No. **Propane:** No. **Internal Roads:** Paved, in good condition. **RV Service:** No. **Market:** 1.5 mi. east in West Salem. **Restaurant:** 1.5 mi. east in West Salem. **General Store:** Yes. **Vending:** Yes. **Swimming Pool:** No. **Playground:** Yes. **Other:** Shelter house, 4-acre fishing pond, shuffleboard, volleyball, canoe landing, state bike trail. **Activities:** Fishing, biking, scheduled twice-monthly activities. **Nearby Attractions:** Biking, hunting, birdwatching, golf, Onalaska Historical Society Museum, historic homes, aquatic center w/ 200-ft. water slide, antique shops. **Additional Information:** Onalaska Center for Commerce & Tourism, (800) 873-1901.

## RESTRICTIONS

**Pets:** Leash only. **Fires:** Fire ring only. **Alcoholic Beverages:** At sites only. **Vehicle Maximum Length:** None.

## TO GET THERE

From the junction of I-90 and CR C, drive 1.5 mi. north and west on CR C, then 2 mi. west on Hwy. 16, Roads are wide and well maintained w/ broad shoulders

## WHITE LAKE
### Raft 'N Rest Campground and Rafting

N4327 Hwy. 55, White Lake 54491. T: (715) 882-5613

🚐 ★★                     ⛺ ★★★

| | |
|---|---|
| Beauty: ★★★ | Site Privacy: ★★★ |
| Spaciousness: ★★★ | Quiet: ★★ |
| Security: ★★★★ | Cleanliness: ★★★ |
| Insect Control: None | Facilities: ★★ |

Proximity to river rafting is what Raft 'N Rest Campground and Rafting has going for it. Located two miles east of White Lake, the campground is on rolling terrain with mostly open, grassy sites in a big field for RVs. Wooded tent sites offer more green space and privacy. A limited playground includes swings and a sandbox. Laundry facilities are limited to two dryers. Laid out in a series of loops, the campground has a typical site width of 30 feet, no pull-throughs,

and two seasonal campers. Special activities and parties are sometimes scheduled, such as a pig roast and rafting party with a disc jockey. Beer kegs are available upon request. During the week, the campground is fairly quiet, but it can get rowdy on weekends with camping/rafting groups. Security measures include one entrance/exit, a manager living on site, and regular patrols (including local police) on the weekends.

## BASICS

**Operated by:** Robb & Sharon Rose. **Open:** May 1–Sept. 30. **Site Assignment:** Reservations w/ 1-night deposit; refunds w/ 7-day notice. **Registration:** At campground office. **Fee:** $20 (cash, check, credit cards). **Parking:** At site.

## FACILITIES

**Number of RV Sites:** 12. **Number of Tent-Only Sites:** 33. **Hookups:** Electric (20, 30 amps), water. **Each Site:** Picnic table, fire ring. **Dump Station:** Yes. **Laundry:** 2 dryers only. **Pay Phone:** No. **Rest Rooms and Showers:** Yes. **Fuel:** No. **Propane:** No. **Internal Roads:** Gravel, in poor condition. **RV Service:** No. **Market:** 2 mi. west in White Lake. **Restaurant:** 2 mi. west in White Lake. **General Store:** Yes, limited. **Vending:** No. **Swimming Pool:** No. **Playground:** Yes, limited. **Other:** Volleyball, pavilion, sports field. **Activities:** Scheduled activities sometimes. **Nearby Attractions:** Wolf River, rafting, hiking & biking trails, Nicolet National Forest, golf, casinos, fish hatchery, horseback riding, fishing, swimming, hunting. **Additional Information:** Troutland Assoc., (715) 882-8901.

## RESTRICTIONS

**Pets:** Leash only. **Fires:** Fire ring only. **Alcoholic Beverages:** Permitted. **Vehicle Maximum Length:** None.

## TO GET THERE

From the junction of Hwy. 64 and Hwy. 55, drive 0.4 mi. south on Hwy. 55. Roads are wide and well maintained w/ broad shoulders.

## WHITE LAKE
### River Forest Rafting Campground

N2755 Sunny Waters Ln., White Lake 54491.
T: (715) 882-3351; www.wolfriverrafting.com; riverfor@aol.com.

🚐 ★                      ⛺ ★★★

| | |
|---|---|
| Beauty: ★★★ | Site Privacy: ★★★★ |
| Spaciousness: ★★★★ | Quiet: ★★★★ |

Security: ★★★     Cleanliness: ★★
Insect Control: None     Facilities: ★

River Forest Rafting Campground has so much going for it. It is located by Wolf River, six miles southeast of White Lake, in the midst of a natural wonderland. A narrow dirt and gravel road leads uphill to the wilderness campsites, like camping in a state forest. When we visited one bathroom and one shower were out of order. Sites are mostly shady and level with no seasonals. Quiet time is from 10 p.m. to 7 a.m., and the speed limit is five mph. Be aware that no pets are permitted. Security includes one entrance road past the office and a campground gate that may be locked at 11 p.m. Cars arriving after that hour will be parked near the registration building and campers should carry a flashlight with them to assist on the walk back to camp.

## BASICS

**Operated by:** John Stecher. **Open:** May 1–Sept. 15. **Site Assignment:** Reservations w/ $5 per person deposit; refund (minus $5) w/ 10-day notice. **Registration:** At campground office. **Fee:** $6.25 per person. **Parking:** At site.

## FACILITIES

**Number of RV Sites:** 9. **Number of Tent-Only Sites:** 31. **Hookups:** Electric (20 amps). **Each Site:** Picnic table, fire ring. **Dump Station:** Yes. **Laundry:** No. **Pay Phone:** No. **Rest Rooms and Showers:** Yes. **Fuel:** No. **Propane:** Yes. **Internal Roads:** Gravel, in fair condition. **RV Service:** No. **Market:** 6 mi. northwest in White Lake. **Restaurant:** 0.25 mi. south. **General Store:** Yes, limited. **Vending:** Yes. **Swimming Pool:** No. **Playground:** No. **Other:** Hiking trails, river. **Activities:** River swimming, fishing, boating (rental canoes & kayaks available), rafting (rental rubber rafts available). **Nearby Attractions:** Nicolet Forest, ATV trail, lakes, hunting, mountain biking, trout streams, horseback riding, golf, casinos, fish hatchery. **Additional Information:** Troutland Assoc., (715) 882-8901.

## RESTRICTIONS

**Pets:** Not allowed. **Fires:** Fire ring only. **Alcoholic Beverages:** Permitted. **Vehicle Maximum Length:** 38 ft.

## TO GET THERE

From the junction of CR WW and Hwy. 55, drive 300 feet north on Hwy. 55. Roads are wide and well maintained w/ broad shoulders.

## WHITE LAKE

## Wolf River-Nicolet Forest Campground and Outdoor Center

N3116 Hwy. 55, White Lake 54491. T: (715) 882-4002

 🚐 ★★       ⛺ ★★★★

Beauty: ★★★     Site Privacy: ★★★★
Spaciousness: ★★★★     Quiet: ★★★★
Security: ★★★★     Cleanliness: ★★★
Insect Control: None     Facilities: ★★

First off, Wolf River-Nicolet Forest Campground and Outdoor Center is not affiliated with Nicolet National Forest Campgrounds. It is a private campground located 8.5 miles southeast of White Lake and nestled in the Nicolet National Forest. It offers secluded, wooded, primitive campsites near a river. Sites with electric hookups are mostly grassy and shaded, with three pull-throughs and six seasonal campers. For rafters, the Wolf River is 1.5 miles away. A rustic trail takes about 15 minutes to walk from the campground to the river. The campground also offers a "pet-sitting" service for rafters and other campers. For a donation, the pet is walked and tied up outside the office while campers are gone rafting or enjoying other area activities. During the winter season, the campground is plowed, so campers can stay while enjoying local snowmobiling and cross-country skiing. Security measures include one entrance/exit, an owner who lives on site, and regular patrols, including local police who drive through the campground frequently.

## BASICS

**Operated by:** Janet Williams. **Open:** All year. **Site Assignment:** Reservations w/ 1-night deposit; refund w/ 14-day notice. **Registration:** At campground office. **Fee:** $16 (cash, check, credit cards). **Parking:** At site.

## FACILITIES

**Number of RV Sites:** 12. **Number of Tent-Only Sites:** 30. **Hookups:** Electric (30 amps). **Each Site:** Picnic table, fire ring. **Dump Station:** No. **Laundry:** Yes. **Pay Phone:** Yes. **Rest Rooms and Showers:** Yes. **Fuel:** No. **Propane:** Yes. **Internal Roads:** Gravel, in fair condition. **RV Service:** No. **Market:** 8 mi. northwest in White Lake. **Restaurant:** 1.5 mi. south. **General Store:** Yes, limited. **Vending:** Yes. **Swimming Pool:** No. **Playground:**

Yes. **Other:** Volleyball, arcade room, mini golf, rental cabins, rental rooms, rental camper, horseshoes, nature trails, basketball, pool table. **Activities:** Hiking, scheduled weekend activities. **Nearby Attractions:** Wolf River, hiking & biking trails, Nicolet National Forest, golf, casinos, fish hatchery, horseback riding, fishing, rafting, swimming, hunting, snowmobiling. **Additional Information:** Troutland Assoc., (715) 882-8901.

## RESTRICTIONS

**Pets:** Leash only. **Fires:** Fire ring only. **Alcoholic Beverages:** Permitted. **Vehicle Maximum Length:** None.

## TO GET THERE

From the junction of Hwy. 64 and Hwy. 55, drive 5 mi. south on Hwy. 55. Roads are wide and well maintained w/ broad shoulders.

# WILTON

## Tunnel Trail Campground

Rte. 1, Box 185, Wilton 54670. T: (608) 435-6829; www.tunneltrail.com; questions@tunneltrail.com.

| 🚐 ★★★★ | 🏕 ★★★★ |
|---|---|
| Beauty: ★★★★ | Site Privacy: ★★★ |
| Spaciousness: ★★★ | Quiet: ★★★★ |
| Security: ★★★★ | Cleanliness: ★★★ |
| Insect Control: None | Facilities: ★★★★ |

A rural campground adjacent to the Elroy-Sparta State Bicycle Trail, Tunnel Trail Campground offers terraced, shaded sites in a valley. Located four miles east of Wilton, the campground has nine pull-throughs and a typical site width of 30 feet. Sites are level and grassy in a quiet, park-like setting. Besides the convenient access from the highway, the campground has a major plus in its proximity to the popular bike trail, formerly the old Chicago-Northwestern railroad bed. The trail is 32 level miles in length and passes through three tunnels and the beautiful hills of the Coulee Region. For campers who don't feel like hauling bikes, the campground rents well-maintained mountain bikes, hybrids, bike trailers, thirdwheels, tandems, and recumbent bikes. The campground is also blessed by being relatively free of mosquitos without having to use insecticides. Quiet hours are from 10:30 p.m. to 7 a.m., with all radios required to be off after 10:30 p.m.

## BASICS

**Operated by:** Scott & Julie Grenon. **Open:** May 1–Oct. 15. **Site Assignment:** Reservations w/ $40 deposit, 2-night min. on weekend, 3-night min. on holidays; refund (minus $5) w/ 2-week notice. **Registration:** At campground office. **Fee:** $25 (cash, check, credit cards). **Parking:** At site.

## FACILITIES

**Number of RV Sites:** 63. **Number of Tent-Only Sites:** 12. **Hookups:** Electric (20, 30 amps), water. **Each Site:** Picnic table, fire ring. **Dump Station:** Yes. **Laundry:** Yes. **Pay Phone:** Yes. **Rest Rooms and Showers:** Yes. **Fuel:** No. **Propane:** No. **Internal Roads:** Paved/gravel, in good condition. **RV Service:** No. **Market:** 4 mi. west in Wilton. **Restaurant:** 4 mi. west in Wilton. **General Store:** Yes, limited. **Vending:** Yes. **Swimming Pool:** Yes. **Playground:** Yes. **Other:** Mini golf, horseshoes, volleyball, basketball, game room, trails, rental cabins, pavilion, badminton, sports field, adults room. **Activities:** Swimming, hiking, biking (rental bikes available). **Nearby Attractions:** Kickapoo River, horseback riding, canoeing, fishing, Amish community, scenic drive, antiques, arts & crafts. **Additional Information:** La Crosse Area CVB, (800) 658-9424.

## RESTRICTIONS

**Pets:** Leash only. **Fires:** Fire ring only. **Alcoholic Beverages:** Permitted. **Vehicle Maximum Length:** None.

## TO GET THERE

From the east junction of Hwy. 131 and Hwy. 71, drive 1 mi. east on Hwy. 71. Roads are wide and well maintained w/ broad shoulders.

# WYEVILLE

## Holiday Lodge Golf Resort

10555 Freedom Rd., Tomah 54660. T: (608) 374-4390

| 🚐 ★★★ | 🏕 n/a |
|---|---|
| Beauty: ★★★ | Site Privacy: ★★★ |
| Spaciousness: ★★★ | Quiet: ★★★★ |
| Security: ★★★ | Cleanliness: ★★★ |
| Insect Control: None | Facilities: ★★★ |

The name says it all. Holiday Lodge Golf Resort caters to golfers or campers looking for a quiet overnight stay. No other activities are offered. Located six miles east of Tomah, the campground is across the street from an 18-hole golf course, a well-stocked pro shop, and a lounge serving sandwiches and drinks. The 71-par course offers gas carts, rental clubs, and watered fairways. Thirty-six holes per day, which includes green fees and a cart, cost $36 per person with a discount for campground guests. The campground's flat, shaded sites are generally spacious (36 feet wide) with 14 full hookups and 14 pullthroughs. The most popular sites are 12–22 because they are larger pull-throughs. The campground offers good security, with one entrance, a manager who lives on site, and a night patrol. For someone who wants to golf and sleep, Holiday Lodge Golf Resort is a popular destination.

## BASICS

**Operated by:** Holiday Lodge Inc. **Open:** Apr. 15–Oct. 15. **Site Assignment:** Reservations accepted w/ no deposit. **Registration:** At campground office. **Fee:** $17 (cash, check, credit cards). **Parking:** At site.

## FACILITIES

**Number of RV Sites:** 30. **Number of Tent-Only Sites:** 0. **Hookups:** Electric (30 amps), water, sewer. **Each Site:** Picnic table, fire ring. **Dump Station:** Yes. **Laundry:** Yes. **Pay Phone:** Yes. **Rest Rooms and Showers:** Yes. **Fuel:** No. **Propane:** No. **Internal Roads:** Gravel, in good condition. **RV Service:** No. **Market:** 6 mi. west in Tomah. **Restaurant:** 6 mi. west in Tomah. **General Store:** No. **Vending:** Yes. **Swimming Pool:** No. **Playground:** No. **Other:** Golf course, pro shop. **Activities:** Golfing. **Nearby Attractions:** Telecommunications Historical Museum, tractor pull, bicycle trails, cranberry fest,. **Additional Information:** Warrens Area Business Assoc. (608) 378-4878.

## RESTRICTIONS

**Pets:** Leash only. **Fires:** Fire pits only. **Alcoholic Beverages:** Permitted. **Vehicle Maximum Length:** None. **Other:** No tents allowed.

## TO GET THERE

From the junction of I-94 and Hwy. 21, drive 6 mi. east on Hwy. 21, then 0.75 mi. south on Excelsior Ave. Roads are wide and well maintained w/ broad shoulders.

# Supplemental Directory of Campgrounds

### Algonquin
Buffalo Park, 4 Alan Dr., 60102. T: (847) 658-9640. RV/tent: 170. $15. Hookups: water, electric (30 amps).

### Amboy
Mendota Hills Resort, 642 US 52, 61310. T: (815) 849-5930. F: (815) 849-9037. RV/tent: 198. $30. Hookups: water, electric (30, 50 amps) sewer, phone.

### Arcola
Arcola Camper Stop, 472 Davis St., 61910. T: (217) 268-4616. RV/tent: 30. $14. Hookups: water, electric (20, 30 amps), sewer, cable TV.

Campalot, 55 Industrial Dr., 61910. T: (217) 268-3563. RV/tent: 10. $15. Hookups: water, electric (20, 30, 50 amps), sewer.

### Atlanta
Hickory Lane Camping, RR 2, 61723. T: (217) 648-2778. RV/tent: 178. $15. Hookups: water, electric (20, 30, 50 amps), sewer.

### Barstow
Lundeen's Landing (East Moline), P.O. Box 182, 61236. T: (309) 496-9956. RV/tent: 68. $15. Hookups: water, electric (30 amps).

### Belvidere
Holiday Acres, 7050 Epworth Rd., 61038. T: (815) 547-7846. RV/tent: 520. $25. Hookups: water, electric (20, 30 amps).

Outdoor World-Pine Country Campground, 5710 Shattuck Rd., 61008. T: (800) 222-5557. F: (815) 544-8019. www.campoutdoor.com. RV/tent: 107. $15. Hookups: water, electric (30 amps), sewer.

### Benton
Gun Creek Recreation Area, 12220 Rend City Rd., 62812. T: (618) 724-2493. RV/tent: 100. $18. Hookups: electric (20, 30, 50 amps).

North Sandusky Creek Recreation Area, State Rd. 154, 62812. T: (618) 625-6115. RV/tent: 141. $18. Hookups: water, electric (30 amps), sewer.

South Marcum Recreation Area, 11623 Trail Head Ln., 62812. T: (618) 435-3549. RV/tent: 143. $14. Hookups: electric (50 amps).

South Sandusky Creek Recreation Area, Red Oak Ln., 62812. T: (618) 625-3011. RV/tent: 121. $18. Hookups: water, electric (50 amps), sewer.

### Biggsville
Hend-CoHills, Rte. 34, 61418. T: (309) 627-2779. RV/tent: 34. $15. Hookups: water, electric (20, 30 amps), sewer.

### Bourbonnais
Kankakee River State Park, 5314 West Rte. 102, 60914. T: (815) 933-1383. F: (815) 933-9809. RV/tent: 250. $15. Hookups: Electric (30 amps).

### Bushnell
Timberview Lakes Campground, 23200 North 2000 Rd., 61422. T: (309) 772-3609. F: (309) 772-3609. timberviewlakes@aol.com, www.timberview lakes.com. RV/tent: 108. $18. Hookups: water, electric (20, 30, 50 amps), sewer, phone.

### Byron
Lake Louise, 8840 Rte. 2, 61010. T: (815) 234-8483. F: (815) 234-2503. www.lakelouise.com. RV/tent: 317. $28. Hookups: water, electric (20, 30, 50 amps), sewer.

### Cahokia
Cahokia RV Parque, 4060 Mississippi Ave., 62206. T: (618) 332-7700. cahokiarv@aol.com. RV/tent: 116. $25. Hookups: water, electric (30, 50 amps), sewer.

## ILLINOIS (continued)

### Cambridge

Gibson's RV Park and Campground, 10768 East 1600 St., 61238. T: (309) 937-2314. gibsons cmp@msn.com, www.hometown.aol.com/gibson cmp. RV/tent: 190. $17. Hookups: water, electric (20, 30 amps).

### Carbondale

Crab Orchard Lake Campground, 10067 Campground Dr., 62901. T: (618) 997-3344. RV/tent: 250. $12. Hookups: water, electric (20, 30 amps).

Little Grassy Campground and Boatdock, 788 Hidden Bay, 62958. T: (618) 457-6655. RV/tent: 152. $10. Hookups: water, electric (30 amps), sewer.

### Carlyle

Cole's Creek Recreation Area (Boulder), 16225 Coles Creek Rd., 62231. T: (618) 226-3211. RV/tent: 148. $15. Hookups: water, electric (30, 50 amps), sewer.

Dam West Recreation Area, 801 Lake Rd., 62231. T: (618) 594-4410. RV/tent: 113. $20. Hookups: electric (30 amps).

Eldon Hazlet State Park, 20100 Hazlet Park Rd., 62231. T: (618) 594-3015. RV/tent: 363. $20. Hookups: electric (30, 50 amps).

McNair Campground, 801 Lake Rd., 62231. T: (618) 594-2484. RV/tent: 25. $20. Hookups: water, electric (30 amps).

### Carmi

Burrell Park Campground, Sixth & Stewart Sts, 62821. T: (618) 382-2693. RV/tent: 25. $18. Hookups: water, electric (30 amps), sewer.

### Champaign

D & W Camping and Fishing Lake, 411 West Hensley Rd., 61821. T: (217) 356-3732. RV/tent: 60. $15. Hookups: water, electric (20, 30, 50 amps), sewer.

### Clayton

Siloam State Park, RR 1 Box 204, 62324. T: (217) 894-6205. RV/tent: 230. $11. Hookups: electric (30 amps).

### Clinton

Weldon Springs State Park, RR 2 Box 87, 61727. T: (217) 935-2644. RV/tent: 98. $11. Hookups: electric (30 amps).

### Crete

Emerald Trails Campground, 3132 East Goodnow Rd., 60417. T: (800) 870-8357. RV/tent: 94. $25. Hookups: water, electric (30 amps), sewer.

### Danville

Kickapoo State Park, 10906 Kickapoo Park Rd., 61858. T: (217) 442-4915. RV/tent: 201. $11. Hookups: electric (30 amps).

### De Witt

Clinton Lake-Mascoutin State Recreation Complex, R. R. 1 Box 4, 61735. T: (217) 935-8722. RV/tent: 308. $11. Hookups: Electric (20, 30, 50 amps).

### Durand

Sugar Shores Camping Resort, 9938 West Winslow Rd., 61024. T: (815) 629-2568. RV/tent: 90. $17. Hookups: water, electric (20, 30, 50 amps), phone.

### East St. Louis

Casino Queen RV Park, 200 South Front St., 62201. T: (618) 874-5000. www.casinoqueen.com. RV/tent: 90. $15. Hookups: water, electric (50 amps), cable TV, Internet.

### Edwardsville

Red Barn Rendezvous, 3955 Blackburn Rd., 62025. T: (618) 692-9015. RV/tent: 45. $18. Hookups: water, electric (20, 30, 50 amps), sewer.

### Effingham

Lake Sara Campground and Beach, 70 Wildwood Dr., 62401. T: (217) 868-2964. RV/tent: 315. $20. Hookups: water, electric (20, 30 amps), sewer.

### Fithian

Five Bridges Campground, State Hwy. 49 North, 61844. T: (217) 583-3200. RV/tent: 37. $20. Hookups: water, electric (30 amps).

### Gages Lake

Gages Lake Camping, 18887 West Gages Lake Rd., 60030. T: (847) 223-5541. F: (847) 223-5564. RV/tent: 100. $29. Hookups: water, electric (30 amps).

### Garden Prairie

Paradise Park, 11122 Station St., 61038. T: (815) 597-1671. www.paradiservpark.com. RV/tent: 170. $25. Hookups: water, electric (15, 20, 30, 50 amps).

### Genesco

Geneseo Campground, 22978 Illinois Hwy. 82, 61254. T: (309) 944-6465. w6465@geneseo.net; www.fultiming-america.com/genesco. RV/tent: 63. $16. Hookups: water, electric (20, 30, 50 amps), sewer, phone, Internet.

Spirit in the Oaks, 27340 East 1350 St., 61254. T: (309) 944-3889. RV/tent: 90. $22. Hookups: water, electric (20, 30, 50 amps), sewer.

### Glenarm

Holiday RV Center & Trav-L-Park, 9683 Palm Rd., 62629. T: (219) 483-9998. RV/tent: 110. $18. Hookups: water, electric (50 amps), sewer.

### Golconda

Dixon Springs State Park (Dixon), RR 2, 62938. T: (618) 949-3394. RV/tent: 50. $10. Hookups: electric (30 amps).

## ILLINOIS (continued)

### Goreville

Ferne Clyffe State Park, P.O. Box 10, 62939. T: (618) 995-2411. RV/tent: 65. $11. Hookups: electric (30 amps).

Hilltop Campgrounds, 255 Baker Ln., 62939. T: (618) 995-2189. RV/tent: 52. $16. Hookups: water, electric (30, 50 amps), sewer.

### Grafton

Pere Marquette State Park, P.O. Box 158, 62037. T: (618) 786-3323. RV/tent: 117. $11. Hookups: electric (30 amps).

### Havana

Evening Star Camping Resort, 16474 Walker Rd., 61567. T: (309) 562-7590. estar@casscomm.com. RV/tent: 403. $15. Hookups: water, electric (20, 30, 50 amps), sewer.

Havana Park District Riverfront Park Campground, South Schrader Ave., 62644. T: (309) 543-6240. RV/tent: 12. $12. Hookups: water, electric (30 amps).

### Ina

Sherwood Camping Resort, 411 Main St., 62846. T: (618) 437-5530. RV/tent: 81. $15. Hookups: water, electric (30 amps), sewer.

### Joliet

Martin Campground, 725 Cherry Hill Rd., 60433. T: (815) 726-3173. RV/tent: 110. $25. Hookups: water, electric (20, 30 amps) sewer.

### Le Roy

Moraine View State Park, R. R. 2, 61752. T: (309) 724-8032. F: (309) 724-8039. RV/tent: 199. $15. Hookups: electric (30 amps).

### Leland

Hi-Tide Recreation, 4611 East 22nd Rd., 60531. T: (815) 495-9032. RV/tent: 33. $23. Hookups: water, electric (20, 30, 50 amps), sewer, phone.

### Lincoln

Camp-A-While, 1779 1250 Ave., 62656. T: (888) 593-5102. camp-a-while@yahoo.com. RV/tent: 27. $16. Hookups: water, electric (20, 30, 50 amps), sewer.

### Litchfield

Kamper Kompanion Campground, 18388 East Frontage Rd., 62056. T: (217) 324-4747. RV/tent: 24. $15. Hookups: water, electric (20, 30 amp), sewer.

### Mackinaw

Kentuckiana Campground (Hopedale), 27585 Kentuckiana Rd., 61755. T: (309) 449-3274. RV/tent: 330. $17. Hookups: water, electric (20, 30, 50 amps), sewer.

### Makanda

Giant City State Park, 235 Grant City Rd., 62958. T: (618) 457-4836. RV/tent: 99. $7. Hookups: electric (20, 30, 50 amps).

### Marengo

Best Holiday Lehman's Lakeside RV Resort, 19609 Harmony Rd., 60152. T: (877) 242-8533. RV/tent: 290. $30. Hookups: water, electric (20, 30, 50 amps), sewer, cable TV, phone.

### Marion

Motel Marion Campground, 2100 West Main St., 62959. T: (618) 993-2101. RV/tent: 25. $15. Hookups: water, electric (30, 50 amps), sewer.

### Marseilles

Illini State Park, 2660 East 2350th Rd., 61341. T: (815) 795-2448. RV/tent: 102. $15. Hookups: electric (30 amps).

Whispering Pines Campground, 2776 East 2625 Rd., 61341. T: (815) 795-5720. RV/tent: 400. $20. Hookups: water, electric (15, 20, 30, 50 amps), sewer.

### Marshall

Mill Creek Park Campground, 20482 North Park Rd. Entrance, 62441. T: (217) 889-3601. F: (217) 889-3601. RV/tent: 139. $15. Hookups: electric (20, 30 amps).

### Mendon

Whispering Oaks Campground, 2124 East 1300th Place, 62351. T: (217) 936-2500. RV/tent: 197. $15. Hookups: water, electric (30 amps).

### Millbrook

Yogi Bear Jellystone Camp-Resort Chicago-Millbrook, 8574 Millbrook Rd., 60536. T: (800) 438-9644. www.jellystonechicago.com. RV/tent: 356. $37. Hookups: water, electric (20, 30, 50 amps), sewer.

### Miller City

Horseshoe Lake State Conservation Area (Cairo), P.O. Box 85, 62962. T: (618) 776-5689. RV/tent: 178. $11. Hookups: electric (30 amps).

### Mt. Vernon

Quality Times, 9746 East IL Hwy. 15, 62864. T: (618) 244-0399. F: (618) 244-7422. RV/tent: 43. $17. Hookups: water, electric (20, 30 amps), sewer, phone.

## ILLINOIS (continued)

### Murphysboro
Lake Murphysboro State Park, 52 Cinda Hill Dr., 62966. T: (618) 684-2867. RV/tent: 74. $11. Hookups: electric (50 amps).

### Nauvoo
Nauvoo Campground, 2205 Mulholland St., 62354. T: (217) 453-2263. F: (217) 453-2253. Ajbate@aol.com. RV/tent: 28. $15. Hookups: water, electric (20, 30, 50 amps), sewer.

### New Windsor
Shady Lakes Camping & Recreation, 3355 75th Ave., 61465. T: (309) 667-2709. F: (309) 667-2809. shadylak@winco.net; www.web.winco.net/~shadylak. RV/tent: 253. $16. Hookups: water, electric (20, 30, 50 amps).

### Oakland
Hebron Hills Camping, 14349 North City Rd. 2350 E, 61943. T: (217) 346-3385. www.HebronHills.com. RV/tent: 55. $16. Hookups: water, electric (20, 30, 50 amps), sewer, phone.

### Onarga
Lake Arrowhead, Frontage Rd. North, 60955. T: (815) 268-4849. RV/tent: 61. $15. Hookups: water, electric (30 amps).

### Oquawka
Delabar State Park, R. R. 2, 91469. T: (309) 867-3671. RV/tent: 124. $8. Hookups: electric (30 amps).

### Oregon
Hansen's Hide Away Ranch & Family Campground, 2936 Harmony Rd., 61061. T: (815) 732-6489. RV/tent: 102. $16. Hookups: water, electric (20, 30 amps), sewer.

### Pearl City
Emerald Acres Campground, 33351 South Mill Grove Rd., 61062. T: (815) 443-2550. RV/tent: 60. $22. Hookups: water, electric (30 amps).

### Peoria
Mt. Hawley RV Park, 8327 North Knoxville Ave., 61615. T: (309) 692-2223. RV/tent: 90. $20. Hookups: water, electric (30, 50 amps), sewer.

### Plainview
Beaver Dam State Park, 14548 Beaver Dam Ln., 62676. T: (217) 854-8020. RV/tent: 84. $11. Hookups: electric (30 amps).

### Rochester
KOA Springfield (Springfield), 4320 KOA Rd., 62563. T: (800) 562-7212. RV/tent: 96. $20. Hookups: water, electric (20, 30 amps), sewer, phone.

### Rock
Cave-In-Rock State Park, New State Park Rd., 62919. T: (618) 289-4325. F: (618) 289-4315. RV/tent: 48. $10. Hookups: electric (30 amps).

### Rock Falls
Leisure Lake Campground, 2304 French St., 61071. T: (815) 626-0005. RV/tent: 68. $16. Hookups: water, electric (20, 30 amps), sewer, phone.

### Rock Island
Camelot Campground & Recreation, 2311 78 Ave. West, 61201. T: (309) 787-0665. F: (309) 787-1320. RV/tent: 158. $17. Hookups: water, electric (30, 50 amps), sewer, phone.

### Rockford
Blackhawk Valley Campground, 6540 Valley Trail Rd., 61109. T: (815) 874-9767. RV/tent: 170. $20. Hookups: water, electric (30 amps), sewer.

### Salem
Stephen A. Forbes State Park, 4577 Rte. 84N, 61074. T: (618) 547-33381. RV/tent: 146. $11. Hookups: electric (30 amps).

### Shelbyville
Bo Wood Recreation Area, R. R. 4, 62565. T: (217) 774-2014. RV/tent: 82. $14. Hookups: electric (30 amps).

### Sheridan
Mallard Bend Campground & RV Park, 2838 North 4351st St., 60551. T: (815) 496-2496. F: (630) 964-6487. www.mallardbend.com. RV/tent: 168. $25. Hookups: water, electric (20, 30, 50 amps), sewer.

### Sheridan
Rolling Oaks Campground, 2743 North4251 1st Rd., 60551. T: (815) 496-2334. RV/tent: 670. $17. Hookups: water, electric (20, 30 amps), sewer.

### Spring Grove
Chain O'Lakes State Park, Oak Point (Fox Lake), 8916 Wilmot Rd., 60081. T: (847) 587-5512. RV/tent: 206. $11. Hookups: electric (30 amps).

### St. Elmo
Bell's Timberline Lake Campground, P. O. Box 15, 62458. T: (618) 829-3383. RV/tent: 100. $14. Hookups: water, electric (30 amps), sewer.

### Sumner
Red Hills Lake State Park (Lawrencville), R. R. 2, 62466. T: (618) 936-2469. RV/tent: 247. $11. Hookups: electric (20, 30 amps).

### Tinley Park
Windy City Campground & Beach, 18701 South 80th Ave., 60477. T: (708) 720-0030. F: (708) 720-0431. RV/tent: 100. $25. Hookups: water, electric (20, 30, 50s), sewer, phone.

## ILLINOIS (continued)

### Union

KOA-Chicago Northwest (Marengo), 8404 South Union Rd., 60180. T: (800) KOA-2827. RV/tent: 138. $25. Hookups: water, electric (15, 20, 30, 50 amps), phone.

### Wilmington

Fossil Rock Campground, 24615 West Strip Mine Rd., 60481. T: (815) 476-6784. F: (815) 476-6704. RV/tent: 275. $25. Hookups: water, electric (20, 30, 50 amps), sewer, phone.

### Windsor

Wolf Creek State Park (Findlay), R. R. 1 Box 99, 61957. T: (217) 459-2831. RV/tent: 406. $11. Hookups: electric (30 amps).

### Yorkville

Hide-A-Way Lakes, 8045 Van Emmon Rd., 60560. T: (630) 553-6323. RV/tent: 800. $20. Hookups: water, electric (20, 30, 50 amps), sewer, phone.

## INDIANA

### Albion

Chain O'Lakes State Park, 2355 East 75S, 46701. T: (219) 636-2654. RV/tent: 413. $11.00. Hookups: electric (30 amps).

### Anderson

Mounds State Park, 4306 Mounds Rd., 46017. T: (765) 642-6627. RV/tent: 75. $11. Hookups: electric (30 amps).

### Andrews

Lost Bridge West S.R.A. Salamonie Lake, 9214 West Lost Bridge W, 46702. T: (219) 468-2125. RV/tent: 276. $11. Hookups: electric (30 amps).

### Angola

Camp Sack-In, 8740 E 40S, 46703. T: (219) 665-5166. RV/tent: 170. $20. Hookups: water, electric (30 amps).

Circle B Park, 340 Ln. 100, 46703. T: (219) 665-5353. RV/tent: 250. $24. Hookups: water, sewer, electric (50 amps).

Cook's Happy Acres RV Park, 1940 South 300W, 46703. T: (888) 318-8797. RV/tent: 100. $24. Hookups: water, sewer, electric (50 amps).

Pokagon State Park, 450 Ln. 100 Lake James, 46703. T: (219) 833-2012. RV/tent: 273. $11. Hookups: electric (30 amps).

### Attica

Summers Campground, 5509 North 200E, 47918. T: (765) 762-2832. RV/tent: 100. $18. Hookups: water, electric (30 amps).

### Birdseye

Newton-Stewart S.R.A. Patoka Lake, RR 1, 47513. T: (812) 685-2464. RV/tent: 563. $8. Hookups: electric (30 amps).

### Bloomington

Paynetown State Recreation Area, 4850 South SR 446, 47401. T: (812) 837-9546. RV/tent: 320. $8. Hookups: electric (30 amps).

### Bluffton

Quabache State Park, 4930 East SR 210, 46714. T: (219) 824-0926. RV/tent: 124. $11. Hookups: electric (30 amps).

### Boonville

Scales Lake Park, 800 West Tennyson Rd., 47601. T: (812) 897-6200. RV/tent: 141. $13. Hookups: electric (30 amps), sewer.

### Borden

Deam Lake State Recreation Area, RR 2, 47106. T: (812) 246-5421. RV/tent: 286. $11. Hookups: electric (30 amps).

### Bremen

Rupert's Resort Campground, 3408 West Shore Dr., 46506. T: (219) 546-2657. RV/tent: 120. $20. Hookups: water, electric (30 amps).

### Brookville

Mounds State Recreation Area, Brookville Lake, P.O. Box 100, 47012. T: (765) 647-2657. RV/tent: 379. $10. Hookups: water, electric (30 amps), sewer.

### Cedar Lake

Cedar Lake Bible Conference, 13701 Lauerman, 46303. T: (219) 374-5941. RV/tent: 40. $22. Hookups: water, sewer, electric (30 amps).

### Charlestown

Charlestown State Park, P.O. Box 38, 47111. T: (812) 256-5600. RV/tent: 219. $13. Hookups: water, sewer, electric (30 amps).

### Chesteron

Indiana Dune State Park, 1600 North 25E, 46304. T: (219) 926-1952. RV/tent: 286. $11. Hookups: electric (30 amps).

Sand Creek Campground, 1000 North 350E, 46304. T: (219) 926-7482. RV/tent: 146. $20. Hookups: water, sewer, electric (50 amps).

## INDIANA (continued)

### Cicero
White River Campground, 11299 East 234th St., 46034. T: (317) 984-2705. RV/tent: 116. $22. Hookups: water, sewer, electric (30 amps).

### Clarksville
Louisville Metro KOA Kampground, 900 Marriott Dr., 47129. T: (812) 282-4474. RV/tent: 92. $21. Hookups: water, electric (50 amps), sewer.

### Cloverdale
Blackhawk Campground, 2046 West CR 1050S, 46120. T: (765) 795-4795. RV/tent: 158. $20. Hookups: water, electric (30 amps), sewer.

### Colfax
Broadview Lake, 4850 South Broadview Rd., 46035. T: (317) 324-2622. RV/tent: 170. $20. Hookups: water, sewer, electric (30 amps).

### Dillsboro
Brownings Camp, 3622 East CR 200S, 47018. T: (812) 689-6464. RV/tent: 281. $15. Hookups: water, sewer, electric (50 amps).

### Edinburgh
Driftwood Camp-RV Park, 12180 US 31N, 46124. T: (812) 526-6422. RV/tent: 62. $13. Hookups: water, electric (30 amps), sewer.

### Elkhart
Elkhart Campground, 25608 CR 4E, 46514. T: (219) 264-2914. RV/tent: 450. $20. Hookups: water, sewer, electric (50 amps).

### Fort Wayne
Gordon's Camping, 1010 Ansely Dr., 46804. T: (219) 351-3383. RV/tent: 321. $30. Hookups: water, electric (50 amps).

### Frankton
Miami Camp, 8851 West 400N, 46044. T: (765) 734-1365. RV/tent: 100. $18. Hookups: water, electric (30 amps), sewer.

### Garrett
Indian Springs Campground, P.O. Box 216, 46738. T: (219) 357-5194. RV/tent: 365. $25. Hookups: water, electric (50 amps), sewer.

### Geneva
Amishville USA, 844 East 900S, 46740. T: (219) 589-3536. RV/tent: 284. $15. Hookups: water, electric (30 amps).

### Granger
South Bend East KOA, 50707 Princess Way, 46530. T: (219) 277-1335. RV/tent: 80. $25. Hookups: water, electric (30 amps).

### Greenfield
Heartland Resort, 1613 West 300N, 46140. T: (317) 326-3181. RV/tent: 309. $25. Hookups: water, sewer, electric (50 amps).

Mohawk Campground & RV Park, CR 375N, 46140. T: (317) 326-3393. RV/tent: 104. $18. Hookups: water, sewer, electric (30 amps).

### Hartford City
Wildwood Acres Campground, 520 West 300N, 47348. T: (765) 348-2100. RV/tent: 169. $15. Hookups: water, sewer, electric (50 amps).

### Indianapolis
Indiana State Fairgrounds Campground, 1202 East 38th St., 46205. T: (317) 927-7510. RV/tent: 170. $15. Hookups: water, electric (20 amps).

### Jasonville
Shakamak State Park, 6265 West SR 48, 47438. T: (812) 665-2158. RV/tent: 196. $11. Hookups: electric (30 amps).

### Knox
Bass Lake State Park, 5838 South SR 10, 46534. T: (219) 772-3382. RV/tent: 60. $11. Hookups: electric (30 amps).

### Kokomo
Springhill Campground, 623 South 750 W, 46901. T: (765) 883-7433. RV/tent: 122. $16. Hookups: water, sewer, electric (30 amps).

### Kouts
Donna-Jo Camping Area, 1255 South CR 350E, 46347. T: (219) 766-2186. RV/tent: 75. $20. Hookups: water, electric (50 amps).

### Liberty
Whitewater Memorial State Park, 1418 South SR 101, 47353. T: (765) 458-5565. RV/tent: 279. $11. Hookups: electric (30 amps).

### Lincoln City
Lincoln State Park, P.O. Box 216, 47552. T: (812) 937-4710. RV/tent: 270. $11. Hookups: electric (30 amps), water.

### Logansport
France Park, 4505 US 24W, 46947. T: (219) 753-2928. RV/tent: 300. $12. Hookups: water, electric (30 amps).

Tall Sycamore Campground, 355 South CR 600E, 46947. T: (219) 753-4898. RV/tent: 125. $16. Hookups: electric (50 amps), water.

### Loogootee
West Boggs Park, P.O. Box 245, 47553. T: (812) 295-3421. RV/tent: 220. $18. Hookups: electric (30 amps), water, sewer.

## INDIANA (continued)

### Lynnville
Lynville Park, P.O. Box 309, 47619. T: (812) 922-5144. RV/tent: 47. $12. Hookups: water, electric (30 amps), sewer.

### Marshall
Turkey Run State Park, P.O. Box 37, 47859. T: (765) 597-2635. RV/tent: 253. $11. Hookups: electric (30 amps).

### Michigan City
Michigan City Campground, 1601 US 421N, 46360. T: (219) 872-7600. RV/tent: 150. $20. Hookups: water, electric (30 amps), sewer.

### Middlebury
Elkhart Co./Middlebury Exit KOA, 52867 SR 13, 46540. T: (219) 825-5932. RV/tent: 120. $30. Hookups: water, electric (50 amps), sewer.

### Mitchell
Spring Mill State Park, P.O. Box 376, 47446. T: (812) 849-4129. RV/tent: 224. $13. Hookups: electric (30 amps).

### Modoc
Kamp Modoc, 8773 South 800W, 47358. T: (765) 853-5290. RV/tent: 260. $20. Hookups: water, electric (30 amps).

### Montgomery
Glendale State Fish & Wildlife Area, P.O. Box 300, 47558. T: (812) 644-7711. RV/tent: 121. $10. Hookups: electric (30 amps).

### Monticello
Arrowhead Campground, CR 400 East, 47960. T: (219) 583-5198. RV/tent: 194. $25. Hookups: water, electric (30 amps), sewer.

Holiday Resort, Lakeside Dr., 47960. T: (219) 583-7396. RV/tent: 36. $20. Hookups: water, electric (30 amps).

Indiana Beach Camp Resort, 5224 East Indiana Beach Rd., 47960. T: (219) 583-8306. RV/tent: 301. $30. Hookups: water, sewer, electric (50 amps).

### Nashville
Brown County State Park, P.O. Box 608, 47448. T: (812) 988-6406. RV/tent: 412. $12. Hookups: electric (30 amps).

Westward Ho Campground, 4557 East SR 46, 47448. T: (812) 988-0008. RV/tent: 122. $25. Hookups: water, electric (50 amps), sewer.

### New Carlisle
Mini Mountain Camp Resort, 32351 State Rd. 2, 46552. T: (219) 654-3307. RV/tent: 199. $22. Hookups: water, sewer, electric (50 amps).

### New Castle
Summit Lake State Park, 5993 North Messick Rd., 47362. T: (765) 766-5873. RV/tent: 125. $11. Hookups: electric (30 amps).

Walnut Ridge Resort Campground, 408 North CR 300W, 47362. T: (765) 533-6611. RV/tent: 150. $20. Hookups: water, electric (30 amps).

### New Harmony
Harmonie State Park, 3451 Harmonie State Park Rd., 47631. T: (812) 682-4821. RV/tent: 200. $12. Hookups: electric (30 amps).

### North Liberty
Potato Creek State Park, 25601 SR 4, 46554. T: (219) 656-8186. RV/tent: 287. $11. Hookups: electric (30 amps).

### Orland
Manapogo Park, 5495 West 760 North, 46776. T: (219) 833-3902. RV/tent: 300. $30. Hookups: water, sewer, electric (30 amps).

### Pendletown
Glowood Campground, 9384 West 700S, 46064. T: (317) 485-5239. RV/tent: 100. $23. Hookups: water, electric (30 amps).

### Peru
Mississinewa Lake-Miami Recreation Area, Box 194, 46970. T: (765) 473-6528. RV/tent: 620. $15. Hookups: water, sewer, electric (50 amps).

### Pierceton
Yogi Bear's Jellystone Park Camp-Resort, 1916 North 850E, 46562. T: (219) 594-2124. RV/tent: 150. $35. Hookups: water, electric (30 amps), sewer.

### Portland
Hickory Grove Lakes Campground, 7424 South 300E, 47371. T: (219) 335-2639. RV/tent: 152. $20. Hookups: water, sewer, electric (30 amps).

### Richmond
Deer Ridge Camping Resort, 3696 Smyma Rd., 47374. T: (765) 939-0888. RV/tent: 64. $24. Hookups: water, electric (30 amps), sewer.

Grandpa's Farm, 4244 SR 227 North, 47374. T: (765) 962-7907. RV/tent: 55. $20. Hookups: water, sewer, electric (30 amps).

Indiana-Ohio KOA Kampground, 3101 Cart Rd., 47374. T: (765) 962-1219. RV/tent: 75. $25. Hookups: water, electric (30 amps), sewer.

### Rockville
Covered Bridge Campground, 211½ South Erie St., 47872. T: (765) 569-3911. RV/tent: 100. $22. Hookups: water, sewer, electric (30 amps).

## INDIANA (continued)

### Rockville (continued)

Raccoon State Recreation Area, 160 South Raccoon Parkway, 47872. T: (765) 344-1412. RV/tent: 350. $12. Hookups: electric (30 amps).

### Scottsburg

Hardy Lake State Recreation Area, Box 174, 47170. T: (812) 794-3800. RV/tent: 167. $10. Hookups: electric (30 amps).

Yogi Bear's Jellystone Park at Raintree Lake, 4577 West SR 56, 47170. T: (812) 752-4062. RV/tent: 91. $35. Hookups: water, electric (30 amps), sewer.

### Shelbyville

Fairland Recreation Park, 3779 North Frontage Rd., 46176. T: (317) 392-0525. RV/tent: 44. $22. Hookups: water, electric (30 amps).

### Shipshewana

Riverside Campground, 5910 North CR 450W, 46565. T: (219) 562-3742. RV/tent: 30. $18. Hookups: water, electric (30 amps).

Shipshewana Campground & Amish Log Cabin Lodging, P.O. Box 172, 46565. T: (219) 768-7770. RV/tent: 45. $28. Hookups: water, sewer, electric (30 amps).

Shipshewana Campground South, 1105 South Van-Buren St., 46565. T: (219) 768-4669. RV/tent: 68. $25. Hookups: water, electric (30 amps).

### Spencer

McCormick's Creek State Park, RR 5 Box 282, 47460. T: (812) 829-2235. RV/tent: 289. $11. Hookups: electric (30 amps).

### St. Paul

Hidden Paradise Campground, 802 East Jefferson St., 47272. T: (765) 525-6582. RV/tent: 168. $20. Hookups: water, sewer, electric (50 amps).

### Terre Haute

Terre Haute KOA, 5995 East Sony Dr., 47802. T: (812) 232-2457. RV/tent: 77. $35. Hookups: water, sewer, electric (30 amps).

### Thorntown

Old Mill Run Park, 8544 West 690N, 46071. T: (800) 874-7343. RV/tent: 385. $25. Hookups: water, sewer, electric (30 amps).

### Unionville

Riddle Point Park on Lake Lemon, 7599 North Tunnel Rd., 47468. T: (812) 332-5220. RV/tent: 100. $16. Hookups: water, electric (30 amps).

### Vallonia

Starve Hollow State Recreation Area, 4345 South County Rd. 275W, 47281. T: (812) 358-3464. RV/tent: 185. $12. Hookups: electric (30 amps).

### Valparaiso

Candy Stripe Campsite, 446 West Division Dr., 46383. T: (219) 462-0784. RV/tent: 100. $22. Hookups: water, sewer, electric (50 amps).

### Warsaw

Hoffman Lake Camp, 7638 West 300N, 46582. T: (800) 289-8256. RV/tent: 193. $22. Hookups: water, sewer, electric (30 amps).

Pic-A-Spot Campground, 6402 East McKenna Rd., 46580. T: (219) 594-2635. RV/tent: 172. $20. Hookups: water, electric (30 amps).

Pike Lake Campground, 117 East Canal St., 46580. T: (219) 269-1439. RV/tent: 110. $14. Hookups: water, electric (30 amps).

### Winamac

Tippecanoe River State Park, 4200 North US 35, 46996. T: (219) 946-3213. RV/tent: 122. $11. Hookups: electric (30 amps).

Williams Broken Arrow Campground, RR 1 Box 391, 46996. T: (219) 946-4566. RV/tent: 990. $22. Hookups: water, sewer, electric (50 amps).

## MICHIGAN

### Acme

Traverse Bay RV Park, P.O. Box 515, 49610. T: (231) 938-5800. RV/tent: 133. $25. Hookups: water, sewer, electric (50 amps).

### Alanson

Crooked River RV Park, 5397 Cheboygan St., 49706. T: (231) 548-5534. RV/tent: 15. $15. Hookups: electric (30 amps).

### Alger

Greenwood Campground, 636 West Greenwood Rd., 48610. T: (989) 345-2778. RV/tent: 45. $22. Hookups: water, sewer, electric (50 amps).

### Algonac

Algonac State Park, 8732 River Rd., 48039. T: (810) 765-5605. RV/tent: 300. $15. Hookups: electric (30 amps).

## MICHIGAN (continued)

### Aloha

Aloha State Park, 4347 Third St., 49721. T: (231) 625-2522. RV/tent: 287. $14. Hookups: electric (30 amps).

### Alpena

Thunder Bay RV Park & Campground, 4250 US 23 South, 49707. T: (989) 354-2528. RV/tent: 45. $18. Hookups: water, electric (30 amps).

### Alto

Tyler Creek Golf Club & Campground, 13495 92nd St., 49302. T: (616) 868-6751. RV/tent: 206. $25. Hookups: water, electric (30 amps).

### Atlanta

Clear Lake State Park, 20500 M-33, 49709. T: (517) 785-4388. RV/tent: 200. $12. Hookups: electric (30 amps).

### Au Gres

Pt Au Gres Marina & Fish Camp, 2325 Green Dr., 48703. T: (989) 876-7314. RV/tent: 44. $20. Hookups: water, electric (30 amps).

### Augusta

Fort Custer Recreation Area, 5163 West Fort Custer Dr., 49012. T: (616) 731-4200. RV/tent: 217. $12. Hookups: electric (30 amps).

Shady Bend Campground, 15320 Augusta Dr., 49012. T: (616) 731-4503. RV/tent: 62. $18. Hookups: water, electric (30 amps).

### Baraga

Baraga State Park, 1300 US 41S, 49908. T: (906) 353-6558. RV/tent: 119. $11. Hookups: electric (30 amps).

### Bark River

Bayside Resort & Campground, 376 Hwy. M-35, 49807. T: (906) 786-7831. RV/tent: 30. $20. Hookups: water, sewer, electric (30 amps).

### Bay City

Bay City State Park, 3582 State Park Dr., 48706. T: (517) 684-3020. RV/tent: 193. $12. Hookups: electric (30 amps).

### Bay View

Petoskey KOA, 1800 NorthUS 31, 49770. T: (231) 347-0005. RV/tent: 206. $25. Hookups: water, sewer, electric (50 amps), phone, cable TV.

### Beaverton

Lost Haven Campground, 5300 Townhall Rd., 48612. T: (989) 435-7623. RV/tent: 100. $20. Hookups: water, electric (30 amps).

### Bellaire

Chain-O-Lakes Campground, 7231 S M-88, 49615. T: (231) 533-8432. RV/tent: 78. $24. Hookups: water, sewer, electric (50 amps).

### Belmont

Grand Rogue Campground/Canoe & Tube Livery, 6400 West River Dr., 49306. T: (616) 361-1053. RV/tent: 82. $25. Hookups: water, electric (30 amps).

### Benzonia

Timberline Campground, 2788 Benzie Hwy, 49616. T: (231) 882-9548. RV/tent: 190. $18. Hookups: water, electric.

### Beulah

Turtle Lake Campground, 854 Miller Rd., 49617. T: (231) 275-7353. RV/tent: 59. $15. Hookups: electric (30 amps).

### Birch Run

Pine Ridge RV Campground, 11700 Gera Rd., 48415. T: (517) 624-9029. RV/tent: 157. $30. Hookups: water, sewer, electric (50 amps), phone.

### Bitely

Pettibone Lake, Pettibone Lake Rd., 51408. T: (231) 689-2021. RV/tent: 16. $10. Hookups: electric (30 amps).

Pickerel Lake Lakeside Campground & Cottages, 12666 North Woodbridge, 49309. T: (231) 745-7268. RV/tent: 42. $14. Hookups: electric (30 amps).

### Boyne City

Young State Park, 2280 Boyne City Rd., 49712. T: (231) 582-7523. RV/tent: 240. $15. Hookups: electric (30 amps).

### Breckenridge

River Ridge Campground, 1989 West Pine River Rd., 48615. T: (989) 842-5184. RV/tent: 82. $24. Hookups: water, sewer, electric (50 amps).

### Brighton

Brighton State Recreation Area, 6360 Chilson Rd., 48116. T: (313) 229-6566. RV/tent: 213. $12. Hookups: electric (30 amps).

### Brimley

Brimley State Park, 9200 West 6 Mile Rd., 49715. T: (906) 248-3422. RV/tent: 269. $12. Hookups: electric (30 amps).

### Buchanan

Three Braves Campground, 400 Able Rd., 49107. T: (616) 695-9895. RV/tent: 156. $19. Hookups: water, electric.

### Buckley

Traverse City South KOA, 9700 M-37, 49620. T: (800) 249-3203. RV/tent: 110. $38. Hookups: water, sewer, electric (50 amps).

## MICHIGAN (continued)

### Byron Center

Dome World Campground, 400 84th St. Southwest, 49315. T: (616) 878-1518. RV/tent: 50. $20. Hookups: water, sewer, electric (30 amps), phone, cable TV.

Woodchip Campground, 7501 Burlingame Southwest, 49315. T: (616) 878-9050. RV/tent: 108. $19. Hookups: water, electric (30 amps).

### Cadillac

Birchwood Resort and Campground, 6545 East M-115, 49601. T: (231) 775-9101. RV/tent: 28. $25. Hookups: water, sewer, electric (50 amps).

Mitchell State Park, 6093 E-M115, 49601. T: (231) 775-7911. RV/tent: 215. $15. Hookups: electric (30 amps).

### Calumet

McLain State Park, RT 1 Box 82, M-203, 49930. T: (906) 482-0278. RV/tent: 103. $14. Hookups: electric (30 amps).

### Carp Lake

Wilderness State Park, 898 Wilderness Park Dr., 49718. T: (231) 436-5381. RV/tent: 250. $15. Hookups: electric (30 amps).

### Caseville

Sleeper State Park, 6573 State Park Rd., 48725. T: (517) 856-4411. RV/tent: 223. $15. Hookups: electric (30 amps).

### Cedar River

J. W. Wells State Park, North 7670 Hwy. M-35, 49813. T: (906) 863-9747. RV/tent: 178. $12. Hookups: electric (30 amps).

### Cedar Springs

Duke Creek Campground, 15190 White Creek Ave., 49319. T: (616) 696-2115. RV/tent: 114. $22. Hookups: water, sewer, electric (30 amps).

### Cedarville

Cedarville RV Park & Campground, Box 328, 49719. T: (800) 906-3351. RV/tent: 57. $20. Hookups: water, sewer, electric (50 amps).

Lazy Days Campground, 266 Mary, 49719. T: (888) 813-2564. RV/tent: 22. $16. Hookups: water, electric (30 amps).

### Champion

Van Riper State Park, P.O. Box 88, 49814. T: (906) 339-4461. RV/tent: 189. $12. Hookups: electric (30 amps).

### Cheboygan

Cheboygan State Park, 4490 Beach Rd., 49721. T: (231) 627-2811. RV/tent: 78. $11. Hookups: electric (30 amps).

### Chelsea

Waterloo State Recreation Area Portage Campground, 16345 McClure Rd., 48118. T: (734) 475-8307. RV/tent: 194. $14. Hookups: electric (30 amps).

Waterloo State Recreation Area Sugarloaf Campground, 16345 McClure Rd., 48118. T: (734) 475-8307. RV/tent: 180. $12. Hookups: electric (30 amps).

### Clare

Herrick Recreation Area, 6320 East Herrick Rd., 48617. T: (517) 772-0911. RV/tent: 73. $11. Hookups: electric (30 amps).

### Clarkston

Holly State Recreation Area, 8100 Grange Hall Rd., 48442. T: (248) 634-8811. RV/tent: 159. $12. Hookups: water, electric (30 amps).

### Clinton

W. J. Hayes State Park, 1220 Wampler's Lake Rd., 49265. T: (517) 467-7401. RV/tent: 185. $15. Hookups: electric (30 amps).

### Clyde

Fort Trodd Family Campground Resort, Inc., 6350 Lapeer Rd., 48049. T: (810) 987-4889. RV/tent: 120. $22. Hookups: water, sewer, electric (50 amps).

### Cooks

Fish Dam Campground, Box 24, 49817. T: (906) 644-7660. RV/tent: 19. $14. Hookups: electric (30 amps).

### Coopersville

Conestoga Grand River Campground, 9720 Oriole Dr., 49404. T: (616) 837-6323. RV/tent: 81. $25. Hookups: water, sewer, electric (50 amps).

### Copper Harbor

Fort Wilkins State Park, P.O. Box 71, 49918. T: (906) 289-4215. RV/tent: 165. $14. Hookups: electric (30 amps).

Lake Fanny Hooe Resort & Campground, P.O. Box 31, 49918. T: (800) 426-4451. RV/tent: 64. $25. Hookups: water, sewer, electric (50 amps), cable TV.

### Crystal Falls

Bewabic State Park, 1933 US 2 W, 49920. T: (906) 875-3324. RV/tent: 144. $11. Hookups: electric (30 amps).

Pentoga Park, 1630 CR 424, 49920. T: (906) 265-3979. RV/tent: 100. $12. Hookups: water, electric (30 amps).

## MICHIGAN (continued)

### Dafter

Clear Lake Campground, 13301 South Mackinaw Trail, 49724. T: (906) 635-0201. RV/tent: 60. $20. Hookups: water, electric (30 amps).

### Davison

Timber Wolf Campground, 7004 North Irish Rd., 48463. T: (734) 736-7100. RV/tent: 196. $17. Hookups: water, sewer, electric (30 amps).

Wolverine Campground, G-7698 North Baxter Rd., 48506. T: (810) 736-7100. RV/tent: 195. $16. Hookups: electric (30 amps).

### Dundee

Wilderness Retreat Campground, 1350 Meanwell Rd., 48131. T: (734) 529-5122. RV/tent: 44. $20. Hookups: water, electric (30 amps).

### East Tawas

East Tawas City Park, 407 West Bay, 48730. T: (517) 362-5562. RV/tent: 170. $20. Hookups: water, sewer, electric (30 amps), cable TV.

Tawas Point State Park, 686 Tawas Beach Rd., 48730. T: (517) 362-5041. RV/tent: 205. $15. Hookups: electric (30 amps).

### Elk Rapids

Vacation Village Campground, 509 Lake St., 49629. T: (231) 264-8636. RV/tent: 31. $21. Hookups: water, sewer, electric (30 amps).

### Emmett

Beech Grove Family Campground & RV Park, 3864 Breen Rd., 48022. T: (810) 395-7042. RV/tent: 100. $20. Hookups: water, electric (30 amps).

### Escanaba

Park Place of the North, E4575 Hwy. M-35, 49829. T: (906) 786-8453. RV/tent: 25. $15. Hookups: water, electric (30 amps).

### Evart

Muskegon River Camp & Canoe, 6281 River Rd., 49631. T: (231) 734-3808. RV/tent: 116. $20. Hookups: water, sewer, electric (30 amps).

### Farwell

Evergreen Acres Campground & RV Park, 78 West Ludington Dr., 48622. T: (517) 588-9702. RV/tent: 25. $22. Hookups: water, sewer, electric (30 amps).

### Fenton

Seven Lakes, 2220 Tinsman, 48430. T: (810) 634-7271. RV/tent: 71. $12. Hookups: electric (50 amps).

### Forester

Forester Park, 2820 North Lakeshore Dr., 48419. T: (810) 622-8715. RV/tent: 120. $16. Hookups: electric (30 amps).

### Fountain

Timber Surf Campground, 6575 Dewey Rd., 48410. T: (231) 462-3468. RV/tent: 75. $19. Hookups: water, sewer, electric (30 amps).

### Frankfort

Betsie River Campsite, 1923 River Rd., 49635. T: (231) 352-9535. RV/tent: 100. $18. Hookups: water, electric (20 amps).

### Garden

Fayette State Park, 13700 13.25 Ln., 49835. T: (906) 644-2603. RV/tent: 61. $9. Hookups: electric (30 amps).

### Gaylord

Gaylord Alpine RV Park & Campground, 1315 M-32 W, 49735. T: (517) 731-1772. RV/tent: 130. $14. Hookups: water, sewer, electric (30 amps).

Otsego Lake State Park, RT. 3 Box 414, 49735. T: (517) 732-5485. RV/tent: 156. $14. Hookups: electric (30 amps).

### Germfask

Big Cedar Campground & Canoe Livery, P.O. Box 7, 49836. T: (906) 586-6684. RV/tent: 52. $20. Hookups: water, electric (30 amps).

Northland Outfitters Camping Resort, Hwy. M-77, 49836. T: (800) 808-3FUN. RV/tent: 15. $20. Hookups: water, electric (30 amps).

### Gladwin

River Valley RV Park, 2165 South Bailey Lake Ave., 48624. T: (517) 386-7844. RV/tent: 68. $23. Hookups: water, sewer, electric (30 amps).

### Glennie

Alcona Park-Modern Area, 2550 South Au Sable Rd., 48737. T: (517) 735-3881. RV/tent: 104. $13. Hookups: electric (30 amps).

Alcona Park-Full Service Area, 2550 South Au Sable Rd., 48737. T: (517) 735-3881. RV/tent: 48. $18. Hookups: water, sewer, electric (50 amps).

### Gordonville

River Ridge Campground, 1989 West Pine River Rd., 48615. T: (517) 842-5184. RV/tent: 73. $19. Hookups: water, sewer, electric (50 amps).

### Gould City

Michihistrigan Campground, HCR Box 20, 49838. T: (906) 477-6983. RV/tent: 34. $18. Hookups: water, sewer, electric (30 amps).

### Gowen

Camp Concordia, 13400 Pinewood Northeast, 49326. T: (616) 754-3785. RV/tent: 38. $15. Hookups: electric (50 amps).

## MICHIGAN (continued)

### Grand Haven

Grand Haven State Park, 1001 Harbor Ave., 49417. T: (231) 798-3711. RV/tent: 174. $14. Hookups: electric (30 amps).

Yogi Bear's Jellystone Park Camp—Grand Haven, 10990 US 31 North, 49417. T: (616) 842-9395. RV/tent: 165. $37. Hookups: water, sewer, electric (50 amps), phone.

### Grant

Chinook Camping, 5471 West 112th St., 49327. T: (231) 834-7505. RV/tent: 56. $18. Hookups: water, electric (30 amps).

Salmon Run Campground & Vic's Canoes, 8845 Felch Ave., 49327. T: (231) 834-5494. RV/tent: 80. $21. Hookups: water, electric (30 amps).

### Grass Lake

Applecreek Resort & RV Park, 11185 Orban Rd., 49240. T: (517) 522-3467. RV/tent: 95. $22. Hookups: water, electric (30 amps).

Hideaway RV Park, 3500 Updyke Rd., 49240. T: (517) 522-5858. RV/tent: 55. $25. Hookups: water, sewer, electric (50 amps).

### Grayling

Hartwick Pines State Park, 4216 Ranger Rd., 49738. T: (517) 348-7068. RV/tent: 100. $14. Hookups: electric (30 amps).

### Greenville

Three Seasons RV Park, 6956 Fuller Rd., 48838. T: (616) 754-5717. RV/tent: 25. $18. Hookups: water, electric (30 amps).

### Gwinn

Horseshoe Lake Campground, 840 North Horseshoe Lake Rd., 49841. T: (906) 346-9937. RV/tent: 125. $20. Hookups: water, sewer, electric (30 amps).

### Hanover

Twin Pines Campground & Canoe Livery, 9800 Wheeler Rd., 49241. T: (517) 524-6298. RV/tent: 81. $15. Hookups: water, electric (30 amps).

### Harbor Beach

North Park Campground, 836 North Huron Ave., 48441. T: (517) 479-9554. RV/tent: 184. $16. Hookups: water, sewer, electric (50 amps), cable TV.

### Harrisville

Harrisville State Park, P.O. Box 326, 48740. T: (517) 724-5126. RV/tent: 200. $14. Hookups: electric (30 amps).

### Hastings

Camp Michawana, 5800 Head Lake Rd., 49058. T: (616) 623-5168. RV/tent: 54. $22. Hookups: water, sewer, electric (30 amps).

### Hesperia

Leisure Haven Campground, 3056 E M-20, 49421. T: (231) 861-7262. RV/tent: 47. $14. Hookups: electric (30 amps).

### Hillman

Heine's Landing, 24650 Landing Rd., 49746. T: (517) 742-4029. RV/tent: 62. $14. Hookups: electric (30 amps).

Sorensen's Grass Lake Resort, 18680 Sorensen Rd., 49746. T: (989) 742-3412. RV/tent: 20. $20. Hookups: water, electric (30 amps).

### Holland

Drew's Country Camping, 12850 Ransom Rd., 49424. T: (616) 399-1886. RV/tent: 75. $20. Hookups: water, electric (30 amps).

Holland State Park, Lake Michigan Campground, 2215 Ottawa Beach Rd., 49424. T: (616) 399-9390. RV/tent: 310. $15. Hookups: electric (30 amps).

### Holly

Groveland Oaks County Park, 14555 Dixie Hwy., 48442. T: (248) 634-9811. RV/tent: 269. $23. Hookups: water, electric (50 amps).

### Hopkins

Miller Lake Campground, 2130 Miller Lake Rd., 49328. T: (616) 672-7139. RV/tent: 42. $22. Hookups: water, sewer, electric (50 amps).

### Indian River

Burt Lake State Park, 6635 State Park Dr., 49749. T: (231) 238-9392. RV/tent: 333. $12. Hookups: electric (30 amps).

### Interlochen

Interlochen State Park, SR 137, 49647. T: (231) 276-9511. RV/tent: 490. $14. Hookups: electric (30 amps).

### Ionia

Ionia Recreation, 2880 David Hwy., 48846. T: (616) 527-3750. RV/tent: 100. $12. Hookups: electric (30 amps).

### Iron Mountain

Lake Antoine Park, N3393 Lake Antoine Rd., 49801. T: (906) 774-8875. RV/tent: 90. $8. Hookups: water, electric (30 amps).

Summer Breeze, LLC, W8576 Twin Falls Rd., 49801. T: (906) 774-7701. RV/tent: 65. $20. Hookups: water, sewer, electric (30 amps).

### Irons

Leisure Time Campground, 9214 West 5 Mile Rd., 49644. T: (800) 266-8214. RV/tent: 100. $24. Hookups: water, sewer, electric (50 amps).

## MICHIGAN (continued)

### Ironwood
Curry Park, Cloverland Dr., 49938. T: (906) 932-5050. RV/tent: 56. $9. Hookups: water, sewer, electric (30 amps).

### Jackson
Greenwood Acres, 2401 Hilton Rd., 49201. T: (517) 522-8600. RV/tent: 1160. $25. Hookups: water, sewer, electric (50 amps).

Pleasant Lake County Park & Campground, Styles Rd., 49201. T: (517) 769-2401. RV/tent: 69. $18. Hookups: water, electric (30 amps).

Swains Lake County Park & Campground, South Concord Rd., 49201. T: (517) 524-7666. RV/tent: 60. $18. Hookups: water, electric (30 amps).

### Jones
Camelot Campground LLC, 14630 M-60, 49061. T: (616) 476-2473. RV/tent: 101. $22. Hookups: water, sewer, electric (50 amps).

### Kinross
Kinross RV Park East, Riley Rd., 49783. T: (906) 495-5504. RV/tent: 174. $12. Hookups: water, sewer, electric (30 amps).

### Laingsburg
Sleepy Hollow State Park, 7835 East Price Rd., 48848. T: (517) 651-6217. RV/tent: 181. $12. Hookups: electric (30 amps).

### Lake City
Maple Grove Campground, East Union St., 49651. T: (231) 839-4429. RV/tent: 23. $20. Hookups: water, electric (30 amps).

### Lansing
Lansing Cottonwood Campground, 5339 South Aurelius Rd., 48911. T: (517) 393-3200. RV/tent: 110. $21. Hookups: water, sewer, electric (30 amps).

### Lapeer
Hilltop Campground, 1260 Piper Dr., 48446. T: (810) 664-2782. RV/tent: 60. $20. Hookups: water, electric (20 amps).

### Leonard
Addison Days, 1480 West Romeo Rd., 48367. T: (248) 693-2432. RV/tent: 133. $22. Hookups: water, electric (30 amps).

Family Park Campground, 120 Yule Rd., 48367. T: (248) 628-4204. RV/tent: 30. $22. Hookups: water, electric (20 amps).

### Lewiston
Lewiston Shady Acres Campground & Cottages, 4329 North Red Oak Rd., 49756. T: (800) 357-2494. RV/tent: 40. $25. Hookups: water, sewer, electric (50 amps), cable TV.

### Lexington
Lexington RV Resort, 7181 Lexington Blvd., 48450. T: (810) 359-2054. RV/tent: 30. $15. Hookups: water, sewer, electric (50 amps).

### Linwood
Hoyle's Marina & Campground, 135 South Linwood Beach Rd., 48634. T: (989) 697-3153. RV/tent: 78. $24. Hookups: water, sewer, electric (50 amps).

### Ludington
Kibby Creek Travel Park, 4900 Deren Rd., 49431. T: (231) 843-3995. RV/tent: 113. $22. Hookups: water, sewer, electric (30 amps).

Lakeview Campsite, 6181 Peterson Rd., 49431. T: (231) 843-3702. RV/tent: 60. $22. Hookups: water, sewer, electric (30 amps).

Ludington State Park, P.O. Box 709, 49431. T: (231) 843-8671. RV/tent: 341. $15. Hookups: electric (30 amps).

Mason County Campground, 5906 West Chauvez Rd., 49431. T: (231) 845-7609. RV/tent: 50. $15. Hookups: electric (30 amps).

Tamarac Village Mobile Homes & RV Park, 2875 North Lakeshore Dr., 49431. T: (231) 843-4990. RV/tent: 20. $15. Hookups: water, sewer, electric (30 amps).

### Mackinaw City
Mackinaw City KOA, 566 Trailsend Rd., 49701. T: (231) 436-5643. RV/tent: 110. $29. Hookups: water, sewer, electric (50 amps).

### Mancelona
Rapid River Campground/Cabins, 7182 US 131, 49659. T: (231) 258-2042. RV/tent: 63. $19. Hookups: electric (30 amps).

### Manistee
Orchard Beach State Park, 2064 Lakeshore Dr., 49660. T: (231) 723-7422. RV/tent: 168. $12. Hookups: electric (30 amps).

### Manistique
Indian Lake Travel Resort, HC-01 Box 3286, 49854. T: (906) 341-2807. RV/tent: 50. $15. Hookups: water, sewer, electric (30 amps).

Kewadin Inn Campground, Rte. 1 Box 1938, 49854. T: (906) 341-6911. RV/tent: 40. $18. Hookups: water, sewer, electric (30 amps).

Matson's Big Manistee River Campground, 2680 Bialik Rd., 49660. T: (888) 556-2424. RV/tent: 55. $22. Hookups: water, sewer, electric (50 amps).

Woodstar Beach Campground, Little Harbor Rd., 49854. T: (906) 341-6514. RV/tent: 41. $14. Hookups: electric (30 amps).

## MICHIGAN (continued)

### Marenisco

Lake Gogebic State Park, HC 1 Box 139, 49947. T: (906) 842-3341. RV/tent: 127. $11. Hookups: electric (30 amps).

### Marquette

Gitche Gumee RV Park & Campground, 2048 SR 28E, 49855. T: (906) 249-9102. RV/tent: 55. $28. Hookups: water, sewer, electric (50 amps).

Marquette Tourist Park & Campground, CR 550, 49855. T: (906) 228-0465. RV/tent: 110. $13. Hookups: water, sewer, electric (30 amps).

### Martin

Schnable Lake Family Campground, 1476 115th Ave., 49070. T: (616) 672-7367. RV/tent: 62. $17. Hookups: water, sewer, electric (50 amps).

### Mears

Hide-A-Way Campground/Waterslide, 9671 West Silver Lake Rd., 49436. T: (231) 873-4428. RV/tent: 86. $20. Hookups: water, electric (30 amps).

Silver Hills Camp/Resort, 7594 West Hazel Rd., 49436. T: (800) 637-3976. RV/tent: 105. $25. Hookups: water, electric (50 amps).

Silver Lake II Campground, 1786 North 34th Ave., 49436. T: (800) 359-1909. RV/tent: 270. $20. Hookups: water, electric (30 amps).

Silver Lake State Park, Rte. 1 Box 67, 49420. T: (231) 873-3083. RV/tent: 156. $15. Hookups: electric (30 amps).

Yogi Bear's Jellystone Park Silver Lake, 8329 West Hazel Rd., 49436. T: (231) 873-4502. RV/tent: 180. $34. Hookups: water, sewer, electric (30 amps).

### Mecosta

Blue Gill Lake Campground, 15854 Pretty Lake Dr., 49332. T: (231) 972-7410. RV/tent: 60. $15. Hookups: water, electric (20 amps).

School Section Lake Park, SR 20, 49332. T: (231) 972-7450. RV/tent: 90. $14. Hookups: water, electric (30 amps).

### Mesick

Mesick RV Park, 285 Manistee River Dr., 49668. T: (231) 885-1199. RV/tent: 190. $15. Hookups: water, electric (30 amps).

### Metamora

Metamora-Hadley Recreation Area, 3871 Hurd Rd., 48455. T: (810) 797-4439. RV/tent: 220. $12. Hookups: electric (30 amps).

### Middleville

Gun Lake Parkside Park, 2430 Briggs Rd., 49333. T: (616) 795-3140. RV/tent: 25. $15. Hookups: water, sewer, electric (30 amps).

Yankee Springs State Recreational Area, 2104 Gun Lake Rd., 49058. T: (616) 795-9081. RV/tent: 345. $10. Hookups: electric (30 amps).

### Milford

Proud Lake State Recreation Area, 3500 Wixom Rd., 48382. T: (248) 685-2433. RV/tent: 130. $15. Hookups: electric (30 amps).

### Mio

Mio Pines Acres, 1215 West 8th St., 48647. T: (800) 289-2845. RV/tent: 90. $20. Hookups: water, electric (30 amps).

### Monroe

Harbortown RV Resort, 14931 LaPlaisance Rd., 48161. T: (734) 384-4700. RV/tent: 250. $30. Hookups: water, sewer, electric (50 amps).

Sterling State Park, 2800 State Park Rd., 48161. T: (734) 289-2715. RV/tent: 288. $14. Hookups: electric (30 amps).

### Montague

White River Campground, 735 Fruitvale Rd., 49437. T: (231) 894-4708. RV/tent: 182. $25. Hookups: water, electric (30 amps).

### Morley

Mecosta Pines RV Park, 550 South Talcott, 49336. T: (231) 856-4556. RV/tent: 30. $20. Hookups: water, electric (50 amps).

### Mount Pleasant

Coldwater Lake Family Park, 1703 North Littlefield, 48893. T: (517) 772-0911. RV/tent: 95. $20. Hookups: water, electric (30 amps).

### Munising

Buckhorn/Otter Lake Campground, HC 50, 49862. T: (906) 387-3559. RV/tent: 72. $15. Hookups: electric (30 amps).

• Wandering Wheels Campground, P.O. Box 419, 49862. T: (906) 387-3315. RV/tent: 100. $22. Hookups: water, sewer, electric (30 amps).

### Munith

The Oaks Resort, 7800 Cutler Rd., 49259. T: (517) 596-2747. RV/tent: 65. $18. Hookups: water, electric (30 amps).

### Muskegon

Hoffmaster State Park, 6585 Lake Harbor Rd., 49441. T: (231) 798-3711. RV/tent: 293. $15. Hookups: electric (30 amps).

Muskegon KOA, 3500 North Strand, 49445. T: (231) 766-3900. RV/tent: 82. $24. Hookups: water, sewer, electric (30 amps).

### Nashville

Camp Thornapple Inc., 5625 Thornapple Lake Rd., 49073. T: (517) 852-9645. RV/tent: 143. $20. Hookups: water, sewer, electric (50 amps).

## MICHIGAN (continued)

### New Era

Stony Haven Campground, 8079 West Stony Lake Rd., 49446. T: (800) 962-1117. RV/tent: 45. $20. Hookups: water, electric (30 amps).

### New Hudson

Green Valley Park, P.O. Box 298, 48165. T: (248) 437-4136. RV/tent: 32. $22. Hookups: water, sewer, electric (30 amps).

Haas Lake Park, 25800 Haas Rd., 48165. T: (248) 437-0900. RV/tent: 110. $30. Hookups: water, sewer, electric (50 amps).

### Newaygo

Ed H. Henning Park, 500 East Croton Rd., 49337. T: (231) 652-1202. RV/tent: 60. $11. Hookups: electric (30 amps).

Little Switzerland Resort and Campground, 254 Pickeral Lake Dr., 49337. T: (231) 652-7939. RV/tent: 80. $20. Hookups: water, electric (30 amps).

Muskallonge Lake State Park, P.O. Box 245, 49868. T: (906) 658-3338. RV/tent: 175. $11. Hookups: electric (30 amps).

Mystery Creek Campground, 9419 Wisner, 49337. T: (231) 652-6915. RV/tent: 65. $20. Hookups: water, electric (30 amps).

Northcountry Campground & Cabins, RR 1 Box 94, 49868. T: (906) 293-8562. RV/tent: 50. $18. Hookups: water, sewer, electric (30 amps).

### Newberry

Newberry KOA, Box 783 M-28, 49868. T: (800) 562-5853. RV/tent: 130. $22. Hookups: water, electric (50 amps).

### Niles

Spaulding Lake Campground, 2305 Bell Rd., 49120. T: (616) 684-1393. RV/tent: 120. $20. Hookups: water, sewer, electric (50 amps).

### North Branch

Sutter's Recreation Area, 1601 Tozer Rd., 48461. T: (810) 688-3761. RV/tent: 40. $19. Hookups: water, sewer, electric (30 amps).

### North Muskegon

Muskegon State Park, 3560 Memorial Dr., 49445. T: (231) 744-3483. RV/tent: 284. $14. Hookups: electric (30 amps).

### Omer

Big Bend Campground, 513 Conrad Rd., 48658. T: (517) 653-2267. RV/tent: 70. $19. Hookups: water, electric (20 amps).

Riverbend Campground & Canoe Rental, P.O. Box 6, 48749. T: (517) 653-2576. RV/tent: 80. $20. Hookups: water, sewer, electric (30 amps).

Russell's Canoe & Campground, 146 Carrington, 48749. T: (517) 653-2644. RV/tent: 30. $16. Hookups: electric (30 amps).

### Onaway

Onaway State Park, Rte. 1 Box 112, 49765. T: (517) 733-8279. RV/tent: 98. $11. Hookups: electric (30 amps).

### Onsted

Lake Hudson Recreation Area, 1220 Wampler, 49265. T: (517) 445-2265. RV/tent: 50. $9. Hookups: electric (30 amps).

### Ossineke

Paul Bunyan Campgrounds, 6969 North Huron, 48762. T: (517) 471-2921. RV/tent: 80. $17. Hookups: water, sewer, electric (30 amps).

### Otter Lake

Genesee Otterlake Campground, 12260 Farrand Rd., 48464. T: (810) 793-2725. RV/tent: 129. $18. Hookups: water, electric (30 amps).

### Paradise

Tahquamenon Falls State Park, Lower Falls, P.O. Box 57, 49768. T: (906) 492-3415. RV/tent: 171. $14. Hookups: electric (30 amps).

Tahquamenon Falls State Park, River Mouth Unit, P.O. Box 57, 49768. T: (906) 492-3415. RV/tent: 130. $14. Hookups: electric (30 amps).

### Paris

Paris Park Campground, US 131, 49512. T: (231) 796-3420. RV/tent: 68. $13. Hookups: water, sewer, electric (30 amps).

### Pentwater

Hill & Hollow Campground, 8915 North Business 31, 49449. T: (231) 869-5811. RV/tent: 150. $28. Hookups: water, sewer, electric (30 amps).

Mears State Park, P.O. Box 370, 49449. T: (231) 869-2051. RV/tent: 179. $15. Hookups: electric (30 amps).

### Perry

Hickory Lake Camping, 11433 South Beardslee Rd., 48872. T: (517) 625-3113. RV/tent: 62. $17. Hookups: water, sewer, electric (30 amsp).

### Petoskey

Petoskey State Park, Rte. 4 Box 121 A, 49770. T: (231) 347-2311. RV/tent: 170. $15. Hookups: electric (30 amps).

### Pinckney

Pinckney Recreation Area, 8555 Silver Hill, 48169. T: (734) 426-4913. RV/tent: 225. $14. Hookups: electric (30 amps).

## MICHIGAN (continued)

### Port Austin

Port Crescent State Park, 1775 Port Austin Rd., 48467. T: (517) 738-8663. RV/tent: 135. $15. Hookups: electric (30 amps).

### Port Huron

Lakeport State Park, 7605 Lakeshore Rd., 48060. T: (810) 327-6224. RV/tent: 284. $14. Hookups: electric (30 amps).

### Rapid River

Camper's Paradise Resort, 8733 EE 25 Rd., 49878. T: (906) 474-6106. RV/tent: 19. $18. Hookups: water, electric (30 amps).

Vagabond Resort & Campground, 8935 CR 513T, 49878. T: (906) 474-6122. RV/tent: 50. $25. Hookups: water, sewer, electric (50 amps).

Whispering Valley Campground & RV Park, 8410 US 2, 49878. T: (906) 474-7044. RV/tent: 26. $22. Hookups: water, sewer, electric (50 amps).

### Riverdale

Half Moon Lake Campground & RV Park, 11394 Lumberjack Rd., 48877. T: (989) 833-7852. RV/tent: 42. $24. Hookups: water, electric (30 amps).

### Riverside

Benton Harbor KOA, 3527 Coloma Rd., 49084. T: (616) 849-3333. RV/tent: 113. $32. Hookups: water, sewer, electric (30 amps).

### Rogers City

Hoeft State Park, US 23 North, 49779. T: (517) 734-2543. RV/tent: 144. $11. Hookups: electric (30 amps).

### Roscommon

Great Circle Campground, 5370 Marl Lake Rd., 48653. T: (800) 272-5428. RV/tent: 45. $20. Hookups: water, sewer, electric (30 amps).

Higgins Hills RV Park, 3800 West Federal Hwy, 48653. T: (800) 478-8151. RV/tent: 98. $22. Hookups: water, sewer, electric (30 amps).

Higgins Lake Family Campground & Mobile Resort, 2380 West Burdell Rd., 48653. T: (517) 821-6891. RV/tent: 35. $17. Hookups: water, electric (20 amps).

North Higgins Lake State Park, RR 1 Box 436, 48653. T: (517) 821-6125. RV/tent: 195. $14. Hookups: electric (30 amps).

Paddle Brave Campground & Canoe Livery, 10610 Steckert Bridge Rd., 48653. T: (517) 275-5273. RV/tent: 45. $16. Hookups: electric (30 amps).

South Higgins Lake State Park, RR 2 Box 360, 48653. T: (517) 821-6374. RV/tent: 395. $14. Hookups: electric (30 amps).

### Rose City

Rifle River State Recreation Area, P.O. Box 98, 48635. T: (517) 473-2258. RV/tent: 181. $12. Hookups: electric (30 amps).

### Rothbury

Back Forty Ranch at the Double JJ Resort, 5900 Water Rd., 49452. T: (800) DOUBLE JJ. RV/tent: 50. $25. Hookups: water, sewer, electric (50 amps).

### Saugatuck

Saugatuck RV Resort, P.O. Box 683, 49453. T: (616) 857-3315. RV/tent: 195. $35. Hookups: water, sewer, electric (50 amps).

### Sault Ste. Marie

Chippewa Campground, P.O. Box 786, 49783. T: (906) 632-8581. RV/tent: 100. $22. Hookups: water, sewer, electric (50 amps).

### Sawyer

New Life Campground, 12033 Red Arrow Hwy., 49125. T: (616) 426-4971. RV/tent: 110. $21. Hookups: water, sewer, electric (30 amps).

Warren Dunes State Park, 12032 Red Arrow Hwy., 49125. T: (616) 426-4013. RV/tent: 280. $15. Hookups: electric (30 amps).

### Scottville

Crystal Lake Campground, 1884 West Hansen Rd., 49454. T: (231) 757-4510. RV/tent: 130. $26. Hookups: water, sewer, electric (30 amps).

Scottville Riverside Park, 105 North Main St., 49454. T: (231) 757-4729. RV/tent: 52. $12. Hookups: water, electric (30 amps).

### Sears

Merrill Lake Park, SR 66, 49679. T: (517) 382-7158. RV/tent: 74. $13. Hookups: water, electric (30 amps).

### Shepherd

Salt River Acres Inc., 926 Greendale Rd., 48883. T: (989) 631-7659. RV/tent: 88. $15. Hookups: water, electric (30 amps).

### Silver City

Porcupine Mountains Wilderness State Park, 412 South Boundry Rd., 49953. T: (906) 885-5275. RV/tent: 188. $14. Hookups: electric (30 amps).

### South Boardman

Ranch Rudolf Campground, 6841 Brownbridge Rd., 49686. T: (231) 947-9529. RV/tent: 25. $30. Hookups: water, electric (30 amps).

### South Haven

Van Buren State Park, Rte. 3 Box 122B, 49090. T: (616) 637-2788. RV/tent: 220. $12. Hookups: electric (30 amps).

## MICHIGAN (continued)

### St. Ignace
Lakeshore Park, 416 Pte LaBarbe Rd., 49781. T: (800) 643-9522. RV/tent: 100. $22. Hookups: water, sewer, electric (50 amps).

Straits State Park, 720 Church St., 49781. T: (906) 643-8620. RV/tent: 275. $14. Hookups: electric (30 amps).

Tiki Travel Park, 200 South Airport Rd., 49781. T: (906) 643-7808. RV/tent: 100. $17. Hookups: water, sewer, electric (30 amps.

### Stanwood
Brower County Park, 8 Mile and Old State Rd., 49346. T: (231) 823-2561. RV/tent: 230. $15. Hookups: water, electric (50 amps).

### Sterling
Rifle River AAA Canoe Rental, 2148 South School Rd., 48659. T: (989) 654-2333. RV/tent: 65. $20. Hookups: water, electric (30 amps).

River View Campground and Canoe Livery, 5755 Townline Rd., 48659. T: (988) 654-2447. RV/tent: 250. $22. Hookups: water, sewer, electric (30 amps).

### Sturgis
Green Valley Campgrounds, 25499 West Fawn River Rd., 49091. T: (616) 651-8760. RV/tent: 220. $19. Hookups: water, electric (20 amps).

### Tawas City
Brown's Landing RV Park, 1129 Dyer Rd., 48763. T: (989) 362-3737. RV/tent: 74. $24. Hookups: water, sewer, electric (50 amps).

Tawas RV Park, 1453 Townline Rd., 48673. T: (989) 362-3848. RV/tent: 39. $25. Hookups: water, sewer, electric (30 amps).

### Tecumseh
Indian Creek Camp & Conference Center, 9415 Tangent Hwy, 49286. T: (517) 423-5659. RV/tent: 47. $25. Hookups: water, sewer, electric (30 amps).

### Thompson
Indian Lake State Park, South Campground, Rte. 2 Box 2500, 49854. T: (906) 341-2355. RV/tent: 302. $15. Hookups: electric (30 amps).

### Tipton
Ja Do Campground, 5603 US 12, 49287. T: (517) 431-2111. RV/tent: 100. $25. Hookups: water, electric (20 amps).

### Traverse City
Traverse City State Park, 1132 US 31 North, 49686. T: (231) 922-5270. RV/tent: 342. $15. Hookups: electric (30 amps).

### Tustin
Cadillac KOA, 13163 M-115, 49688. T: (231) 825-2012. RV/tent: 35. $27. Hookups: water, electric (30 amps).

### Union
Hollywood Shores Resort, 70901 Wayne St., 49130. T: (616) 641-7307. RV/tent: 28. $18. Hookups: water, electric (20 amps).

### Union City
Rustic Potawatomie Recreation Area, 1126 Bell Rd., 49094. T: (517) 278-4289. RV/tent: 70. $18. Hookups: water, sewer, electric (50 amps).

### Vassar
Ber-Wa-Ga-Na Campground, 3526 Sanilac Rd., 48768. T: (517) 673-7125. RV/tent: 74. $22. Hookups: water, sewer, electric (30 amps).

### Vicksburg
Oak Shores Resort Campground, 13496 28th St., 49097. T: (616) 649-4689. RV/tent: 90. $23. Hookups: water, sewer, electric (50 amps).

### Wakefield
Sunday Lake Trailer Park, M28, 49968. T: (906) 229-5131. RV/tent: 84. $12. Hookups: water, electric (30 amps).

### Walkerville
Pine Haven Campground, 7792 North 186th Ave., 49459. T: (231) 898-2722. RV/tent: 25. $20. Hookups: water, sewer, electric (30 amps).

### Waterford
Pontiac Lake State Recreation Area, 7800 Gale Rd., 48054. T: (248) 666-1020. RV/tent: 176. $11. Hookups: electric (30 amps).

### Wellston
Sportsman's Port Canoes & Campground, 10487 West M-55 Hwy, 49689. T: (888) 226-6301. RV/tent: 51. $15. Hookups: electric (30 amps).

Twin Oaks Campground, 233 Moss Rd., 49689. T: (231) 848-4124. RV/tent: 60. $15. Hookups: electric (30 amps).

### West Branch
Lake George Campground, 3070 Elm Dr., 48661. T: (517) 345-2700. RV/tent: 97. $24. Hookups: water, sewer, electric (30 amps).

Troll Landing Campground & Canoe Rental, 2660 Rifle River Trail, 48661. T: (989) 345-7260. RV/tent: 25. $14. Hookups: electric (30 amps).

### White Cloud
Big Bend Park Hardy Dam, 2000 Beech St., 49349. T: (231) 689-6325. RV/tent: 230. $15. Hookups: water, electric (30 amps).

## MICHIGAN (continued)

### White Cloud (continued)

Pettibone Lake County Park, P.O. Box 885, 49349.
T: (231) 652-9191. RV/tent: 16. $9. Hookups:
electric (30 amps).

White Cloud City Campground, 620 Wilcox, 49349.
T: (231) 689-2021. RV/tent: 103. $11. Hookups:
electric (30 amps).

### Williamsburg

Ever Flowing Waters, 5481 Brackett Rd., 49690.
T: (231) 938-0933. RV/tent: 52. $14. Hookups:
electric (30 amps).

### Winona

Twin Lakes State Park, Rte. 1 Box 234, 49965.
T: (906) 482-0278. RV/tent: 62. $11. Hookups:
electric (30 amps).

### Wolverine

Circle S Campground, 15247 Trowbridge Rd.,
49799. T: (231) 525-8300. RV/tent: 65. $20.
Hookups: water, electric (30 amps).

Elkwood Campground, 2733 Lance Lake, 49799.
T: (231) 525-8373. RV/tent: 55. $16. Hookups:
water, electric (30 amps).

### Ypsilanti

Detroit-Greenfield KOA Resort Kamp, 6680
Bunton Rd., 48197. T: (734) 482-7722. RV/tent:
217. $32. Hookups: water, sewer, electric (50
amps).

## MINNESOTA

### Adrian

Adrian Campground and Recreation Park, P.O. Box
187, 56110. T: (507) 483-2820. RV/tent: 120. $15.
Hookups: electric (30 amps), sewer.

### Aitkin

Big "K" Campground, RR 2 Box 965, 56431. T: (218)
927-6001. RV/tent: 55. $19. Hookups: water, elec-
tric (30 amps), sewer.

Edgewater Resort & RV Park, RR 3 Box 890, 56431.
T: (800) 639-4337. RV/tent: 47. $25. Hookups:
water, electric (50 amps), sewer.

Farm Island Lake Resort & Campground, Rte. 2 Box
225, 56431. T: (218) 927-3841. RV/tent: 40. $18.
Hookups: water, electric (30 amps), sewer.

### Albert Lea

Myre Big Island, Rte. 3 Box 33, 56007. T: (507)
379-3403. RV/tent: 99. $13. Hookups: electric
(30 amps).

### Alexandria

Hillcrest RV Park, 715 Birch Ave., 56038. T: (320)
763-6330. RV/tent: 55. $20. Hookups: water, elec-
tric (30 amps), sewer.

### Andover

Bay Shore, 7124 Pymatuning Lake Rd., 44003.
T: (440) 293-7202. RV/tent: 250. $35. Hookups:
water, electric (30 amps), sewer.

Pymatuning State Park, P.O. Box 1000, 44003.
T: (440) 293-6030. RV/tent: 373. $14. Hookups:
electric (20 amps).

Wildwood Acres, RD 1 Marvin Rd., 44003. T: (440)
293-6838. RV/tent: 102. $18. Hookups: water, elec-
tric (30 amps).

### Ashtabula

Hide-A-Way Lakes Campground, 2034 South Ridge
W, 44004. T: (440) 992-4431. RV/tent: 100. $24.
Hookups: water, electric (30 amps).

### Aurora

Silverhorn Camping Resort, 250 Treat Rd., 44202.
T: (330) 562-4423. RV/tent: 300. $32. Hookups:
water, electric (30 amps).

Woodside Lake Park, 2256 Frost Rd., 44241. T: (330)
626-4251. RV/tent: 125. $24. Hookups: water, elec-
tric (30 amps).

### Bainbridge

Paint Creek State Park, 14265 US Rt 50, 45612.
T: (937) 365-1401. RV/tent: 199. $14. Hookups:
electric (20 amps).

Pike Lake State Park, 1847 Pike Ln. Rd., 45612.
T: (740) 493-2212. RV/tent: 213. $12. Hookups:
electric (20 amps).

### Baltimore

Rippling Stream Campground, 3640 Reyn-Bait Rd.,
43105. T: (740) 862-6065. RV/tent: 132. $14.
Hookups: water, electric (20 amps).

### Bellefontaine

Eagles Club of Ohio-Alken Lakes, 5118 US 68
North, 43311. T: (937) 593-1565. RV/tent: 263.
$15. Hookups: water, electric (30 amps).

## MINNESOTA (continued)

### Bellville
Yogi Bear's Jellystone Park Camp-Resort, SR 546 at Black Rd., 44813. T: (419) 886-2267. RV/tent: 90. $30. Hookups: water, electric (50 amps), sewer.

### Belmont
Barkcamp State Park, 65330 Barkcamp Park Rd., 43718. T: (740) 484-4064. RV/tent: 150. $12. Hookups: electric (50 amps).

### Blue Rock
Muskingum River Campgrounds, 11206 South River Rd., 43720. T: (740) 674-6918. RV/tent: 24. $10. Hookups: water, sewer, electric (30 amps).

### Bowerston
Clow's Marina & Campground, 4131 Deer Rd. Southwest, 44695. T: (740) 269-5371. RV/tent: 88. $13. Hookups: electric (20 amps).

### Buckeye Lake
Buckeye Lake KOA, 4460 Walnut Rd., 43008. T: (740) 928-0706. RV/tent: 205. $35. Hookups: water, sewer, electric (50 amps).

### Camden
Cross's Campground Inc., 7777 SR 127, 45311. T: (937) 452-1535. RV/tent: 55. $14. Hookups: water, electric (30 amps).

### Canfield
Dreamiee Acres, 9727 Columbiana-Canfield Rd., 44406. T: (330) 533-9366. RV/tent: 24. $15. Hookups: water, electric (20 amps).

### Carrollton
Camper's Paradise Campground, 4105 Fresno Rd. Northwest, 44615. T: (330) 753-3220. RV/tent: 55. $14. Hookups: water, electric (30 amps).

Cozy Ridge Campground, 4145 Fresno Rd. Northwest, 44615. T: (330) 735-2553. RV/tent: 70. $15. Hookups: water, sewer, electric (30 amps).

Petersburg Boat Landing, 2126 Azalea Rd. Southwest, 44615. T: (330) 627-4270. RV/tent: 78. $12. Hookups: electric (30 amps).

Twin Valley Campground, 2330 Apollo Rd. Southeast, 44615. T: (330) 739-2811. RV/tent: 130. $22. Hookups: water, sewer electric (50 amps).

### Chillicothe
Scioto Trail State Park, 144 Lake Rd., 45601. T: (740) 663-2125. RV/tent: 75. $13. Hookups: electric (30 amps).

### Circleville
A.W. Marion State Park, 7317 Warner-Huffer Rd., 43113. T: (740) 474-3386. RV/tent: 59. $13. Hookups: electric (20 amps).

### Clyde
Traveland Family Campground, 3681 CR 213, 43410. T: (419) 626-1133. RV/tent: 300. $31. Hookups: water, sewer, electric (50 amps).

### College Corner
Hueston Woods State Park, Rte. 1, 45003. T: (513) 523-6347. RV/tent: 491. $15. Hookups: electric (30 amps).

### Conneaut
Evergreen Lake Park, 703 Center Rd., 44030. T: (440) 599-8802. RV/tent: 100. $20. Hookups: water, electric (50 amps).

### Deersville
Tappan Lake Park Campground, US 250, 44693. T: (740) 922-3649. RV/tent: 550. $21. Hookups: electric (30 amps).

### Delaware
Delaware State Park, 5202 US 23N, 43015. T: (740) 369-2761. RV/tent: 214. $15. Hookups: electric (20 amps).

### East Rochester
Bob Boord's Park, 25067 Buffalo Rd., 44625. T: (330) 894-2360. RV/tent: 250. $21. Hookups: water, sewer, electric (30 amps).

Paradise Lake Park, 6940 Rochester Rd., 44625. T: (330) 525-7726. RV/tent: 200. $20. Hookups: water, electric (30 amps).

### East Sparta
Bear Creek Ranch KOA, 3232 Downing St. Southwest, 44626. T: (330) 484-3901. RV/tent: 103. $31. Hookups: water, electric (50 amps), sewer.

### Fayette
Harrison Lake State Park, 26246 Harrison Lake Rd., 43521. T: (419) 237-2593. RV/tent: 193. $14. Hookups: electric (20 amps).

### Fort Loramie
Hickory Hill Lakes, 7103 SR 66, 45845. T: (937) 295-3820. RV/tent: 121. $20. Hookups: water, electric (30 amps).

### Frankfort
Lake Hill Campground, 2466 Mussieman Station Rd., 45628. T: (740) 998-5648. RV/tent: 100. $16. Hookups: water, electric (50 amps), sewer.

### Freeport
Clendening Lake Marina Campground, 79100 Bose Rd., 43973. T: (740) 658-3691. RV/tent: 100. $15. Hookups: electric (30 amps).

Piedmont Lake Marina & Campground, SR 8, 43973. T: (740) 658-3735. RV/tent: 67. $18. Hookups: electric (30 amps).

## MINNESOTA (continued)

**Freeport** (continued)

Twin Hills Park, 77720 Cummins Rd., 43973.
T: (740) 658-3275. RV/tent: 100. $13. Hookups:
water, electric (30 amps).

**Fresno**

Forest Hill Lake & Campground, 52176 CR 425,
43824. T: (740) 545-9642. RV/tent: 76. $18.
Hookups: water, electric (20 amps).

**Geneva**

Audubon Lakes Campground, 3935 North Broadway, 44041. T: (440) 466-1293. RV/tent: 125. $20.
Hookups: water, electric (30 amps).

Geneva State Park, P.O. Box 429, 44041. T: (440)
466-8400. RV/tent: 91. $18. Hookups: electric
(20 amps).

Kenisee's Grand River Camp & Canoe, 4680 RT.
307E, 44041. T: (440) 466-2320. RV/tent: 120. $22.
Hookups: water, electric (50 amps).

R & R Camping, 4455 Rte. 307, 44041. T: (440)
466-2550. RV/tent: 120. $22. Hookups: water,
sewer, electric (30 amps).

**Geneva-On-The-Lake**

Indian Creek Camping & Resort, 4710 Lake Rd.
East, 44041. T: (440) 466-8191. RV/tent: 573. $32.
Hookups: water, sewer, electric (50 amps).

**Granville**

Lazy R. Campground, 2340 Dry Creek Rd. Northeast, 43023. T: (740) 366-4385. RV/tent: 195. $19.
Hookups: water, sewer, electric (50 amps).

**Green**

Pine Valley Lake Park, 4936 South Arlington Rd.,
44720. T: (330) 896-1381. RV/tent: 90. $23.
Hookups: water, electric (30 amps), sewer.

**Greenville**

Wildcat Woods Campground, 1355 Wildcat Rd.,
45331. T: (937) 548-7921. RV/tent: 78. $18.
Hookups: water, electric (30 amps), sewer.

**Homerville**

Wild Wood Lake Campground, 11450 Crawford
Rd., 44235. T: (330) 625-2817. RV/tent: 60. $19.
Hookups: water, electric (50 amps).

**Howard**

Kokosing Valley Camp & Canoe, 25860 Coshocton
Rd., 43028. T: (740) 599-7056. RV/tent: 170. $18.
Hookups: water, electric (20 amps).

**Hubbard**

Homestead Campground, 1436 Brookfield Rd.,
44425. T: (330) 448-2938. RV/tent: 30. $18.
Hookups: water, sewer, electric (30 amps).

**Jefferson**

Buccaneer Campsites, P.O. Box 352, 44047. T: (440)
576-2881. RV/tent: 170. $20. Hookups: water,
sewer, electric (30 amps).

**Kings Mill**

Paramount's Kings Island Campground, 6300 Kings
Island Dr., 45034. T: (513) 754-5901. RV/tent: 349.
$41. Hookups: water, sewer, electric (30 amps).

**Lakeside**

East Harbor State Park, 1169 North Buck Rd.,
43440. T: (419) 734-4424. RV/tent: 570. $17.
Hookups: electric (330 amps).

**Lakeview**

Indian Lake State Park, 12744 SR 235 North, 43331.
T: (937) 843-2717. RV/tent: 443. $14. Hookups:
electric (30 amps).

**Lancaster**

Lakeview RV Park and Campground, 2715 Sugar
Grove Rd., 43130. T: (740) 653-4519. RV/tent: 100.
$25. Hookups: water, sewer, electric (50 amps).

Lancaster Campground, 2151 West Fair Ave., 43130.
T: (740) 653-2119. RV/tent: 24. $15. Hookups:
water, electric (30 amps).

**Latham**

Cave Lake Park, 1132 Bell Hollow Rd., 45133.
T: (937) 588-3252. RV/tent: 300. $19. Hookups:
water, electric (30 amps).

Long's Retreat Family Resort, 50 Bell Hollow Rd.,
45133. T: (937) 588-3725. RV/tent: 450. $14.
Hookups: water, sewer, electric (20 amps).

**Laurelville**

Tar Hollow State Park, 16396 Tar Hollow Rd.,
43135. T: (614) 887-4818. RV/tent: 113. $15.
Hookups: electric (50 amps).

**Lebanon**

Cedarbrook Campground, 760 Franklin Rd., 45036.
T: (513) 932-7717. RV/tent: 150. $21. Hookups:
water, sewer, electric (50 amps).

**Lisbon**

Lock 30 Woodlands RV Campground Resort, 45529
Middle Beaver Rd., 44432. T: (970) 424-9197.
RV/tent: 65. $30. Hookups: water, electric (50
amps), sewer.

**Logan**

Hocking Hills State Park, Old Man's Cave, 20160 SR
664, 43138. T: (614) 385-6165. RV/tent: 170. $17.
Hookups: electric (30 amps).

Scenic View Campground, 29150 Pattor Rd., 43138.
T: (740) 385-4295. RV/tent: 70. $37. Hookups:
water, sewer, electric (30 amps).

## MINNESOTA (continued)

### Lore City
Salt Fork State Park, 14755 Cadiz Rd., 43725.
T: (740) 439-3521. RV/tent: 212. $16. Hookups:
electric (50 amps).

### Loudonville
Camp Toodik Family Campground & Canoe Livery,
7700 TR 462, 44842. T: (419) 994-3835. RV/tent:
153. $17. Hookups: water, electric (50 amps),
sewer.

Lake Wapusun, 10787 Molter Rd., 44676. T: (330)
496-2355. RV/tent: 150. $17. Hookups: water,
electric (30 amps).

Long Lake Park & Campground, 8974 Long Lake
Dr., 44638. T: (419) 827-2278. RV/tent: 75. $22.
Hookups: water, electric (30 amps).

Mohican Campground & Cabins, 3058 SR 3, 44842.
T: (419) 994-2267. RV/tent: 146. $27. Hookups:
water, sewer, electric (30 amps).

Mohican State Park, 3116 SR 3, 44842. T: (419)
994-5125. RV/tent: 167. $20. Hookups: electric
(50 amps).

River Run Family Campground, 3064 Wally Rd.,
44842. T: (419) 994-5257. RV/tent: 98. $24.
Hookups: water, electric (50 amps).

### Mansfield
Charles Mill Lake Park Camp Area, 1271 SR 430,
44903. T: (419) 368-6885. RV/tent: 527. $19.
Hookups: electric (30 amps).

### Marietta
Camp Civitan, 922 Front St., 45750. T: (740) 373-
7937. RV/tent: 42. $15. Hookups: water, electric
(30 amps).

### Marion
Hickory Grove Lake Family Campground, 805 Hoch
Rd., 43302. T: (740) 382-8584. RV/tent: 88. $19.
Hookups: water, electric (50 amps), sewer.

### McArthur
Lake Hope State Park, 22331 SR 278, 45651.
T: (740) 596-4938. RV/tent: 126. $13. Hookups:
electric (30 amps).

### Medina
Pier-lon Park, 5960 Vandemark Rd., 44256. T: (330)
667-2311. RV/tent: 150. $20. Hookups: water,
sewer, electric (50 amps).

### Milan
Milan Trav-L-Park, 11404 SR 250N, 44846. T: (419)
433-4277. RV/tent: 142. $30. Hookups: water,
sewer, electric (50 amps).

### Mineral City
Atwood Lake Park, 4956 Shop Rd., 44656. T: (330)
343-6780. RV/tent: 569. $23. Hookups: electric
(30 amps).

### Minster
Lake Loramie State Park, 11221 SR 362, 45865.
T: (937) 295-2011. RV/tent: 166. $14. Hookups:
water, electric (30 amps).

### Montville
Tri-County Kamp Inn, 17147 Gar Hwy, 44064.
T: (440) 968-3400. RV/tent: 155. $24. Hookups:
water, electric (30 amps).

### Mount Gilead
Dogwood Valley, 4185 Twp Rd 99, 43338. T: (419)
946-5230. RV/tent: 95. $22. Hookups: water, sewer,
electric (30 amps).

Mount Gilead State Park, 4119 SR 95, 43338.
T: (419) 946-1961. RV/tent: 60. $12. Hookups:
electric (50 amps).

### Mount Sterling
Deer Creek State Park, 20635 Waterloo Rd., 43143.
T: (740) 869-3124. RV/tent: 232. $16. Hookups:
electric (30 amps).

### Mount Vernon
Rustic Knolls Campsites, 8664 Keys Rd., 43050.
T: (740) 397-9318. RV/tent: 150. $14. Hookups:
water, electric (30 amps), sewer.

### Nashport
Dillon State Park, 5265 Dillon Hills Dr., 43830.
T: (740) 453-4377. RV/tent: 195. $15. Hookups:
electric (20 amps).

Wild Bill's Resort, 6819 Newark Rd., 43830. T: (740)
452-0113. RV/tent: 150. $18. Hookups: water, elec-
tric (30 amps), sewer.

### Navarre
Baylor Beach Park, 8725 Manchester Southwest,
44662. T: (330) 767-3031. RV/tent: 50. $20.
Hookups: water, electric (30 amps).

### Nelsonville
Happy Hills Family Campground, 22245 SR 278,
45764. T: (740) 385-6720. RV/tent: 63. $20.
Hookups: water, electric (30 amps).

### Nevada
Foxfire Family Fun Park, 3699 Crawford-Wyandot
Rd., 44849. T: (740) 482-2190. RV/tent: 120. $30.
Hookups: water, electric (30 amps), sewer.

### New London
Indian Trail Campground, 1400 US 250S, 44851.
T: (419) 929-1135. RV/tent: 176. $25. Hookups:
water, sewer, electric (30 amps).

### New Paris
Arrowhead Campground, 1361 Thomas Rd., 45347.
T: (937) 996-6203. RV/tent: 33. $21. Hookups:
water, sewer, electric (30 amps).

## MINNESOTA (continued)

### New Washington
Auburn Lake Park, 555 Michael Ave., 44854. T: (419) 492-2110. RV/tent: 28. $18. Hookups: water, electric (30 amps).

### Newbury
Punderson State Park, 11755 Kinsman Rd., 44065. T: (440) 564-2279. RV/tent: 201. $15. Hookups: electric (20 amps).

### Newton Falls
Ridge Ranch Campground, 5219 SR 303 Northwest, 44444. T: (330) 898-8080. RV/tent: 176. $20. Hookups: water, electric (30 amps), sewer.

### Oak Harbor
Paradise Acres, 4225 North Rider Rd., 43449. T: (419) 898-6411. RV/tent: 74. $15. Hookups: water, sewer, electric (30 amps).

### Oberlin
Schaun Acres Campground, 51468 SR 303, 44074. T: (440) 775-7122. RV/tent: 53. $21. Hookups: water, electric (30 amps), sewer.

### Oregon
Maumee Bay State Park, 1400 State Park Rd., 43618. T: (419) 836-7305. RV/tent: 256. $16. Hookups: electric (20 amps).

### Oregonia
Olive Branch Campground, 6985 Wilmington Rd., 45054. T: (513) 932-2267. RV/tent: 138. $22. Hookups: water, sewer, electric (50 amps).

### Orwell
Pine Lakes Campground, 3001 Hague Rd., 44076. T: (440) 437-6218. RV/tent: 70. $16. Hookups: water, electric (30 amps).

### Oxford
Camp America, Box 47, 45056. T: (800) 818-2267. RV/tent: 24. $15. Hookups: water, electric (30 amps).

### Parkman
Kool Lakes Family Camping & Recreation Resort, P.O. Box 673, 44080. T: (440) 548-8436. RV/tent: 97. $19. Hookups: water, electric (50 amps), sewer.

### Paulding
Woodbridge Campground, 8656 Rd. 137, 45879. T: (419) 399-2267. RV/tent: 65. $19. Hookups: water, electric (30 amps).

### Peebles
Mineral Springs Lake Resort, 162 Bluegill Rd., 45660. T: (937) 587-3132. RV/tent: 53. $26. Hookups: water, sewer, electric (30 amps).

### Perrysburg
Stony Ridge KOA Campgrounds, 24787 Luckey Rd., 43551. T: (419) 837-6848. RV/tent: 58. $26. Hookups: water, sewer, electric (30 amps).

### Perrysville
Pleasant Hill Lake, 3431 SR 95, 44864. T: (419) 938-7884. RV/tent: 382. $20. Hookups: electric (30 amps).

### Pioneer
Funny Farm Campground, 19452 CR 12, 43554. T: (419) 737-2467. RV/tent: 200. $22. Hookups: water, sewer, electric (30 amps).

Lazy River Campground, 12-808 SR #20, 43554. T: (419) 485-4411. RV/tent: 350. $23. Hookups: water, sewer, electric (30 amps).

### Port Clinton
Cedarlane Campground, 2926 Northeast Catawba Rd., 43452. T: (419) 797-9907. RV/tent: 175. $26. Hookups: water, electric (50 amps).

Tall Timbers Campground, 340 Christy Chapel Rd., 43452. T: (419) 732-3938. RV/tent: 150. $22. Hookups: water, electric (30 amps).

### Portsmouth
Shawnee Village RV Park & Campground, 13610 US 52, 45663. T: (740) 858-5542. RV/tent: 100. $22. Hookups: water, electric (30 amps).

### Randolph
Friendship Acres Campground, 2210 SR 44, 44201. T: (330) 325-9527. RV/tent: 150. $22. Hookups: water, electric (30 amps).

### Ravenna
Country Acres Campground, 9850 Minyoung Rd., 44266. T: (330) 358-2774. RV/tent: 100. $22. Hookups: water, electric (50 amps), sewer.

### Republic
Clinton Lake Camping, 4990 East Twp Rd 122, 44867. T: (419) 585-3331. RV/tent: 50. $17. Hookups: water, electric (30 amps).

### Rogers
Camp Frederick, P.O. Box 258, 44455. T: (330) 227-3633. RV/tent: 11. $20. Hookups: water, electric (30 amps).

### Rushsylvania
Back Forty Ltd, 959 CR 111E, 43347. T: (937) 468-7492. RV/tent: 52. $18. Hookups: water, electric (30 amps).

## MINNESOTA (continued)

### Salem

Chaparral Family Campground, 10136 Middletown Rd., 44460. T: (330) 337-9381. RV/tent: 230. $23. Hookups: water, sewer, electric (30 amps).

Timashamie Family Campground, 28251 Georgetown Rd., 44460. T: (330) 525-7054. RV/tent: 55. $21. Hookups: water, electric (50 amps), sewer.

### Sandusky

Bayshore Estates Campground, 2311 Cleveland Rd., 44870. T: (419) 625-7906. RV/tent: 380. $35. Hookups: water, sewer, electric (50 amps).

Crystal Campground, 710 Crystal Rock Rd., 44870. T: (419) 684-7177. RV/tent: 124. $28. Hookups: water, sewer, electric (30 amps).

### Senecaville

Seneca Lake Marina Point, SR 313, 43780. T: (740) 685-6013. RV/tent: 320. $14. Hookups: electric (30 amps).

### Shelby

Wagon Wheel Campground, 6787 Baker, 44875. T: (419) 347-1392. RV/tent: 50. $20. Hookups: water, sewer, electric (50 amps).

### South Bloomingville

Top O' The Caves Family Campground/Resort, 26780 Chapel Ridge Rd., 43152. T: (740) 385-6566. RV/tent: 200. $22. Hookups: water, electric (30 amps), sewer.

### Southington

Valley Lake Park, 3959 SR 305, 44470. T: (330) 898-1819. RV/tent: 22. $15. Hookups: water, sewer, electric (30 amps).

### Spencer

Sunset Lake Campground, 5566 Root Rd., 44275. T: (330) 667-2686. RV/tent: 80. $19. Hookups: electric (30 amps) water.

### Springfield

Buck Creek State Park, 1901 Buck Creek Ln., 45502. T: (937) 322-5284. RV/tent: 100. $16. Hookups: electric (30 amps).

### St. Mary's

Grand Lake-St. Mary's State Park, P.O. Box 308, 45885. T: (419) 394-3611. RV/tent: 206. $14. Hookups: electric (50 amps).

### Streetsboro

Mar-Lynn Lake Park, 187 SR 303, 44241. T: (330) 650-2522. RV/tent: 120. $32. Hookups: electric (50 amps), sewer, water.

### Thompson

Heritage Hills Campground, 6445 Ledge Rd., 44086. T: (440) 298-1311. RV/tent: 150. $23. Hookups: water, electric (50 amps), sewer.

### Tiffin

Walnut Grove Campground, 7325 South Twp Rd 131, 44883. T: (419) 448-1014. RV/tent: 30. $18. Hookups: water, sewer, electric (30 amps).

### Toronto

Austin Lake Park & Campground, 1002 Twp Rd 285A, 43964. T: (740) 544-5253. RV/tent: 55. $20. Hookups: water, electric (50 amps).

### Urbana

Meadow Lake Resort, 4739 Woodville Pike, 43078. T: (937) 652-3400. RV/tent: 300. $23. Hookups: water, sewer, electric (50 amps).

### Van Wert

Pleasant Grove Campground, 10856A Liberty-Union Rd., 45891. T: (419) 238-1124. RV/tent: 53. $19. Hookups: water, sewer, electric (30 amps).

### Versailles

Cottonwood Lakes, 8549 Althoff Rd., 45380. T: (419) 582-2610. RV/tent: 40. $14. Hookups: water, electric (30 amps).

### Wellington

Rustic Lakes Campground, 44901 New London Eastern Rd., 44880. T: (440) 647-3804. RV/tent: 100. $23. Hookups: water, electric (30 amps).

### Williamstown

Sulphur Lake Camp, P.O. Box 19, 45897. T: (419) 365-5374. RV/tent: 100. $20. Hookups: water, sewer, electric (50 amps).

### Wilmington

Beechwood Acres, P.O. Box 227, 45177. T: (937) 289-2202. RV/tent: 95. $16. Hookups: water, electric (50 amps).

### Winesburg

Amish Country Campsite, 1930 US 62, 44690. T: (330) 359-5226. RV/tent: 60. $15. Hookups: water, electric (30 amps).

### Zanesville

Campers Grove, Hopewell National Rd. RT. 40, 43701. T: (740) 453-3973. RV/tent: 45. $12. Hookups: water.

Wolfies Family Kamping, 101 Buckeye Dr., 43701. T: (740) 454-0925. RV/tent: 39. $16. Hookups: electric (30 amps), sewer, water.

## OHIO

### Andover
Bunker Hills Campground, 550 Bunker Lake Blvd., 55304. T: (612) 757-3920. RV/tent: 50. $20. Hookups: water, electric (30 amps).

### Annandale
Schroeder County Park, 9201 Ireland Ave. Northwest, 55302. T: (320) 274-8870. RV/tent: 50. $15. Hookups: electric (30 amps).

### Apple Valley
Lebanon Hills Regional Park, 12100 Johnny Cake Ridge Rd., 55124. T: (612) 454-9211. RV/tent: 92. $20. Hookups: electric (30 amps).

### Argyle
Old Mill State Park, Rte. 1 Box 43, 56713. T: (218) 437-8174. RV/tent: 26. $10. Hookups: electric (30 amps), water.

### Ashby
Sundown RV Park & Campground, Rte. 1 Box 145, 56309. T: (218) 747-2931. RV/tent: 30. $18. Hookups: water, electric (30 amps), sewer.

### Babbitt
Timber Wolf Lodge, 9130 Escape Rd., 55706. T: (218) 827-3512. RV/tent: 15. $28. Hookups: water, electric (30 amps).

### Backus
Barrett Lake Resort & Campground, 3781 State 87 Northwest, 56435. T: (320) 528-2598. RV/tent: 34. $16. Hookups: water, electric (50 amps), sewer.

Eagle Wing Campground, 1588 36th Ave. Southwest, 56435. T: (218) 587-2090. RV/tent: 45. $20. Hookups: water, electric (30 amps).

Lindsey Lake Campground, 3781 State 87 Northwest, 56435. T: (218) 947-4728. RV/tent: 40. $15. Hookups: water, electric (30 amps).

### Barnum
Bent Trout Lake Campground, 2928 Bent Trout Lake Rd., 55707. T: (218) 389-6322. RV/tent: 30. $17. Hookups: water, electric (30 amps).

### Battle Lake
Battle Lake Sunset Beach Resort & Campground, RR 3 Box 181, 56515. T: (888) 583-2750. RV/tent: 20. $20. Hookups: water, electric (30 amps), sewer.

### Baudette
Zippel Bay Resort, HC2 Box 51, 56686. T: (800) 222-2537. RV/tent: 57. $20. Hookups: water, electric (30 amps).

### Bemidji
Hamilton's Fox Lake Campground, 2555 Island View Dr. Northeast, 56601. T: (218) 586-2231. RV/tent: 35. $20. Hookups: water, electric (30 amps).

Lake Bemidji State Park, 3401 State Park Rd. Northeast, 56601. T: (218) 755-3843. RV/tent: 98. $15. Hookups: electric (30 amps.).

### Bena
New Leech Lake Campground, HC 1 Box 75, 56626. T: (800) 272-3785. RV/tent: 73. $23. Hookups: water, electric (30 amps), sewer.

### Big Lake
Shady River Campground, 21535 CO 5, 55309. T: (612) 263-3705. RV/tent: 75. $18. Hookups: water, electric (50 amps).

### Bigfork
Scenic State Park, HCR 2 Box 17, 56628. T: (218) 743-3362. RV/tent: 117. $9. Hookups: electric (30 amps).

### Blackduck
Lost Acres Resort & Campground, HC 3 Box 162D Kitchi Lake, 56630. T: (800) 835-6414. F: (218) 835-6414. RV/tent: 8. $20. Hookups: water, electric (30 amps).

### Blooming Prairie
Brookside Campground, 52482 320th St., 55917. T: (507) 583-2979. RV/tent: 60. $20. Hookups: water, electric (30 amps).

### Brainerd
Crow Wing State Park, 7100 State Park Rd. Southwest, 56401. T: (218) 829-8022. RV/tent: 61. $13. Hookups: electric (30 amps).

Hidden Paradise Resort & Campground, 1388 Ojibwa Rd. North, 56401. T: (218) 963-3180. RV/tent: 10. $27. Hookups: water, electric (50 amps), sewer.

Lum Park Campground, 1619 Northeast Washington St., 56401. T: (218) 828-2320. F: (218) 828-2791. RV/tent: 25. $15. Hookups: water, electric (30 amps), sewer, cable TV.

### Breezy Point
Highview Campground & RV Park, HC 83 Box 1084, 56472. T: (877) 543-4526. F: (218) 543-4526. RV/tent: 132. $22. Hookups: water, electric (30 amps), sewer.

### Burtrum
Big Swan Lake Resort, RR 1 Box 256, 56318. T: (320) 732-6065. RV/tent: 21. $20. Hookups: water, electric (30 amps), sewer.

### Caledonia
Beaver Creek Valley State Park, Rte. 2 Box 57, 55921. T: (507) 724-2107. RV/tent: 42. $13. Hookups: electric (30 amps).

Dunromin' Park, RR 1 Box 146, 55921. T: (800) 822-2514. F: (507) 724-5560. RV/tent: 90. $22. Hookups: water, electric (30 amps).

## OHIO (continued)

### Canby
Stonehill Regional Park, Box 2, 56220. T: (507) 223-7586. RV/tent: 40. $14. Hookups: water, electric (30 amps).

### Cannon Falls
Cannon Falls Campground, 30365 Oak Ln., 30365. T: (507) 263-3145. RV/tent: 100. $21. Hookups: water, electric (50 amps).

Lake Byllesby Regional Park Campground, 7650 Echo Point Rd., 55009. T: (507) 263-4447. RV/tent: 57. $17. Hookups: electric (30 amps).

### Carlos
Lake Carlos State Park, 2601 CO 38 Northeast, 56319. T: (320) 852-7200. RV/tent: 126. $15. Hookups: electric (30 amps).

### Cass Lake
Cass Lake Lodge Resort & RV Park, 16293 60th Ave. Northwest, 56633. T: (218) 335-6658. RV/tent: 49. $20. Hookups: water, electric (30 amps), sewer.

Marclay Point Campground, Rte. 2 Box 80, 56633. T: (218) 335-6589. RV/tent: 75. $18. Hookups: water, electric (30 amps).

### Center City
Wild River State Park, 39755 Park Trace, 55012. T: (651) 583-2125. RV/tent: 96. $15. Hookups: electric (30 amps).

### Clearwater
St. Cloud-Clearwater KOA, 2454 CO 143, 55320. T: (320) 558-2876. RV/tent: 93. $27. Hookups: water, electric (50 amps), sewer.

### Cokato
Collinwood Regional Park, 17251 70th St. Southwest, 55320. T: (320) 286-2801. RV/tent: 50. $15. Hookups: electric (30 amps).

### Crane Lake
Beddow's Campground, 7516 Bayside Dr., 55725. T: (218) 993-2389. RV/tent: 22. $20. Hookups: water, electric (30 amps), sewer.

### Cromwell
Island Lake Campground, 1391 Middle Rd., 55726. T: (218) 644-3543. RV/tent: 15. $20. Hookups: water, electric (50 amps).

### Currie
Lake Shetek State Park, 163 State Park Rd., 56123. T: (507) 763-3256. RV/tent: 108. $15. Hookups: electric (30 amps).

Schreler's on Shetek, 35 Resort Rd., 56123. T: (507) 763-3817. RV/tent: 110. $17. Hookups: water, electric (50 amps), sewer.

### Cushing
Fish Trap Campground, RR 1 Box 17, 56443. T: (218) 575-2603. RV/tent: 90. $26. Hookups: water, electric (50 amps), sewer.

Fish Trap Lake Campground, 30894 Fish Trap Lake Dr., 56443. T: (218) 575-2603. RV/tent: 47. $25. Hookups: water, electric (30 amps), sewer.

### Dassel
Lake Dale Campground, 24473 CSAH 4, 55325. T: (320) 275-3387. RV/tent: 45. $15. Hookups: electric (30 amps).

### Deer River
Jessie View Resort & Campground, 45756 CO 35, 56636. T: (218) 832-3678. RV/tent: 37. $20. Hookups: water, electric (30 amps), sewer.

Lake Winnibigoshish Recreation Area, 34385 US Hwy. 2, 56636. T: (218) 326-6565. F: (218) 326-6565. RV/tent: 44. $12. Hookups: electric (30 amps).

### Deerwood
Camp Holiday Resort & Campground, 17467 Round Lake Rd., 56444. T: (218) 678-2495. RV/tent: 40. $21. Hookups: water, electric (30 amps), sewer.

Sisselbagamah RV Resort on Bay Lake, 685 Katrine Dr. Northeast, 56444. T: (218) 678-3393. RV/tent: 35. $20. Hookups: water, electric (30 amps), sewer.

### Detroit Lakes
American Legion Campground, 810 West Lake Dr., 56501. T: (218) 847-3759. RV/tent: 97. $19. Hookups: water, electric (30 amps), sewer, cable TV.

### Duluth
Duluth Tent & Trailer Camp, 8411 Congdon Blvd., 55804. T: (218) 525-1350. RV/tent: 64. $19. Hookups: water, electric (30 amps), sewer.

Indian Point Campground, 902 South 69th Ave., 55807. T: (218) 624-5637. RV/tent: 70. $20. Hookups: water, electric (30 amps), sewer.

### Elbow Lake
Tipsinah Mounds Campground & Park, Rte. 2 Box 52A, 56531. T: (218) 685-5114. RV/tent: 68. $20. Hookups: water, electric (30 amps), sewer.

### Elk River
Wapiti Park Campground, 18746 Troy St., 55330. T: (612) 441-1396. RV/tent: 142. $20. Hookups: water, electric (30 amps), sewer.

### Ely
Canoe Country Campground & Cabins, Box 30, 55731. T: (800) 725-2306. RV/tent: 15. $20. Hookups: water, electric (30 amps), sewer.

## OHIO (continued)

### Erskine

Lake Cameron RV Park & Campground, RR 3 Box 24, 56535. T: (218) 687-4555. RV/tent: 36. $18. Hookups: water, electric (50 amps), sewer, cable TV.

### Esko

Knife Island Campgrounds, 234 Hwy. 61 Box 361, 55733. T: (218) 879-6063. RV/tent: 20. $16. Hookups: water, electric (30 amps).

### Fairfax

Valley View Campground, 60861 State Hwy. 4, 55332. T: (507) 426-7420. RV/tent: 42. $22. Hookups: water, electric (30 amps).

### Fairmont

Dawson's Lakeside Campground, 248 Cottonwood Rd., 56031. T: (507) 235-5753. RV/tent: 140. $20. Hookups: water, electric (50 amps), sewer.

Flying Goose Campground, 2521 115th St., 56031. T: (507) 235-3458. RV/tent: 95. $20. Hookups: water, electric (50 amps), sewer.

### Faribault

Camp Faribo, 21851 Bagley Ave., 55021. T: (507) 332-8453. RV/tent: 62. $19. Hookups: water, electric (50 amps), sewer.

Camp Maiden Rock, 22661 Dodge Court, 55021. T: (800) 657-4776. RV/tent: 100. $21. Hookups: water, electric (30 amps), sewer.

Roberds Lake Resort & Campground, 18192 Roberds Lake Blvd., 55021. T: (800) 879-5091. RV/tent: 40. $24. Hookups: water, electric (50 amps), sewer.

### Fergus Falls

Elks Point, P.O. Box 502 Rte. 1, 56537. T: (218) 736-4292. RV/tent: 40. $20. Hookups: water, electric (30 amps).

### Fifty Lakes

Fifty Lakes Campground, P.O. Box 158, 56448. T: (218) 763-2616. RV/tent: 82. $22. Hookups: water, electric (50 amps), sewer.

### Forest Lake

Timm's Marina & Campground, 9080 North Jewel Ln., 55025. T: (612) 464-3890. RV/tent: 30. $20. Hookups: water, electric (30 amps), sewer.

### Frazee

Birchmere Family Resort & Campground, 18346 Birchmere Rd., 56544. T: (800) 642-9554. RV/tent: 30. $20. Hookups: water, electric (30 amps), sewer.

### Garden City

Shady Oaks Campground, P.O. Box 284, 56034. T: (507) 546-3986. RV/tent: 55. $20. Hookups: water, electric (30 amps), sewer.

### Garfield

Oak Park Campground, 9561 CO 8 Northwest, 56332. T: (320) 834-2345. RV/tent: 55. $17. Hookups: water, electric (30 amps), sewer.

### Garrison

Wilderness of Minnesota, Box 387, 56450. T: (320) 692-4347. RV/tent: 132. $15. Hookups: water, electric (50 amps), sewer.

### Glenwood

Chalet Campground, Hwy. 104, 56334. T: (651) 634-5433. RV/tent: 36. $16. Hookups: water, electric (30 amps), sewer.

### Grand Marais

Grand Marais RV Park & Campground, P.O. Box 820, 55604. T: (218) 387-1712. F: (218) 387-1310. RV/tent: 200. $30. Hookups: water, electric (50 amps), sewer.

Gunflint Pines Resort & Campground, 217 South Gunflint Lake Rd., 55604. T: (218) 388-4454. RV/tent: 20. $25. Hookups: water, electric (15 amps).

### Grand Rapids

Birch Cove Resort & Campground, 32382 Southwood Rd., 55744. T: (218) 326-8754. RV/tent: 14. $19. Hookups: water, electric (20 amps), sewer.

Pokegama Recreation Area, 34385 US Hwy. 2, 55744. T: (218) 326-6128. F: (218) 326-6565. RV/tent: 40. $16. Hookups: electric (30 amps).

Sal's Campground, P.O. Box 363, 55744. T: (218) 492-4297. RV/tent: 44. $20. Hookups: water, electric (30 amps), sewer.

### Hackensack

Quietwoods Campground, 4755 Alder Ln. Northwest, 56452. T: (218) 675-6240. RV/tent: 20. $15. Hookups: water, electric (20 amps).

### Ham Lake

Ham Lake Campground, 2400 Constance Blvd., 55304. T: (612) 434-5337. RV/tent: 130. $19. Hookups: water, electric (50 amps).

### Hastings

St. Croix Bluffs Regional Park Campground, 10191 St. Croix Trail, 55033. T: (651) 430-8240. F: (651) 430-8239. RV/tent: 73. $18. Hookups: water, electric (50 amps).

### Hawick

Old Wagon Campground, 21611 132nd St. Northeast, 56246. T: (320) 354-2165. RV/tent: 25. $19. Hookups: water, electric (30 amps).

### International Falls

Arnold's Campground & RV Park, Hwy. 53 and 21st St., 56649. T: (218) 285-9100. RV/tent: 24. $15. Hookups: water, electric (30 amps), sewer.

## OHIO (continued)

### Isanti
Country Camping RV Tent & RV Park on the Rum River, 750 273rd Ave., 55040. T: (612) 444-9626. RV/tent: 58. $16. Hookups: water, electric (30 amps).

### Isle
Father Hennepin State Park, P.O. Box 397, 56342. T: (320) 676-8763. RV/tent: 103. $15. Hookups: electric (30 amps).

### Jackson
Jackson KOA Campground, 2035 Hwy. 71, 56143. T: (507) 847-3825. RV/tent: 60. $22. Hookups: water, electric (30 amps), sewer.

Loon Lake Campground, 405 4th St., 56143. T: (507) 847-2240. RV/tent: 80. $20. Hookups: water, electric (30 amps).

### Jasper
Split Rock Creek State Park, 336 50th Ave., 56144. T: (507) 348-7908. RV/tent: 28. $13. Hookups: electric (30 amps).

### Jordan
Minneapolis S.W. KOA, 3315 West 166th St., 55352. T: (612) 492-6440. RV/tent: 111. $26. Hookups: water, electric (50 amps).

### Kabetogama Lake
Cedar Cove Campsites & Resort, 9940 Gappa Rd., 56669. T: (218) 875-3851. RV/tent: 30. $25. Hookups: water, electric (30 amps), sewer.

### Kandiyohi
Kandiyohi County Park No. 3, 6920 CO 4, 56251. T: (612) 974-8520. RV/tent: 65. $16. Hookups: electric (30 amps).

### Kelliher
Rogers' On Red Lake Campground & RV Park, HC 78 Box 20, 56650. T: (800) 678-1871. RV/tent: 51. $16. Hookups: water, electric (30 amps), sewer.

### Kerrick
Hoffman's Oak Lake Campground, HC1 Box 80, 55756. T: (218) 496-5678. RV/tent: 14. $18. Hookups: water, electric (30 amps), sewer.

### Knife River
Depot Campground, P.O. Box 115, 56149. T: (218) 834-5044. RV/tent: 32. $18. Hookups: water, electric (30 amps).

### Lake Benton
Hole-in-the-Mountain County Park, Hwy. 14 W, 56149. T: (507) 368-9350. RV/tent: 70. $11. Hookups: water, electric (30 amps).

### Lake Bronson
Lake Bronson State Park, Box 9, 56734. T: (218) 754-2200. RV/tent: 194. $13. Hookups: electric (30 amps).

### Lakefield
Kilen Woods State Park, Rte. 1 Box 122, 56150. T: (507) 662-6258. RV/tent: 33. $13. Hookups: electric (30 amps).

### Lanesboro
Sylvan Park, P.O. Box 333, 55949. T: (507) 467-3722. RV/tent: 42. $13. Hookups: electric (30 amps).

### Le Roy
Lake Louise State Park, 12385 766th Ave., 55951. T: (507) 324-5249. RV/tent: 22. $13. Hookups: electric (30 amps).

### Le Sueur
Peaceful Valley Campsite, 213 Peaceful Valley Rd., 56058. T: (507) 665-2297. F: (612) 388-5605. RV/tent: 38. $18. Hookups: water, electric (50 amps), sewer.

### Lindstrom
Hillscrest RV Park, 32741 North Lakes Trail, 55045. T: (651) 257-5352. RV/tent: 70. $20. Hookups: water, electric (30 amps), sewer.

### Lino Lakes
Rice Creek Campground, 7401 Main St., 55038. T: (612) 757-3928. RV/tent: 78. $20. Hookups: water, electric (30 amps).

### Mahnomen
Shooting Star Casino Hotel & RV Park, 777 Casino Dr., 56557. T: (800) 453-STAR. RV/tent: 47. $13. Hookups: water, electric (30 amps), sewer.

### Mankato
Minneopa State Park, RR 9 Box 143, 56001. T: (507) 389-5464. RV/tent: 62. $13. Hookups: electric (30 amps).

### Maple Plain
Baker Park Reserve, 2931 CO 19, 55359. T: (612) 479-2258. RV/tent: 213. $17. Hookups: electric (30 amps).

### Marine on St. Croix
William O'Brien State Park, 16821 O'Brien Trail North, 55047. T: (651) 433-0500. RV/tent: 125. $15. Hookups: electric (30 amps).

### Mazeppa
Ponderosa Campground, RR 1 Box 209, 55956. T: (800) 895-0328. RV/tent: 80. $17. Hookups: water, electric (50 amps).

## OHIO (continued)

### McGregor

Sandy Lake Recreation Area, HCR 4 Box 362, 55760. T: (218) 426-3482. F: (218) 426-4815. RV/tent: 110. $18. Hookups: electric (30 amps).

Savanna Portage State Park, HCR 3 Box 591, 55760. T: (218) 426-3271. RV/tent: 72. $13. Hookups: electric (30 amps).

### Merrifield

Shing Wako Resort & Campground, HC 87 Box 9580, 51465. T: (218) 765-3226. RV/tent: 33. $21. Hookups: water, electric (30 amps), sewer.

Sunset Bay Resort & Campground, HC 86 Box 1000, 56465. T: (800) 715-2267. RV/tent: 75. $25. Hookups: water, electric (30 amps), sewer.

### Montevideo

Lac Qui Parle State Park, Rte. 5 Box 74A, 56265. T: (612) 752-4736. RV/tent: 66. $13. Hookups: electric (30 amps).

### Moorhead

Buffalo River State Park, P.O. Box 352, 56547. T: (218) 498-2124. RV/tent: 44. $13. Hookups: electric (30 amps).

Fargo-Moorhead KOA, Rte. 4 Box 168, 56560. T: (218) 233-0671. RV/tent: 95. $30. Hookups: water, electric (50 amps), sewer, cable TV.

### Mora

Camperville, 2351 310th Ave., 55051. T: (320) 679-2326. RV/tent: 49. $20. Hookups: water, electric (50 amps).

Captain Dan's Crow's Nest Resort, 2743 Hwy. 65, 55051. T: (320) 679-1977. RV/tent: 51. $22. Hookups: water, electric (30 amps), sewer.

### Morton

Jackpot Junction Casino Hotel Campground, 39375 CO 24, 56270. T: (507) 644-3000. F: (507) 644-2648. RV/tent: 42. $12. Hookups: water, electric (30 amps), sewer.

### Nerstrand

Nerstrand Big Woods State Park, 9700 170th St. East, 55053. T: (507) 334-8848. RV/tent: 68. $13. Hookups: water, electric (30 amps).

### Nevis

Whispering Pines Resort & Campgrounds, Rte. 1 Box 83, 56467. T: (218) 652-4362. RV/tent: 10. $23. Hookups: water, electric (30 amps), sewer.

### New London

Hide-Away Campground, 199th Ave. Northeast, 56273. T: (320) 354-2148. RV/tent: 11. $18. Hookups: water, electric (30 amps).

Sibley State Park, 800 Sibley Park Rd., 56273. T: (320) 354-2055. RV/tent: 138. $15. Hookups: electric (30 amps).

### New Ulm

Flandrau State Park, 1300 Summit Ave., 56073. T: (507) 233-9800. RV/tent: 90. $13. Hookups: electric (30 amps).

### Ogema

Woodland Trails Resort & Campground, Rte. 1 Box 71 E, 56569. T: (218) 983-3230. RV/tent: 35. $15. Hookups: water, electric (30 amps), sewer.

### Orr

Cabin O'Pines Resort & Campground, 4378 Pelican Rd., 55771. T: (800) 757-3122. RV/tent: 30. $20. Hookups: water, electric (30 amps).

Pine Acres Resort & Campground, 4498 Pine Acres Rd., 55771. T: (218) 757-3144. RV/tent: 80. $20. Hookups: water, electric (30 amps), sewer.

### Ortonville

Big Stone Lake State Park, RR 1 Box 153, 56278. T: (612) 839-3663. RV/tent: 40. $13. Hookups: electric (30 amps).

### Osage

R&D Resort & Campground, 54097 Grant St., 56570. T: (218) 573-3182. RV/tent: 26. $10. Hookups: water, electric (30 amps).

### Osakis

Black's Cresent Beach, P.O. Box 416, 56360. T: (320) 859-2127. RV/tent: 10. $22. Hookups: water, electric (30 amps), sewer.

Midway Beach Resort & Campground, 1821 Lake St., 56360. T: (320) 859-4410. RV/tent: 9. $20. Hookups: water, electric (30 amps), sewer.

### Owatonna

Owatonna Campground, 2554 Southwest 28th St., 55060. T: (507) 451-8050. RV/tent: 142. $20. Hookups: water, electric (50 amps), sewer.

### Park Rapids

Breeze Camping & RV Resort on Eagle Lake, HCO 5 Box 321, 56470. T: (218) 732-5888. RV/tent: 69. $22. Hookups: water, electric (20 amps), sewer.

### Pelican Rapids

Pelican Hills Park, RR 4 Box 218B, 56572. T: (800) 430-2267. RV/tent: 83. $20. Hookups: water, electric (30 amps), sewer.

### Pengilly

Swan Lake Campground & Resort, 29995 East Shore Dr., 55775. T: (218) 885-3385. RV/tent: 24. $15. Hookups: water, electric (30 amps).

## OHIO (continued)

### Perham

Golden Eagle Vacationland, Golden Eagle Rd., 56573.
T: (218) 346-4386. RV/tent: 131. $18. Hookups:
water, electric (30 amps), sewer.

### Preston

Forestville Mystery Cave State Park, Rte. 2 Box 128,
55965. T: (507) 352-5111. RV/tent: 73. $15.
Hookups: electric (30 amps).

### Prior Lake

Dakotah Meadows Campground, 2341 Park Place,
55372. T: (800) 653-CAMP. F: (612) 496-6857.
RV/tent: 48. $22. Hookups: water, electric (50
amps), sewer.

### Red Wing

Haycreek Valley Campground, 31673 Hwy. 58 Blvd.,
55066. T: (651) 388-3998. RV/tent: 122. $22.
Hookups: water, electric (50 amps).

### Richmond

Cozy Corners, 19897 Hwy. 22, 56368. T: (320) 597-
3587. RV/tent: 17. $24. Hookups: water, electric
(30 amps).

Your Haven Campground, 18337 SR 22, 56368.
T: (320) 597-2450. RV/tent: 18. $20. Hookups:
water, electric (30 amps), sewer.

### Rochester

Brookside RV Park, 516 17th Ave., 55901. T: (507)
288-1413. F: (507) 288-3166. RV/tent: 25. $25.
Hookups: water, electric (50 amps), sewer, cable
TV, telephone.

### Roger

Minneapolis Northwest/Maple Grove KOA, 10410
Brockton Ln., 55374. T: (612) 420-2255. RV/tent:
160. $29. Hookups: water, electric (50 amps),
sewer, phone.

### Roseau

Roseau City Park, 900 11th St. Southeast, 56751.
T: (218) 463-1791. RV/tent: 20. $16. Hookups:
water, electric (30 amps).

### Rutledge

Pine River Campground, 7201 Hwy. 61, 55795.
T: (320) 233-7678. RV/tent: 70. $18. Hookups:
water, electric (30 amps).

### Sandstone

Banning State Park, P.O. Box 643, 55072. T: (612)
245-2668. RV/tent: 39. $13. Hookups: electric
(30 amps).

### Savage

Town and Country Campground, 12630 Boone
Ave., 55378. T: (612) 445-1756. RV/tent: 46. $25.
Hookups: water, electric (30 amps), sewer.

### Sebeka

Sebeka Municipal Park, P.O. Box 305, 56477. T: (218)
837-5773. RV/tent: 10. $16. Hookups: electric
(30 amps).

### Silver Bay

Northern Exposure Campground, 5346 Hwy. 61,
55614. T: (218) 226-3324. RV/tent: 55. $20.
Hookups: water, electric (30 amps), sewer.

### South Haven

Timberwoods Resort & Campground, 10255
Nevens Ave. Northwest, 55382. T: (320) 274-5140.
RV/tent: 40. $20. Hookups: water, electric
(30 amps), sewer.

### South Isle

South Isle Family Campground, 39002 SR 47, 56342.
T: (320) 676-8538. RV/tent: 47. $18. Hookups:
water, electric (30 amps).

### Starbuck

Glacial Lakes State Park, 25022 CO 41, 56381.
T: (320) 239-2860. RV/tent: 46. $13. Hookups:
electric (30 amps).

### Tenstrike

Gull Lake Campground, Rte. 1 Box 28, 56683.
T: (218) 586-2842. RV/tent: 92. $20. Hookups:
water, electric (30 amps), sewer.

Moen's Birch Haven Campground & Resort, Rte. 1
Box 138, 56683. T: (218) 586-2863. RV/tent: 42.
$16. Hookups: water, electric (30 amps).

### Thief River Falls

Thief River Falls Tourist Park, Oakland Park Rd.,
56701. T: (218) 681-2519. RV/tent: 64. $13.
Hookups: water, electric (30 amps), sewer.

### Two Harbors

Burlington Bay Campsite, 522 1st Ave., 55616.
T: (218) 834-2021. RV/tent: 111. $16. Hookups:
water, electric (30 amps), sewer.

Penmarallter Campsite, 725 Scenic Dr., 55616.
T: (218) 834-4603. RV/tent: 19. $18. Hookups:
water, electric (30 amps).

### Walker

Waters Edge RV Park, 10634 SR 371, 56484. T: (218)
547-3552. RV/tent: 10. $16. Hookups: water, elec-
tric (30 amps), sewer.

## OHIO (continued)

### Warroad
Warroad Campground, P.O. Box 50, 56763. T: (218) 386-1004. RV/tent: 153. $18. Hookups: water, electric (30 amps), sewer.

### Waterville
Sakatah Lake State Park, RR 2 Box 19, 56096. T: (507) 362-4438. RV/tent: 68. $13. Hookups: electric (30 amps).

### Waubun
Elk Horn Resort & Campground, Rte. 2 Box 323, 56589. T: (218) 935-5437. RV/tent: 24. $20. Hookups: water, electric (30 amps), sewer.

### Woodbury
St. Paul East KOA, 568 Cottage Grove Dr., 55129. T: (651) 436-6436. RV/tent: 76. $30. Hookups: water, electric (50 amps), sewer, telephone.

### Zimmerman
Camp in the Woods, 14791 289th Ave., 55398. T: (612) 427-5050. RV/tent: 78. $25. Hookups: water, electric (30 amps), sewer.

### Zumbrota
Shades of Sherwood Camping Park, 14334 Sherwood Trace, 55992. T: (507) 732-5100. RV/tent: 140. $20. Hookups: water, electric (30 amps).

# WISCONSIN

### Algoma
Ahnapee River Trails Camp Resort Inc., 6053 West Wilson Rd., 54201. T: (920) 487-5777. RV/tent: 65. $18. Hookups: water, electric (30 amps).

### Alma Center
KOA Hixton/Alma Center, North 9657 State Hwy. 95, 54611. T: (715) 964-2508. RV/tent: 66. $24. Hookups: water, electric (30 amps), sewer.

### Amherst Junction
Lake Emily Park, 3961 Park Dr., 54407. T: (715) 346-1433. RV/tent: 49. $13. Hookups: electric (30 amps).

### Arbor Vitae
Arbor Vitae Campground, 10545 Big Arbor Vitae Dr., 54568. T: (715) 356-5146. RV/tent: 90. $20. Hookups: water, electric (30 amps), sewer.

Fox Fire Campground, 11180 Fox Fire Rd., 54568. T: (715) 356-6470. RV/tent: 50. $23. Hookups: water, electric (30 amps), sewer.

### Ashland
Evergreen Acres Campground, Rte. 3 Box 353, 54806. T: (715) 682-4658. RV/tent: 20. $16. Hookups: water, electric (20 amps).

Kreher RV Park, 601 Main St. W, 54806. T: (715) 682-7071. RV/tent: 35. $15. Hookups: electric (20 amps).

Prentice Park, 601 Main St. W, 54806. T: (715) 682-7071. RV/tent: 25. $15. Hookups: electric (20 amps).

### Athelstane
Kosir's Rapid Rafts, W 14073 Cty Hwy. C, 54104. T: (715) 757-3431. RV/tent: 32. $11. Hookups: water, electric (20 amps).

McCaslin Mountain Campground, W 15720 County F, 54104. T: (715) 757-3734. RV/tent: 114. $15. Hookups: water, sewer, electric (20 amps).

### Augusta
Coon Fork Lake Campground, CR CF, 54722. T: (715) 839-4738. RV/tent: 88. $13. Hookups: electric (30 amps).

Sandy Hill Campground, E2100 ND Rd., 54722. T: (715) 286-2495. RV/tent: 28. $15. Hookups: water, electric (30 amps).

### Babcock
Country Aire Campground, P.O. Box 88, 54413. T: (715) 884-2300. RV/tent: 39. $17. Hookups: water, electric (30 amps).

### Balsam Lake
Apple River Campground North, 956 165th Ave., 54810. T: (715) 268-8980. RV/tent: 28. $12. Hookups: water, electric (30 amps).

### Baraboo
Baraboo Hills Campground, E 10545 Terrytowne Rd., 53913. T: (608) 356-8505. RV/tent: 180. $25. Hookups: water, sewer, electric (50 amps).

Devil's Lake State Park, 5975 Park Rd., 53913. T: (608) 356-8301. RV/tent: 407. $15. Hookups: electric (30 amps).

Fox Hill RV Park, 11371 North Reedsburg Rd., 53913. T: (608) 356-5890. RV/tent: 50. $27. Hookups: water, electric (30 amps).

Mirror Lake State Park, 10320 East Fern Dell Rd., 53913. T: (608) 254-2333. RV/tent: 148. $15. Hookups: electric (30 amps).

Nordic Pines, E11740 County DL, 53913. T: (608) 356-5810. RV/tent: 140. $20. Hookups: electric (20 amps).

## WISCONSIN (continued)

### Baraboo (continued)

Red Oak Campground, South 2350 US Hwy. 12, 53913.T: (608) 356-7304. RV/tent: 121. $18. Hookups: water, sewer, electric (50 amps).

Rocky Arbor State Park, 10320 Fern Dell Rd., 53913.T: (608) 254-8001. RV/tent: 48. $21. Hookups: electric (30 amps).

### Barron

Barron Motel & RV Campground, 1521 East Division Ave., 54812.T: (715) 637-3154. RV/tent: 17. $14. Hookups: water, sewer, electric (30 amps).

### Bayfield

Apostle Islands Area Campground, HC 64 Box 8, 54814.T: (715) 779-5524. RV/tent: 59. $22. Hookups: water, sewer, electric (50 amps).

Buffalo Bay Campground & Marina, P.O. Box 529, 54814.T: (715) 779-3743. RV/tent: 50. $15. Hookups: water, electric (30 amps).

### Belmont

Lake Joy Campground, 24192 Lake Joy Ln., 53510. T: (608) 762-5150. RV/tent: 78. $18. Hookups: water, electric (30 amps).

### Big Flats

Pineland Camping Park, 916 Hwy. 13, 54613.T: (608) 564-7818. RV/tent: 175. $20. Hookups: waters, sewer, electric (50 amps).

### Birchwood

Doolittle Park, P.O. Box 6, 54817.T: (715) 354-3300. RV/tent: 34. $14. Hookups: electric (30 amps).

Spider Lake Resort & Campground, N2603 CTH T, 54817.T: (715) 354-3723. RV/tent: 45. $16. Hookups: water, electric (20 amps).

### Black River Falls

Black River State Forest, Castle Mound Rec. Area, 910 Hwy. 54 East, 54615.T: (715) 284-4103. RV/tent: 38. $15. Hookups: electric (30 amps).

Jamboree Campground, Hwy. 12, 54615.T: (715) 284-7138. RV/tent: 200. $25. Hookups: water, sewer, electric (30 amps).

### Blair

Riverside Memorial Park, P.O. Box 147, 54616. T: (608) 989-2517. RV/tent: 24. $11. Hookups: electric (30 amps).

### Blue Mounds

Blue Mounds State Park, 4350 Mounds Park Rd., 53517.T: (608) 437-5711. RV/tent: 123. $14. Hookups: electric (30 amps).

### Blue River

Eagle Cave Natural Park, 16320 Cavern Ln., 53518. T: (608) 537-2988. RV/tent: 50. $15. Hookups: water, electric (15 amps).

### Briggsville

Lake Mason Campground, 4035 First Ln., 53920. T: (608) 981-2444. RV/tent: 50. $16. Hookups: water, sewer, electric (30 amps).

Wagon Wheel Campground, 4016 1st Dr., 53920. T: (608) 981-2161. RV/tent: 150. $16. Hookups: water, sewer, electric (30 amps).

### Brodhead

Crazy Horse Campground, N3201 Crazy Horse Ln., 53520.T: (608) 897-2207. RV/tent: 196. $18. Hookups: water, sewer, electric (30 amps).

Sweet Minni Ha Ha Campground, N4697 County E, 53520.T: (608) 862-3769. RV/tent: 117. $20. Hookups: water, electric (30 amps).

### Bruce

Bruce Park, P.O. Box 238, 54819.T: (715) 868-2185. RV/tent: 8. $10. Hookups: electric (20 amps).

### Brule

Brule River Motel & Campground, P.O. Box 126, 54820.T: (715) 372-4815. RV/tent: 65. $15. Hookups: water, electric (30 amps), sewer.

### Burlington

Meadowlark Acres Campground, N 5146 North Rd., 53105.T: (262) 763-7200. RV/tent: 84. $22. Hookups: water, electric (30 amps).

### Butternut

Butternut Lake Campground, Rte. 1 Box 129 A, 54514.T: (715) 769-3448. RV/tent: 24. $19. Hookups: water, sewer, electric (20 amps).

### Camp Douglas

Mill Bluff State Park, 15819 Funnel Rd., 54651. T: (608) 427-6692. RV/tent: 21. $10. Hookups: electric (20 amps).

### Cascade

Hilly Haven Campground, N 2827 Dusty Ln., 53011. T: (920) 528-8966. RV/tent: 70. $20. Hookups: water, sewer, electric (50 amps).

Hoeft's Resort & Campground, W9070 Crooked Lake Dr., 53011.T: (262) 626-2221. RV/tent: 96. $17. Hookups: water, electric (50 amps).

### Cassville

K-7 Korral, 10895 Jack Oak Rd., 53806.T: (608) 725-2267. RV/tent: 35. $20. Hookups: water, electric (30 amps).

Nelson Dewey State Park, County Trunk VV, 53806. T: (608) 725-5374. RV/tent: 43. $15. Hookups: electric (30 amps).

### Chetek

Northern Exposure Resort & Campground, P.O. Box 222, 54728.T: (715) 859-2887. RV/tent: 20. $18. Hookups: water, electric (30 amps).

## WISCONSIN (continued)

### Chetek (continued)

Six Lakes Resort & Campground, 25358 8th Ave., 54728.T: (800) 203-4624. RV/tent: 180. $20. Hookups: water, sewer, electric (30 amps).

### Chippewa Falls

Lake Wissota State Park, 18127 CR O, 54729. T: (715) 382-4574. RV/tent: 81. $15. Hookups: electric (30 amps).

Pine Harbor Campground, 7181 185th St., 54729. T: (715) 723-9865. RV/tent: 26. $14. Hookups: water, electric (30 amps).

### Conover

Buckatabon Lodge & Lighthouse Inn, 5630 Rush Rd., 54519.T: (715) 479-4660. RV/tent: 51. $19. Hookups: water, sewer, electric (20 amps).

### Cornell

Brunet Island State Park, 23125 255th St., 54732. T: (715) 239-6888. RV/tent: 69. $12. Hookups: electric (30 amps).

### Cumberland

Camp Brigadoon, 2554 4th St., 54829.T: (800) 715-BRIG. RV/tent: 131. $18. Hookups: water, electric (30 amps).

### De Pere

Brown County Fairgrounds, Ft. Howard Ave., 54115. T: (920) 336-3283. RV/tent: 40. $15. Hookups: water, electric (30 amps), sewer.

Happy Hollow Camping Resort, 3831 CR U, 54115. T: (920) 532-4386. RV/tent: 125. $23. Hookups: water, sewer, electric (30 amps).

### De Soto

Blackhawk Park, RFD 1, 54624.T: (608) 648-3314. RV/tent: 175. $16. Hookups: electric (30 amps).

### Deerbrook

Veterans Memorial Park, P.O. Box 460, 54409. T: (715) 623-6214. RV/tent: 41. $10. Hookups: electric (30 amps).

### Delavan

Snug Harbor Inn Campground on Turtle Lake, W7772-2C Wisc Pkwy, 53115.T: (608) 883-6999. RV/tent: 43. $35. Hookups: water, electric (50 amps).

### Dells

American World RV Park & Resort, 400 Wisconsin Dells Parkway, 53965.T: (608) 253-4451. RV/tent: 52. $54. Hookups: water, sewer, electric (50 amps).

Arrowhead Resort Campground, P.O. Box 295, 53965.T: (608) 254-7344. RV/tent: 285. $28. Hookups: water, sewer, electric (30 amps).

Blue Lake Campground, 3531 Hwy. G, 53965. T: (608) 586-4376. RV/tent: 45. $20. Hookups: water, sewer, electric (30 amps).

Bonanza Campground, P.O. Box 453, 53965.T: (608) 254-8124. RV/tent: 150. $22. Hookups: water, sewer, electric (50 amps).

Dell-Boo Campground, P.O. Box 407, 53965.T: (608) 356-5898. RV/tent: 138. $31. Hookups: water, sewer, electric (30 amps).

Erickson's Tepee Park Campground, 10096 Trout Rd., 53965.T: (608) 253-3122. RV/tent: 113. $25. Hookups: water, sewer, electric (30 amps).

Holiday Shores Campground & Resort, 3901 River Rd., 53965.T: (608) 254-2717. RV/tent: 140. $26. Hookups: water, electric (30 amps).

K & L Campground, 3503 County Rd. G, 53965. T: (608) 586-4720. RV/tent: 96. $25. Hookups: water, sewer, electric (30 amps).

Lake of the Dells Camping Resort, 3879 Hwy. 13, 53965.T: (608) 254-6485. RV/tent: 200. $30. Hookups: water, sewer, electric (50 amps).

River Bay Resort Campground, Marina and RV Park, P.O. Box 456, 53965.T: (608) 254-7193. RV/tent: 158. $31. Hookups: water, sewer, electric (50 amps).

Sherwood Forest Campground, 352 Hwys 12 & 16, 53965.T: (608) 254-7080. RV/tent: 189. $31. Hookups: water, sewer, electric (50 amps).

Stand Rock Campground, 570 Hwy. N, 53965. T: (608) 253-2169. RV/tent: 140. $25. Hookups: water, sewer, electric (30 amps).

Wisconsin Dells KOA, 235 Stand Rock Rd., 53965. T: (608) 254-4177. RV/tent: 147. $40. Hookups: water, sewer, electric (50 amps).

### Denmark

Shady Acres Campsites, 5422 Shady Acre Ln., 54208.T: (920) 863-8143. RV/tent: 25. $17. Hookups: water, sewer, electric (30 amps).

### Dodgeville

Governor Dodge State Park, 4175 SSR 23N, 53533. T: (608) 935-2315. RV/tent: 268. $15. Hookups: electric (30 amps).

### Eagle

Kettle Moraine State Forest-Southern Unit Head-quarters, 39091 West Hwy. 59, 53119.T: (262) 594-6200. RV/tent: 260. $15. Hookups: electric (30 amps).

### Eagle River

Chain-O-Lakes Resort & Campground, 3165 Campground Rd., 54521.T: (715) 479-6708. RV/tent: 100. $20. Hookups: water, electric (30 amps).

### Elkhart Lake

Plymouth Rock Camping Resort, 7271 North Lando St., 53073.T: (920) 892-4252. RV/tent: 270. $30. Hookups: water, sewer, electric (50 amps).

## WISCONSIN (continued)

### Elton
Glacier Wilderness Campground, P.O. Box 5, 54430. T: (715) 882-4781. RV/tent: 11. $20. Hookups: water, electric (30 amps).

### Exeland
Windfall Lake Family Camping, 632 North SR 40, 54835. T: (715) 943-2625. RV/tent: 25. $13. Hookups: electric (15 amps).

### Fish Creek
Peninsula State Park Campgrounds, P.O. Box 218, 54212. T: (920) 868-3258. RV/tent: 469. $14. Hookups: electric (30 amps).

### Florence
Keyes Lake Campground, HCI Box 162, 54121. T: (715) 528-4907. RV/tent: 35. $15. Hookups: water, electric (30 amps).

### Fort Atkinson
Pilgrim's Campground LLC, W 7271 Hwy. C, 53538. T: (920) 563-8122. RV/tent: 103. $27. Hookups: water, sewer, electric (50 amps).

### Fremont
Blue Top Resort & Campground, 1460 Wolf River Dr., 54940. T: (920) 446-3343. RV/tent: 50. $21. Hookups: water, electric (30 amps).

### Galesville
Pow-Wow Campground, W 16751 Pow-Wow Ln., 54630. T: (608) 582-2995. RV/tent: 128. $18. Hookups: water, electric (30 amps).

### Glidden
Northern Lure Resort & Campground, P.O. Box 5, 54527. T: (715) 264-3677. RV/tent: 19. $20. Hookups: water, sewer, electric (30 amps).

### Gordon
Adventureland, 7440 E CR Y, 54838. T: (715) 376-4528. RV/tent: 50. $18. Hookups: water, electric (30 amps).

### Grantsburg
Cedar Point Resort & Campground, 12480 Cedar Point Ln., 54840. T: (715) 488-2224. RV/tent: 30. $18. Hookups: water, sewer, electric (30 amps).

James N. McNally Campground, 316 South Brad St., 54840. T: (715) 463-2405. RV/tent: 38. $15. Hookups: water, sewer, electric (50 amps).

### Green Lake
Green Lake Campground, W2360 Hwy. 23, 54941. T: (920) 294-3543. RV/tent: 200. $30. Hookups: water, sewer, electric (30 amps).

### Greenbush
Westward Ho Camp Resort, 5456 North Division Rd., 53023. T: (920) 526-3407. RV/tent: 175. $35. Hookups: water, sewer, electric (50 amps).

### Hayward
The Hayward KOA, 11544 North Hwy. 63, 54843. T: (715) 634-2331. RV/tent: 142. $35. Hookups: water, sewer, electric (50 amps).

Nelson Lake Lodge, 12980 North Lodge Rd., 54843. T: (715) 634-3750. RV/tent: 52. $27. Hookups: water, sewer, electric (30 amps).

Revelle's Landing Resort & Campground, 15249 W. Bills Rd., 54843. T: (715) 634-4216. RV/tent: 48. $16. Hookups: water, sewer, electric (30 amps).

Sisko's Pine Point Resort, 8677 North County Rd. CC, 54843. T: (715) 462-3700. RV/tent: 33. $19. Hookups: water, sewer, electric (30 amps).

Sunrise Bay Campground & RV Park, 16269 W. Jolly Fisherman Rd., 54843. T: (715) 634-2213. RV/tent: 51. $18. Hookups: water, sewer, electric (30 amps).

Trail's End Resort & Campground, 8080 North CR K, 54843. T: (715) 634-2423. RV/tent: 65. $30. Hookups: water, sewer, electric (30 amps).

### Hazelhurst
Cedar Falls Campground, 6051 Cedar Falls Rd., 54531. T: (715) 356-4953. RV/tent: 42. $18. Hookups: electric (20 amps).

### Hilbert
Calumet County Park, 6150 City EE, 54129. T: (920) 439-1008. RV/tent: 71. $16. Hookups: electric (30 amps).

### Hiles
Hiles Pine Lake Campground, 8896 West Pine Lake Rd., 54511. T: (715) 649-3319. RV/tent: 80. $18. Hookups: water, electric (30 amps).

### Hixton
Triple R Resort, N11818 Hixton-Levis Rd., 54635. T: (715) 964-8777. RV/tent: 25. $21. Hookups: water, electric (50 amps).

### Holmen
Sandman's Campground, 8905 Hwy. 53 & 93, 54636. T: (608) 526-4956. RV/tent: 50. $14. Hookups: water, electric (30 amps).

### Horicon
The Playful Goose Campground, 2001 South Main St., 53032. T: (920) 485-4744. RV/tent: 192. $26. Hookups: water, sewwer, electric (30 amps).

### Hudson
Willow River State Park, 1034 CR A, 54016. T: (715) 386-5931. RV/tent: 55. $15. Hookups: electric (30 amps).

### Iola
Iola Pines Campground Inc., 100 Fairway Dr., 54945. T: (715) 445-3489. RV/tent: 50. $16. Hookups: water, sewer, electric (30 amps).

## WISCONSIN (continued)

### Iron River
Wildwood Campground, RR 2 Box 18, 54847.
T: (715) 372-4072. RV/tent: 25. $14. Hookups:
water, sewer, electric (30 amps).

### Jefferson
Bark River Campground, 2340 W. Hansen Rd.,
53549. T: (262) 593-2421. RV/tent: 250. $20.
Hookups: water, sewer, electric (30 amps).

### Kansasville
Bong State Recreation Area, 26313 Burlington Rd.,
53139. T: (262) 878-5600. RV/tent: 192. $15.
Hookups: electric (30 amps).

### Kewaskum
Kettle Moraine State Forest, Mauthe Lake Recre-
ation Area, CR Hwy. G, 53010. T: (262) 626-4305.
RV/tent: 147. $14. Hookups: electric (30 amps).

Kettle Moraine State Forest-North, 1765 CR Hwy.
G, 53010. T: (262) 626-2116. RV/tent: 341. $14.
Hookups: electric (30 amps).

### Kewaunee
Mapleview Campsites, N1460 Hwy. B, 54216.
T: (920) 776-1588. RV/tent: 75. $21. Hookups:
water, electric (30 amps).

### Kieler
Rustic Barn Campground, 3854 Dry Hollow Rd.,
53812. T: (608) 568-7797. RV/tent: 58. $18.
Hookups: water, electric (30 amps).

### Kingston
Grand Valley Campground, 5855 CR B, 53926.
T: (920) 394-3643. RV/tent: 200. $21. Hookups:
water, electric (30 amps).

### La Crosse
Bluebird Springs Recreation Area, N 2833 Smith
Valley Rd., 54601. T: (608) 781-CAMP. RV/tent:
148. $20. Hookups: water, sewer, electric (50
amps).

Goose Island Camp, Hwy. 35, 54601. T: (608) 788-
7018. RV/tent: 400. $15. Hookups: electric (30
amps).

Pettibone Resort & Campground, 333 Park Plaza
Dr., 54601. T: (608) 782-5858. RV/tent: 170. $28.
Hookups: water, electric (50 amps).

### Lac Du Flambeau
Lac Du Flambeau Tribal Campground, P.O. Box 67,
54538. T: (715) 588-9611. RV/tent: 72. $18.
Hookups: water, sewer, electric (30 amps).

### Ladysmith
Flambeau River Lodge, N7870 Flambeau Rd., 54848.
T: (715) 532-5392. RV/tent: 25. $15. Hookups:
water, sewer, electric (30 amps).

Thornapple River Campground, N6599 Hwy. 27,
54848. T: (715) 532-7034. RV/tent: 25. $17.
Hookups: water, electric (30 amps).

Westcove Campground, 1011 Edgewood Ave., Hwy.
8, 54848. T: (715) 532-7812. RV/tent: 15. $14.
Hookups: waters, sewer, electric (30 amps).

### Lake Delton
Yogi Bear's Jellystone Park Camp-Resort, 51915
Ishnala Rd., 53940. T: (608) 254-2568. RV/tent: 229.
$58. Hookups: water, sewer, electric (50 amps).

### Lake Geneva
Coachman's Terrace Park, W 3540 SR 50W, 53147.
T: (262) 248-3636. RV/tent: 63. $25. Hookups:
water, sewer, electric (30 amps).

### Lancaster
Klondyke Secluded Acres, 6656 Pine Knob Rd.,
53813. T: (608) 723-2844. RV/tent: 37. $18.
Hookups: water, electric (30 amps).

### Land O'Lakes
Borderline RV Park, P.O. Box 552, 54540. T: (715)
547-6169. RV/tent: 25. $19. Hookups: water, sewer,
electric (30 amps).

### Lodi
Crystal Lake Campground, P.O. Box 188, 53555.
T: (608) 592-5607. RV/tent: 65. $32. Hookups:
water, electric (30 amps).

Smokey Hollow Campground, Inc., 9935 McGowan,
53555. T: (608) 635-4806. RV/tent: 100. $19.
Hookups: water, electric (30 amps).

### Lyndon Station
Bass Lake Campground, 1497 Southern Rd., 53944.
T: (608) 666-2311. RV/tent: 50. $30. Hookups:
water, electric (30 amps).

Yukon Trails Camping, 2330 Hwy. HH, 53944.
T: (608) 666-3261. RV/tent: 65. $30. Hookups:
water, sewer, electric (30 amps).

### Lynxville
River Hills Estates Campground, Box 171, 54626.
T: (608) 874-4197. RV/tent: 40. $15. Hookups:
water, sewer, electric (30 amps).

### Manawa
Bear Lake Campground, N4715 Hwy. 22-110,
54949. T: (920) 596-3308. RV/tent: 150. $24.
Hookups: water, electric (30 amps).

### Maribel
Devil's River Campers Park, 16612 CTH R, 54227.
T: (920) 863-2812. RV/tent: 80. $25. Hookups:
water, electric (30 amps).

## WISCONSIN (continued)

### Marion
Kastle Kampground, N11301 Kinney Lake Rd., 54950. T: (715) 754-5900. RV/tent: 365. $23. Hookups: water, sewer, electric (50 amps).

### Markesan
Shady Oaks Campground, N 2770 Park Rd., 53946. T: (920) 398-3138. RV/tent: 151. $20. Hookups: water, sewer, electric (30 amps).

### Marquette
Sportsman's Resort LLC, 222 Lyon St., 53947. T: (920) 394-3421. RV/tent: 30. $25. Hookups: water, sewer, electric (50 amps).

### Mauston
Bavarian Campsites, W 4796 Hwy. G, 53948. T: (608) 847-7039. RV/tent: 70. $20. Hookups: electric (20 amps).

### Mellen
Copper Falls State Park, RR 1 Box 17AA, 54546. T: (715) 274-5123. RV/tent: 56. $18. Hookups: electric (30 amps).

### Menomonie
Menomonie KOA, 2501 Broadway St. North, 54751. T: (715) 235-6360. RV/tent: 94. $30. Hookups: water, sewer, electric (30 amps).

Twin Springs Resort Campground, 530th St., 54751. T: (715) 235-9321. RV/tent: 75. $24. Hookups: water, sewer, electric (50 amps).

### Mercer
Lake of the Falls, County Trunk FF, 54547. T: (715) 561-2695. RV/tent: 30. $9. Hookups: electric (30 amps).

### Merrill
Council Grounds State Park, N1895 Council Grounds Dr., 54452. T: (715) 356-8773. RV/tent: 55. $15. Hookups: electric (30 amps).

### Merrimac
Merry Mac's Camp'N, E 12540 Halweg Rd., 53561. T: (608) 493-2367. RV/tent: 110. $22. Hookups: water, electric (30 amps).

### Milton
Blackhawk Campground, 3407 Blackhawk Dr., 53563. T: (608) 868-2586. RV/tent: 50. $27. Hookups: water, electric (30 amps).

### Montello
Lake Arrowhead Campground, 781 Fox Court, 53949. T: (920) 295-3000. RV/tent: 115. $27. Hookups: water, sewer, electric (30 amps).

Lakeside Campground, N3510 East Tomahawk Trail, 53949. T: (920) 295-3389. RV/tent: 95. $30. Hookups: water, sewer, electric (50 amps).

Wilderness County Park, N 1499 State Hwy. 22, 53949. T: (608) 297-2002. RV/tent: 159. $15. Hookups: electric (30 amps).

### Mosinee
Lake DuBay Shores Campground, 1713 DuBay Dr., 54455. T: (715) 457-2484. RV/tent: 150. $26. Hookups: water, sewer, electric (30 amps).

### Mountain
Chute Pond Park, 12436 Chute Dam Rd., 54149. T: (715) 276-6261. RV/tent: 100. $18. Hookups: water, electric (30 amps).

### Mukwonago
Country View Campground, 26400 Craig Ave., 53149. T: (262) 662-3654. RV/tent: 150. $26. Hookups: water, sewer, electric (30 amps).

### Muscoda
Riverside Park, P.O. Box 293, 53573. T: (608) 739-3786. RV/tent: 36. $10. Hookups: electric (30 amps).

### Necedah
Buckhorn Campground Resort Inc., 8410 CR G, 54646. T: (608) 565-2090. RV/tent: 24. $20. Hookups: water, electric (50 amps).

Ken's Marina, Campground & Pontoon Rental, W4240 Marina Ln., 54646. T: (608) 565-2426. RV/tent: 35. $15. Hookups: water, electric (30 amps).

St. Joseph Resort, P.O. Box 467, 54646. T: (608) 565-7258. RV/tent: 40. $18. Hookups: water, electric (30 amps).

### Neillsville
Greenwood Park, Hwy. 73, 54456. T: (715) 743-5140. RV/tent: 24. $12. Hookups: electric (30 amps).

Mead Lake Park, CR G, 54456. T: (715) 743-5140. RV/tent: 75. $12. Hookups: electric (30 amps).

Rock Dam Park, Rock Dam Lake, 54456. T: (715) 743-5140. RV/tent: 140. $17. Hookups: water, sewer, electric (30 amps).

Russell Memorial Park, County Trunk J, 54456. T: (715) 743-5140. RV/tent: 200. $20. Hookups: water, sewer, electric (30 amps).

Sherwood Park, County Trunk Z, 54456. T: (715) 743-5140. RV/tent: 38. $12. Hookups: electric (30 amps).

Snyder Park, US 10, 54456. T: (715) 743-5140. RV/tent: 37. $12. Hookups: electric (30 amps).

### Nekoosa
Deer Trail Park Campground, 13846 CR Z, 54457. T: (715) 886-3871. RV/tent: 160. $19. Hookups: water, electric (50 amps).

## WISCONSIN (continued)

### New Lisbon

Fischer's Campground, 7989 Hwy. 80, 53950.
T: (608) 562-5355. RV/tent: 50. $20. Hookups:
water, electric (30 amps).

### Oakdale

Oakdale KOA, P.O. Box 150, 54649. T: (608) 372-
5622. RV/tent: 84. $22. Hookups: water, sewer,
electric (50 amps).

### Oconto

Holtwood Campsite, Holtwood Way, 54153. T: (920)
834-7732. RV/tent: 150. $18. Hookups: water, elec-
tric (30 amps).

North Bay Shore Park, County Trunk Y, 54153.
T: (920) 834-6825. RV/tent: 33. $17. Hookups:
water, electric (30 amps).

### Osceola

Schillberg's Brookside Campground, 409 10th Ave.,
54020. T: (715) 755-2260. RV/tent: 120. $17.
Hookups: electric (30 amps).

### Oshkosh

Circle R Campground, 1185 Old Knapp Rd., 54902.
T: (920) 235-8909. RV/tent: 100. $19. Hookups:
water, sewer, electric (30 amps).

Hickory Oaks Fly In and Campground, 555 Glendale Ave., 54901. T: (920) 235-8076. RV/tent: 50.
$18. Hookups: water, electric (30 amps).

### Palmyra

Circle K Campground, W 1316 Island Rd., 53156.
T: (262) 495-2896. RV/tent: 80. $20. Hookups:
water, sewer, electric (30 amps).

### Pardeeville

Duck Creek Campground, 6560 County Hwy. G,
53954. T: (608) 429-2425. RV/tent: 50. $20.
Hookups: water, electric (30 amps).

Indian Trails Campground, 6445 Haynes Rd., 53954.
T: (608) 429-3244. RV/tent: 168. $21. Hookups:
water, electric (30 amps).

### Pelican Lake

Weaver's Resort & Campground, 1001 Weaver Rd.,
54463. T: (715) 487-5217. RV/tent: 9. $25.
Hookups: water, sewer, electric (30 amps).

### Pembine

Tranquil Vista Campground, P.O. Box 98, 54156.
T: (715) 324-6430. RV/tent: 25. $12. Hookups:
water, electric (30 amps).

### Phillips

Solberg Lake County Park, 104 South Eyder Ave.,
54555. T: (715) 339-6371. RV/tent: 45. $15.
Hookups: electric (30 amps).

### Plover

Ridgewood Campground, 4800 River Ridge Rd.,
54467. T: (715) 344-8750. RV/tent: 70. $22.
Hookups: water, electric (30 amps).

### Portage

Kamp Dakota, W 10670 Tritz Rd., 53901. T: (608)
742-5599. RV/tent: 125. $18. Hookups: water,
sewer, electric (30 amps).

Pride of America Camping Resort, 7584 W. Bush
Rd., 53901. T: (608) 742-6395. RV/tent: 120. $27.
Hookups: water, sewer, electric (50 amps).

Sky High Camping Resort, 5740 Sky High Dr.,
53901. T: (608) 742-2572. RV/tent: 100. $30.
Hookups: water, sewer, electric (50 amps).

### Prairie Du Chien

Wyalusing State Park, 13081 State Park Ln., 53801.
T: (608) 996-2261. RV/tent: 82. $15. Hookups:
electric (30 amps).

### Rapids

Dexter Park, Hwys 80 & 54, 54494. T: (715)
421-8422. RV/tent: 96. $13. Hookups: electric
(30 amps).

North Wood County Park, CR A, 54494. T: (715)
421-8422. RV/tent: 91. $13. Hookups: electric (320
amps).

South Wood Park-Lake Wazeecha, CR W, 54494.
T: (715) 421-8422. RV/tent: 71. $13. Hookups:
electric (20 amps).

### Redgranite

Flanagan's Pearl Lake Campsite, W 4585 South Pearl
Lake Rd., 54970. T: (920) 566-2758. RV/tent: 100.
$17. Hookups: water, electric (50 amps).

### Reedsburg

Lighthouse Rock Campground, 2330 CR V, 53959.
T: (608) 524-4203. RV/tent: 98. $21. Hookups:
water, sewer, electric (30 amps).

### Reedsville

Rainbow's End Campground, 18227 US Hwy. 10,
54230. T: (920) 754-4142. RV/tent: 40. $18.
Hookups: water, electric (30 amps).

### Rhinelander

Lake George Campsites, 4008 Bassett Rd., 54501.
T: (715) 362-6152. RV/tent: 37. $16. Hookups:
water, electric (30 amps).

West Bay Camping Resort, 4330 South Shore Dr.,
54501. T: (715) 362-3481. RV/tent: 79. $18.
Hookups: water, sewer, electric (50 amps).

### Richland Center

Alana Springs Lodge & Campground, 22628
Covered Bridge Rd., 53581. T: (608) 647-2600.
RV/tent: 23. $20. Hookups: water, electric
(20 amps).

## WISCONSIN (continued)

### Rio

Little Bluff Campground, N4003 Traut Rd., 53960. T: (920) 992-5157. RV/tent: 135. $19. Hookups: water, sewer, electric (30 amps).

Silver Springs Campsites, N5048 Ludwig Rd., 53960. T: (920) 992-3537. RV/tent: 300. $26. Hookups: water, sewer, electric (30 amps).

Willow Mill Campsite, 5830 CR SS, 53960. T: (920) 992-5355. RV/tent: 60. $26. Hookups: water, electric (30 amps).

### Saxon

Frontier Bar & Campground, HC 1 Box 477, 54559. T: (715) 893-2461. RV/tent: 25. $16. Hookups: water, sewer, electric (30 amps).

### Shawano

Brady's Pine Grove Campground, N5999 Campground Rd., 54166. T: (715) 787-4555. RV/tent: 200. $24. Hookups: water, electric (30 amps).

Shawano County Park Campground, CR H, 54166. T: (715) 524-4986. RV/tent: 90. $10. Hookups: electric (30 amps).

### Sheboygan

Kohler/Andre State Park, 1520 Old Park Rd., 53081. T: (920) 451-4080. RV/tent: 95. $15. Hookups: electric (30 amps).

### Sherwood

High Cliff State Park, 7650 State Park Rd., 54169. T: (920) 989-1106. RV/tent: 83. $15. Hookups: electric (30 amps).

### Solon Springs

Swanson's Motel & Campground, P.O. Box 296, 54873. T: (715) 378-2215. RV/tent: 21. $16. Hookups: water, sewer, electric (30 amps).

### Somerset

River's Edge Camp Resort, P.O. Box 67, 54025. T: (715) 247-3305. RV/tent: 277. $20. Hookups: water, electric (30 amps).

### Spooner

Country House Lodging & RV Park, 717 South Hwy. 63, 54801. T: (715) 635-8721. RV/tent: 21. $18. Hookups: water, electric (30 amps).

Highland Park Campground, 8050 Carlton Rd., 54801. T: (715) 635-2462. RV/tent: 45. $30. Hookups: water, sewer, electric (30 amps).

Totogatic Park, CR 1, 54801. T: (715) 466-2822. RV/tent: 71. $13. Hookups: electric (30 amps).

### Spring Green

Highland Ridge Campground, P.O. Box 190, 54767. T: (715) 778-5562. RV/tent: 45. $14. Hookups: electric (30 amps).

### Valley RV Park

Valley RV Park, E5016 Hwy. 14 & 23, 53588. T: (608) 588-2717. RV/tent: 18. $19. Hookups: water, sewer, electric (30 amps).

### Spruce

Holt Park, 9601 Holt Park Rd., 54174. T: (920) 842-4433. RV/tent: 50. $7. Hookups: water, electric (30 amps).

### Stevens Point

Collins Park, CR 1, 54481. T: (715) 346-1433. RV/tent: 25. $11. Hookups: electric (30 amps).

Dubay Park, CR E, 54481. T: (715) 346-1433. RV/tent: 31. $11. Hookups: electric (30 amps).

Jordan Park, SR 66, 54481. T: (715) 346-1433. RV/tent: 25. $13. Hookups: electric (30 amps).

### Stoughton

Kamp Kegonsa, 2671 Circle Dr., 53589. T: (608) 873-5800. RV/tent: 100. $23. Hookups: water, electric (30 amps).

Lake Kegonsa State Park, 2405 Door Creek Rd., 53589. T: (608) 873-9695. RV/tent: 80. $14. Hookups: electric (30 amps).

Viking Village Campground & Resort Inc., 1648 County Trunk N, 53589. T: (608) 873-6601. RV/tent: 77. $29. Hookups: water, sewer, electric (50 amps).

### Sturgeon Bay

Door County Yogi Bear's Jellystone Park, 3677 May Rd., 54235. T: (920) 743-9001. RV/tent: 175. $25. Hookups: water, sewer, electric (50 amps).

Monument Point Camping, 5718 West Monument Point Rd., 54235. T: (920) 743-9411. RV/tent: 84. $20. Hookups: electric (30 amps).

### Sturtevant

Cliffside Park, 14200 Washington Ave., 53177. T: (262) 886-8440. RV/tent: 92. $13. Hookups: water, electric (30 amps).

Travelers' Inn Motel and Campground, 14017 Durand Ave., 53177. T: (262) 878-1415. RV/tent: 25. $17. Hookups: water, electric (30 amps).

### Superior

Pattison State Park, 6294 South SR 35, 54880. T: (715) 399-3111. RV/tent: 50. $15. Hookups: electric (20 amps).

### Tilleda

Tilleda Falls Campground, P.O. Box 76, 54978. T: (715) 787-4143. RV/tent: 40. $21. Hookups: water, electric (30 amps).

### Tomah

Holiday Lodge Golf Resort & RV Park, 10558 Freedom Rd., 54660. T: (608) 372-9314. RV/tent: 28. $17. Hookups: water, sewer, electric (30 amps).

## WISCONSIN (continued)

### Tomahawk

Birkensee Resort & Camping, 9350 CR H, 54487.
T: (715) 453-5103. RV/tent: 45. $20. Hookups:
water, sewer, electric (30 amps).

Terrace View Campsites, W5220 Terrace View Rd.,
54487. T: (715) 453-8352. RV/tent: 42. $18.
Hookups: water, electric (30 amps).

### Trego

Bay Park Resort & Campground, 8347 Bay Park Rd.,
54888. T: (715) 635-2840. RV/tent: 52. $25.
Hookups: water, sewer, electric (30 amps).

Eagle Lodge Resort & Campground, 8234 Bald Eagle
Dr., 54888. T: (715) 466-2728. RV/tent: 17. $25.
Hookups: water, sewer, electric (30 amps).

Trego Town Park & Campground, 5665 Trego Park
Rd., 54888. T: (715) 635-9931. RV/tent: 49. $15.
Hookups: water, electric (30 amps).

### Trempealeau

Perrot State Park, P.O. Box 407, 54661. T: (608)
534-6409. RV/tent: 97. $15. Hookups: electric
(30 amps).

### Tripoli

Buck Snort Resort & Campground, 5129 Boyle Rd.,
54564. T: (715) 564-2262. RV/tent: 33. $18.
Hookups: water, sewer, electric (30 amps).

### Two Rivers

Point Beach State Forest, 9400 CTHO, 54241.
T: (920) 794-7480. RV/tent: 127. $15. Hookups:
water, sewer, electric (30 amps).

### Viola

Banker Park, P.O. Box 38, 54664. T: (608) 627-1831.
RV/tent: 45. $5. Hookups: electric (30 amps).

### Wabeno

Ham Lake Campground, 3490 Hwy. 32, 54566.
T: (715) 674-2201. RV/tent: 31. $23. Hookups:
water, sewer, electric (30 amps).

### Washington Island

Washington Island Campground, RR 1 Box 144,
54246. T: (920) 847-2622. RV/tent: 80. $33.
Hookups: water, electric (30 amps).

### Waupaca

Deerhaven Campground, N 3185 Butts Dr., 54981.
T: (715) 256-1412. RV/tent: 40. $18. Hookups:
water, sewer, electric (30 amps).

Royal Oaks Golf Resort Inc., N4440 Oakland Dr.,
54981. T: (715) 258-5103. RV/tent: 25. $17.
Hookups: water, sewer, electric (30 amps).

Rustic Woods, E 2585 Southwood Dr., 54981.
T: (715) 258-2442. RV/tent: 164. $23. Hookups:
water, sewer, electric (30 amps).

Wapaca Camping Park, 2411 Holmes Rd., 54981.
T: (715) 258-8010. RV/tent: 133. $24. Hookups:
water, sewer, electric (30 amps).

### Wausau

Dells of the Eau Claire Park, CR Y, 54401. T: (715)
449-2293. RV/tent: 26. $8. Hookups: electric (30
amps).

Marathon Park, SR 29 W, 54401. T: (715) 261-1570.
RV/tent: 45. $11. Hookups: electric (30 amps).

Rib Mountain State Park, 4200 Park Rd., 54401.
T: (715) 842-2522. RV/tent: 40. $11. Hookups:
electric (20 amps).

### Wautoma

Land of the Woods Campground, 9070 14th Ave.,
54982. T: (920) 787-3601. RV/tent: 150. $23.
Hookups: water, electric (20 amps).

### Webster

Wagner's Port Sand, 4904 Hwy. 70, 54893. T: (715)
349-2395. RV/tent: 60. $20. Hookups: water, sewer,
electric (30 amps).

### White Lake

River Forest Rafts & Campground, N2765 Sunny
Waters Ln., 54491. T: (715) 882-3351. RV/tent: 45.
$6. Hookups: electric (15 amps).

### Whitewater

Scenic Ridge Campground, W7991 R& W Townline
Rd., 53190. T: (608) 883-2920. RV/tent: 187. $9.
Hookups: water, electric (30 amps).

### Wild Rose

Evergreen Campsites, W5449 Archer Ln., 54984.
T: (920) 622-3498. RV/tent: 400. $20. Hookups:
water, electric (30 amps).

### Wonewoc

Chapparal Campground & Resort, S320 Hwy. 33,
53968. T: (888) 283-0755. RV/tent: 72. $24.
Hookups: water, sewer, electric (50 amps).

### Woodruff

Hiawatha Trailer Resort, P.O. Box 590, 54568.
T: (715) 356-6111. RV/tent: 60. $30. Hookups:
water, sewer, electric (50 amps).

Indian Shores Resort & RV Sales, P.O. Box 12,
54568. T: (715) 356-5552. RV/tent: 150. $26.
Hookups: water, sewer, electric (30 amps)

# Index

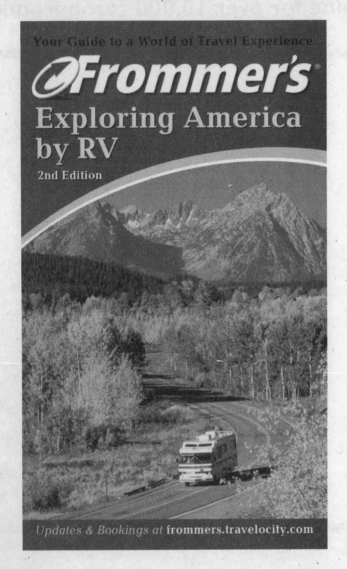